Peter Bemko
(908) 872-7324

W9-CBR-279

PEOPLE AT WORK
HUMAN RELATIONS IN ORGANIZATIONS

Fourth Edition

PEOPLE AT WORK
HUMAN RELATIONS IN ORGANIZATIONS

Fourth Edition

PAUL R. TIMM
Brigham Young University

BRENT D. PETERSON
Brigham Young University

WEST PUBLISHING COMPANY
Minneapolis/St. Paul • New York • Los Angeles • San Francisco

Copy Editor: Marilynn Taylor
Composition: Parkwood Composition
Cover Photo Credits: background from © Superstock; at left © New England Stock Photo; at center © Henley & Savage/The Stock Market; at right © Robert Neumann/The Stock Market

WEST'S COMMITMENT TO THE ENVIRONMENT
In 1906, West Publishing Company began recycling materials left over from the production of books. This began a tradition of efficient and responsible use of resources. Today, up to 95 percent of our legal books and 70 percent of our college and school texts are printed on recycled, acid-free stock. West also recycles nearly 22 million pounds of scrap paper annually—the equivalent of 181,717 trees. Since the 1960s, West has devised ways to capture and recycle waste inks, solvents, oils, and vapors created in the printing process. We also recycle plastics of all kinds, wood, glass, corrugated cardboard, and batteries, and have eliminated the use of styrofoam book packaging. We at West are proud of the longevity and the scope of our commitment to the environment.

Production, Prepress, Printing and Binding by West Publishing Company.

Photo credits follow the index.

COPYRIGHT © 1982,
1986, 1990
COPYRIGHT © 1993

By WEST PUBLISHING COMPANY
By WEST PUBLISHING COMPANY
610 Opperman Drive
P.O. Box 64526
St. Paul, MN 55164–0526

Printed in the United States of America

00 99 98 97 96 95 94 93   8 7 6 5 4 3 2 1 0

Library of Congress Cataloging-in-Publication Data

Timm, Paul R.
  People at work : human relations in organizations / Paul R. Timm,
Brent D. Peterson. — 4th ed.
      p.   cm.
    Includes bibliographical references and index.
    ISBN 0-314-00901-9
    1. Organizational behavior   2. Communication in organizations.
  I. Peterson, Brent D.   II. Title
  HD58.7.T55   1992
  658.4'092—dc20   92-35569
                                                    CIP ∞

CONTENTS

▼ CHAPTER 3

HUMAN NEEDS AND MOTIVATION: WHAT MOTIVATES PEOPLE AT WORK?   43

▼ CHAPTER 4

EMPOWERING PEOPLE AT WORK BY UNBLOCKING GOALS   67

▼ Chapter 5
How Organizations Arrange People
To Accomplish Work   87

▼ Chapter 6
The Human Side of Organizations   115

▼ Part IV
The Driving Force: Leadership   137

▼ Chapter 7
The Nature of Leadership   139

▼ CHAPTER 8
DEVELOPING A LEADERSHIP STYLE THAT WORKS   160

▼ CHAPTER 9
HOW LEADERS CAN BOOST EFFECTIVENESS WITH APPROPRIATE REWARDS   183

▼ PART V
THE MEDIUM: COMMUNICATION   215

▼ CHAPTER 10
UNDERSTANDING MANAGERIAL COMMUNICATION: THE HUMAN TRANSACTION   217

▼ CHAPTER 11
INTERPERSONAL COMMUNICATION:
BEING EFFECTIVE WITH PEOPLE   239

▼ CHAPTER 12
COMMUNICATION IN SMALL GROUPS:
EFFECTIVE TEAMWORK IN ORGANIZATIONS   264

▼ PART VI
WORKFORCE ISSUES: DIVERSITY, SOCIALIZATION,
TECHNOLOGICAL CHANGE, AND STRESS   293

▼ CHAPTER 13
PERSPECTIVES ON CULTURAL DIVERSITY   295

▼ CHAPTER 14
WOMEN AS MANAGERS AND CO-WORKERS   327

▼ CHAPTER 15
PERSPECTIVES ON SPECIAL WORK GROUPS   357

▼ CHAPTER 16
COPING WITH PERSONAL STRESS   387

▼ PREFACE

It has been more than a decade since the first edition of this book was published. Although much has happened in the world of organizations since the early 1980's, the importance of human relations has not diminished. If anything, healthy, productive human relationships have become more important and challenging as our world shrinks. Today, more than ever before, we thrive and grow through our interdependence with humanity worldwide.

Among the changes, much remains the same. We still see evidence that people can develop the technical ability to solve almost any of the complex tasks facing humanity. Feeding people, cleaning up pollution, producing sufficient energy, and curing major diseases are accomplishments within the technical grasp of people. The roadblocks to such accomplishments, however, lie in the problems of human relationships. Without cooperation, little can be accomplished; with cooperation, all things are possible.

This book is about people in the workplace. It focuses on the many psychological and social pressures that people experience when they interact with each other. But more importantly, the emphasis of the book is on you, the reader. Human relationships play an important part in daily life. Understanding these relationships can help you accomplish your goals in all types of organizations.

Many of you are, or shortly will be, in a leadership position in which you deal with other people. We think you will find a great deal of information in this book that will help you succeed. We also believe you will find it enjoyable reading. The book includes examples and illustrations from a variety of sources, and each contributes to the overall flavor. You will find cartoons, illustrations, quotes, and even a few poems. These items are placed throughout the text to enhance your understanding of the subject matter.

We believe that this book should be read—and used; therefore, we have included self-evaluative exercises and learning projects. We encourage you to complete the exercises and use some of the techniques as you interact with other people. You may be pleasantly surprised at the results.

Throughout this book we have used fictitious names for individuals and companies. Any similarity between those names and real people or organizations is coincidental and unintentional. The situations described in our cases and examples, however, are drawn from real-life experiences.

What have we done to upgrade and enhance this fourth edition of *People at Work?* We have included many new and updated activities such as "The NWNL Workplace Stress Test." These new activities appear under the heading "Activity" within the chapters. In many chapters we have written new cases for the "A Case in Point" section. "The Downsizing of ABC Learning, Inc." is a good example of the new cases. We have inserted approximately one fourth new readings in the "Another Look" sections at the end of each chapter. "Achieving Access for the Disabled" is illustrative of the kinds of additions we have made.

In sum, we feel very good about the changes in this edition. We particularly like the content changes we have included regarding communicating in the organization, managing diversity in the workplace, working with workers with disabilities, enhancing opportunities for women at work, and reducing workplace stress. We have tried our best to update and enhance without tampering with the feel and excitement we have created in the first three editions. We are certain that you will find this edition to be a true learning experience. One that will lead you to a greater understanding of *People at Work.*

Many people have helped us prepare this book. We especially thank Denise Simon of West Educational Publishing for her active and insightful involvement in the development of the manuscript. Special thanks also go to Beth Kennedy, our production editor, whose attention to detail made this a better book and to Mary Taylor, who worked closely with us in checking the myriad details associated with this project. Their help was invaluable. We also appreciate Jim Stead who helped develop the excellent instructor's supplement and test questions.

In addition, we thank the people who reviewed earlier editions of the book and provided constructive suggestions for this revision:

- Professor Thomas R. Allen
  Appalachian State University
- Professor Bob Amundson
  Ulster County Community College
- Professor Hal Babson
  Columbus State Community College
- Professor Kathryn Barchas
  Skyline College
- Professor Bonnie R. Chavez
  Santa Barbara City College
- Professor Ron Herrick
  Mesa Community College
- Professor Donald N. Kelly
  North Hennepin Community College
- Professor David Leland
  Red River Community College
- Professor Paula K. McNeil
  Cameron University

Furthermore, we appreciate the hundreds of instructors and thousands of students who used our first three editions and made this revision possible.

We acknowledge, too, the many people who inspired us to write this book. During our years of consulting, training, teaching, and working in business organizations, we have come to know countless people who have taught us important principles of human relations.

Sometimes their teaching came through great example; sometimes their example taught us what not to do.

We dedicate this book to those who sacrificed time with their husband or dad in order to allow us to work on this project. To our wives, Helen and Arlene and to our children: Charlie, Erika, Monika, Jamie (the Timm clan) and Amy, Dan and Caroline Peterson.

Paul R. Timm
Brent D. Peterson

THE SUBJECT:
HUMAN RELATIONS IN ORGANIZATIONS

HUMAN RELATIONS: A KEY TO PROFESSIONAL AND PERSONAL SUCCESS

This chapter answers several all-important questions.

- What is the study of human relations?

- How does human relations differ from earlier management approaches?

- What is the significance of the Hawthorne studies to the field of human relations in the workplace?

- How do modern management approaches, such as systems theory, contingency management, QWL, and self-

managing teams, rely on human relations skills to succeed?

- How can an understanding of human relations affect our personal and professional lives?

- Why are *caring* and *trust* the cornerstone values of human relations?

The answer to these and other questions are coming up next in chapter 1 ....

▼ WHY STUDY HUMAN RELATIONS?

More careers have been damaged by poor human relations skills than by any other cause. Having great technical ability but poor people skills is a formula for disaster. Knowing how to do a job isn't enough. To produce results in any modern organization requires depending on others and knowing how to work with people. Even top executives—*especially* top executives—need to understand relationships among people. You seldom hear of a top manager losing his or her job because of a lack of technical skills. You regularly hear of people failing because they simply can't get along with others.

This book provides the background for developing skills in the crucial art of human relations. It identifies key forces and tools everyone needs to strengthen their relationships with others, especially in the work environment.

To understand and to relate constructively with people are the greatest of all human skills.

▼ SOMETHING MORE THAN PERSONNEL

To some people, human relations is just the name of a department at work. It's the place where you go to get a job or apply for benefits. Some companies still call it the personnel department.

But human relations is much more than a name on an office door. The way human relations are handled becomes the heart and soul of any organization. Just as an individual's personality is assessed by the way he or she interacts with others, so is an organization's culture—personality—determined by its policies and behaviors in human relations.

■ An organization's personality is determined by its human relations policies and behaviors.

Well-managed companies care about their people. Their actions say loudly and clearly that people are seen as the most important of all resources. Poorly managed companies may talk about human relations, but their words are mostly just noise.

Modern organizations are much more than offices and factories, plants and equipment. They consist of more than departments with names like procurement, production, staffing, finance, accounting, sales, research and development, or marketing.

Although all those departments may show up on the organization chart, the soul of a company, hospital, government agency, or non-profit group is the collective body of *people* who make it all work. The people who staff the offices, work on the production lines, sell the products, provide the services, and operate the machines give life to the organization. They define the character of the organization.

With the technological developments of the past decades, and especially the computer revolution of the 1980s, it is easy to fall into the trap of undervaluing the importance of people and of human relations to the success of a corporation. Today, as much as, or even more than ever, the human side of organizations is critical to success.

▼ WHAT DOES THE FIELD OF HUMAN RELATIONS MEAN TO YOU?

On a personal level, the study of human relations can make the difference between success and failure in all that you do. Dr. Elwood Chapman, a longtime scholar in human behavior, feels that most employees underestimate the importance of human relations. He encourages us to work to become "human relations smart."

More careers have been damaged through faulty human relations skills than through a lack of technical ability. Many people are technically smart but human relations dumb because they seem unaware that simply knowing *how to do a job is not the key to success.* To produce results, most of us depend on others, and this requires knowing *how to work with people.* Before this can be done successfully, many human relations skills need to be learned and practiced.

Some individuals underestimate the problems that poor human relations can get them into. They persist in concentrating on personal productivity and fail to acknowledge that they are part of a complicated team structure that can only operate efficiently when human relationships are given proper attention.

To be human relations smart, it is essential to maintain cooperative relationships with all members of an organization, from co-workers to superiors. Communication must be open and healthy. The quality of any relationship will influence the productivity from that individual.[1]

The human relations-smart person understands and applies the ideas discussed in this book. The payoff for those who make the effort to use this information is the ability to establish cooperative relationships with others. Communication can be open and healthy; the quality and productivity of relationships can improve.

> ■ Lack of human relations skills can quickly damage your career.

▼ HOW HUMAN RELATIONS SMART ARE YOU?

The following is a self-test that can give you a sense of how well you already practice some key human relations principles.

▼ ACTIVITY: HUMAN RELATIONS SELF-TEST

Although human relations skills are not as easy to identify or quantify as technical skills, they are extremely important to your career progress. The more you practice positive human relations, the less co-workers and superiors will misinterpret your goals, and the more supportive they will be.

Twenty human relations competencies are listed below. *Check only those you practice daily.* The exercise will demonstrate why it is

ACTIVITY *continued*

difficult to be considered "human relations smart."

I consistently:

☐ Deal with all people in an honest, ethical, and moral way.

☐ Remain positive and upbeat even while working with others who may be negative.

☐ Send out positive verbal and nonverbal signals in all human interactions, including over the telephone.

☐ Refuse to be involved in any activity that might victimize another person.

☐ Build and maintain open and healthy working relationships with everyone in the workplace. I refuse to play favorites.

☐ Treat everyone, regardless of ethnic or socioeconomic differences, with respect.

☐ Work effectively with others, regardless of their sexual orientation.

☐ Permit others to restore a damaged relationship with me; I don't hold a grudge.

☐ Maintain a strong relationship with my immediate superior without alienating co-workers.

☐ Am a better-than-average producer while contributing to the productivity of co-workers.

☐ Refuse to initiate or circulate potentially harmful rumors.

☐ Maintain a good attendance record, including being on time to work.

☐ Show I can live up to my productivity potential without alienating co-workers who do not live up to theirs.

☐ Acknowledge mistakes or misjudgments, rather than hiding them.

☐ Refuse to allow small gripes to grow into major upsets.

☐ Am an excellent listener.

☐ Keep a good balance between my home and career lives so that neither suffers.

☐ Look for, and appreciate, the good characteristics of others.

☐ Keep my business and personal relationships sufficiently separated.

☐ Make only positive comments about those not present.

SCORE ☐

(Add five points for each square checked)

A score of 70 or above indicates you are practicing a substantial number of recognized human relations skills; a score of under 50 suggests a review of current practices may be in order.

SOURCE: Reprinted with permission. Elwood N. Chapman, *Winning at Human Relations* (Los Altos, Calif.: Crisp Publications, 1989), p. 3.

▼ A BRIEF LOOK AT THE HISTORY OF HUMAN RELATIONS IN ORGANIZATIONS

People at work have not always been as valued as they are today. Today's sense of caring about the individual has emerged over a period of many years.

A study of management history is also a study of philosophy. Many of the great philosophers made contributions to the way people think about leadership and management. Machiavelli, for example, in 1513 developed a handbook on how to rule over people. He assumed that all people were lazy and self-centered and that tricking them into working made good sense. He believed that the end

■ A study of management history also reflects changes in philosophy over the years.

justified the means. Indeed, we have come to associate his name with the process of manipulation.

Throughout history, people were assumed to be members of various classes. Some were rulers (kings, nobility, and trusted aristocrats) and many were followers. If one assumed that people of lower social status should be subservient, management of them would likely rely on exerting power or force. Managers with such assumptions did not give much thought to human relations—after all, lower-class people were barely seen as human.

The eventual breakdown of the rigid class system with the advent of democratic thinking called for new and different ways to manage. The notion that people are "created equal and endowed with certain inalienable rights," as Thomas Jefferson asserted, was a radically different way of thinking about human relationships. Today's manager must be concerned with "the human element" instead of dictating to people as the ancient aristocrat did.

▼ THE SCIENTIFIC MANAGEMENT APPROACH

By the late 1800s, the Industrial Revolution was picking up a great deal of steam. More jobs were being mechanized. Investors, engineers, and chemists were coming up with products people had only dreamed of. *Science* was being viewed as the great answer to most of humanity's problems. And managers were beginning to look at ways to apply scientific methods to the study and improvement of work efficiency.

Although many researchers were involved with scientific management, Frederick W. Taylor is generally regarded as the father of this new approach to management. Briefly, Taylor felt that through science, a careful worker or manager could find the one best way to do any job. This right way would emerge from careful scientific observation, standardized measurements, and systematic trial-and-error experiments.

People known as efficiency experts began to come into prominence. These experts would carefully observe people at work (sometimes using a modern technological device, such as the motion picture), measure each movement, examine the tools being used, and even attempt to scientifically select the "first-class person" for the job. This was all done in search of the one best way to accomplish a task, and great improvements in efficiency often came about from these efforts.

■ Using observation, measurement, and trial and error, scientific managers sought the one best way to do any job.

During this search to study management scientifically, supervisors sought to establish work rates, set standards of performance (all determined scientifically through observation), and define a full and fair day's labor for each task.

Taylor defined *management* as "knowing exactly what you want [people] to do, and then seeing that they do it in the best and cheapest way." To accomplish this, managers felt that they could simply exchange people, the way we would spare parts on a machine, and

Early scientific management sought the "one best way" to combine people and machinery for maximum results.

maintain or improve the output. This rather simplistic picture of human nature was the Achilles' heel of scientific management, as we'll see in a moment.

▼ THE HUMAN RELATIONS APPROACH TO MANAGEMENT

In the late 1920s and early 1930s, a new approach to management theory was born. A researcher named Elton Mayo and his associates conducted a series of experiments at the plant of the Western Electric Company in Hawthorne, Illinois. Those experiments proved to be the transition point from scientific management to the early human relations style of management.

Mayo originally adhered to the scientific management approach. He and his associates had conducted many scientific investigations of such things as worker fatigue, the use of rest periods, changes in physical surroundings of the workplace, and their effects on worker output. In fact, Mayo's team was involved in a series of such experiments when a chance discovery gave birth to what we now call human relations.

▼ A CHANCE DISCOVERY AT THE HAWTHORNE PLANT

Mayo and his associates were using experiments to study the relationships between physical work environment and worker productivity when a breakthrough occurred.

The researchers were looking at the relationship between the brightness of light in the workplace and the efficiency of the workers, as measured by their output. They found that by making the workplace slightly brighter, they could increase output. So they cranked up a carefully measured increase in candlepower and found that the output increased even more. But being good scientific researchers, they also decided to check the other direction by reducing illumination. Output again went up. They reduced it even further. Output continued to *increase!* What was happening? They found that by either increasing *or* decreasing illumination, sometimes even dimming the lights to the brightness of a moonlit night, they almost always got *increases* in productivity. (See Figure 1.1.) Something that couldn't be accounted for in terms of their scientific measurements was taking place.

■ Researchers discovered that something more than the physical work environment affected worker productivity.

After considerable analysis, the researchers determined that the very fact *the workers were being observed* by the research team seemed to affect their output. The workers enjoyed being the center of the research team's attention and responded by producing more. What resulted is now known as the *Hawthorne effect,* a situation created when managers or researchers pay special attention to workers that seems to result in improved worker output. But from a scientific management perspective, paying attention to people shouldn't have caused them to work better. After all, they weren't being *paid* any more money! Other forces must have been at work.

■ Paying attention to worker needs seemed to affect work output.

FIGURE 1.1
The results of the Hawthorne Studies in which researchers measured the brightness of light (illumination) in relation to worker performance (productivity).

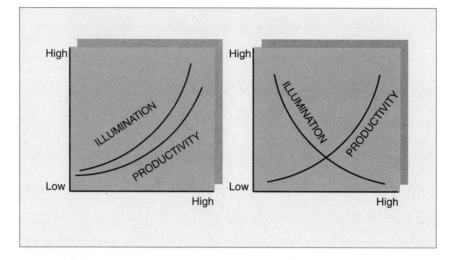

Mayo and his group hypothesized that the increased production resulted from changed social situations of the workers (workers received more attention), modifications in worker motivation and satisfactions, and altered patterns of supervision. Social and psychological factors were seen as playing a major role in determining worker satisfaction and productivity.

- Social and psychological factors were found to play an important role in determining worker satisfaction.

Over the next decades, many other researchers got involved in studying the human relations approach. There emerged a genuine sense of "industrial humanism." Managers became increasingly aware of the importance of designing the work environment to restore workers' dignity. The human relationist soon concluded that most people were working for more than just money; other things motivated them.

Over the years, much research has focused on human behavior in the workplace. Among the findings of these studies are the following:

- People are motivated by a variety of things, not just money.

- Individuals are motivated by a wide variety of social and psychological factors, not just earnings.
- Worker behavior is affected by feelings, sentiments, and attitudes. People, after all, are not machines.
- Informal work groups play an important role in determining the attitudes and performance of individual workers.
- Leadership behaviors that overemphasize the need to command workers should often be modified. Let people participate in decisions, rather than excluding them.
- Worker satisfaction is associated with productivity; satisfied workers are likely to be more effective.
- Communication channels were recognized as being important. Information does not only flow through the formal organization structure; it also flows in many informal ways.
- Worker participation in decision making is important to healthy organizations.
- Management requires effective social skills as well as technical skills; management is both an art and a science.

▼ THE BEHAVIORAL MOVEMENT TAKES MANAGEMENT BY STORM

By the 1950s and 1960s, behavioral scientists were busily conducting research and training programs in all types of businesses. Many of these researchers moved into business colleges and began teaching others their approach. Not since Taylor at the turn of the century has an approach to study had such an effect on management.

Some of the major impacts of the human relations approach on management are as follows:[2]

- The role of the manager became much more people-oriented.
- Considering management as the problem of getting work done through people opened up the whole question of incentives and source of motivation.
- Skills of supervision were expanded to encompass the ability to communicate, develop an understanding of others, and be effective in gaining cooperation.
- In organization structure, there was less emphasis on authority and a move toward power equalization.
- Leadership styles played down autocratic behavior and emphasized participation and freedom for subordinates.
- Organizations were viewed as social systems in which the informal relationships that emerged within the group were often more compelling than the formal rules of the company.
- The goal of the firm was viewed no longer as exclusively that of profit or efficiency. Fostering social goals became part of the measure of performance.
- The supervisor's role was not just to monitor operations but also to manage conflict and change.

There Were Critics of Human Relations, Too

Despite the fact that the human relations approach to management has had a major impact upon management thought, there have been criticisms of it. Some people have called human relationists the "happiness boys" and criticized them for being so concerned with making contented workers without placing an equal emphasis on the importance of productivity. Also disparagingly referred to as "cow sociologists," human relationists are accused that their only goal is to produce "contented cows," not productive workers. Others have criticized the movement for using certain human relations techniques, such as worker participation, to manipulate workers.

- Some critics labeled human relationists as "happiness boys" or "cow sociologists."

It would be unfair to end this discussion of the human relations school on a negative note. Much of what we have learned—and continue to learn—through this approach is most valuable to the study of people at work. Indeed, many chapters in this book will deal with principles learned through the research of human relationalists conducted in the last half century.

Where Management Theory Stands Today

■ Modern management theory recognizes that our world is constantly changing and requires a combination of approaches to cope with management challenges.

Management thinking continues to evolve, of course. We will never reach an ultimate theory to explain and predict all that managers would like to know. Recent trends have led toward what might be called integrative approaches—theories that combine the best of what is known to try to cope with management challenges in today's world. These approaches recognize that our world is constantly and rapidly changing and that we are all more interdependent—dependent upon each other—than ever before. Interdependence is highlighted in the *systems theory* approach; change is accounted for in *contingency approaches.* Another modern trend focuses on the *quality of work life* approach. Below is a quick look at these.

▼ THE SYSTEMS THEORY APPROACH

In the 1960s, a general *systems theory* emerged from a convergence of many sciences. A basic assumption was that nothing in nature exists in a vacuum—everything is interrelated with everything else at some point. *Systems* emerge from this interconnectedness. Every system has:

■ Input

■ Transformation

■ Output

Any action taken affecting one system must have ripple effects on other systems.

The study of ecology uses systems theory to show interrelatedness. In the early 1970s, ecologists were successful in obtaining a ban on certain aerosol sprays because of the damage to the earth's ozone layer allegedly caused by fluorocarbon propellants. Many people were amazed that chemicals released by their underarm spray deodorants (input) could destroy the ozone (transformation), thus allowing more rays of the sun to penetrate the earth and perhaps cause additional skin cancer in people (output). The ecologists used a systems approach to explain interrelatedness in ways people never dreamed of.

Let's try another example. Suppose you set up a business to manufacture waterbeds. Your simplified organizational system might include the system shown in Figure 1.2.[3]

Systems theory holds, however, that such a description is grossly oversimplified and that managers must be able to account for interrelationships. What affects part of the system (i.e., a shortage of one raw material, a serious argument among workers, or a weakened market for finished products) affects the entire system and all interconnected systems.

Let's think for a moment about what we might learn about people at work from such a point of view:

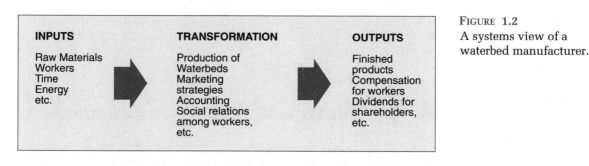

FIGURE 1.2
A systems view of a
waterbed manufacturer.

- Mistreating one employee may result in "ripple effects" throughout the work force. Supervisor-worker relationships are not isolated, one-on-one interactions.

- A new business opening nearby may hire away your best workers unless something is done to retain them.

- Government regulations, enforced by agencies that are systems in themselves, can affect input, transformation, and/or output of your system.

- Organizations have multiple purposes, objectives, and functions, some of which will naturally be in conflict. Supervisors need to strive for a balance among the competing wants of subgroups.

Systems theory provides a more broad-based view of the management process than does scientific or human relations approaches taken alone. However, it has not yet produced as many specific techniques for managing people as have the scientific management (time studies, work measurement) and human relations (participation in decisions) approaches.

▼ THE CONTINGENCY APPROACH

Management theorists have been frustrated by an inability to agree upon one broad theory to unite the field—an approach that would be useful in all circumstances. This search may have been an offshoot of Taylor's implicit belief that there is one best way.

The role of a manager in *contingency* or *situational theory* is different. This approach accepts the idea that there is a need for, as the cliche goes, "different strokes for different folks." For example, the manager's job is like a golfer's. He or she faces two tasks: (1) determining where he or she is on the course in relation to the green and (2) deciding what club to use to get the best results. Where you are and the tools you have available determine what must be done in the particular situation. There is no "one best way" applicable for all circumstances. Flexibility is called for in adjusting to changing conditions.

The primary emphasis of this approach is recognizing that no two situations are exactly alike since the world is in constant flux and that different management actions are often called for in different

■ Contingency
approaches stress the
need to use different
techniques in
different situations.

situations. There are no pat answers applicable to any and all situations. We'll talk more about a contingency approach to leadership in Chapter 8.

▼ THE QUALITY OF WORK LIFE APPROACH

First introduced in the late 1960s, the *quality of work life* concept refers to the degree to which work should provide opportunities to satisfy a wide variety of workers' needs.

The quality of work life (QWL) approach seeks ways to make participation in work activities both gratifying and productive. Instead of breaking jobs down into mindless, repetitive tasks, advocates of QWL suggest redesigning workers' jobs so that they can complete a whole unit of work (such as assembling a whole product), instead of just performing isolated tasks, such as attaching one part of an assembly. Much more satisfaction arises from completing a whole job. Pilot programs in auto manufacturing plants showed impressive reductions in absenteeism, quality defects, and other indicators or dissatisfaction when workers' jobs were redesigned in such ways.

One successful approach to redesigning jobs and improving the quality of work life has been the *quality circle.* This method uses employee participation to determine how jobs should be redesigned for the best results.

Quality Circles Provide One Approach to Improving QWL

A quality circle is a group of eight to ten people who meet periodically (often once a week) to spot and solve problems in their work area. The idea of using small groups of workers to solve work-related problems was popularized by U.S. management consultants and then adopted by the Japanese after World War II. U.S. companies, stunned by dwindling productivity, then borrowed the idea from the Japanese, who believe that such groups are partly responsible for the spectacular productivity gains they have made since the war.

A quality circle selects and analyzes a problem, develops a solution, and presents its findings to management, which generally accepts the group's recommendations.

Based on the findings to date, quality circles appear to be quite successful, from the point of view of both management and labor.

The workers themselves (1) often share in any cost savings (some companies, for example, paid circle members approximately 10 percent of any cost savings) and (2) get a feeling of accomplishment from tackling a challenging task; therefore, they, too, benefit from the quality circles. On the whole, the circle idea appears to be an effective one for harnessing the performance-stimulating potential in a work group.

▼ JAPANESE MANAGEMENT AND QWL

In the past few decades, many Japanese companies have been successful for a number of complex reasons. Among these is the highly effective application of QWL managerial approaches. But success is not limited to Japan. Many companies could achieve greater productivity by making improvements in:

- Job security for workers (freedom from fear of being laid off).
- Opportunities for personal growth for workers.
- Opportunities for worker participation in decisions
- Open communication among all levels and departments.
- Trust among workers and groups because they all have the same goals—the organization's well-being.
- Cooperation, not competition, as the basis for relationships within the company.

▼ THE USE OF SELF-MANAGING TEAMS

Self-managing teams (SMTs) have evolved from the idea of quality circles. In quality circles, employees are well trained in teamwork and problem-solving, but they often have little power beyond calling attention to problems or suggesting ideas for change. SMTs go far beyond quality circles. As part of an SMT, employees are trained to use their skills daily to schedule, assign tasks, coordinate with other groups (and sometimes customers and suppliers), set goals, evaluate performance, and address discipline issues. Project management and participative management are SMT cousins, as each emphasizes sharing tasks and teamwork. SMT members contract to learn and share jobs usually performed by a manager. They do, indeed, self-manage.

The use of SMTs is based in the following beliefs:[4]

- **Employees are an organization's greatest resource.** Increasingly, organizations are giving employees more ownership and autonomy. They find that employees work harder and need less hand-holding when they have more control of their jobs and more freedom to choose how they will do them. Recent statistics indicate that organizations that encourage employee involvement are increasing productivity by 30 percent and more. Workers who participate in self-directed work groups (self-managing teams) report higher motivation, increased self-worth, and greater pride in their work.

- **SMTs "self-correct" quickly.** Forward-looking organizations emphasize quality and excellence. They need skilled people who can perform several tasks and respond quickly to changes. SMT members are trained to "self-correct." In other words, they identify problems and correct them quickly. As organizations eliminate layers of management and staff to increase cost effectiveness and improve communication, SMTs are replacing managers by doing the job themselves.

- **SMTs provide today's work force with a means of self-expression.** Intelligent people want psychological enrichment and control of their lives. One common complaint among employees is that they are frustrated in achieving organizational needs because management erects too many barriers. SMTs provide opportunities for people to put their cards on the table and take responsibility for their actions. They are a logical way to group people who want to remain in an organization but value working creatively. As organizations struggle with the problem of too few people in the work force, SMTs are serving as training grounds for learning multiple tasks.

▼ THE BOTTOM LINE IN HUMAN RELATIONS TODAY: CARING AND TRUST

As we move through the final decade of the twentieth century, a review of current problems in both public and private organizations reveals that there is an imperative need to continue to grow in our understanding—and application—of the principles of human relations.

Some indicators suggest, however, a reduced interest in others; a self-centered attitude that disdains the need for cooperative interaction among people. In his well-known report on higher education, *The Closing of the American Mind,* Allan Bloom concludes that "students these days are pleasant, friendly, and, if not great-souled, at least not particularly mean-spirited. *Their primary preoccupation is themselves, understood in the narrowest sense* [italics added]."[5]

In the best-seller *In Search of Excellence,* Tom Peters and Robert Waterman repeatedly emphasize the importance of human relations. They argue that the number-crunching, coldly analytical manager is inappropriate for today's business environment: "The numerative, rationalist approach to management [that dominates at most business schools] teaches us that well-trained managers can manage anything. It seeks a detached, analytical justification for all decisions. It is right enough to be dangerously wrong, and it has arguably led us seriously astray."[6]

■ A sense of caring is the foundation of human relations success.

Indeed, it is the sense of caring about others that forms the foundation of human relations and organizational success. Buck Rodgers, former vice-president of marketing for IBM Corporation, describes this as "the blue that binds." He states that "the important thing [for effective organizations] is to get all your people, particularly the behind-the-scenes ones, involved in working with the customer and developing a partnership relationship."[7]

▼ A WORKING DESCRIPTION OF HUMAN RELATIONS

When relationships are healthy, open, fun and mutually rewarding, they enhance our lives.

So, what is this field of human relations in organizations? A sterile definition would satisfy few people, but some common characteristics are generally agreed upon.

First, human relations is a body of study that has deep roots. The need to better gain cooperation of others has been present ever since the first human sought to do a job that was too big to do alone.

Second, human relations has evolved as an area of study. A breakthrough came when managers and scholars realized that people are not like machines or interchangeable parts. Some other factors besides the laws of physics affect people at work.

Third, we now see human relations as an ever-evolving field of study involving virtually all aspects of human behavior, mental and physical. As the nature of work changes (e.g., from mostly physical to more "knowledge" work), new understandings about the nature of people at work must be considered.

Finally, the root values underlying the study of human relations are *caring* and *trust.* The self-centered person will never master human relations. The successful human relations manager knows that we win by helping other people win. We get what we want by showing others how to get what they want. All humanity is a part of a larger whole. And trust, cooperation, and mutual caring are critical elements in all success.

■ Relationships we create with others are the treasures of life.

Ultimately, the relationships we create and maintain with others, whether at work or in our personal lives, are the treasures of our lives; the jewels of living. As Elwood Chapman says, "When relationships are healthy, open, fun, and mutually rewarding they can enrich your life far beyond material possessions. Good relationships will sustain you in hard times."

Chapman goes on to caution that "interpersonal human dealings are fragile and demand tender loving care. Even when they seem strong, they can never be taken for granted. Those who become skillful at creating and maintaining on-going positive relationships enjoy more successful careers and happier personal lives. We sometimes refer to these individuals as being 'human relations smart.'"[8]

People at Work can help you become human relations smart. We encourage you to undertake the journey with an open mind and a happy heart. We think you'll enjoy the experience.

▼ SUMMARY OF KEY IDEAS

- Human relations is much more than a department or separate function of an organization.
- An organization's personality—culture—is determined by its policies and behaviors in human relations.
- Even with increasing emphasis on technology, the importance of understanding human behavior has never diminished.
- People in organizations were not always valued as much as they are today. The scientific management approach, for example, tended to take a rational, analytical look at industry. People were seen as physical parts of the overall machinery.
- Elton Mayo's Hawthorne experiments revealed the importance of understanding the human element in a broader sense: socially, psychologically, and physically.
- Modern management approaches, such as QWL and self-managing teams, require ever-increasing human relations skills.
- On a personal level, human relations skills can make the difference between success and failure in all we do.
- The object of this book is to help make you human relations-smart.
- The underlying value in human relations is a sense of caring about others. Self-centered people find it more difficult to become human relations smart.

▼ KEY TERMS, CONCEPTS AND NAMES

Caring	Ripple effects
Hawthorne experiments	QWL
Human relations smart	Self-Managing team

Elton Mayo
Scientific management
Systems theory

Contingency approach
Quality circles

▼ NOTES

1. Elwood N. Chapman, *Winning at Human Relations* (Los Altos, Calif.: Crisp Publications, 1989), p. 2.

2. Adapted from Howard M. Carlisle, *Management Essentials* (Chicago: Science Research Associates, 1989).

3. This example is adapted from Paul R. Timm, *Supervision,* 2d ed., (St. Paul: West Publishing 1992), pp. 30–31.

4. Robert F. Hicks and Diane Bone, *Self-Management Teams* (Los Altos, Calif: Crisp Publications, 1990), p. 5.

5. Allan Bloom, *The Closing of the American Mind* (New York: Simon and Schuster, 1987), p. 83.

6. Thomas J. Peters and Robert H. Waterman, Jr., *In Search of Excellence: Lessons from America's Best-Run Companies* (New York: Harper and Row, 1982), p. 29.

7. Buck Rodgers, *The IBM Way* (New York: Harper and Row, 1986), p. 58.

8. Chapman, *Winning at Human Relations,* p. iii.

ANOTHER LOOK: IF YOU CARE ENOUGH

Cynics suggest that people don't care as much as they once did. Others say that people care too much (especially about themselves). To complicate the matter, even social scientists admit that there are a lot of unanswered questions related to simple caring. For instance: How do we learn it? When do we show it? Who are the caregivers? Does it apply to big business? Can caring be taught? And most important of all, what is it?

Some define care as the necessary ingredient that unites families and personal relationships, guaranteeing both friendships and quality work. It is the emotional fabric which allows individuals to get along, to relate, and to help each other. Simply put, care is any positive, personal attention designed to protect and to promote one's self, another person, or a thing. Without it, emotional and physical growth suffer; with it, one can move mountains.

Everyone has people and things that they care about. Whether it's stuffed animals or pets, people or products, caring attachments develop.

Gail Melson, Ph.D., [a] professor ... at Purdue University, and one of the experts in the field, has been studying care since the early 1980s. When asked how her interest began, Dr. Melson says, "That's a little hard for me to answer. I've always been interested in what determines successful and effective parenting, and I

began to think about what childhood experiences are related to care. Clearly, there are many influences on what makes an effective caregiver, and how children learn to care is a neglected area."

To better understand the overall psychology of care, Melson adds, "We look at children and their lives to study caring for others. For example, a child's behavior around a younger brother or sister or watching a child encounter a baby in a waiting room or grocery store. You can see caring involvement."

Melson's findings are provocative. In one of her studies, she simply watched 71 preschool boys and girls. One by one, each child was led into a playroom where a six-to-eight-month-old infant was either seated in a chair or on the floor. The baby's mother was off to the side, reading. Other than saying, "hello," the mother was instructed not to interact with the children. It did not take long for the children to interact with each other.

The children soon started looking at the baby. About one-third of the children came close, smiled, and offered the baby a toy. Half of the children got down face-to-face with the infant. About 15 percent actually touched the baby. The most important finding came when comparing the reactions of boys and girls.

According to Melson, "Surprisingly, there were no differences between boys and girls in how much they looked at, touched, or interacted with the baby. Prior to age five, little boys and girls are equally interested in babies and their care. They begin to diverge around that age. Boys decrease in their interest; girls maintain the same or increased interest. This finding holds through adolescence into adulthood."

Do males and females differ in this ability to care? Yes. But it is believed that current social changes will require everyone to assume a role as caretaker. Children require care outside the home, and people are living longer. Moreover, enlightened businesses are beginning to realize that there must be a symbiotic care relationship between employer and employee. Without it, productivity suffers. As a result, a 21st Century trend is evident. More and more people of both genders will be required to care for others. To learn how, people must care to learn.

Melson defines care as "fostering the development of another." Jack Beasley, Ph.D., ... [a] professor ... at Georgia Southern College (Statesboro), agrees and takes it a step further. He says, "The ability to care is also associated with one's willingness to see—or want to see, for that matter—another person's point of view or needs and act accordingly."

ANOTHER LOOK *continued*

Beasley, also a corporate consultant on this and other family issues, believes that caring is a skill. As he says, "Learning how to care is a life-long process. Even if you didn't experience caring in childhood, you can learn how to care in adulthood. In fact, many of the techniques associated with childhood caring maximize productivity and improve relations." If you want to better care for the people or pets you love, no matter the environment, he offers the following techniques.

(1) Provide individuals with opportunities where they can practice caring. One way children learn how is by taking care of pets. Another is by tending seeds in a garden, or perhaps taking care of an elderly relative. Assigning or taking on business projects (even protégés) requires much the same nurturing as new-seed growth. Practicing care is also one form of cooperation which reduces competition and increases positive good-will.

(2) Role-model caring. As Beasley puts it, "It is important that everyone see both men and women as role models of sensitive caring. Show your care. By doing so, you say to them, 'It's okay to care.' Often, what you are, what you model, what you do, speaks so loudly that people do not even hear what you're saying. Of course, telling people what you care about indirectly gives them permission to recipro-

cate and tell you what they care about. Not only is it important for children to see both parents as nurturing, it is equally important for employees to see their supervisors as caring."

(3) Do not smother. When children are learning how to interact with babies, they often engage in inappropriate smothering, picking up the baby, playing with the child as if he or she were a doll. They have the idea of caring, but have no concept of hurting the young child. Beasley reminds that "part of caring is knowing when to 'hold back.' Give what is appropriate to the care and need of the individual, but don't overkill. Don't do for someone what they can do for themselves. If you do too much, the individual will devalue both you and their own abilities."

(4) Care enough to allow people to learn from logical consequence. Beasley takes the previous point a step further and suggests, "It's like 'tough care.' Both adults and children need to be allowed to experience natural and logical consequence. You can tell people what will happen, but occasionally they have to experience it to believe it. Care enough to let them experience it, but step in when appropriate to minimize the hurt."

(5) Keep your needs in check. It is important to care for people, but when one does it for one's own gain, then care turns to selfishness. Beasley

believes, "Care is a by-product of self-esteem. Individuals who are content with themselves and their abilities don't have as much to prove as someone who is struggling to determine who they are and what they stand for. One way to foster the development of another and keep your own needs in check is to give them the encouragement to enhance their own abilities. Then they can take all the credit."

6. Finally, care for yourself. Beasley says, "Caring for yourself is not selfish. As trite as it sounds, you can't show your care for others if you don't care for yourself."

REFERENCES

Beasley, J.J., & Flynn, T. An experimental study of the effects of competition on the self-concept. (Winter 1980). *Adolescence,* 15, 799–806.

Melson, G.F., & Fogel, A. Learning to Care. (January, 1988). *Psychology Today,* 22, 39–45.

Shafii, T. The prevalence and use of transitional objects: A study of 230 adolescents. (November 1986). *Journal of the American Academy of Child Psychiatry,* 25, 805–808.

SOURCE: Perry W. Buffington, Ph.D. Adapted from *SKY* (May 1989), pp. 79–84. This article has been reprinted/republished through the courtesy of Halsey Publishing Co., publishers of Delta Airlines' *SKY* magazine.

▼ A CASE IN POINT: MEETING THE STANDARD

Custom Canvas Products makes awnings, hammocks and lawn furniture for distribution throughout the Sun Belt states. The company name arose from the special service it provides: customers can request customized canvas products of all sorts. Special orders are the norm.

Because of these special orders, Custom has been unwilling to automate—to purchase machines to make their products. Instead, most work is done with hand tools.

In one section of the plant, a crew of nine workers use a hand-held machine to attach metal eyelets to the canvas so that the material does not tear when hung. Frank Bixby is supervisor over this work team and is a part owner in the company. To maximize productivity, Frank recently had a consultant do a time-and-motion study to determine how many eyelets each worker should be able to install per day. The expert reported that the "standard" (the ideal number of installations per day) should be 5,312 eyelets.

The problem is that the workers are actually installing only 4,000 to 4,600 eyelets per day.

After careful observation, Frank suspects that his workers are deliberately working below the standard. He suspects that the work group has established its own productivity standard. He has also noted that people who tended to work faster than the group pace were subject to ridicule, sarcasm, and other harassment by co-workers. On one occasion, a newer employee came to Frank to report that he'd been told outright to slow down or he may have an unfortunate "accident."

But people who worked slower than the norm were also pressured by the group to increase production.

On days when the group's production was high, they would report lower figures and slow down the next day so as to smooth out the production run. Frank doesn't know exactly what to do. The standard doesn't seem unreasonable and every day the workers fall below it the company risks losing customers.

QUESTIONS

1. Why do you think the group is restricting production?
2. How would the scientific management expert deal with this problem?
3. How would a human relations expert look at the issue?
4. How do the workers demonstrate their caring for each other?
5. What is the dilemma between people and productivity?

SOURCE: Reprinted by permission from pages 36–37 of *Supervision* (2d ed.) by Paul R. Timm. Copyright © 1992 by West Publishing Co. All rights reserved.

THE RESOURCE: PEOPLE

CHAPTER

2

HUMAN PERCEPTION AND HUMAN RELATIONS

This chapter answers several all-important questions:

■ What is human perception?

■ What is the impact of human perception on people relationships?

■ How does the perception/truth fallacy cause problems in human relations?

■ What is perpetual expectancy?

■ Why do fellow employees see the same situation in different ways?

■ How can we help ourselves avoid the pitfalls of seeing situations inaccurately?

■ How can awareness of differences in interpretation help us be more effective in dealing with others?

The answer to these and other questions are coming up next in chapter 2 ....

CHAPTER 2

Source: 1960 United Features Syndicte, Inc.

What is going on in the Peanuts cartoon? What do three little kids studying the clouds have to do with human relations? Well, when those kids are from the Peanuts gang, you can bet there's a message in what they say. And that message serves to introduce the topic of this chapter: human perception.

When we look at the clouds, we tend to be much like Linus and Charlie Brown. What we see reflects our experiences, our expectations, and our interests. No two people see the clouds (or, for that matter, any other object or idea) in exactly the same way. We perceive—that is, we make sense out of things—according to our own points of view.

These different points of view can often cause trouble in human relations. Organizations provide many examples of some employees seeing a problem as a ducky and others seeing it as a map of the Caribbean.

■ This chapter seems to help us overcome problems of perception.

The purpose of this chapter is twofold: (1) to help us be more aware of the problems associated with the unique ways we each see the world and (2) to help us effectively deal with such problems. It is hoped that we will be better employees and more efficient members of society by becoming aware of such differences.

▼ THE PERCEPTION/TRUTH FALLACY

Perception is the process of becoming aware of objects and other data through the medium of the senses. It is from our perceptions that we gain knowledge. The quality of that knowledge varies with the accuracy of our perceptions.

People have a strong tendency to believe that the way they see the world is closer to "the truth" than the way others see it. We tend to assume that people who see things differently from the way we do are wrong. This assumption leads frequently to misunderstandings and occasionally to major conflicts. One rule to keep in mind when dealing with people is this: *Do not accept all situations at their face value. The truth and what we see may not be the same.*

We usually see only the things we are looking for—so much that we sometimes see them where they are not.
Eric Hoffer

Avoid assuming that you always see things accurately while assuming that others are more often wrong. The problem is that the things or events we perceive—accurately or not—become reality for us. We then act on these "truths" as we deal with other people.

Here's an example. Suppose you walk into the machine shop of a small company. Three people are there. One person is sitting next to a machine, leaning against the wall. Another employee is fixing a child's bicycle. The third person is talking on the phone to someone he addresses as "Honey." It is 9:30 A.M. on a Tuesday. What do your immediate impressions tell you about this scene?

"A bunch of goof-offs," you say. "I'll bet their supervisor is away. I'd probably fire them if they worked for me!"

Perhaps your perceptions are accurate. But if you act on this picture of "reality" without further investigation, you could be making a big mistake.

■ Misperceptions can lead to big mistakes.

Here is what was really happening in that machine shop. The first employee had worked all night to get out a rush order. He hadn't slept in over twenty-six hours, and he was taking a fifteen-minute break. The man on the phone had also been at work through the night. This was the first chance he'd had to call his wife to see how their sick four-year-old daughter was responding to new medication. The third worker was taking time on her day off to work on the company-sponsored "Toys for Poor Kids" Christmas project.

Does that change your perceptions of this scene a bit? What might have happened if you had just been appointed as a new supervisor and you'd ordered everyone "back to work"?

The point is this: *Don't take initial perceptions at face value.* Get as much information as possible before you firm up perceptions into opinions that influence your actions. A good way to avoid such misperceptions is to better understand how the perception process works. We'll examine this process more closely now.

▼ PERCEPTUAL EXPECTANCY

Magicians use it to fake us out. Teachers and other professional communicators use it to preview the message they'll give us.

ACTIVITY: THE WAY IN WHICH A PERSON VIEWS AN EVENT DETERMINES HOW HE OR SHE REACTS TO IT

How do you react to some everyday situations? How intense are your feelings about some typical events? Read each of the short incidents described below and select the word that best describes what you would imagine your first reaction would be. Write the word in the space provided. You may use the same word more than once. Do not make an in-depth analysis of the situation; just read it quickly and give your first impression.

1. alarm	12. happiness
2. anger	13. humiliation
3. concern	14. interest
4. curiosity	15. irritation
5. disapproval	16. joy
6. disinterest	17. kindness
7. envy	18. love
8. excitement	19. resentment
9. fear	20. sadness
10. gladness	21. worry
11. gratitude	

I. While riding the subway, you see a man with three small boys ranging in ages from about two to six. The boys run up and down the aisles, yelling and screaming. The father sits totally oblivious of the behavior of his kids.

_____

II. You are heading home after a hard day's work. You are passed on the freeway by a couple driving a car similar to yours. They are obviously close to each other; in fact, you wonder if he can safely drive the car while she tousles his hair and nibbles his earlobes.

_____

III. While attending the company's family picnic, you overhear a child saying to his parent: "I hate you! You are so mean to me! I hate the way you treat me!"

_____

IV. At lunch time you decide to walk a few blocks for a quick sandwich. As you are crossing the street at a busy intersection, a car races through the intersection, apparently trying to beat the red light.

The car comes so close that you literally jump out of the way to avoid being hit.

_____

V. You are on a committee for your service club to interview and select a citizen of the year. During the interviews of candidates, you are informed that a real hero has been nominated and will arrive for an interview shortly. He saved a drowning child last summer and donated the reward money to create a CPR training program for youth leaders. He is kind and courteous.

_____

Before considering your first responses, we'd like you to react to the incidents again, but from a slightly different point of view. Do the same as you did before: read the vignette and select the word that best describes what you think your first response would be. Use the list of words from the preceding page, writing the appropriate word in the space provided. Feel free to use the same words more than once.

I. While riding the subway, you see a man with three small boys ranging in ages from about two to six. The boys run up and down the aisles, yelling and screaming. The father sits totally oblivious of the behavior of his kids. They are on the way home from the hospital where his wife died after weeks of suffering from cancer.

_____

II. You are heading home after a hard day's work. You are passed on the freeway by a couple driving a car similar to yours. They are obviously close to each other; in fact, you wonder if he can safely drive the car while she tousles his hair and nibbles his earlobes. The passenger is your spouse, and it is your car.

_____

III. While attending the company's family picnic, you overhear a child saying to his parent: "I hate you! You are so mean to me! I hate the way you treat me!" The

ACTIVITY *continued*

child is your son, speaking to your spouse.

_____

IV. At lunch time you decide to walk a few blocks for a quick sandwich. As you are crossing the street at a busy intersection, a car races through the intersection, apparently trying to beat the red light. The car comes so close that you literally jump out of the way to avoid being hit. The driver is your eighty-year-old mother, who recently had an eye operation.

_____

V. You are on a committee for your service club to interview and select a citizen of the year. During the interviews of candidates, you are informed that a real hero has been nominated and will arrive for an interview shortly. He saved a drowning child last summer and donated the reward money to create a CPR training program for youth leaders. He is kind and courteous, but he was accused of sexually molesting your child, although evidence at the trial was insufficient to convict him.

_____

Advertisers use it to lure us into the new-car showroom. What is "it"? It's *perceptual expectation,* the mental anticipation so natural to our everyday actions. We constantly make mental guesses about how people, events, or things will be. Sometimes we are right. Other times we are wrong. And sometimes we are deliberately misled.

Perceptual expectations create a mental set in us that causes us to anticipate future behaviors or events. For example, the new manager in a clothing company was described to her employees as very energetic, very autocratic, out to make money, cold, and standoffish. As you may suspect, the people who were going to be managed by this person felt some anxiety. Their perceptual expectancy was that they were going to have a new leader that would be pretty difficult to work for.

But when the new manager took over, her demeanor, behavior, and treatment of the employees were exactly the opposite of their expectations. The workers were, at first, a little uncomfortable. Their expectations were *not* being met. "When is she going to get mean?" they wondered.

After getting to know the "truth" about this manager, the work group became very close and the organization functioned well. Fortunately, in this case, the negative expectations evaporated as the workers got to know the *real* new manager. But in many circumstances where workers have strong expectations about a new boss, barriers to communication and relationships can be difficult to overcome. The organization and the people involved suffer.

The expectancies we have as a result of our perceptions influence the way we get along with others and the way we respond to them. This is the problem we face with perception.

■ Our mental set causes us to anticipate future behaviors or events.

The following diagrams illustrate the concept of perceptional expectancy:

Does the diagram represent a spiral? We expect it does—but, does it?

Which person is the tallest? What were your initial expectations?

■ To perceive is to attach meaning to experience.

■ Four key elements of the perception process are :
selection
motives
organization
interpretation

▼ A SIMPLE READING EXERCISE

The triangles below contain some common sayings. Read them aloud.

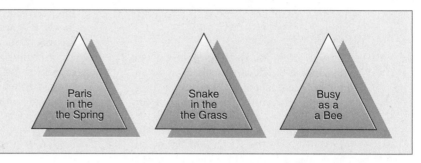

Now look at them carefully. In the first statement, you should have read, "Paris in *the the* spring." In the second statement, you should have read, "Snake in *the the* grass." In the third statement you should have read, "Busy as *a a* bee." If you did not read these statements accurately, you did not perceive the information correctly. If you misread the statements, your previous experience likely led you to expect to see only one *the* or *a*.

One way to reduce the number of mistaken perceptions is to become more aware of just how perception works.

▼ KEY ELEMENTS OF THE PERCEPTION PROCESS

We said earlier that to perceive is to make sense out of things. Another way to describe perception is as a process of *attaching meaning to experience.* As we experience raw data through seeing, hearing, feeling, tasting, smelling, and the like, we mentally organize these sensations into something that has meaning for us.

For example, let's say you are walking down a busy city sidewalk and see a crowd of people assembled near an intersection. As you get closer, you hear unusual sounds—the rhythm of steel drums. Eventually you assemble these sights and sounds and attach meaning: A street band is playing Jamaican music—an advertising gimmick for a travel agency.

First you pay attention to raw information: sights and sounds. Then you mentally organize these impressions into a meaningful event and label it "Jamaican street band." That's perception.

The perception process has four key elements: selection, motives, organization, and interpretation. Let's look at each of these.

1. **Selection.** As we interact with people, we are constantly exposed to a barrage of meanings and innuendos. In fact, we become over-exposed. We receive too much data to deal with. We select only

Perception is the process of attaching meaning to sights, sounds, and other stimuli.

What do you see? A young woman? A grouchy old clown? Turn the book upside down and then respond again.

■ Intensity increases the probability of selection.

key information from all the raw data. We select what seems important to *us*. Why do some messages seem more important than others? Intensity and repetition cause people to be attracted to some messages while they ignore others.

The more *intense* a message, the higher the probability that we will attend to it. For example, at a cocktail party, the more boisterous and outgoing people have a greater probability of being heard. You may think a loud person is obnoxious or you may enjoy his or her antics, depending on your feelings toward the person. In either case, the probability is high that owing to the intensity of the person's actions, you will pay attention to him or her.

People often pay more attention to an exceptionally tall or unusually short person than to a person of average size. Furthermore, the person with the loud Hawaiian shirt is difficult to forget—especially when the other partygoers are in business suits! Simply said, intensity of the message in our environment has a direct impact on whether we perceive the message or not.

The rhythm of the steel drum music in the earlier example, as well as the unusually large number of people assembled, made

PERSONNEL HAS ASKED US TO LOOK AT THIS SLIDE PRESENTATION ABOUT ALL THE CHANGES IN EMPLOYEE BENEFITS...

UH-OH... THE PERFESSER'S FIRST LAW OF SLIDE PRESENTATIONS:

"THE MORE COLOR IN THE GRAPHICS—THE WORSE THE NEWS."

■ Repetition increases the chance of selection.

you select this event for further investigation.

Just as people are attracted to a stimulus that is intense, people are also attracted to a stimulus *that is repetitious, that is repetitious, that is repetitious.* If we listen to a recording on a record player and a groove is out of line, the record player continues to play the same message over and over again. We are very quickly attracted to the sound; we want to correct it before it drives us nuts!

Have you ever tried to block out of your mind the drip of a leaky faucet at night? Its maddening repetition holds your attention whether you want it to or not.

■ Our motives can cause us to perceive one thing while ignoring others.

2. **Motives.** Why do people do the things they do? We'll talk a lot more about this subject in the next five chapters. For now, it is enough to say that personal motives—wants, interests, and desires—affect perceptions.

One young man had been driving across the country and was very hungry. On passing through a small town, he saw the sign over a Dairy Queen ice cream stand ahead. Licking his chops, he drove up and jumped eagerly out of the car, only to discover that the sign actually said Dry Cleaner. His motive—to satisfy hunger—had led to a *mis*perception.

Similarly, if you had just been in a serious automobile accident, you would be likely to perceive the white-jacketed paramedic rushing to your aid as a fine person. Yet if you were not motivated by a need for medical help and you saw this same individual in a restaurant or shop, your perception might be totally different: "That person looks like a weirdo to me." Same person—different perceptions.

Our motives affect the ways we perceive.

■ Perceptions make sense as we organize them.

3. **Organization.** A perception is almost never of a single bit of raw data. Even the faucet dripping in the night is not taken alone. The *context* in which it occurs—late at night, you're trying to sleep, there are no other sounds in the house, you need to be alert in the morning for a big exam, and so on—adds to your awareness of the drip (and, in this case, the annoyance of it).

Likewise, the street band example begins to make sense as you put together in your mind the various perceptions: a large crowd, unusual music, and travel agency motive.

As we interact with people, we often organize our perceptions of them according to variables such as physical attractiveness, age, educational background, religion, and race. How much better might human relationships be if we did not organize people into groupings in this way? Once people are categorized in our minds, these perceptions can have wide-ranging effects on how we deal with people.

■ Interpretation adds further meaning to perceptions.

4. **Interpretation.** Once we select and organize perceptions, we draw further conclusions about their meaning through *interpretation.*

Consider this example: A new and very attractive employee smiles at you. You are faced with a task of interpreting that smile.

What does it mean? Is the smile out of politeness? Is the smile an indication of a romantic interest? Is the smile directed at the crazy sweatshirt you are wearing? Interpretation deals with the meaning you make of the smile.

Ron Adler and Neal Towne present a variety of factors that affect the way people interpret messages:[1]

■ *Past experience.* What meanings have similar events held? If, for example, you've been gouged by landlords in the past, you might be skeptical about an apartment manager's assurances that careful housekeeping will ensure the refund of your cleaning deposit.

■ *Assumptions about human behavior.* "People generally do as little work as possible to get by." "In spite of their mistakes, people are doing the best they can." Beliefs such as these will shape the way a person interprets another's actions.

■ *Expectations.* Anticipation shapes interpretations. If you imagine that your boss is unhappy with your work, you'll probably feel threatened by a request to "see me in my office first thing Monday morning." However, if you imagine that your work is especially good, your weekend will probably be a pleasant one as you anticipate a reward from the boss.

■ *Knowledge.* If you know that a friend has been jilted by a lover or had a disagreement with a friend, you'll interpret his or her aloof behavior differently from the way you would if you were unaware of what had happened. If you know that an instructor speaks sarcastically to all students, then you won't be as likely to take his or her remarks personally.

■ *Personal moods.* When you're feeling insecure, the world is a very different place than it is when you're confident. The same goes for happiness or sadness, anger or bliss, or any other opposing moods.

> ■ Other factors affect the way we interpret perceptions:
> Experience
> Assumptions
> Expectations
> Knowledge
> Moods

▼ OTHER FACTORS THAT SHADE THE FILTERS OF OUR MINDS

In addition to the four key elements that affect perception (selection, motives, organization, and interpretation), other factors have also helped make us all unique individuals who perceive things differently. These personality influencers color the lenses of the "glasses" through which we see the world. Among them are heredity, environment, friendships and peers, and sensory organs.

> ■ A few other factors that influence our view of the world:
> Heredity
> Environment
> Friendships and peers
> Sensory organs

Heredity

Heredity plays a fairly important role in the way we see our world. We have little opportunity to choose our parents, our grandparents, or the families we come from. But our genes have a tremendous

SOURCE: Reprinted with special permission of King Features Syndicate, Inc. © King Features Syndicate, Inc. World rights reserved.

impact on whether we are able to see with twenty-twenty vision, for example, whether we have hearing defects, whether we are color blind, or whether we are left-handed or right-handed.

It's hard to understand how the world looks to other people who have been endowed with other physical characteristics.

Environment

The environment in which people grow up directly affects how they see present situations. If you have grown up in a home where Mom and Dad are heavily involved in physical fitness and jogging, you are likely to see nonjoggers as people who do not care about their bodies and who tend to be overweight. If you grew up in a small farming community, the way you see people who live in a large city is different from the way you see those who grew up as you did.

Some neighborhoods have a very pleasant feeling of community, of neighbors who care for each other. Some neighborhoods are marred by violent gangs, and people who live there constantly feel afraid to go outside. Our assumptions about people are likely to be very different depending on our home environment.

Friendships and Peers

People tend to see life in much the same way their peers would like them to see life. In fact, a variety of studies have been done on the impact that peers have on their friends. The studies show that once a peer group has made a decision or taken a stand—even if that decision or stand is wrong—individual group members will frequently go along. This tendency to go along will depend on the strength of the group and the individual's desire to be a member of it.

Young people are particularly susceptible to peer-group pressures. Junior high schools are filled with kids who act, dress, and even think as they do primarily because of peer pressures.

Sensory Organs

Taste buds cause some people to love the taste of liver, while others dislike it.* Some people enjoy the taste of wine or liquor, while others dislike it immensely. Taste buds affect perception.

Likewise, a variety of smells affect us. A fragrance that is pleasant to one person may be unpleasant to another person.

Smell, taste, tolerance for temperature changes, and tolerance for loud noises are examples of sensory differences. These, too, affect perceptions.

SOURCE: Reprinted with special permission of King Features Syndicate, Inc.

*It was six men of
    Indostan
  to learning much
    inclined,
Who went to see the
    elephant
  Though all of them
    were blind
That each by observa-
    tion
  Might satisfy his
    mind.*

*The first approached
    the elephant
  And, happening to
    fall
Against the broad and
    sturdy side,
  At once began to
    bawl;
"Why, bless me! But the
    elephant
  Is very like a wall!"*

*The second, feeling of
    the tusk,
  Cried: "Ho! What
    have we here
So very round and
    smoother and
    sharp?
  To me, 'tis very
    clear,
This wonder of an ele-
    phant
  Is very like a spear!"*

*The third approached
    the animal,
  And, happening to
    take
The squirming trunk
    within his hands
  Thus boldly up he
    spake:
"I see," quoth he, "the
    elephant
  Is very like a snake!"*

▼ A Summary: Six Blind Men and One Elephant

Our experience in teaching and training has taught us that the best way to help people deal with the problems of perception is to make them aware of the process and elements of perception. We hope that as you have read this chapter, you have had an opportunity to reflect on your own life and on the various problems that you have had in perceiving the environment in which you live and work.

The well-known parable about six blind men who came to check out an elephant brings to a close our discussion of perception.

▼ Summary of Key Ideas

- Our experiences, expectations, and interests influence what we see, and what we see may actually differ from the truth.
- Perceptual expectations occur when we see what we expect to see.
- The four key elements of the perceptual process include selection, motives, organization, and interpretation.
- The five primary factors that affect the way we interpret perceptions are experience, assumption, expectations, knowledge, and moods. Additional factors include heredity, friendship and peers, environment, and sensory organs.

▼ KEY TERMS, CONCEPTS, AND NAMES

Assumptions   Organization
Environment   Perception
Peer-group pressures   Perceptual expectancy
Interpretation   Perception/truth fallacy
Knowledge   Selection
Motives

▼ QUESTIONS AND EXERCISES

1. Look at the box with nine dots. With a pencil, connect the nine dots in the square, using four straight lines. Don't lift the pencil from the paper. Do not retrace any lines!

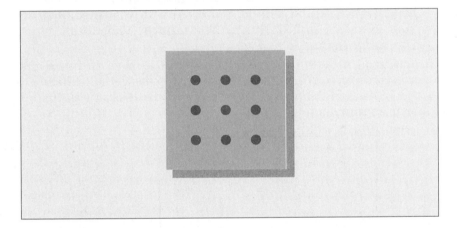

   Don't give up too quickly! Could you get it? If not, you may be having a perceptual problem. Your previous experience with the words used in our instructions may have influenced your expectations. We never said your lines needed to stay within the square, but you may have assumed that. Unless you go outside the square, you cannot complete the exercise. Look at the top of the next page to see how to complete the exercise.

2. Explain how your heredity, sensory organs, and past experience may influence your perceptions toward the following:

   Dogs   Company presidents
   Rhubarb   Retail clerks
   Advanced mathematics   Auto mechanics
   Middle-aged women   Hairdressers
   Democratic Party leaders   Fashion designers
   Snow   Textbook authors
   Jogging   Life
                                Death
                                Religion

The fourth reached out his eager hand
And felt about the knee:
"What most this wonderous beast is like
Is very plain," quoth he:
"Tis clear enough the elephant
Is very like a tree!"

The fifth who chanced to touch the ear
Said: "E'en the blindest man
Can tell what this resembles most—
Deny the fact who can:
This marvel of an elephant
Is very like a fan!"

The sixth no sooner had begun
About the beast to grope
Than, seizing on the swing tail
That fell within his scope,
"I see," quoth he, "the elephant
Is very like a rope!"

And so these men of Indostan
Disputed loud and long.
Each in his own opinion
Exceeding stiff and strong;
Though each was partly in the right,
And all were in the wrong.
John G. Saxe

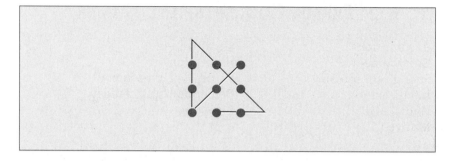

3. Using the same terms as in exercise 2, predict how a friend of yours may react to each. Then compare your guesses with how she or he really perceived these.

4. Repeat exercise 3 with a new acquaintance—perhaps someone you've recently met in class. How accurate were you? How much better (or worse) did you do, compared with your predictions of your friend's view? What does this result say about the role of knowledge in interpreting perceptions.

5. The man in the following cartoon seems to have an interesting self-perception. What motives might have caused the politician to see himself in this way? How would you be likely to respond to such an introduction?

"Hi! I'm a phony politician and a complete jerk. I hope you'll vote for me . . ."

Reprinted by Permission of Newspaper Enterprise Association, Inc.

6. Can you control your perceptions of events? Look at the figure below, then answer the following questions?
   A. What do you see when you interpret the figure as a cooking utensil?
      Answer: _____
   B. What do you see when you interpret the figure as a weapon of war?
      Answer: _____
   C. What do you see when you interpret the figure as a person?
      Answer: _____
   D. What do you see when you interpret the figure as an animal?
      Answer: _____

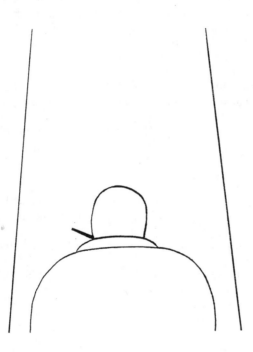

7. Answer the introductory questions at the beginning of this chapter.

 # NOTES

1. Adapted from *Looking Out/Looking In,* 3d ed., by Ronald B. Adler and Neal Towne. Copyright © by Holt, Rinehart and Winston, Inc., reprinted by permission of the publisher. For further ideas on how perception can affect work relationships, see Judith Jaffe, "Of Different Minds," *Association Management,* October 1985, pp. 120–24.

▼ A CASE IN POINT: LEMKIRK TRAINS NEW EMPLOYEES

Harvey Lemkirk, a manufacturing plant foreman, was asked to teach a new employee how to work a machine. The new worker was a young man, a member of a minority race, who had been hired under a special program intended to train difficult-to-employ people.

Lemkirk, who did not sympathize with such special hiring programs, begrudgingly took the young man to the machine and instructed him how to run it: "Each time this metal part comes down this assembly line here, you pull it off, stick it under the press so that the edges line up here, and then push this foot pedal so the drill bit will come down and put the hole in the right place. Be careful to keep your hands away from the drill bit when you are doing it. Any moron should be able to do this. Got any questions?"

"No, sir," replied the new worker.

"Okay, then, go to it. And good luck. If you have any problems, let me know."

In the foreman's mind, there was little likelihood this employee would develop into a particularly effective worker. He had seen many minority employees hired under affirmative action who simply couldn't seem to cut it. And, frankly, he didn't understand exactly why it was like this. He treated them the same as anyone else. In fact, he made it a point to use exactly the same language to explain this simple procedure to all new employees.

In a few days, Lemkirk's new employee fell seriously behind on both the quantity and quality of his work. Lemkirk was not surprised.

Let's look at how things worked for a second worker trained by Lemkirk:

The second new employee, a young man who Lemkirk seemed to think looked pretty sharp, was given essentially the same verbal instructions as the first worker. This new man, perhaps sensing that the foreman seemed to like him, took the "any moron should be able to do this" comment in stride and asked for a few clarifying pointers, which he got. Soon he was on his way to meeting his production quota just like the old pros who had been there for some time.

QUESTIONS

1. How did the perceptions of both Lemkirk and the first new employee influence the outcome of this situation?
2. How could either man change the situation?
3. How did perceptions affect the outcome for the second worker?
4. What perceptions were different?

A CASE IN POINT: "I JUST GOOFED" OR "WE ALL SAW WHAT WE WANTED TO SEE"

NEWS ITEM, HOUSTON. A short circuit fought off more than 60 police officers along the Houston ship channel before it was finally subdued. Uniformed and plain clothes officers spent the predawn hours chasing what they thought was someone peppering them with gunfire from atop one of the tanks. One officer said he had been shot in the heel of the shoe. Another graphically described slugs slamming into a road paved with oyster shells. Police threw themselves to the ground with each loud crack.

Fire trucks stood ready, and police lobbed tear gas bombs into spots where they thought a sniper was hiding. In the first light of dawn, two sheriff's deputies and four journalists came upon the culprit—a one-inch piece of pipe. The "shots" were nothing more than the popping noise produced by water dripping through an opening into a conduit pipe, seeping through insulation tape, and shorting out a piece of No. 8 electrical wire. "I just goofed," said the electrician who was called to silence the wire.

The personnel and equipment used to hunt down the "sniper" cost Harris County and the city of Houston an estimated $3,000.

QUESTIONS

1. What appears to be the main problem in this incident? What should have been done to alleviate this problem?
2. What principles of perception were at play in this situation? List as many as you can.
3. How does this type of incident relate to you in your work and in your relations with others?

SOURCE: Excerpted from *The Human Side of Organizations,* by Stan Kossen. Copyright © 1978 by the author. Reprinted by permission of Harper & Row, Publishers, Inc.

CHAPTER

3

HUMAN NEEDS AND MOTIVATION: WHAT MOTIVATES PEOPLE AT WORK?

This chapter answers several all-important questions:

- What is motivation and how can managers help people become and remain motivated?

- What does the organization achieve by getting its members to be motivated?

- What is motivation?

- What motivates *you*?

- Are there many different kinds of needs? Which ones motivate people best?

- How do people's expectations affect motivation?

- How does the hierarchy of needs affect the way people behave, according to Maslow?

- What emerging motivators seem to be present more strongly in the 1990s?

The answer to these and other questions are coming up next in chapter 3 ....

■ Can you become an
expert motivator?

Some people have an oversimplified notion of what will motivate workers. They feel that by giving people extra wages, productivity will automatically increase. They are also convinced that paying special attention to workers or watching the workers more closely will result in more motivated employees. Although any of these techniques may work in certain circumstances, none of them is a blanket solution.

In reality, motivation is a highly personal matter, and the influence a manager can have on someone else's motivation is quite limited. This chapter will explain some fundamentals of the motivating process.

Can a manager *really* bring about long-lasting motivation in workers? Before you answer yes, no, or maybe, take a careful look at the material in this chapter. You'll find a number of ideas about the nature of motivation and techniques for using the motives of others to get work done.

Can you become an expert motivator after reading this? Probably not. But you are likely to become more aware of what it takes to motivate. The best preparation for motivating others is like training in the art of painting: Get acquainted with the range of available techniques, train your judgment, experiment, and learn from the results.

▼ Why Motivation Is the Manager's Challenge

One of the things that makes it so difficult for managers to motivate others is the fact that *motivation itself is not visible or measurable.* What we can measure is human behavior (productivity, quality of work, absenteeism, etc.). Motivation itself is a mental process. It is unique to every individual and extremely complex.

Whether or not motivation is taking place must be *inferred* from behaviors that are observed. Specifically, if you see a particular behavior taking place, you can make guesses about why the employee is acting that way.

Sometimes the relationship between the motivation and the behavior is pretty clear. For example, if you see a person leave the office and go to the company cafeteria for lunch (that's the behavior observed), you can assume that the person is motivated by hunger. Of course, you cannot see hunger, but you can see the behavior of going to get some food. But even simple examples like this can be wrong. Maybe the worker goes to the cafeteria for social reasons—to talk with co-workers—even though he or she is not particularly hungry.

Therein lies the motivation problem. Understanding the motivation of employees and then doing something to affect that motivation are complicated by the fact that we cannot directly observe motivators. We can only observe behavior and from that behavior presume what motivates it.

The Best Indicators of Motivation

In most work situations, worker motivation (or lack of it) is expressed through behaviors, such as:

- Productivity—amount of work accomplished
- Quality of work
- Promptness
- Absenteeism
- Grievances expressed
- Accidents (as a result of carelessness)
- Turnover (number of workers quitting or fired)
- Agreement or disagreement among workers

Observing such behaviors, of course, may lead to errors of interpretation. We cannot always accurately identify specific motives from outcomes. For example, how can we know when a highly productive worker is being motivated by his or her pay or by some inner drive to be the fastest worker in the plant? The simple answer is that we can't know for sure. But understanding the nature of motivation can help us make more accurate guesses and probably be more effective at creating conditions that motivate people.

▼ A DEFINITION OF MOTIVATION

Motivation can be described as the **need** *or* **drive** *that incites a person to some action or behavior.* The verb *motivate* means to provide *reasons for action*. Motivation, then, provides a reason for exerting some sort of effort. This motivation spring forth from individual needs, wants, and drives. It provides a reason for behaving a certain way.

■ Motivation provides motives for action; reasons for exerting effort.

To motivate others involves a process of providing *motives for action*. Motivation, then, *provides a will to do or a reason for exerting some sort of effort.* This motivation springs from individual needs, wants, and drives.

We all constantly respond to needs, wants, and drives in our daily lives. When we first awake in the morning, we are likely to experience a need to satisfy hunger that has built up during the night. Most of us are motivated by wants such as career advancement, material goods, or pleasant relationships with others.

All *motivation,* then, *is directed toward some desired goal or reward.* We exert the effort to make breakfast because we anticipate the payoff: the satisfaction of our need for food. Likewise, we make certain efforts on the job because we anticipate the possibility of being rewarded with higher pay, status, praise, and the like. So, one key characteristic of motivation is that it is *goal-oriented*—it is motivation toward some desired end.

■ Motivation is directed toward some payoff.

Sometimes the desired payoff is the avoidance of something unpleasant. We step outside for some fresh air to escape the stuffy

office. Likewise, we may be motivated to seek a new job to reduce the stress we are experiencing in our present position.

In this way, our motives show up in our behavior. That is, when we are motivated, we *do* something that we might not do if we were not motivated. *Activity is the basic outcome of motivation.*

▼ WHAT MANAGERS MUST MOTIVATE PEOPLE TO DO

The manager's most important work is to motivate and direct human behavior. If there were no coordinated efforts of people seeking common goals, orchestrated by effective leadership, humanity would be doomed to accomplish no more than what could be done by one person, working alone.

At the heart of any enterprise lies member motivation. To succeed, the organization, through its leaders, must help its people to be motivated to do the following:

1. Join and remain active in the group.
2. Produce dependable behavior—that which fulfills their designated roles and contributes to the planned, organizational tasks.
3. Innovate and adapt to changing organizational needs, going beyond their role requirements.

Creating conditions under which these kinds of behavior can flourish is the job of the effective manager. These conditions determine the extent to which *motivation* will occur.

▼ UNDERSTANDING THE NATURE OF MOTIVATION

■ Understanding human motivation is a key to successful management.

Understanding the nature of human motivation is a key to successful management. Management is the process of getting productive work done with and through the efforts of other individuals. To do this effectively, the manager must answer this question: "What will motivate people to willingly and productively work toward organizational goals?" The manager must predict, with reasonable accuracy, the kinds of behavior that result when different motivators are present. To make these predictions, the manager needs to understand what *motives* or *needs* are more likely to evoke productive behaviors in individuals at a particular *time.*

The better you understand motivation, the better you will be able to predict behavior accurately. You will come to know that when you as a manger do certain things, you might expect certain responses from the people you are managing.

In this text, our focus is on behaviorism—an approach to psychology that assumes that observed behavior provides the only valid data of psychology. This approach studies what people *do* and infers from those actions what *caused* them to act that way.

The motivation of individual employees can be *influenced* but cannot be *controlled* by organizational leaders, especially over the long run. Managers who think they consistently have direct control on the motivation of others are probably being unrealistic. Managers can attempt to *influence individual motives,* but they cannot control the motivation of other people. The individual nature of people makes motivation complicated and often unpredictable.

■ Can managers really expect to directly affect the motivation of others?

One simple way to look at motivation suggests three emotions that can lead to behavior change:

■ Fear
■ Duty
■ Love

When motivated by fear, we behave because we *have* to. We are compelled to do something. Such motivation is short-lived.

When motivated by a sense of duty (or loyalty or obligation), we are responding because we *ought* to. For most people, this motivation is rather short-lived.

■ The motivation process is very complicated and unpredictable.

When we respond to the emotion of love, we act because we *want* to. The emotion of love provides for the strongest, most long-lasting motivation and behavior change—we do something because we truly love to do it.

▼ WHAT MOTIVATION IS NOT

We have discussed a number of things that motivation is. Now let's talk about some of the things that motivation is *not.* We have already suggested that *motivation is not totally susceptible to outside control,* such as that exerted by an employee's supervisor. Motivation comes from within the individual. So, the act of telling someone what to do or threatening someone is not, in itself, motivation.

■ Motivation comes from within; it is not just telling someone what to do.

Here are three more "nots" that apply to motivation:

1. *Motivation is not always based on conscious, "obvious" needs.*
   Some people are motivated by the darnedest things! Although we managers may feel that we're providing ample rewards for

employee behavior, in fact our efforts may not work. We cannot be sure that others will perceive the reward as worth the effort.

■ Why might some people *prefer* to fail?

2. *We are sometimes motivated by forces we are not even aware of.* In recent years, there has been much concern about the ways some advertisers are using *subliminal* or subconscious appeals to get people to buy their products. Careful examination of magazine ads reveals sexual symbolism and suggestive illustrations designed to "grab" your unconscious mind, thus getting the sales message across.

   Sometimes people do not care to admit subconscious motivations. A common example is the individual who has a low self-image and who *prefers* to fail or to do a poor job. By doing so, that individual reinforces his or her negative self-image. The effect is a somewhat perverse sense of satisfaction in realizing that "I was right about myself; I am a failure."

3. *Motivation is not the same as job satisfaction.* Some people are very satisfied on their jobs and yet are not motivated by the work. The manager who attempts to motivate employees by providing a more comfortable work environment, more friendly relationships between supervisors and employees, and even additional money may in fact be influencing job satisfaction, but not motivation. (The distinction between satisfiers and motivators is discussed in chapter 4). Employees may be satisfied but *not* motivated. Likewise, employees may be motivated but not satisfied.

Motivation, then is:

1. Not totally susceptible to a supervisor's control, especially since it takes different things to motivate even the same worker at different times;
2. Not always the same for all people; and
3. Not the same as job satisfaction.

One other "not" should be added to this list: *Motivation is not simple to understand or apply on the job.* It is far more complicated than it may appear at first glance. To use principles of motivation as a manager, one must become aware of some of the needs that motivate people at work.

Before you read on, complete the questionnaire entitled "Things That Motivate Me" on page 49. We'll get back to it later.

▼ NEEDS MOTIVATE, AND EVERYBODY NEEDS SOMETHING

All people have needs. And as noted earlier, those needs are unique for each person. Nevertheless, we all have some *basic needs.* All human beings need water, food, sleep, air to breathe, and a satisfactory temperature in which to live. Yet even among these basic needs, there are individual differences. Some people need more

ACTIVITY: THINGS THAT MOTIVATE ME

Circle the numbers of the *six* items from the following list that you believe are most important in motivating you to do your best work. Then rank the six selected items, with the most important item being 1, the second most important item 2, and so on.

1. _____ Having steady employment
2. _6_ Being respected as a person
3. _____ Having adequate rest periods or coffee breaks
4. _3_ Receiving good pay
5. _____ Working in good physical conditions
6. _5_ Having a chance to turn out quality work
7. _____ Getting along well with others on the job.
8. _____ Having a job close to home
9. _____ Having a chance for promotion
10. _4_ Having an opportunity to do interesting work
11. _____ Receiving pensions and other security
12. _____ Not having to work too hard

13. _____ Knowing what is going on in the organization
14. _____ Feeling my job is important
15. _____ Having an employee council
16. _____ Having a written job description
17. _____ Being told by my boss when I do a good job
18. _____ Getting a performance rating
19. _____ Attending staff meetings
20. _____ Agreeing with the organizations objectives
21. _2_ Having an opportunity for self-development and improvement
22. _____ Having fair vacation arrangements
23. _____ Knowing I will be disciplined if I do a bad job
24. _____ Working under close supervision
25. _1_ Having a large amount of freedom on the job (not working under direct or close supervision.

After you have completed this chapter *and* Chapter 4 (not now!), compare your answers with others in your class.

---

sleep than others, some eat more, some become acclimated to higher or lower temperatures.

People also have a variety of *secondary needs.* Some would argue that these needs are really *wants.* These needs or wants include the desire to be accepted by other people, the desire to achieve certain goals or objectives, or the need for prestige or status. Again, these vary widely among people.[1]

Let's consider some human needs as described by well-known theorists.

▼ NEED FOR ACHIEVEMENT

David C. McClelland has spent a lifetime studying the human urge to achieve. His research has led him to believe that the need for achievement is a distinct human motive that can be identified in certain people. The need for achievement has been studied in a

■ Do some people have an exceptionally high need to achieve?

Achievement-motivated people gain satisfaction from the accomplishment itself.

wide range of experiments. One typical experiment went something like this:[2]

Participants in the experiment were asked to play a ringtoss game. Their objective was to throw the rings so that they would hook on a peg. That was essentially the only instruction. The variable that the experimenters looked for was how close to the peg the individual subject stood when tossing the rings. The subjects could stand anywhere they wanted to.

Most people tended to throw randomly, first standing very close and later perhaps stepping back. The people with a high need for achievement seemed to carefully measure where they were most likely to get a sense of mastery—not too close to make the task ridiculously easy, or too far back to make it impossible. They set moderately difficult but potentially achievable goals.[3]

McClelland found that people with a high need for achievement tend not to be gamblers. They *prefer to work on a problem, rather than leave the outcome to chance.* They don't mind taking moderate risks, but they want to have as much control as possible over the outcome.

■ Characteristics of people with a high need for achievement:

Prefer to work on the problem

Gain satisfaction from achievement itself

Appreciate concrete feedback

Come from families where parents held high expectations

Another characteristic of achievement-motivated people is that *they gain satisfaction from the accomplishment itself.* They do not reject rewards, but the rewards are not as essential as the achievement itself. Such people get a bigger kick out of winning or solving a difficult problem than from the money, praise, or other rewards they may receive.

Another finding about these people is that they enjoy and *appreciate receiving concrete feedback.* They respond favorably to getting information on how well they are doing on the job. However, they tend to resent comments from supervisors about their personalities, their physical appearance, or other information not directly relevant to the work. They want task-relevant feedback. They want to know the score.

Finally, McClelland found that achievement-motivated people *are more likely to come from families where parents held high expectations for their children.* Some people tend to achieve because their parents expected them to achieve.

From this description, one can see that achievement-motivated people would be very desirable in organizations. As managers, however, high achievers may be overly demanding or have unrealistically high expectations of others. This can result in leadership problems.

▼ NEED FOR AFFILIATION

Another secondary need identified in individuals is the need for affiliation. Some people have an unusually high desire to be accepted by others. *They tend to conform to what they believe other people want from them.* If the work group has high goals, effective work habits, and other organizationally desirable characteristics, the group will tend to pull the individual member up to a high level of performance. Likewise, low performance can result from group pressures in the opposite direction.

■ Do some people have an exceptionally high need to be accepted?

Research on affiliation needs suggests that a common goal among people who have a high need for affiliation is social interaction and communication with others. Such people dislike being alone.

In some cases, affiliative behavior is linked with the need to reduce anxiety. People may interact with others because they have fears or stresses that can be relieved in part by other people. It's the "misery loves company" idea. In other cases, individuals simply enjoy being with people.

Whatever the nature of the need for affiliation, the behavior it tends to produce is similar. *People with a high need for affiliation seek the company of others and take steps to be liked by them.* They try to project a favorable image, and they will work to smooth out disagreeable tensions in meetings and so forth. They help and support others and want to be liked in return.

▼ NEED FOR POWER

The final type of secondary need considered here is the need for power. Some individuals have a strong need to win arguments, to persuade others, to prevail in every situation. These people are likely to be driven by a high need for power. They feel uncomfortable without this sense of power.

■ Do some people have an exceptionally high need to exert power?

The concept of a need for power is not new. Machiavelli, a sixteenth-century philosopher and politician, was a master at using power to get his way. In fact, his name has become synonymous with a personality type that likes to manipulate others. A strong

■ A strong power drive is not necessarily undesirable.

power drive, however, is not necessarily undesirable or reflective of a character defect. In its positive sense, power can reflect the process by which persuasive and inspirational behavior on the part of a leader can evoke "can-do" feelings of power and ability in subordinates. Power can build confidence in people. The active leader who helps a group form goals and who helps the members attain their goals constructively uses power.

■ Managers should strive to recognize the effects of secondary needs on people.

There is nothing wrong with having a high need for power, a high need for affiliation, or a high need for achievement. Each can be useful and productive to an organization. The key thing is for the manager to recognize the influence of these secondary needs on the behavior of employees.

▼ THE EXPECTANCY THEORY OF MOTIVATION

Expectancy theory takes into account both personal needs and opportunities to solve those needs as it tries to explain and predict how and why people do what they do. This theory also contends that human beings are both emotional (seeking satisfaction of needs) and reasonable (thinking through what alternative action will satisfy needs) at the same time. Each person tries to predict, "If I do this particular thing, will it lead to that particular payoff for me?"

■ An expectancy model shows relationships between needs and motivation.

Victor Vroom is credited with developing an expectancy theory that considers these different needs and motivators (see figure 3.1).[4] In essence, the model states that an individual will expend effort (that is, will be motivated) when he or she believes that

■ the effort will result in favorable performance.
■ favorable performance will result in a desired reward.
■ the reward will satisfy an important need.
■ the desire to satisfy that need is strong enough to make the effort worthwhile.

Notice that the model includes the variable *ability*. If an employee is motivated and expends effort but lacks in ability (skills, knowledge, training, etc.), he or she may fail to achieve favorable performance. Organizations bear some responsibility for seeing that employee ability is appropriate to the tasks required for "favorable performance."

Expressed another way, this model says that people ask themselves three questions in response to a motivator:

1. What's in it for me?
2. How hard will I have to work to get what's in it for me?
3. What are my *real* chances of getting that reward if I do what you (or they) want?

If a student wanted a grade of A for a particular course, for example, his or her *motivation* to study would be a function of

1. how badly the student *desired* the grade and
2. the level of *expectancy* that study would result in achieving it.

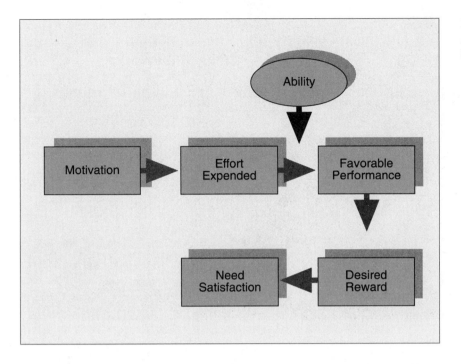

FIGURE 3.1
An expectancy model of motivation.

If a manager offers a sales representative a five hundred-dollar cash bonus for selling twenty automobiles this month, the employee may or may not be motivated, depending on how he or she answers questions such as "Is five hundred dollars an appropriate reward for such an effort?" "How hard will it be to sell twenty cars?" or "If I do sell twenty automobiles, will the boss really pay me the five hundred dollars?"

▼ HOW MOTIVES CHANGE

Motives do not always affect people with the same strength. At any given time, many needs are competing for attention. People pay attention to the need with the greatest strength at that particular moment. This need most influences behavior at that time. Keep in mind that behavior or the activities people engage in are related to some sort of goals (conscious or unconscious). These goals are hoped-for rewards toward which motives are directed. The successful manager provides an environment in which *appropriate* goals are available for need satisfaction.

Management theorists Paul Hersey and Kenneth Blanchard make a distinction between goal-directed activities and goal activities. They suggest that *goal-directed activities* are motivated behaviors based on expectations that the goal is, in fact, attainable, worthwhile, and desirable. This ties in with the expectancy theory we just discussed. The need strength of goal-directed activities *increases* as a person engages in them. That is, as a person gets closer to some goal, the strength of the motivating needs increases. Anyone who has attempted to jog long distances might be aware of this principle.

■ How do goal-directed and goal activities change as the objective gets nearer?

Active leaders construc-
tively use power to help
others build confidence.

As one sees the last mile marker in a long-distance race, one tends to be even more motivated, knowing that the finish line is not far ahead. Students frequently experience additional motivation near the end of a course when the hoped-for goal of getting an A seems just around the corner. It seems to be human nature to want to sprint that last little distance and finish in a blaze of glory. This is the nature of goal-directed activity, according to Hersey and Blanchard.

Goal activities, however, involve engaging in the goal itself. They are "consuming" activities (see figure 3.2). A goal-directed activity might be going to a restaurant and ordering a pizza; the corresponding goal activity would be the act of eating the pizza. Unlike the need strength of goal-directed activities, the need strength of a goal activity *decreases* as one engages in it. The more pizza we eat, the less we are motivated by a desire for food.

■ Should we switch between goal activities and goal-directed activities?

Long-term, ongoing motivation occurs when people alternate between goal-directed and goal-consuming activities. Goal-directed motivation stimulates people to work for a desired reward. But if one never got to "consume" that reward—to relish its achievement—one would eventually tire of exerting the goal-directed effort. The expectation of goal attainment would evaporate, and the person would no longer have a reasonable target for efforts. Likewise, if someone engages only in goal-consuming behaviors and the goal is not challenging, lack of interest and apathy will develop and motivation will dissipate. The worker who is required to attain a production level that is too easy to reach is not likely to be motivated by that aspect of the job.

A continuous cycle between goal-directed and goal-consuming opportunities is most likely to result in long-term motivation.

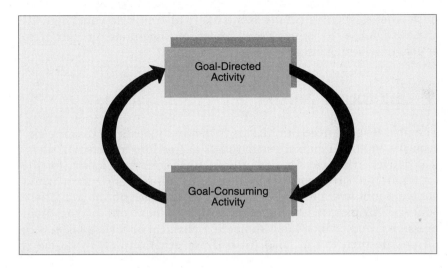

FIGURE 3.2
A continuous cycle can lead to long-term motivation.

▼ THE HIERARCHY OF NEEDS

When a need has been satisfied, it no longer motivates. At least, not for the time being. But let's look a little more closely at the common situation in which a need is only partially satisfied and is replaced by another. To understand that, we need to note the hierarchical arrangement of needs.

Abraham Maslow formulated his famous *hierarchy of needs* back in the 1940s. It was then, and continues to be, a major contribution to the understanding of motivation. Maslow was one of a number of psychologists who, believing that behavior can best be explained in terms of individuals seeking need satisfaction, sought to establish a list of "universal needs" that affect everyone.

In his research, Maslow saw that different needs work on people at different times and that some needs are more basic to all people than others. Until such basic, or "lower-order needs," are satisfied (at least to the extent that another need replaces them), "higher-order needs" cannot and will not motivate a person.[5]

Maslow boiled down his list of needs to five. These were survival, security, belonging, prestige, and self-fulfillment.

■ Maslow's hierarchy of needs was a major contribution to our understanding of motivation.

■ Why was Maslow's theory such an important step in improving our understanding of motivation?

▼ SURVIVAL NEEDS

The human need to be physically comfortable is the most basic type of need, according to Maslow. Whenever we put on mittens in cold weather, replenish our body with food and water after exercise, or step outside for a breath of fresh air, we are seeking to satisfy these physiological needs.

Most of us can understand how difficult it would be to pay attention to other types of needs if such basic needs are not met. Consider trying to concentrate on your studies, for example, while you are extremely hungry or very uncomfortable in a hot, stuffy room. These

■ We cannot be motivated by higher-level needs if these most basic needs are not met.

unsatisfied physiological needs are likely to dominate your thoughts and behavior, even though you'd prefer to concentrate on your higher goal of studying effectively.

▼ SECURITY NEEDS

The next level of needs in Maslow's hierarchy deals with safety and security. Included here are such things as freedom from fear of physical danger, the need for self-preservation, and the concern for the future. In the early years of the industrial United States, many workers, no doubt, were fearful of injury or even death on the job. These concerns, in part, led to the organization of labor unions and other pressure groups. Once their immediate physical needs are taken care of, people turn to the need for self-preservation and to thoughts about the future.

■ We may quit a job we see as too dangerous.

People respond to needs for security in a number of ways. We may quit a job we view as being too physically dangerous. We may be especially motivated to observe certain safety precautions to reduce the chance of accident or injury. We may save some money from paychecks for the eventuality that income may be cut off. And we may do a number of other things to reflect our concern for self-preservation and our concern for the future. Once we feel reasonably secure, still higher needs become primary motivators.

▼ BELONGING NEEDS

People are social animals. We all have a need for acceptance by other people. In modern society, there are few real hermits.

■ Most people need good relationships with others.

Social needs, like any others, vary widely among different individuals. Some of us do prefer to be left alone, but most people have a basic yearning for meaningful relationships with others. We need only to look at people who are imprisoned, such as the prisoners of war in the Vietnam War, to recognize how much affiliation is needed. Many of these prisoners relate that after being kept in isolated captivity for months and months, they were finally permitted the opportunity to communicate with other prisoners. They reacted ecstatically to the fulfillment of this need. As another example, studies have shown that employees who work away from others, such as bank tellers who work in isolated, drive-in banking facilities, tend to be less satisfied on the job. They typically cite the lack of interaction with other employees as a source of their dissatisfaction.

▼ PRESTIGE NEEDS

■ Recognition and rewards can satisfy our need for prestige.

People have varying needs to be recognized by others and to have clear self-images. We all like to receive "strokes" that tell us, "Your efforts are recognized, and you are regarded as a person of value."

Organizational rewards can often fill these esteem needs. Even subtle rewards, such as private offices, carpeting, or a more desirable location in a workroom, can convey this recognition and sense of worth to individual employees. Unfulfilled esteem needs can very quickly lead to dissatisfied employees.

Such things as organizational titles, or status symbols such as a new automobile and expensive clothing, are attempts to meet our esteem needs.

▼ SELF-FULFILLMENT NEEDS

Maslow coined the term *self-actualization* to identify the highest level of needs that motivate people. This is described as the need to maximize one's potential. According to Maslow's theory, the individual who has achieved a reasonable degree of satisfaction in the four lower-level needs can now focus energies on self-actualization. The result is usually a high degree of professional development and accomplishment. The artist who produces her very best painting and the author who creates what he regards as a literary masterpiece are examples of self-actualized people.

■ Self-actualization arises from doing your very best.

The employee who seeks to satisfy self-actualization needs strives to produce the best possible job. This employee is best motivated by supervisors who are supportive by providing an environment where self-directed work may take place.

▼ WE ALL "LIVE" AT DIFFERENT NEED LEVELS

Maslow's theory has become a cornerstone in the literature of management and psychology. The key to its value lies in its recognition of the ever-changing needs that motivate us all. One implication of Maslow's theory is that we all "live" at different levels of existence; we find our most consistent needs to be at one or two levels.

In general, we are motivated most strongly by our strongest unfulfilled needs. People who are reading this book are likely to be successful individuals. You are likely to be either a manager or training to become a manager. By and large, you find your lower-order needs easily satisfied, so you concentrate on higher ones. This is not to say that you are not occasionally motivated by physical hunger or desires, but you are not compelled to seek satisfaction from hunger as a *primary* activity of your day. Physical needs, safety needs, and probably your social needs are generally satisfied. Your need satisfaction efforts focus on the higher-order needs, such as esteem and self-actualization.

Remember, however, that other people are not in exactly the same position. To assume that all workers are likely to be motivated by higher-order needs would probably get the supervisor into considerable trouble.

ACTIVITY: WHERE ARE YOU ON THE LADDER?

Maslow's hierarchy of needs shows that all humans have the same basic needs. How do these needs get satisfied in the average job? Put an X on the level where you think you spend most of your time. Are you at the survival level or closer to self-fulfillment? Or do you (like most people) operate mostly in the security or prestige levels?

Look again at the triangle. Circle your X and then place new Xs with the initials of others you work with where you think they fit.

SOURCE: Twyla Dell, *An Honest Day's Work* (Los Altos, Calif.: Crisp Publications, 1988), p. 12. Reprinted with permission.

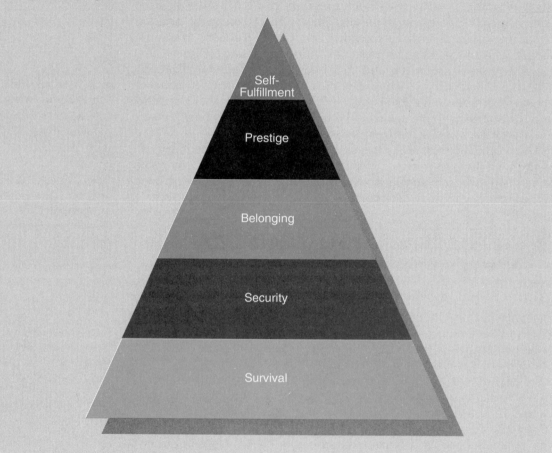

In this chapter, we've talked about human needs and how they related to motivation. Each theory described (Maslow's, McClelland's, Hersey and Blanchard's, Vroom's, and so on) suggests ways to better understand what happens as people experience and respond to different needs.

Although we have suggested that people, at times, seem to be driven by external forces, we do not mean to minimize free will. Human beings are not like the salivating dogs or rats in a maze so often used in psychology experiments. We maintain a higher sense of values, which can and do influence our behaviors. We are not totally self-centered nor constantly seeking only self-gratification. We often develop a larger sense of worth by giving of ourselves for a larger, common good.

▼ THE GROWING TREND TOWARD SELF-ACTUALIZATION

One distinct trend of the 1990s is the movement toward ever more emphasis on self-actualization. This trend is marked by several shifts in what had been traditional thinking.

The first shift is that people are looking to work as a source of more than just financial income. In their book *Re-inventing the Corporation,* John Naisbitt and Patricia Aburdene explain the trend this way:

■ Today, work is seen as more than just a source of income.

> There is a new ideal about work emerging in America today. For the first time, there is a widespread expectation that work should be fulfilling—that work should be fun.
>
> Thirty years ago, that would have been an outrageous notion.... Nevertheless, people know intuitively that work ought to be fun and satisfying, even when it is not.
>
> Today ... the same forces which are re-inventing the corporation are transforming this deep human need into a realistic expectation in the workplace. The economic demands of the information society together with the new values of the baby boom generation are fostering the "work should be fun" idea.[6]

The second shift in traditional thinking lies in the ways people view job security. Today, relatively few people can expect to join a corporation upon graduation from school and remain securely there until retirement. With so many companies being restructured, being taken over, and simply going out of business, old-fashioned job security with a big corporation is largely a myth.

As a result, more people are recognizing that job security is achieved by developing excellent and marketable skills that are in demand. In addition, a sharply increasing number of people are starting their own businesses. Entrepreneurs often gain feelings of control over their own destiny and freedom that are not available in traditional organizations.

The final shift is that people are rethinking the broader issue of balancing career and other life activities. People need to feel fulfilled in all areas: career, family or relationships, self-development, and so forth. People are increasingly recognizing the need for self-management and life balance.

As one author put it, "We have the same amount of mental energy and the same number of hours in a day as people of other generations and other locations, but we have so many more demands, so many more things. We live in the first time and place in the world's history and geography where challenges stem not from scarcity but from surplus, not from oppression but from options, and not from absences but from abundance."[7]

The senior editor of *Training* magazine, Ron Zemke, sums up a shift toward different motivators in the 1990s in his editorial comment that appears as "Another Look" at the end of this chapter. His summarizing comment: "Personal growth and life satisfaction are back [as important motivators]."[8]

Psychological theories help us understand much of what motivates, but they cannot explain all human behavior. The challenge to those who would seek to motivate others is to understand what has been known to work in some situations and to make judgments about what may be helpful in the future.

In chapter 4, we'll suggest some things that supervisors and managers can do to create a climate where individual needs can be satisfied and motivation can flourish.

▼ SUMMARY OF KEY IDEAS

- Management is the process of getting productive work done with and through the efforts of other individuals; thus, understanding human motivation is essential for managerial success.

- Motivation comes from individual needs, wants, and desires, which provide motives for action. Motives are the reason for exerting effort.

- Motivation is directed toward achieving a goal or reward.

- The three emotions that can lead to behavior change are fear, duty, and love, which has the strongest influence.

- Research on human motivation has shown that characteristics of people vary depending on their need for achievement, affiliation, and power.

- Victor Vroom's expectancy theory of motivation helps explain the interaction between needs and motivation.

- A major contribution to motivation theory is Abraham Maslow's hierarchy of needs, which includes (in ascending order) survival, security, belonging, prestige, and self-fulfillment needs.

▼ KEY TERMS, CONCEPTS, AND NAMES

Basic needs	David C. McClelland
Behaviorism	Motivation
Belonging needs	Need for achievement
Expectancy theory of	Need for affiliation
Job satisfaction	Need for power
Abraham Maslow	Prestige needs
Maslow's hierarchy of needs	Goal-consuming activity

Goal-directed activity

Job satisfaction

Life balance

Secondary needs

Security needs

Self-fulfillment

Motivation

Socialneeds

Survivial needs

Victor Vroom

▼ QUESTIONS AND EXERCISES

1. List several examples of each of Maslow's five levels of needs.

2. What are some of your key personal goals? What are the key goals of the organization you work (or have worked) for? Are they compatible?

3. Summarize McClelland's description of the person with a high need for achievement. To what extent does this describe your own behaviors and attitudes? (If you don't fit this description very well, don't feel bad. Only a tiny percentage of all people studied by McClelland's researchers fit the "high-achiever" profile exactly.)

4. How well do you fit the description of one having a high need for affiliation? How well do you fit the description of a person having a high need for power?

5. Summarize in your own words Vroom's expectancy theory of motivation. Cite examples that support or seem to contradict this theory.

6. To what degree do you agree that people today are rethinking their ideas of security and self-actualization? Give examples.

7. Answer the introductory questions at the beginning of this chapter.

▼ NOTES

1. Kenneth A. Kovach, "What Motivates Employees? Workers and Supervisors Give Different Answers," *Business Horizons*, September–October 1987, p. 30.

2. David C. McClelland et al., *The Achieving Society* (Princeton, N.J.: Van Nostrand, 1961).

3. Paul Hersey and Kenneth H. Blanchard, *Management of Organizational Behavior*, 3d ed. (Englewood Cliffs, N.J.: Prentice-Hall 1977), p. 43.

4. Victor H. Vroom, *Work and Motivation* (New York: Wiley, 1964).

5. Abraham Maslow, *Motivation and Personality* (New York: Harper and Row, 1954).

6. John Naisbitt and Patricia Aburdeen, *Re-inventing the Corporation* (New York: Warner Books, 1985), p. 79.

7. Linda and Richard Eyre, *LifeBalance* (New York: Ballantine Books, 1987), p. 16.

8. Ron Zemke, "Dusting off the '60s in the '90s," *Training*, June 1991, p.8.

▼ ANOTHER LOOK: DUSTING OFF THE '60S IN THE '90S

It's official. The thirtysome-thing-turning-fortysomething gang has looked around and decided there must be more to life than clinging to the corporate ladder, eyes riveted on the feet of the lad or lass one rung above, plotting one's personal advancement and hoping against hope to find sweet air and rosebuds at the top.

Time magazine, America's semiofficial chronicle of what's hot and what's not, decreed in April that the yupster boomers, pop publishing's most enduring cover kids, are letting go of the rungs and seeking asylum in "The Simple Life." They're turning away from the 1980s' "obsession with gaudy dreams and godless consumerism."…

Out are: conspicuous consumption, greed, self-aggrandizement and 20-hour-a-day careerism. Adios, Beamers and Rolexes. Farewell, furs and diamonds and designer originals. Bye-bye, braces, bow ties, hyper-thyroid titles and inflated paychecks. So long, Lee Iacocca and Steven Jobs.

In are: frugality, value, greening, charitable instincts, introspection, self-doubt, and evenings at home with family and friends. Hello, K-Mart and Sears, Bean and Land's End, tithing and good works. Hello, making ends meet and doing without. Hello, pleasant jobs and being a part of something worthy. Hello, Scrabble.

All a mere counter-fad? A reaction to the economy? Perhaps. But the sociologists—the same ones who have made those Americans born between 1946 and 1964 the most "lavishly analyzed, dramatized, mythologized and agonized over" generation in history, as Tom Wolfe describes it—think not. "This is real and has staying power," the sociologists swore to *Time*.

And already there are implications for human resources development…. Personal growth and life satisfaction are back on the menu, listed not as appetizers but as entrees. De-yuppiing boomers are rushing to be the first in their social circles to enroll in seminars on "Life Goaling" and "New Directions."…

At the core of this alleged greening of the boomers, there is no doubt a bit of fundamental truth: It's time to put some living back into life. There is more to "being" than worrying about "six sigma" quality and niche markets and one's position in the hierarchy of replaceable cogs in a commercial machine. The lawyer for those workers at a Washington-state papermill who sued their employer for making them wear beepers—off the job—had the right idea when he said, "A job is a job, not your life." Unless I miss my guess, more of us have the stirring than are yet willing to admit it out loud and in public.

SOURCE: Adapted from *Training,* June 1991. Reprinted with permission.

▼ ANOTHER LOOK: MONEY ISN'T EVERYTHING

The 1980s may have been the decade of conspicuous consumption and the worship of money, but a lot of people are still taking jobs for the rewards of fighting the good fight. For them, the payoff is in "psychic income," not in bigger investment portfolios—careers that allow them to pursue a dream, perform a public service or simply spend more time with their families than at the office.

Schoolteachers are a case in point. According to a recent poll by the National Center for Education Information, 90 percent of public-school teachers are satisfied with their jobs even though 55 percent feel they are underpaid.

"There's a day-to-day feeling of accomplishment with the children that only teaching gives me. I very much enjoy it," says Julianne McGlone, a seventh-grade social-studies teacher in Indian Mills, N.J., who earned $19,800 this year. McGlone quit a better-paying job as a postal carrier in 1979 to do what she had always wanted to do. Even with next year's raise, to $21,300, she'll still earn less than she did delivering mail.

But the time she can take off during the school breaks more than makes up for the financial sacrifice. "They can't pay me enough for my time," says McGlone, who finds the long summer break and other holidays essential for "recharging" and enjoying her family.

The desire for more time with her husband and two young sons led Washington, D.C., lawyer Karen Telis, 37, to take a $40,000-a-year pay cut. "The money is out there—I just decided I didn't need it," says Telis, who now works three days a week, a welcome change from the 14-hour days plus weekends that were routine at the prestigious law firm where she worked until 1982.

"It was career vs. marriage; it really came down to that. Marriage won out," she says.

Improving his fellow man's quality of life—not chasing a six-figure income—is what attracted Clarence Ditlow to a staff attorney's job with Ralph Nader in 1971 and then, in 1976, to the Center for Auto Safety in Washington, an influential consumer-advocacy group that spun off from the Nader operation. "I wanted to make a difference in society," says Ditlow, who earns less than $25,000 as the center's executive director. He has repeatedly done battle with the auto industry over safety issues and is proud of his label, "the $200 million man," earned for his role in forcing Firestone to recall one of its tire models.

Besides, it's fun. "You have to enjoy it, or you'd leave immediately because, from a monetary standpoint, there are certainly greener pastures," Ditlow says.

After years of climbing to the top of the corporate ladder, a growing number of executives are leaping off. "They've reevaluated what is giving them satisfaction in life. They've reached a point where they want to do something to benefit the others," says Ann Powers Kern of executive-search firm Korn/Ferry International. Although nonprofit salaries have improved in recent years, a move to such an organization often entails a pay cut.

Russell Palmer, for example, was the chief executive officer of the international accounting firm Touche Ross for 10 years. Three years ago, he accepted a seven-year appointment as the dean of the Wharton School of Business at the University of Pennsylvania. "I wanted to give something back to the system that had allowed me to rise to the top of my profession, and I couldn't think of a better way of doing that than by helping young people get a running start in what they want to accomplish," says Palmer, 51, about the move away from the Big Eight firm to academia. He says he has no regrets. "It's the only time in my life I'll ever take more than an 80 percent cut in compensation, and it was worth every penny."

SOURCE: Carey W. English, copyright June 23, 1986, *U.S. News and World Report.*

A CASE IN POINT: YOU CALL THIS FAIR PLAY?

"Can you believe this?" exclaimed Frank during the morning coffee break. He had been reading a copy of the daily newspaper. "It says here that the city garbage collectors' new contract calls for minimum pay of twenty-eight thousand dollars a year! I can't believe I'm reading this!"

Frank wasn't the only person upset after reading that. "That really burns me up," interjected Rosalee. "I work my tail off at this factory forty hours a week, and I don't make anywhere near that much money. What do those guys think they are trying to prove?"

"If a garbage collector is worth twenty-eight grand, then I'm worth more than that," exclaimed Jose as he pounded on the table. "We need to do something about this. Let's go talk to Charlie and demand some raises."

Coincidentally, Charlie, their supervisor, walked into the break room about this time.

"What are you demanding now?" he asked calmly. All three of the workers immediately started telling him about the newspaper article reporting the garbage collectors' pay.

"I can see why you folks might be a little upset. Let's cool off a bit and talk about this at our meeting later on today," said Charlie. "But don't get your hopes up."

QUESTIONS

1. What do you think is motivating these employees to complain about their pay?
2. Discuss the employees' complaint in terms of Maslow's hierarchy of needs.
3. Assume that the average earnings of each employee are nineteen thousand dollars a year. If you were Charlie, what would you say to these employees at the team meeting this afternoon?

 A CASE IN POINT: CHANGING LIFE-STYLES

Steve Wozniak was the cofounder of the Apple Computer Company. Throughout the 1970s and 1980s, Wozniak and his associates lived in the fast lane of high-tech. Their company came from nowhere to be one of the industry giants.

In 1989, newspaper stories described a different Steve Wozniak. They told how he was currently spending much more of his time bicycling across Yellowstone Park and reading books. Wozniak was quoted as saying that he "reclaimed a life from the high-pressure world of high-tech...." He said, "I want to change my life to where I have a normal life after ten years of being chased by everyone in the world.... I've been a very patient person with all the things that have gone on for many years. I've been very accessible. I've been giv-

ing. But in the last year and a half, it really started to bother me. I'm ready to be me."

Since he had fulfilled his childhood dream of designing a computer, Wozniak was ready to try his hand at teaching. He had no full-time teaching job, but he enlisted as a volunteer at a tiny school in the Santa Cruz Mountains. He wanted to teach children to follow creative urges, to be more nonconformist and unconventional.

Of course, Wozniak left Apple with $100 million in stock, which makes it quite easy for him to be a free spirit.

QUESTIONS

1. What do Wozniak's actions say about the way needs change?

A Case in Point *continued*

2. What seem to be the primary motivators for Wozniak now as compared with ten years ago?

3. Do you know of other people who have made similar dramatic shifts in what appear to be their dominant motivators? Describe such situations.

4. How do you think your needs will change over the next twenty years? What will be likely to motivate you in the future that doesn't motivate you now? What motivates you now that may not be so strong a motivator in ten years? Twenty years? Fifty years?

CHAPTER

4

EMPOWERING PEOPLE AT WORK BY UNBLOCKING GOALS

This chapter answers several all-important questions:

- What is empowerment, and how does it relate to goals and motivation?

- What happens when people's goals are blocked from achievement?

- What is cognitive dissonance, and why is it so uncomfortable?

- How do programmed limitations cause us to fall short of goals?

- How can managers realistically influence motivation?

- What is the key to a motivating climate?

- How can job enrichment provide motivation for workers?

- Are there any surefire ways to motivate?

- What does it mean to say that "everyone can be a VIP"?

- What is motivational faith?

The answer to these and other questions are coming up next in chapter 4....

CHAPTER 4

Empowerment has become a major buzzword in the 1990s. The process of empowerment involves giving—or helping people discover—the power within themselves to satisfy their needs and wants.

For empowerment to grow, organizational leaders need to create conditions for motivation. This is done in large part by unblocking goals—by removing the stumbling blocks to employee need satisfaction. In this chapter, we'll talk about what happens when people's needs are left unmet. We'll also suggest some ways that the manager who is sensitive to employee needs can help develop a climate where workers can be motivated—and empowered.

SHOE   JEFF MACNELLY

SOURCE: Reprinted by permission: Tribune Media Services.

The needs that create motivation are highly individual in nature. No two people experience exactly the same feelings or desires.

Because understanding human motivation—an important aspect of human relations—is a key to successful organizations, it is useful to know what happens when people's needs are blocked.

▼ WHAT HAPPENS WHEN GOALS ARE BLOCKED?

What happens when a goal seems both achievable and desirable, but for some reason we are blocked from gaining it? Typically, we respond with one or a combination of the following behaviors.

Coping

Coping means that people struggle or contend with the problem, often by trial and error, until they achieve some degree of satisfaction. One approach to coping is to simply adjust to that which we cannot control. When prices of a product go up sharply, people cope by buying a cheaper substitute or buying less. This is one way of coping with a blockage (in this case, a loss of purchasing power).

Substitution of Another Goal

When a goal clearly becomes blocked from achievement, people may seek out a substitute goal. The basketball player who realizes that success at a major college is not likely because he or she is a foot or two shorter than all the other players may try a different sport. The worker who sees little opportunity for promotion may change jobs. And the loon who can't get accepted to the navy flight school may try crop dusting.

Workers who can't find much satisfaction on the job often channel their efforts into off-the-job goals. The active civic club member or the avid hobbyist may be substituting such activities for job-related satisfactions.

Resignation, Repression, or Retaliation

Simply giving up the pursuit of a goal is another option. Some people repress their goals or put them to the back of their mind until another time. Occasionally, people retaliate against the person or force that is blocking achievement of the goal. The citizen who fights city hall or the upset employee who files a grievance with a labor union may be retaliating.

Retaliation often takes other forms in business. Unhappy employees take more sick days, tell others what a lousy company they work for, or sometimes even sabotage work output.

While retaliation is almost always destructive, resignation can be either destructive or healthy. When being resigned to blocked goals

> ■ When our goals are blocked, we usually respond with one or more of these behaviors:
> Coping
> Substitution of another goal
> Resignation, repression, or retaliation
> Fixation or obsession
> Rationalization
> Cognitive dissonance
> Frustration

festers a sense of helpless resentment, it is, of course, detrimental. When employees are resigned to an uncontrollable goal blocker and make the best of a less than ideal situation, they may simply have a realistic view of the world. Such a view can be healthy.

Fixation or Obsession

One unhealthy response to a blocked goal is fixation or obsession. This involves focusing on the goal and continuing to "beat one's head against a wall" in a futile effort to accomplish the blocked goal. Such behavior differs from coping behaviors in that the person who is fixated seldom tries any new approaches to the problem. The person becomes obsessed but also becomes incapable of rationally working toward the goal.

Some argue that an obsession can be a positive thing, like an obsession for excellence or for quality. Perhaps. But in those contexts, the word *obsession* is being used as a synonym for a drive or ongoing effort. Obsessive behaviors imply an *irrational* pursuit, not a conscious, sustained, thoughtful effort.

Rationalization

The attitude that "I didn't really want to achieve that anyhow" illustrates rationalization. A response to a blocked goal may simply be to very convincingly tell ourselves that we didn't really want to obtain that goal anyhow.

Another form of rationalization is to identify scapegoats. Here, we blame an outside force over which we have no control—such as the economy or our competitor—for blocking our goal achievement.

Cognitive Dissonance

whole

Leon Festinger developed a psychological theory in the 1950s called *cognitive dissonance*.[1] His theory deals with the ways people respond to new information or experiences, especially those that differ from what was previously believed to be true.

We all have developed a complex network of attitudes and emotions based on our experiences against which we evaluate new information or experiences. If the new data fit what we already "know," there is no problem. The network is reinforced and strengthened. If, however, we experience something that seems inconsistent with what we already "know," an imbalance is created in our minds. Something just doesn't seem to fit.

According to Festinger's theory, people seek a balance or an equilibrium between their thoughts and experiences. Put another way, people want the world to make sense to them. When people feel some psychological discomfort, they will act to deal with it.

■ People seek a balance in their thoughts and experiences.

Here's an example of cognitive dissonance. Suppose that your supervisor has been riding you pretty hard and seldom seems to have a good word for anything you do. You are convinced that your supervisor dislikes you—and the feeling is mutual. This is information already "known" to you.

One day, you overhear this same supervisor vigorously arguing for a big raise for you! Your supervisor is telling the boss that you are definitely the best worker on the crew and that there is a lot of promotion potential in you. This new bit of information (the overheard conversation) doesn't fit with what you already "know" (that your supervisor thinks you're a bum).

Cognitive dissonance theory would suggest that you'll probably change your view in some way. Perhaps you'll adjust your thinking: "Maybe my supervisor really does appreciate me. Maybe my supervisor's not so bad but just has trouble expressing appreciation to others."

Or you may adjust for this dissonance by thinking, "My supervisor's just trying to throw weight around and impress the boss with apparent 'concern' for workers. The raise for me is not really important. This is just an attempt at a power play."

Cognitive dissonance frequently results when one realistically thinks that a particular goal can be achieved, but for some reason that goal is not achieved. The results of cognitive dissonance can be a change in attitude, perhaps toward how reachable the original goal really is or toward oneself ("I am a failure").

Your response to dissonance can be one of the following:

1. Ignore it.
2. Discount the new information or experience.
3. Change your attitude.

Frustration

One final result of blocked needs is individual frustration. Frustration exists within the mind of the person. Frequently, blockages that people perceive, and are frustrated by, are *programmed limitations* that people have in their own minds.

We all have programmed our self-perception of what we can or cannot achieve. A blocked goal may serve to reinforce those limitations, even though the only blockage is in our own mind. Some interesting stories are told about such mentally programmed limitations.

■ What are programmed limitations?

For example, elephants used in setting up circus tents are trained to have certain programmed limitations from a very early age. When an elephant is very small (say, only a half ton or so), it is tied with a very heavy rope to a large stake. Although it may frequently pull and tug at that rope, there is no way it can get away from the stake. When this elephant gets older and much more powerful, easily strong enough to pull up such a stake, it does not do so. In fact, some circus trainers simply put a leg iron around the elephant's foot, with no rope attached at all. Simply having the leg iron in place causes the elephant to stay put. The animal "knows" it cannot wander.

Mental limitations
become real when we
accept them as such.

Other examples of programmed limitations are found in the world
of sports. Before the early 1950s, many people believe that no
human being could run a mile in less than four minutes. Then Roger
Bannister broke the "magical" four-minute mile. Within only a few
months, several other people also ran a mile in less than four minutes. The limitation seemed to have been socially dictated, rather
than to have been a real, physical barrier.

Advocates of the "power of positive thinking" see such programmed limitations as sources of frustration. The frustrations that
grow out of goal blockages only serve to reinforce these limitations.

▼ HOW MANAGERS CAN INFLUENCE MOTIVATION

While understanding the nature of motivation and some of its effects
on people is very useful, even more important is knowing how to

"Hey! The carrot's for the horse!"

create situations where motivation can work for managers and for their organization. The following paragraphs describe several ways that a manager can use the information in this chapter to help empower employees to become motivated.

Have Realistic Expectations

Managers cannot motivate anyone. A manager's input to the motivating situation is limited and, at best, bears indirectly on the performance of others. This does not mean that managers should ignore opportunities to help people motivate themselves. What the manager can most profitably do is seek to understand what motivates the individual employee at a particular point in time. And there is only one realistic way to do that: communicate.

Communicate about Wants, Needs, and Goals

The effective manager seeks to understand what motivates others through *listening* and encouraging free expression of employee wants. Because motivation is goal-oriented, managers and their employees must *clarify* both organizational and work group goals, as well as the individual objectives of the employee. Managers need to see where each person fits. In most cases, individual wants and goals can mesh effectively with the needs of the organization.

Kenneth Blanchard and Spencer Johnson described a simple but effective goal-setting process in their book *The One Minute Manager*.[2] The six steps to setting and using goals are as follows:

1. Agree on your goals.
2. See what good behavior looks like.
3. Write out each of your goals on a single sheet of paper using less than 250 words.
4. Read and reread each goal, which requires only a minute or so each time you do it.

■ Managers can influence motivation by doing the following:
  Having realistic expectations
  Communicating about wants, needs, and goals
  Understanding the difference between motivators and maintenance factors
  Creating a motivational climate
  Using the reward system

Agreement on goals is a critical first step in management.

5. Take a minute every once in a while out of your day to look at your performance.

6. See whether or not your behavior matches your goal.

■ Managers and workers get on the same wavelength by clarifying goals.

By talking through this process and coming to agreement about the desirability and description of goals and their related behaviors, managers and employees get on the same wavelength and can move toward goal accomplishment.

Understand the Difference between Motivators and Maintenance Factors

■ Herzberg's two-factor theory of motivation contrasts motivators and hygiene or maintenance factors.

Over two decades ago, Frederick Herzberg put forth a two-factor theory of motivation. He suggested that the things that can motivate people appeal to the higher-order needs as described by Maslow.[3] These include opportunities for achievement, recognition, challenging work, responsibility, and advancement. Many managers, however, spend a great deal of time trying to motivate people by appealing to their lower-level needs. For instance, providing people with more comfortable work environments, more money, an office with a view, or even pleasant relationships with supervisors can, and probably will, lead to worker *satisfaction*.

■ The two factors are satisfaction and motivation. They are not the same.

The two-factor theory identifies motivation and satisfaction as two different, and often unrelated, things. Where working conditions are tolerable or better, managers waste a great deal of time trying to get motivation out of satisfiers. If minimum standards are not met, however, workers can be highly dissatisfied, and this can have disastrous effects on their productivity.

One critic of Herzberg's work, Abraham K. Korman, feels that this research erred by assuming that most, if not all, individuals are at

▼ TABLE 4.1 A COMPARISON OF MASLOW'S AND
            HERZBERG'S THEORIES

MASLOW	HERZBERG
Higher-Order Needs	**Motivators**
Self-fulfillment	Work itself
	Achievement
	Responsibility
Prestige	Recognition
	Advancement
Lower-Order Needs	**Hygiene or Maintenance Factors**
Belonging	Interpersonal relations
	Technical supervision
Security	Company policy and administration
Survival	Job security
	Working conditions
	Salary
	Personal life

the higher-level needs.[4] That criticism may be valid, because people do function at different levels of needs. Otherwise, the theories of Maslow and Herzberg support each other. As shown in table 4.1, *motivators* relate to the higher-level needs. Similarly, dissatisfiers, or what Herzberg called *hygiene* or *maintenance factors,* relate to lower-level needs. Herzberg contended that only appeals to the higher-level needs can be motivating. Efforts to stimulate workers through the lower-level needs will, at best, simply reduce the probability of worker dissatisfaction.

The sensitive manager recognizes that to motivate people, the work itself—the job being done by the individual—must generate some degree of interest and provide some opportunity for the individual to attain self-actualization.

Create a Motivational Climate

To create a motivational climate, there must be openness between managers and subordinates. Each must have a clear understanding of both the organization's goals and, to the degree possible, the individual employee's goals. The manager must be flexible, creative, and receptive to new ideas from subordinates. The only way this can be conveyed is through effective communication and positive interpersonal relationships.

■ Openness between managers and subordinates is a key to a motivating climate.

Sometimes employees find it difficult to express personal goals. Many have never considered what their life objectives are. Effective supervisors will help employees formulate their goals through discussion and training. These efforts can pay off handsomely in motivating organization members.

One effective way of creating motivational climate is through job enrichment. According to Herzberg, *job enrichment* is a process

Activity: What Motivates Your Employees?

Think of yourself as a manager. (Use your part-time or full-time job as a point of reference.) If you were the manager, would you know what your employees really want? Their answers could surprise you. A survey of 2,000 workers and their immediate supervisors found that what managers think employees want and what employees really want are often at opposite ends of the spectrum.

Rank the following most common motivators in terms of how effective they would be for motivating you and your employees:

Motivator	Ranking for You	Ranking for Your Employees
Money		
Job security		
Promotion		
Personal development		
Working conditions		
Interesting work		
Loyalty from the company		
Tactful disciplining		
Appreciation		
Flexibility about personal needs		
Feeling informed		

In responding to the survey, managers consistently saw themselves as being motivated by different factors than their employees. They felt that the best ways to motivate employees were the traditional trio of motivators: job security, financial rewards, and job advancement.

The problem is that the traditional motivators are scarce resources for a company. There is not an unlimited amount of these to pass around. They cannot always be provided. So the majority of employees would remain unsatisfied if these were the supervisor's primary means of motivation.

EVERYONE CAN BE A VIP

There is some good news, however. The survey also asked all the employees in the company to say what really motivated them. They picked a very different set of motivators as most effective. In fact, the traditional trio of motivators were the bottom three of their list.

The primary motivators of the empowered workplace are what we call the VIP motivators:

VALIDATION

- Respect for employees as people
- Flexibility to meet personal needs
- Encouragement of learning, growth, and new skills

INFORMATION

- Knowing why things are being done
- Getting inside information about the company

PARTICIPATION

- Employees having control over how they do their work
- Involvement in decisions that affect them

ACTIVITY *continued*

Validation:

_____

Information:

_____

Participation:

_____

SOURCE: Adapted from Cynthia D. Scott and Dennis T. Jaffe, *Empowerment* (Los Altos, Calif.: Crisp Publications, 1991),

SOURCE: Reprinted with permission. Elwood N. Chapman, *Winning at Human Relations* (Los Angeles, Calif.: Crisp Publications, p. 3.

where, through talking together, subordinates and their supervisors come to an understanding of how the job could be made more meaningful.

The manager's primary task is to create a climate of trust, so that a subordinate will feel comfortable in offering suggestions about the nature and scope of the worker's job. Once the trust is created, the supervisor and worker can systematically discuss the nature and duties of the subordinate's job with suggestions of how that job could be enriched—that is, how the *responsibilities* of the job can be increased. Most, but not all, people are motivated by more responsible jobs over which they have control.

■ Job enrichment means increasing job responsibility.

▼ FOSTERING MOTIVATIONAL FAITH

Alan L. Wilkins talks about building *motivational faith* in his book *Developing Corporate Character.* People will be motivated to the extent that they have faith in their organization and belief in its future.

> Employees use their understanding of history, the promises made to them, and their own predisposition to trust others to decide how much effort they will give to the organization. If they have faith in the fairness and in the ability of the organization and in their own ability to make valued contributions, then they are very likely to be motivated to work for the good of the organization. They assume that their own excellent contributions to the organization will be rewarded appropriately. They therefore spend little time worrying about how to protect themselves and work hard to cooperate with others to make the organization succeed.[5]

Wilkins goes on to describe the elements of motivational faith:

1. *Faith in the fairness of leaders*—belief that management plays fair and gives equal opportunities.
2. *Faith in the fairness of employees*—belief that other workers carry their share of the workload.
3. *Faith in the ability of the organization*—belief that it can deliver on its leaders' promises.
4. *Faith in one's own ability*—belief that one's job will make a difference and that one has the capability to do what is asked.[6]

Use the Reward System

A key management tool is the allocation of rewards. What you reward others for is what you get more of. The rewards or resources that a manager can allocate include such obvious things as pay, benefits, and promotions but also some other things that are more subtle. For example, virtually all supervisors can dispense the reward of *verbal* approval to their employees. Each time supervisors tell employees that they are doing a good job or "stroke" them for some special efforts they have made, they are using part of the organizational reward system.

Likewise, rewards managers can provide may take the form of qualities that people want from their jobs. One survey found that the following ten qualities were most sought after. Arranging for workers to do any of them can be construed as rewarding.[7]

■ What do people most want from their jobs?

1. Work for efficient managers
2. Think for themselves
3. See the end result of their work
4. Be assigned interesting work
5. Be informed
6. Be listened to
7. Be respected
8. Be recognized for their efforts
9. Be challenged
10. Have opportunities for increased skill development

Managers need to be conscious of the systematic ways in which they reward people. In an ideal world, rewards would never be haphazardly distributed. But this is not the way it is. Managers are not perfect. In fact, it is not unusual for managers to reward behavior that is actually counterproductive to the organization.

■ Managers motivate best when they catch people doing something *right*.

Blanchard and Johnson recognize the value of carefully praising effective worker behavior. They encourage managers to "help people reach their full potential [by catching] them doing something *right*."[8] Reward positive behavior immediately, and you'll get more of it.

Empowerment and Unblocking Goals Boost Self-Esteem

People spend one-third of their waking lives at work. For many, the workplace is the most important community they live in. Empowerment builds and enhances self-esteem. People who feel good about themselves give more to their work. They are also physically healthier. The outcome is healthy people in healthy places.

In situations where people are not free to work at the maximum effectiveness and their self-esteem is constantly under attack, stress claims, illness, and absenteeism go up. Morale goes down. Productivity plummets. We can look at health, productivity, and satisfaction with work as three interlocking circles:[9]

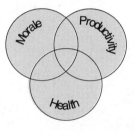

Workers need to be encouraged to find their satisfaction in how well they do their jobs. The key to motivation in an empowered environment is to understand that what gives people the most personal satisfaction is doing a good job. When people are given information, skills, tools, and responsibility, they thrive. Self-esteem is enhanced when people are allowed to exercise more judgment in their work.

Self-esteem is nurtured by achieving goals. The successful organization needs to create a structure and a climate in which people may be successful. Unblocking goal achievement leads to empowerment, which leads to healthy organizations.

▼ CAUTION: THERE IS NO EASY, SUREFIRE WAY TO MOTIVATE

A final thought about motivation is offered by organizational psychologists Daniel Katz and Robert L. Kahn. They suggest three ways that people oversimplify their thinking about motivation in organizations and thus get into trouble.[10]

1. People tend to rely too heavily on the use of *blanket motivation*—the same approach to motivating all organization members. "What's good for the goose is good for the gander" may work on fowl—but not on people.

2. People believe in a concept of *global morale*—an overall assessment of organizational spirit without regard to individual differences. The *average* depth of a river may be only four feet. But that doesn't mean someone can walk across it.

■ People oversimplify motivation attempts in three ways.

3. People tend to emphasize motivation of the individual while neglecting the formal structure of the organization. They fail to account for the ways the organization itself affects the individual members. An enthusiastic worker in a poorly designed job—one with too much or too little work to do, for example—soon gets *de*motivated.

Avoiding such oversimplifications can be very difficult. Because efforts to motivate don't always bring about the desired results, the manager must be able to tolerate a degree of frustration. Indeed, the only managers who can hope to succeed are those who can deal with uncertainty, aggravation, and ongoing battles that are never won but only fought well. *Employee motivation (and self-motivation, too!) requires constant managerial attention.*

▼ SUMMARY OF KEY IDEAS

- Empowerment grows when stumbling blocks to employee need satisfaction are removed.
- The seven responses to blocked goals are coping; goal substitution; resignation, repression, or retaliation; fixation; rationalization; cognitive dissonance; and frustration.
- Although managers cannot actually motivate anyone, they can influence motivation by having reasonable expectations, communicating wants and goals, understanding the difference between motivators and maintenance factors, creating a motivational climate, and using a reward system.
- Frederick Herzberg's two-factor theory describes factors that motivate (e.g., recognition, challenging work, and responsibility) and those that satisfy (e.g., work environment, money, and relationship with peers).
- Three ways in which people oversimplify motivation are by relying on one motivational program, failing to account for individual differences, and neglecting structural barriers to motivation.
- Empowerment can boost employee self-esteem, leading to better morale, productivity, and health.
- People develop a sense of motivational faith based on their belief in (1) the fairness of leaders, (2) the fairness of employees, (3) the ability of the organization, and (4) their own abilities to contribute.

▼ KEY TERMS, CONCEPTS, AND NAMES

Cognitive dissonance   Empowerment
Coping   Leon Festinger

Fixation or obsession
Frustration
Frederick Herzberg
Hygiene factors
Job enrichment
Job satisfaction questionnaire

Motivational faith
Programmed limitations
Rationalization
Two-factor theory of motivation
Alan L. Wilkins

▼ QUESTIONS AND EXERCISES

1. Review your answers in the activity "What Motivates Your Employees?" Discuss why you ranked the items as you did. How do your rankings compare with those of your classmates? What might account for differences? To what extent are you motivated by maintenance factors? By motivational factors?

2. Think of a recent example where one of your personal goals has been blocked from achievement. (We all have occasional blockages, so don't feel bad.) How, specifically, did you respond to that blockage? What alternatives might you have used?

3. We've discussed the concept of programmed limitations in this chapter. Do you believe that we are limited by such things? If so, suggest some other examples of this process. If not, how might the examples we've suggested be explained?

4. Think of a job you have worked on. How, specifically, could that job be enriched?

5. Why are openness and faith between managers and subordinates the keys to creating a climate for motivation?

6. Describe specific examples of the "VIP" qualities most sought by people at work. How do your responses to the activity on page 49 relate to the VIP idea?

7. Answer the introductory questions at the beginning of this chapter.

▼ NOTES

1. Leon Festinger, *A Theory of Cognitive Dessonance* (Stanford, Calif: Stanford University Press, 1957).

2. Kenneth Blanchard and Spencer Johnson, *The One Minute Manager* (New York: Morrow, 1982), p. 34.

3. Frederick Herzberg, B. Mausner, and Barbara Snyderman, *The Motivation to Work,* 2d ed. (New York: Wiley, 1959).

4. Abraham K. Korman, *Organizational Behavior* (Englewood Cliffs, N.J.: Prentice-Hall, 1977), especially pp. 140–145.

5. Alan L. Wilkins, *Developing Corporate Character* (San Francisco; Jossey-Bass, 1989), p. 27.

6. Ibid., pp. 28–29.

7. The survey was conducted by the Public Agenda Foundation and is reported in Twyla Dell, *An Honest Day's Work* (Los Altos, Calif.: Crisp Publications, 1988), p. 13.

8. Blanchard and Johnson, *The One Minute Manager,* p. 37.

9. Cynthia D. Scott and Dennis T. Jaffe, *Empowerment* (Los Altos, Calif.: Crisp Publications, 1991), p. 46.

10. Based on Daniel Katz and Robert L. Kahn, *The Social Psychology of Organizations,* 2d ed. (New York: Wiley, 1978).

▼ Another Look: Empowerment Is Not a Gift

It was my first division meeting with my new boss, Joe. "I called this meeting to announce we are starting participative management in the division," he barked. "I've decided that participative management is the wave of the future. You will participate, by God, or I'll fire your butt!"

He was not kidding.

I've thought a lot about Joe as I've watched the reactions of managers who have had a "close encounter of the empowerment kind." The phenomenon is similar to a religious conversion. Some experienced it while listening to a passionate motivational speaker. Some got it from a book or an article. And some never got it at all; they just heard about others who got it and thought they'd better act like they got it, too.

These managers are assembling empowerment committees and task forces. They're demanding new empowerment policies. Just like Joe, they want to do the right thing. Trouble is they've missed the point.

"How do I empower my employees?" is a question as flawed as "How do I motivate my employees?" In fact, it's even more flawed: Eliminating boss control is at the core of empowerment. The "how do I" part of the question, no matter how well-intended, still reeks of boss control. Empowerment can never be achieved through managers who act as if it is their gift to bestow

upon disenfranchised workers.

What is empowerment? It's the self-generated exercising of judgments. It is doing what needs to be done rather than simply doing what one is told. From the manager's perspective, it's the process of releasing the expression of personal power. Because personal power is already present within the individual, empowerment is not a gift one gives another. Rather, one can release power by removing the barriers that prevent its expression.

Empowerment benefits both customers and employees. Benjamin Schneider at the University of Maryland has demonstrated through extensive research that the No. 1 variable affecting customer relations is employee relations. At Disney World the philosophy is: Our guests (customers) will only receive the quality of service our cast members (employees) receive.

If employees come to the job with adequate power to act with responsible freedom, what prevents them from using this power? One of the primary barriers is their anticipation of pain. Jerry Harvey, an iconoclastic professor at George Washington University, once declared that resistance to change is a myth. "It is not change people resist; it is the prediction of pain. We can effectively implement change if we can accurately determine people's predic-

tions about what will produce discomfort," he wrote.

So it is with empowerment. If you ask employees to walk out on the high wire of risk, where's the managerial net that will catch them if they slip and fall? Where there is no protection, there is only a prediction of pain.

Most organizations have "red rules" and "blue rules." Red rules are the laws or quasi-laws that, if broken, risk grave consequences to the organization. Blue rules are policies, procedures and guidelines that organizations adopt to make work more efficient, consistent or cost-effective. For example, bank tellers have certain check-cashing limits because of government regulations. Violations of that rule could result in a bank losing its charter. On the other hand, a bank might have a policy of running a teller machine tape on every transaction to make auditing more efficient. One is a red rule—a "law"; one is a blue rule—a "guideline."

In a lot of organizations, however, the law and the guideline get equal treatment in the thick three-ring binder of policies and procedures. Very quickly, employees begin to treat guidelines as laws, especially if anyone in the organization ever violates a red rule. Punish an infraction and, if you are not careful, you create a long-standing precedent.

If protection is the safety net, then permission is the encouragement employees

ANOTHER LOOK *continued*

need to get on the high wire. A manager's attitude and actions can engender in people the confidence and courage to act with responsible freedom and rational boldness.

Protection and permission aren't all there is to it, of course. If employees are to do what's needed, rather than just do as they're told, they also need a sense of *purpose,* a vision of what the organization is trying to accomplish. They need *proficiency:* Disney doesn't give its street sweepers four days of training because street sweeping is complex; Disney wants sweepers who are able to answer guests' questions about the park. And finally, employees will need a *payoff:* What's in it for them, materially or emotionally, to go the extra mile on behalf of the company?

But beware: This all has to do with actions, not words. As Will Rogers said, "People learn more from observation than conversation." You won't get far with empowerment if, to paraphrase the old song, your memos tell them "yes, yes," but there's "no, no" in your eyes.

SOURCE: Chip R. Bell, *Training,* December 1991.

▼ ANOTHER LOOK: ARE SOME WORKERS BOUND TO BE UNHAPPY

Traditional thinking holds that companies can increase employee job satisfaction if they do things like give a worker more autonomy. But in recent years many academic researchers have concluded that sometimes an unhappy worker is inherently an unhappy worker—and little can change that.

In a 1985 study, for instance, researchers at the University of California at Berkeley found the job satisfaction of 5,000 middle-age men changed little in five years, regardless of changes in job, pay or job status.

A study there a year later examined the personality characteristics and job attitudes of people who had been followed over a 50-year period. Those who had unhappy dispositions early in life tended to report the least job satisfaction; those with happy dispositions, the most satisfaction.

Going a step further, Richard D. Arvey, a University of Minnesota management professor, recently found that genetics may play a part. In his study, identical twins who were reared separately had similar scores on certain job-satisfaction measures, like how much feeling of accomplishment they got from their jobs.

Researchers caution that the studies don't suggest companies should abandon efforts to improve job satisfaction; environmental factors—quality of a boss, for instance—clearly play a role. But, says Barry Staw, a management professor at the University of California at Berkeley, "what it means is that influencing job attitude is a hell of a lot harder than we thought it was. You can't put in a weekend program and expect the world to change."

To be sure, many human-resources managers aren't sold. "I take this with a grain of salt," says Ronald Pilenzo, president of the American Society for Personnel Administration. Job-enrichment programs, he adds, have "turned on" a lot of workers.

SOURCE: Wall Street Journal, 18 April 1988, p. 25.

▼ A CASE IN POINT: FOSTER'S BLUEBIRD TERRITORY

At first, Xonyx Corporation was hesitant about hiring Kris Foster. She was attractive and bright, but her education seemed totally unrelated to the competitive business world. She had graduated from a small liberal arts college and had majored in, of all things, humanities.

At the time Foster applied for the job of sales representative, the corporation was under considerable pressure to hire more women. Other women had been employed in the past, but most had not worked out very well. But Foster was different. In her first full year in her sales territory, she made seven thousand dollars more than any other first-year sales representative. Top management was happy to see her succeeding and wanted to give her every opportunity.

Xonyx Corporation is a major manufacturer and distributor of office products. Its word processors, copiers, and duplicators are well known for high quality and very good service. Each sales representative covers a geographic territory. He or she is responsible for following up on the present customers to make sure their equipment needs are being met and for getting additional sales within that area. Often this follow-up requires frequent visits to the offices of customers and potential customers.

Occasionally, sales territories are realigned to meet an increasing demand for Xonyx products. Although every effort is made to give each sales representative an equal opportunity to make commissions, some territories are simply more lucrative than others. Foster's territory, for example, includes several large office complexes. In addition, a major corporation will soon locate in her territory. Other sales representatives on the team good-naturedly kidded her about having a "bluebird" territory: "The bluebirds just come float ing in the window bringing her little orders." And, in fact, Foster did receive many more orders over the phone than did the other sales reps.

After a while, though, the ribbing became less good-natured, and the references to her bluebird territory started getting under Foster's skin. She felt she had to work just as hard for each order as did any other sales rep. The situation was aggravated further when the economy took a downturn, and many of the other sales reps had considerable difficulty in meeting their quotas.

Just this morning, Foster came into your office and appeared to be very upset. She recognized that her sales results for the last two months were far lower than in the earlier part of the year. But she seemed to be agitated by something more than just her results.

After a short discussion with you, her manager, in which she expressed her frustrations, Foster shrugged her shoulders and went back to work. But she hinted in her comments that she may not want to stay with the company too much longer. You are concerned about this. She is a good producer, and her long-term relationship with the company would be very beneficial.

QUESTIONS

1. What do you think motivates Foster?
2. What types of needs are being fulfilled or being left unfulfilled on her job?
3. How would you, as her manager, help her overcome this slump?
4. What long-range issues need to be addressed to maintain high morale, job satisfaction, and productivity for your sales team?

THE PLACE: ORGANIZATIONS

CHAPTER

5

HOW ORGANIZATIONS ARRANGE PEOPLE TO ACCOMPLISH WORK

This chapter answers several all-important questions:

- Why do people form organizations?

- What trade-offs must people face as they join or are pulled into organizations?

- Is there one best way to design an organization?

- What features of organizations can be designed by managers?

- What does the acronym KISS mean, and how can it apply to organization theory?

- What are the six principal types of departmentalization?

- In what ways do organizations seek to control individual behavior?

- What are some modern alternatives to traditional organization patterns?

- What is "intrapreneuring" and how can organizations foster it?

The answer to these and other questions are coming up next in chapter 5....

CHAPTER 5

In this chapter, we introduce some basics of organization theory—some issues that affect people at work. We focus on characteristics of organizations—the arrangements of people and other resources.

We begin with a warning: Organizations tend to be far more complex than they appear. Neat pyramids of little boxes tell us very little about organizations.

Likewise, comparing organizations to machines (well oiled or otherwise) is an oversimplification. Such a mechanistic view implies that if something goes wrong, one can simply replace the malfunctioning "part" and—voilà—the machine purrs on once again. But people are not interchangeable parts.

■ Organizations are far more complicated than machines.

Human organizations are far more complex than any machine. Human interaction is influenced by countless factors: intelligence, social skills, experience, attitudes, emotions, and technical abilities, just to name a few. And no two people are alike.

▼ THE ONE BEST WAY TO ORGANIZE: AN ELUSIVE CREATURE

Is there an *ideal* way to build an organization? The search for that elusive butterfly, "the one best way," has been going on for a long time.

In the nineteenth century, Max Weber thought he had found the perfect organizational system. He called it bureaucracy. In a purely theoretical sense, bureaucracy probably could work. But as we all know, the term has now become synonymous with organizational ineffectiveness.

Indeed, no one organizational structure can be perfect for every situation. Just as no two people are exactly alike, neither are any two organizations the same. Every organization has its own peculiar purpose and task. Each has its own distinct culture, or set of acceptable behaviors and values. Therefore, to say that a certain "perfect structure" could be imposed on any organization would be unrealistic.

▼ HOW ORGANIZING BENEFITS MEMBERS

Picture this scene: You just signed on with Moose Lips Corporation, a manufacturer of camping equipment. On your first day, you arrive at the plant, but no one there tells you what you are expected to do. You notice that other people come to work whenever they wish, take long coffee breaks, and generally seem to wander around aimlessly. The work they occasionally do accomplish seems to be of poor quality. No one seems to care much.

■ Lack of organization is frustrating to workers.

This behavior could get very frustrating, especially if you want to be an effective worker—if you want to contribute to the company's goals. The chaotic situation would lead to very little job satisfaction for you. And the company's objectives—if there were any to begin with—would very likely not be met. (All this probably explains why you don't see Moose Lips products in the stores!)

"For what it's worth, the new organization chart is out, and you're not in your box."

Organizing seeks to reduce such confusion. It helps members of an organization to understand what they are to do, whom they are to report to and receive instructions from, and how their efforts relate to the company's objectives. An effective organization pattern helps employees to gain job satisfaction.

▼ HOW ORGANIZING BENEFITS THE ORGANIZATION

Organizations exist for the purpose of accomplishing things that cannot be done by individuals working alone. From the day the earliest cave dweller discovered that a large boulder could not be moved by one person and the help of others was needed, people have organized efforts. As the tasks at hand became more and more complicated, the organization structure also became more complex. Today, with such enormous tasks as building elaborate missile systems, nuclear power generators, water conservation systems, and ambitious space exploration programs, the need for sophisticated organizations is greater than ever.

The benefits of organizing do not, however, come free. People pay a price when they join or form an organization.

■ The fundamental reason for any organization is to accomplish work that cannot be accomplished by one person working alone.

▼ TRADE-OFFS: THE PRICE OF ORGANIZATIONS

We are all members of many organizations. In our modern world, we all spend a major portion of our lives in some sort of organized activity. At birth, we are introduced to an organization called the hospital staff. Within a few days, we actively join an organization called the family. For the rest of our lives, our needs and wants are fulfilled directly or indirectly by organizations. Manufacturing, farming, mining, and distribution organizations bring products to satisfy material needs. Schools, churches, clubs, and informal social groups serve needs for information, understanding, personal growth, and affiliation. Governments are organized to provide essential services for the public good.

■ Ninety percent of us work in organizations.

About 90 percent of us work in organizations. In contemporary society, there are few real hermits. Being a recluse from organizational life is difficult, if not impossible.

■ People pay a price for the benefits of an organization: some freedom.

Nevertheless, people pay a price to join or exist in organizations. The price is some personal freedom. People cannot do everything they wish once they are members of organizations.

In the largest organization of which we all are members—society—the price of membership is conformity to social standards. As citizens, we agree to obey the laws, even though we may not want to obey them. Failure to obey the laws, even ones we disagree with, results in punishment.

When we enroll in school, we agree to behave in organizationally acceptable ways—even though we may prefer to act otherwise. We're quiet when we'd rather talk; we sit still when we'd rather jump up and down.

For every organization of which we are members, the trade-off is some decrease in personal freedom—some restraint on what we might like to do—in exchange for the benefits that organization provides.

▼ HOW ORGANIZATIONS SEEK TO CONTROL PEOPLE

■ What are some examples of organizational controls?

One important aspect of an organization's design is the way *controls* are imposed on its members. The number and types of controls used vary.

Examples of organizational controls include budgets, interviews, quality inspections, performance reports, product specifications, time clocks, and checks on progress toward goals. The controls imposed on the assembly crew producing a nuclear missile would be very different from the controls imposed on traveling journalists for *National Geographic* magazine.

In the missile production crew, the tasks would require strict adherence to specifications, safety procedures, and instructions from the engineers. Imagine what disastrous consequences could

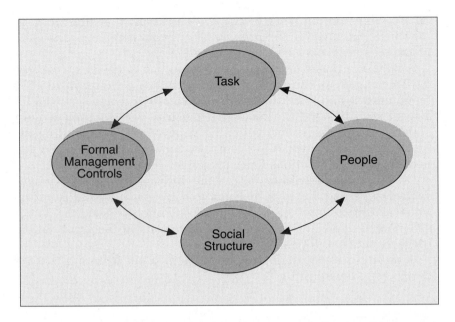

FIGURE 5.1
Each organization must
find a workable fit
between these elements.

result if a crew didn't follow assembly instructions precisely: the crew could start a new (and final) world war with a single mistake! Strict controls, such as frequent inspections, engineering tests, and detailed work rules, would be essential in the missile assembly process.

On the other hand, the tough missile assembly rules could never fit the creative atmosphere needed for effective journalism. Here, the task requires adherence to facts—but not to strict and detailed production inspections. Lives are not usually at stake in writing magazine articles. Besides, if a supervisor from *National Geographic* frequently hovered over the journalists' desks, the independent-minded writers might quit because the close control was intrusive and insulting.

Clearly, the type of organizational structure and controls must *fit* the people, social structure, and task of the organization (see figure 5.1).

▼ LINE AND STAFF

When organizations first emerge, all members are likely to be *line workers*. The line organization is made up of workers and their supervisors who are directly involved in producing the goods or services that the organization exists to produce.

Let's say that you have set up shop to manufacture and sell hang gliders. At first, only three people are involved in producing your brand of hang glider, the Gooneybird. Demand for your product is strong, and you all work long hours to keep your distributors stocked with Gooneybirds. You are all line workers.

Eventually, you add more workers and decide to specialize. Some employees build the frames; others put on the skin. You set up separate departments. One group focuses on buying raw materials; another is in charge of shipping the Gooneybirds to dealers; and so

■ *Line* employees produce the goods or services.

on. To this point, all workers can still be classified as line workers; they are all involved in the *primary* task of your company—the manufacture and sale of Gooneybird hang gliders.

Finally, the organization grows so large that it needs *specialized assistance.* When one of your customers flies a Gooneybird off a mountainside and is injured on the canyon floor, you see a need for a legal staff to fight the resulting lawsuit. The number of your employees increases, and your line supervisors are spending too much time hiring, explaining company benefits, and so on. So you need to add staff functions like a personnel department.

■ *Staff* personnel advise and assist the line organization.

Staff personnel advise and assist the line organization. They have special expertise, but they normally do not have authority to tell line managers or workers what to do. They offer advice; they do not give orders. Typically, the larger and more complex an organization, the more staff employees it will have.

In addition to the staff-line distinction, other factors affect the design of an organization.

▼ FACTS THAT AFFECT ORGANIZATIONAL DESIGN

At least five key factors play a major part in determining the design of an organization: task specialization, task integration, chain of command, location of decisions, and distribution of and access to information.

Task Specialization

■ Five key factors affect the design of an organization:

Task specialization
Task integration
Chain of command
Location of decisions
Distribution of and access to information

One important question in organizational design is "How specialized should each position or job be?" Organizational designers would say, "How 'differentiated' should the organization be?" Let's look into this more deeply.

Going back to the hang glider company example, we can see how task specialization might work in two different ways. Suppose the success of the Gooneybird hang glider has been so great the company is now a major manufacturer. Such a company would become more differentiated; task specialties would emerge. One group of workers would deal full-time with the process of procuring raw materials. Other specialized areas might be the quality control inspectors, the research and development staff, the sales staff, and the like.

The result is that each of these specialized groups becomes expert in dealing with a specific segment of the organization's overall mission. Each group may become so expert—and isolated from other parts of the organization—that the differentiated unit may develop different ways of thinking and even different emotional orientations as it works in those specialized areas. Sometimes its members get carried away and lose sight of the larger organization's intentions.

If the organization becomes too differentiated, the right hand may not know what the left hand is doing. Salespeople may aggressively sell Gooneybirds, while production people are turning out many

As the organization soars to new heights, differentiation becomes necessary

more of your new, improved model, the Albatross. The specialized purchasing department may buy a ten-year supply of fabric, while your research people have just discovered a cheaper but stronger substitute product.

Task specialization affects the organization's efficiency in another way. Mass production techniques, especially the use of assembly lines, are based on the notion of task specialization. The thinking is that as a person repeats a relatively simple procedure over and over again, he or she becomes very efficient at accomplishing that task. This efficiency can pay off for the organization so long as there is adequate coordination of this job with other related tasks. This leads to the next feature of organizational design: task integration.

■ Efficiency results when specialized tasks are carefully coordinated.

Task Integration

Job specialization, as just described, can be very useful to the organization so long as its benefits can be *integrated* into the overall organizational task. The degree of effectiveness of this coordination is another feature of organizational design over which managers have some influence. Once task specialization has occurred, coordination must take place to ensure a smooth operation.

■ The greater the specialization, the greater the need for integration.

In successful firms, the states of integration and differentiation go hand in hand. The more differentiation there is, the greater the need for collaboration and coordination.

Picture a manufacturing operation where one section is assembling the electronic parts for portable radios and the other section is producing cases for the same radios. If the group producing the radios' innards assembles six hundred units a day while the other group can only produce three hundred cabinets for those radios, the result will be an unbalanced operation. The manager's function here would be to balance the amount of work between the two groups—preferably without sacrificing efficiency. This coordination is a typical organizational design function.

Chain of Command

■ Span of control is the number of people reporting to a manager.

FIGURE 5.2
Tall and flat organization structures. Note: Each dot represents one worker.

The arrangement of organizational authority is known as the *chain of command.* It determines who reports to whom. The size of an organization and the number of levels of authority—how many different "ranks" you have—determine the shape of that organization. Some organizations are described as "tall"; others are "flat." Each supervisor's *span of control* helps determine the organization's shape. The span of control indicates how many people report to an individual supervisor. In a *tall* organization, *few people report to each manager,* but there are many levels of management. In a *flat*

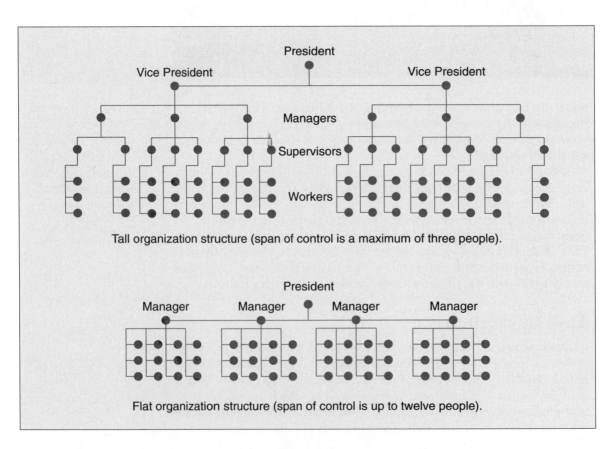

Tall organization structure (span of control is a maximum of three people).

Flat organization structure (span of control is up to twelve people).

organization, the span of control is quite broad; *many people report to a given manager.* Figure 5.2 illustrates these two organizational arrangements.

Each type of structure has advantages and disadvantages. The task, the total number of employees, and several other factors can affect the shape of an organization. When the span of control is narrow (as in a tall organization), each supervisor or manager can work on an individual basis with subordinates. The manager who has, say, five people reporting to him or her can get to know and work closely with each employee.

Tall organizations may have more communication problems. As information flows from level to level in a tall organization, messages get distorted. The more levels, the greater the distortion problem. A message from the top executive officer of the company coming down the organization through many levels runs a far greater risk of being distorted than would the same message in a flat organization.

The flat organization with a wide span of control (where one supervisor has many subordinates) poses some other communication and coordination problems. Typically, a manager in a flat organization may have difficulty developing a close relationship with the workers—there are too many people to get to know.

Furthermore, when the organization has few different levels, there may be less incentive to work for promotions. The organization that has, say, only three different levels of authority offers fewer opportunities to advance. This may affect the workers' motivation.

Location of Decisions

Who makes important decisions in the organization? This question can in part be determined by the organizational design. Some organizations *centralize* decision making at a very high level. Even relatively routine decisions are made only by top-level management. Other organizations create subunits in the organization where decisions may be made. These units may be called profit centers and may exist as separate entities for organizational decision making. They plan their own strategies, carry out plans, and are totally responsible for the outcomes of their own efforts.

As discussed in chapter 4, job enrichment—which is becoming more widespread in organizations—deals with increased responsibility and decision making. Organizations are frequently allowing workers, even at lower-level jobs, to make decisions relevant to their jobs. However, job enrichment is difficult when the tasks to be done are highly specialized or closely regulated. For example, the worker on a timed assembly line has little opportunity for creativity or personal decision making on that job. This limitation in part accounts for the criticism of assembly lines as dehumanizing.

Distribution of and Access to Information

Modern organizations are becoming more and more "information intensive." This means that the need for crucial information is

- Tall organizations permit managers to work with employees on an individual basis.

- Tall organizations may have more communication problems, resulting from the many levels information flows through.

- Managers may have difficulty getting to know all their workers in flat organizations with a large span of control.

- Profit centers are subgroups responsible for their own decisions.

SOURCE: From the *Wall Street Journal*—permission, Cartoon Features Syndicate. Reprinted by permission: Tribune Media Services

■ Information can be a source of power and control.

becoming more important to the organization. Information is power. People who are located in positions where they have access to great amounts of information are likely to control organizational functioning. This form of power need not follow the formal organization chart. In many organizations, for example, an executive secretary to a top-level manager may be very powerful because he or she has access to organizational scuttlebutt—informal information—as well as control over who gets in to see the boss.

▼ DEPARTMENTALIZATION: ANOTHER APPROACH TO ORGANIZING

■ Large organizations can be broken down into subunits in six ways.

Departmentalization involves grouping together similar types of activities and responsibilities into sections, divisions, branches, or departments. We use the term *department* in a general sense to refer to any such subunit of the organization.

We can break down the large work organization in one of at least six different ways, or we can use a combination of the six. The principal types of departmentalization are as follows:[1]

1. Function
2. Territory
3. Product
4. Customer
5. Time
6. Equipment or process

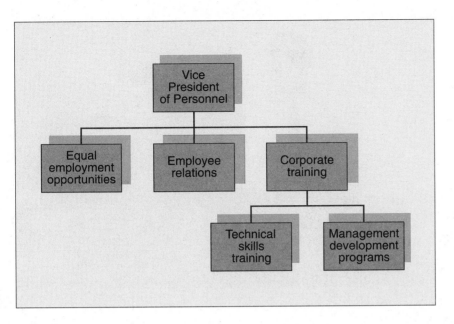

FIGURE 5.3
Function departmental-
ization.

Function

Probably the most common form of departmentalization is by function. Specialized needs of a company are met by specialized departments such as research and development, finance, personnel, marketing, and manufacturing.

Large, complex organizations often create many functional divisions with subfunctions under each. For example, the function called *personnel* may eventually add further specialized units, such as equal opportunity employment, employee relations, and corporate training. Even these areas may be further departmentalized, as illustrated in figure 5.3.

Territory

Some firms organize along *territorial* or *geographic* lines. Local banks, for example, often find they can serve their customers better and gain more customers by establishing branch banks in different neighborhoods. Similarly, companies set up regional offices around the country or around the world to be closer to their customers, suppliers, or transportation facilities.

Product

As organizations grow, they often broaden their lines of products or services. A cosmetics manufacturer may expand into costume jewelry; a food distributor may add a line of paper products. Creation of a jewelry division or paper products division may now make sense. Employees in such divisions can focus their attention on the unique characteristics of their specific products.

Some firms organize along geographic lines.

Customer

The type of customer served provides another opportunity for departmentalization. Some organizations set up specialized sales forces that sell only to major industrial accounts or to government agencies.

Department stores often create divisions based on the customers served. A bargain basement may serve cost-conscious buyers, while a catalog service offers a wide range of goods to people who prefer not to come to the store.

Wise companies clarify their marketing niche—the specific people at whom they target their sales effort—to maximize productivity. If the target market is senior citizens with above-average income, the company wastes no time on teenagers.

Time

Some organizations work around the clock. The use of shifts is an example of time departmentalization. Sometimes a completely different organization with different reporting relationships and responsibilities goes into effect during, for example, the graveyard shift (midnight to 8 A.M.). Equipment breakdowns may be reported directly to the maintenance manager at night, rather than to a lower-level supervisor, as on the day shift.

Equipment or Process

The nature of the equipment or process used provides another common departmentalization opportunity. For example, in a modern printing plant, one department may produce only four-color printing on high-speed presses. Another department in the same plant may print one-color work or do binding, camera work, platemaking, or some other specialized process.

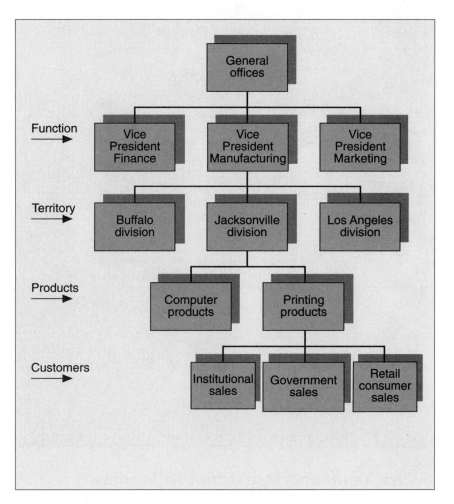

FIGURE 5.4
Departmentalization on several levels. *SOURCE:* Adapted from Stan Kossen, *Supervision* (New York: Harper and Row, 1981), p.225.

Not all firms use all these types of departmentalization, but often a firm will use several. An organization chart illustrating the combination of several forms of departmentalization is shown in figure 5.4.

Although departmentalization such as we've described often provides for a more streamlined organization, it can have drawbacks. Perhaps the major one is that departments tend to become competitive and sometimes uncooperative. These smaller work units often fight for their "fair share"—or perhaps a bit more than their fair share—of the organization's resources. They also tend to blame other departments for foul-ups or delays.

■ Departmentalization can have drawbacks.

▼ MODERN ALTERNATIVES TO TRADITIONAL ORGANIZATIONS

In recent years, companies have more often experimented with organization patterns that differ from the traditional ones described thus far. Among these innovations are work teams, matrix organizations, and "intrapreneuring" organizations.

Small, autonomous
work teams can offset
the drawbacks of larger,
traditional organization
structures.

Work Team and Individual Autonomy

One attempt to overcome the drawbacks of traditional organization structures is a return to the smaller work groups. The work group in such cases is an autonomous group of employees who are collectively responsible for their output. Perhaps a classic example of this approach was carried out by two Scandinavian auto manufacturers beginning in the 1960s. Work at the Saab and Volvo plants in Sweden was redesigned so that different work teams are responsible for specific installations on the car (for example, the entire electrical system, controls, and instrumentation). One first-level supervisor and one industrial engineer or technician oversee two or four teams. Supervision focuses primarily on overall quality and on making certain that each team has the necessary equipment.[2]

■ Some work teams build entire products from the ground up.

A number of other manufacturing organizations have also begun to use small work teams, sometimes giving them the responsibility for building an entire product from the ground up. The result has been, for some employees, additional opportunities, responsibilities, and a higher level of motivation. Quality of the products produced by these teams has been generally very good.

Carrying the team approach one step further, some organizations allow individual workers to build an entire product from the parts provided. Here, the manager's responsibility is simply to see that

Organizational Resources (Instructors)	Organizational Needs (subjects)					
	Grade 7 History	Grade 8 History	Grade 7 Math	Grade 8 Math	Grade 7 Science	Grade 8 Science
Mrs. Parker						
Mr. Little						
Ms. Jones						
Mr. Davis						

FIGURE 5.5
A school's matrix organization.

necessary parts are available and to check the quality. One organization using this approach is the Western Electric Corporation, where some employees build electronic switchboard systems from the ground up. The firm's television advertisements extoll the virtues of this return to individual craftsmanship and describe the assembly process as a "virtuoso performance." Opportunities for personal satisfaction do exist in such an arrangement. However, not all workers may be ready to be artisans.

Matrix Organizations

A matrix may be used as an alternative organizational design for the overall company structure or for special projects. The matrix design is organized around function and basically replaces the pyramid structure of traditional management organizations. For example, a school's faculty organization might be organized in a matrix design. The functional areas of education—that is, the various subjects taught—could form one axis of the matrix, with the instructors forming the other axis (see figure 5.5).

This faculty's organization could be shifted or revised each term or school year to match the school's varying needs with the instructors having the most applicable training. For example, in the first year, Mrs. Parker heads the math instruction for both seventh grade and eighth grade. In the second year, Mrs. Parker shifts to take over science instruction, having taken advanced courses in science during the summer. Now Ms. Jones and Mr. Davis take over seventh- and eighth-grade math instruction to fill the void created by Mrs. Parker's shift to teach science. In addition to working in their functional subject areas, all faculty members report to the principal's office on administrative issues.

A matrix form of organization is often used when special projects must be undertaken. For example, in the aerospace industry, companies create teams made up of employees from different departments for special short-term projects. One such company may want to prepare a major proposal to bid for a government contract. A team is pulled together including engineers, drafters, financial specialists, technical writers, and artists. A project director becomes their boss for as long as they work on the project. When the proposal is completed, the workers return to their regular departments and report again to their departmental bosses.

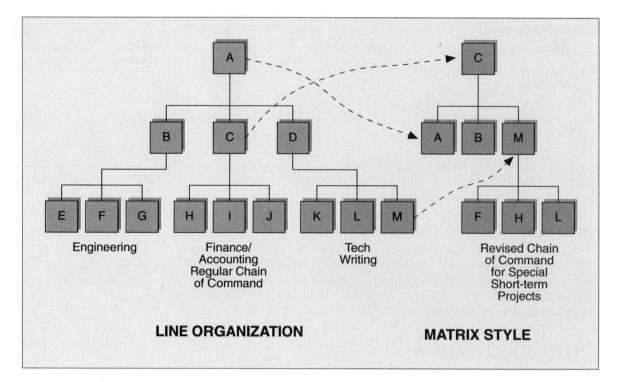

Engineering

Finance/
Accounting
Regular Chain
of Command

Tech
Writing

Revised Chain
of Command
for Special
Short-term
Projects

LINE ORGANIZATION

MATRIX STYLE

FIGURE 5.6
A matrix organization.

■ The matrix becomes a
separate entity super-
imposed on the larger
organization.

■ Matrix organizations
violate the unity-of-
command principle.

■ The flexible, self-
confident worker will
be most comfortable
in a matrix.

In some cases, people of lower rank in the formal organization
become bosses in the matrix team. Figure 5.6 shows how person C
becomes temporary boss over person A when representatives from
various functions are assembled into a project team.

A project manager is chosen to coordinate the effort of this work
team but may have no *permanent* authority over these workers. In
effect, the matrix organization is a separate entity superimposed on
the larger organization. The project leader may temporarily supervise employees who are above, below, or on the same hierarchical
level.

Once the project is complete—say, the government bid document
is prepared and submitted—the project team is disbanded, and the
workers return to their original departments.

Although specialized teams assembled into matrix organizations
can be very effective, they also have some disadvantages. For one
thing, matrix organization members usually continue to report to
their permanent department supervisor as well as to the project
leader. This violates an old principle of organizations called *unity of
command*—the believe that each individual should report to only
one boss.

If the matrix approach is to be successful, both project supervisors
and permanent supervisors must resolve any conflicts in their orders
to subordinates. The employee must not be required to choose between managers.

Probably the most important determinant of satisfaction in a
matrix is a worker's flexibility and self-confidence. Rigid or insecure
employees are likely to be uncomfortable in such an arrangement.

"Intrapreneuring"

Modern organizations are increasingly recognizing the need many people have for the satisfaction gained from building or creating their own products or services. This need manifests itself in thousands of people who leave established organizations to create their own businesses—to become entrepreneurs.

For many companies, the response to this trend is to encourage entrepreneurial experiences within the organizational structure. "Creative corporate mavericks" are being given more space to work through their own ideas for the good of the company. These people are called *intrapreneurs*.[3]

Intrapreneurs bridge the gap between manager and inventor. They are team builders who have a firm grasp of the marketplace realities. They can make fast decisions without much data or guidance and are mainly action-oriented. Furthermore, intrapreneurs don't like to take no for an answer and will do anything, even the mundane tasks, necessary to move a project along.

To tap the power of the intrapreneur, corporations must provide appropriate rewards for risk taking and extraordinary contributions to the company. One reward intrapreneurs crave is recognition for their success in moving a project from inception to realization. Intrapreneurs are also motivated by an atmosphere that allows them freedom to explore and pursue various options without undue pressure to conform or meet time deadlines. This feeling of freedom includes the freedom to make mistakes and is crucial to successful intrapreneurship.

In the most innovative companies, small intrapreneurial business units are allowed to grow and mature by retaining some of the money they have earned for the company. They then use that money as capital for new ideas. The result: innovation flourishes.

Many innovative companies build intrapreneurs. Companies like 3M and most high-tech manufacturers have allowed people within to create and champion their pet projects. One classic case is the Post-it note designed by an intrapreneur within 3M. The company's willingness to allow freedom of inquiry led to an enormously profitable new product.

> ■ Many companies encourage innovation by giving more freedom to "creative corporate mavericks."

From Pyramid to Circle

Bureaucratic or rigidly structured organizations are marked by highly specialized functions, clear departmental boundaries, limited job descriptions, and close supervisory control to make sure that the work gets done. Cynthia Scott and Dennis T. Jaffe see modern organizations moving away from pyramid structures to "circles" that permit greater employee empowerment.

They see the following as characteristics of the pyramid:

- Decisions are made at the top.
- Each person is clearly responsible only for his or her job.
- Change is slow and rare and comes only from the top.
- Feedback and communication come from the top down.

- Movement and communication between divisions is minimal.
- If you do your job, you can expect job security and promotions as the organization expands.
- People focus attention upward, and the person above you is responsible for your results.
- Managers say how things are done and what is expected.
- Employees are not expected to be highly motivated, so it is necessary to keep tight control over their behavior.

Until recently, most organizations operated roughly according to those principles.

But now, more organizations are evolving into a new organizational environment characterized by high commitment, high involvement, and self-management. One way to look at the shift toward empowerment is to think of two basic ways to structure the organization.

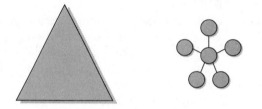

The traditional organization is the pyramid, while the new, empowered organization can be thought of as looking more like a circle, or a network. The new organization form is called the circle or network, because it can be thought of as a series of coordinating groups or teams, linked by a center, rather than an apex. The following are characteristics of the circle:

- The customer is in the center.
- People work cooperatively together to do what is needed.
- Responsibility, skills, authority, and control are shared.
- Control and coordination come through continual communication and many decisions.
- Change is sometimes very quick, as new challenges come up.
- The key skill for an employee, and a manager, is the ability to work with others.
- There are relatively few levels of organization.
- Power comes from the ability to influence and inspire others, not from your position.
- Individuals are expected to manage themselves and are accountable to the whole; the focus is on the customer.
- Managers are the energizers, the connectors, and the empowerers of their teams.[4]

The logical extension of the circle organization is the self-directed work team. In the Another Look article beginning on page 108, Bob Hughes shows how organizations can best implement such teams.

▼ EFFECTS OF TECHNOLOGY ON ORGANIZATIONS

Finally, traditional organization structures can be drastically changed by adapting to changing technology. Many manufacturing organizations are becoming more aware of the economic advantages of using robots to accomplish organizational work. The cost of human labor is often extremely high when compared with the operating costs of the increasingly available, electronically guided machines. Although few people think that machines will entirely replace human labor, machines do pose an alternative for some firms.

■ The cost of human labor is often far greater than the cost of machines.

Another impact of technology is increased sophistication in communications. Today, a growing number of people are members of organizations but never have any physical contact with their fellow members. Via computer networks, modems, fax machines, and the like, more people work at home or other widely disbursed locations. The organization is based almost entirely in the commonness of purpose, not in any physical structure.

Up to this point, we've emphasized (1) factors that determine a need for organizations and (2) factors that shape organizations from within. But organizations also are shaped by outside forces, some of which they may have little control over.

▼ OTHER FORCES THAT ORGANIZATIONS MUST FACE

Organizations do not exist in a vacuum. They are constantly interacting with many different environmental forces. These forces include the society in which they exist, the political climate, and the availability of needed resources, all of which provide opportunities and challenges to organizational leaders.

Organizations have recognized that they need not be simply *acted on* by their environment. Frequently, an organization may do better to reach out and try to influence environmental forces. For example, many corporations have become very active in the political arena. Their intent is to affect legislation that in turn affects their businesses. So, instead of sitting back and having the government act on the organization with regulations and legislation, organizations reach out and attempt to influence those governmental actions.

■ Organizations realize the value of reaching out to influence their environment.

Similarly, organizations are sensitive to social problems and changes. Many companies have initiated aggressive social action programs. In part, they do this to avoid government regulation. But in many cases, they simply recognize the public relations and humane benefits of such activities.

■ Organizations seek to influence social changes, political actions, sources of resources, and so forth.

For example, some major companies, such as Xerox, IBM, and Wells Fargo, offer their employees *social service leaves of absence.* Under this program, selected employees are given full pay and benefits while they perform volunteer service for a year or more. Often the volunteer service is coordinated through a social services agency or charitable group. The advantages for the company are public recognition as well as a program that can boost employee morale and help workers gain new skills.

The idea of influencing the environment is not new. Early manufacturers recognized the importance of controlling resources for their companies. Near the beginning of the twentieth century, Ford Motor Company bought mines, foundries, and railroads to ensure that raw materials for its automobiles would not be interrupted. Today, many organizations contribute generously to colleges and universities to ensure a continued supply of trained labor.

The point is that few organizations can sit back and be acted on by external forces. It makes sense for them to reach out and to activate, influence, and control important forces such as government, social pressure groups, and suppliers of vital materials.

▼ SUMMARY OF KEY IDEAS

- Organizations are complex social systems that provide order and direction for individuals through a structure that helps the organization accomplish its goals.
- With organization come some necessary limitations on personal freedom.
- Despite the years of research on how to organize, no one has found one best way that is appropriate in all situations.
- People are controlled in varying degrees by the formal management controls, task requirements, and social structure of an organization.
- Line employees are concerned with production of the organization's goals or service, while staff personnel provide assistance and counsel to the line employees.
- Five actors affecting organizational design are task specialization, task integration, chain of command, location of decisions, and distribution of and access to information.
- Departments may be organized by function, territory, product, customer, time, and equipment or process. Any combination of the six may also be found.
- Three modern alternatives to traditional organizations are work teams, matrix organizations, and intrapreneurial organizations.
- Modern organizations are moving away from pyramid structures toward circle or network structures.
- People are often connected via communication technology and have no physical contact with the organization.

▼ KEY TERMS, CONCEPTS, AND NAMES

Centralized decision making   Circle or network organizations
Chain of command   Customer departmentalization

Equipment or process
   departmentalization
Flat versus tall organizations
Function departmentalization
Intrapreneurs
Matrix organizations
Mechanistic view of
   organizations
Product departmentalization
Profit center

Pyramid structures
Self-directed work teams
Span of control
Task integration
Task specialization
Territory departmentalization
Time departmentalization
Work teams

▼ QUESTIONS AND EXERCISES

1. Describe some ways in which specific organizations reach out to influence their environments. How effective are they? How could they do more?

2. Draw up an organization chart for your school or organization. Show any departmentalization. Explain whether the organization is tall or flat. How could it be rearranged?

3. What are some of the effects of a tall organization? Of a flat organization? How are these types of organization structures likely to affect workers on the job? Which type of organization would you prefer to work in? Why?

4. Describe a case in which work teams, matrix organizations, and intrapreneurial organization structures would be effective.

5. Read the "Another Look" articles on the following pages. Then answer the introductory questions at the beginning of this chapter.

▼ NOTES

1. The discussion of departmentalization was adapted in part from Stan Kossen, *Supervision* (New York: Harper and Row, 1981), pp. 224–29.

2. Edgar F. Huse, *The Modern Manager* (St. Paul: West, 1979), p. 353.

3. The term *intrapreneur* was popularized in Gifford Pinchot III, *Intrapreneuring* (New York: Harper and Row, 1985).

4. Cynthia D. Scott and Dennis T. Jaffe, *Empowerment* (Los Altos, Calif.: Crisp Publications, 1991), p. 12.

5. Ibid., p. 15.

ANOTHER LOOK: CUMMINS ENGINE

When Cummins Engine was founded in 1919, the company explicitly highlighted individual worth and ingenuity as the core of its values, but over the years these were gradually forgotten. As the company grew, they hired managers from Detroit's large automotive firms instead of developing managers from within. These new supervisors, who were not steeped in Cummins's values, neglected the many talents the line workers had to offer; instead, they operated by a management system developed at the height of the Industrial Revolution when the assembly line had been broken down into simple tasks the undereducated, mostly immigrant workers of that day could understand. As a result, by the time James Henderson joined Cummins, the company had had seven strikes within a three-year period.

"Accountants and production managers loved that old management system," says Henderson, now Cummins's president, "because they could easily count bolts and widgets as they came along the line." That became the measure of productivity, and it created an ever-widening chasm between the worker and management. It was time for Cummins to return to the basics.

The first step was to develop a set of core values that employees could use to measure their own performance—and be measured by. The list the Cummins team came up with focused on the people:

- trust, respect, and equity for workers

- a commitment to the worker's full potential

- training as a keystone for ataining organizational excellence

- the worker's participation in decision making

Cummins decided to test their new approach in a model plant in South Carolina, and it worked better than Henderson and his associates dared hope. Quality rose, and so did the workers' sense of commitment. For example, two women began drawing a rose on each engine they assembled. Although the artwork was hidden when the engine was painted, the rose was the women's unique statement of their commitment to quality.

In the model plant, jobs were no longer broken down into narrowly defined tasks. This took some getting used to, as Jim Henderson learned the day he called the plant manager's office several times and no one answered. When he finally reached the manager at his home later in the evening, Henderson learned that the manager, his secretary, the receptionist, and every other available person in the building had been down on the assembly line all day filling a rush order.

SOURCE: Chuck Colson and Jack Eckerd, *Why America Doesn't Work* (Dallas: Word Publishing, 1991), pp. 125–26. Reprinted with permission.

ANOTHER LOOK: TWENTY-FIVE STEPPING STONES FOR SELF-DIRECTED WORK TEAMS

There is an old story about three men of the cloth fishing on a small lake: a Protestant minister, a Catholic priest and a rabbi. The priest watches in astonishment as his companions, one after the other, climb out of the rowboat and walk across the water to the concession stand. Assuring himself that his faith is as great as theirs, he steps from the boat and promptly sinks. The minister turns to the rabbi and says, "Do you suppose we should have shown him where the rocks are?"

The idea of converting a classic hierarchical organization into a network of self-directed work teams has received so much glowing press, and has proven so successful for some companies, that the process begins to sound like a simple matter of stepping out of the old rowboat and strolling into a glorious new future. As many organizations have learned to their chagrin, life doesn't work that way. The fact is, self-directed teams represent a sweeping organizational change, and you'll have much better luck if you know where the rocks are. Here are some of the stepping stones discovered so far by companies that have braved the attempt.

1. I have already demonstrated the first common error. I described work teams as "self-directed." Newly formed teams are not self-directed, nor will they be for some time, probably two or three years. Everyone needs to understand that team development is evolutionary. Describing fledgling teams as self-directed establishes unrealistic expectations. Forget the adjectives. Just call them "work teams."

2. Awareness training should occur early in the process so that stakeholders (workers, supervisors and managers) share a common vision. This is a critical step in managing expectations. There will be many misconceptions concerning what "teams" will be, what they'll do, how much authority and responsibility they'll have—and how quickly the master plan will unfold.

3. There are no bread crumbs in the forest. Either the birds ate them or those who went before us were so unsure of the path that they did not leave any. Attempting to duplicate some other organization's effort will not work. Implementation of work teams is unique to each location. What worked in a company in North Carolina may not work in the same company in New Jersey. Both the people and the organizational culture are probably different. Even divisions or departments at the same site can differ significantly. Implementation in these divisions may not follow parallel paths.

4. Not everyone will welcome this "empowering" effort. Some pundits have estimated that 25 percent to 30 percent of working Americans, from top to bottom do not want to be empowered. That is, they don't want more responsibility on the job than they've already got.

5. All stakeholders must understand that this evolution takes time. How much? Rensis Likert said it takes three to five years of concentrated effort to change an organization. Ralph Stayer, CEO of Johnsonville Foods in Sheboygan WI, says it takes less. Hope for Stayer's timetable—but build expectations around Likert's.

6. All stakeholders must be assured—and it must be true—that they will not ultimately suffer as a result of the improvements in performance brought about by this change. Managers must ask and answer questions that seem, from a hard-nosed business perspective, almost blasphemous. For instance, "Suppose we achieve the 20 percent or 30 percent improvement in output advertised as a realistic goal for self-directed teams: Can current or future demand support such an increase without laying people off?"

7. Team development will not follow a straight path. There will be ups and downs as teams move along the development continuum toward self-direction.

8. It is still widely assumed that if we call any group of employees a "team," they will function as a team and our organization will begin to reap all the vaunted benefits of "teamwork"—higher quantity, bet-

ANOTHER LOOK: TWENTY-FIVE STEPPING STONES FOR SELF-DIRECTED WORK TEAMS *continued*

ter quality and so on. It just doesn't happen that way. Groups must go through some process—some sort of team-building or developmental activity—to begin to function as teams. Group members will need training in areas such as self-awareness (perhaps using instruments such as the Myers-Briggs Type Indicator) and how to reach consensus in decision making ("Desert Survival," for instance, is a well-known consensus-building exercise). The team will also need help in establishing a direction—a mission and vision. And during this educational process, team members should determine future training and development needs.

9. For each step teams take toward self-direction, managers must take one step back. If this doesn't happen, someone's toes will be stepped on and the credibility of the whole idea will suffer. Employees will ask, "Is management serious about this or not?"

10. Forget the fanfare and the banners. Do not announce "D-day." Consultant Peter Block, author of *The Empowered Manager* and other books, tells us that organizational culture is "changed through a series of moments." This change will not occur on any given day. To most workers, kickoff speeches and pep rallies don't signal management commitment; they signal a new "program of the month."

11. Managers should be prepared to model the behavior they want to see; workers will insist on it. Gandhi said, "We must be the changes we wish to see in the world." One of the paradoxes in this whole slippery business surfaces here: Although employees at all levels will demand to see "model" behavior from their bosses, nobody must use the fact that "My manager doesn't manage me that way" as a cop-out. As Block advises us, "It is unrealistic to expect our bosses to live up to our expectations."

12. Beware of managers who pay lip service to the Great Team Scheme. They can cause much more damage than those who are honest enough to oppose it openly. Their subordinates will be quick to notice that nothing is really changing, and that all the team-building activities amounted to "just another training program." Credibility, once shattered, is doubly hard to rebuild.

13. The development of some work teams may be thwarted by a perception paradox on the part of the manager responsible for the team. As the manager, I may believe that my actions are perfectly aligned with the organization's vision, when in reality I am overly directive. I show no inclination to change; why would I when I see no need? I need some feedback. If I don't get it—or if I do get it but don't accept it and act on it—I'll become

a wreck on the highway of this transformation the organization is undergoing. We all know what happens to car wrecks on the freeway: They have to be removed so that traffic can proceed. It was a perceptive manager who once said, "It's sometimes easier to change *people* than it is to *change* people." And what if the "car wrecks" form a majority? Will work teams ever succeed in that organization? The jury is still out.

14. That last problem also occurs in reverse. Some managers, in an effort to be "participative" or to model the desired management style, overcompensate and fail to be directive when direction is needed. Ken Blanchard makes a compelling case for applying his Situational Leadership II model, which has been widely used with individual workers, when supervising developing teams. Initially, new teams are a lot like new hires. They are often highly motivated but don't know what to do. They need direction at this point. The catch is that managers have to be a little bit smarter than the teams in order to tell them what they need to do.

15. Do not neglect or forget first-line supervisors. They are the key to making the whole thing work—and yet they have the most to lose. They must be convinced that, while their roles will change, they will still have jobs. Involve them in steering committees, design

ANOTHER LOOK *continued*

teams and other important activities.

16. With a greenfield operation (a plant start-up that uses work teams from the beginning), it is better to overstaff initially and move the extra people to other locations or divisions as both the technical and social sides of the new organization solidify. The "extras" should be promoted, not demoted, as they are transferred from the greenfield site. Though most people would agree that it's easier to implement work teams in a greenfield plant than to retrofit an established culture, it may not be that much easier. The technical side of the new operation must be perfected, and product must go out the door if the bills are to be paid.

17. The membership of steering committees and design teams should represent diagonal slices of the organization; that is, members should come from different functions and different levels of authority. Personal qualifications should include open-mindedness, good communication skills and candor. You want people who will say what they think. But beware of including members who value the status quo excessively.

18. Steering committees and design teams must operate under one ground rule: "Don't assume anything." If these critical groups are paralyzed by the old paradigm and are unwilling to consider new methods, little will be gained from sociotechnical redesigns.

19. Provisions should be made for work teams to remove ineffective team leaders. Some organizations have team members rotate through the leader position. Others name several members who serve as facilitators with responsibilities for different areas such as safety, quality/production, communication and team development. Most important: In perception and in fact, team leaders must be members of the team and not surrogate supervisors.

20. Some decisions are tougher than others. Profound statement, right? Do not allow teams to start with the hard ones—hiring, firing or peer appraisal, for example. A good exercise is to list all the different sorts of decisions that teams might make, and arrange them in a hierarchy. Let young teams learn to make the easy decisions before they have to make the tough ones. "Easy," however, must not be a synonym for "inconsequential," particularly not in the perception of team members.

21. Visits to other organizations that use work teams are crucial for members of steering committees and design teams. They need to ask, "What worked and what didn't?" They need to get a feel for the environment of an organization that runs on work teams. And it's important for members of these critical decisionmaking bodies to realize that it is possible to make this idea work. If others can do it, they can too. There is, however, a growing problem with the idea of learning from other organizations. Just as companies have always protected the information and processes that make up the technical side of their operations, some team-based organizations, realizing the competitive value of their investments in the social side, have started guarding those secrets as well. Proprietary walls are going up, for example, around innovative selection, appraisal and compensation systems.

22. As teams develop, systems, policies and procedures will need to be changed, or they may form a "glass ceiling." Teams will mature to the point where they have increased the company's productivity by, say, 30 percent. Then workers may ask: "What's in it for us? We're making the company all this extra money, and we're still drawing the same old wage." A valid question. Some team-based organizations are using compensation plans where as much as one-third of a team member's wages are determined by individual and team performance.

ANOTHER LOOK: TWENTY-FIVE STEPPING STONES FOR SELF-DIRECTED WORK TEAMS *continued*

23. When designing pay-for-skill or pay-for-knowledge compensation programs, be sure to include objective criteria for advancement. Competency-based training should be developed for each group of skills (or "skill cluster"). Satisfactory achievement on written or performance tests (the latter whenever feasible) should be required for promotion to the next higher grade.

24. At the risk of sounding trite, communication is paramount. Everything must be communicated, and always through two-way channels; memos are unsatisfactory. Open communication builds trust, which is often lacking at the onset of a work-team transformation.

25. Managers must understand that leading this change, and later managing in this environment, will be as difficult as anything they've ever undertaken. And if you promise them it will also be deeply rewarding, don't forget to mention what, exactly, will be so rewarding about it.

One final thought: The winning organizations have always been the ones with the best people. This principle will become even more obvious over the next several years. The critical challenge right now is not only to recruit the best, but also to keep them. We know that, in addition to the work itself, the work environment and the quality of supervision have an enormous effect on job satisfaction. Organizations structured around work teams are generally seen as more desirable places to work. We're all competing for the same labor pool. Work teams may provide an edge.

As companies in increasing numbers struggle to forge work teams into vehicles of empowerment and competitive advantage, the rocks that support this strategy become more obvious. And we all know that it helps to know where the rocks are.

SOURCE: Bob Hughes, *Training, December, 1991.*

▼ A CASE IN POINT: MOTO-WIZ GOES MATRIX

Sandra Dudley was generally happy in her job as an electrical engineer working for a medium-sized, but rapidly growing, specialized motors manufacturer. She had been with Moto-Wiz for eight months, having been hired fresh out of college. She had a good boss, one who was very careful in giving her clear instructions for each task assigned to her. But she now got the impression that all that would soon change.

Moto-Wiz had been invited to bid on a government contract for specialized plastic motors to be used in the armament system of the new B-2 bomber. Winning the contract could result in enormous profits for Moto-Wiz. It would be, by far, the company's largest contract.

Top management had decided to set up a special team to prepare a proposal, complete with design specifications to be submitted. They assigned as project director a man from the research and development department. Dudley was selected for the project, along with people from marketing, finance, technical writing, and the art department. The project was to be completed in thirty days. This would require a lot of overtime and a lot of very hard work.

Dudley knew the project manager vaguely, but the rest of the team members were unknown to her.

She was more than a little uncomfortable about the upcoming project.

QUESTIONS

1. How do you think Dudley is likely to react to this new assignment?
2. As Dudley's department head, what would you do to help her in this change in her work arrangement?
3. What could the project director do to help employees like Dudley to be successful in this matrix organization?
4. What are the probable advantages and disadvantages faced by Moto-Wiz in its decision to use a matrix organization?
5. How might the matrix organization affect work climate, employee satisfaction, and worker motivation?

CHAPTER

6

THE HUMAN SIDE
OF ORGANIZATIONS

This chapter answers several all-important questions:

■ How do the ways people really act create an informal organization?

■ How do formal organizations tend to inhibit people from normal growth and development?

■ What are seven developmental dimensions along which people grow?

■ What is organizational climate, and how can we measure it?

■ How do values of the organization's culture manifest themselves?

■ Why is it important for a manager to recognize the effects of organization structures on employees?

The answer to these and other questions are coming up next in chapter 6....

CHAPTER 6

■ The *informal* organization may look quite different from the formal one.

■ Often, the *real* power resides in people who do not hold formal leadership positions.

We looked at reasons for organizing and the pros and cons of various organizational structures in chapter 5. Next, we'll look more closely at *human* aspects that determine organizational effectiveness. Organizations are never as clear-cut and mechanical in reality as they appear on paper. Organizational charts can be misleading.

The human side of organizations—the ways people *really* interact—creates an *informal organization.* Organizations and suborganizations (departments, work teams, and the like) develop personalities of their own. An informal organization arises, and it often contradicts the established "real" organization.

For example, a simple formal organization chart might look like figure 6.1. But *informal* reporting patterns may look quite different. The president's secretary may be far more influential (in part because he or she can control access to the president), and the accounting manager may seldom make a move without checking with the marketing manager. The informal organization chart might look like figure 6.2

Managers who assume that the formal organization chart accurately describes all reporting arrangements may be in for a surprise. Often the real power resides in people who do not occupy key spots in the organization. Consider the case of the chief executive officer (CEO) of a medium-sized company whose office workers "ran" her. She light-heartedly introduced her secretary to outsiders as her "boss." While everyone laughed during such introductions, workers within the company knew there was much truth to the designation. The secretary had been with the company longer than the CEO, and she made sure everyone in the office followed procedures the secretary's way. It was even said that vice-presidents occasionally fetched the mail or a cup of coffee for the CEO's secretary—the boss's "boss." For a glance at where this informally powerful secretary fits in, see figure 6.3.

▼ FACTORS THAT CAN GIVE PEOPLE INFORMAL AUTHORITY

Many factors tend to give people informal authority in organizations. In the preceding case of the CEO's secretary, seniority (years

FIGURE 6.1
A simple formal organization chart.

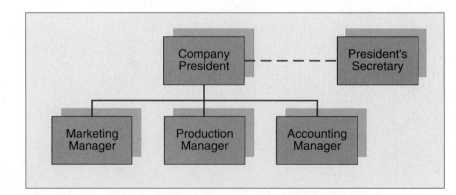

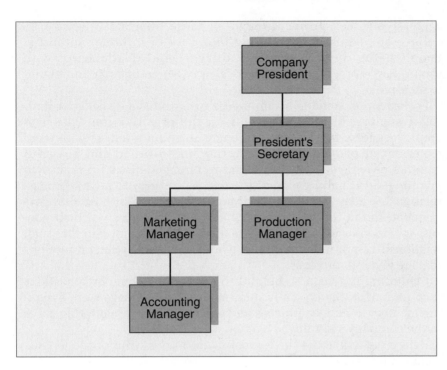

FIGURE 6.2
An informal organization chart.

with the company) and familiarity with company procedures provided a basis for her power. Other important factors might include access to other powerful people in the organization, aggressive or intimidating behavior, experience in the area of the organization's work, and general credibility or believability among peers. Clearly, looking at the boxes in a company's organization chart doesn't tell us who *really* has power and influence.

Seeing others attempting to gain or use informal authority in organizations upsets some people. In their anger and disgust, they call this power seeking "company politics," "brownnosing," the "corporate rat race," and so on. While we don't encourage anyone to

■ Many factors tend to give people informal authority in organizations.

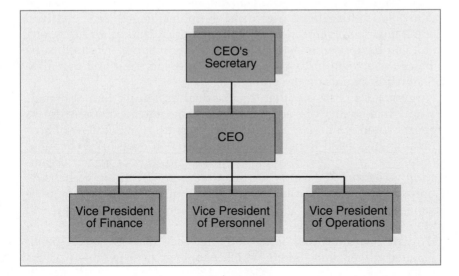

FIGURE 6.3
The boss's 'boss'—an informal organization chart.

aggressively seek power through all these informal ways, we do believe one can't avoid running into a lot of informal authority. People naturally form informal alliances and relationships with each other—sometimes in an ethical way, sometimes in an attempt to manipulate.

■ Mentors can convey informal authority on their protégés.

For example, some new employees seem to have a knack for finding a mentor, or helper-teacher, in the organization. The new employees form friendships and enjoy common interests with more experienced people. As a result, the more learned and powerful mentors provide contacts, tips, and recommendations for their own favorite (and usually younger) friends or protégés. A mentor-protégé relationship may last for years. Many top leaders in business, government, the military, and other fields attribute much of their success to a mentor who helped them along. Others complain that such relationships are unfair to those who are passed by for promotions that are given to protégés.

Mentoring has been so helpful to people that some organizations now formalize this typically informal activity. Managers are assigning mentors to new employees and even explaining mentoring skills in the company's employee handbook.[1]

Before we talk about the human factor in organizations, let's look at a broader issue.

▼ THE DILEMMA OF BEING HUMAN AND BEING ORGANIZED

The organizations we belong to influence our way of behaving and, often, our ways of thinking. We change to conform to what the organization wants or needs. To some degree, we cease to be individuals and become part of a larger creature: the organization.

■ Organizations can have detrimental effects on people.

Organizational theorist Chris Argyris wrote an article entitled "Being Human and Being Organized" that illustrates a key dilemma of the relationship between organizations and people. The thesis of his article is this: Being organized is important—in fact, civilized people must be organized—yet too much organization, or the wrong kind, can have serious detrimental effects on people. There must be a balance between individual needs on the one hand and organizational requirements on the other.

■ Formal organizations often inhibit people from normal growth.

Argyris goes on to say that the classical design for formal organizations has some very serious flaws. The nature of these flaws appears when we set two pictures side by side: "First, a view of how human beings need to behave in our society in order to be healthy, productive, growing individuals; and second, how a formal organization (a factory, business, or hospital) requires them to behave. Comparing these pictures, we see that the organization's requirements, as presented by 'classical' descriptions, are sharply opposed to the individual's needs."[2]

Argyris continues his thesis by citing what he calls "seven developmental dimensions" along which people grow (see table 6.1). As

▼ TABLE 6.1 ARGYRIS'S SEVEN DEVELOPMENTAL DIMENSIONS

CHILDLIKE BEHAVIORS	MATURE, ADULT BEHAVIORS
Being passive	Being active
Being dependent on others	Being relatively independent of others
Reacting with few types of behaviors	Reacting with many types of behaviors
Having shallow, brief, erratic interests	Having intense, long-term, coherent commitments
Accepting brief, unconnected jobs	Searching for long-term challenges that link the past and the future
Being content with low status	Searching for advancement
Having little self-awareness, being impulsive	Having self-awareness and self-control

children become adults, their behavior changes significantly. The seven dimensions reflect typical changes.

1. People grow from being *passive* as infants toward being *active* as adults.

2. People grow from being *dependent* on others toward being relatively *independent* of others. The adult develops an ability to "stand on his or her own two feet."

3. Children react to situations with relatively *few types of behaviors;* adults develop *many.* A small child may throw temper tantrums or cry when things don't go his or her way; adults learn to cope with disappointments in a wider variety of ways.

4. Children typically have rather *shallow, brief, and erratic interests.* Their attention span is quite short. As they grow into adulthood, their attention span grows, as does their ability to be more intense, to *deal with the long term,* and to *hold coherent commitments.* The deepening interests of adulthood require increasingly varied challenges. Adults want their tasks to be not easy but challenging, not simple but complex, not a collection of separate little things but a variety of parts that they can put together.

5. As people grow from childhood to adulthood, they are less satisfied with *brief and unconnected jobs.* Instead, they seek *long-term challenges* that *link the past and the future.* Adults want to see where their work fits in, to get a vision of the "big picture."

6. The adult is no longer content to be at the bottom of the organizational totem pole, as a child may be. Adults seek *advancement opportunities.*

7. Children are *not very self-aware;* they tend to be *impulsive and to seek instant gratification* of their needs. As we mature into adulthood, most of us learn to be *more self-aware* and *more self-controlled.* Self-control helps us develop a sense of integrity and self-worth.

People change behaviors in seven ways as they mature.

The maturation process Argyris describes is quite obvious in most people. The question is "How does such a developing self fit into a typical organization?" Think back to some of the principles of organizational design discussed earlier. How do they coincide with this natural development of people? Argyris contends that there is a direct conflict in many cases.

■ How does the traditional organization hinder normal growth?

The classical organization structure often serves to *restrain* adult activeness; to *foster continued dependence* on others; to demand only few and often *repetitive* types of *behaviors;* to require only *shallow, brief interests;* to *discourage self-development and advancement* and a view of the overall organizational picture. The dilemma is obvious and real.

What can we do about this? Argyris says that "there is only one real way to improve the sad picture described ... by decreasing the *dependency,* decreasing the *subordination,* and decreasing the *submissiveness* expected of employees. It can be shown that making a job 'bigger'—not more specialized and small—will help do these things; and that employee-centered (or participative) leadership also will improve the situation."[3]

Argyris concludes his article with a call for action. He encourages those who engage in organizational design to recognize this dilemma, this deadening effect on individual growth caused by overly restrictive organizational design: "No organization can be maximally efficient that stunts its own vital parts."[4]

To accuse all organizations of stunting the growth of their people would be unfair and inaccurate. Nevertheless, there are tendencies to be too restrictive and to exert too much control over workers. The degree to which those forces are at work in an organization can be determined by studying the *climate* of the firm.

Reprinted with special permission of King Features Syndicate, Inc.

▼ ORGANIZATIONAL CLIMATE

Climate is a rather slippery concept to define. This is true whether one is referring to the weather (just exactly how does one describe the climate of, say, Chicago?) or to the environment within a company.

Organizational climate arises from a composite impression people get from such things as the way managers treat their workers, the corporate "philosophy," the work atmosphere, and the types of objectives the organization is chasing.

Many management theorists feel that the climate of an organization is more important to success than the management techniques used. Even careful planning, organizing, staffing, motivating, and controlling can fall flat if the organization's climate is poor.

A key point to keep in mind is that climate arises from the perceptions and impressions of the people who work in the organization, not directly from some way of organizing or managing the work.

One researcher who has studied the concept of climate extensively is W. Charles Redding. He identifies five components that, taken together, determine the organizational climate. These are

1. The degree to which management is *supportive* of its employees' efforts
2. The extent of *participative decision making* used
3. The degree of *trust* employees have in management
4. The amount of *freedom to communicate* openly
5. The firm's degree of emphasis on *high performance goals.*

▼ EXCELLENCE AND ORGANIZATIONAL CLIMATE

The well-known book *In Search of Excellence,* by Thomas Peters and Robert H. Waterman, cites numerous characteristics of the exceptional company. Many of these characteristics are closely relat-

■ Organizational climate is often hard to define.

■ Climate arises from the members' impressions of the work environment.

ed to what we have been calling organizational climate. Among the attributes found in top companies were organizational systems designed to:

- produce lots of winners by boosting employee self-worth;
- celebrate the winning once it occurs;
- make extraordinary use of nonmonetary incentives—especially "hoopla" and applause;
- permit people to feel that they have control over their own destinies;
- encourage fertile talk and an "action bias" (they *do* things; they don't talk ideas to death);
- encourage "fluid" organizations with rich ways of communicating informally;
- promote open communication where people get in contact with each other regularly; and
- encourage friendly, internal competition.[6]

These qualities can be considered a major part of the organization's climate. They also constitute critical dimensions of the organizational *culture,* which we will describe in a moment.

▼ WHAT WOULD AN IDEAL ORGANIZATIONAL CLIMATE BE LIKE

- Six factors are essential to a strong organizational climate.

We're not positive that there is a perfectly "ideal" organization anywhere on Earth. But we do feel, and the research supports, that the following are essential to a strong organizational climate:

1. *Trust.* Personnel at all levels should make every effort to develop and maintain relationships in which trust, confidence, and credibility are sustained by statement and act. *All* personnel should be treated as if they could be trusted.

2. *Participative decision making.* Employees at all levels in the organization should be communicated to and consulted with on organization policies relevant to their positions. Employees at all levels should be provided with avenues of communication and consultation with management levels above theirs for the purpose of participating in decision-making and goal-setting processes.

3. *Supportiveness.* A general atmosphere of candor and frankness should pervade relationships in the organization, with employees being able to say what's on their minds regardless of whether they are talking to peers, subordinates, or superiors.

4. *Openness in downward communication.* Except for necessary security information, members of the organization should have relatively easy access to information that relates directly to their immediate jobs, that affects their abilities to coordinate their work with that of other people or departments, and that deals broadly with the company, its organization, leaders, and plans.

Celebrating organizational successes reinforces the corporate climate.

5. *Listening in upward communication.* Personnel at each level in the organization should listen with open minds to suggestions or reports of problems made by personnel at each subordinate level in the organization. Information from subordinates should be viewed as important enough to be acted on until demonstrated otherwise.

6. *Concern for high performance goals.* Personnel at all levels in the organization should demonstrate a commitment to high performance goals (high productivity, high quality, low cost), as well as a high concern for other members of the organization.

Of all these items, which seems to be the most important? Careful statistical analysis indicates that the single most important ingredient of good organizational climate is *trust* among organizational members.

Traditional organizational structure, with its heavy emphasis on hierarchy and control over people—indicating a low level of trust—seldom produces a good organizational climate. Perhaps the lack of trust in organizations has been a catalyst accelerating the search for new organizational structures.

■ Trust among organization members is the most important ingredient of a good climate.

▼ EXAMINING CULTURE IN ORGANIZATIONS

Over time, every organization develops unwritten rules of behavior that its members are expected to obey. The values and norms of the most influential leaders—formal *or* informal leaders—eventually become adopted by most members of the organization. This whole set of pervasive values, norms, and attitudes is called the *culture* of the organization.

When you join an existing organization, no one hands you a data sheet describing the organization's culture. In fact, it may take days—even weeks—to learn a culture well enough to describe it. Yet everyone would do well to investigate the culture of an organization before committing to join it.

Why is culture so important—and how does one discover what an organization's culture is? Culture constitutes rules and norms that determine who will succeed, fail, gain power, or gain influence in an organization. Employees who are working for a company while ignorant of its culture are like foreigners trying to drive autos in a distant land without any knowledge of the traffic laws there. They haven't taken the time to learn the rules!

■ The "rules" of a culture are often unwritten but are still enforced.

While the "rules" of a culture are usually unwritten, they are still enforced. One must try to learn them through observation and by asking questions. For example, to observe what behaviors are practiced by those who are successfully rewarded or promoted is to observe culture. Asking "What would I be expected to continually do in this company to eventually be promoted to vice-president?" would probably help one learn about a culture. The rules, expectations, and acceptable behaviors in an organization are its outward manifestations of its "private" culture.

Let's look at an example that took place in a Goodyear auto service center. A newly hired mechanic named Jim was told that *"superior service to the customer"* was the creed of the whole shop. Jim's supervisor emphasized that if he would just remember this, Jim would do well as a mechanic in the company.

Being well trained in basic auto mechanics, Jim worked hard to please customers during his first morning on the job. When the lunch break came, he was exhausted. Jim was happy to see that there were no customers in sight, and his supervisor shut several doors to the service stalls. Taking his sack lunch and a soda pop, Jim found a clean spot on the shop floor, sat down, and began to eat. He was glad it was lunchtime, as his legs ached from standing all morning.

But as soon as Jim had seated himself comfortably on the shop floor, his supervisor startled him with a curse and loud yelling—directed straight at Jim! "What! Get off yer butt, Jim! I thought I told you there's never any sittin' around here. Imagine what would happen if the regional store director stopped by and saw you just sittin' there!"

Jim was shocked! Jumping up, he protested to his supervisor that he had worked harder than any other mechanic that morning, that his legs were tired, and that the shop had no chairs in it. Then his

Every organization develops a culture of its own.

supervisor explained that it "just didn't look right" to have a uniformed mechanic sitting on the shop floor—even during lunch break. Jim learned that one had to go into a back room or outside to be able to sit.

The unwritten rule about never sitting on the shop floor was an outward manifestation of the values and norms of the service center. Workers always had to appear to be actively in the service of the customer. That was a big part of the culture. The "no sitting" rule was merely an outward sign of the internal value of the culture.

Jim learned about the culture in the service center the hard way. If another mechanic would have just given him a few hints, Jim could have avoided this unpleasant experience on his first day at work.

Alan L. Wilkins, a leading authority on organizational cultures today, explains why learning a culture is so important for new employees:

> For the new employee, learning the organization is like learning how to fit in and avoid major blunders in a foreign culture. When traveling in a foreign country, it is of course useful to have a map which shows you how to get from one place to another. However, avoiding social blunders and really understanding the foreign culture requires another kind of map—a social map. You need to know how to get where you want to go socially....
>
> Shortly after starting a new job, most new employees learn that the policy handbook and the standard operating procedures only go so far. New employees soon learn that there are exceptions to the rules. Some rules can be violated without great repercussions and others are sacred. Even more important, the new employee learns that certain ways of thinking and acting (we are a "conservative company," "look busy," "don't kill a new product idea") are really more important to know than rules.[7]

▼ ORGANIZATIONAL CHARACTER: GOING BEYOND CULTURE

Wilkins now argues that it is time to look beyond culture. He prefers the term *character* rather than *culture*. He feels that culture has been overused and "trivialized because so many have written about 'managing culture,' 'managing myths,' or 'creating meaning' without serious attention to just how difficult it is to manipulate these complex social processes. [In addition] culture has been used to talk about almost everything organizational, and it has therefore lost much of its special meaning."[8]

■ An organization's character is created from its people's skills, habits, and personal commitment.

An organization's character may be described as ideas, beliefs, and hopes of people both inside and outside the organization about the appropriate role for the organization and about how it should fulfill that role. Character is created from the skills, habits, and personal commitments that make fulfillment of these role expectations possible.

Specifically, Wilkins identifies the following components of organizational character:

■ Organizational character arises from a shared vision.

1. *Shared vision:* a common understanding of organizational purpose; a sense of "who we are":
2. *Motivational faith:*
   ■ in the fairness of the leaders and others
   ■ in the ability of personnel and the organization
3. *Distinctive skills:* the tacit customs, the networks of experts, and the technology that add up to the collective organizational competence.[9]

The "corporate character" approach to understanding organizations is relatively new, and its usefulness remains to be seen. Nevertheless, the focus on these key components seems to be promising as we seek to better understand a complex, yet vitally important, dimension of organizations.

▼ WHEN ORGANIZATIONAL STRUCTURES CHANGE

Organizational structures are not fixed and permanent. If anything, they are more flexible and changeable now than ever before in histo-

Reprinted with permission of Tribune Media Services, Inc.

ry. No set of skills can be used forever. The needs of people and organizations change constantly. Wise leaders recognize and appreciate this need for change. Wise managers also spend the effort to learn how best to manage the inevitable change process.

The process of reorganizing a company is complex—much more so than many managers realize. Even relatively minor changes can lead to disruptions, friction, and heavy expenses. By nature, people tend to resist change. They see threats in the unknown and are usually more comfortable with the status quo.

When it is necessary to change the structure of an organization (either a whole company or small subgroups within a company), the process must be carefully planned and executed. Two experts in such change, Cynthia D. Scott and Dennis T. Jaffe, offer these basic guidelines:

1. *Have a good reason for making the change.* Changes are not fun. Take them seriously. Be sure to understand the reasons making the change necessary.

2. *Involve people in the change.* By being involved, people understand the need for changes and are less resistant to them.

3. *Put a respected person in charge of the process.* The change leader should be seen in a positive light by the people to be affected by the change.

4. *Create transitions management teams.* Assemble a team to plan, anticipate, troubleshoot, coordinate and focus the change efforts.

5. *Provide training in new values and behavior.* Guide the people through the new ways things are expected to be done.

6. *Bring in outside help.* An objective, third-party consultant can often anticipate unforeseen problems and reinforce the direction you want to go.

7. *Establish symbols of change.* Encourage the development of newsletters, new logos or slogans, and/or recognition events to help celebrate and reflect the change.

8. *Acknowledge and reward people.* As change begins to work, take time to recognize and recall the achievements of the people who made it happen.[10]

■ Organizational change must be carefully planned and executed.

▼ HOW DOES ORGANIZATION STRUCTURE AFFECT PEOPLE AT WORK?

Leaders need to be aware of the impact of organizational patterns on the people involved. Traditional structures—those emphasizing a pyramid arrangement of clearly defined positions—stifle people's normal development. Likewise, organization structures contribute to employee perceptions of the work climate. Climate and culture are heavily influenced by opportunities to communicate and by the trust engendered by such interactions. Traditional organizations, with emphasis on controlling people's behavior, seldom develop feelings of trust, which are a crucial part of organizational climate.

■ Managers need to be aware of the trade-offs encountered when changing organizational structure.

In summary, the manager needs to be aware of the trade-offs encountered when making decisions about organizational design. The astute manager will continue to seek greater understanding of how organizational issues affect human beings. This manager will be sensitive to and aware of the impact of changes in organizational structure, climate, and culture on people at work.

▼ SUMMARY OF KEY IDEAS

■ The informal organization is structured more around personalities and norms than around organizational positions and procedures.

■ Five contributors to one's informal power are seniority, access to key organizational people, aggressive behavior, experience, and credibility among peers.

■ Argyris's seven developmental dimensions describe how people change from children to adults. Many organizations disregard this growth by failing to treat workers as mature adults.

■ Redding's five components of organizational climate are supportiveness, participation in decision making, trust, open communication, and concern for high performance goals.

■ The eight characteristics of excellent companies identified by Peters and Waterman are considered part of an organization's climate.

■ Culture includes the pervasive values, norms, and attitudes for the whole organization; climate, then, is one aspect of organizational culture.

■ Corporate character is defined by shared vision, motivational faith, and distinctive skills.

▼ KEY TERMS, CONCEPTS AND NAMES

Chris Argyris	Organizational climate
Corporate character	Organizational culture
Developmental dimensions	Charles Redding
Downward communication	Supportiveness
Employee involvement	Trust
Horizontal communication	Unity of Command
Mentor	Upward communication
"Mop Bucket Attitude (MBA)"	Alan Wilkins

▼ QUESTIONS AND EXERCISES

1. List and describe the developmental dimensions identified by Argyris. How do organizations set up roadblocks to human development? Be specific, and give examples.

2. Pick a particular job you are familiar with. How could this job be redesigned using one or more of the alternatives to traditional design? What would be the effects on the people involved? On the organization?

3. Why is it important for the manager to be aware of organizational culture?

4. Does the notion of corporate character seem potentially more fruitful than the older notion of organizational culture? Defend your view.

5. Imagine that you see a need to reorganize the department you manage in XYZ Corporation. Assume that your boss gives you the go-ahead. How would you go about implementing a change?

6. Answer the introductory questions at the beginning of the chapter.

▼ NOTES

1. Michael Maxtone-Graham, "Put a Mentor in Your Manual," *Training,* June 1991, pp. 12–13.

2. Chris Argyris, "Being Human and Being Organized," *Trans-action* 1 (1964): 3.

3. Ibid., p. 6.

4. Ibid.

5. W. Charles Redding, *Communication within the Organization* (New York: Industrial Communication Council, 1972), p. 139 ff.

6. Thomas J. Peters and Robert H. Waterman, *In Search of Excellence* (New York: Harper and Row, 1982).

7. Alan L. Wilkins, "Business Stories," *Exchange* (Fall 1981), p. 26.

8. Alan L. Wilkins, *Creating Corporate Character* (San Francisco: Jossey-Bass, 1989), pp. xi–xii.

9. Ibid., p. 3.

10. Cynthia D. Scott and Dennis T. Jaffe, *Managing Organizational Change* (Los Altos, Calif.: Crisp Publications, 1989), p. 9.

Another Look: Set the Stage for Employee Involvement

The success of employee involvement (EI) lies in the ability to develop an organizational climate that will supports its growth. Unfortunately, many organizational leaders fail to seriously consider the steps needed to successfully graft the EI process onto their work environment.

Managers sometimes erroneously believe that EI will automatically occur once employees and managers receive basic education on what EI is and how they and their companies can benefit from it. In reality, many employees and managers often resist organizational EI efforts because they don't understand their organizations' EI goals, or their expected roles in the process.

Managers, in particular, often resist EI programs because they view them as a threat to their status and power. Additionally, senior managers may attempt to implement EI because they want to get more out of their employees, without truly developing partnerships or a team. If this occurs, the EI process will eventually break down, and subsequent attempts to improve the work climate will be significantly more difficult because of the loss of employee trust.

Finally, organizations may inadvertently create roadblocks that make it difficult for employees and managers to become more fully involved in their work, and which lead them to question whether their organizations are fully committed to the concept of EI.

Lack of Support

Organizational support can be illustrated through the case of a leading customized software supplier that initiated an EI program by having its senior managers outline key organizational values on which to base the EI process. One important value was encouraging employees to be risk takers who would not be afraid to "challenge accepted ways of doing things" within the company. Another key value was company support of the "open sharing of information between employees and managers."

A few months after the program's implementation, the organization's HR department began a series of departmental-wide meetings to facilitate open communication between managers and employees. In one of the first of these meetings, two employees asked their senior manager some hard questions about the company's intended strategy for dealing with recently surfaced problems in one of its newest products.

The department manager's responses made it apparent he didn't like dealing with difficult questions. Shortly after the meeting, the two employees received counseling from their immediate managers concerning the wisdom of posing potentially embarrassing questions to their senior management. News of this incident quickly spread across the plant to other employees. The managers found that in subsequent meetings employees were very reluctant to voice their questions and concerns.

This incident is representative of the problems that can occur when no attempt is made to set the stage for employee involvement. The situation could have been avoided had the HR manager and senior managers met early in the planning process to agree on guidelines they would follow in conducting these meetings. As it was, the organization lost an important opportunity to initiate EI.

Where to Begin

First, training and viable role models should be provided so employees and supervisors can develop new organizational roles. For example, supervisors can benefit from training that helps them develop coaching skills; encourage teamwork and self-management; and promote employee initiative.

Employees should receive training that shows them how to self-manage their work; assume greater leadership roles within their team; develop decision-making and problem-solving skills; and aggressively look for work improvement opportunities.

Second, redesign organizational systems to ease the

ANOTHER LOOK *continued*

pain of change for employees and management and to remove organizational roadblocks to EI. While the importance of training to EI programs is often discussed, relatively little attention is paid to the importance of redesigning organizational systems to support EI. The envisioning session and the organizational audit are two very useful tools for setting the stage for EI.

The Envisioning Session.
This is a one- to two-day facilitated session that is designed to provide senior managers with answers to the following questions:

- How would we like to see our organization function five years from now?

- What organizational values and philosophy would help us create a work environment that would support these desired changes?

- What role could an EI program play in helping us to create our desired corporate environment?

- What options are we willing to consider in building EI? (Task forces, cross-functional improvement teams, quality circles, company-wide suggestion systems, self-directed work teams, etc.)

- How do we currently measure the success of our organization and how will we measure the success of an EI process?

A necessary part of the envisioning process involves identifying industry-specific models for evaluating the comparative feasibility of different involvement options, such as self-directed work teams or cross-functional improvement teams. One of the best means of doing this is to allow managers and employees to visit companies within their fields that have successfully implemented EI Programs, and to use the envisioning session as a means of identifying EI program elements from other companies that can be successfully adopted.

The Organizational Audit.
A second critical step in setting the stage for EI is to conduct an organizational audit, which provides a snapshot of how the organization is currently performing.

An organizational audit serves three purposes: It enables you to compare desired organizational values, leadership practices and employee behaviors with those currently existing within your organization; it helps you identify those existing organizational systems that support or discourage the growth of EI; and it can provide you and your senior managers with the information required to decide on EI efforts, such as self-directed work teams or job-redesign projects, that can significantly affect organizational resources, work

processes and reporting structures.

The organizational audit can help you determine the degree of change that will be required to move your organization toward EI, as well as determine the level and type of resistance to an EI program you are likely to encounter from managers and employees.

An organizational audit answers these questions:

- How does our current performance compare with our desired performance?

- To what degree do our managers and employees want to see EI implemented within our company?

- What roadblocks will we need to overcome to successfully implement an EI program?

- What options are available to us for overcoming these roadblocks?

There are three principal types of organizational systems that should be reviewed in the audit: The rules and guidelines that determine the degree of authority and discretion employees are given to do their jobs, and the framework within which employees are expected to operate to produce value-added results; the behaviors that get rewarded and punished in the organization, and the degree to which rewards and punishments are effectively administered; and special communication, incentives

ANOTHER LOOK: SET THE STAGE FOR EMPLOYEE INVOLVEMENT
continued

and educational programs that could be put in place, or modified, to support EI.

A number of vehicles exist for performing organizational audits. For example, existing organizational databases, such as information collected through exit interviews or through employee complaints, can provide useful knowledge about adverse effects that policies and procedures may be having on EI.

Organizational surveys can tell you the degree to which EI-related leadership practices and organizational values are both desired and practiced by managers and employees. For example, a survey format might ask respondents to describe the degree to which they want to and are encouraged to:

- Take on responsibilities beyond their formal job descriptions.
- Call their supervisors' attention to problems in their work areas.
- Challenge antiquated or ineffective work methods.
- Take part in team decisions.
- Present their suggestions to senior management.

Focus sessions can be conducted with small groups of 15 to 20 employees and supervisors to anticipate organizational factors that are likely to pose the greatest roadblocks to the EI process., In these sessions, participants are introduced to five key values that drive commitment cultures and are

shown a variety of examples of how these values operate within successful EI-directed organizations. These values are:

- **Employee ownership.** Employees should be encouraged to view themselves as owners in their organization's successes and challenges.

- **Employee self-direction and personal growth.** Employees should take the initiative to formulate their own career goals and development plans.

- **Open communication.** There should be fluid communication between managers and employees and across work functions. Employees should have free access to the types of information needed to do their jobs effectively.

- **Risk taking and innovation.** Employees should aggressively look for ways to improve their team's performance, and question outmoded or ineffective methods and procedures.

- **Teamwork.** Employees and managers should foster mutual support and common effort within their work groups and across work functions.

Focus session participants are then encouraged to identify all possible roadblocks that could keep employees from acting on these values, and to generate suggestions for overcoming these road-

blocks. Exhibit 1 provides examples of roadblocks and suggestions that are frequently identified by session participants.

Focus sessions not only provide the benefit of surfacing potential obstacles to the EI process, but also provide participants with opportunities to explore change options for removing these obstacles at the team, departmental and organizational levels. Focus sessions also enable participants to learn about the EI techniques other departments and work units are using.

CONCLUSION

Employee involvement can never be successful if viewed simply as an educational or communication program. Before beginning an EI program, management needs to identify any roadblocks that may prevent employees and supervisors from committing to full involvement. Then, as a team, managers and employees can explore options for overcoming these roadblocks.

The envisioning session and organizational audit are useful tools for identifying and removing potential roadblocks to EI before they damage the EI process. By taking the time to use them, you can ensure your EI program's success, and take a solid step toward developing your employees' commitment and involvement.

SOURCE: Robert W. Barner and J. Jackson Fulbright, *Human Resources,* May 1991, pp. 73–78.

▼ A CASE IN POINT: WENDY'S SUCCESSFUL 'MOP BUCKET ATTITUDE'

After feasting on success for more than 15 years, Wendy's Old Fashioned Hamburgers restaurants developed heartburn in the mid-1980s. Costs soared, sales dropped, and formerly enthusiastic analysts waxed gloomy about Wendy's prospects, convinced our company had lost focus.

I came on as president in 1986 and found we had indeed lost our focus—on people. We had such a fear in our hearts about numbers, about the power of computer printouts and going by the book, we'd managed to lose sight of our customers and employees both.

There's a special purgatory for service businesses that forget their business starts with people. What happened to us was typical: Managers weren't getting the respect they needed and were passing their frustrations along to the crew. The crew, feeling unappreciated, made the customer feel the same. And the customers voted with their feet—as customer are wont to do.

As sales fell, store labor was cut and sales fell ever further. Morale took a nose dive, quality became spotty, and consistency in operations was nonexistent. It was time, clearly, to heave the charts and the printouts and to concentrate once more on the basics. Beginning with the most basic tenet of them all: Mop Bucket Attitude, or M.B.A.

Mop Bucket Attitude says that all the business sophistication in the world pales before the "wisdom" of a clean floor. Fancy price-cost tabulations or quarterly earnings have no meaning to the customer, but quality food, variety and atmosphere do. Those had traditionally been our strengths, and they hadn't lost one bit in value; we just weren't playing to them any more. With our priorities now firmly in hand, we turned to our employees.

Ours is an industry once defined by high employee turnover. It was viewed as normal if not inevitable. We questioned that view, and decided the best way to become the customer's restaurant of choice was to become the employer of choice. Our plan on this front was two-pronged: to work harder to develop the potential of the people we already had, and to move aggressively to attract and retain the best people we could find.

We began by raising employee training to uniformly high standards, seeing that everyone, from the newest kid on fries all the way up to the manager, received the same basic training. (Previously, anyone with two weeks on the job might train the last person in the door.) Then we worked to make "manager" truly a status position, giving managers more control and latitude in day-to-day decisions.

Still, we knew young people of ambition might forsake us the first chance they got for "real" jobs with benefits to match. So we improved base compensation, offered a package of top-flight benefits and a cash bonus paid out each quarter. We created an employee stock option plan called "We-share" to give our employees a larger stake in the company. And, reflecting the special concerns of our founder, Dave Thomas, we included paid leave and reimbursed medial and legal costs for company employees who adopt children.

It worked. Our turnover rate for general managers fell to 20% in 1991 from 39% in 1989, while turnover among co- and assistant managers dropped to 37% from 60%—among the lowest in the business. With a stable—and able—work force, sales began to pick up as well. To win back repeat business, though, we would have to concentrate not just on this transaction, but the next.

We know it's easy to increase store traffic and sales short term. You flood the market with coupons, let fly with a few specials, maybe go for a splashy new ad campaign. But if you get customers in the door and disappoint them, it's a disaster. Not only must you offer customers quality, value and a pleasant experience: You must offer it consistently.

With the aim of increasing consistency throughout the 3,800 Wendy's restaurants world-wide, we launched "Sparkle" in 1989—a program that is part incentive, part strategy for elevating standards and measuring quality, service and cleanliness on a daily basis. We refocused our managers and crew to look at their restaurants from the customer's point of view.

We also looked at our menu lineup and added more products to the premium side of the business, an acknowledged area of our

A CASE IN POINT: WENDY'S SUCCESSFUL 'MOP BUCKET ATTITUDE' *continued*

strength. At the same time, we reached out to our cost-conscious customers with a Super Value menu of nine items priced at 99 cents—not just on Wednesdays or for a "limited time only," but every day of the year.

The customers who'd deserted us began to come back. I won't say it was a flood; more of a trickle at first. When we started these programs in 1987, we made just five cents a share. In 1991, by contrast, we reported earnings of 52 cents a share. Amid flat sales in the rest of the industry and a recession that wouldn't go away, Wendy's realized a 31% rise in earnings last year for a profit of $51 million—its best year since 1985.

I wish I could say there was some kind of magic wand behind all of this. In fact, the "magic wand" approach was the first thing to go. The main reason we have sustained 12

consecutive quarters of sales gains over the prior year—and look to continue it into the next 12 and beyond—is because we returned to the solid, unmagical principles of management that put us on the map in the first place.

These are the principles that focus on people—and never go out of fashion.

QUESTIONS

1. What actions by management indicate an awareness of the importance of the human side of organizations?

2. What can we learn about people in organizations from this case?

SOURCE: James W. Near, *Wall Street Journal*, 27 April 1992, p. A16.

▽ A CASE IN POINT: THE ELECTRONIC GAMES DIVISION

The electronic games division of Toys R Fun Corporation, a large toy manufacturer, was organized along functional lines. Each department, or function, worked pretty much on its own. There were departments of research, new product design, manufacturing, marketing, finance, and personnel. The division manufactured a variety of electronic games, all of which were selling quite well. It was somewhat less successful at coming up with competitive new products in this fast-changing industry.

Because the division had experienced some turbulent business conditions and had seemed to lose much of its competitive edge, the general manager called in a consultant to discuss what he saw as problems in intergroup relations. The manager felt that there were too many conflicts among the various groups. He believed those conflicts were hindering the division from keeping on top of the very rapidly changing market. Specifically, he

was afraid that the conflicts were hampering the division's product development efforts, efforts that required coordination and cooperation among all the functional groups.

A university-based consultant, Arlene Steinberg, came to the organization and decided to do a thorough analysis before she made any recommendations. Her efforts included interviewing virtually every manager in the plant, administering questionnaires to many of the workers and supervisors, and carefully analyzing the organizational structure of the plant.

Steinburg found that the division was highly specialized and that the managers and others were highly motivated. But the overall design of the division needed to be improved. The primary coordination of departments was through the division manager, who held frequent meetings with his top staff to discuss and coordinate all product development activities in the division. This was not sufficient, however. Poor intergroup relations were symptoms; poor organizational design, Steinburg concluded, was a cause. The different functional groups simply were not communicating with each other.

The consultant suggested that a new organizational structure be tried. She suggested that new product developments be carried out by teams made up of one or more individuals from each of the different functions in the plant. This, she felt, would bring about better coordination.

The consultant stayed on to train key people who would coordinate and assemble these teams for new product development. The project teams designed all phases of the new products, including design, financing, and marketing. Once a team's project had been launched, the team itself was disbanded and people went back to their own organizations. Typically, this took about six months.

Two years after this reorganization, follow-up studies were done to see if the new system was working. It was found that in the year after the implementation of the program, nine complex and highly profitable new products had been developed. This compared with a total of five new products in the previous five years. The friction among groups apparently had been reduced, morale was better, and the company's profits were up.

QUESTIONS

1. What were some of the key organizational design problems with the old way that Toys R Fun was working?

2. What principles of effective orgnization structure had been violated by the old way of doing things?

3. Specifically, how did organizational design seem to affect the people involved in this company? How did the design changes affect the way people interacted and communicated?

PART

IV

THE DRIVING FORCE: LEADERSHIP

CHAPTER

7

THE NATURE OF LEADERSHIP

This chapter answers several all-important questions:

■ What are some popular myths about leadership?

■ Are there certain personal traits that make a person a good leader?

■ Are leaders born or made?

■ What personal characteristics will eliminate a person from consideration for leadership positions?

■ What four factors most influence the leadership situation?

■ How do assumptions or expectations affect leadership style?

■ What did Douglas McGregor mean by Theory X and Theory Y?

■ What is a self-fulfilling prophecy, and how can it affect leadership?

■ What is power, and how can it influence leadership?

■ Who is Arthur Friedman, and what was his "outrage"?

The answers to these and other questions are coming up next in chapter 7....

Leadership is the pivotal force behind successful organizations ... leadership is necessary to help organizations develop a new vision of what they can be. The new leader is one who commits people to action, who converts followers into leaders, and who may convert leaders into agents of change.
Warren Bennis and Burt Nanus, Leaders: The Strategies for Taking Charge *(New York: Harper and Row, 1985), pp. 3–4.*

Chapter 7

Leadership. It's a term we apply to the movers and shakers of this world—the people who have the amazing power to get others to do things. We see Teddy Roosevelt charging up San Juan Hill, and Norman Schwarzkopf and Colin Powell orchestrating operation Desert Storm. We see James Brady quietly pursuing gun control laws, and Jimmy Carter helping build homes for the homeless. We see professional athletes leading antidrug campaigns and AIDS-prevention efforts. We see courageous leaders in political, moral, religious, and educational causes. Our lives are constantly bumping against people we designate as true leaders.

But true leadership does not require news media exposure. Great leadership happens every day in millions of contexts. We have true leaders among parents, students, teachers, citizens, and people in all walks of life.

In this chapter, we present an overview of the nature of leadership. In the following chapter, we'll show you how to develop an effective leadership style.

▼ The Myths of Leadership

The whole subject of leadership is permeated with myths. Before we discuss leadership and its applications, it would be useful to puncture a few of those myths.

Myth 1: Leadership Is a Rare Skill

REALITY:
- Nothing could be farther from the truth; everyone has leadership potential.
- There are millions of leadership roles throughout the world, and many are filled by capable leaders.
- People may be leaders in one organization and followers in another.
- Leadership opportunities are plentiful and within the reach of most people.

Myth 2: Leaders Are Born, Not Made

REALITY:
- Biographies mislead by sometimes portraying great leaders as unpredictable superhumans with unique charisma and almost mystical genius.
- Leadership is not a gift of grace too abstract to be defined, much less learned.
- Because the title of leader is often attributed to those whose actions take place in the most dramatic realms of human endeavor (e.g., Mahatma Gandhi, Napoleon, Winston Churchill, Nelson Mandela), we sometimes assume they were destined to lead.
- This myth perpetuates myth 3.

- A wide range of people can become leaders.

Myth 3: Leaders Are Created by Extraordinary Circumstances and Great Events

REALITY:

- This myth would have us believe that leaders emerge suddenly, during times of great conflict and chaos, as did Martin Luther King, Jr. This is true only sometimes.
- This myth limits the opportunities for leadership still further. It indicates that leadership is only associated with some sort of grand cataclysm or rise and fall of power; we have no opportunity to exercise leadership skills under normal circumstances. But leadership is exercised by all kinds of people in all kinds of situations everyday.

> ■ Leadership is exercised in everyday situations, not just during great conflict.

Myth 4: Leadership Exists Only at the Top of an Organization

REALITY:

- We feed this myth by focusing on top leadership when organizations have thousands of leadership roles available to employees.
- Corporations are moving in the direction of creating more leadership roles through empowerment and self-directed work teams within the organization.

Myth 5: The Leader Controls, Directs, Prods, Manipulates

REALITY:

- Perhaps this is the most damaging myth of all.
- Leadership is not so much the exercise of power itself as the ability to empower others.

> ■ True leaders empower others.

- Leaders align their energies with others: they pull, rather than push; they inspire, rather than command.
- Managers may command people, use a system of rewards and punishments, maintain control through intimidation—but a leader's tools are very different.
- Some managers try to substitute management for leadership.
- Often organizations are overmanaged and underled.
- Management is never a substitute for leadership.

Myth 6: Leaders Are Charismatic

REALITY:

- Some are, most are not.
- There are always a few leaders who correspond to our fantasies of "divine inspiration" and "grace under pressure" (e.g., John F. Kennedy), but most leaders are all too human—fallible, flawed,

with no particular charm that separates them externally from their followers.

- Charisma is the result of effective leadership—not the other way around. It is often the ability to articulate the felt needs of an emerging group of people.

Myth 7: It Is Immoral to Seek Power

REALITY:

- Those who recognize that power is a key requisite for change may feel revulsion toward it.
- Power has been maligned and misunderstood.
- Power is often associated with greed and selfish ambition.
- Power is associated with those who abuse and misuse it, rather than with those who use it wisely.
- We confuse power with subjugation and with control. In doing so, we reject power, whether consciously or unconsciously, and thereby restrict our own opportunities for leadership.
- Power is a means to an end.
- Power is energy, and as with any form of energy, its value lies in how we use it. Until used, power is neutral—it is neither benign nor corrupting.

▼ UNDERSTANDING LEADERSHIP

The preceding seven myths have been perpetuated through centuries of folklore and superstition. This may be the reason why leadership is misunderstood.[1]

SyberVision, a producer of audiotape and videotape learning programs, has elaborated on the leadership studies of Walter Bennis and Burt Nanus. Its findings are based on interviews with over ninety outstanding leaders in the corporate and public sectors and the fine arts. Sixty of those interviews were with chief executive officers, presidents, or board leaders. One of SyberVision's findings was that leadership is simply the ability to turn a dream, a vision of a desired future state into a reality—with and through the cooperation of other people.

A few basic principles can be applied to leadership:

- Leadership can be understood—it can be defined.
- Leadership is not an unsolvable riddle; there is no cosmic mystery behind the men and women who emerge as strong, powerful leaders.
- The ability to lead is based on the application of practical skills and experience that can be developed by anyone.
- Leadership is the marshaling of skills possessed by a majority but used by a minority.
- Leadership can be learned. The principles behind leadership are accessible and attainable and can be acted upon by everyone.

Leaders admit their skills were not inborn. They worked hard—diligently and tirelessly—to apply the skills and principles that enabled them to lead their organizations.[2]

▼ LEADERS REQUIRE WILLING FOLLOWERS

A young man walks into the late-night convenience store, pulls out a pistol, and orders the clerk to put her hands over her head.

"Open the cash register," he commands, "and then walk into the storage room."

The clerk does exactly what she's told. The man locks her in the back room, scoops the money out of the cash drawer, and pours himself a large cherry cola Slurpee.

"Stay in that room for ten minutes," he shouts as he heads for the door, "or I'll blow your head off." He jumps into his car and roars off.

Is this armed man a leader? He did get the clerk to do what he wanted, didn't he?

Yes, he did, but he used *coercion* (actually, direct threat), rather than *leadership.* Leadership of the type we are concerned with in organizations cannot be based on threats—at least not over the long run.

A leader is a person who has in some way gained the loyalty of others who are *willing* to follow. The willingness to follow arises from people's perceptions of the leader's position and personal characteristics. Sometimes, people are "thrust into positions of leadership." More often, people earn the right to lead by developing useful skills and attributes. Alluding to such skills, Henry Ford made this often-quoted observation: "The question 'Who ought to be boss?' is like asking 'Who ought to be the tenor in the quartet?' Obviously the man who can sing tenor."

■ People earn the right to lead by developing skills and aptitudes.

▼ LEADERSHIP TACTICS

The person who can lead will be called on to do so. But how can people assure their own success as leaders? First, they should recognize the range of choices in leadership tactics available. They should also recognize that each tactic has its price.

Figure 7.1 presents a realistic range of possible behaviors available to leaders who have organizational authority.[3] Note the effect on subordinates' freedom (and opportunity for growth, as discussed in chapter 4) offered by each managerial approach.

With boss-centered tactics, the boss makes decisions and simply announces them. The leadership style can be quick but also offers subordinates virtually no freedom or involvement in choices. The price of such a dictatorial style can be worker resistance to the decision and resentment of the leader.

At the opposite end of the scale is a high degree of participation by workers in making decisions. This participative approach has benefits that we'll discuss at length later.

The greatest mistake made in selecting managers is to become impressed with an individual's ability to do things himself as opposed to getting things done through other people. The best managers are those who get things done through other people.
E. B. Barnes, president, Dow Chemical Company

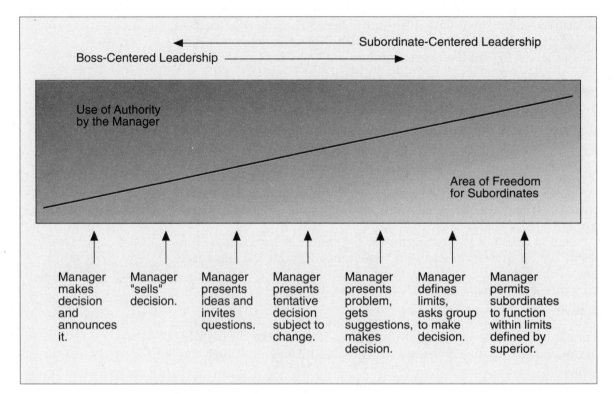

FIGURE 7.1
A continuum of leader-
ship tactics.
SOURCE: R. Tannenbaum, I.
Weschler, and F. Massarik,
Leadership and Organization
(New York: McGraw-Hill,
1961), p. 69.

Combining an appropriate mix of boss-centered and subordinate-
centered leadership poses a major challenge for any manager. How
can people maximize their own leadership potential? We'll suggest
several skills and approaches later in this chapter. But first, let's
consider leadership in a more general way. For starters, where does
leadership come from?

▼ ARE LEADERS BORN OR MADE?

Although now mostly discredited, the "born leaders" school of
thought once prevailed. For many years, social scientists attempted
to define specific personal traits or characteristics in individuals
that made them effective leaders. This research approach was based
on the underlying assumption that leaders are somehow different
from ordinary people. If people could only identify what makes
leaders different, people would be able to "scientifically" select the
best leaders. One early study indicated that tall people tended to be
better leaders than short people. (Napoleon would have been surprised to hear that!) Other studies looked at such attributes as general intelligence, self-confidence, persuasiveness, and intuition as
these relate to leadership.

■ Are leaders somehow
different from
ordinary people?

Several problems arose from this avenue of study. For one thing,
some of the labels for the traits being studied were unclear. Just how
does one define something like *intuition* or *attractiveness*? A more

important criticism of this research approach is that the findings were largely inconclusive when applied to different leadership *situations*. An effective sales manager may not be successful as a railroad crew supervisor. A military commander may function poorly as a cleric or as a political leader.

Social scientists who saw the need to study individual situations began to regard the search for *universal* leadership traits as virtually worthless. Before we write off more than fifty years of research studies, however, let's consider a massive review of such studies prepared by Ralph Stogdill. Stogdill's analysis of almost three hundred studies concluded that leaders, when compared with nonleaders, possessed some almost universal characteristics. They were almost always goal-directed, venturesome, self-confident, responsible, tolerant of stress and frustration, and capable of influencing others. Stogdill also concluded that when a person has only one or two of these traits, one cannot reliably predict whether or not that individual will be a good leader. For example, a self-confident, goal-directed person who does not also possess several other leadership characteristics could not automatically be assumed to be a good leader. However, when a combination of most of these characteristics was present, they tended to indicate a personality appropriate to the person seeking the responsibilities of leadership.[4]

Perhaps one reason some people discredit the traits approach to leadership studies is that it seems to imply that a leader either does or doesn't have the desired characteristics—an implication that questions the value of leadership training. If you have leadership traits, you don't need the training; if you don't have them, the training probably won't help. That could be depressing for those who don't have the "right" traits.

Clearly, the trait studies have problems. But to completely deny the existence of some prominent leadership traits could be an overcorrection. Although personal traits do not in themselves make a leader, they are a part of the larger, more complex set of forces working in any leadership situation.

John Geier used a sort of reverse traits approach that is potentially useful to our understanding of leadership.[5] He found that certain personality traits consistently *eliminate* an individual from leadership consideration in almost all situations. The individual who is seen as (1) uniformed about issues important to the group, (2) a very low participator, or (3) very rigid in thinking is passed over when groups select leaders.

■ Are there any universal leadership traits?

■ Does leadership training do any good?

■ Some traits seem to disqualify people from leadership positions.

▼ FACTORS THAT AFFECT LEADERSHIP SUCCESS

Social science research has not been overly successful in predicting who would be a good leader. It has, however, been successful in determining the kinds of factors that affect leadership success.

Doonesbury 1979 G. B. Trudeau. Reprinted with permission of Universal Press Syndicate. All rights reserved.

■ Four factors, in addition to the leader's personality traits, affect leadership success.

Among these are the personal characteristics or traits we've already discussed. But at least four other factors are equally, if not more, important:

1. Leader's expectations or assumptions about human behavior
2. Nature of the task(s) to be accomplished
3. Leader's power
4. Leader's style

Assumptions about Others: You Get What You Expect

We all tend to make assumptions about other people we encounter. The leader is no exception. leaders see their subordinates, as a group or individually, in favorable, neutral, or negative ways. More specifically, they *assume* that their subordinates can and will do some things but cannot or will not do others. These perceptions are likely to change, but the assumptions leaders hold about others affect the ways they work with those others. These leadership attitudes, or expectations of how others will react, affect how one leads others. In a very real sense, people act in certain ways because one expects them to.

Complete the following activity before you read further. The theory behind this questionnaire will be explained later in the chapter.

THEORY X AND THEORY Y

In 1960, Douglas McGregor published a classic book in the field of management entitled *The Human Side of Enterprise.* The book was based on considerable research about human nature and human motivation. McGregor found that leaders in organizations tended to hold a set of assumptions about their followers, which he labeled Theory X*. These assumptions were, by and large, negative:

1. Work is inherently distasteful to most people.
2. Most people are not ambitious, have little desire for responsibility, and prefer to be directed.
3. Most people have little capacity for creativity in solving organizational problems.
4. Motivation occurs only at what Maslow called the survival and security levels.
5. Most people must be closely controlled and often coerced to achieve organizational objectives.

McGregor felt that these assumptions were held by most traditional managers. He questioned, however, whether or not they are really true. Can one realistically say that most people are basically lazy, or that they are self-centered and have little concern for organizational goals? McGregor thought not. He then developed an alternate set of assumptions, which he labeled Theory Y:

1. Work is as natural as play, if the conditions are favorable.
2. Self-control of the individual is often indispensable in achieving organizational goals.
3. The capacity for creativity in solving an organization's problems is widely distributed throughout the organization.

Effective leadership must comprise many elements, three of which are essential—integrity, enterprise, and service; and of these, integrity is first among equals.
Rawleigh Warner, Jr., chairman of the board, Mobil Oil Corporation

■ Most traditional managers seemed to hold Theory X assumptions.

---

*Over the years, the label Theory X has led to some confusion. It is not really a theory—in the sense of a set of guidelines that explain and help people predict—but is rather a *listing of key assumptions* that people hold with regard to others. These assumptions are paraphrased here for easy reading.

ACTIVITY: WHAT ARE YOUR ASSUMPTIONS ABOUT YOUR COWORKERS?

This instrument is designed to help you better understand the assumptions you make about people and human nature. There are ten pairs of statements. Assign a weight from 0 to 10 to *each statement* to show the relative strength of your belief in the statements *in each pair.* The points assigned for each pair must in each case total 10. Be as honest with yourself as you can, and resist the natural tendency to respond as you would "like to think things are." This instrument is not a test. There are no right or wrong answers. It is designed to be a stimulus for personal reflection and discussion.

1. It's only human nature for people to do as little work as they can get away with. _____ (a)

   When people avoid work, it's usually because their work has been deprived of its meaning. _____ (b)
   10

2. If employees have access to any information they want, they tend to have better attitudes and behave more responsibly. _____ (c)

   If employees have access to more information than they need to do their immediate tasks, they will usually misuse it. _____ (d)
   10

3. One problem in asking for the ideas of employees is that their perspective is too limited for their suggestions to be of much practical value. _____ (e)

   Asking employees for their ideas broadens their perspective and results in the development of useful suggestions. _____ (f)
   10

4. If people don't use much imagination and ingenuity on the job, it's probably because relatively few people have much of either. _____ (g)

   Most people are imaginative and creative but may not show it because of limitations imposed by supervision and the job. _____ (h)
   10

5. People tend to raise their standards if they are accountable for their own behavior and for correcting their own mistakes. _____ (i)

   People tend to lower their standards if they are not punished for their misbehavior and mistakes. _____ (j)
   10

6. It's better to give people both good and bad news, because most employees want the whole story, no matter how painful. _____ (k)

   It's better to withhold unfavorable news about business, because most employees really want to hear only the good news. _____ (l)
   10

7. Because a supervisor is entitled to more respect than those below him or her in the organization, it weakens his or her prestige to admit that a subordinate was right and he or she was wrong. _____ (m)

   Because people at all levels are entitled to equal respect, a supervisor's prestige is increased when he or she supports this principle by admitting that a subordinate was right and she or he was wrong. _____ (n)
   10

8. If you give people enough money, they are less likely to be concerned with such intangibles as responsibility and recognition. _____ (o)

   If you give people interesting and challenging work, they are less likely to complain about such things as pay and supplemental benefits. _____ (p)
   10

9. If people are allowed to set their own goals and standards of performance, they tend to set them higher than the boss would. _____ (q)

   If people are allowed to set their own goals and standards of per- _____ (r)
   10

ACTIVITY *continued*

formance, they tend to set them lower than the boss would.

10. The more knowledge and free- ____ (s)
dom a person has regarding his or her job, the more controls are needed to keep him or her in line.

The more knowledge and free- ____ (t)
dom a person has regarding his $\frac{}{10}$ or her job, the fewer controls are needed to ensure satisfactory job performance.

Now add up the points you assigned as follows. The higher score reflects your predominant orientation.

Theory X score = Sum of a, d, e, g, j, l, m, o, r, and s

Theory Y score = Sum of b, c, f, h, i, k, n, p, q, and t

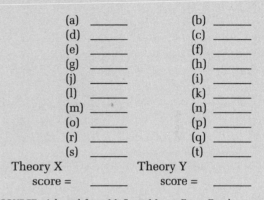

(a) ____	(b) ____
(d) ____	(c) ____
(e) ____	(f) ____
(g) ____	(h) ____
(j) ____	(i) ____
(l) ____	(k) ____
(m) ____	(n) ____
(o) ____	(p) ____
(r) ____	(q) ____
(s) ____	(t) ____
Theory X	Theory Y
score = ____	score = ____

SOURCE: Adapted from M. Scott Myers, *Every Employee a Manager* (New York: McGraw-Hill, 1970), pp. 122–23.

4. Motivation occurs at the belonging, prestige, and self-fulfillment levels, as well as the survival and security levels.

5. People can be self-directed and creative at work if properly motivated.[6]

Don't be confused by the letters X and Y. McGregor intentionally used these nondescriptive names to avoid implying that one set of assumptions is absolutely better than the other. Although Theory X does represent a more pessimistic view of people, Theory Y is not always preferable or more appropriate. For this reason, McGregor avoided calling the two approaches "good" assumptions versus "bad," or "pessimistic" versus "optimistic."

The point of McGregor's work is that the assumptions we hold about others affect the way we behave toward others. A manager who holds Theory X assumptions is likely to treat people very differently from the way a manager who holds Theory Y assumptions would treat people. Although the assumptions themselves do not *cause* a manager to act in a particular way, they do *influence* the behavior of that manager.

If a manager subscribes to Theory X's rather pessimistic view and believes that people basically dislike work and will try to avoid it whenever they can, he or she is likely to act to prevent them from avoiding work. The result is closer supervision and probably a more dictatorial style. If, however, a manger subscribes to Theory Y assumptions and sees others as *potentially* enjoying their work, he or she will try to help them do so. If a manager views workers as having imagination and creativity on the job, he or she will likely

Theory X assumes that people dislike work and have little capacity for solving problems.

- Theory Y managers are not always nice.

- Theory X managers are not always bad.

- People develop Theory X and Theory Y assumptions based on experience.

- How can you make Theory Y work?

give them opportunities to exercise that creativity. So, outlook affects management style.

Don't assume, however, that the manager who holds Theory Y assumptions is *necessarily* the nice, easygoing leader. By the same token, don't assume that the Theory X manager is a dictator or an ogre. Some managers who hold Theory X assumptions are very friendly and very nice to their workers. Often this friendliness is based on a paternalistic attitude—a sense of "I'll take care of you, you're not bright enough to take care of yourself."

McGregor believed that most people have the *potential* to be mature and self-motivated workers. However, don't jump to the conclusion that Theory Y expectations are always appropriate. Some people simply do not live up to their potential. Positive assumptions do occasionally lead to disappointments. But by and large, giving the benefit of the doubt seems to be a good managerial approach.

The sets of expectations described by Theory X and Theory Y are *attitudes* or *predispositions* toward people. As with other attitudes, we develop them in part through our experiences. Although holding Theory Y assumptions about people may be useful, be aware that some people will let you down. Don't let the few sour your assumptions about the many.

Some workers do drive managers to Theory X assumptions. But few managers can be driven to where they don't want to go. Look into yourself. Do you want to think the best of others? Or is it more comfortable to subconsciously use disappointments of the past as excuses for holding negative assumptions about others?

The only way to reap the benefits of positive assumptions about others is simply to *make the Theory Y assumptions* guides to your behavior. Stick to them. Don't attach conditional clauses, and probably your workers will eventually respond by living up to your expectations.

SELF-FULFILLING PROPHECIES

Theory X assumptions tend to be based on a rather pessimistic view of subordinates. Theory Y is more optimistic. Business leaders who have sought to apply McGregor's concepts contend that the only way one can confirm Theory Y assumptions is to go ahead and use them. The whole secret to applying Theory Y is to make those assumptions and give them an opportunity to prove useful. As one industrialist has put it (and as more than one great spiritual leader has stated in slightly different words), "Make the same assumptions about others that you make about yourself, and then behave accordingly."

Psychologists have been very interested in the effects of expectations on people's behavior. Robert K. Merton, Robert Rosenthal, and others extensively studied such "self-fulfilling prophecies." They found that our expectations of others seem to *cause* those others to behave in certain ways.

A popular training film, *Productivity and the Self-fulfilling Prophecy: The Pygmalion Effect,*[7] shows how expectations can be either useful or destructive tools in the hands of managers. A number of experiments are discussed in the movie. In the experiments, teachers of both children and adults were told that several of their students had been shown to have exceptionally high aptitude or intelligence. In reality, those students were chosen at random and did not possess any unusual abilities. The experimenter was creating an expectation. Nevertheless, after the classes were completed, students who had been identified as having high aptitude scored significantly better on all measurements of achievement. When the instructors in the classes were told that this was an experiment and that there were no differences among students, they were shocked. They honestly thought that they had given no special treatment to the so-called high-aptitude students. The only factor that was manipulated in the experiment was the *teacher's expectation* of certain students.

These studies provided a dramatic illustration of the notion of "What you expect is what you get." This notion can work negatively, too. Often people hold negative assumptions about others because of appearance, race, gender, or virtually any other characteristic. These stereotypes have a way of becoming self-confirming. We may *expect* the female employee to be more emotional or the boss's son to be less concerned about doing a good job. If we believe these expectations, we are likely to behave differently toward the individuals because of the expectations.

■ Stereotypes can become self-confirming.

People are just beginning to understand the concept of the self-fulfilling prophecy. No one fully understands all the forces at work. Expectations may be transmitted to others through subtle, nonverbal cues. Perhaps once one gets an idea, one's brain works overtime to seek confirmation of that idea. Perhaps a worker's behavior is not really so bad—but a manager may go out of the way (unconsciously) to gather examples that better "fit" with a preconceived negative opinion of that worker.

■ How can we avoid problems of negative self-fulfilling prophecies?

People who have studied self-fulfilling prophecies recommend that we all withhold judgments on other individuals as much as possible—that we keep our expectations rather loose; that we don't let our assumptions about what a person can or cannot do interfere with the way we work with that person.

Task to Be Accomplished

The nature of the work that needs to be done also has an impact on choosing appropriate leadership styles. In the military service, for example, leadership training tends to emphasize an autocratic style. This style seems to be based on Theory X assumptions about the nature of people. It seldom recommends opportunities for participation in decision making. At least, this is the popular view of the military leader accustomed to following orders.

This style of leadership may be used because the nature of the military task is unique. Few other jobs openly suggest that followers may be called on to give the ultimate sacrifice: their lives. There is little time for participative decision making on the battlefield.

On a more day-to-day level, the nature of the tasks being accomplished by a company also affects appropriate leadership styles. If the organization is primarily concerned with assembling or manufacturing something, the work to be done is clearly identified and easily measured. For example, the manager may ask the worker to insert wheels on skateboards or bumpers on automobiles. The job is

■ A clearly defined, step-by-step job is high in task structure.

clearly designed and not very flexible. A job with this degree of clarity is referred to as being high in *task structure.* The step-by-step details permit little variation in how the work is to be done.

In other situations, tasks may be much more vague—low in structure. Some organizations such as research laboratories, universities, public relations firms, or governmental review boards carryout tasks that are much less well defined. The supervisor on the assembly line seldom needs to be overly concerned with defining exactly *what* is to be done, but leaders in think-tank organizations spend a great deal of time doing so. So the nature of the task does affect the leader's job and style.

Typically, the higher one goes in the organizational hierarchy, the less task structure one finds. Top managers spend more time conceptualizing—thinking about what should be done—than actually doing or directing the job.

The Leader's Power

Leaders bring two types of power to any situation: *personal* power and *position* power. *Personal power* given to an individual is based on how others perceive that individual. It usually emerges when one is seen as having expertise, skills, ability, or other characteristics

■ Leaders can have two types of power: personal and position.

that the group considers important. There is a natural attraction to people with high personal power.

Position power is conferred on an individual by someone in a higher level of authority. It depends on rank, position, status, ability, or a combination of these to provide others with rewards or punishments. In short, position power is *authority.*

The newly announced political candidate may run initially on personal power (personality, appearance, experiences, and so on), until position power in the form of endorsements and party nomination is granted. After being elected, the officeholder has position power (having been legitimately selected by the voters), which adds significantly to the potential for leadership effectiveness.

Think for a moment about these two forms of power. Some characteristics of personal power are

- It is incremental—it grows as people see the individual exercising it well.
- It can be expanded over time.
- It can be shared. Holders of personal power can give of their credibility and power by showing that others are with them.

Authority or position power is more formal and cannot be "grown":

- It is limited by the "job description."
- It cannot normally be shared.
- It works best when used the least.

Successful leaders exert their authority sparingly. To do otherwise conveys a dictatorial attitude of "Do it this way because I'm the boss." The leader using personal power would convey an attitude of "Do it this way because you recognize my experience, judgment, and ability."

The Leader's Style

The final determinant of leadership success is *personal style.* This is a vague term. Styles can be as unique as the individuals who develop them. But one thing is certain: Style is heavily influenced by the other three factors we've already discussed—expectations, the tasks to be accomplished, and power. In the next chapter, we focus on how to develop styles that work.

▼ CONCLUSION

We all have opportunities to be leaders. All that's really required is that we cultivate some willing followers. Whenever we attempt to lead—that is, to get someone to do what we require—we choose from various tactics available to us. The use of physical threat, as in the convenience store holdup case, is not leadership. It's coercion. It will not produce lasting results.

Managers must evaluate the effects on their followers' freedom resulting from orders or requests. The dictator permits no freedom for subordinates; the participative leader permits a great deal. There is a place for both approaches—and for all those in between. The

SOURCE: Reprinted with special permission of King Features Syndicate, Inc.

exact place is determined by the leader's and the followers' personality traits, the leader's expectations and assumptions, the nature of
the task to be accomplished, and the leader's power.

▼ SUMMARY OF KEY IDEAS

- The study of leadership has been permeated with many myths.
- The personality characteristics or traits of a leader are only one of
  the factors that contribute to effective leadership. Other factors
  include the leader's expectations about human behavior, the
  leader's power, and the nature of the task.
- McGregor believes that people's actual behavior is often consistent with the way we expect them to act, people's behavior may
  not reflect their full potential, and people develop their Theory X
  or Theory Y assumptions based on their own experience.
- To reduce the possibility of self-fulfilling prophecies, we should
  withhold judgments as much as possible, keep our expectations
  loose, and avoid letting our assumptions about a person interfere
  with the way we work with that person.
- The task structure varies from flexible to rigid and requires a variety of leadership responses.
- The two types of power that a leader brings to any situation are
  personal power based on the individual's personal style and position power based on the authority conferred by the organization.

▼ KEY TERMS, CONCEPTS, AND NAMES

Authority	Self-fulfilling prophecies
Warren Bennis	Subordinate-centered leadership
Boss-centered leadership	Task structure
Douglas McGregor	Theory X
Robert K. Merton	Theory Y
Myths of leadership	Traits approach to leadership
Burt Nanus	studies

▼ QUESTIONS AND EXERCISES

1. Discuss the pros and cons of a traits approach to studying leadership. What alternatives would you suggest?

2. Describe several situations where expectations seem to have affected outcomes. (These examples need not be related to on-the-job activities.)

3. Review your score on the assumptions-about-workers questionnaire. What does this reveal about you? How might your assumptions affect the way you lead others?

4. How can leaders apply Theory Y assumptions? To what degree is the approach realistic?

5. Interview a leader in an organization in such a way as to determine that person's assumptions about his or her subordinates. To what extent could this person's comments be regarded as Theory X or Theory Y assumptions?

6. Think of a situation in which you feel that others expected you to fail or succeed. How did their expectations influence your behavior?

7. Read the following two "Case in Point ..." articles and then answer the introductory questions at the beginning of this chapter.

▼ NOTES

1. SyberVision Seminar Systems, *Leaders: The Strategies of Taking Charge,* based on the work of Warren Bennis and Burt Nanus (Pleasanton, Calif.: SyberVision, 1989).

2. Ibid.

3. R. Tannenbaum, I. Weschler, and F. Massarik, *Leadership and Organization* (New York: McGraw-Hill, 1961), p. 69.

4. Ralph M. Stogdill, *Handbook of Leadership* (New York: Free Press, 1974), pp. 81–82.

5. John Geier, "A Trait Approach to the Study of Leadership," *Journal of Communication,* 17 (1967):316–23.

6. This summary of McGregor's assumptions is adapted from Paul Hersey and Kenneth H. Blanchard, *Management of Organizational Behavior,* 3d ed. (Englewood Cliffs, N.J.: Prentice-Hall, 1977), p. 55.

7. *Productivity and the Self-fulfilling Prophecy: The Pygmalion Effect* (New York: McGraw-Hill Films, 1975).

ANOTHER LOOK: THE LEADERSHIP CHALLENGE

Considering the complex tasks of the information era and its elite labor force, the business leader's job is quite a challenge.

He or she possesses no authority over people whatsoever. The military puts deserters in jail. In business, when you are deserted, you get two weeks' notice. Maybe. Disobey a military order and you face a court-martial. In a seller's market, if your first lieutenant disagrees with your approach to the client, he or she can go out tomorrow and get another job that probably pays better anyhow.

A CORPORATION IS A VOLUNTARY ORGANIZATION

Managing through authority is out of the question. Workaholics simply burn themselves out. Loyalty is a quaint memory of the industrial past, a bone in the throat of hundreds of thousands of auto and steelworkers who thought it went both ways.

THE MILITARY MANAGEMENT MODEL CAN COMMAND AUTHORITY; BUSINESS LEADERSHIP MUST WIN LOYALTY, ACHIEVE COMMITMENT, AND EARN RESPECT.

If people are not loyal and you have no authority over them anyhow, how do you accomplish anything?

Paradoxically, people who are difficult to supervise and free to leave, people who think for themselves, who question authority, are a leader's best source of information and only hope for achieving organizational goals.

This sophisticated resource cannot be ordered, but it does respond to democratic leadership, financial incentives, and a company that recognizes that people also belong to another institution—the family.

THE NEW WORKFORCE WILL HELP YOUR COMPANY ACHIEVE OBJECTIVES, IF IT CAN ACHIEVE ITS OWN PERSONAL GOALS AS PART OF THE BARGAIN.

An effective leader creates a vision that tells people where a company is going and how it will get there and becomes the organizing force behind every corporate decision: Will this action help us achieve our vision?

"We learned that you cannot expect an employee to function at his optimum unless the manager has been successful in conveying the big picture to him," says T.

Stephen Long, vice-president of marketing at Trans Hawaiian, a $26 million-a-year tourism and transportation company in Honolulu.

More important is "selling" that vision to the people who will actualize their own goals—for achievement, security, and creativity—by achieving the corporation's. Without their energetic participation, little can be accomplished.

Incredibly, some "experts" and business gurus believe that treating people like partners and team members is patronizing or that the whole, enormous paradigm shift from authority to commitment, from management to leadership is merely a "trend." Pretty soon, they tell the hapless old-line managers who long for the past, the dust will settle and we'll be back to good old-fashioned coercion.

Revisionists in academia and the media fail to recognize what people who run businesses face every day: A highly skilled specialist can leave the company *anytime* to work for the competition or raid the client list and start his or her own business.

SOURCE: John Naisbitt and Patricia Aurdene, *Megatrends 2000* (New York: William Morrow and Company, 1990), pp. 222–23.

▼ A CASE IN POINT: ARTHUR FRIEDMAN'S OUTRAGE: EMPLOYEES DECIDE THEIR PAY

One thing for sure, Arthur Friedman will never become the chairman of the board at General Motors.

It is not just because the modish, easygoing Oakland appliance dealer does not look the part—Hush Puppies, loud shirts, and denim jackets tend to clash with the sober decor of most executive suites. And it certainly is not because he is an incompetent administrator— the Friedman-Jacobs Co. has prospered during the 15 years of his stewardship.

It is mainly because Art Friedman has some pretty strange ideas about how one runs a business.

Five years ago, he had his most outrageous brainstorm. First he tried it out on his wife, Merle, and his brother Morris.

"Here he goes again," replied Merle with a sign of resignation, "Another dumb stunt."

"Oh, my God," was all that Morris could muster.

His idea was to allow employees to set their own wages, make their own hours and take their vacations whenever they felt like it.

The end result was that it worked.

Friedman first unleashed his proposal at one of the regular staff meetings. Decide what you are worth, he said, and tell the bookkeeper to put it in your envelope next week. No questions asked. Work any time, any day, any hours you want. Having a bad day? Go home. Hate working Saturdays? No problem. Aunt Ethel from Chicago has dropped in unexpectedly? Well, take a few days off, show her the town. Want to go to Reno for a week, need a rest? Go, go, no need to ask. If you need some money for the slot machines, take it out of petty cash. Just come back when you feel ready to work again.

His speech was received in complete silence. No one cheered, no one laughed, no one said a word.

"It was about a month before anyone asked for a raise," recalls Stan Robinson, 55, the payroll clerk. "And when they did, they asked Art first. But he refused to listen and told them to just tell me what they wanted. I kept going back to him to make sure it was all right, but he wouldn't even talk about it. I finally figured out he was serious."

"It was something that I wanted to do," explains Friedman. "I always said that if you give people what they want, you get what you want. You have to be willing to lose, to stick your neck out. I finally decided that the time had come to practice what I preached."

Soon the path to Stan Robinson's desk was heavily traveled. Friedman's wife, Merle, was one of the first; she figured that her contribution was $1 an hour more. Some asked for $50 more a week, some $60. Delivery truck driver Charles Ryan was more ambitious; he demanded a $100 raise.

In most companies, Ryan would have been laughed out of the office. His work had not been particularly distinguished. His truck usually left in the morning and returned at five in the afternoon religiously, just in time for him to punch out. He dragged around the shop, complained constantly, and was almost always late for work. Things changed.

"He had been resentful about his prior pay," explains Friedman. "The raise made him a fabulous employee. He started showing up early in the morning and would be back by three, asking what else had to be done."

Instead of the all-out raid on the company coffers that some businessmen might expect, the 15 employees of the Friedman-Jacobs Co. displayed astonishing restraint and maturity. The wages they demanded were just slightly higher than the scale of the Retail Clerks union, to which they all belong (at Friedman's insistence). Some did not even take a raise. One service man who was receiving considerably less than his co-workers was asked why he did not insist on equal pay. "I don't want to work that hard," was the obvious answer.

When the union contract comes across Friedman's desk every other year, he signs it without even reading it. "I don't care what it says," he insists. At first, union officials would drop in to see how things were going, but they would usually end up laughing and shaking their heads, muttering something about being put out of a job. They finally stopped coming by.

The fact is that Friedman's employees have no need for a union; whatever they want, they

A CASE IN POINT: ARTHUR FRIEDMAN'S OUTRAGE: EMPLOYEES DECIDE THEIR PAY *continued*

take and no one questions it. As a result, they have developed a strong sense of responsibility and an acute sensitivity to the problems that face the American worker in general that would have been impossible under the traditional system.

George Tegner, 59, an employee for 14 years, has like all his co-workers achieved new insight into the mechanics of the free enterprise system. "You have to use common sense; no one wins if you end up closing the business down. If you want more money, you have to produce more. It can't work any other way. Anyway, wages aren't everything. Doing what you want to is more important."

Roger Ryan, 27, has been with the company for five years. "I know about inflation, but I haven't taken a raise [in several years]. I figure if everybody asks for more, then inflation will just get worse. I'll hold out as long as I can."

Payroll clerk Stan Robinson: "I'm single now. I don't take as much as the others, even though I've been here longer, because I don't need as much. The government usually winds up with the extra money anyway."

Elwood Larsen, 65, has been the company's ace service man for 16 years. When he went into semi-retirement last year, he took a $1.50 cut in pay. Why? Larsen does not think a part timer is worth as much. "I keep working here because I like it. We all know that if the Friedmans make money, we do. You just can't gouge the owner."

In the past five years, there has been no turnover of employees. Friedman estimates that last year his 15 workers took no more than a total of three sick days. It is rare that anyone is late for work, and even then there is usually a good reason. Work is done on time, and employee pilferage is nonexistent.

"We used to hear of lot of grumbling," says Robinson. "Now, everybody smiles."

As part of the new freedom, more people were given keys to the store and the cash box. If they need groceries, or even some beer money, all they have to do is walk into the office, take what they want out of the cash box, and leave a voucher. Every effort is made to ensure that no one looks over their shoulder.

There has been only one discrepancy. "Once the petty cash was $10 over," recalls Friedman. "We never could figure out where it came from."

The policy has effected some changes in the way things are done around the store. It used to be open every night and all day Sunday, but no one wanted to work those hours. A problem? Of course not. No more nights and Sundays. ("When I thought about it," confesses Friedman, "I didn't like to work those hours either.")

The store also handled TVs and stereos—high profit items—but they were a hassle for all concerned. The Friedman-Jacobs Co. now deals exclusively in major appliances such as refrigerators, washers, and dryers.

Skeptics by now are chuckling to themselves, convinced that if Friedman is not losing money, he is just breaking even. The fact is that net profit has not dropped a cent in the last five years; it has increased. Although volume is considerably less and overhead has increased at what some would consider an unhealthy rate, greater productivity and efficiency have more than made up for it.

None of this concerns Friedman, though. He keeps no charts, does not know how to read cost-analysis graphs, and does not have the vaguest idea what cash flow means. As long as he can play golf a couple of times a week, and make money to boot, he could not be happier.

Encouraged by his success, Friedman decided to carry his revolution beyond labor relations. If it worked there, he figured, it should work with customer relations as well. So policy changes resulted in such innovations as the following "last bill" notice, that dread purveyor of bad tidings:

"For some reasons which we really cannot understand, you have decided not to pay the bill that you owe us.

"This letter officially cancels that bill and you are no longer under any obligation to pay us. We have decided not to give this bill to a collection agency, as our gain would be small compared to your loss.

"We would appreciate it, however, if you would take a moment to tell us why you

A CASE IN POINT *continued*

made the decision not to pay us. It would be very helpful to us and the rest of our customers."

As cute as this may appear, it could hardly be expected to work. But Friedman claims that delinquent accounts are no more frequent today.

"We don't collect any more money than we did before, but we don't collect any less either. The difference is that you learn a lot more about the problem. Anyway, it's a lot more pleasant way of doing business," says Friedman.

QUESTIONS

1. How does Friedman's "outrage" relate to our discussion of McGregor's Theory X and Theory Y?
2. To what extent could Friedman's approach be used in other organizations?
3. What would limit its application?
4. What do your answers to the preceding questions say about your assumptions about workers.

SOURCE: Reprinted by permission of *the Washington Post* from Martin Koughan, *The Washington Post,* Sunday, February 23, 1975. Copright *The Washington Post.*

▼ A CASE IN POINT: UNDERSTANDING YOUR EMPLOYEES

Immediately after college, Karen had joined the telephone company in its management training program. She had been identified as a potentially "fast-track" manager and had been working in the Miami office for only four months when an opening for a unit manager came about. At first, the district manager thought about hiring someone from outside or transferring a more experienced manager. But because Karen was already available and to avoid recruiting or moving costs, he decided to let Karen have a chance at the job. In the new job, she would have seven supervisors reporting to her. Each supervisor directed five or six customer service representatives who talked directly to customers all day.

Shirley, the most experienced of the supervisors, had been filling in as acting manager for the past few weeks. She seemed to know pretty well what she was doing, and because of her many years working in the office, she knew each employee well.

The first day on he job, she sat down with Karen and briefed her on which employees were indifferent, which were plain lazy, which were marginal performers, and which had personality problems. Her list seemed to include almost all the employees! Along with her assessment of the workers, this supervisor gave Karen some tips on how to "handle" certain members of the staff. The two women spent all morning discussing these things.

Usually, Karen diplomatically turned a deaf ear to this kind of advice. But because she was so new on the job and knew no one in the office, she was more susceptible to suggestion. Although Shirley seemed pretty negative, Karen felt that generally the advice was probably sound. This office was going to need quite a bit of shaping up, concluded Karen.

QUESTIONS

1. How would the advice received from this experienced supervisor be likely to affect Karen's management style?
2. What would you do in a similar situation if an employee gave you some unsolicited appraisals of all the workers who were to report to you?
3. How do the potential problem of self-fulfilling prophecies and the discussion of McGregor's Theory X and Theory Y apply to this case?

DEVELOPING A LEADERSHIP STYLE THAT WORKS

This chapter answers several all-important questions:

■ Why is the manager's choice between decisiveness and participation so important?

■ What are some potential advantages to be gained from employee participation in decisions?

■ What are some potential disadvantages of participation?

■ Which leadership style is right?

■ What is the difference between task and maintenance activities?

■ What is Fiedler's leadership contingency model, and how can it be used?

■ What key ingredients determine an employee's or group's development level?

■ What does Likert mean by the linking-pin function of management?

■ Why is feedback and flexibility important for leaders?

The answers to these and other questions are coming up next in chapter 8....

CHAPTER 8

Congratulations! You've just been elected president of the Discovery Club, a service organization. You've been active in the club for several years and feel strongly about the importance of its goal: to strengthen relationships between students and the community via civic service projects. You have lots of good ideas, and now you are in a position to get things rolling in a new direction. But you're a little concerned about being a "boss." What kind of leadership should you use?

In the previous chapter, we discussed the nature of leadership and emphasized key variables that affect the leadership process. In this chapter, we suggest some ways to apply such information in leading others. Before we go on, however, let's look at your potential as a leader. Answer the questions in the following "test" of your leadership potential. Be honest.

▼ ACTIVITY: TEST YOUR LEADERSHIP POTENTIAL

	Usually	Sometimes	Rarely
1. I look for positive challenges during periods of change.	_____	_____	_____
2. I'm willing to take risks and learn from mistakes.	_____	_____	_____
3. I regularly acknowledge others' accomplishments.	_____	_____	_____
4. I reflect the values I claim to believe in.	_____	_____	_____
5. I look for ways to share power.	_____	_____	_____
6. I delegate tasks with authority and decisiveness.	_____	_____	_____
7. I have written long-range plans, and I am committed to them.	_____	_____	_____
8. I know how to motivate other people.	_____	_____	_____
9. I know how to promote team effort and spirit.	_____	_____	_____
10. I regularly give honest, constructive feedback to my team.	_____	_____	_____
11. I make decisions in a timely manner.	_____	_____	_____

Striving to answer "Usually" on each of these questions is a worthy goal for any leader. Any questions you answered with "Sometimes" or "Rarely" should become your goals as you study this book.

Make a list of your leadership goals; for instance, "I will look for opportunities to be more decisive."

SOURCE: Marilyn Manning with Patricia Haddock, *Leadership Skills for Women* (Los Altos, Calif.: Crisp Publications, 1989), p. 3.

▼ YOUR LEADERSHIP STYLE: DECISIVENESS VERSUS PARTICIPATION

Probably the most important problem most managers face is that of creating an appropriate balance between *decisiveness* and *participation*. Ultimately, managers need to make decisions. Once a problem has been carefully thought through, being decisive is a great virtue. Nevertheless, the chief advantage of having others participate in decision making is that the decision arrived at by group participation is more likely to be accepted. Resistance to new ideas is greatly reduced when people have had a chance to participate in decisions.

The way one mixes decisiveness with participation opportunities says much about one's general leadership style. Keep in mind that most managers adjust styles depending on the people they are leading and on other issues that we'll talk more about later.

Studies of leadership suggest that there are at least four commonly recognized styles: autocratic, consultative, participative, and laissez-faire (see figure 8.1). All but the autocratic style are regarded as democratic to some degree in that the followers participate in leader decisions.

■ Four general styles of leadership are autocratic, consultative, participative, and laissez-faire.

Autocratic

The *autocratic* leader is decisive and permits little, if any, follower participation in the decision-making process. Such individuals simply weigh the information, make the decision, and impose that decision on their followers. This may sometimes be necessary, such as in an emergency. If a restaurant patron is choking on food and you are the only person who knows the Heimlich maneuver, it's appropriate

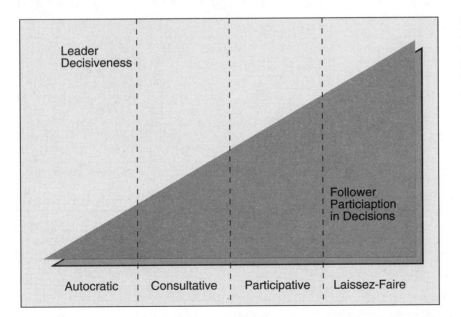

FIGURE **8.1**
Degrees of leader decisiveness and follower participation under four leadership styles.

for you to jump in and take charge. Likewise, in warfare, military leaders make command decisions, some of which are not popular.

Successful autocrats (and there are some) make short-term expectations clear and leave no doubt about the rewards of conforming and the costs of not conforming. Then they deliver the rewards or punishments as promised.

In most organizations, the consistently autocratic leader is disliked and ultimately becomes ineffective. People spend a great deal of energy attempting to get around or defeat the purposes of the autocratic leader.

Consultative

The *consultative* leader tends to be fairly high in decisiveness but allows followers more participation in the decision-making process by allowing them to assume more responsibility for their own future as well as preparing them for more responsible positions within the company.

Herman Sundays by Jim Unger Kansas City: Andrews and McMeel, Inc., 1986

Laissez-faire

Loosely translated from the French, *laissez-faire* means "let them do anything that they want to." The exceptionally "laid back" leader may have happy employees but probably will not have very productive employees—although, again, there are exceptions. When subordinates are self-motivated and highly interested in what they are doing, this free-rein style may be appropriate. Under this approach, the leader acts principally as a representative of the work group. The leader's job is to be sure there are necessary resources so that the group can accomplish its tasks. In essence, the leader is saying, "You know what needs to be done and how to do it, so I'll keep out of your way. Let me know if you need anything."

- A laissez-faire leader represents the group and obtains the resources it needs.

A certain type of follower is needed to work effectively under laissez-faire leadership. Workers who are self-motivated and experienced enjoy such hands-off leadership. Workers who are not so sure of themselves may resent what they perceive as a lack of direction, or they may simply avoid doing anything productive. Later in this chapter, we will show how you can determine if this style is likely to work.

The autocratic leader uses a top-down approach.

The consultative or laissez-faire leader does more to serve and support the followers in a bottom-up manner:

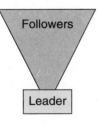

Participative

The *participative* manager is likely to work from Theory Y assumptions. Participative leaders assume that subordinates are creative and have worthwhile ideas that can be applied on the job. They seek out insights and ideas and use them—usually *before* a decision has been made.

- Is a participative style always best?

Tremendous advantages can arise from participation. More and better ideas can emerge. Resistance to changes is likely to dissipate. And, in general, the work climate and employee morale can improve with group involvement.

Participation has disadvantages, however, especially when overused. Some decisions do not lend themselves to a participative approach. For example, decisions about individual compensation or about highly personal matters should not be discussed widely. Similarly, decisions that need to be made quickly often cannot be made with a participative approach.

In addition, the leader must keep in mind that participation can be expensive. It ties up a number of people in meetings (which too often are poorly run), and the costs in time and money can be enormous. Nevertheless, the quality of decisions reached may well offset these costs.

A participative style spreads the responsibilities of leadership among all involved. This can pay big dividends in developing your workers by allowing them to assume more responsibility for their own future as well as preparing them for more responsible positions within the company.

Some argue that the bottom-up versus top-down philosophy is what distinguishes leadership from management. A leader is one who serves and supports others (bottom-up), while a manager pushes down an agenda of work to be done.

▼ WHICH STYLE IS RIGHT?

The question is, "When should the different leadership styles be used? What works best?"

Before we can answer that, we need to review some of what has already been covered and add a few more ingredients to the soup.

To make good guesses about which leadership style is likely to work best, people need to understand something about *situational variables* (factors in the environment that are likely to change). One such variable is the mixture of task and maintenance activities needed by the work group.

Getting the Job Done versus Feeling Good about It

In any work situation, two types of activities are influenced by the leader: *task activities* and *maintenance activities*. *Task* has to do with *what* the group is doing; *maintenance* is concerned with *how* the group members do it. Clarifying work group goals is primarily a task activity, while establishing a pleasant, creative, supportive work climate is mostly a maintenance activity.

Most leaders understand their task roles; they see a job to be done and know they're responsible to see that it is accomplished. Some, however, underestimate the importance of maintenance. One can go too far with either activity, and the degree of emphasis is an important management judgment.

Although the task activities get the job done, neglect of maintenance can lead to serious dissatisfaction that could undermine the entire process. The manager who rams through a solution may face group resentment that eventually will more than offset the "victory." And sometimes maintenance activities are the most important outcome of a meeting, making participants feel good about the opportunities for affiliation and participation in group work. The manager who is sensitive to a healthy balance between getting the job done and making that experience rewarding to the workers is likely to be more successful in the long run than one who overemphasizes one factor. Group members will appreciate an appropriate mix of task and maintenance efforts. They are far more likely to go along with the manager who balances these activities.

- The manager who rams through a decision may face resentment that offsets the "victory."

The Leadership Contingency Approach

Fred E. Fiedler developed a *leadership contingency model* that helps determine the best leadership style by looking at three variables: *leader-member relations, task structure,* and *position power.*

- Fiedler sees three key leadership variables: Leader-member relations Task structure Position power

Fiedler's research suggests that the degree to which a leader should emphasize task versus maintenance activities can be determined by the *favorableness of the situation.* This he defines as "the degree to which the situation enables the leader to exert his or her influence over the group."[1]

In the most *favorable situation,* the leader

- is well liked by the group,
- is directing a clearly defined task, and
- has recognized status or position power.

In an *unfavorable* situation,

- the leader is not well liked,
- the task is not very clear, and
- the group does not recognize the leader's right to power.

Some mixture of positives and negatives would put the leader in a *mixed situation.*

Fiedler's research concludes that when the situation is either very favorable *or* very *unfavorable* to the leader, the leader would do well to stress task activities and not be overly concerned with relationship activities. When the favorableness of the situation is intermediate, the leader needs to be more concerned with the building of good relationships (see figure 8.2).

Stated simply, when the situation is highly favorable (you are liked, the task is clear, and you have position power), you can afford to be a little bossy. Likewise, when the situation is highly unfavorable (you are disliked, the task is ambiguous, and you don't have position power), you might as well be bossy—you have little to lose. But when the situation is somewhere in the middle (you are liked but the task is unclear and you have only moderate position power), you'd be wise to stress maintenance activities—that is, relationship building.

FIGURE 8.2
Fiedler's leadership contingency model.

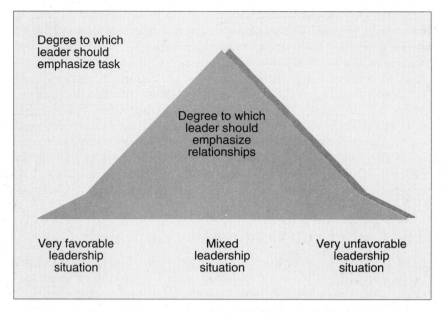

Degree to which leader should emphasize task

Degree to which leader should emphasize relationships

Very favorable leadership situation

Mixed leadership situation

Very unfavorable leadership situation

■ A skilled leader switches emphasis from task to maintenance as needed.

A skillful leader should be capable of switching emphasis as needed. As changes appear in, say, task clarity and relationships with group participants, a marked increase in situational favorableness may call for a shift in emphasis from maintenance (building rapport and so on) to task activities.

▼ SITUATIONAL LEADERSHIP: GETTING AT THE BEST APPROACH

Management theorists Paul Hersey and Kenneth H. Blanchard have built on the ideas of Fiedler and a number of others to develop their *situational leadership theory* (SLT). According to their approach, a leader can determine an appropriate mixture of relationship building and task directing to increase the probability of effectiveness. "To determine what leadership style is appropriate in a given situation, a leader must first determine the *development level* of the individual or group in relation to a specific task that the leader is attempting to accomplish through their efforts."[2]

■ Development level is determined by four characteristics.

What is *development level?* According to SLT, the development level of a person or group can be diagnosed by considering four characteristics of the group *in relation to the specific job the group is called on to accomplish.* These characteristics are as follows:

1. The capacity to set high but attainable goals
2. The willingness and ability to take on responsibility
3. Education, experience, or both, relevant to the task
4. Personal maturity on the job in combination with a psychological maturity or self-confidence and self-respect

These characteristics can be categorized under two headings: *competence* and *commitment.*

Let's look at an example. You have been asked to lead a committee to recommend a marketing strategy for a new product line. In gathering information about those who will work on the committee, you determine the following:

1. The participants have a good record for reaching ambitious yet realistic targets for themselves (commitment).
2. The participants have shown an eagerness to work on the committee and to take responsibility for marketing this new product line in a vigorous manner (commitment). If the product goes over well, they expect to get credit; if it flops, they expect to shoulder the blame.
3. Each participant has been in on the new product development from the ground floor. The participants know how the product is made and why it's built the way it is, and they have a good idea of potential markets, based on past experience (competence).
4. The participants are seasoned professionals in their fields. They are interested in success, and they have proven track records (competence).

The preceding committee is at a very high development level. But what if the team consists of quite another group? Let's say that the participants

1. tend to take excessive risks (have a record of "biting off more than they can chew");
2. want credit if their plan works but won't accept blame if it fails;
3. have never worked on a committee like this one before; and
4. are "rookies" in this business.

Under this second set of circumstances, the leader's job is likely to be quite different. The second group's development level is very low.

Most groups are likely to fall somewhere in between these two examples. Figure 8.3 indicates how the effective leadership style would be determined. Once the development level of the participants is identified (or realistically guessed at), "the appropriate leadership style can be determined by constructing a right (90°) angle from the point on the continuum that represents the development level of the follower(s) to a point where it intersects the [curve] in the style-of-leader portion of the model. The quadrant in which that intersection takes place suggests the appropriate style to be used by the leader in that situation with follower(s) of that maturity level."[3]

Or, we could say that the leader's predominant behavior changes in relation to the group's development level. The leader also tends toward a different leadership style under each condition, as illustrated in table 8.1.

Directing, coaching, supporting, and delegating each calls for a different mix of communication skills. The ways in which leaders communicate with the low-development employee or group should be different from the way leaders talk to a high-development-level employee or group.

FIGURE 8.3
Situational leadership.

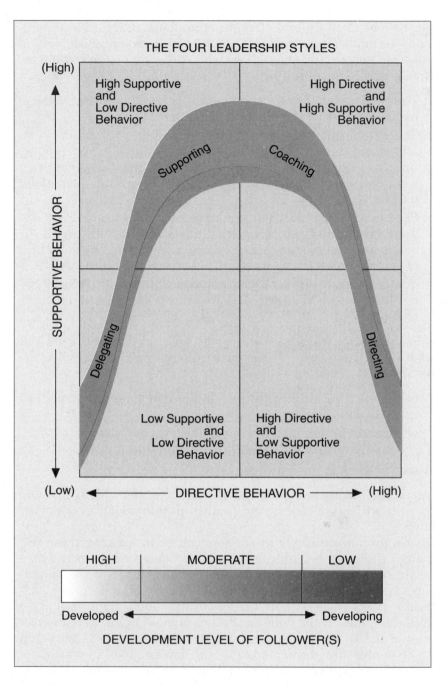

The appropriate leadership style will probably be more autocratic with low-development workers. Managers will direct these workers more and will not expect much participation—at least not at first. The highly developed work group—the self-motivated, personally responsible, experienced team with a success record—may well thrive under a leader who lets the group do its own thing (so long as it continues to work toward organizational goals).

▼ TABLE 8.1 WORKERS' DEVELOPMENT LEVEL AFFECTS LEADERSHIP STYLE AND COMMUNICATION APPROACH

GROUP'S TASK-RELEVANT MATURITY LEVEL	LEADERSHP STYLE	LEADER'S PREDOMINANT BEHAVIOR
Low	Autocratic	Directing
Moderately low	Consultative	Coaching
Moderately high	Participative	Supporting
High	Laissez-faire	Delegating

As Kenneth Blanchard, Patricia Zigarmi, and Drea Zigarmi said, "In determining what style to use with what development level, just remember that *leaders need to do what the people they supervise can't do for themselves at the present moment.*"[4] An objective of any manager should be to move the work group toward increasing development. The payoff includes more motivated, stimulated workers who work on their own without close supervision. Such workers tend to be productive even when their managers aren't monitoring them.

▼ HOW ORGANIZATIONS SHIFT TO PARTICIPATIVE, LAISSEZ-FAIRE STYLES

Management consultant Ed Yeager explains that successful organizations must eventually grow into participative, self-directing units:

> Here is how the most successful organizations make the shift. The focus in the organization moves from vertical or hierarchical to horizontal. The emphasis shifts from accountability of "the boss" to accountability of the team. Empowerment, a currently popular but badly misunderstood term, becomes pervasive. The orientation of everyone is up- and downstream, working with co-workers, rather than up and down the channels and "chain of authority."
>
> To be empowered, a person, or better, a team, must have the authority to make virtually any decision or initiate any action that comes to him or her with no escalation, no higher-order approvals, and no second-guessing. Teams of operators, professionals, and specialists are organized around responsibilities or outputs directed toward their internal or external customers. They are trained in the basic team skills, communication skills, problem solving, service improvement, quality management, performance measurement techniques, etc.[5]

Coaching, he says, becomes the primary focus as people master skills and become fully responsible for their own work and that of the team.

FIGURE 8.4
The linking-pin role.

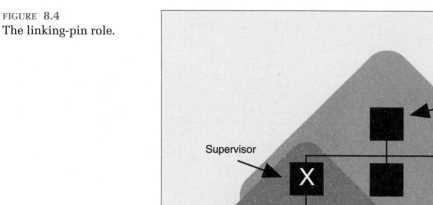

▼ BECOMING A LINKING PIN

Boosting workers' development level allows the leader to take on a new role. The leader can become a liaison between workers and top management, acting as the workers' advocate to get resources and rewards. This is what management theorist, Rensis Likert, calls the *linking-pin function* of management. The manager becomes the link (or linking pin) that ties the group that he or she manages to the next higher group in the organization (see figure 8.4). Likert describes this function as follows: "The capacity to exert influence upward is essential if a leader (or manager) is to perform his ... functions successfully. To be effective in leading his own boss, that is, he needs to be skilled both as a supervisor and a subordinate."[6]

Every supervisor is a member of two work groups: the one he or she is responsible *for* and the one he or she is responsible *to.* When workers become more mature, their supervisor need not supervise them closely and can spend more time in the linking-pin role.

As the work group evolves toward higher development levels over time, the leader must be ready to adjust his or her behaviors accordingly. As communication scholar Franklin Haiman said almost thirty years ago, "The man officially called leader performs only those tasks which the group itself is not yet mature enough, intellectually or emotionally, to handle for itself. The leader's goal is to work himself out of a job."[7]

▼ THE IMPORTANCE OF FEEDBACK AND FLEXIBILITY

As our discussion implies, leaders wear several hats. They serve and are served. They direct, coach, support, and delegate. To be effective

1991 United Feature Syndicate. *Build a Better Life By Stealing Office Supplies: Dogbert's Big Book of Business.* Reprinted with permission, Pharos Books, New York, N.Y.

in these many functions, leaders must be sensitive to feedback and willing to adjust as needed.

To charge blindly ahead with an inappropriate leadership style is folly.

In an "Another Look" article entitled "How to Get 'No' for an Answer" at the end of this chapter, Mortimer Feinberg suggests ways to critically evaluate the courses of action selected.[8] Modern organization cannot survive with a bunch of yes-men and yes-women.

▼ LEADERSHIP STYLES: A WRAP-UP

How does one develop a style that works? This chapter suggests that one can recognize different leadership styles by the mix between decisiveness and participation. Each of the four general styles—autocratic, consultative, participative, and laissez-faire—may be appropriate in certain cases. These styles come to life as leaders direct, coach, support, and delegate to followers.

The leader's situation is influenced by the tasks to be accomplished, the followers' needs for both task and relationship guidance, the personalities of both leader and followers, and the position power of the leader.

Leaders become representatives of their people to higher management.

As leaders help followers achieve higher development levels, the boss's role becomes one of a linking pin—a representative of the workers to higher management instead of primarily a supervisor.

When group members grow under appropriate leadership, everybody wins.

▼ SUMMARY OF KEY IDEAS

- The four general leadership styles are autocratic, consultative, participative, and laissez-faire.
- The two types of activities that are influenced by a leader are task and maintenance.
- Task behavior focuses on getting the job done, whereas maintenance behavior concentrates on making the work experience rewarding for the employee.
- The three key variables of Fiedler's contingency approach are leader-member relations, task structure, and position power.
- Fiedler suggests that when the leadership situation is highly favorable or highly unfavorable, the leader should emphasize task, and when the situation is mixed in favorability, the leader should focus on relationships.
- The curvilinear relationship among Hersey and Blanchard's four situational leadership styles flows from *directing* to *coaching* to *supporting* to *delegating*, depending on the follower's development level, which is based on competence and commitment.
- According to Likert, the successful manager serves as a linking pin between subordinates and superiors and has some degree of upward influence with superiors.

▼ KEY TERMS, CONCEPTS, AND NAMES

Autocratic style	Consultative style
Kenneth Blanchard	Linking-pin function
Development level	Maintenance activities
Favorableness of the situation	Participative style
Fred E. Fiedler	Position power
Paul Hersey	Situational leadership theory (SLT)
Laissez-faire style	Task activities
Leadership contingency model	Task structure

▼ QUESTIONS AND EXERCISES

1. Observe a leader at work. How would you characterize this person's style? How does he or she adjust to situational variables?

2. List a series of activities you engage in on the job or in school. Now categorize these into either *task* or *relationship* activities. If your activities include leading others, study your task-relationship mix. Is it appropriate?

3. Describe in your own words the concept of *development level.* How does this concept help us determine appropriate leadership behaviors?

4. What are some implications of being a linking pin?

5. What does Fiedler mean by "favorableness of the situation"? How does the degree of favorableness affect the way a leader should lead?

6. Discuss the statement, "The leader's goal is to work himself or herself out of a job." What are the potential benefits of such a goal? Is this goal attainable?

7. Read the following "Another Look ..." articles and then answer the introductory questions at the beginning of this chapter.

▼ NOTES

1. Fred E. Fiedler, *A Theory of Leadership Effectiveness* (New York: McGraw-Hill, 1967), p. 13.

2. Situational leadership theory was articulated by Paul Hersey and Kenneth H. Blanchard in *Management of Organizational Behavior,* 3d ed. (Englewood Cliffs, N.J.: Prentice-Hall, 1977). The term *development level* was originally called *task-relevant maturity.* A recent updating of the theory using simpler terms is found in Kenneth Blanchard, Patricia Zigarmi, and Drea Zigarmi, *Leadership and the One Minute Manager* (New York: William Morrow, 1985).

3. Blanchard, Zigarmi, and Zigarmi, *Leadership and the One Minute Manager,* p. 68.

4. Ibid., p. 69.

5. Ed Yeager "Organizations Embrace Power of Teamwork," Salt Lake City *Desert News,* 17 March 1991, p. B10.

6. Rensis Likert, *New Patterns of Management* (New York: McGraw-Hill, 1961), p. 14.

7. Franklin S. Haiman, *Group Leadership and Democratic Action* (Boston: Houghton Mifflin, 1951), pp. 38–39.

8. Mortimer R. Feinberg, "How to Get 'No' for an Answer," *Wall Street Journal,* 30 December 1991, p. A–12.

▼ ANOTHER LOOK: HOW TO GET 'NO' FOR AN ANSWER

Today it's more important than ever to get "no' for an answer from the people in your organization—if "no" is what it takes to avoid damaging mistakes, plug costly leaks and make vital course changes.

That's not easy, even when times are good. People tend to observe the unwritten law that the glass is always at least half full. But it's a lot harder for people to be negative when things are tough. They figure the boss has enough trouble without hearing more bad news. And, being human, they may think of the declaration attributed to Louis B. Mayer: "I don't want yes-men around me. Tell me what you think even if it costs you your job!"

So today it takes more than merely saying, "My door is always open." Astute managers are doing everything possible to elicit the truth—even when it's unpleasant—by creating a positive atmosphere for negative feedback, by rewarding nay-sayers as well as yea-sayers, and by setting an example of self-criticism.

Here's a sampling of useful techniques for emphasizing the necessary negative.

- *Remove the "Made by the Boss" label.* People speak more freely if they don't think they're knocking the boss's pet project. Lorian Mariantes, senior vice president of the Rockefeller Group, says: "Don't admit it's your

idea at first. I say something like, 'Here are two or three possible approaches. What do you think?'" If the idea holds up under discussion, the senior executive can "buy into it" without admitting total authorship.

- *Hold a "negative brainstorming" meeting.* James Wesley, president and CEO of Summit Communications Group, says, "Don't let a bad idea get past the first meeting." Sometimes managers go through a charade of consideration of an unworkable notion to avoid looking autocratic. Subject each scheme to an acid test. Hold a session at which people are encouraged to take their best shots. Subject all ideas to this routine, whether their origins be high or low.

- *Build an atmosphere of trust.* "People must know they have nothing to fear when they bring bad news," observes a major oil company chairman. He emphasizes the importance of staying calm even when the news is hair-raising. "Impress on them that delay in reporting bad news is the cardinal sin." This atmosphere of confidence and openness can't be built overnight. It's built up over the years. And it can be destroyed in one moment if the boss hits the roof when confronted with a not-so-hot report.

- *Help people say "no" to their own shaky proposals.* Constructive criticism should begin at home. People who are used to analyzing their own ideas will not only produce better ideas; they will be more adroit at and confident about criticizing the ideas of others, including the boss. Carl Dargene, president and CEO of Amcore Financial, uses some key questions to get people to subject their own proposals to rigorous testing. For example:

  "Have you considered this aspect (with particulars)?"

  "What's the downside contingency?"

  "Would you spend your own money on it?"

- *Relax the chain of command.* John McGlynn, president of Agfa Technical Imaging Group, says, "I encourage people at the lowest ranks to pick up the phone and call me with their ideas and reactions." Mr. McGlynn knows some of his managers are uncomfortable with this short-circuiting of the chain of command. But the idea is to have employees at all levels talking with each other with the mutual purpose of doing a better job.

- *Make allowances for the times.* Executives who are accustomed to free speech from team members when business is good may assume that employees will feel just as uninhibit-

ANOTHER LOOK *continued*

ed when things are tight. That often runs counter to psychological impulses.

William Fabian, executive vice president of Morey La Rue, a textile rental company, had been discussing possible down-sizing implications with a key manager. As he usually did with the manager—a trusted associate for many years—Mr. Fabian spoke in a theoretical vein, wondering aloud about a 30% reduction in payroll. The manager took this as a directive. Mr. Fabian had to step in to reverse plans that would have led to a harmful slashing of staff. The manager thought the notion was a bad idea—but he inferred that the boss wanted it done. Now Mr. Fabian makes it a point to draw out objections that might be withheld because of the economic environment.

Executives can't dictate personal feelings. But they can make it clear that their people have the paramount obligation to beam the top candlepower of their brains onto every issue that comes before them, and to say "no" when no is the word that should be said.

Positive thinking is still, on balance, the best policy. But "on balance" is the operative phrase. The optimum mode is productive, positive attitudes tethered to reality by the occasional tug of the negative. "No," after all, is not a four-letter word.

SOURCE: Mortimer R. Feinberg, *Wall Street Journal,* 30 December 1991, p. A-12.

ANOTHER LOOK: THE LEADERSHIP CHALLENGE

Great leaders get extraordinary things done in organizations by inspiring and motivating others toward a common purpose. Their effectiveness isn't magical or beyond the reach of mortals. They rely on specific practices to turn challenging opportunities into remarkable successes. Those methods and techniques can be learned and applied to great advantage.

SEEK NEW OPPORTUNITIES

The quest for change is an adventure. It tests our skills and brings forth dormant talents. It is the training ground for leadership. Here are some suggestions for how you can search for opportunities in your leadership role:

- *Treat every job as an adventure.* Identify projects you have always wanted to undertake but never have. Ask your team members to do the same. Pick one major project per quarter. Implement one smaller improvement every three weeks. Figure out how to do all of this within the budget you now have, or [with] the money you will save or earn when the project succeeds. If you still need money, just like any adventurer, go out and raise it from your supporters. Your new projects don't have to be ones that change the world. They can be anything that gets your organization moving on the road to ever greater heights.

- *Treat every new assignment as a turnaround, even if it isn't.* There is no magic to making a previously poorly performing unit a high-performing one. Often the critical difference is a leader who sees within the existing group untapped energy and skill and who assumes that excellence can be achieved. Ask for a tough assignment. Ask your superiors to give you an opportunity to take on that losing operation. Challenge calls forth leadership. There's no better way for you to test your own limits than to place yourself voluntarily in difficult jobs.

- *Add adventure to every job.* Ask people to join

you in solving problems and volunteering creative ideas. Delegate more than just the routine jobs. But be sure to find out what motivates each of your team members. Different people find different things challenging. Get to know each person's skill levels.

- *Break free of the routine.* Make a list of your daily routines. Keep those that help you find opportunities for improvement, and get rid of the hindrances. Each day, break one useless old habit and start a new one. Call some new people. Read a new book. Visit a new place.

EXPERIMENT: TAKE RISKS

Leaders are experimenters, trying new approaches to old problems. They use their "outsight"—their ability to perceive external realities—to discover useful ideas for themselves. Innovation is always risky, and wise leaders recognize this necessary fact. But instead of punishing failure, they encourage it. Rather than fix blame for mistakes, they learn from them. Here are some ways to help people take charge of change.

- *Institutionalize processes for collecting innovative ideas.* Gather suggestions from customers, employees, suppliers, and other stakeholders. Use focus groups, advisory boards, suggestion boxes, breakfast meetings, brainstorm-

ing sessions, customer evaluation forms, mystery shoppers, mystery guests, and visits to competitors to collect ideas. Each is a way to open your eyes and ears to the world outside the boundaries of the organization.

- *Put idea gathering on your own agenda.* Devote 25 percent of every weekly staff meeting to listening to ideas for improving process technologies and developing new products or services. Invite people from other departments— even customers—to offer their suggestions on how your unit can improve. Call three customers who haven't purchases anything from you in a while and ask them why. Ride a route with one of your sales or delivery people. Work the counter and ask customers what they like and don't like. Shop at a competitor's store. Better yet, anonymously shop for your own product and see what the salespeople in the store say about it.

- *Renew your teams.* Never let them get disconnected from outside information. Make sure members attend professional conferences, participate in training programs, and visit colleagues in other parts of the organization. Add a new member or two to the group every couple of years. New people, especially those who haven't been socialized into your way of doing

things, can help you get a new perspective. Put everybody through a creativity course. Give them the knowledge, skills, and tools they need to generate new ideas.

- *Analyze every failure, as well as every success.* At the completion of a project, or at periodic intervals during it, take the team off site and do a review. Build the agenda around: What did we do well? What did we do poorly? What did we learn from this? How can we do better the next time? Make sure that everyone contributes. Type all the notes and make them available to everyone. Take immediate action when you return.

FOSTER COLLABORATION

Fostering collaboration is all about getting people to work together, a process that must be nurtured, strengthened, and managed. Leaders who champion collaboration search for integrative solutions—ways of settling problems by concentrating on what everyone has to gain. To find integrative solutions, change people's thinking from an either/or (or zero-sum) mentality to a positive perspective on working together. Get people to be clear about their needs and interests, but frame differences so that participants recognize that the greatest gain comes from cooperating with each other. To promote

ANOTHER LOOK *continued*

integrative solutions:

- *Seek many inputs.* By their very nature, integrative solutions begin with diverse opinions. Active listening is the source of considerable inspiration. It allows people to put their cards on the table and feel a part of the decision.

- *Meet one-on-one.* This lets people know that you value their input and forces them to focus their remarks. If you expect opposition, face-to-face communications improves the likelihood of developing understanding between competing perspectives.

STRENGTHEN PEOPLE

Leaders are motivated to use their power in service of others because empowered people perform better. When others are strengthened to accomplish extraordinary things on their own, the leader's own sphere of influence is enhanced. Empowering others is essentially the process of turning followers into leaders. Leaders build and enhance power when their people work on tasks that are critical to the organization's success, when they exercise discretion and autonomy in their efforts, when their accomplishments are visible and recognized by others, and when they are well connected to other people of influence and support. There

are several strategies you can use to build more power for yourself and for others:

- *Use your power in service of others.* Ask the people who work for you what they need to do their jobs most effectively, then go get it for them. Your challenge is to give your power away: Paradoxically, the more you give away, the more you get for yourself.

- *Enlarge people's sphere of influence.* One way to give some of your power away is to increase the amount of autonomy and discretion others have. Delegate. Form quality circles and other problem-solving groups. Enable people to make top-priority decisions without consulting you. One caution: Provide people with the training to make use of their decision-making power and discretionary tasks. Give them all the necessary resources to perform autonomously— materials, money, time, people, and information.

PLAN SMALL WINS

Problems that are conceived of too broadly overwhelm people because they defeat our capacity even to think about what might be done, let alone begin doing something about them. Leaders face a similar challenge in trying to achieve extraordinary accomplishments. So how do they do it? One hop

at a time. The most effective processes of change are incremental—they break down big problems into small, doable steps and get a person to say *yes* numerous times, not just once. Leaders help others to see how progress can be planned by splitting things into measurable milestones.

Here are strategies for getting, and keeping, people committed through a small-wins approach:

- *Make a plan.* First, your planning should be driven by your values and vision, not by technique. Second, involve in the planning process as many as you can of the people who will have to implement the plan. Third, break the project into manageable chunks. Fourth, use the planning process to walk people through the entire journey. This act of visualizing enables people both to anticipate the future and imagine their success.

- *Make a model.* Select one site or program with which to experiment to serve as a model of what you'd like to do in other programs or locations. Use it as an aid in teaching people about the principles of achieving excellence; then challenge them to improve on it.

- *Take one hop at a time.* Once you've set your sights, move forward in incremental steps. Don't

ANOTHER LOOK: THE LEADERSHIP CHALLENGE *continued*

attempt to accomplish too much at once, especially in the beginning. Provide orientation and training at the start of every new project, since the group may never have worked together before. The key to getting started is *do-ability*. Identify something that people feel they can do with existing skills and resources. Keep people focused on the meaning and significance of your plan, but remind them to take it one day at a time. It's a lot more productive to make a little progress daily than to attempt to do the whole task at once. Be certain to make progress very visible. And schedule opportunities for people to discuss progress and problems.

■ *Reduce the cost of saying yes.* If you want people to experiment, expect mistakes. It's easier for people to say yes when you minimize the costs of their potential failures.

■ *Give people choices and make those choices highly visible.* Unless they have choices to make, people aren't really exercising responsibility. If you've established a clear vision and have a consensus about the right way to do things, then people on your team have autonomy, but understand which decisions and responsibilities must be carried out. By publicizing the choices made by the team, you create binding-in-forces that increase the energy and drive to succeed in the task.

SOURCE: James M. Kouzes and Barry Z. Posner. Adapted by *Success* (April 1988) from J. M. Kouzes and B. Z. Posner, *The Leadership Challenge* (San Francisco: Jossey-Bass, 1987). Used with permission.

▼

There are several different ways a leader can give instructions to a subordinate. Compare the difference in approach used by two office managers as they handed out the same assignment.

Office Manager 1 "Call the Wilson Office Equipment Store as well as Ajax Office Supply. Get them to quote you prices on all the office dictation equipment they carry. Ask them to arrange for a demonstration. Invite two managers to that demonstration—make it Cribbs and Giroux—and let them try out the equipment. Get them to put their reactions on paper. Then prepare me a report with the costs and specifications of each of the pieces of equipment. Oh, yes, be sure to ask for information on repair costs, too...."

Office Manager 2 "I'd like to do something about our stenographic system. A lot of the managers who don't have secretaries of their own are complaining it takes them too long to get a secretary who can handle their dictation. The secretaries are also complaining because dictating to them eats up a lot of their time. Could you check up on some of the various kinds of dictating machines, find their prices, advantages, and disadvantages, and give me a recommendation as to what we should do? I think we can spend about three thousand dollars. Possibly you could talk to some of the managers to get their ideas."

QUESTIONS

1. Compare the approaches of these two man-

A CASE IN POINT *continued*

agers as they delegated this assignment. In terms of the situational leadership approach we've discussed in this chapter, how effective would these two styles be?

2. Assume that one of your subordinates has a low development level. Which of the approaches just described would likely be more appropriate when instructing this subordinate?

3. Assume that the employee to whom you are giving some instructions has a very high development level. Which of the approaches just described would be more appropriate for this individual?

4. Assume that you have been given the instructions by office manager 1. What are your reactions? How do you feel about the task assigned to you?

HOW LEADERS CAN BOOST EFFECTIVENESS WITH APPROPRIATE REWARDS

This chapter answers several all-important questions:

- What are the traditional ways rewards can be used to create motivation?

- What determines the results of motivating through the use of money?

- What is equity theory, and what can it teach us about rewards?

- How do people respond when they feel they are unfairly treated?

- What is the difference between direction and control, and how do they work together?

- What is goal congruity, and why is it important?

- What can supervisors do about job design to improve employee motivation?

- Why is it important to provide rewards in some systematic way?

- What is behavior modification, and how can a supervisor use this approach to help motivate others?

- How do different schedules of reinforcement work?

- When can participative decision making most profitably be used? When should it be avoided?

- Why does management sometimes reward the wrong thing?

- What is the problem in "rewarding A while hoping for B," and how can it be avoided?

The answers to these and other questions are coming up next in chapter 9....

Chapter 9

Imagine that as you approach graduation from school, a rich uncle asks you to join his staff at The Italian Gourmet, a frozen pizza manufacturing company that he just purchased. The plant has been operating fairly well, but your uncle believes that the workers are not as motivated as they might be. Absenteeism is consistently 10 to 12 percent, and productivity as measured by output fluctuates by 15 to 20 percent each week, causing frequent delays in product delivery.

Your uncle knows that you have studied human relations. He asks you to design a rewards system that can be used at The Italian Gourmet to motivate workers in a positive way. What are some of the rewards and benefits that you might employ?

In chapter 3, we discussed needs, wants, and desires and how these affect people's behavior. In chapter 4, we looked at ways to create conditions for motivation by unblocking goals. In chapters 7 and 8, we discussed leadership and how you can develop a leadership style that will work for you. In this chapter, we tie together the information from these previous chapters and describe a number of options that are available to a leader who seeks to motivate others. We also discuss specific applications and strategies for rewarding.

▼ EXTERNAL REWARDS

■ How do leaders create conditions for motivation?

A leader can encourage workers toward organizational goals in at least five traditional ways. When appropriately used, these rewards can create conditions where motivation can result. Supervisors attempt to "motivate" through the following:

- ■ Compensation
- ■ Direction and control
- ■ Job design

North America Syndicate, Inc., 1991.

- Benevolence
- Communication

We put the word *motivate* in quotation marks to remind you that we don't really motivate others; we can only motivate *ourselves.*

These methods are stimuli that attempt to help people to be motivated. Often, we refer to them as motivators. That's okay so long as we keep in mind that there is no surefire cause-and-effect relationship between offering a stimulus and getting a specific outcome. The degree to which any of these may work depends on the individual and his or her needs.

Much of what motivates people comes from internal reinforcements, such as pride in a job well done, satisfaction in achieving something of significance, and so on.

Meanwhile, back to the external rewards that leaders can dispense in an attempt to help employees to be motivated....

Compensation

When people speak of rewards, most listeners immediately think of money. For most people, compensation means bucks. But pay as we know it today is a comparatively recent invention, dating back only 200 years or so to the dawn of the Industrial Revolution. Throughout most of history, people generally lived, toiled, and died without pay, at least in a monetary form. Some unknown managerial genius, probably a mill superintendent in the midlands of England, invented the wage, and it has been with us ever since.[1]

HOW PAY CAN CREATE MOTIVATION: IT'S NOT JUST THE MONEY, IT'S THE PRINCIPLE

Pay may well be overrated as a motivator. Although money is indispensable for survival in a cash economy, most advanced societies

- Is pay overrated as a motivator?

Money is a very complex motivator.

provide income even for those who do not work. Few people in modern industrial nations have to fear that they might starve to death for
lack of money. This has not been true historically, however.

■ Money motivates best
at the survival or
security levels.

The power of money to motivate is strongest when there isn't
enough of it to ensure a decent standard of living. In this sense,
money ties in with what Maslow called survival and security
needs. Once these lower-order needs are met by money, the motivating power of cash decreases for most people.

When a person has enough money to survive, the importance of
money as a motivator shifts in two ways, according to management
theorist Saul Gellerman.[2]

First, for most (but not all) people, money loses a good deal of its
power to compete against other needs. It must be stressed that in
very few cases does money become unimportant; for most people, it
simply becomes *less* important. Other needs, which previously
might have been sacrificed for the sake of enhancing income, now
tend to take precedence over pay. For example, workers may no
longer be willing to sacrifice leisure time to work overtime, even for
double the normal wage. Likewise, employees may refuse to tolerate unpleasant or unsafe working conditions regardless of the
money paid.

Indeed, some social commentators see free time and work flexibility as the "status symbols" of the 1990s, as opposed to the
emphasis on money in the 1980s.

Second, money changes from a relatively simple motivator to a
very complex one. This is because once survival seems assured, a
whole host of needs, varying widely among individuals, tends to
surface. Thus, for one person newly raised to the rank of the afflu-
ent, money may mean security; for another, it may mean an opportunity to invest and grow richer; and for still another, it may mean
independence. In brief, our ability to predict how any given individual or group will react to pay diminishes sharply as the pay
rises above the subsistence level.

■ Once income rises
above the "decent
standard of living"
level, money rewards
have a less
predictable effect on
worker performance.

PAY AS A MEASURE OF FAIRNESS·

For many people, pay is regarded as a measure of *fairness*. The
money received from one's employer is regarded as a fair trade for
the work one does. If one puts in more effort, accomplishes greater
results, or helps the organization to be more profitable, one expects
more pay.

■ Sometimes a pay raise
is appreciated as a
sign of recognition
more than for the
actual cash increase.

Assuming that wages are sufficient to provide workers with their
basic needs, an increase in pay may be seen as a sign of recognition—a way of "keeping score." Conversely, when workers see
inequities in the way they are paid—when they feel they are being
shortchanged—serious morale problems can arise.

■ Perceptions of
fairness affect the
ways people react to
rewards.

EQUITY THEORY AND PAY: RESEARCH FINDINGS

Much research has been done in the area of social psychology to
help managers understand how people react to what they see as
unfair situations. One approach, developed in the 1960s by J. Stacy
Adams, has become known as *equity theory*.[3] This theory seeks to

predict how people will respond when they find themselves in "unjust relationships."

Suppose, for example, that you were hired by the Comatose Waterbed Corporation as a quality inspector. Your training in marine biology and your six years with another waterbed manufacturer made you a natural for this position.

After a few months on the job, you discover, quite by accident (you were snooping through some old files), that Herm Talbutt, the other quality inspector, is earning eighty dollars a week more than you. He does exactly the same job you do, and he doesn't even have a marine biology degree!

You may suddenly perceive your employment as an unjust relationship, and you may be pretty upset. Equity theory predicts that you'll respond to the perceived unfairness in one of five ways. You might do any of the following:

1. Simply endure the distress: "It's a crummy deal, but I'll just have to live with it."

2. Demand compensation or restitution: "I'll go to the boss and demand a raise."

3. Retaliate against the perceived cause of the inequity: "I'll start letting defective waterbeds pass. That'll fix the company."

4. Psychologically justify or rationalize the inequity: "Herm has a bigger family than mine. He needs the money."

5. Withdraw from the inequitable relationship: "I'm gonna quit this lousy company."

Any response to perceived unfairness can be detrimental to an organization. Supervisors must be aware of the possible effects but at the same time be realistic about avoiding them. Because equity is in the eye of the beholder, there are wide differences among what people see as fair. Although managers should make every effort to be fair, inevitably someone will feel slighted.[4]

In many cases, pay is a potential motivator only in the sense of telling the employee, "You are of worth to the organization." In using compensation as a reward, the supervisor should be particularly sensitive to the issue of fairness.

Direction and Control

Two other traditional motivators are direction and control. *Direction means telling someone what to do and what not to do. Control means making sure the person does as told.* Therefore, the two must be considered together. Direction is provided in many different ways in an organization: through policy manuals, operating procedures, oral instructions, and the like. Ultimately, however, leaders are responsible for seeing that followers are given direction. The way leaders provide those instructions can profoundly affect employee morale. Situational leadership, discussed in Chapter 8, provides guidelines for the type and amount of direction and control you should give.

Work consists of whatever a body is obliged to do, and Play consists of whatever a body is not obliged to do.
Mark Twain, The Adventures of Tom Sawyer

■ The way supervisors give directions can have a strong impact on employee performance and morale.

LEVEL OF ABSTRACTION IN DIRECTIONS

Another factor that affects success in giving direction and control is the *level of abstraction* of the words used.

At a low level of abstraction, words are precise and usually clear. For example, "Pick up that *sixteen-pound sledgehammer* leaning against the *north wall* of the *toolshed,* and bring it to me." This instruction will be clear to almost everyone. The terms are concrete; they describe things one can point to.

More abstract terms communicate less clearly. For example, "I want you to *clean up* the *work area*." This instruction is subject to several interpretations. "What does 'clean up' mean?" "Should we just pick up the scrap, or should we sweep, too?" "Or should we mop the floor and wash the windows, too?" "And just how far does the 'work area' extend?"

Even higher levels of abstraction are used in instructions, such as "How about *orienting* these new employees to our *corporation philosophy.*"

You are likely to get very different results from different types of instructions.

GOALS, OR "EVERY TIME YOU AIM NOWHERE, YOU GET THERE"

You can't provide effective direction if you don't know where you're going. Two sets of goals are important to the supervisor: the organization's and the employee's. Simply stating goals in itself is not a motivator. But when people become *committed* to goals—preferably ones they have had some part in setting—accomplishment of the goals can be very rewarding.

The ideal situation is to have individual members' goals pulling in the same direction as the organization's objectives. When the objectives of both individual and organization are clear and understood, the manager can determine whether or not they can coincide.

Goals, like targets, will never be hit until aimed at.

"In his mysterious way, God has given each of us different talents, Ridgeway. It just so happens that mine is intimidating people."

SOURCE: From *The Wall Street Journal*—permission, Cartoon Features Syndicate.

If the worker's goals and the company's goals are pulling in opposite directions, there is little sense in going on. If they seem partially compatible, further clarification and commitment to each other can be a catalyst for success.

A simple example of a problem in *goal congruity* is when a salesperson's personal goal is to continue selling low-price equipment produced by the company, while the organization's objective is to focus on the more expensive products. If the salesperson feels uncomfortable selling more expensive equipment or does not wish to do so, a discussion of goal congruity is needed.

■ What is goal congruity?

The leader should point out the areas of congruity (both the salesperson and the company want to earn a profit) and try to get the salesperson to see and strive for the common ground between what's good for the organization and for the individual.

If congruity cannot be established, the employee may be better off in another organization.

SUMMARY

Both direction and control provide traditional ways to motivate employees. Although control is often viewed rather negatively, it is generally necessary to be sure that direction is carried out. Failure to follow up may imply to employees that the instructions given are not that important. People prefer to have their work checked, especially when they are accomplishing what was sought for.

Direction and control can sometimes lead to supervisor-worker conflicts. Nonetheless, clear direction and well-understood goals ensure that unreasonable or counterproductive demands will not be made on subordinates.

Job Design

In chapter 5, we discussed various organization patterns and their effects on individual workers. One way to motivate people is to arrange their jobs so that they can gain a sense of satisfaction from the work. That is often easier said than done. Some jobs necessary to the organization are going to be unpleasant or boring to most people.

One attempt to reduce turnover in such jobs is to hire people who have mental limitations or perhaps lower expectations regarding work. Specifically, some companies have had considerable success in employing mentally retarded workers to do repetitive tasks generally found to be too boring for other workers.

Another approach, used especially in manufacturing, has been to automate—to get machines to replace human labor. Again, this is best when the task is repetitive and relatively simple. Don't assume that automation only involves sophisticated electronic robots. In many companies, countless tasks can be done by simple machines. The classic case is the collator, or sorting machine, attached to a photocopier. Many a secretary has complained loud and long about the time wasted sorting copies when a low-cost sorter could be purchased or rented.

Job enrichment—expanding the responsibilities associated with a job—is another viable alternative in many situations.

Some organizations have tried to *distract* workers from dull work by using such things as music, frequent rest periods, or more attractive facilities. These are not likely to have long-term positive effects.

- Fitting employee abilities to the demands of the job helps to motivate.

Companies are increasingly concerned with job design, because the nature of today's work force *demands* change. Today's workers tend to be better educated and are far less likely to put up with a dull or meaningless job. Reactions to dull or menial jobs (as perceived by the worker) include increased waste, low-quality work, poor efficiency, absenteeism, and high employee turnover. Many workers will not tolerate a menial job as an alternative to collecting unemployment insurance. Collectively, these reactions to dullness produce a significant drag on organizational productivity.

Fitting the job to the individual and the individual to the job is no longer just a nice thing to try to do. It is necessary for the continuing well-being of an organization.

Benevolence

Another traditional motivator supervisors can use is benevolence: attempts to make the workers happy. The employer who gives workers turkeys at Christmastime or sets up company athletic activities and so on is using this motivational approach. The underlying belief is that happy workers are more productive than unhappy workers. This, however, is an oversimplification. The relationship between happiness and productivity works in complex ways and is subject to many exceptions.

- Is a happy worker always a more productive worker?

The same gesture of benevolence may be interpreted in widely different ways. Back in the 1950s, a company picnic may have been deeply appreciated. Today, the same picnic may be viewed as paternalism, which could be resented.

Again, the issue of fairness must be considered. Giving to one employee or to one group of employees some special benefit or gift may be resented by those who don't get the same reward. The results of giving gifts in an effort to distract, entertain, please, or placate employees have been mixed at best. Although such rewards may be regarded as nice gestures by the workers, their ability to develop long-term motivation is limited.

Saul Gellerman concludes that "there is little, if any, evidence that being nice to people, or providing them with enjoyable off-the-job experiences, has a significant or lasting effect on productivity. On the other hand, they don't hurt either; and when used in conjunction with more effective measures (such as appropriate job design and equitable pay), they no doubt help to ease some of the inevitable everyday strains of working in an organization."[5]

Communication

Communication with workers can in itself be regarded as a form of reward. Positive communication with one's boss is often associated with job satisfaction. A supervisor can use communication in at least four ways to motivate and encourage employees. These are (1) giving recognition through the use of praise and criticism, (2) being receptive to workers' ideas, (3) providing timely information, and (4) systematically reviewing employee performance.

■ The quality of communication can itself be a motivator.

PRAISE AND CRITICISM
Sometimes praise is embarrassing, and so-called constructive criticism can make one mad. Both praise and criticism can be broken down into two types. Type 1 praise consists of statements that have little effect on the performance of the receiver. They slide off the receiver just as water runs off a duck's back. Type 2 praise consists of statements that may have a positive effect on performance under certain circumstances. Some examples of Type 1 and Type 2 praise are offered in Table 9.1.

A similar classification of criticism is illustrated in Table 9.2. Type 1 criticism results in defensiveness and deterioration of performance. Type 2 criticism is at least potentially constructive, because it may result in improved future performance.

RECEPTIVENESS TO WORKERS' IDEAS
Another way to motivate employees is to be receptive to the ideas they offer. This requires the supervisor to have well-developed listening skills. Such listening involves *active effort* on the part of the message receiver. It also involves *responding* in appropriate ways to the person who is speaking.

Receptive listening means being willing to receive, process, and deal with incoming information from workers. Receptiveness encourages risk—up to a point. To be genuinely receptive, the manager must recognize that employees can and do have worthwhile

■ Effective listening requires active effort and appropriate responses.

■ Receptiveness goes beyond listening.

ideas—that they can creatively contribute to the organization. (Sounds a little like Theory Y, doesn't it?)

▼   **Table 9.1 Ineffective versus Effective Praise**

Type 1 praise has little effect on performance of the receiver.	**Type 2 praise may have a positive effect on performance and build an authentic relationship.**
1. Generalized praise—such as, "You're doing a good job, Charlie." This is meaningless and it generally rolls off the back of the individual without effect. It is often seen as a "crooked" stroke.	1. Specific praise—such as, "Charlie, you did a great job handling that unpleasant customer with a complaint this afternoon." This communicates to the receiver that the boss has actually observed or heard about the praised action …
2. Praise with no further meaning. There is no analysis of why a praised behavior is being commended. This "discounts" the persons being praised by assuming they will respond with higher productivity and better morale merely as a response.	2. Continuing with, "The reason I think it was such a good job is because you acted interested, asked questions, wrote down the facts, asked the customer what she thought we should do to make it right." Analysis of this kind permits the employee to internalize the learning experience.…
3. Praise for expected performance, when it may be questioned. Mabel, who always gets in on time and is met one morning with, "Mabel, you're sure on time today, you're doing great," from her boss, may wonder what's really going on.	3. Praise for better than expected results … for coming in over quota … exceeding the target … putting out extra effort.
4. The "sandwich" system—praise is given first to make the person be receptive to criticism (the real reason for the transaction), which is then followed by another piece of praise, hoping thereby to encourage the person to "try harder" next time [and] feel better about the criticism.	4. Praise, when deserved, given by itself is believable; when mixed with critique, it is suspect. Authentic relations develop better when people talk "straight." When positive conditional recognition is in order, do so; when critique is deserved, do so. Don't mix the two.
5. Praise perceived by the receiver as given in the nature of a "carrot," mainly to encourage the receiver to work even harder in the future.	5. Praise that is primarily to commend and recognize, and does not seek to put a mortgage on the future.
6. Praise handed out lavishly only when the "brass" or higher-ups are present. Employees soon recognize the boss is trying to impress superiors with what a good human being he or she really is in dealing with subordinates.	6. Praise given when it is deserved, not just on special occasions [or] when it seems to build the image of the praiser to some third party.

---

source: James H. Morrison and John J. O'Hearne, *Practical Transactional Analysis in Management* (Reading, Mass.: Addison-Wesley, 1977), pp. 118–19. Reprinted with permission.

▼   TABLE 9.2 DESTRUCTIVE VERSUS CONSTRUCTIVE CRITICISM

Type 1 criticism tends to produce a defensive reaction in the receiver and worsen performance.	**Type 2 criticism is a type of constructive criticism that may improve performance.**
1. Criticism that involves use of the personal "you," e.g., "You're having too many accidents on the lift truck, Bill. What's the matter with you anyway?" It is almost always seen as a "discount" or put down by the receiver....	1. Criticism using a situational description, e.g., "Bill, we're experiencing an increase in lift-truck accidents. What's going on?" This indicates the manager is open to looking at all the facts leading to the unfavorable result.
2. Criticism that is unanalyzed. The subordinate then tends to rationalize the criticism as a personal opinion of the manager.... Or, the manager is viewed as unable to analyze the problems effectively.	2. Discussion of cause and effect with the unfavorable condition perceived by both as the result of one or more causal factors, one of which might even be the manager!
3. If the situation has been properly assessed, some managers are at a loss to provide coaching necessary for the subordinate to improve. This may be the result of ignorance or lack of competency in deciding on the corrective steps.	3. If steps 1 and 2 above have been properly accomplished, it is important for solutions to be outlined and agreed on. If the subordinate can't do this, the manager must provide, or arrange, for a resource that can develop corrective measures.
4. Critique of an individual in public is not only regarded as humiliating by the subordinate involved, but sometimes even more so by other members of the organization.	4. Individual criticism given in private is usually more acceptable. "Saving face" is almost as important in Western cultures as it is in the Orient.
5. Criticism given *only* in the interests of the boss (to get the boss recognition, promotion, or raise) or the organization (more profit or status in the marketplace). These may all be legitimate interests, but *authentic* relationships are not likely to develop.	5. Criticism given *also,* or even chiefly, in the interests of the employee (to provide greater competencies, future achievements, or a more secure future with the organization).
6. The manager does all the critiquing which sets the stage for a Parent-Child (relationship).	6. The subordinate participates in the critiques, even to the point of taking the lead role in defining the unsatisfactory condition, analyzing causes, and suggesting corrective steps.
7. Criticism used as a (calculated) game to justify withholding raises or promotions.	7. Game-free criticism leading toward candor (and authentic interactions).

SOURCE: *James H. Morrison and John J. O'Hearne,* Practical Transactional Analysis in Management, (Reading, Mass.: Addision-Wesley, 1977), pp. 120–21. Reprinted with permission.

Being receptive also involves being *supportive.* The notion of *supportiveness* and risk encouragement can be clarified by looking at the opposite notion: *defensiveness.*

When people feel threatened—primarily by threats to their self-esteem—a defensive climate develops. Jack Gibb studies the kinds of behaviors seen in defensive people. He concluded that when a working relationship is characterized by defensiveness, some of the following symptoms are likely to appear.[6]

1. People undergo frequent *evaluation;* organization members feel that they are being subjected to "good" or "bad" judgments.
2. A high degree of *control* over member behaviors is attempted by the leaders in the organization; people feel manipulated and burdened by lots of rules, regulations, and rigid procedures.
3. Leaders employ *strategies*—gimmicks or tricks—aimed at such things as getting the employee to think he or she is participating in important decisions when in fact the boss is making the decision alone.
4. Superiors tend to maintain their status by talking down to the "little people" in the organization; leaders tend to be dogmatic and preachy.

The supportive environment does not have such defensive characteristics. Instead, some of the following are found:

1. Objective *descriptions* of problems replace evaluative comments.
2. Leaders take a *problem orientation,* not simply calling up the rule or policy to stifle a difficulty, but getting to the root of the issue and seeking out underlying causes.
3. The climate is marked by *spontaneity* and *empathy* for others.
4. There is a sense of *equality* and *fairness.*
5. Dogmatism or preaching is replaced by *provisionalism*—a sense of not yet being certain of the answer but reflecting a continuing search for solutions.

■ Workers communicate more openly in a supportive environment.

In supportive environments, workers are more willing to share their thoughts and ideas, and supervisors are more willing to receive those thoughts. Members can feel safe in participating without a threat to their egos or their sense of self-worth. Risk taking and the freedom to make mistakes are accepted as normal states of affairs. Consequently, growth possibilities are broadened for the employee.

These broadened growth possibilities provide for job enrichment and long-lasting motivation within the organization. Without supportiveness and encouragement, communication becomes a power contest, rather than a search for better ways of doing things. The waste of human resources by defensive organizations can be enormous.

TIMELINESS OF INFORMATION

Have you ever had the feeling that you are the last to know about some change or some new procedure in the organization? It's an

uncomfortable feeling. Most people want to be kept current on changes and organizational procedures, policies, goals, and the like—especially those that affect them on their jobs.

One way a supervisor can motivate people is by providing them with *timely* information. Effective managers tell their workers what they *need* to know to do their job *and what they may want to know* to establish closer relationships and feelings of belongingness in the organization. No one likes to go about groping in the dark.

■ People want to be kept current with timely information.

"One nice thing about this company, though.
They almost never fire anybody.

SOURCE: Chuck Vadun. Reprinted with the permission of Chuck Vadun.

Again the concept of *equity* enters in here. When some people are consistently "in the know" and others are left without needed information, the situation is clearly inequitable. When people feel they are being treated unfairly, they will retaliate, withdraw, and respond in other detrimental ways.

- Information can be a form of status.

Information is in itself a form of status. Power often arises from key information. The classic example found in many organizations is the secretary to a top corporate leader. This person has little formal authority but enormous informal clout. This power comes from the secretary's access to confidential and important information.

The effective leader will seek to see that followers have all the information they need, on a timely basis.

- Regular performance reviews are *vital* to the management of people.

PERFORMANCE REVIEWS

One powerful communication tool is the performance review. An effective appraisal session with employees can clarify expectations and objectives for both supervisors and workers and can provide a base for supportive, mutually beneficial relationships. A poorly prepared or improperly conducted performance review can undo in an hour all the good manager-employee relationships that have developed over a period of months or even years.

Ideally, periodic performance reviews combine information *giving* with information *getting*. They are not talking *to* subordinates,

▼ TABLE 9.3 GUIDE TO EMPLOYEE PERFORMANCE APPRAISAL

PERFORMANCE FACTORS	FAR EXCEEDS JOB REQUIREMENTS	EXCEEDS JOB REQUIREMENTS	MEETS JOB REQUIREMENTS	NEEDS SOME IMPROVEMENT	DOES NOT MEET MINIMUM REQUIREMENTS
Quality	Leaps tall buildings with a single bound	Must take running start to leap over tall buildings	Can leap over short buildings only	Crashes into buildings when attempting to jump over them	Cannot recognize buildings at all
Timeliness	Is faster than a speeding bullet	Is as fast as a speeding bullet	Not quite as fast as a speeding bullet	Would you believe a slow bullet?	Wounds self with bullet when attempting to shoot
Initiative	Is stronger than a locomotive	Is stronger than a bull elephant	Is stronger than a bull	Shoots the bull	Smells like a bull
Adaptability	Walks on water consistently	Walks on water in emergencies	Washes with water	Drinks water	Passes water in emergencies
Communication	Talks with God	Talks with the angels	Talks to himself	Argues with himself	Loses those arguments

they are talking *with* subordinates. The manager's role is, and must be, that of an evaluator, but the review should not be judgmental in matters going beyond the work context. Statements such as "The accuracy with which you write up your sales orders needs to be improved" would normally be appropriate in an appraisal interview. Statements such as "You need to change your hairstyle and stop living with your boyfriend" would probably be out of line. Stick to the work-related evaluations.

A performance review can be used to accomplish the following:

1. Let employees *know where they stand.*
2. *Recognize and commend* good work.
3. Provide workers with *directions* on how they could best improve their work.
4. Develop employees in their present jobs by suggesting ways to *enrich* or *enlarge* their tasks.
5. Provide *training opportunities* so employees might be qualified for higher-rated jobs.
6. Let subordinates know the direction in which they may *progress in the organization.*
7. *Record* assessment of the department or unit as a whole and show where each person fits into the larger picture.
8. Officially *warn* certain employees that they must improve.[7]

While employees receive valuable information from an effective performance appraisal, leaders also gain. Unfortunately, some people responsible for performance appraisals often assign low priority to them because they have not thought about the benefits of a good appraisal session. Managers and supervisors report the following advantages of doing a good job with an appraisal:

1. Performance appraisals give me valuable insights into the work being done and those who are doing it.
2. When I maintain good communication with others about job expectations and results, opportunities are created for new ideas and improved methods.
3. When I do a good job appraising performance, anxiety is reduced because employees know how they are doing.
4. I increase productivity when employees receive timely corrective feedback on their performance.
5. I reinforce sound work practices and encourage good performance when I publicly recognize positive contributions.
6. When I encourage two-way communication with employees, goals are clarified so they an be achieved or exceeded.
7. Regular appraisal sessions remove surprises about how the quality of work is being perceived.
8. Learning to do professional performance appraisals is excellent preparation for advancement and increased responsibility.[8]

■ Stumbling blocks to effective performance reviews.

Supervisors must be aware of possible stumbling blocks to effective performance reviews. Certain attitudes on the part of the supervisor can set the stage for failure. Among those are the following:

1. *Failing to accept the subordinate as a person, unconditionally.* A fundamental respect for the worth of people is required for effective performance appraisals to take place. This does not mean that the manager accepts the subordinate's behavior or value system. Instead, it means that the subordinate's potential and intrinsic worth to the organization is recognized.
2. *Being overly concerned with why the subordinate behaves as he or she does, rather than with what can be done to improve.* Overemphasizing specific causes tends to elicit excuses by the subordinate. When this approach is carried too far, the manager may be playing amateur psychologist. Diagnosing a psychological condition and giving it a label such as "poor self-image," "lack of aggressiveness," or "too hot-tempered" can lead to self-fulfilling prophecies. Once a manager has identified a problem in such a way, he or she is likely to see more and more evidence that supports the diagnosis as correct. The manager will selectively pay attention to examples of hot temper or apparent lack of self-assurance so he or she can say, "Aha—just as I thought!"
3. *Harboring an underlying belief that appraisal sessions should be used to punish the employee.* If you find yourself thinking, "Wait till the performance review—I'll get that SOB then," you are missing the point. Confrontive review sessions are seldom productive. The wise supervisor pays special attention to creating a supportive climate so that performance reviews result in improved performance as well as evaluation.

▼ ALLOCATING REWARDS: A LEADERSHIP TASK

Leaders have a choice of either (1) distributing rewards haphazardly or (2) thinking through and developing *strategies* for reward allocation. If managers accept the first option, they may or may not motivate useful behaviors in others. They also run a far higher risk of falling into the common trap of rewarding the wrong behaviors and thus encouraging inappropriate actions from others. Furthermore, they risk the sin of omission: failure to reward that which is good.

In this chapter, we encourage you to consider the advantages of using the second option when rewarding others. Although systematic strategies apply equally to tangible rewards, such as money, office space, and other clearly recognized benefits, we will focus on the kinds of rewards that leaders at any level can realistically allocate: social rewards, such as recognition, opportunities for participation in organizational decisions, and opportunities to gain self-actualization through accomplishing objectives.

■ Use systematic strategies when rewarding others.

■ Although organizations restrict what some levels of management can do to reward workers, some rewards are available to all supervisors.

▼ A RECOGNITION STRATEGY

Systematic approaches for expressing verbal approval have produced remarkable results. In one division of a major corporation, a program of simply complimenting and thanking employees for work well done—*in a systematic, not haphazard, manner*—led in one year to cost savings of about $3.5 million. And these savings did not include improvements in employee morale, which is difficult to measure.

This systematic approach is known by several names: *behavior modification* (a term that may conjure up Orwellian manipulation for some people), *operant conditioning* (you may picture rats in a maze), or the more acceptable—*performance improvement.* Regardless of the name, the approach seems to work.

Companies implement such a performance improvement program this way. The first step is to hold a series of meetings in which managers and employees discuss mutual needs and problems as well as potential solutions. The discussion session provides a base for determining job performance standards and how they will be met. The meetings also identify reinforcers that managers may use to "modify" the employee's behavior. One company, for example, held a three-day session that revealed the following:

■ A strategy for thanking and complimenting workers can lead to improvements in reaching organizational productivity goals.

■ How companies implement a performance improvement program.

> What workers, such as clerk typists, want most is a sense of belonging, a sense of accomplishment, and a sense of teamwork.... In return, managers ask for quicker filing of reports and fewer errors.

The second step is to arrange for worker performance to be observed with a reliable follow-up. The third step is to give feedback often, immediately letting employees know how their current levels of performance compare with the levels desired. At an airline company, for instance, five telephone reservation offices employing about eighteen hundred people keep track of the percentage of calls in which

Recognition should
never be haphazard.

callers make flight reservations. Then they feed back the results daily
to each employee. At the same time, supervisors are instructed to
praise employees for asking callers for their reservations. Since the
program started, the ratio of sales to calls has soared from one in four
to one in two.[9] Whatever the name of the program, the objective is to
provide stroking rewards in such a way that they motivate performance and reduce dissatisfaction.

At the heart of any such performance improvement efforts is the
premise that *future behavior is influenced by the outcomes of past
behavior.* If the outcome immediately following something one does
is in some way rewarding, one is likely to repeat the behavior. If the
response is punishing, one is likely to not do the behavior again
(unless one prefers punishment to other outcomes).

■ A basic premise:
Future behavior is
influenced by the
outcomes of past
behavior.

We can provide three types of responses to behaviors: positive
reinforcement, negative reinforcement, or no observable reinforcement at all. The effects of each on the behavior it follows are shown
in table 9.4

There are some questions about how far one can go with verbal
approval as a motivator. Theoretically, it should work indefinitely
so long as an appropriate *schedule of reinforcement* is used. The two
main reinforcement schedules are *continuous* and *intermittent.*

■ Different schedules of
reinforcement
produce different
results.

Continuous reinforcement means the individual receives reinforcement (a compliment or supportive statement) *every time* he or
she does the desired behavior. Continuous reinforcement is useful
when the person is being taught a new behavior and needs to be
shored up to develop confidence in this new ability. People learn
very quickly at least initially, under continuous reinforcement. You
may see this when teaching a child how to do something like catch-
ing a ball. Every time the ball is caught, you praise the child, and the
child will usually develop the skill very quickly. The principle generally holds for employees working on unfamiliar tasks.

▼   TABLE 9.4 BEHAVIOR RESPONSES TO DIFFERENT REINFORCEMENT

TYPES OF RESPONSES TO EMPLOYEE BEHAVIOR	EFFECTIVE ON THE RECURRENCE OF THE BEHAVIOR
Positive reinforcement	Tends to increase or strengthen the recurrence of such behavior
Negative reinforcement	Tends to decrease or weaken the recurrence of such behavior *unless* the employee is *seeking* negative reinforcement
Reinforcement withheld	Tends to decrease or weaken the recurrence of such behavior; can lead to extinction of the behavior

SOURCE: Paul R. Timm, *Managerial Communication: A Finger on the Pulse,* 2d ed. (Englewood Cliffs, N.J.: Prentice-Hall, 1986), p. 135. Reprinted by permission.

Three main problems arise with continuous reinforcement, however. First, it takes too much time and effort. It is not feasible to always compliment each job done; you might as well do the task yourself!

■ Continuous reinforcement has drawbacks.

Second, there is a problem of "inflation." Just as dollars lose value when too many are in circulation, verbal approval is cheapened by overuse.

Third, once continuous reinforcement is expected, one has a hard time weaning people away from it without certain risks. If a leader suddenly stops continuous reinforcement—that is, no longer expresses verbal approval for each good behavior—the message to workers may be that the behavior is no longer appropriate and should be stopped. In short, the manager may extinguish the desired behavior.

The drawbacks of continuous reinforcement can be overcome by using *intermittent reinforcement.* Instead of expressing approval by every good action, express approval at intervals, such as each time a unit of work, say a day's or week's quota, is completed.

■ Intermittent reinforcement can overcome drawbacks of continuous reinforcement.

Another intermittent reinforcement approach is to provide rewards at completely random times. Much of the lure of slot machine gambling comes from the anticipated random windfall. The anticipation keeps players engaged in the "desired behavior" (putting money in the slot). Under random intermittent reinforcement, the worker doesn't know exactly when he or she will be rewarded. So long as there remains any hope of eventually receiving a reward, extinguishing of the desired behavior is delayed. If the rewards are too far apart, the worker will not continue to produce unless he or she is particularly good at working hard today for some far-off, but certain-to-be-worthwhile reward. Relatively few workers today are content to "get their reward in heaven."

The best approach is to use continuous reinforcement when new behaviors are being developed and then to gradually move to an intermittent schedule to maintain the desired performance.

▼ PARTICIPATION IN DECISION MAKING

Participation is becoming more widely recognized for its motivational value. When workers feel that they are participating in decisions, some interesting things happen.

More and more, effective managers are giving workers the opportunity to help make decisions that will affect them on the job. Participation in decision making by workers can have a number of key advantages for the organization. It also has some drawbacks, however. Let's first look at the advantages.[10]

Advantages of Participation in Decision Making (PDM)

■ Successful PDM calls for idea sharing and resolving differences among people in constructive ways.

Because an individual's range of experiences is limited, it follows that several people working on the same problem, issue, or decision can bring more relevant information to light. Each participant represents a unique frame of reference—an individual way of looking at the world—that may provide the key to a better solution. The usefulness of all these ideas is limited by the extent to which the group can tie the different viewpoints together into a high-quality decision. To be successful, the group must develop procedures for (1) sharing ideas and perspectives, so that members may build on one another's insights, and (2) resolving differences among group members that, if left unattended, could prevent eventual agreement. We discuss some of the problems and opportunities of such group communication in greater detail in chapter 10.

■ The key advantages to PDM are potentially better decisions and less resistance to implementation.

In addition to bringing many minds to focus on the problem, PDM has a second important advantage. There is likely to be a *higher degree of commitment to a group decision* and a *reduction in resistance or hostility to it,* at least among those who participated. Similarly, if those who participated in making the decision are the same people who will execute the decision, they will do so more faithfully, because they understand why and how the decision was reached.

The significant advantages of PDM are thus (1) potentially better quality decisions and (2) less resistance to implementation.

PDM Works Better on Some Kinds of Problems

The nature of the group's task seems to affect the degree to which a group's decision or solution is likely to be better than an individual's. Research by behavioral scientists suggests that groups handle certain kinds of problems best:

1. Studies show that groups are better at solving problems that require the making of relative rather than absolute judgments. That is, groups can better solve problems for which there is no single correct solution.

2. Groups tend to be more successful than individuals working

alone when the problem is complex, has many parts, and requires a number of steps to solve.

3. Groups also seem better at dealing with controversial or emotionally charged problems.

When the problem is relatively simple or noncontroversial or involves routine legal tasks, group discussion does not seem to offer major advantages.

Disadvantages of PDM

Sometimes supervisors or managers call for participative decision making for the wrong reasons. They use it as a substitute for making tough decisions. This *tendency to stall* by taking the problem to a committee is one drawback to PDM.

A second general disadvantage is that participation can *cost a lot of money.* A group decision inevitably takes more time than an executive action. And the costs of such time can readily add up. Taking a group of workers off their regular task for an hour or so to hash out a problem is likely to cost many hundreds of dollars.

A third disadvantage is that sometimes PDM produces *lower-quality decisions.* In some situations, the group process may backfire and produce a worse decision than might be made by an individual. This can occur (1) when the group members lack sufficient expertise to deal with the problem and (2) when pressures block the free flow of information. In the former case, the solution will reflect pooled ignorance. In the latter situation, the quality of the group's decision is distorted either by members' overwillingness to agree with each other or by too much dominance of the discussion by one person or faction.

■ The key disadvantages to PDM are that it is sometimes used to put off decisions, it costs a lot of money, and lower-quality decisions sometimes result.

Sometimes the group's decision involves excessive risk. No one feels obligated to take responsibility for the decision, and therefore all members feel more comfortable in taking far more risk than they normally would. When the social pressures toward risk taking are great, a lynch-mob mentality can result.

Individual dominance is also a serious problem. If one or two people involved in the decision are unusually articulate, persuasive or powerful, PDM may degenerate into simply a way of ratifying decisions already made by the dominant person or subgroup.

A final disadvantage of PDM is that it is sometimes inappropriate because of a need for swift choices imposed by the problem. A battle group in combat cannot use PDM while the enemy awaits the solution. Similarly, in business, some decisions must be made quickly. Delaying a decision may squander a potential opportunity.

Although there are both advantages and disadvantages to participative decision making, most organizations have many opportunities for using PDM effectively. Again, from the perspective of this chapter, perhaps the most significant advantage is that *workers who participate* in making decisions in the organization *feel better about the organization.* PDM is potentially a motivating opportunity for them.

▼ Problems of Rewarding the Wrong Things

■ People too often reward one kind of behavior while hoping for another, often opposite, behavior.

Despite their best intentions, many leaders fall into the trap of rewarding the wrong kinds of behavior. They often do this without thinking. Most organizations offer innumerable examples of reward systems that pay off for one behavior, even though the management hopes for another, often the opposite, kind of behavior. For example, the common practice of paying people by the hour encourages filling up of time, rather than productive use of effort. The mechanic who fixes a machine so well that it never breaks down again may soon be out of a job. The doctor who ostensibly is paid to make patients well can make much more money if patients stay sick and continue treatment. Few people take advantage of such situations, but the reward system is not tied directly to the desired behavior. Instead, it rewards behaviors that are irrelevant or even counterproductive.

How many times has an ambitious junior executive suggested a remedy for a problem and been instructed to "write up a report on it"? For a potentially useful suggestion, the reward is to do more work! Or a clothing store owner constantly encourages the sales force to cooperate with each other—to share ideas with each other. Yet for a sales promotion, the boss offers an award only to *the* (one) top producer of *sales.* The results: salespeople tripping over each other to get to the customer, causing distrust and conflict among themselves. Or at a staff meeting, the member who suggests additional study of a problem is inevitably nominated to do the work.

It often makes sense to have the person who makes a suggestion "write up a report." But that person should be given assistance or at least time off from other responsibilities to avoid being burdened with additional work.

Here is another example. As a staff supervisor at a large corporation, I (Paul Timm) shared responsibility for evaluating employee suggestions. For each suggestion, I had three options:

1. Accept the suggestion (in which case I would then need to see that it was implemented).
2. Reject the suggestion (I would not have to do anything further).
3. Refer the suggestion to a higher organizational level where my counterpart would have the same options.

I had little or no real incentive to approve suggestions even if they were pretty good. If I did accept a suggestion, my work had just begun. I would then have to go to all our offices and teach the new procedure, create needed forms or equipment, arrange budget expenditures, and so on. A rejection avoided all that work. Finally, *my work evaluation was in no way affected by the number of employee suggestions I approved.* In fact, these suggestions were simply extra work piled on my "regular" duties.

No reward was provided for doing what the organization would *like* to have had done. The organization wanted to accept as many suggestions as would possibly work, yet the reward system discouraged it.

This problem is fairly common. Managers advocate employee openness until the first person speaks up and is quickly labeled as having an "attitude problem." Managers tell people to cooperate and avoid unnecessary intergroup conflict but do not reward helping behavior and often unintentionally encourage friction or "friendly competition." The "Another Look" article entitled "On the Folly of Rewarding A, While Hoping for B" at the end of this chapter builds on this line of reasoning. We think you'll enjoy it.

▼ SUMMARY OF KEY IDEAS

- The five traditional ways that a leader encourages employees to work for organizational goals are compensation, direction and control, job design, benevolence, and communication.

- Equity theory seeks to predict our response to an unjust relationship; the five typical responses to an unjust situation are to endure, demand compensation or restitution, retaliate, rationalize, or withdraw.

- Direction tells the individual what to do, while control ensures that the person does as told.

- The four ways in which communication may be used to motivate and encourage employees are (1) giving recognition through the use of praise and criticism, (2) being receptive to workers' ideas, (3) providing timely information, and (4) systematically reviewing employee performance.

- The defensive environment is characterized by personal evaluations, control of organizational members, strategies and games, and impersonal climate; in contrast, the supportive environment is characterized by objective descriptions of problems (not people), problem orientation, spontaneity and empathy for others, equality and fairness, and provisionalism.

- The eightfold purpose of performance reviews includes letting employees know where they stand, recognizing and commending superior work, providing direction for improvement, suggesting ways to enrich or enlarge the job, providing training opportunities, letting employees know where they may progress in the company, helping employees understand where they fit in the larger picture, and providing official warnings to specific employees who must improve.

- Three stumbling blocks to good performance reviews are failing to accept the subordinate as a person, being preoccupied with why the subordinate's behavior is inadequate while forgetting to focus on improvements, and believing that the performance review should be used to punish the employee.

- In spite of organizational restraints, supervisors can systematically allocate social rewards such as recognition, and encourage participation in organizational decisions.

- A recognition strategy is a plan for complimenting workers in order to encourage them to make continued improvements in reaching organizational goals. The strategy is based on the premise that the outcomes of past behavior influence future behavior.

- The two major advantages of participative decision making are potentially better decisions and less resistance to implementation.

- Three key disadvantages to PDM are postponement of decision making, monetary cost of involving others, and possibility of low-quality decisions.

- Reward systems can fail when the organization is rewarding the wrong behavior.

▼ KEY TERMS, CONCEPTS, AND NAMES

Behavior modification
Benevolence
Continuous reinforcement
Direction and control
Equity theory
Extinguishing behaviors
Saul Gellerman
Goal congruity
Intermittent reinforcement
Job design
Steven Kerr

Participation in decision making (PDM)
Performance reviews (or appraisals)
Receptiveness to ideas
Supportive versus defensive relationships
Timely information
Transactional analysis
Type 1 and Type 2 criticism
Type 1 and Type 2 praise

▼ QUESTIONS AND EXERCISES

1. Write down five key personal goals. Ask your boss (or instructor) to write down five key goals of your organization (business or school). Be specific. To what extent do you have goal congruity? What can you do about goals that do not seem to coincide?

2. Why does company benevolence seem to be a less effective motivator than it may have been in years past? What social or personal factors affect benevolence as a motivator?

3. Read the "Another Look ..." article entitled "On the Folly of Rewarding A, While Hoping for B." Do you agree with the author's thesis that managers often reward the wrong behaviors? Give some examples you have seen (within or outside the work environment), and suggest ways to rearrange the reward system to be more effective.

4. Describe some cases of participative decision making you have been involved in. How good was each decision? How did it compare with a decision made by an individual working alone? Was the difference in decision quality worth the extra cost of the group process?

5. In this chapter, we described examples of how a reward system can affect the employee suggestion process. Have you seen similar difficulties in your organizations? Give examples.

6. Answer the introductory questions at the beginning of this chapter.

▼ NOTES

1. Saul W. Gellerman, *The Management of Human Resources* (Hinsdale, Ill.: Dryden Press, 1976), pp. 17–18.

2. Ibid., pp. 19–20.

3. The basic premises of equity theory can be found in J. Stacy Adams, "Toward an Understanding of Inequity," *Journal of Abnormal Social Psychology*, 67 (1963): 422–36. Later studies are summarized in Lenoard Berkowitz and Elaine Walster, ed., *Advances in Experimental Social Psychology*, vol. 9 (New York: Academic Press, 1976).

4. For some recent research dealing with equity theory in a managerial context, see Sherron B. Kenton, "The Role of Communication in Managing Perceived Inequity," *Management Communication Quarterly*, (1989): 536–43.

5. Gellerman, *The Management of Human Resources*, p. 33.

6. Jack Gibb, "Defensive Communication," *Journal of Communication* (1961): 141–48.

7. Paul R. Timm, *Managerial Communication*, 2d ed. (Englewood Cliffs, N.J.: Prentice-Hall, 1986), p. 133.

8. Robert B. Maddux, *Effective Performance Appraisals* (Los Altos, Calif.: Crisp Publications, 1987), p. 9.

9. Timm, *Managerial Communication*, pp. 131–32.

10. For a more detailed discussion, see Paul R. Timm, "We Can't Go on Meeting Like This," *Communicator's Journal*, 2 (1984): 54–58.

ANOTHER LOOK: GUIDELINES FOR THE ETHICAL ADMINISTRATION OF REWARD SYSTEMS

Many incentive systems have been designed by organizations wanting to reward their employees for above-average performance. Unfortunately, these systems often fall prey to unethical administrative practices. If this happens, employees are penalized and the intent of the process is destroyed.

Managers charged with the administration of merit and bonus budgets, for example, often are unwilling to differentiate between employees on the basis of performance. They simply divide rewards equally, or nearly so, among performers who may range from inadequate to outstanding. When this happens they end up reinforcing poor performance while penalizing superior work.

Some managers are afraid if they recognize good performance one year, they are locked into giving similar recognition next year, earned or not. Some also feel it is necessary to give an adequate performer a raise every year. Still others feel giving a substandard performer an increase might motivate better performance. Then, of course, there are a few who want to reward only their friends. All of the above approaches are seriously flawed, and filled with ethical pitfalls.

Incentive systems are designed to reward people on the basis of performance and their overall contribution to the organization. Managers must be honest. They must understand the

work being performed and be able to differentiate clearly between levels of performance by individuals. They must also have some personal convictions about what is right and wrong, as well as the courage to stand behind their decisions.

The following self-evaluation can help you recognize important issues faced by leaders as they use rewards. If you are now in a leadership position, complete the survey and total your score. If you are not yet a leader, study the statements to better understand the potential pitfalls in reward allocation.

Circle the number that best represents you. A 5 is a perfect score on each item.

WHEN I ADMINISTER REWARD SYSTEMS	High				Low
1. I lay ground work by insuring there is mutual understanding with each employee about what is expected in terms of performance.	5	4	3	2	1
2. I update job descriptions as changes occur and insist that the salary grades of my employees remain appropriate to their positions.	5	4	3	2	1
3. I consistently monitor performance against expectations and give all employees appropriate feedback.	5	4	3	2	1
4. I am alert for both superior or inferior performance as related to goals and standards.	5	4	3	2	1
5. I note, and communicate to others, employee efforts to develop and increase their potential.	5	4	3	2	1
6. I refuse to let nonperformance factors like friendship, race, religion, family background, sex, or age influence my decisions.	5	4	3	2	1
7. I test my decisions to be sure they are based on facts and not just assumptions or impressions.	5	4	3	2	1

ANOTHER LOOK *continued*

8. I make my decisions on objective data and push aside any unwillingness to help my employees face reality.	5	4	3	2	1
9. When I observe others who are unethical in distributing awards, I resist the same impulse in myself.	5	4	3	2	1
10. I strive to maintain equity between employees and am prepared to justify with facts my decisions to anyone.	5	4	3	2	1

TOTAL _____

A score below 40 suggests you need to do some hard work to improve the ethical administration of your reward systems.

SOURCE: Reprinted with permission from Robert B. Maddux and Dorothy Maddux, *Ethics in Business* (Los Altos, Calif.: Crisp Publications,

---

▼ ANOTHER LOOK: ON THE FOLLY OF REWARDING A, WHILE HOPING FOR B

Whether dealing with monkeys, rats, or human beings, it is hardly controversial to state that most organisms seek information concerning what activities are rewarded, and then seek to do (or at least pretend to do) those things, often to the virtual exclusion of activities not rewarded. The extent to which this occurs of course will depend on the perceived attractiveness of the rewards offered, but neither operant nor expectancy theorists would quarrel with the essence of this notion.

Nevertheless, numerous examples exist of reward systems that are fouled up in that behaviors which are rewarded are those which the rewarder is trying to *discourage,* while the behavior he desires is not being rewarded at all.

SOCIETAL EXAMPLES

Politics. The American citizenry supposedly wants its candidates for public office to set forth operative goals, making their proposed programs "perfectly clear," specifying sources and uses of funds, etc. However, since operative goals are lower in acceptance, and since aspirants to public office need acceptance (from at least 50.1 percent of the people), most politicians prefer to speak only of official goals, at least until after the election. They of course would agree to speak at the operative level if "punished" for not doing so.

The electorate could do this by refusing to support candidates who do not speak at the operative level.

Instead, however, the American voter typically punishes (withholds support from) candidates who frankly discuss where the money will come from, rewards politicians who speak only of official goals, but hopes that candidates (despite the reward system) will discuss the issues operatively. It is academic whether it was moral for Nixon, for example to refuse to discuss his 1968 "secret plan" to end the Vietnam war, his 1972 operative goals concerning the lifting of price controls, the reshuffling of his cabinet, etc. The point is that the reward sys-

ANOTHER LOOK: ON THE FOLLY OF REWARDING A, WHILE HOPING FOR B *continued*

tem made such refusal rational.

War. If some oversimplification may be permitted, let it be assumed that the primary goal of the organization (Pentagon, Luftwaffe, or whatever) is to win. Let it be assumed further that the primary goal of most individuals on the front lines is to get home alive. Then there appears to be an important conflict in goals—personally rational behavior by those at the bottom will endanger goal attainment by those at the top.

But not necessarily! It depends on how the reward system is set up. The Vietnam War was indeed a study of disobedience and rebellion, with terms such as "fragging" (killing one's own commanding officer) and "search and evade" becoming part of the military vocabulary. The difference in subordinates' acceptance of authority between World War II and Vietnam is reported to be considerable, and veterans of the Second World War often have been quoted as being outraged at the mutinous actions of many American soldiers in Vietnam.

Consider, however, some critical differences in the reward system in use during the two conflicts. What did the GI in World War II want? To go home. And when did he get to go home? When the war was won! If he dis-

obeyed the orders to clean out the trenches and take the hills, the war would not be won and he would not go home. Furthermore, what were his chances of attaining his goal (getting home alive) if he obeyed the orders compared to his chances if he did not? What is being suggested is that the rational soldier in World War II, *whether patriotic or not,* probably found it expedient to obey.

Consider the reward system in use in Vietnam. What did the man at the bottom want? To go home. And when did he get to go home? When his tour of duty was over! This was the case *whether or not* the war was won.

In light of the reward system used in Vietnam, would it not have been personally irrational for some orders to have been obeyed? Was not the military implementing a system which *rewarded* disobedience, while *hoping* that soldiers (despite the reward system) would obey orders?

Universities. Society *hopes* that teachers will not neglect their teaching responsibilities but *rewards* them almost entirely for research and publications. This is most true at the large and prestigious universities. Clichés such as "good research and good teaching go together" notwithstanding, professors often find that they must choose between teaching and

research oriented activities when allocating their time. Rewards for good teaching usually are limited to outstanding teacher awards, which are given to only a small percentage of good teachers and which usually bestow little money and fleeting prestige. Punishments for poor teaching also are rare.

Rewards for research and publications, on the other hand, and punishments for failure to accomplish these, are commonly administered by universities at which teachers are employed. Furthermore, publication oriented resumés usually will be well received at other university, whereas teaching credentials, harder to document and quantify, are much less transferable. Consequently, it is rational for university teachers to concentrate on research, even if to the detriment of teaching and at the expense of their students.

By the same token, it is rational for students to act based upon the goal displacement which has occurred within universities concerning what they are rewarded for. If it is assumed that a primary goal of a university is to transfer knowledge from teacher to student, then grades become identifiable as a means toward that goal, serving as motivational, control, and feedback devices to expedite the knowledge transfer. Instead however, the grades them-

ANOTHER LOOK *continued*

selves have become much more important for entrance to graduate school, successful employment, tuition refunds, parental respect, etc., than the knowledge or lack of knowledge they are supposed to signify.

It therefore should come as no surprise that information has surfaced in recent years concerning fraternity files for examinations, term paper writing services, organized cheating at the service academies, and the like. Such activities constitute a personally rational response to a reward system which pays off for grades rather than knowledge.

BUSINESS-RELATED EXAMPLES

Ecology. Assume that the president of XYZ Corporation is confronted with the following alternatives:

1. Spend $11 million for antipollution equipment to keep from poisoning fish in the river adjacent to the plant; or

2. Do nothing, in violation of the law, and assume a one in ten chance of being caught, with a resultant $1 million fine plus the necessity of buying the equipment.

Under this not unrealistic set of choices, it requires no linear program to determine that XYZ Corporation can maximize its probabilities by flouting the law. Add the fact that XYZ's president is probably being rewarded (by creditors, stockholders, and

other salient parts of his task environment) according to criteria totally unrelated to the number of fish poisoned, and his probable course of action becomes clear.

Evaluation of Training. It is axiomatic that those who care about a firm's well-being should insist that the organization get fair value for its expenditures. Yet it is commonly known that firms seldom bother to evaluate a new [training] program, or whatever, to see if the company is getting its money's worth. Why? Certainly it is not because people have not pointed out that this situation exists; numerous practitioner oriented articles are written each year to just this point.

The individuals (whether in personnel, manpower planning, or wherever) who normally would be responsible for conducting such evaluations are the same ones often charged with introducing the change effort in the first place. Having convinced top management to spend the money, they usually are quite animated afterwards in collecting [compliments and] anecdotes about how successful the program was. The last thing many desire is a formal, systematic, and revealing evaluation. Although members of top management may actually *hope* for such systematic evaluation, their reward systems continue to *reward* ignorance in this area. And if the personnel department

abdicates its responsibility, who is to step into the breach? The change agent himself? Hardly! He is likely to be too busy collecting anecdotal "evidence" of his own, for use with his next client.

Miscellaneous. Many additional examples could be cited of systems which in fact are rewarding behaviors other than those supposedly desired by the rewarder. A few of these are described briefly below.

Most coaches disdain to discuss individual accomplishments, preferring to speak of teamwork, proper attitude, and a one-for-all spirit. Usually, however, rewards are distributed according to individual performance. The college basketball player who feeds his teammates instead of shooting will not compile impressive scoring statistics and is less likely to be drafted by the pros. The ballplayer who hits to right field to advance the runners will win neither the batting nor home run titles, and will be offered smaller raises. It therefore is rational for players to think of themselves first and the team second.

In business organizations where rewards are dispensed for unit performance or for individual goals achieved, without regard for overall effectiveness, similar attitudes often are observed. Under most Management by Objectives (MBO) systems, goals in areas where quantifi-

ANOTHER LOOK: ON THE FOLLY OF REWARDING A, WHILE HOPING FOR B *continued*

cation is difficult often go unspecified. The organization therefore often is in a position where it *hopes* for employee effort in the areas of team building, interpersonal relations, creativity, etc., but it formally *rewards* none of these. In cases where promotions and raises are formally tied to MBO, the system itself contains a paradox in that it "asks employees to set challenging, risky goals, only to face smaller paychecks and possibly damaged careers if these goals are not accomplished."

It is *hoped* that administrators will pay attention to long run costs and opportunities and will institute programs which will bear fruit later on. However, many organizational reward systems pay off for short run sales and earnings only. Under such circumstances, it is personally rational for officials to sacrifice long term growth and profit (by selling off equipment and property or by stifling research and development) for short term advantages. This probably is most pertinent in the public sector, with the result that many public officials are unwilling to implement programs which will not show benefits by election time.

Conclusions. Modern organization theory requires a recognition that the members of organizations and society possess divergent goals and motives. It therefore is unlikely that managers and their

subordinates will seek the same outcomes. Three possible remedies for this potential problem are suggested.

Selection. It is theoretically possible for organizations to employ only those individuals whose goals and motives are wholly consonant with those of management. In such cases the same behavior judged by subordinates to be rational would be perceived by management as desirable. State-of-the-art reviews of selection techniques, however, provide scant grounds for hope that such an approach would be successful.

Training. Another theoretical alternative is for the organization to admit those employees whose goals are not consonant with those of management and then, through training, socialization, or whatever, alter employee goals to make them consonant. However, research on the effectiveness of such training programs, though limited, provides further grounds for pessimism.

Altering the Reward System. Managers who complain that their workers are not motivated might do well to consider the possibility that they have installed reward systems which are paying off for behaviors other than those they are seeking. This, in part, is what happened in

Vietnam, and this is what regularly frustrates societal efforts to bring about honest politicians, civic-minded managers, etc. This certainly is what happened in both the manufacturing and the insurance companies.

A first step for such managers might be to find out what behaviors currently are being rewarded. Chances are excellent that these managers will be surprised by what they find—that their firms are not rewarding what they assume they are. In fact, such undesirable behavior by organizational members as they have observed may be explained largely by the reward systems in use.

By altering the reward system the organization escapes the necessity of selecting only desirable people or of trying to alter undesirable ones.

REFERENCES

1. Barnard, Chester I. *The Functions of the Executive* (Cambridge, Mass.: Harvard University Press, 1964)

2. Blau, Peter M., and W. Richard Scott, *Formal Organizations* (San Francisco: Chandler, 1962).

3. Fiedler, Fred E. "Predicting the Effects of Leadership Training and Experience from the Contingency Model," *Journal of Applied Psychology,* Vol. 56 (1972), 114–119.

ANOTHER LOOK *continued*

4. Garland, L. H. "Studies of the Accuracy of Diagnostic Procedures," *American Journal Roentgenological, Radium Therapy Nuclear Medicine,* Vol. 82 (1959), 25–38.

5. Kerr, Steven. "Some Modifications in MBO as an OD Strategy," *Academy of Management Proceedings,* 1973, pp. 39–42.

6. Kerr, Steven, "What Price Objectivity?" *American Sociologist,* Vol. 8 (1973), 92–93.

7. Litwin, G. H., and R. A. Stringer, Jr. *Motivation and Organizational Climate* (Boston: Harvard University Press, 1968).

8. Perrow, Charles. "The Analysis of Goals in Complex Organizations" in A. Etzioni (Ed.), *Readings on Modern Organizations* (Englewood Cliffs, N.J.: Prentice-Hall, 1969).

9. Scheff, Thomas J. "Decision Rules, Types of Error, and Their Consequences in Medical Diagnosis," in F. Massarik and P. Ratoosh (Eds.), *Mathematical Explorations in Behavioral Science* (Homewood, Ill.: Irwin, 1965).

10. Simon, Herbert A,. *Administrative Behavior* (New York: Free Press, 1957).

11. Swanson, G. E. "Review Symposium: Beyond Freedom and Dignity," *American Journal of Sociology,* Vol. 78 (1972), 702–705.

12. Webster, E. *Decision Making in the Employment Interview* (Montreal: Industrial Relations Center, McGill University, 1964).

SOURCE: Condensed from the original article. Steven Kerr, "On the Folly of Rewarding A, while Hoping for B," *Academy of Management Journal,* 18 (1975): 769–83.

▼ A CASE IN POINT: SETTING TEAM GOALS

Susan had called her entire team together to review goals and objectives for the coming year. She said, "We all know the importance of goal setting. We've heard that over and over again in this company. I trust that each of you are setting personal objectives that are tough to reach, goals that really will stretch your efforts. In fact, I think that is so important that I'm going to sit down with each of you individually in the next day or so and go through your personal goals."

Some of the members of the team turned and looked at each other and scowled. Susan picked up on that and said, "What's the problem back here? You guys do have goals set, don't you?"

"May I be perfectly frank with you?" asked Mark. "I've been selling for this outfit longer than you've been alive. I've been constantly producing good results. I've probably made millions of dollars for this organization. And you know what? I think goal setting is the pits, I'm so sick and tired of hearing about how important it is to set these stupid goals! Why don't you just get off our backs, let us go out and sell the best we can, and forget about all this nonsense."

Susan was flabbergasted. She had always known that goal setting was the only way to gain self-motivation. But here is one of her best salespeople saying he hates goal setting. Several of the other salespeople immediately chimed in. They too felt that goal setting had been carried to a ridiculous extreme, and that it really didn't make much difference to the results obtained.

"Don't you get sick of some of this 'rah-rah' stuff that the company gives us all of the

A CASE IN POINT: SETTING TEAM GOALS *continued*

time?" asked Mark. "I sure do. Why not just do this: Tell us to go out and do the best we can in selling. And you sit back and accept the results that we get. It would take a lot of anxiety off of everybody. The pressures of goal setting and trying to achieve these ridiculous goals simply aren't worth it to a lot of us who have been around selling for quite a while."

"Okay, okay. I'll try not to preach too much about goal setting," said Susan. "You guys go ahead and get the results any way you can. *But* I've prepared a list of our team goals, and I expect that we will reach these goals this year. In fact, I expect that we'll exceed them. I've spent a lot of time planning these out, and despite your objections, I'm going to give copies of them to each of you, and I expect each of you to do your share. Complain if you will, but we are going to achieve the objectives for this team that are listed on this sheet of paper."

With this, the team manager passed out a list of six key targets. The sales representatives in the team looked them over and said absolutely nothing about them. The meeting was adjourned.

QUESTIONS

1. Why do you think the experienced salesman had some complaints about the process of goal setting? What kinds of experiences might he have had that turned him off to the goal-setting process? How do you feel about goal setting?
2. What do you think of the way the sales manager handled the objections to the goal-setting process? Was she wise to pass out the list of team goals?
3. What alternatives to the team manager's approach might have been used? What do you think the results might have been?
4. Is it important for this team manager to convince all of the sales representatives of the value of goal setting? In trying to convince them, what arguments does she have going for her? What arguments might be working against her?

▼ A CASE IN POINT: WHAT UPSET JESS?

Darcy just completed a performance appraisal discussion with one of her employees and is upset about it. She told another supervisor at lunch, "I appraised Jess this morning. I had to call him out of the budget meeting because I remembered all of my appraisals were due today. I couldn't believe his reaction. He said he had no time to prepare and expected me to have an example to support each criticism I made. About all he did, really, was to criticize my position on a couple of issues. I told him several things I didn't like about his performance and then was good enough to tell him how to correct his faults. All I got back was anger and silence. You would think he would be grateful for some feedback, but I guess people today don't really care about improving. Normally, he's a pretty good employee, but he was sure upset during the appraisal. What do you suppose is wrong with him anyway?"

QUESTIONS

1. Why was Jess upset?
2. What unspoken messages could have been conveyed to Jess by Darcy's style of handling the appraisal?
3. If you were Darcy's boss, how would you counsel with her to improve her skills in appraising performance?
4. How would you design a performance program for Jess?

SOURCE: Robert B. Maddux, *Effective Performance Appraisals* (Los Altos, Calif.: Crisp Publications, 1987), p. 35.

THE MEDIUM: COMMUNICATION

UNDERSTANDING MANAGERIAL COMMUNICATION: THE HUMAN TRANSACTION

This chapter answers several all-important questions:

- What are the essential principles of understanding communication?

- What is the role of a symbol in communication?

- What does the concept of transaction have to do with effective communication?

- What are the three major aspects of communication theory presented in this chapter?

- How do human values and human personality affect human communication?

- Why is it important to understand people if one wants to be a good communicator?

- It is often said that meanings exist only in people. What does this mean?

- What are the differences between verbal and nonverbal symbols?

- Why is it important to be aware of the environment in which communication takes place?

The answer to these and other questions are coming up next in chapter 10 ....

CHAPTER 10

One's ability to communicate effectively is based on one's understanding of how people communicate and why they fail to communicate. The Latin root word for communication is *communicare,* which means "to make common." So the degree to which a message sender and receiver have a *common understanding* of a message is the measure of how effective the communication process has been. Effective communication tends to produce success in understanding and influencing co-workers. By studying the principles of communication, we can learn to express concern, help others, get needed information, and develop good working relationships.

Through communication, people find, establish, and foster close relationships; corporations make decisions that affect millions of people; supervisors coordinate the efforts of employees to produce goods and services; employees are hurt and helped; and organizational success or failure is established. Clearly, communication—especially effective communication—matters. Nevertheless, effective communication is not easy to achieve nor to maintain. "Communication breakdown" has just about taken the place of original sin as an explanation for the ills of the world—and perhaps with good cause. As our world becomes more complex and as we spend more time in organized activities, the need for interpersonal understanding has never been greater. And just as important, the cost of failure has never been higher.[1]

"It's not really all that important that we understand each other ... just that *you* understand *me.*"

SOURCE: From *The Wall Street Journal*—permission, Cartoon Features Syndicate.

▼ COMMUNICATION AND MAKING SENSE

What essential principles can help us understand communication? What is the essence of communication? These questions have been considered by many different communication theorists who generally agree that communication occurs when a person is able to make sense out of something. This means that one sees some connection among aspects of a situation. Communication is, therefore, a wholly human activity performed by people. When two people come together, each tries to make sense of the other and of the environment into which they have come together. Making sense is aided by the use of symbols.

Brent D. Peterson, Gerald M. Goldhaber, and R. Wayne Pace say,

> A symbol is something that stands for something else. A word, for example, is a symbol when it refers to an object. To communicate, a person must be able to evolve a mental picture of something (create a concept), give it a name, and develop a feeling about it. Effective communication with another person implies that the concept, the name, and the feeling are similar to what that person has in mind. In other words, effective communication means that you and I refer to the same things when we talk. We share understanding.[2]

■ A symbol is something that stands for something else.

If effective communication is taking place between us and you say to me, "Meet me at my office at seven o'clock tomorrow," then I should visualize the same office as you do, the same time of day as you do, and about the same purpose for the meeting as you do.

How do we know what other people mean when they talk to us? How can we make certain that other people know what we mean when we talk to them? We might ask each other, "What do you mean?" If we can physically point to what we are talking about, we have a better chance of discovering what we mean. Many things that we talk about, however, are difficult to point to physically; for example, feelings, plans, and experiences are difficult to point to. How can we determine what a message means when we cannot look at it directly? We must describe to each other the concepts we have inside each of us.

The problem with describing what is in each of us is outlined by Peterson, Goldhaber, and Pace:

> We ought to remember, however, that communication is a process in which events are not controlled to any great extent. As I say something to you, for example, I interpret your behavior; you react nonverbally to some parts of what I say and verbally to others. While you are reacting, you are also formulating what you will say when I finish. You might even interrupt me. At the same time, I might react to a concept inside of me that sprang to prominence by some movement you made and that is somewhat unrelated to our immediate conversation. The moments when we respond directly to what each of us means are few and precious. Effective communication depends in part upon our abilities to sense and respond to these fleeting revelations at just the right moment.[3]

■ Communication begins when a person has a purpose for communicating.

Communication begins when a person has a purpose or a reason for communicating. A person's purposes are expressed through symbols—verbal or language symbols and nonverbal or behavior symbols—that, when combined into units, becomes messages. A person's messages are interpreted by another person.

■ Three major aspects of communication must be understood for effectiveness.

Three major aspects of communication must be understood for anyone to be an effective communicator: (1) people, (2) messages, and (3) the environment. First, in communication, the person, or both *people*, is the focus of understanding. Communication represents people in the act of transacting. Second, although the people are of primary importance in a study of communication, it is through the sending and receiving of messages that people make sense of one another. Third, communication takes place in a social environment. An organization where one works can be a major environment in which one communicates.

When these components merge, they create a communication event. Effective communication occurs through a process of human transactions in which people share symbolic messages in social environments for the purpose of achieving effective human relationships. For example, a one-to-one communication event is a transaction in which both people are simultaneously engaged in producing messages and responding to each other's messages.

▼ PEOPLE

■ People are the keys that unlock the mysteries of communication.

People are the keys that unlock the mysteries of communication. To comprehend communication, we must discover some of the factors that affect the creation of meaning in people. Factors such as personality and values seem to be critical to understanding people. Other aspects of understanding could be studied, but we will focus on these two.

To be effective communicators, we each must know how others see us. Often someone asks: "How do the workers I supervise see me as a manager or as a leader?" Other questions that might be asked are "How do I see myself, how do I feel about myself as a person, and how do I feel about myself as a managing, communicating human being?"

It is essential to comprehend clearly one's own personality and to sense how one perceives and understands one's own values and the values of others. Self-understanding is the first step toward evaluating the quality of one's own contribution to a communication relationship. By better understanding people, one begins to develop understandings that make communication more beneficial to all concerned. Discovering your own communicating personality will help you understand human values.

Our thoughts and especially our feelings about ourselves influence our thoughts and feelings about, and our communication with, others. Self-evaluation is therefore important. We need to mentally look into a full-length mirror from time to time—to take a long look at ourselves and to consider how others see us. What kind of communicators are we? Do people see us as effective communicators or as ineffective communicators? Is the way others see us different from the way we see ourselves?

Objectivity is sometimes difficult for people when they analyze themselves. Therefore, we have included a questionnaire entitled "Attitudes toward Interacting with People." It may help you learn how others might see you. Complete it and see how you do. However, remember that questionnaires may or may not be accurate. Keep your eyes open to see how others react to you.

▼ ACTIVITY: ATTITUDES TOWARD INTERACTING WITH PEOPLE

University of Connecticut psychologist Kenneth Ring and his associates have developed a test designed to show a person's attitudes about interacting with people. Here is an adaptation of Ring's test, with simplified scoring and analysis.

Consider each statement carefully. Then circle T or F to indicate whether you find it true or false. Each item is designed to bring out the presence of specific attitudes about working with people.

T F 1. I often feel like telling people what I really think of them.

T F 2. I would be uncomfortable in anything other than fairly conventional dress.

T F 3. I enjoy being with people who are suave and sophisticated.

T F 4. When in a new and unfamiliar situation, I am usually governed by the behavior of others present.

T F 5. In social situations, I often feel tense and constrained.

T F 6. At times I suspect myself of being too easily swayed by the opinions of others, and perhaps too openminded and receptive to other people's ideas.

T F 7. I usually have trouble making myself heard in an argument.

T F 8. I don't like formality.

T F 9. I feel I can handle myself pretty well in most social situations.

T F 10. I like to meet new people.

T F 11. I don't mind playing a role or pretending to like something I really don't like if it serves some good purpose.

T F 12. I enjoy "putting people on" sometimes, and playing conversational games.

T F 13. I usually find it difficult to change someone else's opinion.

T F 14. I like to do things that other people regard as unconventional.

T F 15. I enjoy being the host (or hostess) of a party.

T F 16. I think a person should adapt his or her behavior to the group that he or she is with at the time.

T F 17. I often find it difficult to get people to do me favors, even when I have the right to expect them to.

ACTIVITY: ATTITUDES TOWARD INTERACTING WITH PEOPLE *continued*

T F **18.** I would like to belong to several clubs or lodges.

T F **19.** I think it is important to learn obedience.

T F **20.** I like to avoid situations that do not permit me to do things in an original way.

T F **21.** Just the thought of giving a talk in public scares me.

T F **22.** I can fit in pretty easily with any group of people.

T F **23.** In general, I find that I dislike nonconformists.

T F **24.** It is usually easy for me to persuade others to my own point of view.

T F **25.** I like to go to parties.

T F **26.** I prefer to listen to other people's opinions before I take a stand.

T F **27.** When in a group of people, I have trouble thinking of the right things to talk about.

T F **28.** If I am with someone I do not like, I am usually diplomatic and do not express my real feelings.

T F **29.** I have the knack of recognizing people's talents and abilities and putting them to the best purpose.

T F **30.** I like to follow instructions and do what is expected of me.

Now total the number of A's, B's, and C's that you scored. If you have more A's than anything else, you are predominantly a Type A in your attitudes toward management. A score of mostly B's indicates strong Type B tendencies, and a majority of C's indicates you are basically a Type C. Of course, few people fit wholly and completely into only one of these categories, but most people are predominantly one or the other. The more one letter outnumbers the other, the more completely your tendencies lie in the direction of that type. The number of eggs you have in all three baskets indicates the extent to which you share characteristics of all three types.

SCORING AND ANALYSIS

Item	If Your Answer Was	Letter	Item	If Your Answer Was	Letter	Item	If Your Answer Was	Letter
1	False	C	11	False	A	21	False	B
2	False	B	12	True	B	22	False	A
3	False	A	13	False	B	23	True	C
4	True	C	14	False	C	24	True	B
5	True	A	15	True	B	25	False	A
6	True	C	16	True	C	26	True	C
7	False	B	17	False	B	27	True	A
8	False	C	18	False	A	28	False	A
9	False	A	19	True	C	29	True	B
10	True	B	20	True	A	30	True	C

ACTIVITY *continued*

TYPE A ATTITUDES

Type A people are highly individualistic, strongly opinionated, and have little patience with sham or pretense. People in this category are by nature frank and outspoken; they believe in saying exactly what they think. They are not socially adept or skilled in the subtleties of diplomacy. The roundabout approach is completely foreign to them. They are uncomfortable in situations where they cannot be forthright and direct. They want to be "themselves" at all times, and they expect others to do the same. Their tendency to be independent-minded may alienate people. Type A people would think nothing of telling an irate client to go to hell.

Type A people are happiest and most successful in situations where they can be their own bosses or where they can be selective about their clientele and do not have to meet the public at large. Such people may have many talents, and they possess strength of character, but they tend to lack skill in interpersonal relations and the ability to get along harmoniously with all types of people in various situations. Type A people would be least happy in public contact situations.

TYPE B ATTITUDES

Typically, Type B people are highly skilled in interpersonal relations. They get along well socially. They have an innate understanding of people. They are quick to grasp the underlying motivations of other people. This insight serves them in excellent stead when they wish to gain the support of others who may have conflicting views. They not only understand people but also enjoy them. They rarely feel at a loss in any circumstance where people are involved.

Type B people have ability as strategists, which makes them highly effective in influencing others. Type B people are happiest and function most effectively in public contact situations. A Type B person could easily and happily manipulate an irate client.

TYPE C ATTITUDES

One secret of getting along in this world is the ability to adjust to conditions, roll with the punches, make allowances for other people's faults, and appreciate their virtues. Type C people can get along with almost anybody, in any setting, and can exhibit admirable patience even with difficult people under trying circumstances. They "pour oil on troubled waters rather than make waves." They are often found saying to clients, "I'm sorry, I only work here."

They are respectful of the rights of others and go out of their way to avoid antagonizing others. They are interested in what other people think, their concepts and ideas. A Type C person would exhibit great understanding and empathy in dealing with an irate customer. Type C people can work quietly, efficiently, and competently in practically any field that does not require them to be aggressive, impose their will on others, or mold others' opinions. They tend to be uncomfortable in jobs that require them to order people around, enforce discipline, and become involved in conflicts of will.

Now that you have scored and analyzed your test, you might say to yourself, "I'm an excellent communicator. The way I scored on this test is simply wonderful." Others might say, "The way I scored on this test stinks, I feel terrible." And some may say, "It's just a dumb test. We ought to get rid of it. It should never have been put in the book." It's okay for you to think any way you wish. The important thing is for you to say to yourself, "Whether the test is good or bad, let me watch the people with whom I work and see how they treat me and see if I can determine how other people see me in terms of my communication personality. Do I enhance situations with my personality, or do I cause problems because of the way I communicate?

By permission of Johnny Hart and Field Enterprises, Inc.

▼ MESSAGES

The term *message* is often used in a popular sense to refer to the form in which language symbols are used. Technically, a message represents the meanings that people assign to things, but the term *messages* can also be used in a nontechnical sense to refer to the form in which the symbols are presented. The materials presented in this section deal with the way people assign meanings to verbal and nonverbal symbols.

■ Words alone have no meaning; people assign meaning to them.

We assign meaning to events in our lives, the people we work for, the things we see on television, and so on. When we listen to another person talk, the meanings we assign to what that person says make up the messages we are creating. Messages develop inside of us. It is often said that *meanings exist only in people.* This can also be said about messages. A message is simply a group of meanings assigned to some experience.

The creation of a message depends on a person's ability to use symbols. The two most common types of symbols are verbal and nonverbal. The term *verbal* refers to language symbols. The study of how people use language is a study of verbal symbols. *Nonverbal* symbols are nonlanguage behaviors, appearances, emblems, sounds, silence, and time-space relationships that stand for, represent, or refer to something else. When a person assigns meaning to a nonverbal activity, communication through nonverbal means is taking place.

Verbal Symbols

Simply stated, a *verbal symbol* is a word or arrangement of words that we use to convey our thoughts and experiences to others. We each have developed our own unique way of processing and arranging words, which we call our *language structure.* The number and variety of verbal symbols that we understand and have at our command constitutes our *vocabulary.* Our ability to communicate effectively is mainly determined by our perceptions of reality, our vocabulary, our language structure, and our use of nonverbal symbols.

Reprinted by permission: Tribune Media Services.

Nonverbal Symbols

Nonverbal symbols have tremendous impact on communication. The extent that people are able to control them, or at least take them into account as they speak and listen, is the extent to which people will be successful communicators.

The common expression that a person "cannot not communicate" is derived from the recognition that behavior is the open display of a person's thoughts. Your appearance, for example, is a symbol to others. Approximately 35 percent of the social meaning in a normal conversation is conveyed by the verbal components and approximately 65 percent by the nonverbal components—and these figures are probably conservative. Consider the communication that takes place in the way you style your hair, the type of clothes you wear, the condition of your body, the way you stand, the expression on your face, the eye contact you maintain, the gestures and body movements you use, the way you position yourself in relationship to those with whom you communicate, the tone of voice you use, and so on. Nonverbal communication is taking place constantly.

PERSONAL SPACE AND TERRITORIALITY

The concept of *personal space* can be defined as the distance you allow between yourself and others. According to Edward Hall, people carry their personal space with them and allow it to expand and contract according to the type of communicative encounter in which they are participating.[4] Hall classified personal space in four subcategories related to distance and situation: (1) *intimate,* ranging from actual physical contact to a distance of about 18 inches; (2) *casual personal,* from about 1.5 feet to 4 feet; (3) *social consultative,* from 4 to 12 feet; and (4) *public,* from 12 feet to the limits of visibility.

We all seem to adjust to the proper distance for various communicative situations. If you have just been introduced to the president of a corporation for a job interview, you most likely use the casual personal distance. On the other hand, if you are with your best

■ The extent to which people control and understand nonverbal symbols is the extent to which people will be effective communicators.

■ Physical distance between people communicates meaning.

■ Communication
problems can arise
from invading another
person's space.

friend or sweetheart after a very rough day at school or at work and you need love and sympathy, you will probably use the intimate distance.

Problems of communication can occur when someone invades another's personal space. People do this by not using the proper distance demanded by the other person and the situation. For example, it's probably not a good idea to slap the back of a supervisor or manager on the day you go to work for him or her. However, after you have worked well together for some time and established a positive relationship, he or she might welcome the warmth you show by a slap on the back.

We all take our personal space with us wherever we go. In certain situations, people identify so clearly with a given location or space that they act as if it were their *territory*. Reflect on your territory. Where do you sit in class? Have you stayed in approximately the same place throughout the semester? Do you get upset when someone else sits in your seat? Do you have your own personal study chair in the library? Is there a specific place you sit at the dinner table? Territorial behavior seems to be a standard part of our everyday contact with other people.

■ People protect and
defend their personal
space.

How do you feel when someone invades your personal space or territory? How do you protect your favorite seat in the cafeteria? Some common techniques used to defend territory are as follows:

1. *Markers;* such as books, coats, briefcases, or backpacks
2. *Tenure;* for example, if you continue to come to the same seat or territory over a period of time, everyone finally realizes that the territory is yours and leaves it alone
3. *Friends;* for example, you may say, "Marsha, will you watch my place until I get back with the hamburgers?"

We all define our personal space and territory according to the situation in which we are communicating. The proximity between two individuals who want to establish a friendship can have a major effect on the outcome of their relationship. And we know that some behavior can be explained by the need to stake out and defend territory. The key is to learn as much as possible about these issues, so that we can use them to help us obtain desired responses in others. Understanding personal space and territory can help us be better communicators.

APPEARANCE

■ People strive to send
appearance messages
that meet their own
expectations and the
expectations of
others.

Every morning when we pull ourselves out of bed, we make a series of decisions that affect our appearance and the messages we wish to convey by the way we look. If we are in a hurry and are not concerned about impressing anyone, we might not spend much time with our appearance. If we have a job interview, we might spend considerable time preparing ourselves to look the way we feel the interviewer would want us to look.

In essence, people strive to send appearance messages that correspond with others' expectations. Americans spend millions of dollars on weight-reduction programs, makeup and beauty aids, hair

We communicate through our grooming and the way we dress.

spray, mouthwash, soap, clothes, hair stylists, acne creams, jogging outfits, and many other items just to improve the way they look. Advertisers have a heyday with statements such as "The dry look is in, the wet head is dead," and "Lipstick is not to be seen, it is to be used to make women appear natural."

Attractiveness, body shape, hair, and clothing and other artifacts people place on their bodies all have an impact on behavior. Physical *attractiveness* influences the types of messages people send and receive in a variety of encounters. This is particularly true in persuasive situations. Perceived attractiveness increases the credibility of the speaker and possibly gives that person a persuasive advantage over a less attractive person. What messages do the physical attractiveness and *body shapes* of others send to you? Study your own physical appearance and body shape, and analyze what you might be saying to others.

What can we learn about a person by the clothes he or she wears? Do clothes give us helpful nonverbal cues for understanding others?

■ What can we learn from nonverbal cues?

Personal apparel includes a wide variety of items other than *clothing*. Nonclothing apparel, or *artifacts,* include eyeglasses, cosmetics, and wigs. Most theorists agree that clothing and artifacts contain much information about people.

R. Hoult's research suggests that the clothes we wear have a greater influence on people we do not know than they do on our friends.[5] Hoult found that when subjects knew each other well, changes in clothing did not significantly change the way they rated each other. However, when subjects rated pictures of unknown attractive faces paired with unattractive clothing, the attractive faces' ratings went down. When he paired unattractive faces with attractive clothing, the unattractive faces' ratings went up. According to Hoult, clothing is not a highly influential factor in nonverbal communication when individuals are well acquainted.

Attractiveness, body shape, hair, clothing, and artifacts together create personal appearance. Appearance has a major impact on how others see us and what we think and feel about others.

BODY LANGUAGE

This aspect of nonverbal communication created excitement as a result of the best-selling books *Body Language,* by Julius Fast, and *How to Read a Person Like a Book,* by Gerald Nierenberg and Henry H. Calero. People wanted to be able to detect subtle body movements and stances in others and to determine what they meant. These popular books seemed to be saying, "Read us and learn what your employer really thinks, or read us and know what your date really has in mind for the evening."

■ Body movements need to be studied in concert with other aspects of nonverbal communication.

However, the study of body language is not that precise. Most body movements in and of themselves have little meaning. We must be aware of other aspects of nonverbal communication if we are to be effective symbol readers. Body movements must be studied in concert with other nonverbal cues. We generally respond to nonverbal symbols that are a combination of more than one isolated cue.

TOUCH BEHAVIOR

Touching is an effective means of communicating. By hugging your parents and sincerely telling them that you love them, you strengthen the bonds that hold your family together. Touching seems to work best in combination with other stimuli. The combination of the hug and the words creates a message that is probably more effective than giving the hug alone or just saying the words.

While touching is an effective means of communicating in many circumstances, it can cause innumerable problems if done in an improper way. It is quite acceptable for a quarterback to slap a tackle on the fanny for making a good block. However, a slap on the fanny is quite inappropriate for most other people or in most other settings.

Even though touching is usually used with other types of messages and can often be used inappropriately, it is one of the best methods for creating relationships. The handshake and pat on the back enhance communication.

Smiles communicate friendliness and a desire to get along.

FACIAL EXPRESSIONS AND EYE CONTACT

The face is a major source of messages about how people feel. It reveals much about internal emotional states. The face can show whether a friend is happy or upset. It may be the primary source of messages outside of human speech.

The mouth has received a great deal of research attention, because it is used to frown and smile. As a rule, smiles communicate friendliness and a desire to get along. People smile when seeking approval or in communicating acceptance of others. The smile can be used in a sarcastic way, as well. Looking at other cues from other parts of the face and body can help determine the sincerity of the smile.

The eyes are a major message sender of the face. Eye contact has a great impact on determining who receives and does not receive messages.

Facial expressions are complex and therefore difficult to deal with. But of all the areas of the body, the face can give the best external feedback of internal feelings. Looking a person in the eyes creates a linkage—a sense of communication—not available without such contact.

■ Our faces tell the rest of the world how we feel.

VOCAL CUES (PARALANGUAGE)

Paralanguage is the study of *how* something is said (not what is said) by the words that are used. Sarcasm is an example of paralanguage. The young quarterback who has tossed a pass that resulted in an interception and a touchdown for the other team could hear from his coach words such as "Way to go, Bill. That was the most beautiful pass I have ever seen anyone throw!" If Bill were to listen only to the words of the coach, he would interpret them as a positive reaction. But Bill will probably realize from the coach's tone of voice that he was displeased. Studies of conflicting messages on the vocal and verbal levels indicate that most of the time people read vocal cues accurately.

■ Nonverbal symbols can have a great impact on communication. Keep verbal and nonverbal symbols working together.

Nonverbal symbols have a great impact on communication. We have presented six groups of nonverbal communication variables. These are perhaps the most common variables. If you wish to be an accurate reader of nonverbal communication, you must be sensitive to the entire context in which the nonverbal symbols are being sent. You must read as many cues as possible and then make a composite judgment of their meaning. Therefore, to be effective, you must minimally evaluate the personal space and territory, the appearance, the body movements, the touching behavior, the facial expressions and eye contacts, and the vocal cues as they are used in the communication context. Along with these nonverbal messages, be awake to the words that are being spoken. If you take the entire communication context and all of its variables into account, you will be a much more effective receiver and sender of symbols.

▼ ORGANIZATIONAL ENVIRONMENT

The environmental aspect of human communication concerns the conditions in which communication occurs. The environment is the social context: the physical surroundings, setting, and location. For three employees in a room, the immediate environment might be the room (its shape, size, and furnishings), the air (its circulation, temperature, and humidity), and the sounds (their tone, frequency, and quality). The extended environment can be the entire organization in which you find yourself. This environment consists of many aspects.

People are constantly interacting with a variety of changing cultures and situations. The broad organization is constantly changing and is often in a state of unrest. We will not cover or discuss the impact of the organizational environment here because it has been presented in previous chapters.

▼ SUMMARY OF KEY IDEAS

■ Communication is the process of making sense of (assigning meaning to) symbols. Effective communication occurs when two or more people share a similar understanding of a symbol.

- People, messages, and the environment combine to form a communication event.
- Since communication is a wholly human activity and people are the key to understanding communication, self-evaluation of our personalities is helpful to achieve effective communication.
- The effective communicator is able to control and understand nonverbal symbols.
- Hall's four classifications of personal space based on distance and situation are intimate, casual personal, social consultative, and public.
- The major appearance factors are attractiveness, body shape, clothing, and artifacts.
- Along with appearance, nonverbal cues include body language, touch, facial expressions and eye contact, and vocal cues.

▼ KEY TERMS, CONCEPTS, AND NAMES

Appearance
Assumption
Body language
Communication
Edward Hall
Environment
Eye contact
Facial expressions
Gerald M. Goldhaber
Message

Nonverbal symbols
R. Wayne Pace
Paralanguage
Personal space
Self-fulfilling expectations
Symbol
Touch behavior
Verbal symbols
Vocal cues

▼ QUESTIONS AND EXERCISES

1. List all the new information you have learned about yourself from completing the "Attitudes toward Interacting with People" activity.
2. List the way people behave toward you throughout one day. At the end of the day, look at your list. What have you learned about how people see you?
3. Analyze your nonverbal symbols. How do others see you?
4. Answer the introductory questions at the beginning of the chapter.
5. How can value differences complicate communication?
6. Rank the following values according to their importance to you, with 1 being the most important and 18 the least important. Then compare your rankings with the general American sample on the next page.

_____ Ambitious (hardworking, aspiring)
_____ Broad-minded (open-minded)
_____ Capable (competent, effective)
_____ Cheerful (lighthearted, joyful)

_____ Clean (neat, tidy)
_____ Courageous (willing to stand up for one's beliefs)
_____ Forgiving (willing to pardon others)
_____ Helpful (willing to work for the welfare of others)
_____ Honest (sincere, truthful)
_____ Imaginative (daring, creative)
_____ Independent (self-sufficient, self-reliant)
_____ Intellectual (intelligent, reflective)
_____ Logical (consistent, rational)
_____ Loving (affectionate, tender)
_____ Obedient (dutiful, respectful)
_____ Polite (courteous, well mannered)
_____ Responsible (dependable, reliable)
_____ Self-controlled (restrained, self-disciplined)

Instrumental Values	General American Sample	Instrumental Values	General American Sample
Ambitious	2	Imaginative	18
Broad-minded	5	Independent	14
Capable	10	Intellectual	17
Cheerful	12	Logical	15
Clean	8	Loving	11
Courageous	6	Obedient	16
Forgiving	4	Polite	13
Helpful	7	Responsible	3
Honest	1	Self-controlled	9

▼ Notes

1. Paul R. Timm, "The Way We Word," _Supervisory Management_ 23 (1978):20

2. Brent D. Peterson, Gerald M. Goldhaber, and R. Wayne Pace, _Communication Probes,_ 3d ed. (Chicago: Science Research Associates, 1983), p. 1.

3. Ibid, p.2.

4. Edward T. Hall, _The Hidden Dimension_ (New York: Doubleday, 1966).

5. R. Hoult, "Experimental Measurement of Clothing as a Factor in Some Social Ratings of Selected American Men," _American Sociological Review_ 19 (1954):324–28.

ANOTHER LOOK: THE STANFORD STUDY

Professor Thomas W. Harrell of the Stanford Graduate School of Business* recently completed a twenty-year study relating to career success. While there were no "certain passports to success," Harrell found there were three consistent personal qualities that appeared to have a positive affect on the careers of those studied. These included:

1. An outgoing, ascendant personality

2. A desire to persuade, to talk with, and to work with people

3. A need for power

Although interpersonal communication skills are not necessarily related to the third characteristic, they are certainly intimately intertwined in the first two.

The point is best made with Harrell's conclusion that:

"The consistent variable found which related to management success was the personality trait of social extroversion or sociability. This variable was consistently related to success throughout a twenty year career."

*Stanford University Study: Harrell & Alpert, March 1986

SOURCE: Bert Decker, *The Art of Communicating* (Los Altos, Calif.: Crisp Publications, 1988), p. 12.

ANOTHER LOOK: THE WAY WE WORD

Although we take the whole process of communication pretty much for granted, the way our language works is not well understood by most people.

SOURCE OF MISCOMMUNICATION

First, it may seem ironic that language—the very basis of what many view as real communication—poses one of the most pervasive sources of misunderstanding in our communicative processes, but it does.

Let me explain: We have all developed our own ways of using words and symbols to describe what we mean to others. How we process and arrange words is our personal language structure. Our sensory experiences—that is, our perceptions of the physical world to which we attach words and symbols—can be likened to data cards for a computer. And in these terms, our language structure is analogous to a system program, which tells the computer what to do with the new data. So communication failures often arise between people either because of differences in how they relate words to experiences or because of the way they process the words they speak or hear.

There are two ways to improve verbal communication skills: either increase a person's vocabulary so that more precise "data cards" can be produced, or improve the match between language structures and objective reality. Increasing someone's vocabulary will usually be a far less fruitful approach than working on structures, because only in those situations where there is a seriously inadequate vocabulary—such as when a person is learning a new language—would [an] emphasis on improved vocabulary be significantly valuable. Clarifying language structures by examining our logic and showing discrepancies between the way we "process" words and the way the real world behaves is a far more valuable approach.

Let's look at several assumptions about word use that may be causing some of the more common problems in the ways we process language.

ANOTHER LOOK : THE WAY WE WORD *continued*

FACT VS. ASSUMPTION

Many problems of miscommunication arise when the way we structure our language does not distinguish between fact and assumption. And to presume that people in general—including ourselves—know an absolute fact when they see one is a dangerous presumption.

In truth, the vast majority of information we receive is inference or opinion, not fact. Something we personally observe or experience can be regarded as a fact—at least for us. But just about anything else should be considered inference or opinion. The times that we run into misunderstanding and disagreement with others are when we state inferences or opinions as though they were facts. The problem is that the language we normally use does not automatically make the distinction clear. So we must make an extra effort to do so.

For example, under normal circumstances, we can state direct observations—"I saw Tom leave the plant at five o'clock"—as facts. But if we take the fact about Tom leaving the plant and try to elaborate on it, what we say becomes an inference. For example, when we say, "I saw Tom leaving the plant *to go home,*" we are now adding a new dimension to the message that may or may not be true, in fact. That Tom left the plant can be verified by observation, but that he went home is merely inferential on our part.

An inference is a conclusion based upon incomplete information, and much of what we talk about is based on inference. By necessity, we communicate inferences all the time. But problems arise when our listeners are unclear as to whether we are inferring or speaking of fact. Our language often tends to muddy this distinction, so inferences have a way of coming out sounding awfully factual.

Again, let me restate: There is nothing inherently wrong with drawing inferences. Inferences are necessary for people to make day-to-day sense out of the world. We seldom have the luxury of having *all* available data at our disposal before we draw conclusions. The important thing is that we recognize inferences as such and that we word them in ways that will help us and our listeners avoid confusing them with facts. Failure to do so can often lead to confusion and argument.

For example, if you like the sales manager's dress, and you say, "Hey, I like that dress," fine. That's a fact. You are clearly expressing a factual, "as-it-relates-to-me" statement. You like the dress and there's little room for misunderstanding. If, however, you say, "That's a nice dress you're wearing," you're stating an opinion that sounds like a fact, and there's more room for interpreting what you really mean. Do you like the fact that the sales manager is

wearing a dress instead of her customary pantsuit, which you think is too masculine? Do you like the fact that you can now get a better look at the sales manager's legs? Are you being sarcastic and not really complimentary? There's more room for interpretation in an opinion. (Of course, nonverbal dimensions such as tone of voice and facial expression can clarify the point you are trying to make.)

Nobody can argue about what you "like." If you say, "I didn't like that movie," that's your right and other people will respect it. But if you say, "That was a rotten movie," then others may be put on the defensive, especially if they liked the movie.

HOW TO RESPOND?

When an opinion is not identified as such, the receiver of the message has to make a decision on how to respond—whether to be "nice" and agree with you or be true to his or her feelings and say that it was not a "rotten" movie. If contrary opinions are offered, the risk of starting an argument is increased.

Another example: If I state the opinion that "Frank is stupid," it may appear on the surface that stupidity is an inherent characteristic of Frank, but what, in fact, I am saying is that

■ My personal experience has supplied me with a meaning for the word *stupid.*

ANOTHER LOOK *continued*

- I have perceived Frank's behavior as fitting my view of the concept of "stupidity."
- Therefore, I have concluded that Frank is stupid.

Notice that the words *I* and *me* enter in this analysis throughout. When I conclude that Frank is stupid, I am really talking about my own opinion. I've related these two things, Frank and stupidity, *I* have related them within my world of words. Whether or not they are related in objective reality remains unclear.

So, in essence, every opinion we offer is a statement about ourselves. This is so because:

- We can never say all there is we have to say about any topic, since this would take too long. Therefore …
- Those things we do choose to talk about and those that we choose to ignore involve a selection process on our part, based on our past experiences. Thus whereas …
- Each of us has had totally unique experiences and no two people have experienced the same things, and since …
- We have each created our own unique way of attaching words or labels to our world of experiences—therefore …
- When we combine several of these labels into a message, we are saying

very little about objective reality and instead are describing something that is of great important to us *personally.*

Thus to conclude that "Frank is stupid," is to report on some word associations we have made. This statement doesn't really say much about Frank, but it does say some very interesting things about us. A simple remedy for this problem of expression is by making clear that you recognize this process and by converting these opinions into facts. "*I think that* Frank is stupid" is a fact. Or "I've observed Frank doing things *I consider stupid*" is a fact.

Although this changing of terms often results in additional effort and longer messages, the tradeoff results in greater accuracy and clarity of expression. Failure to so clarify what our message is can lead to considerable embarrassment, incorrect conclusions, and serious harm to our credibility. I suspect his potential breakdown was in S. I. Hayakawa's mind when he said that general semantics—that is, the study of language and its behavioral effects—could more accurately be described as the study of "how not to be a damn fool."

Another common problem in the way we structure language is the tendency to oversimplify the categories into which we mentally sort things. We deal with our life experiences in egg-carton

;fashion, neatly fitting each experience into one of several compartments.

The Either/Or Temptation

The problem with this practice is that people rely too heavily on polar terms, terms that force us to choose between extremes—like good or bad, weak or strong, big or little—and which tend to oversimplify and confuse the issues we are discussing. In reality, most things we encounter in life are more accurately described in terms of probabilities or fine variations among events or experiences than by an either/or categorization. In other words, our experiences represent some shade of gray, rather than black-or-white differentiations. To illustrate, simply ask yourself—and others—questions such as these:

- Are you rich or poor?
- Are you big or little?
- Are you handsome or ugly?
- Are you conservative or liberal?

The appropriate response, of course, to questions like these would be "As compared to whom (or what)?" It can be very helpful to our communicative abilities to train our thinking away from oversimplified categorization, although this does take a more active intellectual effort to talk in terms of degrees or comparisons.

In an industrial organization, this process may mean

ANOTHER LOOK : THE WAY WE WORD *continued*

avoiding the tendency to classify workers as "industrious" or "lazy" or as "productive" or "unproductive." In one company I've heard of, a sales manager actually had a big chart on his office wall with the names of all his salesmen boldly displayed under the headings "Heroes" and "Bums."

The problem with this tendency is that when our language and thinking utilize such either/or logic, other possibilities are overlooked. If we only classify a manager as a "good leader" or "bad leader," we leave out a lot of other possibilities. Maybe he or she is effective in some dimensions of the job while ineffective in others.

Sales representatives and other persuaders often manipulate this either/or orientation to their advantage. "Would you like to take delivery immediately or next week?" attempts to preclude the option of not taking delivery at all. It's the old story of the ice cream shoppe operator who asked each customer whether they wanted one egg or two in their milkshakes. Few people said neither, and he charged extra for each egg, of course.

Another consideration is that our credibility can be seriously damaged when listeners recognize these kinds of oversimplified language structures. While there are legitimately dichotomous categories—such as male or female—most things don't fit so neatly into either/or slots. Or sometimes the categories

themselves become so broad as to be meaningless. Whenever we hear ourselves or others sending either/or messages, it might be wise for us to consider:

- Are all the options covered?
- As compared to what (or whom)?

SELF-FULFILLING EXPECTATIONS

The manager who comes to actually see his subordinates as heroes or bums is obviously not relating to reality. It is far more realistic and hopeful to think in terms of ever-changing individuals who can and will change their work performance. Today's hero may have been yesterday's bum—if we, as managers, have been able to avoid the related problem of self-fulfilling prophecies. Because we usually choose what perceptions we will pay attention to and then mesh these things into our views of reality, there is a strong tendency to only look for the pieces that fit.

Similarly, there are interactive effects between our perceptions and the ways we talk. What we see directly affects what we say. And what we say in turn affects what we see. The filters of our mind develop over time as we label our world of experiences, and these filters then determine what we select to perceive. When we can make no sense out of some thing or event—that is,

if it doesn't fit our world view—we tend to reject it.

It can be quite disconcerting, for example, to find the worker we've labeled "rebellious" suddenly vigorously defending the status quo. It's also unsettling to find the "nice, pleasant" receptionist suddenly shouting angrily at a visitor. We'd prefer to reject or explain away such discrepancies because they just don't jibe with "the way things are" in our mental worlds. The way we label things leads to expectations of how the things will behave in the future.

Furthermore, expectations have a way of becoming self-fulfilling. The supervisor who labels a subordinate "lazy" will undoubtedly find more and more evidence to support the judgment. And in all likelihood, this supervisor's attitude will then be perceived by the worker, thus leading to suspicion and distrust. The overall result: a strong potential for miscommunication. So let's keep our labels—if we must use them—somewhat loose. Let's build into them some flexibility so that unanticipated changes in things, events, and people can be plugged into our mental worlds without throwing us off balance.

NEED FOR CLEAR THINKING

To be credible as a message source, a person must be constantly aware of such things as the pervasiveness of change. In short, we need

ANOTHER LOOK *continued*

to think clearly and communicate clearly. When our ways of thinking become too rigid, we move away from paralleling reality.

In summary, we must remember that words do not have inherent meanings. They are simply labels that we attach in unique and individual ways to our world of experiences. And since labels trigger meanings in others, the degree to which

we achieve true communication is determined in part by how accurate we are in relating these labels to reality. If we are inaccurate, we describe a world that is not there. Carried to the extreme, inappropriate language uses can affect our mental health. Our psychological and sociological well being can depend upon our being aware of the important ways in which language reflects

and influences the way we think and communicate.

Many communication problems arise from a lack of awareness about "the way we word." In fact, when the many pitfalls of language processing are pointed out, it seems amazing that people can communicate at all.

SOURCE: Paul R. Timm, "The Way We Word," *Supervisory Management* 23 (1978):20–26. Copyright © by Paul R. Timm, 1978.

▼ A CASE IN POINT: SCHULTZ AND PETERSON: A DISPUTE

In an effort to control costs of servicing customer accounts, Jim Schultz, manager of systems at Washburn National Bank, was charged with making a study and subsequent recommendations to reduce the operating expense of the department.

Thirty days later, Schultz's recommendations were put into operation; six months later, costs for operating the department were reviewed against costs for the preceding six-month period. It was found that costs had decreased by $2,715. This decrease was due primarily to savings in salaries charged against the customer service department. During the preceding six-month period, 9,037 customers had been provided service. Under the new system, 4,812 customers had been provided service.

The vice-president of the bank reported the savings to the president, Mr. Peterson. Peterson expressed surprise that the vice-president thought a savings had taken place. "In the first place," the president said, "you moved the customer service department from the main floor to the sixth floor so that fewer customers would take the trouble to check

their balances and review their statements; furthermore, you require each customer to show positive identification before they can obtain any information about their accounts; on top of this, you have instructed the personnel in customer service absolutely to refuse to give out any banking information to anyone requesting it over the telephone. It's my opinion that you should revert to the old system and give our customers the kind of service they deserve."

QUESTIONS

1. What should Schultz say?

2. What, if any, communication problems are occurring between Schultz and the vice-president? Between the vice-president and Peterson? Between the bank and its customers?

3. What effects might be occurring inside each of the parties involved in this incident?

4. What should be done now?

CHAPTER

11

INTERPERSONAL COMMUNICATION: BEING EFFECTIVE WITH PEOPLE

This chapter answers several all-important questions:

- What does support listening do?

- How do the open-question, "uh-huh," and content reflection techniques work to create support listening?

- How does retention listening differ from support listening?

- What are the eight points for effective retention listening?

- When is it appropriate to use the skill of accurate understanding?

- How does accurate understanding work?

- What three approaches constitute the conflict-managing technique?

- What do you do to manage each of the following types of conflict: simple conflict, pseudoconflict, and ego conflict?

- What are some circumstances in which the communication conflict approach should be used?

The answer to these and other questions are coming up next in chapter 11 ....

CHAPTER 11

■ Managers need good interpersonal communication skills.

Some problems are associated with communication in organizations. Employees are forced to communicate through other employees who may or may not get the message. Feelings are often crushed. Trust can be lost. Production might fall off. Life can be miserable.

People engaged in managing, supervising, selling, and providing services depend on good interpersonal communication to accomplish their objectives. In this chapter, we deal with skills to help managers more effectively obtain their objectives through efficient interpersonal communication. What kinds of objectives tend to be associated with interpersonal communication? Among other things, a manager should be able to:

1. maintain close relationships without developing feelings of uncertainty or rejection;
2. help others understand themselves and achieve a degree of personal growth;
3. interpret and pass on information to another person with minimal distortion and misunderstanding; and
4. listen so as to create a supportive atmosphere in which another person can talk without being defensive.

During the past twenty or thirty years, many helpful approaches to the study of interpersonal communication have been proposed. The study of transactional analysis (TA), especially, has done much to foster effective interpersonal relationships. TA has been successful because it helps people evaluate their communication effectiveness. Furthermore, and most important, it helps individuals step out of the communication situation, to evaluate how the messages of both the speaker and the listener influence the effectiveness of communication. For communication to be effective, people must stand back and be aware of what they are doing. A casual, unthinking approach results in ineffective communication.

■ Effective communicators are aware of what they do to influence others.

Conversation
i have just wandered back
into our conversation and find that you are still rattling on about something or other
i think i must have been gone at least twenty minutes and you never missed me

now this might say something about my acting ability or it might say something about your sensitivity

▼ SKILLS OF EFFECTIVE COMMUNICATIONS

Besides being aware, you must be concerned about the other person. If you are not, the skills that we are about to present may seem phoney and manipulative. However, they do work if you are aware and concerned and practice them. We will discuss skills of effective listening, accurate understanding and managing communication conflict.

▼ EFFECTIVE LISTENING

As the quiz in the following activity indicates, listening can be a challenging process. A starting point for improvement lies in recognizing that we engage in two types of listening:

1. listening to show support for the other person *(support listening)*,

ACTIVITY: SUPPORT LISTENING QUIZ

Test your listening skills. Select the one best answer among the three given, even though you may feel that all answers may be correct to some degree. See page 242 for comments.

1. A person is a good listener only if he/she
   a. Does not think while the other person is talking
   b. Hears everything the other person has to say
   c. Seeks information as she/he listens about his/her own and the other person's assumptions, viewpoints, and feelings

2. To get a clear picture of the other person as we listen
   a. We have to "tune in" on some things that are never actually voiced
   b. We must concentrate on everything she/he says
   c. We must clear our minds of any prejudices or evaluations we may have made in advance

3. The biggest block to interpersonal communications is
   a. One's inability to listen intelligently, understandingly, and skillfully to another person
   b. One's inability to be logical, lucid, and clear in what one says
   c. The fact that any statement may have several meanings

4. It is necessary for everyone who must deal with other people on important matters to know how to listen with understanding because
   a. In a crucial conversation, false ideas of other people can lead to misunderstanding and disagreement
   b. There will be less argument
   c. People usually try to conceal their real feelings

5. You can determine whether you have communicated with the other person by
   a. Asking him/her questions
   b. Watching her/his facial expressions
   c. Knowing whether he/she should be interested in what you are talking about

6. When we talk to another person, we can assume
   a. That the other person is listening to what we say
   b. That what is important to us may not be important to her/him
   c. That he/she knows and shares our unspoken feelings

7. Three factors enter into our daily person-to-person listening. Which is most important?
   a. Assumptions
   b. Viewpoints
   c. Feelings

SOURCE: Reprinted from *American Business* © Geyer-McAllister Publications. Permission to reprint granted by Elliott Service Company, Mount Vernon, New York.

2. listening to retain and evaluate information *(retention listening)*.

These two types of listening are generally discussed and studied independently by communication theorists. The nondirective counseling approach of psychologists like Carl Rogers exemplifies support listening, while education specialists and communication scholars like Ralph Nichols focus on retention. All approaches assume that people spend a large portion of their lives listening, and that is true. The next section of this chapter presents important ideas and aids dealing with both support and retention listening.

one thing troubles me though
when it is my turn to rattle on for twenty minutes
which i have been known to do
have you been missing too?
Ric Masten

ACTIVITY: "SUPPORT LISTENING QUIZ" COMMENTS

Compare your responses with the following comments about each question:

1. It is not enough to be just a blotter or photographic negative that soaks up everything that is said. Good listening requires active participation on the part of the listener. The correct answer is *c*.

2. It is not enough to concentrate on everything that is said; we have to be actively thinking as we listen. It is actually impossible to cleanse our minds of our prejudices and evaluations, but it helps to "know thyself." The correct answer is *a*.

3. No matter how logical, lucid, or clear the transmitter is, unless the receiver is "tuned in," there can be no communication. The fact that one statement may have several meanings complicates the process of interpersonal communication, but good listening habits can overcome this obstacle. The correct answer is *a*.

4. [Answer] *b* is wrong because elimination of arguments in itself does not mean good communication. [Answer] *c* is also wrong because the purpose of listening with understanding is not just to get at hidden feelings, but to be able to communicate with others. The correct answer is *a*.

5. Many times facial expressions can be very deceiving. Just because a person appears interested in a subject does not mean he/she actually understands. The correct answer is *a*.

6. People often think of something else when someone else is speaking, and these unspoken feelings vary with each individual. It is safest to assume that the other person probably has a different set of values from your own. The correct answer is *b*.

7. Feelings are deeply imbedded in people and are not subject to logical argument. Viewpoints and assumptions are more easily changed by new facts and perspectives. The correct answer is *c*.

SOURCE: Reprinted from *American Business* © Geyer-McAllister Publications. Permission to reprint granted by Elliott Service Company, Mount Vernon, New York.

▼ SUPPORT LISTENING

Support listening consists of hearing and remembering what others say with a minimum of emotion or observable reaction. The idea is to focus on listening to another so as to learn what that person thinks and feels. Avoid speaking except to encourage or cause the other person to speak.

Support listening consists of three responses:

- Open questions
- "Uh-huh"
- Content reflection

Open questions cannot be answered with a simple yes or no statement. "Uh-huh" is the simplest kind of oral response, and consists of saying "uh-huh" or "hmmm" as the other person talks. Content reflection involves repeating, mirroring, or echoing the content of a statement made by another person in the form of a question. Each reaction is designed to cause the speaker to keep speaking and the listener to keep listening.

Support listening places the responsibility for continuing a conversation, dialogue, or interview on the other person. If you ask the question "What do you think about our firm?" and then look intently and inquiringly at the person to whom you addressed the question, the responsibility for continuing the dialogue is placed firmly on the other person. The commitment is equally strong when you simply say "uh-huh" or "hmmm" when the other person makes a comment. The effect is essentially the same when you echo the idea just stated. Support listening establishes that you want the other person to either begin or continue talking. When you respond this way, you create an expectation that can be fulfilled only when the other person talks and when you listen.

■ Support listening puts the responsibility for continuing the conversation on the other person.

Each skill of support listening encourages the other to talk. The following dialogue illustrates support listening:

RITA: Doris, how do you feel about the department? (Open question)

DORIS: Working in this department is extremely difficult.

RITA: Uh-huh ("Uh-huh")

DORIS: What I mean is that I have problems getting along with Dan.

RITA: Hmmm. ("Uh-huh")

DORIS: He just can't accept the fact that I'm his boss.

RITA: Dan can't accept you as his boss? (Content reflection)

DORIS: That's right! He's always making snide comments about women bosses.

RITA: What kinds of things does he say? (Open question)

Support listening is grounded in the theory of positive reinforcement. People like to talk to others who support them or at least do not deny or reject them. Reinforcement theory suggests that a person's behavior is influenced by its consequences. Thus, if you react or respond in a supportive manner to something the other person said, he or she will feel that the comments have been reinforced and will continue to talk. If you begin talking and get positive reactions in return, you will tend to continue talking. Each support listening skill provides positive reinforcement by indicating that you have an interest in what is being said and care enough to listen.

■ Support listening is grounded in positive reinforcement.

What You Must Do

To listen supportively, you need to have concern for the other person and an interest in listening to what he or she has to say.

Although each type of response can be used individually and independently, the techniques of support listening are most effective when they are used together. The open question is often used to open the conversation, after which a content reflection or an "uh-huh" response is given. Thereafter, as the conversation runs through a sequence of interactions involving reflections and "uh-huh" responses, another open question can be asked.

■ Skills and techniques of effective interpersonal communication work only if you care about the other person.

Begin the conversation or interview with an open question:

ARLENE: How have you been getting along with George?

Then look at the other person and lean slightly toward him or her. Indicate that you are listening by nodding your head occasionally as the other talks. Vocalize your support by giving an "uh-huh" response:

SALLY: I really appreciate all that he does for me.

ARLENE: Uh-huh.

SALLY: He really seems to care about me.

ARLENE: Uh-huh.

The "uh-huh" response provides support and indicates that you are following the conversation.

Or you might want to secure more information about a topic. In that case, content reflection and additional open questions are appropriate:

SALLY: But I simply can't stand this place any longer.

ARLENE: You can't stand being here any longer!

SALLY: You said it! If I have to work with George any longer, I'm going to go out of my mind.

ARLENE: Well, how do you feel about the board of directors?

Support listening is a basic technique that shows support and encourages the other person to continue talking. Support listening is essentially nonevaluative—it avoids expressing approval or disapproval—and requires careful hearing of the other.

In using the "uh-huh" response, focus on the other person and verbalize your support by saying "uh-huh," "hmmm," "I see," or some equivalent nonjudgmental comment.

Content reflection responses are provided by echoing or mirroring back the content of what the other person said. Avoid using a questioning tone of voice that makes the reflected question sound like a challenge to and an evaluation of what the other said.

The open question involves asking a free-response inquiry that requires a statement or explanation rather than a simple yes or no answer.

■ Support listening is not a gimmick.

Although the evidence is quite strong in support of the efficacy of the technique of support listening, it depends on the sincere interest of the user to truly hear and remember what the speaker is saying. If the listener is not sincerely interested in what the speaker has to say, then the technique is merely a gimmick. In those instances, the speaker usually recognizes what is happening, refuses to cooperate, and focuses on the technique rather than on communicating. Used wrongly, the technique fails to help the other person to communicate. If this happens, just let the other party take full control of the content of the conversation. Then gradually reinforce the other's comments by using the "uh-huh" response. Introduce new topical areas through an open question, but refrain from content reflections until they can be worked into the conversation unobtrusively.

Keep in mind that the combination of facial expressions, tone of voice, and body language plays a vital role in support listening.

SOURCE: © Field Enterprises, Inc. 1974. By permission of Johnny Hart and NAS, Inc.

▼ RETENTION LISTENING

In an interview with *U.S. News and World Report,* Lyman K. Steil makes the following points about listening for retention:[1]

1. Because of the listening mistakes of workers (and most make several mistakes each week), letters have to be retyped, appointments rescheduled, and shipments rerouted. Productivity and profits decline.

2. A simple ten-dollar mistake by each of the 100 million workers in the United States would add up to a cost of $1 billion.

3. "Good" or effective listening is more than merely "hearing." Effective listening involves:
   a. hearing;
   b. interpreting (which leads to understanding or misunderstanding);
   c. evaluating (weighing the information and deciding how to use it); and
   d. responding (based on what we heard, understood, and evaluated).

4. When all four stages (hearing, interpreting, evaluating, and responding) are considered, people on average listen at an effective rate of 25 percent.

5. The ability to listen is not an inherent trait; it is learned behavior that has to be taught. Unlike reading, writing, speaking, and many other subjects, however, it is not systematically taught in our schools.

6. People have not been taught to listen well. We spend 80 percent of our waking hours communicating and 45 percent of our communication time listening (with speaking, reading, and writing taking up the other 55 percent). Ironically, our schools devote the greatest amount of time to teaching what we do least: writing. The least amount of teaching time is devoted to what we do most: listening.

7. Listening is more complex than reading. If we misread something or are distracted, we can go back and read it again. But listening

put me in your human eye
come taste
the bitter tears
that i cry
touch me
with your human hand
hear me with your ear
but notice me
damn you
notice me
i'm here
Ric Masten

is transient: "The message is written on the wind. If we don't get it the first time, there usually is no going back."

8. According to a recent study, managers rate listening as the most important competency among the abilities they considered critical for their managerial success. "The higher one advances in management, the more critical listening ability and skill become." Most problems in business arise because management fails to listen.

9. Most people recognize the lack of listening skills in others but consider themselves good listeners. Listening exercises usually demonstrate that people are not as good at listening as they thought they were.

What You Must Do

Steil makes eight points that he feels are extremely important for a manager, or anyone, to operate effectively as a retentive listener.[2]

1. *Resist distractions.* This point emphasizes the importance of concentration. Force yourself to keep your mind on what is being said.

2. *Be an opportunist.* Do your best to find areas of interest between you and the speaker. Ask yourself "What's in this for me? What can I get out of what is being said?"

3. *Stay alert.* It is easy to daydream if the speaker is a bit boring. Force yourself to stay alert even if the speaker is slow and boring. If your thoughts run ahead of the speaker, use the extra time to evaluate, anticipate, and review.

4. *Identify the speaker's purpose and adapt to it.* What is the speaker trying to do? Is the speaker informing, persuading, or entertaining? Whatever the speaker's purpose, identify it and adjust to it.

5. *Listen for central themes, rather than for isolated facts.* Too often, people get hopelessly lost as listeners because they focus in on unimportant facts and details and miss the speaker's main point.

6. *Plan to report the content of a message to someone within eight hours.* This forces the listener to concentrate and to remember. It is a good practice technique.

7. *Develop note-taking skills.* There are many approaches to note taking. Whichever approach you use, the simple process of writing things down as you hear them helps you retain what you hear even if you do not read the notes later.

8. *As a listener, take primary responsibility for the success of two-way communication.* Don't blame the other person for your listening inadequacies. Listening is your responsibility, not the speaker's.

The effective communicator can listen both supportively and retentively. Be aware of both types of listening, and practice the skills presented in this section of this chapter.

After people have developed the skills of effective listening, they must determine if they understand what they have heard. The skill of accurate understanding helps make certain that people understand one another.

▼ ACCURATE UNDERSTANDING

Accurate understanding consists of restating in your own words what the other person's statement means to you. With this sort of restatement, the other person can determine whether the message getting through to you is the one intended.

■ Listening is important, but if you do not understand, who cares?

With understanding, you provide the other person with an indication of how you have interpreted his or her statements and feelings. This technique involves more than just repeating what a person says or saying the other person's ideas in some other way. For example, the following conversation between Sue and Bill demonstrates what happens when you repeat or rephrase *without* repeating what it means to you:

SUE: Business management is really a different program.

BILL: You mean business management is not like other programs?

SUE: Yeah. It sure is an awfully different program.

Bill may feel that he understands about a program in business management, but the understanding is illusory because little if anything was expressed. Instead of merely rephrasing Sue's statement, Bill could have asked himself, "What does Sue's statement mean?" Bill could then restate Sue's comment to reveal his understanding of what it means to him. For example, Bill could have said, "You mean business management is a lot more exciting than other programs?" Sue would then verify whether or not Bill had actually understood her comment as she intended it. If the restatement was not an accurate reflection of what Sue meant, she would probably restate the comment in other terms in an effort to communicate more clearly.

Here is a detailed example of how understanding might proceed:

BOB: Majoring in management is fantastic!

RHEA: You mean that the professors in the management department make their courses exciting?

BOB: Yes, partly at least. But studying about how to get people to better complete their jobs is fun.

RHEA: Then you think that a major in management can prepare people to make a difference in their own lives as well as to help others be more successful on the job?

Accurate understanding is not a gimmick or trick. The technique translates the desire to know what the other person means into a simple procedure for checking the meaning of the other's comment. It is done by a simple restatement of what you understood.

The accurate understanding technique is based on the premise that when an individual expresses an idea, that idea is restated in another way by the listener. The initiator of the statement then clarifies, expands on, or further explores the ideas and feelings embodied in the statement. Often the individual moves on to express a new idea or feeling that is now more meaningful to him or her.

What You Must Do

Focus on the other person; listen carefully (use the support listening responses) to what the person is saying, and how it is being said, to catch both verbal and nonverbal cues to what the other person probably means. Ask yourself, "What does the statement mean to me?"

If the other's statement was general, it might suggest something specific to you:

LES: Mahogany office furniture is the best kind.

DELLA: You mean that mahogany wood takes a more brilliant polish than other kinds.

LES: No, mahogany furniture lasts longer.

On the other hand, if the other person's comment was specific, it may elicit a more general interpretation from you:

JILL: I've got to have thirty sheets of lined notepaper right away.

DAN: Do you mean you need something to write on? I have some plain copier paper.

JILL: That will be fine. Anything on which we can write some notes will do.

Use these guidelines to state your accurate understanding of the other person:

1. Restate the other person's expressed ideas and feelings in your own words.
2. Preface your statements with a tentative introductory phrase, such as one of the following:
   - "Are you saying ..."
   - "You mean that ..."
   - "You feel that ..."
   - "You think that ..."
   - "It seems to you that ..."
   - "It appears to you that ..."
3. Avoid any indication of disapproval or approval: refrain from blaming, expressing rejection or strong support; avoid giving advice or persuading.
4. Wait for the other person's response.
5. Where necessary, paraphrase the other's response to secure the most accurate understanding possible.

After you have listened and are certain that you understand, then in many cases the communication process is complete. However, often you must go beyond listening and understanding. One difficult problem of communicating is knowing how to deal with conflict sit-

SOURCE: © Field Enterprises, Inc. By permission of Johnny Hart and NAS, Inc.

uations. The next section deals with skills for effectively managing communication conflict.

▼ INTERPERSONAL COMMUNICATION CONFLICT

Conflict (a state of disharmony or disagreement between two or more persons) is a normal part of our daily lives, at home, at school, or on the job. According to researchers Gerald R. Miller and Mark Steinberg, the three major types of interpersonal conflict are simple conflict, pseudoconflict, and ego conflict.

■ What is interpersonal conflict?

Conflict is almost always associated with communication behavior and is usually prevented, resolved, or alleviated through the use of some type of communication technique. An effective communication conflict-managing technique uses responses that reduce the frequency and likelihood of caustic, angry, defensive, and sarcastic reactions that lead to or aggravate conflict. It allows people to see all sides of a conflict situation and to integrate what they see into their perceptions. This technique involves three response approaches that specifically address the three major types of conflict.[3]

Simple conflict arises when two people or two groups of people know each other's goals but neither side can attain its personal desires without blocking the goal of the other person or group. The *communication conflict-managing approach* is a method of controlling and possibly overcoming simple conflict by using response approaches that keep the conflict simple, that delay the interaction, and that cast the conflict in a mutual noncompetitive frame.

Pseudoconflict may result through ineffective communication. People who agree on an issue but who are unable to communicate their agreement assume they disagree. Your boss wants you to complete the Harper report tomorrow, and you want to complete the Harper report tomorrow; however, from your boss's attitude, you believe she wants you to spend the day tomorrow doing research. Thus, pseudoconflict takes place. The *pseudoconflict-managing approach* is a method of eliminating distortions in communications.

■ What is pseudoconflict?

Ego conflict occurs when people become emotionally involved to the point that there is some threat to their egos. Ego conflicts bring

Conflict is a normal part of life.

What is ego conflict?

people to the point of saving face at any cost by putting others down in order to protect themselves. The *ego conflict-managing approach* is to (1) focus on relevant and factual matters (as opposed to extraneous matters and conclusions), (2) encourage the other person to focus on relevant and factual matters, and then (3) quit talking and let the other person describe the conflict and the reasons for its occurrence.

The communication conflict-managing technique is intended to help people manage their defensive responses so that they build relationships, rather than hinder them. For example, suppose that you want to go to Disneyworld for a vacation, but your spouse wants to visit his or her mother in Oklahoma. You cannot afford to do both, so you may be in a simple-conflict situation. Depending on your relationship, you may or may not get involved in conflict, but the potential exists. The simple conflict-managing approach would work well in this situation, because it allows you to keep the conflict from escalating to the ego conflict stage, and it provides you with responses that can keep the conflict from ever occurring. A possible response might be "It is obvious that we cannot go to both places. Why don't we take a day or so and try to see each other's point of view and then try to make a decision?"

If the conflict escalates beyond the simple conflict stage and in fact becomes a pseudoconflict, the pseudoconflict-managing approach helps the two people realize that they do not have a con-

SOURCE: © Field Enterprises, Inc. By permission of Johnny Hart and NAS, Inc.

flict. A possible response might be "We both want to see your mother, and we both want to take the kids to Disneyworld. Why don't we invite her to go with us?" Conflicts often escalate as people become ego involved with the topics at hand. The ego conflict-managing approach can help to cool off this kind of situation.

The technique of managing communication conflict is based on the notion that conflict is inevitable and that no relationship can expect to be totally free of it. To completely eliminate conflict is impossible. Therefore, it must be managed so that relationships can be continued.

Through conflict, we sometimes learn important things about ourselves, significant others, and how we relate to one another. Conflict is not necessarily destructive as long as we treat people with respect and honestly try to control the conflict. This technique does not offer specific solutions to specific conflicts, but it does suggest some general approaches to problems of conflict. The technique will work when you treat people as they should be treated.

■ Conflict can have positive effects.

In the simple conflict-managing approach, you treat people well by speaking openly and frankly, by not letting your perceptions get in the way of how you relate to others, and by treating both the person and the idea as being equal to you and your ideas.

In the pseudoconflict-managing approach, you treat people well by eliminating the distortions that have occurred between you and the others. This can be done by asking for clarification and by presenting your understanding of the other.

In the ego conflict-managing approach, you treat people well by not letting your own ego push you to respond in negative terms, by letting the other speak his or her piece, and by helping to describe the conflict that exists between the two of you.

What You Must Do

■ Three assumptions
are made regarding
conflict.

The technique of managing communication conflict includes (1) understanding the three major assumptions about interpersonal conflict, (2) being aware of the possible outcomes of conflict management, (3) selecting the form of interpersonal conflict in which you are involved, and (4) using the proper conflict-managing approach to keep the conflict from causing problems or escalating.

To be able to minimize problems associated with conflict and to maximize the value associated with conflict, be aware of the following three assumptions. These will guide you in effectively using any of the three approaches proposed for managing conflict.

1. *Conflict is inevitable.* Keep in mind that people cannot be together without experiencing conflict situations. It is natural for conflict to occur.

2. *Conflict is not a dirty word.* When conflict occurs, it is not a sign that those involved are bad people or that they are less worthwhile as members of our society. On the other hand, conflict can be extremely important and beneficial to relationships.

3. *Conflict arises for many reasons and takes many forms.* Although three approaches to handling conflict are suggested, there are many reasons for people getting involved in conflict and many ways that this conflict can manifest itself. The key is your ability to recognize differences in situations and to adjust your conflict-management approach to the specific conflict.

■ Conflict has at least
five possible out-
comes.

Conflict has many possible outcomes, and they all require different approaches for effective management. To be effective in managing conflict, be aware of at least the following five possible outcomes:

1. *Discontinuing the relationship.* If any given conflict gets too severe and the participants cannot manage it effectively, there is a tendency to give up on the relationship.

2. *Suffering through the relationship.* Because some people are unable to discontinue a relationship, they simply suffer through hoping the relationship will get better without managing it.

3. *Dampening the conflict.* This is a type of conflict managing. Those in conflict thus reduce the pain of the conflict by avoiding it temporarily, but the conflict still exists.

4. *Resolving the conflict.* In simple conflict situations, people are usually able to resolve their problems. They do this by communicating effectively. They use listening and understanding skills.

5. *Managing the conflict.* Occasionally people can manage and handle conflict in a very effective manner. The three approaches presented next identify the skills necessary to manage conflict.

The three approaches to communication conflict are linked to the three forms of conflict discussed previously.

MANAGING SIMPLE CONFLICT

1. *Keep the conflict simple.* Do not let the conflict become pseudo-conflict or ego conflict. Try your best to prevent misunderstand-

Communicating effectively resolves conflicts.

ings, and do not attack the other's pride or ego. Try to state the misunderstanding as clearly as possible. For example, say, "Is the issue here to determine which color of carpet we want? I want dark brown and you want light brown." Try not to use emotional language or attack the other person. For example, do *not* say, "Let's get this clear! The issue seems to be to determine which crummy color of carpet you want. I want a rich dark brown, and for some stupid reason you want an ugly light brown!" Keep the conflict simple by using nonthreatening language and stating the problems as clearly as possible.

2. *Wait a while.* If tensions are beginning to build and you can put off making a decision, let the issue drop for a while. While waiting, analyze your reasons for the point of view you have selected. Perhaps a solution that neither of you thought of will materialize. You might say, at a later time, "I'm glad we selected pink carpet."

3. *Face the problems together.* Do not compete with one another but try to work together as a team. Mutually agree that the outcome of the situation will affect both of you. Try to work together to solve your problem. Nothing stifles problem solving more than a dictatorial approach from one or both sides of a conflict. Work together.

"God grant me the strength to accept the things I cannot change, the courage to change the things I can, and the wisdom to tell the difference."
Serenity Prayer

MANAGING PSEUDOCONFLICT

1. *Verify that the pseudoconflict exists.* The problem in dealing with pseudoconflict is that you do not know it exists. Check the other's perceptions of what is going on, and review in your own mind if something is wrong. Have you done anything to alienate the other? This leads to the second step.

2. *Ask for clarification.* The second step is simple. Ask the other person to help you by telling you what has happened. You might ask, "What do you mean by that?" or "What is on your mind?"

The idea is to get the other to talk and to explain what the pseudoconflict is. This allows for the correction of both sets of perceptions concerning the conflict.

Managing Ego Conflict

■ Communication conflict can be reduced if you never miss an opportunity to keep your mouth shut.

1. *Never miss an opportunity to keep your mouth shut.* When people let their egos get involved in an interaction, they put up barriers to cooperative communication. To manage ego conflicts, lower those barriers. You can bring down barriers by allowing people to express their relevant concerns. However, be careful not to allow these expressions of concern to escalate or cause further problems of conflict. Therefore, let the person speak, but then restrict the person from saying more than necessary.

2. *Do not explain the conflict; instead, describe it.* When the people in conflict are able to talk to each other, have them describe the conflict as best they can. Try not to explain what happened from any point of view; simply describe what happened. Do not allow competition to enter into the descriptions of the conflict.

3. *Determine the sources of conflict.* After you have agreed about what caused the conflict by describing it, then you can begin to determine what the sources of the conflict were. If you can get to this point, you will most likely be able to manage ego conflict. However, getting to this point is extremely difficult in ego conflict situations.

▼ Summary of Key Ideas

■ Effective listening is a two-part process requiring support listening and retention listening.

■ Steil's eight points that aid the retentive listener are: resist distractions, be an opportunist, stay alert, identify and adapt to the speaker's purpose, listen for central themes, plan to report the content of a message within eight hours, develop note-taking skills, and take the primary responsibility for the success of two-way communication.

■ When stating your understanding of a communication, use the following guidelines: restate in your own words, use an introductory phrase, avoid indication of approval or disapproval, wait for the other person's response, and paraphrase when appropriate.

■ The three approaches that constitute the communication conflict technique are: simple conflict, pseudoconflict, and ego conflict. The management techniques used to deal with them will differ depending on the type of conflict.

■ The three assumptions one should remember concerning conflict are that conflict is inevitable, is not necessarily harmful, and arises for many reasons and takes many forms.

■ The five possible outcomes of conflict are: discontinuing the relationship, suffering through the relationship, dampening the conflict, resolving the conflict, and managing the conflict.

▼ KEY TERMS, CONCEPTS, AND NAMES

Accurate understanding
Communication conflict
Content reflection
Effective listening
Ego conflict
Simple conflict
Lyman K. Steil

Interpersonal communication
Managing conflict
Open questions
Pseudoconflict
Retention listening
Support listening
"Uh-huh" technique

▼ QUESTIONS AND EXERCISES

1. Give an example of where and when you might use support listening, and explain how it can help you communicate more effectively.

2. Answer the introductory questions at the beginning of the chapter.

3. Read each of the following statements, and then write a content reflection and an open question for each. Check your answers with a friend to make certain you are responding appropriately.

   a. "Look, we have been having considerable success with this method. Why should we gamble and make a change in critical times like these?"

   b. "Gosh, I think your ideas are terrific. But to tell you the truth, my boss just can't see something new like this. I just don't think he would buy it."

4. In the following dialogues, identify the type of conflict and then structure an appropriate way to manage the conflict:

   a. JOHN: I think this organization stinks. You are a poor manager. In fact, I have an eight-year-old sister who can handle people better than you can.

      BILL: This is a good organization. I can't for the life of me understand why you feel this way. No one else feels this way. Several feel this is the best organization they have worked for.

   b. JOHN: I think you should give me a raise for each good idea I have given this firm.

      BILL: I never give raises for doing your normal job. You were hired to give good ideas.

▼ NOTES

1. Lyman K. Steil, interview with *U.S. News and World Report.* Copyright, May 26, 1980, *U.S. News and World Report.*

2. Ibid.

3. Gerald R. Miller and Mark Steinberg, *Between People: A New Analysis of Interpersonal Communication* (Chicago: Science Research Associates, 1975), pp. 260–70.

ANOTHER LOOK: THE EFFECTS OF [ORGANIZATIONAL] COMMUNICATION SYSTEMS ON MESSAGE CONTENT

"Why can't people get things straight?" How frequently has this question been asked silently or out loud in an organization? Probably as often as employees get together to discuss problems with the boss, or bosses talk about misunderstandings with employees. Routine person-to-person communication is subject to a multitude of pitfalls and processes that have detrimental effects on understanding. Many of the problems stem from the way in which human beings process information. Other sources of misunderstanding are a function of the system by which messages are distributed throughout an organization. Organizational communication is subject to not only the maladies of interpersonal interaction but also to the anomalies of relaying messages through human links in a communication system.

PERSONAL FACTORS THAT DISTORT MESSAGES

We shall discuss a number of principles that reflect personal factors that contribute to the distortion of messages. These factors issue naturally from our concept of communication as the act and process of assigning meaning to displays. A display is anything that activates one of our senses—seeing, hearing, tasting, smelling, feeling. At any moment we are bombarded by a limitless variety of displays originating from inside ourselves as well as

from outside. Hence the first factor that contributes to the distortion of messages is related to our perception of displays.

Principle 1: People Perceive Things Selectively   Our sensory receptors—eyes, ears, fingers, noses, tongues—are physically limited so that they can respond to only a few of the stimuli impinging upon them. Each of us responds to those sensations that get past our natural barriers or limitations, that seem most pertinent to our situation, and that are consistent with our own personal preferences and perspectives. The fidelity, or accuracy, of information is limited by the selective perceptions we make.

Principle 2: People See Things Consistent with What They Believe   Our perceptions are affected by the way we talk about people, things, and events. What we believe changes our perceptions. If we expect to see a friend react in a negative way to a suggestion, we shall no doubt perceive him or her to react negatively. This is sometimes called the *Pygmalion effect*. If we believe that people are very smart and intelligent, we will tend to see their behavior as consistent with our belief. On the other hand, if other people see that we expect great things from them, they will try to behave

consistently with our expectations.

Principle 3: Language Itself Is Inaccurate   Our perceptions of people, things, and events never correspond exactly to reality because we selectively see them and because we tend to see what we believe about people, things, and events. In communicating we use language to represent our perceptions. Our talking involves language that is supposed to portray or describe that about which we are talking. It is through language that we make our private perceptions somewhat public so that others may get some idea of what we mean. Language does not diminish the importance of nonlanguage. Nonverbal signals clue others in to what we mean. In fact, we shall talk more about them later. Nevertheless, we must not lose sight of the basic principle that language symbols do not accurately represent what a person means.

Principle 4: The Meaning of a Message Occurs at Both Content and Relational Levels   A message consists of both verbal or language (oral and written) and nonverbal or nonlanguage (aural and pictorial) symbols. What a person says and how a person behaves combine to make a message-display. Each message can be analyzed at a *content* or

ANOTHER LOOK *continued*

denotative level and at a *relational* or interpretive level....

The content, or denotative, level of meaning concerns the ideas, things, people, events, and happenings to which the message literally refers. You are functioning at the content level when you respond to the information of the message—that is, when you respond to the ideas, attitudes, opinions, and facts referred to by the message, you are dealing with the message at the content level.

The relational, or interpretive, level of meaning concerns how the message is to be taken, for example, lightly or seriously. When you say, "Smile when you say that," you are dealing at the relational level because your comment tells the other person how to interpret the message and what kind of relationship you are to have. The relational level indicates how the information and the relationship is to be understood. Your attitudes toward other people are expressions at the relational level.

Principle 5: Distortions Are Encouraged by Inconsistencies between Verbal and Nonverbal Aspects of a Message A basic axiom of communication theory is that *a person cannot not behave.* Thus as [W. Charles] Redding and [George A.] Sanborn ... have concluded, "Communication is always going on, then, whether one desires it or

not—so long as there is someone to interpret what we say, or fail to say, or do, or fail to do".... It has been estimated that in a conversation involving two people, verbal aspects of a message account for less than 35 percent of the social meaning whereas nonverbal aspects of a message account for 65 percent of the social meaning. On the other hand, [Albert] Mehrabian ... states that "a person's nonverbal behavior has more bearing than his words on communicating feelings or attitudes to others".... He estimates that 7 percent of the total feeling is derived from verbal aspects, 38 percent from vocal aspects, and 55 percent from facial aspects, resulting in 93 percent of the feeling communicated being based on nonverbal features.

Principle 6: Message Ambiguity Often Leads to Distortions *Ambiguity* may be defined as some degree of uncertainty associated with information or actions. If a statement you make seems ambiguous to me, that means that I am uncertain how to take what you say. There are three types of ambiguity that may occur in communication: ambiguity of meaning, ambiguity of intent, and ambiguity of effect....

Ambiguity of meaning concerns the uncertainty of predicting what the originator of a message means. To the extent that you cannot

readily and efficiently determine what a person meant when he or she said or wrote a message, the message will have a degree of ambiguity for you. The greater the ambiguity of meaning, the greater the difficulty you will have in comprehending the message.

Ambiguity of intent concerns the uncertainty of predicting why the originator of a message said or wrote this particular message to you at this particular time in this particular way and under these particular conditions. To the extent that you cannot figure out why the person is communicating with you, the message will be ambiguous to you. For example, suppose you go home and find a note pinned to your bedroom curtain with this message on it: "The president of the university called and wants to talk to you tomorrow morning." Why would the president want to talk to you? What does he or she want? The degree to which you are unable to answer such questions indicates how ambiguous the intent of the message is to you.

Ambiguity of effect concerns the uncertainty of predicting what the consequences of responding to a message might be. You may accurately interpret the meaning of the note about the president's request for a meeting—the president wants you to arrive at his or her office in the morning; you may even predict his or

ANOTHER LOOK: THE EFFECTS OF [ORGANIZATIONAL] COMMUNICATION SYSTEMS ON MESSAGE CONTENT *continued*

her intent fairly accurately—to talk to you about your standing in the university; however, what will be the effect or consequence of understanding the message, arriving at the president's office, and engaging in a conversation about your standing in the university? Of course, nothing may come of it; on the other hand, what might be some possible consequences? The extent to which some of these questions have unclear answers is the extent to which the message involves ambiguity of effect.

Principle 7: Memory Propensities Toward Sharpening and Leveling Details Encourage Distortion to Occur　Some evidence suggests that people may have some patterns associated with their memory systems that lead to distortions in verbal communication. [P.S.] Holzman and [R.W.] Gardner ... developed a schematizing test that differentiated between *levelers* and *sharpeners.* Individuals who are levelers had fewer correct memories of an incident or story and tended to show more loss and modification of the overall structure of the story than did those who were sharpeners. Gardner and [L.J.] Lohrenz demonstrated that the serial reproduction of a story underwent different fates when transmitted through separate chains of levelers and

sharpeners. Levelers lost more themes, lost more of the overall story, and showed increasingly more fragmented messages than did sharpeners. A person may be structured toward leveling information or toward sharpening information. A propensity toward stripping away the details in a verbal message is called *skeletonizing* ..., and a propensity toward the invention of details is called *importing.* Each of us may have a memory propensity that leads toward leveling, stripping away, or skeletonizing details in messages or a memory propensity that leads toward sharpening, inventing, or importing details into messages. In either case a memory propensity may contribute to distortions and lack of fidelity in communication.

Principle 8: Motivational Factors May Encourage Message Distortions　Three basic motivational factors tend to produce changes in messages that result in lack of fidelity: attitudes toward the message content; desires, self-interest, and motives of communicators; and attitudes of intended receivers.

1. *Attitudes toward the message content.* A study by [W.] Johnson and [C.B.] Wood ... demonstrated that subjects who held positive attitudes toward a racial minority tend to "abstract" the positive information

about them from a passage containing both positive and negative information; on the other hand, a subject who had negative attitudes tended to abstract negative information from the same passage. The tendency for communicators to distort information in a message according to their attitudes seems to be well supported by other research....

2. *Desires, self-interest, and motives of communicators.* [Jay M.] Jackson ... suggested that people in organizations communicate or fail to communicate with others in order to accomplish some goal, satisfy a personal need, or improve their immediate situation. [Anthony] Downs ... identified four major biases that produce distortions in the communication of officials in bureaucracies: (1) They tend to distort information by exaggerating data that reflect favorably on themselves and to minimize data that reveal their shortcomings. (2) They tend to prefer policies that advance their own interests and the programs they advocate and to reject those that injure or fail to advance their interests. (3) They tend to comply with directives from superiors that favor their own interests and drag their feet or ignore those that do not. (4) They tend to take on additional work if it is directly beneficial to their own goals and avoid work that weakens their ability to achieve their own goals. [William V.] Haney ...

ANOTHER LOOK *continued*

described three motives that encourage distortions to develop in messages: (1) The desire to convey simple messages. The communication of complex information is difficult and psychologically taxing on the individual; thus organization members tend to simplify messages before or as they pass the information along. (2) The desire to convey a "sensible" message. When a person receives a message that doesn't seem to make sense, the desire is to make sense out of it before passing it along. Most of us tend to avoid sending along messages that seem illogical, incomplete, or incoherent. (3) The desire to make message sending as pleasant (or at least as painless) as possible for the sender. Organization members tend to avoid conveying messages that are painful for them. Instead they make changes that soften the message and make it less painful.

3. *Attitudes of intended receivers.* There is evidence to support the idea that the initiator of a message will tend to distort it in the direction of the announced attitude of whoever is to receive the message. This may be a subcategory of motivational factors, since expressing ideas contrary to those held by an intended receiver may be potentially painful.

ORGANIZATIONAL FACTORS THAT DISTORT MESSAGES

Characteristics of organizations themselves tend to encourage distortions to occur in messages. We shall briefly review a number of organizational factors that contribute to message distortion in organizational communication.

1. *Occupying a position in an organization influences the way a person communicates.* By becoming a functioning member of an organization who occupies a position with duties and authority assigned to it, an individual acquires a point of view, a value system, and develops expectations and limitations that are different from a person who holds a different position or is a member of a different organization entirely. A supervisor, for example, is compelled at times to look at the functioning of the organization differently from subordinates. The supervisor must react to production problems somewhat differently from the way a particular subordinate might react to them. In fact, a supervisor must think about the organization in a different way. The person within the organization sees its operations differently from an outsider. Each position in an organization demands that the person who occupies it must perceive and communicate about things from the perspective of the position. Occupying a position tends to contribute to distortions in organizational communication messages....

2. *Hierarchical—superior-subordinate—relationships influence the way in which a person communicates.* The arrangement of positions in hierarchical fashion suggests to those who occupy the positions that one set of individuals is "superior" and another set is "subordinate." The fundamental difference is one of perceived status. People and positions located higher in the hierarchy have greater control over the lives of those who are located lower in the organization. Lower-downs find it desirable to be cautious in communicating with higher-ups. Information may be distorted because a subordinate is careful to talk about things that his or her superior is interested in hearing and to avoid topics and ways of saying things that are sensitive to the boss. The superior, on the other hand, would not wish to discuss things that tend to undermine his or her position in the organization by reflecting negatively on his or her competence and decision-making abilities. Even between friends, hierarchical relationships affect what can be discussed and the way in which things can be discussed....

3. *Restrictions in who may communicate with whom and who may make decisions influence the way in which a person communicates.* Coordination of activities and the flow of information in an organization require some centralization of decision making. To avoid having members of the organization going in too many different directions,

ANOTHER LOOK: THE EFFECTS OF [ORGANIZATIONAL] COMMUNICATION SYSTEMS ON MESSAGE CONTENT *continued*

making contradictory decisions, and having imbalances in work loads, an organization is structured so that certain decisions are made by a limited number of individuals. We have referred to them in different ways—as liaisons, gatekeepers, people in authority, decision makers, or superiors—but in nearly all cases those individuals get information from a variety of others within and without the organization. When central decision makers receive too much information too fast or have too many decisions to make too quickly, distortions are likely to occur as a result of *overload.*

4. *Impersonalization of organizational relationships influences the way in which a person communicates.* One fundamental characteristic of formal organizations is that relationships are to be formal and impersonal. The impersonalization of relationships leads to the suppression of emotional messages. In order to hide or disown emotional expressions, individuals develop ways of keeping others from expressing their emotions. Eventually organization members avoid or refuse to consider ideas that might allow or encourage the release of feelings. The consequence, in the long run at least, is a lessened awareness of the impact of a person's feelings on others and an inability to predict accurately the emotional reactions of others. Ultimately the organization is comprised of

individuals who cannot communicate their feelings and who substitute rules for solving problems.

5. *The system of rules, policies, and regulations governing thoughts and actions influences the way in which a person communicates.* As a philosophy of impersonal relationships encourages the development of a system of rules that substitutes for authentic problem solving, so the characteristic of having general but definite policies for guiding decisions leads to impersonal relationships. A rigid application of rules and policies to behavior and decisions leads to an inability to make compromises and fosters impersonality and lack of emotional communication. Rules encourage the evolution of rigid, routine, and traditional patterns of communicating. Institutionalization of behavior is the consequence, with remote and distant, rather than face-to-face, interpersonal communication. Positional relationships are reinforced, and interpersonal relationships are discouraged. Information and messages may be distorted to accommodate the rules and maintain impersonality.

6. *Task specialization narrows a person's perceptions and influences the way in which a person communicates.* Although specialization has contributed immensely to national productivity by increasing efficiency, it is also the source of many communication

problems. Individuals identify with their own areas of expertise, learn entire vocabularies unknown to other employees, and often fail to integrate their efforts with other departments. The result is often a bottleneck in the flow of information or a great deal of "buck passing" from one person to another because the client's problem is not in the employee's area of specialization. To some extent specialization fosters conflicts through competition for resources to accomplish narrow objectives. Although competition may help keep employees functioning with alertness, it may lead very quickly to destructive relationships and dysfunctional communication. Specialization may be the source of much of the message distortion that occurs in organizations. Task specialization leads to what some called *trained incapacity,* or a limited ability to perform general organizational functions. Accompanying an incapacity to do varied tasks is the inability to perceive the total picture and act for the good of colleagues and the organization. Such limited perspectives reduce a person's ability to comprehend other's problems, resulting in lower levels of empathy. Without empathy, understanding may be diminished and distortion increased.

ANTIDISTORTION FACTORS

Messages in every organization are subject to a degree of distortion, but formal organi-

ANOTHER LOOK *continued*

zations also have forces that limit the amount of distortion that occurs in communication. Although the antidistortion forces may reduce the level of distortion below that implied by the lengthy list of personal and organizational factors contributing to distortion, they do not entirely eliminate distortion. Downs ... lists four general ways in which organization members attempt to increase the fidelity of information communicated in an organization.

1. *Establish more than one channel of communication.* When an employee (manager or operative) believes that information he or she is receiving may be distorted, one way to counter the distortion is to verify the information through multiple sources of messages.

2. *Develop procedures for counterbalancing distortions.* If we assume that those who work in organizations realize that personal and organizational factors produce distortions, then those who receive information can routinely adjust reports to counteract the distortions contained in them. To the extent that a manager, for example, has accurately identified the distortions, he or she can adjust the information more closely to the original design. When counterbalancing procedures are used throughout the organization, as they tend to be, much of the cumulative effect of personal and organizational distortion factors tends to be reduced. The main distorting effect will be the inaccurate estimate of the source and degree of distortion in the information.

3. *Eliminate the intermediary between the decision maker and those who provide information.* This can be done by maintaining a basically flat organization structure.

4. *Develop distortion-proof measures.* One way to reduce distortion is to create message systems that cannot be altered in meaning during transmission, except through direct falsification. To be distortion-proof, a message must be able to be transmitted without condensation or expansion (skeletonizing or importing) between the source and the terminating point. Obviously only a very small proportion of all messages directed to any individual in an organization can be distortion-proof. Nevertheless, carefully prepared codes and easily quantifiable information may represent messages that are less subject to distortion through selective omission of qualifiers, shifts in emphasis, ambiguous terminology, and other perceptual and language factors that affect many messages.

SOURCE: Excerpted from R. Wayne Pace and Don F. Faules, *Organizational Communication*, 2nd ed. (Englewood Cliffs, NJ: Prentice-Hall, 1989), pp. 148–165. ;

ANOTHER LOOK: FAILURE TO COMMUNICATE CAN DISGRUNTLE WORKERS

All good, effective communication involves understanding the other person and really focusing on the needs of the other party. Focus on what might they be thinking; how they might take this memo or this promotion; what will their attitude be. Sherron Kenton

Maybe it's a disappointing pay raise, or a transfer into an office with an inferior view, or the comparison between your scarred furniture and the new office suite given to your colleague, but *something* has you convinced that life just isn't fair.

When employees start feeling that they are treated unfairly, the business may end up suffering, according to Sherron Kenton, an Emory University School of Business professor who has recently completed a research paper entitled "Communication: A Means of Deterring Retaliation in

ANOTHER LOOK: FAILURE TO COMMUNICATE CAN DISGRUNTLE WORKERS *continued*

the Workplace."

The first and easiest response for employees who feel discriminated against is to talk themselves out of it, Ms. Kenton said. However, if they can't get rid of the nagging feeling that they are being mistreated, they may try to equalize what they perceive as an unfair situation. Work may become sloppy, or expense accounts may be misrepresented, she noted, adding that management begins noticing that the employee just isn't putting his heart into his work anymore.

Ms. Kenton said that after extensive research, she found that careful communication is the key to preventing the deliberate inefficiency of angry workers.

It may sound simple, but many managers don't take the time to explain decisions to employees. "They think: 'Why should I tell you? You work for me—I'm the boss,'" she explained.

Even when intentions are the best, management often mistakenly assumes that employees understand their decisions, she said, citing as an example, a company's transferring an executive to a desirable city and assuming that the executive will interpret the move as an award.

However, according to Ms. Kenton, the employee may feel that management is displeased with his performance and intent on getting rid of him.

"We don't think about other people," she said. "All good, effective communication involves understanding the other person and really focusing on the needs of the other party. Focus on what might they be thinking; how they might take this memo or this promotion; what will their attitude be."

If extra work is necessary or if pay raises can't meet expectations, it's necessary to explain "the big picture," Ms. Kenton said. Management decisions are easier to accept if employees understand why a policy was set and how it may pay off in the future.

It's always better to prepare employees in advance for changes or problems that will be coming up, she added, saying, "Knowing in advance is always better than after the fact."

However, even the most communicative manager can't have complete control over a worker's perception of fairness. Ms. Kenton's search of social psychology literature found that gender often affects how people react to perceived inequity.

Because of early socialization, women can often handle unfairness better than men, Ms. Kenton said. Women tend to assume the blame for problems rather than reacting against the organization, whereas men tend to address inequity more readily, she said.

The literature also indicated that women are often more concerned about the status of long-term relationships than men and are less likely to focus on a quick resolution of immediate issues.

SOURCE: Lisa Crowe, "Failure to Communicate Can Disgruntle Workers, Emory Professor Warns," Business Monday Section *Atlanta Journal— Constitution,* 3 November 1986.

▼ A CASE IN POINT: A HOT TRAVELER AND A HOT MOTEL MANAGER

THE MOTEL MANAGER'S STORY

A fellow from a city several hundred miles away has just checked into your motel. He gives the impression that he is a big-shot government worker. After a short visit to his room, he storms into your office, claiming his air conditioner is faulty. You have recently spent seventy-five dollars to repair the unit in his room. You are certain that he must have banged it with his fist and that he is responsible for the trouble with the unit. You are not about to let him push you around.

THE TRAVELER'S STORY

You have just settled into a rather dumpy motel. It is mid-August, and the temperature is 109 degrees. You flip on the switch to the air conditioner; there is a buzz, a hum, and smoke starts to pour out of the vents of the air conditioner. After several bangs with your fist, the smoke vanishes, but the air conditioner will not work. You are hot and tired, and wish you had selected a finer motel. At that point, you storm into the motel manager's office, inform him that he mans a cheap, dumpy, and poorly cared for motel. You demand that he rush immediately to your room and repair your air conditioner.

QUESTIONS

1. What would you recommend be done by the traveler and the motel manager using the skills and techniques presented in this chapter?
2. What could the traveler do to solve his problem and also be a good communicator?
3. What could the motel manager do to reduce the conflict?

COMMUNICATING IN SMALL GROUPS: EFFECTIVE TEAMWORK IN ORGANIZATIONS

This chapter answers several all-important questions:

■ What makes a good leader in a small group?

■ Why is involvement of all group members so important for the success of a group?

■ Why are cohesiveness and conformity important for a group to function effectively?

■ What are the five steps of problem solving?

■ How does one structure a group?

■ What is the brainstorming approach, and when is it used?

■ What are the four rules of brainstorming?

■ What is the nominal group process?

■ How can criteria help in the decision-making process?

■ How does one state a criterion?

The answers to these and other questions are coming up next in chapter 12....

CHAPTER 12

The use of groups to solve problems is so widespread that most people have questions about how to make group processes more effective. They want to know how to improve group action, how to make leadership more meaningful, and how to get people to work together.

The first characteristic of problem-solving groups is that they focus on tasks—they want to find a solution to a problem. The individuals involved come together to work toward the accomplishment of a task. A typical problem-solving group is a work team in an organization.

The second characteristic of problem-solving groups is that the individual members communicate face-to-face. George C. Homan's definition of a group reveals the essential features of what we mean by a small group: "A number of persons who communicate with one another often over a span of time and who are few enough so that each person is able to communicate with all the others, not at second hand, through other people, but face-to-face."[1]

The combination of the preceding characteristics yields a definition of a small problem-solving group: "Several people, but in small enough numbers to permit communication with all other members, who are assembled face-to-face for the purpose of solving a problem."[2] Small-group communication takes place in a variety of forms and is known by different names. For example, people often talk about committees, teams, panels, conferences, boards, and councils. At the university, committees are appointed; in a government agency, teams are created; in a research foundation, panels are appointed; in a union organization, conferences are called. In all these settings, these small groups are assigned to work at solving a problem.

In this chapter, we focus on how to make group teamwork effective by discussing some general characteristics of groups and by presenting procedures for effective problem solving by groups.

▼ GENERAL CHARACTERISTICS OF GROUPS

Because principles of communication discussed in the previous two chapters apply equally well to interpersonal communication in small groups, we focus attention in this chapter on five basic characteristics of small groups that help explain the behavior of people in small groups. Those characteristics are group leader attitudes, leader behaviors, communication patterns, communication climate, and cohesiveness. Regardless of the group's agenda, or content issues, all small groups have universal process issues.

Leader Attitudes

Leadership in groups or work teams is not always a formally delegated authority. Nevertheless, for groups to excel, especially in problem-solving tasks, the leaders must have seven characteristics:

1. *Trust* in the other group members, regardless of their rank or

leader *n.* a person who makes an important decision,

then sits back,

and answers stupid questions for the rest of his life.

B.C. by permission of Johnny Hart and Field Enterprises, Inc.

position. You can't expect others to go all out for you if they think you don't believe in them.

2. *A vision of what is possible.* Generally, the most profitable vision is the long-term view. Sometimes a quick fix is needed, but the long-term ramifications of a group's efforts must be anticipated by the leader.

3. *A cool head* to deal with difficult, often exasperating pressures and conflicts of opinion in a rational, objective manner.

4. *A willingness to encourage risk.* Nothing discourages group members like the feeling that if they fail in any way, disaster will result. People need the latitude to fail and learn from their mistakes.

5. *Expertise.* Leaders need to know what they are talking about or be willing to learn. Such learning can come from often unpredictable sources.

6. *An openness to dissent.* Group members cannot contribute fully if they cannot speak up. Encourage differing points of view, even when they may be unpopular or poorly expressed.

7. *An ability to simplify* all that has been said into a concise plan of action. You need to see the big picture in order to set a course, communicate it, and maintain it. Don't get tangled in details; keep it simple.[3]

Leader Behaviors

Leadership consists of behaviors that keep a group together and working to solve a problem. Group members' behaviors can be grouped into *roles.* A *role* is the pattern that characterizes an individual's contributions to the group. That is, what an individual does and says in a group can be thought of as either a contribution to or distraction from the functioning of the group.

■ Effective group leaders are people who act like leaders.

People often talk about the role a person is playing in a group. Leadership consists of performing roles that keep a group together and working on a task. So leadership is a combination of roles that are taken by members of a group. Kenneth D. Benne and Paul Sheats compiled a list of *functional roles* of group members that help the group accomplish its task, that promote and maintain group member relationships, and that help meet individuals' needs, although they may on occasion distract from either or both the task and the main-

A strategy meeting in casual-culture office.

tenance goals.[4] Some of the major roles that group members may perform are listed here. Keep in mind that leadership behaviors should contribute to task and maintenance goals.

TASK ROLES: CONTRIBUTE TO SOLVING THE PROBLEM, PERFORMING THE TASK

1. *Initiating.* Suggesting methods, goals, and procedures; starting the group moving in a positive direction by proposing a plan.
2. *Information seeking.* Soliciting ideas, data, personal experiences, and reports.
3. *Information giving.* Offering ideas, data, personal experiences, and factual statements.
4. *Opinion seeking.* Asking for statements of belief, convictions, values, or expressions of feeling.
5. *Opinion giving.* Stating own beliefs, convictions, values, and feelings.
6. *Clarifying.* Interpreting issues, elaborating on ideas expressed by others, giving examples or illustrations.
7. *Coordinating.* Demonstrating relationships between ideas, restating ideas, summarizing, and offering integrated statements for consideration.
8. *Energizing.* Prodding group to greater activity, stimulating others to action.
9. *Procedure developing.* Handling such tasks as making seating arrangements, running the projector, passing out papers.
10. *Recording.* Keeping written record of meeting on paper, recording ideas on chart or chalkboard.

MAINTENANCE ROLES: CONTRIBUTE TO MEMBER SATISFACTION

1. *Supporting.* Praising, expressing warmth, indicating solidarity.
2. *Harmonizing.* Mediating differences among others, conciliating.

3. *Following.* Listening to others, going along, accepting group decisions.

4. *Tension relieving.* Introducing humor, joking, relaxing others, diverting attention from tense situations.

5. *Gatekeeping.* Facilitating participation of everyone in group, bringing in members who might not speak, preventing dominance by one or two members, maintaining permissive atmosphere.

PERSONAL ROLES: MEETING INDIVIDUAL NEEDS AT THE EXPENSE OF THE GROUP

1. *Blocking.* Constantly raising objections, insisting nothing can be done, introducing irrelevant digression.

2. *Aggressing.* Deflating status of others, expressing disapproval and ill will.

3. *Recognition seeking.* Boasting, calling attention to self, seeking sympathy or pity, claiming credit for ideas.

4. *Confessing.* Engaging in personal catharsis and using group as audience for mistakes.

5. *Clowning.* Diverting attention of group to tangents, engaging in horseplay and ridicule, disrupting with cynical comments.

6. *Dominating.* Giving directions, ordering people, interrupting, and insisting on own way.

7. *Special-interest pleading.* Supporting personal projects and interests, pressing others for support, acting as representative or advocate for other groups.

A leader performs more leadership roles than do other members of the group. An organization or formal group often designates a person as its leader or head to represent the group or carry out some of the organizing and mechanical chores that need to be done for the group to complete its work. Groups are sometimes categorized according to the pattern of leadership roles taken in the group. For example, a democratic group is one in which the leadership roles are shared somewhat equally by all members of the group. An autocratic group is one in which the leadership roles are performed almost exclusively by one person. A laissez-faire group is one in which the leadership roles are not performed or are only used minimally. Most problem-solving groups need someone to serve as a designated leader or as a chairperson who can take the initiative in getting the group organized and functioning.

■ A leader is a person who performs the most leadership roles in a group.

Communication Patterns

In problem-solving groups, greater efficiency is likely to be achieved in completing the task if agreement is reached on the communication patterns to be used. In small groups, each member cannot speak whenever he or she wishes. Out of courtesy and the need to hear what others have to say, members of the group take turns talking. Nevertheless, some members of the group tend to contribute more, while others contribute less.

FIGURE **12.1**
Hierarchical communi-
cation pattern.

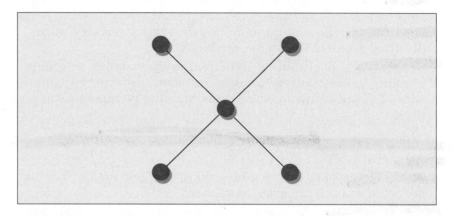

For example, a person of high status in the group may find that he
or she has become the center of interaction, so that other members of
the group speak to the high-status figure and the high-status person
talks to the group as a whole. The result is a *hierarchical* communication pattern (see figure 12.1). In this pattern, the high-status person is in the center and all communications appear to flow to and
from her or him. Little, if any, communication takes place directly
between other group members. Although this is not the preferred
pattern (from a communication point of view), it is sometimes used
by authoritarian leaders with varying degrees of success.

FIGURE **12.2**
Chain communication
pattern.

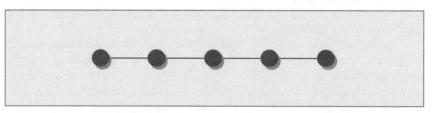

On other occasions, especially with newly formed groups, people
speak only to the people nearest them. There is little interaction and
messages are passed along, creating a *chain* pattern (see figure 12.2).

The chain communication pattern is inefficient and is quickly
replaced by one of a wide range of patterns. Where one group member is reticent (speaking only when drawn into the conversation)
while the other members openly communicate with one another, an
isolate pattern develops (see figure 12.3).

FIGURE **12.3**
Isolate communication
pattern.

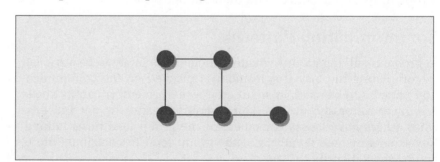

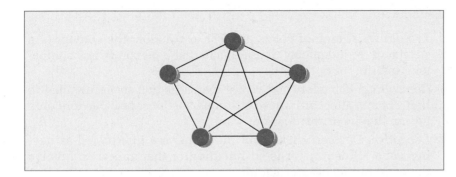

FIGURE **12.4**
Completely connected,
or com-con, communica-
tion pattern.

The isolate communication pattern is also inefficient and may result in some other pattern of communication. In some instances, the group may achieve efficiency by having two or three of its more communicative or outgoing members assigned the task of communicating with the isolates as well as with one another. Many other possible communication patterns exist, but the one that is usually most desirable for small groups is the *completely connected (com—con)* pattern (see figure 12.4). This pattern results when every member of the group makes a significant contribution to the accomplishment of the task and interacts regularly with every other member of the group.

Although the com—con pattern may require more time than other patterns, the cohesiveness and flexibility of the group increases, because members feel they have influenced the group as often as they want to. In general, status, power, influence, and control discrepancies are minimized, and members feel a sense of belonging. Teamwork seems to be heightened.

■ A group is most effective when everyone feels he or she can participate.

Communication Climate

The communication climate of the group is the prevailing atmosphere or conditions regarding the exchange of information, ideas, and feelings within the group setting. The climate is revealed most clearly by the often subtle verbal and nonverbal interactions between group members. The leader has, depending on his or her power and style, a more or less significant influence on the communication climate of the group. The communication style of each member of the group also contributes to the overall climate.

Jack R. Gibb identified individual behaviors that created two different general climates in groups: a defensive climate and a supportive climate.[5] A defensive climate often leads to hostility and destructive group relations. A supportive climate more often leads to helpful, cooperative, positive relationships.

DEFENSIVE

When attitudes, assumptions, and subtle behaviors are perceived by other members of the group as threatening and potentially punishing, especially to a person's sense of self-respect, then the climate is defensive. Behaviors that may be interpreted as threatening include the following:

- *Evaluative.* A tone of voice, a physical reaction, the content of a statement, or judgments that indicate that a person is less competent, inferior, or out of line.
- *Controlling.* Behaviors and verbal messages that seem intended to limit, block, alter, or impose attitudes, feelings, or behaviors on a person that he or she does not want.
- *Deceptive.* Devices, tricks, and ploys that are interpreted as having some hidden or unstated intention or that appear to involve the withholding of information.
- *Noncaring.* Communicative behaviors that indicate a lack of concern for the plight of others, that seem cold, detached, and impersonal.
- *Superior.* Ways of interacting that imply inequality and superiority, especially when tinged with an attitude of arrogance, tending to demean the other.
- *Dogmatic.* Statements, vocal tones, and postures that imply an attitude of absolute certainty or that suggest that no other alternatives are available or none will be considered.
- *Hostile.* Negative evaluations, limitations on and blocks to the accomplishment of goals, deceptiveness and withholding of information, lack of concern about what happens to others, arrogance and demeaning attitudes, and an unwillingness to compromise.

When threats are posed to such an extent that hostility and destructive drives are excited, physical attacks are not uncommon. If a person chooses not to engage in physical violence, he or she might react in one of the following ways:

- Complete avoidance of interaction
- Suppression of topics in the areas of hostility
- Pretense that no threat exists
- Verbal aggression as a substitute for physical violence

None of these avoidance and adjustive reactions is conducive to a positive interpersonal climate; each tends to produce a negative spiral, resulting in distortion and misunderstanding.

SUPPORTIVE

- A supportive climate is effective in a group because all the members feel they can say what they think.

A supportive climate exists when parties in the interaction feel that they have a sense of worth and importance. Supportiveness involves helping others to attain goals that are important to them. Such help is provided by understanding what others want to accomplish and by encouraging them to try new approaches without fear of reprisal. Supportiveness is communicated most clearly by the following types of responses:

- *Descriptive.* Statements that are nonevaluative and that provide reports of information.
- *Problem-oriented.* Ways of reacting that focus on problems to be solved, rather than on what can and cannot be done.

- *Open and honest.* Reactions that communicate to others a willingness and ability to express positive interests and helpfulness as well as reservations about what is happening.

- *Warm and caring.* Expressions and behaviors that indicate understanding and empathy with the goals of the other; listening to understand what the other means so that help can be provided.

- *Egalitarian.* Comments and reactions that suggest attitudes of equality and a willingness to participate in a shared relationship, rather than in a superior/demanding-subordinate/complying one.

- *Provisional.* Communicative behavior that allows for potential error, indicating that both parties are involved in working out ways of helping one another where both can make contributions and be right some of the time.

Cohesiveness

Productivity is usually highest when the group is cohesive. Teamwork, group morale, and team spirit also contribute to cohesiveness. For example, when the spirit of a basketball team is high, members are dedicated to the entire team, they place great value on working hard for the team, and they have a deep sense of belonging to the team. Because of their commitment to the group, members have a concern for one another and are willing to exert great effort to accomplish the goals of the group. Such concern and effort usually result in increased productivity.

- If group members feel like a team and they genuinely care about each other, the group is more productive.

Although cohesiveness tends to produce higher levels of group accomplishment, it also places demands on members of the group. When membership in a group is attractive and important to an individual, the norms or expected and acceptable behaviors exert a strong influence on the individual. The stronger the influence of norms on behavior, the greater the likelihood of a person conforming to group expectations.

As a person comes to feel that a group provides satisfaction and benefits, the group more readily exerts influence over the person. Individuals who deviate from what is expected by the group often find themselves denied some of the benefits they want to have through membership in the group. But adherence to norms and expectations tends to increase acceptance and cohesiveness. Feelings of warmth and confidence increase as acceptance and cohesiveness increase. Finally, membership in highly cohesive groups tends to reduce personal anxieties and increases a sense of personal value. Thus attractiveness leads to cohesion, cohesion leads to productivity, and adherence to norms leads to conformity. Conformity often leads to satisfaction and increased personal value.

In contrast, feelings of cohesiveness may be undermined by conflicts, divisive attitudes, emotional reactions, hostilities toward others, and defensiveness. When these feelings are held privately by group members and influence how individuals work in a group, they constitute a *hidden agenda.* That is, any desires, aspirations, feelings, and motives of group members that cannot be brought into the open and recognized directly operate in the group as hidden

Groups can accomplish tasks that an individual would not attempt.

objectives. Like the formal or public agenda of a group, the hidden agenda is a schedule of desires to be achieved. In a highly cohesive group, members feel free to express their feelings, rather than to suppress them. In an uncohesive group, much time and energy may be wasted on a hidden agenda.

Understanding these four concepts of group interaction is crucial if you wish to be an effective group member. The next section of this chapter deals with procedures for group problem solving.

▼ STEPS OF THE GROUP PROBLEM-SOLVING PROCESS

■ The quality of a good decision is often a function of the process used in making the decision.

The quality of any decision is a function of the process used in arriving at the decision. That is why so much time and effort is put into designing systems and procedures for doing things. For example, law enforcement agencies have been obligated, over the years, to adopt procedures for ensuring that the rights of defendants are protected. How defendants are handled, what is said to them, and when they are to be advised have been specified because the sequence has been found to influence the way in which decisions are made and how human rights are protected.

Problem solving is based on a similar philosophy. The process that a group follows in solving problems affects the quality of the solutions. Group problem solving is at least a five-step process: (1) getting the group together and working, (2) stating and analyzing problem questions, (3) generating ideas for solving the problems, (4) selecting the most useful ideas for a solution, and (5) deciding which ideas will be used. The rest of this chapter systematically reviews these five steps.

Getting the Group Together and Working

Getting a group together to work requires effective group structuring. A technique developed by R. Wayne Pace, Brent D. Peterson, and M. Dallas Burnett lists three specific skills, or activities, that help to get a group organized and functioning properly: (1) planning for the group, (2) acquainting the group members, and (3) orienting the group members.[6]

To *plan* for the group, do the following:

- Prepare a list of important ideas and topics for the group to discuss.

- Prepare an agenda that stimulates the group to act on the important ideas and topics. Include such items as the call to order, roll call, reading and approval of minutes of previous meeting, and introduction of guests. Order items of business according to importance, and be willing to skip low-priority items as necessary to stay on schedule. Allocate time for each item of business and note times on agenda.

- Prepare the physical setting for the expected interaction of the group. Consider such things as seating arrangements, chalkboards, projectors, and handouts.

To *acquaint* the group members, do the following:

- Introduce members to one another. This may be done formally, or informally with each member introducing himself or herself to the group.

- Ask each group member to share experiences and feelings with other group members. This opens the door for the development of genuine relationships.

To *orient* the group, do the following:

- Present the topic, objectives, and work to be completed by the group.

- Present the format to be followed. Group members will know the roles, hows, and whens of expected participation. If the group is to be unstructured, tell group members this so they can act accordingly.

- Discuss whether or not the group is to make decisions and, if so, the decision-making process that will be employed.

B.C. by permission of Johnny Hart and Field Enterprises, Inc.

■ Assign specific roles or duties to each group member, as appropriate.

■ Answer questions before the beginning of group interaction.

This approach takes time initially but saves time ultimately in that it helps groups to quickly organize and begin functioning productively and efficiently. It applies to all types of groups but is vitally important for problem-solving groups.

Once the group is together and ready to work, it can state the problem.

Stating and Analyzing Problem Questions

■ What are the key features of a good problem question?

The second step in group problem solving involves stating and analyzing a problem question. For example, if a labor union is concerned about its image, it might ask, "In what ways might we improve our image?" Let's examine this question to recognize the key features of an acceptable problem question.

First, a creative problem question asks, "Precisely what is to be changed?" In the sample question, the image is to be changed. Second, an effective question indicates what type of change is to occur. The sample question indicates that the image is to be improved—although it could be changed in other ways; for example, it could be reduced, lowered, or made less visible. Third, a creative problem question allows for many alternatives in solving the problem. In the sample question, the phrase "In what ways might" suggests that many alternatives are sought. Fourth, a creative problem question specifies who is expected to solve the problem. In the sample question, the who is "we," referring to the problem-solving group.

After the problem has been stated and accepted by all members of the group, then it is time to move to the third step, generating ideas for solving the problems.

Generating Ideas for Solving the Problems

We shall present two approaches for generating ideas in groups: (1) brainstorming and (2) the nominal group process. Brainstorming is used when you have an interactive group that can talk, work, and get along together. The nominal group process is best used when you can expect only a limited amount of group interaction.

BRAINSTORMING

Brainstorm is used to identify and list as many ideas as possible that could be used in solving a problem. It allows a group to think up ideas for solving a problem without the interference of critical and judgmental reactions. Brainstorming can be used to get ideas on any kind of problem as long as there is a wide range of potential solutions. It can be used to answer questions such as these:

■ "What information do we need?"

■ "How might we get the information?"

- "What guidelines might be used to evaluate the ideas?"
- "What might we do?"
- "How might we put our ideas into effect?"
- "What might be the advantages and disadvantages of what we do?"

Brainstorming can produce large numbers of ideas for use in solving problems. It can also develop attitudes that improve individual idea finding.

The four basic rules governing brainstorming allow each individual in the group to contribute facts and experiences that other group members may not possess. Thus an atmosphere is created in which individual contributors may freely offer unusual ideas without fear of contradiction or evaluation. This enables a large number of possibilities to be produced in a short period of time. The four rules of brainstorming may be summarized as follows:

1. *Criticism is ruled out.* Judgmental thinking inhibits the entire process. Killer phrases—such as "We've never done it that way. It won't work. It's too expensive. That's too hard to administer. It needs more study. Let's be practical. It's not good enough"— should be banished from the session.

2. *Freewheeling is wanted.* The wilder the ideas, the better. Even impractical ideas may trigger practical suggestions from others. Let imagination soar and then bring it down to earth later.

3. *Quantity is wanted.* The larger the number of ideas, the greater the likelihood of usable ideas. Paring down a long list of ideas is easier than expanding a short list. Most likely the best ideas will be far down the list, because the routine ones will tend to be offered easily and quickly.

4. *Combination and improvement are sought.* Be constantly on the alert to piggyback onto the ideas of another person. In addition to contributing ideas of your own, make suggestions concerning how the ideas of others an be turned into better ideas or how two or more ideas can be combined into a still better idea.

When conducting a brainstorming session, follow these steps:

1. Review the problem question that has been previously determined by the group. No questions should be asked once the brainstorming session begins. All questions should be answered before the session begins.

2. Set a specific amount of time for the session to last. Stick with the time limits.

3. Follow all brainstorming rules faithfully. No one should criticize, belittle, or degrade the ideas of anyone else.

4. Throw the floor open to unrestricted presentation of ideas. As recognized by the leader—and leaders, do this quickly—participants should shout out all ideas, crackpot and crackerjack.

5. Record the ideas through a tape recorder or a secretary, and prepare a copy of the list to be given to each participant following the session.

The brainstorming technique is generally used in groups to help them develop new ideas. Whenever a group faces a situation that requires creative problem solving, this technique can be effective. Brainstorming leads to better understanding of problems.

THE NOMINAL GROUP PROCESS

The nominal group process refers to "a structured group meeting in which participants alternate among silently thinking up ideas, listing ideas on a flip chart, and voting on ideas. The decision of the group is secured through ranking or rating of ideas."[7]

The nominal group process is described in detail in the Another Look article entitled "The Nominal Group Process" at the end of this chapter. It is used most effectively where the emphasis is on getting ideas for making decisions. When you want to get information and suggestions from a number of people, the nominal group process is especially appropriate if there are differences in power, rates of interaction, and status. This process tends to equalize such differences and allows group members to contribute their best ideas.

After ideas have been generated, either using the brainstorming approach or the nominal group process, the group can select the most useful ideas for a solution.

Selecting the Most Useful Ideas for a Solution

The fourth step in group problem solving is to select from the ideas generated in step three those that could be combined into a workable solution for the stated problem. One critical task is to develop a list of requirements that indicate the difference between an idea that is desirable and workable and one that is less satisfactory.

■ Decision-making standards or criteria are keys to effective decision making.

Criteria are standards by which one can determine which ideas are the most acceptable for solving a problem. Criteria represent guidelines for mentally testing the acceptability of a proposal or plan. They are phrased as statements that indicate the minimal requirements that any suggestion, idea, plan, or proposal must meet in order to be acceptable.

Criteria should be phrased in the following manner: "Anything that is done (idea or course of action) must meet the following requirements." They consist of declarative statements that specify what must and must not happen for a course of action to be considered acceptable:

■ "The idea must ..."
■ "The idea must not ..."

The clear and explicit statements of criteria bring both so-called logical and emotional reasons for making decisions to the surface for close scrutiny by all group members. In group problem solving, one major difficulty lies in getting all group members to reveal the criteria that they hold. In many cases, you may not even realize that you have a restriction you would like to impose on an idea until the idea is outlined in some detail. Therefore, listing as many criteria as possible may help in locating key restrictions that you and others may have overlooked.

In group problem solving and communication, it is often helpful to rank the criteria after a long list has been compiled. Criteria of high importance can be considered seriously, allowing less important ones to be modified or set aside as part of the process of arriving at agreement.

After the ideas and criteria have been established, the group can finally decide which idea or ideas best solve the problem by meeting the established criteria.

Deciding Which Ideas Will Be Used

The fifth step in group problem solving is to decide which one of the potentially desirable and workable ideas will be used and how it will be put into practice. The group should make certain that all members are satisfied with the idea chosen, because implementation of the idea usually requires full support from the problem-solving group.

In large organizations with professional planners or a "plans" section or department, the task of preparing plans, developing operational procedures, and securing equipment is normally handled by planning professionals. Even with professional planning staff available, however, selecting ideas and a general plan of implementation usually remains the work of the problem-solving group.

WAYS OF MAKING A DECISION

In determining which problem-solving ideas should be used, one must understand the different ways of making decisions so that an appropriate approach can be selected. Occasionally, the issue and the cause unify the group, so that each person fully subordinates personal differences to the interest of the group. The recommended action so captivates the group members that it transcends all differences and impels a *unanimous* decision.

Unanimity occurs only rarely. However, most of the time—provided a reasonably high level of open discussion has prevailed—*consensus* can be achieved. Consensus is achieved by having the group members talk out their differences. Each member of the group must be given a full and uninhibited opportunity to express differences of opinion, to contribute to and influence the form of the action to be taken. Although making decisions by consensus may take more time than do other modes of decision making, it provides for the widest possible base of support and the resolution of as many differences as possible. Group members should, ideally, have at least some areas of strong agreement with the choice to be made, even though they may have some reservations.

Majority decision making is probably the most common method used in most areas of human endeavor, at least in democratic countries. Deliberative bodies usually accept the will of the majority. Decisions are made by identifying members of the majority and the

■ "Majority rules" is the most common decision method, although it is not always appropriate.

A challenging problem commands the attention of the group.

minority points of view. This is accomplished by taking some type of vote or poll. Individuals are asked to indicate their preferences in one of the following ways: by saying aloud "aye" or "nay"; by raising their hands; by writing their preferences on slips of paper; or by a "division of the house," in which the individuals move to either side of the room to indicate their preference.

Decisions made on the basis of a *plurality* represent majority decision making except that the acceptable decision is the one supported by the largest number of individuals. The tally of those who approve and those who disapprove may be taken following the pattern of majority decision making.

Decisions made by a *minority coalition,* by *unilateral action,* and by *inaction* are usually considered to be less desirable than are decisions arrived at through any of the other modes. Nevertheless, occasionally groups can be difficult to move to make a decision, even though a procedure is provided. Under those conditions, an informed minority or a single individual may proceed to make the choice, seeking the concurrence and sustaining vote of the entire group in the process.

SELECTING AN APPROPRIATE WAY

■ How can we select the best decision-making procedure?

Each group must be encouraged to identify and adopt a specific decision-making procedure that is appropriate for the issue under discussion and the climate of the group. When a group is functioning at a high level of involvement and with mutual concern and enthusiasm, seeking unanimity or consensus may be appropriate. When agreement may be more difficult to achieve, majority and plurality procedures may be more appropriate. When the group is indecisive, inhibited, or unable to proceed with majority decisions, it may have to accept the alternatives favored by a strong minority or a well-informed individual. Inaction may be used strategically in making decisions, because it allows a choice to be made without the necessity of anyone's assuming responsibility or blame for the action.

The quality of almost any decision is a function of the procedures one uses in arriving at the decision. For individuals to be committed to a course of action, they must feel that the choice of alternatives was arrived at in an acceptable way.

▼ SUMMARY OF KEY IDEAS

- The five characteristics of a small group are: group leader attitudes, leader behaviors, communication patterns, communication climate, and cohesiveness.

- The three primary types of roles that a group member may assume are: task, maintenance, and personal; a person may be involved in a variety of activities that are subsumed under each role.

- Group communication patterns, which are determined by the direction of communication interaction, may be arranged into four general types: hierarchical, chain, isolate, and com-con.

- The group communication climate may be either defensive or supportive.

- Cohesiveness tends to produce higher levels of productivity but demands that group members adhere to norms in order to achieve a level of conformity.

- The five-step process for group problem solving involves assembling the group, stating and analyzing the problem, generating possible solutions, selecting the most useful solutions, and deciding which solution will be implemented.

▼ KEY TERMS, CONCEPTS, AND NAMES

Brainstorming	Leadership
Cohesiveness	Majority
Communication climate	Nominal group
Conformity	Plurality
Consensus	Roles
Criteria	Small group
Defensive climate	Small-group problem solving
Jack R. Gibb	Supportive climate
Group structuring	Unanimity
Interaction	

▼ QUESTIONS AND EXERCISES

1. Rank the following statements that might describe the characteristics of a good group. Place a 1 in front of the statement that you feel is the most important characteristic of a good group, a 2 in

front of the next most important characteristic, and so on. Place a 12 in front of the statement least descriptive of a good group. When you have ranked all of the statements, discuss with a class-mate why you both ranked them the way you each did.

_____ A healthy competitiveness exists among members.

_____ Everyone sticks closely to the point.

_____ The group avoids conflict situations.

_____ Members perform leadership functions.

_____ Each member gives and receives feeling feedback.

_____ The leader suggests a plan for each group meeting.

_____ Aggression is openly expressed.

_____ Informal subgroups develop spontaneously.

_____ Members freely express negative feelings.

_____ The goals of the group are clearly stated.

_____ Information is freely shared among members.

_____ Members' feelings are considered when tasks are performed.

2. Form a group with some friends and practice brainstorming using the following problems:

a. How can an egg be packaged so that it will not break when dropped from a ladder?

b. What adjustments would our society have to make if there were three sexes instead of two?

c. Select one or two of the following diagrams. What might they be?

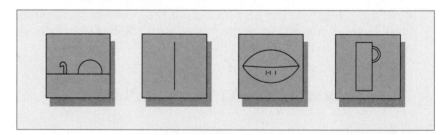

3. Criteria come into play in every situation in which a choice must be made between competing proposals, products, ideas, and even people. One way to learn how to identify and state criteria is to take a problem and make a list of criteria that might be used in judging from among possible ways of solving the problem. For example, suppose you feel that you want a new job. You have several alternatives, such as going to school, changing to a new job, and moving to a new location. What should you do?

On a blank sheet of paper, list all the criteria you can think of that should govern the kind of decision you make. Now look over the list and assign a rank to each criterion. This will give you an opportunity to think about each criterion and to consider the importance of each one in evaluating your plan.

4. Answer the introductory questions at the beginning of the chapter.

▼ NOTES

1. George C. Homans, *The Human Group* (New York: Harcourt Brace Jovanovich, 1950), p. 1.

2. R. Wayne Pace, Brent D. Peterson, and M. Dallas Burnett, *Techniques for Effective Communication* (Reading, Mass.: Addision-Wesley, 1979), p. 137.

3. Adapted from Kenneth Labich, "The Seven Keys to Business Leadership," *Fortune Education Program,* © 1989 Time, Inc.

4. Kenneth D. Benne and Paul Sheats, "Functional Roles of Group Members," *Journal of Social Issues:* Volume 4(2), 41–49.

5. Jack R. Gibb, "Defensive Communication," *Journal of Communication* 11 (September 1961): 141–48.

6. Pace, Peterson, and Burnett, *Techniques for Effective Communication,* pp. 148–54.

7. Ibid., pp. 194–200.

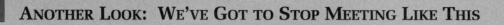

Another Look: We've Got to Stop Meeting Like This

We used to hear people say that the only sure things were death and taxes. Now we seem to have added a third: meetings. Unfortunately, most people view all three with about the same levels of enthusiasm.

Meetings are big business. Michael Doyle, president of Michael Doyle Associates, has discovered that on an average business day, well over 17 million meetings are held!

(I once read that if all the people in the world who are attending meetings right now, at this precise moment, were laid end-to-end—they'd all be a lot more comfortable!)

Far too many meetings miss their mark simply because of a lack of planning or preparation. One recent study of more than 1,000 middle managers identified the top three reasons for failed meetings;

- They get off the subject.
- They lack agendas or goals.
- They last too long.

We've got to stop meeting like this!

TYPES OF MEETINGS

Whether we're talking about training meetings, staff meetings, committee meetings, or board meetings, it might help to review some basics.

First, let's sort meetings into these categories:

- Information. This includes giving and receiving infor-

mation. Many training programs fall into this category. Such meetings can work both ways. Astute trainers can provide two-way communication by encouraging trainees to share experiences.

- Action. This type of meeting could be as brief as two people addressing a problem to get closure and action.

- Problem solving. This could involve a group or team that gets together to attack a single problem.

- Brainstorming. We've seen a real resurgence of the creative group-think process. The typical ground rules (no criticism allowed, the wilder the better, and so forth) are the basis for these creative exercises.

Those categories are not meant to be an exhaustive list. And often, no clear-cut lines distinguish them.

WHY MEETINGS FAIL

We can all relate to the reasons cited earlier for why meetings fail (they stray from their subjects, they have no agenda or goals, and they are too lengthy). But other factors can contribute to ineffective meetings.

- Lack of planning. Even a novice trainer would not run a session without planning. Why then, would anyone think a meeting could be conducted without preparation?

- Lack of objectives. Regardless of the kind of meeting, it is imperative that objectives be stated and "bought into" by the meeting attendees.

- Lack of an agenda.

- Wrong people. Make sure the people attending your meeting are the ones who should be there. Meetings are costly. If some attendees shouldn't be there, the costs rise measurably.

- Wrong place. The wrong site can kill an otherwise effective meeting. Try off-site meetings. With fewer interruptions such as phone calls, the business at hand is usually conducted more efficiently.

- Wrong time. Everyone can recall an ineffective meeting in which bad timing—the wrong day or time—was the culprit. And it is amazing how quickly problems can be handled at an 11:30 A.M. meeting. Better yet, if you really want action, schedule one for Friday at 4:30 P.M.!

MAKING MEETINGS WORK

With all this rhetoric about why meetings fail, how do we make them better? Consider these ideas as starters and you'll see how meetings can really work for you.

The Agenda   Of course, any meeting needs a game plan—an agenda. At the very least, you should have an outline

ANOTHER LOOK *continued*

on a flipchart. But it's far better to send an agenda out in advance to all participants, to help them prepare for discussion on the items that are included.

Expectations   To ensure that the stated objectives are in "sync" with those of the attendees, simply ask them about their expectations. This may not be appropriate for a weekly staff meeting or other event of an hour or so, but it can be an excellent vehicle for longer sessions. It's also a great way for trainers to get trainees to buy into programs. It's usually most effective with 10 to 20 participants.

Here's how it works. After the traditional welcome and introduction, give an overview of the program or schedule. Then identify the objectives and say to the group, "OK, you know my objectives. But to make sure your goals are similar to my goals, tell me your objectives for this meeting. In other words, tell me what has to happen between now and 4 P.M. tomorrow to make sure that your objectives are met."

Participants may hesitate to respond individually, so put them into groups of three or four people and ask them to synthesize their comments. Ask a representative from each group to list two or three of that group's objectives. Post them on a flipchart for all to see. As necessary, make adjustments and add them to the agenda.

Now, your meeting is their meeting.

Facilitation   All but unknown a decade ago, "facilitating" has become the "in" thing for trainers. To paraphrase Carl Rogers, we can't teach anyone anything—all we do is facilitate their learning. Many trainers, in fact, have abandoned their "trainer" hats and term themselves "facilitators" instead.

In a meeting, the role of a facilitator is an important one. Essentially, this role is one of a "chauffeur" who "drives" the meeting in a subtle way. The facilitator, typically from outside the group or organization, plays a neutral role and helps steer the meeting toward its destination—its end objective.

He or she keeps things going and ensures that all sides are heard. Of course, the facilitator has no vote and maintains a middle-ground position.

With an outside facilitator, the person who presides over the meeting can concentrate on the discussion and be an active part of it. She or he doesn't have the worry about the "order" or conduct of the procedures and can give full attention to the motion on the floor.

The Consent Calendar   A consent calendar is an effective and efficient way to handle the multitude of items that may have to be discussed at certain kinds of meetings.

The by-laws of most associations and professional organizations stipulate a variety of items that the board of directors must pass. These might include such day-to-day business as the secretary's report, membership reports, and committee updates. All too often, needless time is wasted on these items, but since it's mandated by policy, the board plows through these, one by one!

As the name implies, a consent calendar requires the consensus or consent of the governing body.

Here's how it works. Well in advance, the president, secretary, or executive vice-president of the association or society considers all the items on the agenda. He or she makes a thoughtful judgment on which items are likely to be passed with little or no discussion. These items are compiled and listed on a "consent calendar."

At the board meeting, announce each item individually. If even one person raises a question or comment on any item, it is automatically removed from the consent calendar. Remember, the purpose of the consent calendar is to save time, not to "railroad" things through. Only the items that are approved without question can stay on the consent calendar, which can be a valuable time saver.

Living Minutes   This tool is an excellent one to use for small groups, sales meetings,

ANOTHER LOOK: WE'VE GOT TO STOP MEETING LIKE THIS
continued

staff meetings, and board or committee meetings. It entails a skilled recorder (not the leader or facilitator) to keep a running (living) document of the discussions.

Using a flipchart, the recorder listens intently to the comments as each item is under discussion. As points are brought out, the recorder succinctly and briefly captures the essence or key words and writes them on the flipchart. The words should reflect the intent of the contributor's comments; the recorder should ensure accuracy by asking, "Is this what you're saying?" or "Is this OK?"

As the outline-type sheets are completed, someone should remove them from the chart and tape them to the walls where everyone can see them.

Walking Meetings   Have you ever been involved in meetings in which things got "hot and heavy"? Here's a tool for such situations.

Say an agenda item proves to be a sensitive or controversial one. Before things get out of hand and pandemonium breaks loose, suggest a "walking meeting." Assign groups of two or three people to a team. If possible, get adversaries on the same

team. Their task for the next 15 to 20 minutes is to "take a walk" with the issue at hand. They should come back at the prescribed time with either a compromise, a suggested solution, or other ideas for reaching consensus.

"Motion Sickness"   Far too many groups catch "motion sickness." Of course, it's important to use parliamentary procedures at many meetings, but don't get carried away. Some items don't require motions. Get agreement and move on.

Start and End Times   Why not call a meeting for 2:03 P.M. rather than 2 P.M., or for 10:37 A.M. rather than 10:30 A.M.? People tend to remember odd starting times more easily; they tend to be more punctual as well.

Above all, state the starting and ending times—and start and end on time!

Stand-Up Meetings   Have you ever walked into a meeting room with no furniture? Try it and you'll be surprised at how fast things move along. Stand-up meetings are great for small groups.

Discussion Time   Limit discussion time on any

issue. A lot of time is wasted on needless "discussion" in which someone takes 15 minutes to echo someone else's position. Research suggests that, when presented with an issue, 60 percent of the group will make up their minds on it within 60 seconds!

Obviously, you shouldn't curtail relevant and necessary discussion, but don't waste time. Differentiate between someone who has something to say and someone who has to say something.

Do your homework   We've got to stop meeting like this! Like training sessions, meetings should be well-planned and well-orchestrated.

Keep in mind the obstacles that may get in the way of effective meetings—and remove them. Do your homework and the results will be positive.

Try some of the proven tools presented above. They work. Discard methods that aren't as effective, and your colleagues will agree: "We've got to *start* meeting like this!"

SOURCE: Edward E. Scannell, *Training and Development*, January 1992.

ANOTHER LOOK: THE NOMINAL GROUP PROCESS

WHAT IT IS

A nominal group is one "in name only," meaning that the processes of face-to-face, oral interaction are restricted. The term *nominal group,* when referring to the technique, indicates a structured group meeting in which participants alternate among silently thinking up ideas, listing ideas on a flip chart, and voting on ideas. The decision of the group is secured through ranking or rating of ideas. Nominal group process (NGP) involves four stages:

- Writing ideas silently
- Recording ideas on a flip chart
- Offering pro, con, and clarifying comments on each idea
- Rank-ordering or rating ideas

NGP is used primarily for creative decision making in which individual judgments need to be secured and combined for the most acceptable decision.

WHAT IT DOES

NGP employs different and appropriate types of group activities for each of the different phases of creative decision making. NGP balances participation among members of the group. Finally, NGP applies the concept of simple mathematics to reduce errors in combining individual judgments into group decisions. NGP

has been demonstrated to be superior as a creative decision-making technique to face-to-face, interacting groups when the group objective is to produce or bring together information on a problem. NGP teams tend to produce a higher average number of unique ideas, a higher average total number of ideas, and a better quality of ideas. It appears that interacting groups inhibit individual contributions and encourage more premature evaluation of ideas, resulting in a decrease in the creativity, originality, and practicality of group decisions.

WHY IT DOES IT

NGP tends to balance the influence of members throughout the decision-making process, allowing equality of participation and consideration of ideas. NGP reduces the tendency for high-status, highly expressive individuals of strong personality to dominate discussion. Thus, it facilitates more open discussion, the contribution of unusual ideas, and the asking of objective questions about controversial ideas. By controlling the amount and kind of interaction, NGP tends to balance socioemotional roles with the performance of task roles and to provide rewards for making quality decisions. High-quality ideas seem to come from the generation of suggestions silently followed by additional thought and

listening during a round-robin discussion of the ideas. NGP provides for a sense of accomplishment by moving systematically from stage to stage, with real results demonstrated through the posting of ideas and their discussion.

HOW TO DO IT

This technique requires preparation and involves approximately four steps.

1. Select and arrange a meeting room large enough to accommodate participants in groups of five to nine members at tables. Seat participants along each side and at one end of a rectangular table so as to create an open U-shape: put a flip chart at the open end of the table.

2. Provide the following supplies:
   a. Worksheets for each participant with question printed on top
   b. A flip chart for each table
   c. A roll of masking tape
   d. A pack of 3" × 5" cards for each table
   e. Felt pens for each table
   f. Paper and pencil for each participant

Note: Since NGP meetings rely heavily on the posting of ideas in front of each small group, it is essential to have a flip chart or some other device of posting ideas for continuous viewing by the

ANOTHER LOOK: THE NOMINAL GROUP PROCESS *continued*

group. A chalkboard is undesirable for this purpose; however, sheets of newsprint, butcher paper, or other kinds of large sheets of paper can be used after they are attached to the wall or to a chalkboard.

3. Welcome participants and explain how the NGP works; stress the importance of the task and each member's contribution.

4. Place an NGP question on the flip chart to elicit ideas or information. Avoid questions that can be answered with a simple yes or no. Avoid questions that ask for decisions, such as whether something should be done. Phrase the question or questions to provide for the largest number of answers possible with such wording as:
   a. What kinds of difficulties are being experienced?
   b. In what ways might we reduce waste?
   c. What are the ways in which we can increase production?

Some guidelines for conducting an NGP session follow:

1. Silent generation of ideas in writing
   a. Distribute sheets with question: read the question aloud and illustrate how specifically ideas should be listed.
   b. Indicate that each member should write ideas in short phrases or statements, working silently and independently.
   c. Give the group five minutes to write ideas without interruption; maintain the rule of silence firmly; discourage any attempts to work together.
   d. Call group up for movement to Step 2.

2. Public portrayal of ideas in writing
   a. A recorder asks for one idea from each member, going one at a time around the table. The recorder writes the idea on a flip chart at the head of the table and proceeds to the next group member in turn.
   b. Each idea is written in a short phrase of three or four words. Continue to record ideas until all ideas are publicly portrayed before the group, omitting duplicate items but listing variations of ideas.
   c. Restrain the group from making any comments about ideas until all suggestions are posted. Make the entire list visible to the group by tearing off sheets as they are filled and taping them to the wall or chalkboard.

3. Serial clarification of each idea.
   a. Serial clarification means taking each idea in the order listed on the sheets and talking about each one in that order.
   b. The purpose of this stage is to clarify the meaning of each of the suggestions, *not* to argue its merits.
   c. During the discussion period, team members should be making notes and recording their judgments of each item.
   d. During the discussion period, participants are encouraged to provide brief analyses of the logic underlying each suggestion and the relative importance of the item in solving the problem.
   e. Individuals should feel free to express agreement or disagreement with the analysis and the relative importance of the items.
   f. The leader should keep the discussion moving so that all items are clarified and some expression of importance attached.

4. Rank-ordering of priority items
   a. Have the group identify, from the entire list of suggestions on the flip chart, a specific number of most important items. Anywhere from four to eight items might be indicated.
   b. Have each group member write his or her priority items on separate 3" × 5" cards and rank-order the cards

ANOTHER LOOK *continued*

from one to seven by placing an appropriate number and drawing a circle around it in the upper left-hand corner of each card. For identification purposes, place the item numbers in the lower right-hand corner of each card.

c. Collect all the cards and shuffle them, recording each idea and its rank-order on a flip chart.

d. Study the rank-ordering and eliminate all items that did not receive any votes.

5. Discussion of initial rank-ordering

a. Since some items may be ranked differently by members of the group, it is advisable

to increase the likelihood of making the most accurate decisions by reducing misinformation, by increasing clarification, and by allowing for the interpretation of items. Following the discussion, a final ranking will take place. Members need not change their original ranking, but they should vote differently if they have a new perspective on the items as a result of the discussion.

b. The discussion should consume no longer than ten minutes and should consist of clarifying statements. Avoid focusing too much attention on the

items discussed so you won't distort perceptions of items not commented upon.

6. Final ranking

a. In order to refine judgments of participants, the final ranking may also include a rating of each of the final-ranked items.

b. Instruct the group to choose the five most important items from the flip chart and list them in rank order on a sheet of paper as shown below.

c. Collect all sheets. Post rankings and ratings on the flip chart for studying the group decisions.

d. Make plans for devising ways to implement ideas.

LIST ITEM IN RANK ORDER (NUMBER)	PHRASE DESCRIBING ITEM ON FLIP CHART	RATING OF ITEM IN TERMS OF RELATIVE IMPORTANCE						
		UNIMPORTANT						VERY IMPORTANT
_____	_____	1	2	3	4	5	6	7
_____	_____	1	2	3	4	5	6	7
_____	_____	1	2	3	4	5	6	7
_____	_____	1	2	3	4	5	6	7
_____	_____	1	2	3	4	5	6	7
_____	_____	1	2	3	4	5	6	7
_____	_____	1	2	3	4	5	6	7
_____	_____	1	2	3	4	5	6	7

SOURCE: R. Wayne Pace, Brent D. Peterson, and M. Dallas Burnett, *Techniques for Effective Communication,* © 1979, Addison-Wesley, Reading, Massachusetts, pp. 194–200.

▼ A CASE IN POINT: A NEW APPROACH TO FINAL EXAMINATIONS AT STATE UNIVERSITY

State University is in the midst of a major discussion concerning how to handle final examination periods. The students have brainstormed and given many suggestions to the administration about how to deal with the final examination period. The basic problem question facing the administration is "What type of final examination period is best for a college or university?"

The examination period might be handled in a number of different ways, including setting aside a week or more at the end of the semester devoted exclusively to giving exams, or giving exams on the final class meeting, or giving exams during the last two or three weeks of class but without a formally designated exam week.

QUESTIONS

1. By brainstorming, list three other solutions.

2. Which of these suggestions would be most acceptable to you? Why? The answer depends on the criteria used to evaluate the proposals. Some potential criteria would require any final exam period to do the following:

- Provide opportunity for an overall evaluation of what students have learned (this may come from a desire or value held about examinations).

- Allow instructors time to meet grading deadlines (to many, this represents a practical consideration).

- Not create a financial burden on the university, staff, and students (this seems to come from the desire to avoid introducing disadvantages).

- Not create scheduling problems (this may come from practical considerations of administering a school).

3. Develop at least six more criteria that could be used to make the best decision about the type of final examination period.

▼ A CASE IN POINT: CUTBACK AT COMMERCIAL AIR

Chuck Stewart's small commuter airline had flourished during the early days of deregulation. When the government lifted many of the restrictions on the cities the airlines could serve, the rates they could charge, and the like, Chuck saw a golden opportunity to set up a business. Commercial Air was born.

Because of its fuel-efficient, short-range jets, Commercial Air soon found itself to be very profitable serving a network of smaller cities in the Midwest. Business travelers used Commercial to link up with the major airlines in Chicago, St. Louis, and Memphis. Stewart had a fast-growing and very lucrative business.

Problems began to arise when a labor union organizer convinced about 25 percent of Commercial's employees that only through unionization could they strengthen their job security and improve benefits. Stewart bitterly fought unionization but eventually realized that some of his workers were dead set on joining the Brotherhood of Airline Workers.

The company's financial position started to deteriorate about eighteen months ago. Higher interest rates on newly purchased equipment and a decline in passengers hurt. Chuck Stewart realizes now that it's time for belt-tightening, or the company could go under. The thought is depressing to Chuck.

Bill Baker, the company's general manager and a close friend of Chuck, was talking with Chuck over a few beers last Thursday after work:

A CASE IN POINT *continued*

CHUCK: I'm not sure exactly what it's going to take, Bill, but I'm going to save this company any way I can. Obviously, we need to trim the work force.

BILL: You're right, Chuck. But I can't see just making blanket cuts. We need a scalpel, not a meat ax.

CHUCK: I'm with you. Say, you're the big believer in participative decision making. Why don't we just get the people together, explain our problem, and let them figure out how to reduce the work force?

BILL: I'm not sure that'll work. We're looking at 20 percent of those people being terminated. How would you feel if you were asked to decide your own fate that way?

CHUCK: I'd feel lousy. But isn't the big advantage of participation supposed to be less resistance to change? Our people are adults. They know the realities of the business world. Let's give them some general guidelines and see what they come up with.

BILL: I suppose it's possible. I could get each work group together—there are sixteen to twenty people in each group—and see if they can draw straws or something.

CHUCK: That sure would take some heat off me. I hate letting people go. Oh yes, and Bill—off the record—I'd sure appreciate if the groups would decide to ax mostly union people.

QUESTIONS

1. What do you think of Chuck's and Bill's approach to decision making?
2. Is participative decision making a good option in this case? Explain your response.
3. What motivations lie behind the decision to use participation?
4. What problems do you foresee in Chuck and Bill's approach?
5. We discussed hidden agenda in this chapter. Describe Chuck's.

VI

WORKFORCE ISSUES: DIVERSITY, SOCIALIZATION, TECHNOLOGICAL CHANGE, AND STRESS

CHAPTER

13

PERSPECTIVES ON CULTURAL DIVERSITY

This chapter answers several all-important questions:

- How do efforts to employ culturally diverse workers reflect the value system of a free society?

- Why do some employers resist hiring a culturally diverse workforce?

- How does the unemployment rate among African American workers compare with that of other workers?

- Why is racial discrimination potentially wasteful?

- What is being done to overcome discrimination against various racial/ethnic groups?

- What is affirmative action, and what does it seek to accomplish?

- What are the four major minority groups in the United States and Canada?

- What special pressures are experienced by many African Americans, Hispanic Americans, Asian and Pacific Island Americans, and Native Americans in our North American culture?

- How does the plight of Native Americans differ from that of other racial/ethnic groups?

- What can we do to reduce cultural misunderstanding and the waste of human energy?

The answers to these and other questions are coming up next in chapter 13....

CHAPTER 13

*Every morning at seven o'clock
There's twenty tarriers aworking on the rock
And the boss comes along and he says
"Keep still,
And come down heavy on the cast iron drill."
And drill, ye tarriers, drill. Drill, ye tarriers, drill.
For it's work all day for sugar in your tay,
Down beyond the rail-way,
And drill, ye tarriers, drill!
And blast!
And fire!
Irish railroad song by
Thomas Casey, 1888*

■ The door to opportunity in the United States has not always been open to all people.

■ Groups that blend into the mainstream culture have more upward mobility than those that do not.

From its early days, the United States has depended on the inexpensive labor of newly arrived people to build its businesses. Black slaves worked on southern plantations; Irish and Chinese workers built the railroads; Polish, Italian, and other groups filled factory, domestic, and other unskilled jobs.

Yet the door to better opportunities was often posted with signs such as "Whites Only" and "No Irish Need Apply." While the past century has seen many European immigrants assimilated into the American "melting pot," some ethnic and cultural groups are still struggling for economic equality. In addition, economic and political conditions abroad have brought new groups of immigrants from Mexico, Southeast Asia, and other areas. Many Hispanic Americans, African Americans, Asian and Pacific Island Americans, Arab Americans, Native Americans, and other ethnic and cultural groups face significant pressures in the workplace.

In this chapter, we focus on issues that minorities face and suggest ways that human relations-smart managers can deal with these issues.

▼ MANAGERS MUST LEARN TO HELP AND DEAL WITH DIVERSITY PROBLEMS

Organizations are expected to reflect the values of the societies in which they function. In the United States and Canada, a key value is the notion of equal opportunity for all people. These countries have long been regarded as the land of opportunity: with hard work, anyone might make his or her fortune; a son or daughter might even become the nation's leader. Indeed, in the 1988, U.S. presidential race, the two major contenders for the Democratic Party nomination were Michael Dukakis, son of Greek immigrants, and Jesse Jackson, son of an African American South Carolina mill worker.

The possibility of upward social mobility has attracted group after group of immigrants from different countries to the United States and Canada. Once they arrived, however, many found obstacles to enjoying real economic opportunity. Each wave of immigrants faced resentment and hostility from those already here. Established citizens—including earlier immigrants—feared that the economic pie could not be cut into ever-smaller pieces, that soon their nation would run out of jobs. In addition, they were often suspicious of those who looked, talked, and acted differently.

Through subsequent generations, Europeans and some other immigrant groups have blended into their new culture and entered the mainstream of U.S. and Canadian business, moving up to white-collar and eventually management and executive positions. But for other, especially visible ethnic and racial groups, such as African Americans, Hispanic Americans, and Asian and Pacific Island Americans, the problems of exclusion from opportunity persist.

U.S. society has taken two approaches to increasing minority employees' opportunities: voluntary action of organizations and

Economic opportunity has attracted group after group of immigrants to the United States.

government legislation. As discussed later in this chapter, the results have been mixed.

▼ ASSISTING THE CULTURALLY DIVERSE BEGINS WITH HELPING THEM GET JOBS

While unemployment rates in the United States dropped and remained low during most of the 1980s, some groups were left out of the economic boom. In particular, the unemployment rate among African American youths has remained exceptionally high. It is a chronic problem with no easy solutions. "We've been working on it for ten years," says the director of equal opportunity programs at a major corporation. "We've had ten years of frustration."

■ High unemployment is a chronic problem for African American youths.

When the economy goes into a recession, or even a temporary slowdown, the unemployment rate rises faster among young African Americans than it does for any other group. During the early-1980s recession, the unemployment rate was nearly 40 percent for African American males ages sixteen to nineteen.

The *Wall Street Journal* noted that the unemployment problem "[affects] just about every aspect of Black life in the U.S.: high youth unemployment is widely seen as an early link to the chain that shackles Blacks to higher crime rates than whites, a higher incidence of family breakups, and a lifelong economic disadvantage."[3]

While lack of education is a major barrier to getting and keeping a job for some groups, other issues compound the problem. A lack of role models, particularly in professional positions, can discourage

■ Many factors limit opportunities for minorities.

youths from seeking job training or a college education. Inadequate basic job skills can also limit opportunities.

▼ PREJUDICE BEGETS DISCRIMINATION

At the root of many problems faced by culturally diverse workers are prejudgment and discrimination. *Prejudice*—an opinion formed without all the facts—often is rooted in misunderstanding or lack of exposure to different types of people. When we prejudge others, we often are led into acts of *discrimination*—into giving unequal and unfair treatment to people different from ourselves.

Such discrimination is unethical and illegal. In addition, it is bad business. As management writer Lawrence L. Steinmetz says,

■ Discrimination is wasteful.

> The problem with prejudice is that it does produce a great deal of waste of resources, just like lighting a cigar with a hundred-dollar bill. It is wasteful even if the person can afford it and also thinks the cigar tastes better because of lighting it with the hundred-dollar bill. In like manner, when employers are prejudiced against certain workers, waste occurs. If a minority individual is capable of doing a job but is prevented from doing it, waste will occur because of not using the minority person's talents on the one hand and having to use someone else's talents (who might even be overqualified) to do that particular job on the other.[4]

▼ ANTIBIAS EFFORTS STIR IRE OF SOME

According to Julia Lawlor in *USA Today:* "Maybe white men can't jump, but they sure can whine. In offices and factories across the country, the complaints from some particularly vocal white men are reaching a crescendo: They can't get hired, they can't get promoted, they can't get a raise, they can't get on the fast track. Women and minorities, they say, are getting all the breaks."[5]

This is generally a misperception as the white man is still king of the hill. According to Lawlor, studies indicate that twenty years after affirmative action changed the face of the workplace for minorities in the United States, women still hold fewer than 5 percent of senior management jobs, and racial and ethnic groups, fewer than 1 percent. Women make seventy-two cents to every dollar a white man makes, African Americans make sixty-eight cents, and Hispanic Americans, sixty cents. However, when employers try to correct this imbalance, it can cause an uproar among white men as they see their privileges disappearing.

■ Robert Hayles's experience in workshops shows diverse groups are more creative.

Robert Hayles, vice-president of cultural diversity for Grand Metropolitan's North American Food Sector in Minneapolis (which includes Pillsbury) is certain that diversity is a noble goal. The more diverse the work group, he maintains, the more different points of view, the higher the creativity of the group and hence the more effective the organization. Hayle's experience in workshops indicates that diverse groups are more creative.

It is interesting to note that of the Fortune 1000 companies, 70 percent recognize diversity as an important issue that they must address. However, currently only a third of them have begun programs to deal with this. The third that has taken the leap lists the following reasons for doing so:

1. Demographics. Today, the work force is 43 percent white men, 35 percent white women, and 22 percent racial and ethnic groups. In the year 2005, the work force will be 32 percent white men, 33 percent white women, and 35 percent racial and ethnic groups.
2. Results. Many have seen higher profitability by enacting long-range affirmative action programs. Hayles's work is cited frequently as a reason for enacting diversity programs.
3. Lawsuits. The average cost of a discrimination suit against a company in the United States is $475,000.[6]

▼ DISCRIMINATION CAN BE OVERCOME

Since the Civil War, many people have worked to break down the barriers of discrimination against racial and ethnic groups. Beginning in the 1950s, the modern civil rights movement, led by such activists as Martin Luther King, brought the problems of racial and ethnic groups, especially African Americans, into the public consciousness. This movement was instrumental in establishing several approaches to reducing discrimination, including legislation and affirmative action programs.

Legal Responses

Congress passed several significant laws during the 1960s to deal with discrimination. The Manpower Development and Training Act of 1962 permitted many individuals to gain occupational training for the first time. The Civil Rights Act of 1964 presented strong support for equal employment opportunities. It "prohibited employers, labor unions, and employment agencies from discriminating against persons on the basis of color, religion, sex or national origin." Smaller organizations, however, were not affected by this legislation, as it applied only to employers with fifteen or more employees.

■ Federal laws seek to overcome discrimination.

The Civil Rights Act of 1991 amended the Civil Rights Act of 1964 to strengthen and improve federal civil rights laws and to provide damages in cases of intentional employment discrimination.

Civil rights legislation has done much to reduce or eliminate the visible, outward acts of discrimination against racial and ethnic groups in jobs and other areas. There are limits, however, to what legislation can accomplish. Laws do not automatically change people's behavior, attitudes, or values. Some people still harbor feelings of hatred toward other groups of people, as can be seen in the rise of various hate groups in the Untied States during the 1980s.

■ Can society legislate morality?

Many people argue that society cannot legislate morality. Some people resist laws that require them to do what is right and fair. After Congress passed the Civil Rights Act of 1964, for example, many companies obeyed the new law only on a token basis. They hired one or two African Americans and put them in highly visible positions to demonstrate compliance with the law. In more recent years, however, many major organizations have responded to additional government pressure by initiating legitimate programs with a sincere desire to provide more opportunities for minority members. The Civil Rights Act of 1991 is a further testament of the seriousness with which the government and our society regard civil rights.

Government Pressures

To supplement the new laws, over the past twenty-five years, the federal government has started many programs to pressure organizations to alleviate racial discrimination. Many of these programs came to be known under the umbrella term *affirmative action.* The implication of affirmative action was that companies would aggressively seek to hire and promote more culturally diverse workers by such methods as special recruitment and training programs. Companies were urged to do something affirmative to compensate for past discrimination.

■ What is the EEOC?

The federal government established the Equal Employment Opportunity Commission (EEOC) to help carry out affirmative action programs. Although there are critics of the EEOC's effectiveness, the agency's efforts have changed hiring policies. Many more racial and ethnic groups now enjoy opportunities for good jobs—jobs with growth potential.

On the other hand, affirmative action has also produced some negative reactions. Some employees have balked at what they see as preferential hiring treatment and arbitrary quotas for racial and ethnic groups, a situation often called *reverse discrimination.*

The 1976 case of Allan Bakke established that discrimination against whites is just as illegal as discrimination against racial and ethnic groups. Bakke, a white male, sued the state of California when his application to a state university medical school was turned down. His suit contended that minorities less qualified than he had been admitted through a special admissions program at the school. The U.S. Supreme Court ruled in his favor, and he was admitted to medical school. In handing down this decision, the Supreme Court pointed out that affirmative action is okay as long as rigid preferential systems are not used. The goal of affirmative action is fine, but quotas are not. In fact, the goal of affirmative action is not quotas.

■ The *Bakke* decision puts business leaders in a bind.

However, as a result of the *Bakke* decision, business leaders face the challenge of creating affirmative action opportunities for racial and ethnic groups while avoiding reverse discrimination. As businesses now face a shrinking labor pool, however, some labor experts say that affirmative action programs will become increasingly important to maintaining a sufficient qualified work force.[7]

The intent of affirmative action programs is to alleviate racial discrimination and provide career opportunities for members of ethnic and racial groups.

▼ RACIAL AND ETHNIC GROUPS FACE PROBLEMS AND MAKE PROGRESS

Members of ethnic and racial groups traditionally have had to start out in the most dangerous, difficult, and unpleasant jobs. The pay, like the skill level, was low. Through years of hard work and education, with the assistance of civil rights legislation, some ethnic and racial groups attained the American dream of successful careers. The top television program of the 1980s, "The Cosby Show," illustrates this progress. It not only depicts a successful African American professional couple, but it has provided a spotlight for African American actors to appear in more than token roles.

Success stories remain more the exception than the rule, however. In 1988, the Commission on Minority Participation in Education and American Life concluded that "America is moving backward, not forward, in its efforts to achieve the full participation of minority citizens in the life and prosperity of the nation."[8]

The 1988 commission was a forty-member panel of business, education, and civic leaders including former presidents Gerald R. Ford and Jimmy Carter. It reported that the four major minority groups— African Americans, Hispanic Americans, Native Americans and Alaskan Natives, and Asian and Pacific Island Americans—potentially will constitute one-third of the United States' population just after the year 2000. "In education, employment, income, health, longevity and other basic measures of individual and social well-being gaps persist and, in some cases, are widening between members of minority groups and the majority population," said the commission.[9]

Although these ethnic and racial groups were listed by the 1988 commission, there are many more diverse ethnic groups in the U.S.

When John Henry was a little baby,
Sitting on his daddy's knee,
He took up a hammer and a little piece of steel
And said, "This hammer's gonna be the death of me,
Lord, Lord, this hammer's gonna be the death of me."
—Ballad about an African American railroad worker killed during construction of a West Virginia tunnel about 1873

■ In many measures of well-being, gaps persist and are widening between members of nondominant cultural groups and the dominant population.

Each has its own specific problems. However, all share some common concerns about education, discrimination, and other matters.

African Americans

■ Civil rights legislation and affirmative action programs have helped increase opportunities for African Americans.

The civil rights legislation and affirmative action programs originally aimed at African Americans, historically the largest and most visible racial and ethnic group, have helped provide increased job opportunities for that group. While working as a Pullman porter was once the best job many African Americans could gain, today young African American people can aspire to management and professional positions.

African American entrepreneurs are also making their mark in the business community. According to an annual survey by *Black Enterprise* magazine, the top one hundred African American-owned businesses in the United States produced $6.75 billion in revenues in 1988.[10] One notable African American entrepreneur is Brady Keys, a former professional football player who now runs a Detroit-based company, The Keys Group. This firm owns or operates thirteen Burger King outlets in Detroit and eleven Kentucky Fried Chicken outlets in Georgia, with sales of $14 million in 1988.[11]

Yet special pressures are placed on African American workers, especially those in predominantly white businesses. There is some evidence that African American professionals are leaving large corporations to work at smaller African American owned companies. One African American bank officer who made the move said some African Americans believe that to succeed in a mostly white business, they must "compromise their identity as Blacks." An attorney who took a pay cut to join a smaller African American law firm said he saw more chance for advancement there than at a large white firm where partnerships may depend on bringing in major corporate clients—who often are still reluctant to hire minority attorneys.[12]

■ Discrimination does not end for African Americans who achieve executive status.

African Americans who work their way into management in largely white organizations often find new challenges. Some white workers may resent having an African American supervisor. Others may constantly second-guess an African American manager and question his or her authority. Some African American executives find white clients reluctant to do business with them.[13]

Hispanic Americans

Hispanics have made up the latest large wave of immigrants to the United States. Most have settled either in Sun Belt states or in large northern cities. More established Hispanic American groups in the United States were originally from Puerto Rico or Cuba. Most recent Hispanic immigrants are refugees from economic and political problems in Mexico and Central America. Of the total Hispanic American population of 19 million, an estimated 12 million are Mexican.

■ New Hispanic immigrants face more challenges than do more established ethnic groups.

The newest Hispanic immigrants, many penniless, face more challenges in the workplace than did the more established groups. For

Educational, cultural, and language barriers create additional pressures on immigrant workers.

example, 17 percent of Cubans have four or more years of college, while only 7 percent of Mexicans do.[14] Unskilled Hispanic Americans, like immigrants before them, have done some of the most difficult and least desirable work, such as domestic, farm labor, and sweatshop-type factory jobs. Some have opened small service businesses in Hispanic American communities.

In addition to educational and language barriers, Hispanic American workers, especially illegal ones, face other pressures. The Immigration Reform Law of 1986 was aimed at reducing the number of illegal aliens in the United States by requiring them to register for temporary residency status. It also makes employers responsible for keeping records on employees' work authorization papers.

Many employers dislike having to be the enforcers of the new law. Intentional or accidental paperwork violations can bring civil fines of up to ten thousand dollars per employee. Such fines are especially hard on owners of small Hispanic American businesses. The *Wall Street Journal* noted that employers found themselves trying "to avoid hiring illegal immigrants without illegally discriminating against applicants with dark skins or a general foreign appearance." Some employers acknowledge they will avoid hiring Hispanic Americans rather than risk fines.[15]

■ Employers dislike being responsible for enforcing immigration laws.

The law provided an eighteen-month residency status to workers who could prove they had lived in the United States since 1982. They then had one year to become permanent residents by passing English and U.S. civics tests. But getting together the necessary documents to prove residency, plus the $185 application fee, were major obstacles for many immigrants. Even Hispanics who qualify for permanent residency may be hesitant to become U.S. citizens, because they feel they are being disloyal to their homeland.[16]

Asian and Pacific Island Americans

Waves of immigrants from various Asian countries have been coming to the United States and Canada for more than one hundred years. Many groups have faced harsh racial prejudice. Over the years, many Asians have become assimilated into the American mainstream while others have chosen to remain in Asian enclaves in large cities. Recent Asian immigrants, sometimes fleeing economic or political hardships, have come mainly from Korea and Southeast Asia.

■ Many immigrants see education as the ladder to success.

Like other racial and ethnic groups, Asians and Pacific Islanders have seen education as one step to becoming successful in their new country. While immigrant parents have often taken blue-collar jobs, many have encouraged their children to enter professional fields. In addition, Asian and Pacific Island American communities have provided social and financial support for newcomers. The Korean custom of the *kye,* for example, has helped finance many small businesses. Friends meet monthly for dinners and pool their available cash, from one hundred to forty thousand dollars. Each month, a different member receives the pot and pays for dinner. Along with hard work, saving, and good business sense, such collective financial help has allowed many Korean-Americans to become successful entrepreneurs.

Native Americans

■ Native Americans have a unique legal and political status.

Native Americans have a unique legal and political status based on special agreements between them and the U.S. government.[18] Unfortunately, this status has not helped Native Americans gain access to the American dream and may even help keep these original Americans largely outside the mainstream of U.S. society and economic life.

To understand the plight of Native Americans, one must know something about their background and history. As the United States developed from the Atlantic coast westward, Indian tribes were removed from their lands in the East to *reservations* in the West. These reservations, which were often wild and arid, are also rich in natural resources that increase in value over time. Today, native Americans generally have a very low economic standing, although many of them live on tribal lands that often contain potentially valuable oil, gas, coal, and uranium deposits as well as timber, fish, water, and highly desirable recreational areas.[19]

In attempting to understand the relative isolation of Native Americans, one must examine their cultural heritage and their historic relationship with the U.S. government. Unlike other ethnic and racial groups, the Native Americans did not leave their cultural homelands to come to the New World. They have largely stayed together as tribes and have sought to maintain their cultural heritage, which is vastly different from that of mainstream America.

Relations between the U.S. government and Indian tribes have ranged from open warfare to a situation in which the tribes are captive nations or internal colonies. The term *captive nation* relates to the limited political autonomy of tribal governments as well as the isolation of the people from the mainstream of society. It has often been used to describe the condition of Eastern European countries under the Soviet Union.[20]

The term *internal colonies* refers to a situation wherein one area, the internal colony, is exploited for the benefit of another.[21] The term has gained increasing use as forces both within and outside the tribes have encouraged tribal leaders to develop the natural resources on reservations in order to improve the socioeconomic status of tribal members and provide resources to outside interests.

Tribal leaders, aware of past exploitation from outsiders as well as the pressure to avoid development that might disrupt the traditional life-style of the tribe, are generally not eager to make major changes rapidly. Nonetheless, some development is taking place. At the same time, some Native Americans are entering the world of business. Among other developments, the Native American Chamber of Commerce of Mid America, an organization to support American Indian businesses, was established in Kansas City, Missouri, in 1986. Forums and workshops have been supported to allow successful Native American businesspeople to share their experiences with other Native Americans. Furthermore, highly successful business enterprises have been established in various tribal locations.[22] The predictions are that as the twentieth century draws to a close, Native Americans will establish a place of prominence for themselves in U.S. society while maintaining their distinctive culture.

> ■ Native Americans are entering the world of business at an increasing rate.

▼ WHAT DOES ALL THIS MEAN FOR HUMAN RELATIONS?

We need powerful beliefs to impel us to accept, respect, and work with others successfully. Some of us have inherited or embraced religious or philosophical beliefs that make this task easier. We learned that we should, "Love our neighbor as ourselves," or that "All are created equal," or to "Have compassion on all sentient beings," or "Live and let live." Such values are often stated in creeds of faith or in the constitutions and anthems of nations. We recite them or sing them on public occasions to remind ourselves of our basic commitments to each other.[23]

The human relations-smart person knows the value of understanding and appreciating differences. We can learn about the cultures of other people in many ways, including books and films. But knowledge about others is not a substitute for getting to know them personally.

> ■ Human relations-smart people know the value of understanding and appreciating differences in others.

The way to get to know people is no mystery. You talk with them. You seek to gain common understanding (our definition of communication discussed earlier). Simons suggests using friendly curiosity, in a respectful, nonjudgmental way. You might want to use questions, such as these:

What does it mean to you when ...?
What do you say to yourself about ...?

ACTIVITY: BEYOND DIVERSITY

Everyone agrees that from time to time a conversation between a man and a woman may as well be in two different languages for all the miscues that occur. Truth is, the miscuing can happen anytime there is communication between people who are much different from you—in looks, beliefs, language or customs. These differences are delicately packaged under the moniker "diversity." The growing diversity of the workforce has caused many migraines for those managers who must encourage interaction and tolerance, which commonly requires reshaping attitudes and behaviors previously set by a more uniform group.

Most of us are not born with the multicultural awareness now needed in the workplace. We have to acquire it along the way. How well are you doing at it?

YOUR DIVERSITY AWARENESS

Check the box next to the phrase that best describes your approach or attitude most of the time. This is an attitude inventory, not a test, so just go with your first inclination, and enjoy yourself!

1. ☐ Follow orders and don't make waves, do as you're told.
   ☐ It's fun to find ways around the rules, to question authority.
2. ☐ Time is a river.
   ☐ Time is money.
3. ☐ Watch what I do; learn by modeling or demonstration.
   ☐ Do as I say; learn by explicit instructions.
4. ☐ Get closer so we can talk.
   ☐ Can we have a little breathing room between us?
5. ☐ The more things change, the more they stay the same.
   ☐ Things are getting better all the time.
6. ☐ I need to take risks.
   ☐ I need to feel secure.

7. ☐ We're all in this together.
   ☐ It's every man for himself.
8. ☐ Doing your duty is most important.
   ☐ Expressing yourself or having fun is most important.
9. ☐ A case-by-case application of rules works best.
   ☐ A uniform application of rules works best.
10. ☐ Relationships are important.
    ☐ Knowing things is important.

Ethnic orientation, racial identification, learning styles, sexual preference, age/life-stage, male/female perceptions—all breed differences in the perspectives and values we bring to shared human problems and goals. While there are no "right" answers to the quiz here, it is important that you compare your attitude with that of your boss and your employees. If an employee has one attitude and you have another, chances are you've been experiencing conflict. Perhaps a different method of motivation will get the results you've been looking for.

IN OR OUT?

Following are some exercises to help you understand your own diversity awareness as well as that within your company. Characterize the dominant group within your company. What are the predominant attitudes? How were they shaped? What are the consequences of such attitudes? Do you fall inside or outside the dominant group?

Rate your ability to perform the following:

1 = Cannot do

2 = Can do with difficulty

3 = Can do reliably

4 = Am truly excellent at this

5 = Could teach others how to do this.

When I Am in the Dominant Culture

____ I am aware that I am part of a dominant culture and know how its dynamics work.

ACTIVITY *continued*

____ I realize that people of other cultures have fresh ideas and different perspectives to bring to my life and my organization.

____ I work to make sure that members of other cultures get heard and are respected for their differences.

____ I coach others on how to succeed in my culture. I tell them the underwritten rules and show them what they need to do in order to function better.

____ I give others my personal support and loyalty even if they are rejected or criticized by members of my culture.

____ I recognize how stress causes individuals to revert to older and narrower beliefs and to make oneself and one's culture right and others wrong.

____ I apologize when I have done something inappropriate that attacks or offends someone of a different background.

____ I go out of my way to recruit, select, train and promote people from outside the dominant culture, despite feeling less comfortable with them. I see this as one of my responsibilities as a manager.

____ I listen to people of other cultures when they tell me how my culture affects them.

When I Am Not in the Dominant Culture

____ I realize that, because of my background, I have something distinctive to contribute to the organization in which I find myself.

____ While I know that I do not have to lose my cultural distinctiveness to fit in, I realize that I may have to learn new information and skills that will enable me to succeed in the dominant culture.

____ I look for members of the dominant culture who will help me "read between the lines" to understand the unwritten rules about "how the system works."

____ When I succeed in the dominant culture I am careful not to make myself an exception and separate myself from others of my background.

____ I share what I learn about the dominant culture with others like myself.

____ I recognize that when the pressure is on I tend to revert to older and narrower beliefs and want to make myself and my culture right and others wrong.

____ I resist the inclination to cluster exclusively with my own kind of people or exclusively with people from the dominant culture when I am in mixed company.

____ I resist blaming the dominant group for everything that goes wrong.

____ I know how to present distinctive features of my culture and its points of view in ways that others can hear and understand.

____ I can respect individuals of other cultures and treat them fairly even though I may be fiercely committed to conflicting political goals.

CRITICAL ISSUES

Below is a list of issues that may be diversity-related. Next to each issue, indicate whether it is a critical issue within your company by writing C for Critical, O for Occasional, N for Nonexistent.

____ Offensive slurs, jokes, stereotyped remarks

____ Insensitive or exclusionary language (sexist, racist, etc.)

____ "We" versus "they" distinctions

____ Sabotage or harassment of minorities

____ Different senses of time and urgency about dealing with diversity

____ Communication, delegation problems

____ Inequities in pay scale, promotion or job definition

____ Dead-end jobs. People forced into narrow, specialized niches

____ Lack of training opportunities

ACTIVITY: BEYOND DIVERSITY *continued*

____ Lack of role models or mentors

____ Double standards

____ Understanding how to use different strengths

____ Lack of management skills

____ Violations of work rules, policies, procedures

____ Lack of motivation/participation

____ Lack of training or resources to deal with diversity

____ Sexual harassment

Look at the issues that you marked C. Do others in your office agree over what is critical? What beliefs and values seem to be at the root of these issues?

SOURCE: "Beyond Diversity," *Executive Female*, May/June 1991, pp. 49–50.

What's it like for you when ...?
What do you imagine when you say ...?
How do you picture it?
Tell me what is important to you ...?

Remember that we each come from but one of many cultures. Racial and ethnic cultures are different, but the solar system does not revolve around the ways of the dominant culture. When you encounter something in another's culture that is unacceptable to you, don't reject or blame the person, even though you need to deal with the things that frustrate you. By blaming, you risk creating hostility, prejudice, and social injustice.

By becoming culture-conscious, you not only can communicate and collaborate better, but you can learn new and interesting ways to do things and look at things. People who are different can bring out the best in us if we allow them to.[25]

▼ SUMMARY OF KEY IDEAS

■ The issues of cultural diversity require special attention by organizational leaders in order to (1) avail the organization of talents and capabilities of racial and ethnic workers, (2) comply with the law, and (3) provide fair opportunities to workers.

■ Prejudice based on what we've been taught and experienced is natural but often poses barriers to effectively working together.

■ When we put ourselves at the center of a cultural solar system, we tend to see those who are different as wrong, bad, ugly, incompetent—as adversaries instead of potential friends.

■ Although results are mixed, voluntary action and legislation serve as the two primary approaches for increasing opportunities for racial and ethnic groups.

- The Civil Rights Act of 1964 made it illegal for an organization to discriminate on the basis of color, religion, sex, or national origin.

- The Civil Rights Act of 1964 was strengthened with the advent of the Equal Employment Opportunity Commission, which enforces equal employment opportunity laws.

- The Civil Rights Act of 1991 amended the Civil Rights Act of 1964 to strengthen and improve federal civil rights laws and to provide damages in cases of intentional employment discrimination.

- African Americans, Hispanic Americans, Asian and Pacific Island Americans, and Native Americans often face difficult social pressures. Sensitivity to these pressures enables a manager to better work with those of different cultural backgrounds.

- The most effective thing the human relations-smart person can do is get to know *individuals* with different backgrounds. This can be done by asking questions and seeking understanding.

▼ KEY TERMS, CONCEPTS, AND NAMES

Affirmative action
Bakke decision
Captive nation
Civil Rights Acts of 1964
   and 1991
Civil rights movement
Discrimination

Diversity
Equal Employment Opportunity
   Commission (EEOC)
Internal colony
Kye
Reverse discrimination
Robert Hayles

▼ QUESTIONS AND EXERCISES

1. How to deal with the dominant culture

   Depending on where we find ourselves, we may sometimes be part of a dominant culture and at other times be an outsider. Use the two checklists below to find out how well you do things which enhance multicultural harmony and collaboration. The first is for those who are in the dominant culture; the second is for those in a different culture.

   Check the items which are true of you.

   Hint: The more true, the better! However, don't kid yourself about how well you see yourself perform in these areas. Get feedback from others as well as rating yourself.

A. When I belong to the dominant culture:

☐ I am aware that I am part of a dominant culture and know how its dynamics work. I listen to people of other cultures when they tell me how my culture affects them.

☐ I have a philosophy of fairness and I let others in my culture know about my commitment.

☐ I realize that people of other cultures have fresh ideas and different perspectives to bring to my life and my organization.

☐ I insure that members of other cultures are heard and respected for their differences.

☐ I coach others on how to succeed in my culture. I tell them the unwritten rules and show them what they need to know to function better.

☐ I insure that my subordinates and colleagues from other cultures are prepared for what they have to do to meet the demands of my culture.

☐ When I train or coach others I do not put them down or undermine the value of their differences.

☐ I give others my personal support and loyalty even if they are rejected or criticized by members of my culture.

☐ I am aware that outsiders to my culture recognize my cultural peculiarities better than I do and I go to them for information about the effect of things that I do and say.

☐ I recognize that when under pressure I tend to revert to narrower beliefs to make myself and my culture right and others wrong.

☐ I apologize when I have done something inappropriate that offends someone of a different background.

☐ When answerable to someone of a different culture, I avoid the tendency to "go over his or her head" to a person of my own culture.

☐ I make others aware of unfair traditions, rules and ways of behaving in my culture or organization that keep them out.

☐ I resist the temptation to make another group the scapegoat when something goes wrong.

☐ I give those from other cultures honest yet sensitive feedback about how they perform on the job.

☐ I distribute information, copies, results etc. to whomever should get them regardless of cultural differences.

☐ I go out of my way to recruit, select, train, and promote people from outside the dominant culture.

B. When I Don't Belong to the Dominant Culture:

☐ I realize that, because of my background, I have something distinctive to contribute to my organization.

☐ Even when rejected, I take pride in my culture. I take steps to build my self-esteem and the self-esteem of others who, like me, do not belong to the dominant culture.

☐ While I know that I do not have to lose my cultural distinctiveness to fit in, I realize that I may have to learn new information and skills to succeed in the dominant culture.

☐ I look for and cultivate members of the dominant culture who will help me "read between the lines" to understand the unwritten rules about "how the system works."

☐ When I succeed in the dominant culture, I am careful not to make myself an exception or separate myself from others of my background.

☐ I share what I learn about the dominant culture with others like myself.

☐ I recognize that when under pressure, I tend to revert to narrower beliefs to make myself and my culture right and others wrong.

☐ I sympathize and collaborate with other non-dominant groups to achieve common objectives in the dominant culture.

☐ I resist the inclination to cluster *only* with my own kind of people or *only* with people from the dominant culture when I am in mixed company.

☐ I resist blaming the dominant group for everything that goes wrong.

☐ I share with members of the dominant culture the distinctive qualities and accomplishments of my own culture.

☐ I know how to present distinctive points of view in ways that others can hear and understand.

☐ I can respect individuals of other cultures and treat them fairly even though I may be fiercely committed to conflicting political goals.

☐ I know how to refresh myself from the wellsprings of my own culture when I am exhausted by trying to understand and work in the dominant culture.[26]

2. What can you do as a manager to reduce problems of minority discrimination?

3. Write a brief article describing what it is like (or what you think it would be like) to work (or study) in an organization in which you are a nondominant culture member.

4. Commit yourself to improving your vision of greater cultural diversity. Pick two people with whom you share your vision during the next week. Make a commitment to do this now. Report your experience.

5. Interview an ethnic and racial group businessperson to gain insights into her or his experiences in the workplace.

6. Answer the introductory questions at the beginning of the chapter.

▼ NOTES

1. George Simons, *Working Together: How to Become More Effective in a Multicultural Organization* (Los Altos, Calif.: Crisp Publications, 1989), pp. 12–14.

2. Ibid., p. 14.

3. "Minority Report," *Wall Street Journal*, 8 September 1980, p. 1.

4. Lawrence L. Steinmetz, *Human Relations* (New York: Harper and Row, 1979), p. 304.

5. "Anti-bias Efforts Stir Ire of Many," *USA Today*, p.   .

6. "Diversity Provides Rewards," *USA Today*, 24 April 1992, p.

7. "Labor Letter," *Wall Street Journal*, 1 November 1988, p. A1.

8. Wiley M. Woodward, "Study Rules Plight of One-Third of a Nation," *Black Enterprise* August 1988, p. 24.

9. Ibid.

10. "Tomorrow, the World," *Black Enterprise,* June 1989, p. 187.

11. Trudy Gallant-Stokes, "Brady Keys Does Franchising Right," *Black Enterprise,* September 1983, p. 63.

12. Frank E. James, "More Blacks Quitting White-Run Firms," *Wall Street Journal,* 7 June 1988, p. 37.

13. "When the Boss Is Black," *Time,* 13 March 1989, pp. 60–61.

14. "Hispanic Groups Sow Wide Diversity," *Wall Street Journal,* 2 November 1988, p. 81.

15. Alfredo Corchado, "New Immigration Law Riles Small Businesses in Places Like El Paso," *Wall Street Journal,* 4 May 1988, pp. 1, 15.

16. Diana Solis, "Amnesty's Next Steps, toward U.S. Citizenship, May Be Long Ones for New Hispanic Immigrants," *Wall Street Journal,* 2 May 1988, p. 52; "Illegal Aliens' Amnesty Program Ends on a Note of Desperation in Some Cities," *Wall Street Journal,* 4 May 1988, p. 15.

17. Matthew Shifrin, "Horatio Alger Kim," *Forbes,* 17 October 1988, p. 92.

18. C. Matthew Snipp, "The Changing Political and Economic Status of the American Indians: From Captive Nations to Internal Colonies," *American Journal of Economics and Sociology* 45 (April 1986): 145.

19. Ibid., p. 146.

20. Ibid.

21. Ibid., p. 150.

22. Victoria S. Long, "Indian Support Group to Be Based in KC," *Kansas City Times,* 30 April 1986, p. 1.

23. Simons, *Working Together,* p. 71.

24. Ibid., p. 70.

25. Ibid.

26. George Simons, *Working Together: How to Become More Effective in a Multicultural Organization* (Los Altos, Calif.: Crisp Publications, 1989), pp. 67–68.

▼ ANOTHER LOOK: RETHINKING DIVERSITY

*The new gospel [of multicul-
turalism] condemns [the traditional American] vision of
individuals of all nations
melted into a new race in
favor of an opposite vision: a
nation of groups, differentiated in their ancestries, invi-
olable in their diverse
identities. The contemporary
ideal is shifting from assimilation to ethnicity, from integration to separatism....*

*Instead of a nation com-
posed of individuals making
their own free choices,
America increasingly sees
itself as composed of groups
more or less indelible in their
ethnic character. The national ideal had once been* e
pluribus unum. *Are we now
to belittle* unum *and glorify*
pluribus? *Will the center
hold? Or will the melting pot
yield to the Tower of
Babel?—Arthur M.
Schlesinger Jr.,* The
Disuniting of America, *1991.*

Managing diversity is
about coping with "unassimilated differences," says R.
Roosevelt Thomas Jr., president of the American
Institute for Managing
Diversity at Morehouse
College in Atlanta. "It's
about managing people who
aren't like you and who
don't necessarily aspire to be
like you."

Thomas and Schlesinger,
then, are philosophical ene-
mies? Not necessarily.
Schlesinger is right, Thomas
says, to worry about the
prospect of "Balkanization,"
the fragmentation of society
by race, culture and even
gender under the banner of

multiculturalism. "But what
he's calling multiculturalism
is not what we're calling
managing diversity,"
Thomas adds. As applied in
a business or government
organization, "managing
diversity means: How do we
build systems and a culture
that unite different people in
a common pursuit without
undermining their diversity?
It's taking differences into
account while developing a
cohesive whole."

Can we achieve *unum*
without asking the *pluribus*
in the melting pot to do quite
so much melting? If that was
ever the plan on college campuses, it doesn't appear to be
working out. From
Schlesinger's book: "The cult
of ethnicity exaggerates differences, intensifies resent-
ments and antagonisms,
drives ever deeper the awful
wedges between races and
nationalities.... Campuses
today, according to open
University of Pennsylvania
professor, have 'the cultural
diversity of Beirut. They are
separate armed camps. The
black kids don't mix with
the white kids. The Asians
are off by themselves.
Oppression is the great status
symbol.'"

Suppose, however, that we
could go at this *pluribus*
business without losing sight
of the fact that *unum* is,
indeed, our goal—a broader,
more inclusive *unum,* to be
sure. Might there not be pay-
offs for everybody?

"Some corporations are
finding," Thomas says, "that
their biggest 'diversity' prob-

lem lies in the differences
between junior white male
managers and senior white
male managers. Young
whites are not intending to
play the success game by the
same rules."

Managing diversity is not a
synonym for equal employ-
ment opportunity (EEO),
Thomas told a group of personnel specialists at a conference last year. Neither is it a
code word for affirmative
action, although he insists
that affirmative action programs must continue for the
next 20 years or so.
Managing diversity isn't
even the same thing as
"valuing differences."

"You can learn to respect
each other, you can like each
other, you can minimize
racism and sexism, you can
have better interpersonal relations. You can do all that and
still not know how to manage
diversity—because people
don't know what manage-
ment *is*," Thomas says.

Until recently, he argues,
"assimilation has made it
unnecessary to learn to manage." The corporation dictated a mold for up-and-comers
to fit: Always arrive early
and work late, never turn
down a transfer to another
city, dress like so, talk like
so, express the right opinions. "Managing" was largely
a matter of enforcing the
mold and rewarding those
who fit it best.

"Unassimilated differ-
ences" have to do only partly
with blacks who don't want
to lose their "blackness" and
women who don't want to

ANOTHER LOOK: RETHINKING DIVERSITY *continued*

give up their "femininity"—but who do want the same shot at promotions, pay hikes and authority as is given to white male Republicans with the right school ties and low golf handicaps. The problem of diversity, Thomas says, is not limited to questions of race, gender, ethnicity, disabilities and sexual orientation. The differences that sap energy and undermine productivity and performance in an organization extend to things like personality styles; your Myers-Briggs type can blind you to the abilities of people with different types. Diversity issues rear their heads whenever different professional mind-sets clash: the accountants vs. the marketers vs. the engineers.

Managing diversity is not primarily about ethics or social responsibility or "doing the right thing," Thomas says. It's about human performance. It's about making a profit. It's about remaining competitive. "The 'managing' is more important than the 'diversity,'" he insists, "because if managers are really managing, diversity will take care of itself."

The widely publicized demographic changes commonly referred to under the heading "Workforce 2000" make it inevitable that more minorities, women and immigrants will be hired, he says. And what about retaining and promoting the ones we hire? If we assume that the current clustering of

women and minorities at the bottom of the organizational pyramid is due to a corporate environment that is somehow unfriendly to them—that the "glass ceiling" reflects bias and not any lack of hard work or intelligence or merit—then what we're talking about is "the underutilization of human resources," Thomas says. "It's a managerial issue as opposed to a legal, social or moral issue."

Quite so, agrees the director of management training at a major insurance company, who asked not to be identified because her company is about to launch a new diversity effort on a worldwide scale. "To a large extent," she declares, "it's what we've been saying about management all along—people are individuals and they have to be managed as individuals. Now we're just saying, 'Hey, we were right. So let's get with it.'" If her company can learn to "manage diversity" well, she says, "That means we'll have created a climate where everyone can contribute to the best of their ability." And "everyone" includes white males.

If this sort of talk about "diversity" doesn't catch practically everybody by surprise today, it would have just a few years ago, says Robert Hayles, vice president of cultural diversity for Grand Metropolitan [North American] Food Sector (formerly Pillsbury Co.) of Minneapolis.

With a handful of exceptions—Digital Equipment Corp., US West and a few other companies—"'diversity,' five years ago, meant protected groups," Hayles says. That is, "diverse people" were members of groups covered by anti-discrimination laws, period. Diversity was, indeed, a code word for affirmative action. Over the past year or two, however, a wider definition has gained much greater currency. Hayles, who, like Thomas, is black, subscribes to the broad view himself.

According to this view, "diversity work" addresses the biases of the male manager who is reluctant to send a female to New York on business because it's too dangerous, thus denying her a fast-track career opportunity. But it also addresses the female—or male—who really *doesn't* want to make business trips to New York. Is there some other way, equally valid or even more so, to give this person the experience and seasoning needed for a promotion?

This broader view of diversity is by no means universal—and by no means universally welcomed. Most of the time, "diversity program" is still used as a synonym for EEO or affirmative action. And in some circles, a view of "diversity" that includes white males is looked upon as blasphemous. Hayles says he catches plenty of heat for his approach: "African-Americans say, 'Hey, our ancestors were brought here by force, we've suffered

ANOTHER LOOK *continued*

from racism for hundreds of years, and statistics say it'll be somewhere between the years 2100 and 3000 before we achieve parity [with whites] in jobs, income and home ownership. If you dilute diversity work, we won't see parity until the year 5000.'"

Along with dismay at the prospect of white males edging in beneath the diversity umbrella comes suspicion. "I know a professor at a university in New York who thinks it's a George Bush plot to do away with progress by women and minorities," says Sivasailam Thiagarajan, adjunct professor in the School of Education at Indiana University in Bloomington. "At universities, it is still politically incorrect to say, 'Let's use a bigger yardstick to measure differences.' It's seen as another sneaky way to get around affirmative action.'

To be sure, affirmative action supporters needn't be paranoid these days to figure that someone is out to get them. Many whites see affirmative action as reverse discrimination, plain and simple. "Quota" has become a dirty word on the national scene. George Bush leads a long list of politicians who have made hay with voters by denouncing racial hiring targets. One of the few things we do know about the Senate-probe-resistant legal views of new Supreme Court Justice Clarence Thomas is that he thinks affirmative action programs are bad news. Other nonwhite writers and professionals have also stepped for-

ward to assert that affirmative action stigmatizes its minority beneficiaries in more ways than it helps them.

There is, however, another way to look at the broadening definition of diversity.

In light of the societal backlash against "political correctness" and the police-state atmosphere said to be enveloping many college campuses, "diversity" may have been on the road to joining "quotas" as a word to be spat out in public with distaste. Something had to change.

> 'Diversity' no longer refers to a range of views on a disputed question but rather entails enlisting in a whole set of ideological causes that are identified as being "for diversity'....
>
> [In 1989], when the University of Pennsylvania was planning to require all freshmen in campus residences to participate in consciousness-raising sessions dealing with racism, sexism, and heterosexism, one undergraduate on the "diversity education" planning committee sent a note to the administration noting her reservations about the program. She expressed her "deep regard for the individual and my desire to protect the freedoms of all members of society." A university administrator sent her note back, with

the word "individual" underlined and the comment, "This is a RED FLAG phrase today, which is considered by many to be RACIST. Arguments that champion the individual over the group ultimately privilege the 'individuals' belonging to the largest or dominant group."—Dinesh D'Souza in "Illiberal Education," *The Atlantic Monthly,* March 1991.

> Today's radicalism-from-above uses administrative power to impose an improved "consciousness" on [college] students. It uses various instruments of indoctrination, from mandatory instruction in officially approved thinking (about race, gender, sexual preference) to codes of permissible speech. This is done in the name of "sensitivity" to the needs of "diversity."—George Will in *Newsweek,* May 6, 1991.

Observations like Will's are sometimes waved aside as part of a "predictable backlash" by a "white-male power structure" terrified at the prospect of having to share any power whatsoever with minorities and women. But for those who do favor advances by minorities and women, there is a nonideological issue at work here also, a straightforward problem of strategy and tactics.

ANOTHER LOOK: RETHINKING DIVERSITY *continued*

Unless I have some sort of gun to hold to your head, I can only exercise a moral claim on you to the degree that you are willing to accept my claim as valid. As a society, our tolerance for the moral claims of others is running low. A lot of people are now saying openly what they've been thinking for some time. In 1991, it was almost as if a dam burst. To wit:

The policies of penance may be most fruitless of all. You can only harangue people and tell them what bad guys and oppressors they are and that they have a debt and better make good on it for so long before they tell you to get lost.—Meg Greenfield in *Newsweek,* Aug. 5, 1991.

As the list of victims and rights expands, and as the special-interest groups that promote them grow increasingly numerous, militant and shrill, the people who constitute what remains of the social mainstream are feeling ever more beleaguered and unsympathetic.

Their well of guilt is running dry, a phenomenon that is known as "compassion fatigue"....—John Taylor in "Don't Blame Me! The New Culture of Victimization," *New York* magazine, June 3, 1991.

What is odd about the PC [politically correct] people ... is their dopey belief that people can be bullied into being kind, good and sensitive to each other, never speaking thoughtlessly to, or thinking unkindly of, people whatever their race, religion, country of national origin, sex or sexual habits.

Mostly the bullying is done by wielding brutish language.... [A]busive epithets are used mercilessly on people whose words or ideas defy the dogma of goodness.... Standard PC epithets include 'racist,' 'elitist,' 'sexist,' 'anti-Semite' and 'homophobe,' each carrying its own built-in exclamation mark. It's a language for people who talk at the top of their lungs.—Russell Baker in a *New York Times* piece syndicated nationally in August 1991.

Those epithets are losing their sting; they don't shut the other guy up as quickly today as they did yesterday. The pointed finger of guilt is less useful as a lever. Blame it on the excesses of PC. Blame it on George Bush cynically fanning racial tensions with Willy Horton in 1988 and with "quotas" ever since.

Or, better, blame it on an economy in which "mainstream people" have increasing reason to fear for their own futures, never mind anybody

else's. Corporate "downsizings" have thrown millions out of work and left millions more clinging fearfully to their jobs. Adjusted for inflation, average weekly earnings have fallen 12 percent over the past 20 years. Confidence in the American Dream is fading. Perhaps for the first time in the nation's history, there is serious, widespread doubt that our children will live better than we do.

In the past few years, ugly white-racist incidents have made headlines in some pretty odd places—not in the Old South but at Stanford and the University of Massachusetts. Between July and November 1991, police recorded 12 separate cases of cross burnings in the yards of black citizens in Dubuque, IA.

As this is written, a badly shaken nation heaved a sigh of uneasy relief as voters in Louisiana decided that they would not, after all, choose as their governor David Duke, erstwhile neo-Nazi and ex-grand wizard of the Ku Klux Klan.

We can blame all of this on just about anything we like. But unless we assume for some reason that the people of Louisiana have not seen a national news magazine or watched a network television broadcast for the past 30 years, we can't blame it on a lack of sermons. The problem simply cannot be that white folks in Louisiana haven't heard the news that racism is bad. It makes no sense any longer to pretend that the answer to the

ANOTHER LOOK *continued*

Duke problem—or the sexism problem or the homophobia problem—is to tell white males one more time, or 1,000 more times, that they are "bad guys and oppressors and that they have a debt and better make good on it."

They've all heard the message. If anything, the message now seems to be exacerbating the very problems it's supposed to solve. The blame game even shows signs of coming full circle and collapsing into comic absurdity. The San Jose *Mercury News* reports that a small group of white Californians has formed to protest stereotypes of whites as oppressors. They will badger people to use the term European-American instead of Anglo or white. One member is quoted as saying, "If someone uses the term 'lily white,' we'll contact them and explain that that shows insensitivity to European ethnic diversity."

Apparently this is earnestness, not social satire.

If we want to build a society with equal opportunity and justice for all—and businesses that function effectively with the diverse employees and customers thrust upon them by demographic changes and the global economy—the road of guilt and blame looks increasingly like a dead end.

"We can't do it the way we've been trying to do it," says Lewis Griggs of Copeland Griggs Productions in San Francisco, producer of the "Valuing Diversity" series of training films. "We've got to go back and come in through a different door."

The risk of expanding the definition of diversity, says Grand Met's Hayles, is that you may contribute to a "state of denial" about the special problems of protected groups. This must be guarded against. The advantage of starting with the premise that *everybody* is diverse, however, is that "you don't make white males the subject of the work rather than part of it."

The idea behind managing diversity is to learn to look at people as individuals, and to see individual strengths and weaknesses instead of merely registering bothersome variances from arbitrary corporate norms. The goal, says Thomas, is an organization that is able to function as productively with heterogeneous workers as it once did with homogeneous ones.

Hayles takes issue with Thomas on that point. He insists that research has established beyond any reasonable doubt that well-managed heterogeneous groups are more productive than homogeneous ones. Managing diversity, therefore, is about improving corporate performance, not just holding the line as the work force becomes less Anglo. To back his claim, Hayles cites research and writings by authorities such as Stuart W. Cook, professor emeritus at the University of Colorado, and Harvard's Rosabeth Moss Kanter. In her 1983 book, *The Change Masters,* for instance, Kanter describes a study showing that companies with "progressive

human resource practices" such as affirmative action and participative management showed unusually high profitability and financial growth over a 25-year period.

Thomas doesn't argue about what such studies have proved or failed to prove. If heterogeneous groups can indeed become more productive than homogeneous ones, he says, "that's icing on the cake. But the first challenge is to get the same level of productivity. We need to learn how to bake the cake before we worry about putting on the icing. And we don't know how to bake the cake yet."

Whether the goal is equal performance or superior performance, both men agree that the way to get there is to stop treating diversity as a moral issue and start treating it as a business issue. This focus helps explain the emphasis in diversity training on teaching lessons that often sound embarrassingly simplistic. Why would anyone over the age of eight need workshops and games and exercises to inform him that everybody is "different" in some way? Where's the blinding revelation in the news that we have all been culturally inculcated with unconscious biases? "The revelation," says Hayles, "is that our problems with differences cost money. They cost productivity."

"The attempt of diversity training is precisely to get out of the guilt cycle," says Adriana Arzac, executive director of the International Society for Intercultural

ANOTHER LOOK: RETHINKING DIVERSITY *continued*

Education, Training and Research (SIETAR). "The point is not to say, 'OK, you white guys, clean up your act and shame on you'.... The same stereotypes the white male has of minorities and women are also working in reverse."

The guilt-free diversity trolley may still jump the track, however, unless we find a better way to conduct discussions about stereotypes and sensitivities. Merely adding white male gripes to the ever-expanding pile of behavioral do's and don'ts is pointless. If the idea behind all this is to help people work together more productively, then learning to respect or "value" differences cannot be a matter of everyone exchanging and memorizing lists of peeves: Joe learns that he must never forget himself and use a term like "salesman" or "chairman" around Betty, and he must always refer to Maya as a "woman of color," to Diana as "black," and to Sam as a "Chinese American" rather than an "Asian American." Betty, Maya, Diana and Sam learn to all Joe a European American but never to call Bob one because Bob thinks the term is extraordinarily silly, although he must never say so or laugh at it because that would transgress against Joe's diversity....

These are not people who will like one another, trust one another, be comfortable with one another or do any creative work together. These are porcupines, bristling with hyper-acute sensitivities, circling one another warily and on tip-toe.

Thiagarajan quotes George Bernard Shaw: "A friend is somebody in whose presence I can do as I damn please." We might expand that sentiment and suggest that a coworker with whom I can accomplish great things is one to whom I can say what I damn well think."

Confronting bigotry is one thing, Hayles declares. But what about all the well-meaning people who are struggling as best they can to work together effectively? Surely there must be something better to offer them than checklists of booby-trapped words and forbidden opinions.

The spirit of the age favors the moralist and the busybody, and the instinct to censor and suppress shows itself not only in the protests for and against abortion or multiculturalism but also in the prohibitions against tobacco and pet birds. It seems that everybody is forever looking out for everybody else's spiritual or physical salvation.... The preferred modes of address number only three—the sermon, the euphenism, and the threat—and whether I look to the political left or the political right I'm constantly being told to think the right thoughts and confess the right sins....

A society in which everybody distrusts everybody else classifies humor as a dangerous substance and entertains itself with cautionary tales.... I see so many citizens armed with the bright shield of intolerance that I wonder how they would agree on anything other than a need to do something repressive and authoritarian.—Lewis H. Lapham in *Harper's*, October 1991.

It is in that spirit of humorless, sermonistic distrust that we have grown used to carrying on the national conversation about stereotypes and biases and who has been thinking the wrong thoughts about whom. Thiagarajan notes ruefully that a national training association has recently begun warning speakers at its conferences that it will not tolerate any attempts at humor that might prove offensive to any individual or group—this in the name of respecting diversity. "So I can't make fun of Hindus?" asks Thiagarajan, who is Hindu. "I can't make fun of stupid people?"

If the goal of diversity work is a high-performance organization rather than just a climate in which nobody's feathers are ever ruffled, we need a different way to talk about the problem of differences.

"We've got to be *more* willing to accidentally offend each other," says Griggs. "Let's know that we're going to make mistakes and try to patch them up instead of trying to ward off all possible mistakes.

ANOTHER LOOK *continued*

That's the wrong tack. If we develop the right attitude of 'standing in neutral' with respect to the likelihood that somebody has a different attitude about something, we won't need lists of wrong words to avoid."

SOURCE: Jack Gordon, "Rethinking Diversity," *Training*, January 1992, pp. 23–30.

ANOTHER LOOK: MANAGING DIVERSITY

Imagine that Chrysler Corporation chairman Lee Iacocca has just named his successor: an African-American woman who is a single parent. The scenario is still so far-fetched that most managers in America can't even envision it. And that's the problem. Two decades of affirmative action at the workplace and a diversifying population at large have changed the complexion of corporate America, adding more women, minorities and immigrants. But now that we've assembled a rainbow workforce, there's only one problem—how to make it work effectively.

Successfully integrating the new employees throughout a company's operations, including the executive suites, is proving more difficult than anyone expected. Often just holding onto these workers can be an accomplishment.

For many Americans, work is the only place where we commingle freely with those from different backgrounds. And while that is theoretically the fulfillment of the American Dream, the result is often a managerial nightmare. Company after company is discovering that the opportunity for person-to-person misunderstanding is so great it threatens productivity. And the white-European-male-oriented corporate culture, which has reigned ever since Adam Smith invented capitalism, simply doesn't encourage all kinds of workers to flourish.

SHAKEN EXECUTIVES

Managing the so-called "demographically diverse" workforce, under normal circumstances, might have been left to the devices of human resources directors. But an extraordinary fact has catapulted concern all the way into the boardroom. A shortage of skilled workers is coming, and competing for a capable workforce is shaking top executives right down to their well-polished wingtips.

The nation's current high unemployment rate of 6.8 percent masks a menacing labor shortage. Between now and 2000, the Bureau of Labor Statistics reports, annual growth in the U.S. workforce will slow to 1.2 percent, down from the 2 percent growth of 1976 to 1988. By 2000, white men (including Hispanics) will account for just 45 percent of the total workforce, down from 48 percent in 1980.

This is a state of affairs William Hanson faced early on, as vice president of manufacturing personnel at Massachusetts-based Digital Equipment Corp. A pioneer in equal employment opportunity, Digital, one of the largest multinational corporations in the U.S., was struggling to absorb new workforce entrants in 1979. The newcomers were competing for jobs traditionally held by white males at the high-tech computer manufacturer. No matter what managers did, blacks and whites were segregating themselves on the work floor and again in the cafeteria.

Alan Zimmerle, Digital's current corporate manager of affirmative action programs, explains: "In those early days, we had a strong EEO program, but white males resented having to 'do something special' for the minorities. The black men were resentful, feeling 'we don't need whites to take care of

ANOTHER LOOK: MANAGING DIVERSITY *continued*

us.' And at meetings, black women felt as if they were 'invisible.'"

With tensions escalating, Hanson called in Barbara Walker as a consultant. The insights she reached and the programs she implemented are now serving as a model for managing diversity across America.

An attorney by training, Walker had spent 17 years in federal agencies ushering in civil rights. Hanson's mandate to Walker: Help manufacturing deal with "the black/white thing." Needing "some people I trusted," Walker set up a small discussion group of seven senior managers, "all of whom had different questions about different things."

Walker quickly sensed that the real issue was: how to divide the goodies in the corporate pie. How would people be judged and promoted? By whose criteria? Clearly, the prevailing view of affirmative action—that some would be promoted at the expense of others—was breeding resentment on the one hand and self-doubt on the other.

The smallness of the group made it safe for people to open up about racial and cultural stereotypes. Getting to the root of "the black/white thing" led to "the male/female thing, the short/tall thing, the Hispanic/others thing....," recalls Walker.

Once she got the executives talking, Walker realized that they held a world of

negative assumptions about the "others," whether they were black, female, Asian or homosexual. "Black and white men and women were making flagrantly negative assumptions about each other, from great social distances. People were working together physically but separated by a huge gulf of misunderstanding."

One woman became enraged as she explained to the group some of the ways her male colleagues put her down. As her voice grew louder and louder, one man finally interrupted: "I don't know what you're complaining about—at least you're white."

"That opened it up," recalls Walker, now the vice president of human resources and human relations at the University of Cincinnati. "Once that got said, we were able to begin to see the dynamics of race and gender."

Another powerful insight: After listening to some members of the group describe certain ways they felt white women were insensitive, one got up, pounded on the table and screamed, "Stop calling me a white woman. I am not a white woman!" Of course she was. But both she and the group members learned how powerfully people resent being slapped with a negative stereotype.

In the competitive milieu of Digital, managers left out of the early group began pressuring Walker to involve them. By the time she had

set up five or so groups, each with seven members from disparate backgrounds, she realized: "Maybe everybody wants to talk about it." The early informal groups have been formalized into a program of "core" groups in which employees are asked (but not required) to participate. Led by employees specially trained to diffuse tension and get honest participation, these groups meet for about 10 weeks to discuss among coworkers specific fears and apprehensions as they arise.

By giving members a period of time to get comfortable with one another, the core groups created a "looseness between black and white." Says Walker: "We were bonding." The groups also have exposed a host of private feelings that typically compromise public performance in the culturally diverse workplace. Walker has found that:

■ When black managers make a point forcefully in a meeting, no matter how justified, whites tend to react as if they have been unduly threatened.

■ Blacks are especially sensitive to "the sacred closet of race." Often raised not to let outsiders know what their experience is like, they may label as "traitors" those who reveal to whites their intimate feelings and experiences. As a result, many have been taught to isolate themselves and mistrust all white people.

ANOTHER LOOK *continued*

■ Latinos often appear clannish because they are drawn together by their common language, even though they may come from a variety of countries and cultures.

The core groups are still going strong at Digital, where an expanded program it calls "Valuing Diversity" also includes a variety of ethnic celebrations. The company has found that the payoff is more than bonding. Affirmative action chief Zimmerle reports that productivity has improved significantly in the manufacturing division. The number of women in management has increased 20-fold in the past 10 years. And there are important competitive advantages as well.

"Diversity breeds innovation in product development and in sales," says Zimmerle. "Understanding differences gives us a competitive edge because, in a global environment, our customer base has changed radically over the past 20 years. Previously, white males made sales calls to other white males. Today's customer may be of any ethnic or racial group, man or woman."

The fact of cultural differences, experienced executives say, has changed the managerial mission. The task is no longer to treat all employees the same and mold them to a monolithic corporate culture, but to see them individually and to open the promotion pipeline to people who change the rules.

How well are you fostering these goals? There are very concrete steps you can take in your own department. Even if your company has paid only lip service to diversity, increasing morale and productivity while slowing turnover can only make you look good.

■ Watch the numbers. By analyzing your workforce composition, you can establish just how well you've done so far. Count the numbers of minorities, women, immigrants and, if possible, homosexuals in your company. How many have been promoted to key positions recently? What is the turnover rate among those groups? Corning Inc., for example, was spurred to action in the mid-1980s when a new CEO realized that women and minorities were leaving the company at twice the rate of white men, costing a painful $3 million a year.

■ Talk diversity issues over with your coworkers. Many companies require employees to attend training sessions that force them to look at their own prejudices. Corning mandates that its managers and professionals attend gender- and racial-awareness seminars. In Digital's Valuing Diversity program, sexual orientation, particularly considering the specter of AIDS, is "a huge emotional issue," says Walker. And while the rhetoric at some of these seminars may sound like psychobabble, training sessions can produce important results. "I learned I wasn't as liberal as I had thought," confesses Susan Whitney, a Digital manager supervising production in a number of countries. If seminars are beyond your budget, hundreds of firms use a series of videotapes (Copeland Griggs Productions, 415-668-4200) produced with funding from America's major corporations.

■ Actively engage diversity by making others aware of it. By definition, diversity brings multiple perspectives, a boon to solving problems. But studies have shown that diversity spurs creativity in problem solving only if coworkers have advance awareness of the attitudinal differences among them. Informing members of a work group that differences exist among them, reports Taylor Cox Jr. of the University of Michigan Business School, fosters creativity in solving problems and making decisions.

■ Thinking interculturally whenever problems develop. If you find yourself frustrated in talking with others, remember that almost all communication problems are culturally influenced,

ANOTHER LOOK: MANAGING DIVERSITY *continued*

advises Sara B. Cegelski, who designs intercultural training programs for Wordsmart, a Rochester, New York, company. Mainstream U.S. culture values conversation that proceeds in a direct manner, from point A to B to C. But people in other cultures prefer to talk in metaphors, weave detours, and touch on tangential issues before they get to a point. They are not less logical or less focused on the task.

- Examine opportunities for mentoring employees of diverse backgrounds at all levels. A number of CEOs are seeking an education from specially formed task forces. Tenneco, for

instance, recently formed eight women-only advisory councils other information with top management and each other to help promote women within the organization.

- Make sure your standards are fluid enough for all achievers. Watching people react to the annual anxiety of performance appraisal can teach you a lot. Whites, particularly men, are afraid they will be held back to make room for someone else. Others may be defeated and defiant before they sit down. Promotions are the ultimate acid test of your diversity policy: If you've always used, say, the number of hours worked

as an important criterion in promotions, it may be time for you to develop standards that are more flexible. You may be ruling out single parents, for example.

- Reward managers who are doing it right. Many companies have instituted salary incentives, bonuses and special recognition for managers who hire, and more importantly, hang on to and promote, workers from a variety of racial backgrounds.

Move over, Lee Iacocca.

SOURCE: Marlene Piturro and Sarah S. Mahoney, "Managing Diversity," *Executive Female*, May/June 1991, pp. 45–48.

▼ A CASE IN POINT: THE DOWNSIZING OF ABC LEARNING, INC.

The ten persons listed below are co-workers at ABC Learning, Inc. Due to general financial problems in the economy, ABC has experienced a drastic reduction in the attendance at its public seminars. Consequently, to be able to keep functioning during what it believes to be a temporary turndown in the economy, it has decided that it must reduce its staff by 30 percent. Your task (given the information listed below) is to select the three employees to be cut.

After you have selected your three, get together with several other students to see if they selected the same three as you. If not, why do you suppose you selected different people? After talking with others, would you change any of your selections?

LIST OF ABC EMPLOYEES:

Sue Winder, president of ABC, raised in Kansas City, Missouri, and a human resource management graduate of the University of Iowa. Started ABC with her brother John in 1978. The company, although small, has been very successful in the public seminar business. Occasionally, she must downsize, and occasionally, she must increase the size of her firm, depending primarily on the state of the economy.

Bill Jonas, vice-president of marketing, a Navajo from Tuba City, Arizona. Bill graduated from Northern Arizona State University in Flagstaff with a degree in marketing. His studies emphasized direct-mail marketing. He has

A CASE IN POINT *continued*

worked with three large direct-mail, public seminar companies prior to coming to work for ABC. He has ten years of experience.

Paul Singh, vice-president of finance, is a graduate of Madras University in accounting who immigrated to the United States in 1980. He has taken a few special finance courses from the University of Phoenix. He is fiscally conservative and is constantly concerned about cash flow.

Jose Gonzales, legal counsel, received his law degree from Pepperdine University. Born and raised in Los Angeles, he has focused his career on small start-up companies, such as ABC. He has been with the company two months and is very concerned about the cutback and the legal problems associated with laying people off.

Chick Sanderson works as the key sales person for ABC and is responsible for making the plans of Bill Jonas work. Chick's dad owned a used car lot and taught him the tricks of the sales trade. Chick knows that if ABC would let him sell his way, he could sell thousands of seminars. Chick went to work for his dad after he graduated from high school. He has been with ABC for two years.

Sally Kozlowski is the secretary. She spent one year at secretarial school and can operate all the company's computer programs. She is especially proficient in WordPerfect and Lotus. Everyone in the company comes to her for any secretarial work.

Roberta Johnson is the receptionist. She graduated from City College of Pomona. She is African American and an excellent employee. Many of those who call the company for a seminar or for help comment on the wonderful treatment they get from the receptionist. Roberta has been with ABC for a month.

Jake Waters graduated from the University of California-Los Angeles in speech communica-

tion and has become the best rated trainer at ABC. He is handsome and intelligent. His blond hair and muscular build attract many interesting comments in his teacher evaluations. He has been considering asking for a raise because he is the most productive trainer at ABC.

Sheldon Brown graduated from the University of Washington with a degree in human resource development. He is an African American with a strong feeling about the importance of education and training. His seminars get good ratings because he spends so much time dealing with the content of the seminars. His delivery is OK, and he comes across as someone who is in the know.

Lola Pongi, was born and raised in Samoa, moving with her family to Oakland, California, when she was ten. Lola attended the University of California-Berkeley for two years and then went to work selling makeup for a local firm, during which time she discovered that she was an excellent presenter. She auditioned with ABC to teach its professional appearance seminar and has been a successful trainer in this area for ten years.

List the three individuals that you would cut from the company. Give at least one reason for each decision.

Person One _____

Reason _____

_____

_____

Person Two _____

Reason _____

_____

_____

Person Three _____

Reason _____

_____

_____

▼ A CASE IN POINT: FRANK'S CHOICE

Frank Santiago was the first Hispanic to be promoted to supervisor at fast-growing Ridgeway Telecommunications. He had always felt that management treated him fairly, but he also recognized that many minority workers seemed to fare less well. At times he wondered if he was a "token" Hispanic promoted to illustrate that the company was fair to minorities. But overall he could find no evidence to support that suspicion. Indeed, Frank was generally seen as a "fast-track" manager destined for higher leadership possibilities.

But now the shoe was on the other foot. Jeff Buchanan, a black worker who had lost his left arm below the elbow while serving in Vietnam, was discouraged about his career opportunities. He wanted the new foreman's position that had opened up, and he had talked for almost an hour to Frank without getting much reassurance. The conversation weighed heavily on Frank's mind as he called Marsha Mason, the personnel manager, for some advice.

"Marsha, I'm confused. I'm well aware that Ridgeway claims to have an affirmative action program, but I'm not sure how I should handle Jeff," he began. "He wants the second shift foreman's job, but frankly he's not the most qualified. But at the same time, every other candidate for the job is white, and he may be pretty upset if he's not selected. How serious are we about this affirmative action stuff, Marsha?"

You are well aware of our AA plan, Frank, but we also have to be realistic about who we promote," said Marsha. "We're not a giant corporation where a few less-effective people can be absorbed without much damage. Who is best qualified?"

"If that's the only question, I'd recommend Billy Joe Hammond. He has more senority than Jeff and I think he's more conscientious," Frank replies.

"Well, you do what you think is best," Marsha responded. "But you probably should be aware that the EEOC people have been in here counting noses and have made it pretty clear to me that they'd like to see a few more dark ones. And with Jeff being handicapped, we'd make a few more points. So if your recommendation of Billy Joe gets overruled, don't take it personally."

QUESTIONS

1. What potential problems would Frank face if he recommended Jeff Buchanan for the promotion?
2. What problems might Frank face if he recommended Billy Joe Hammond?
3. What long term benefits might Ridgeway Telecommunications gain from promoting Jeff?
4. If you were Frank, what would you do?

SOURCE: Paul Timm, *Supervision* (St. Paul: West 1992), p. 364. Reprinted by permission from *Supervision* by Paul R. Timm. Copyright © 1992 by West Publishing Company. All rights reserved.

CHAPTER

14

WOMEN AS MANAGERS AND CO-WORKERS

This chapter answers several all-important questions:

■ How has the role of women in the workplace changed over the last fifty years?

■ What are some traditionally male fields that have opened to women?

■ Why should women seek line-management positions in a company?

■ Why are mentor relationships important?

■ What are some specific issues faced by working parents?

■ What are some effective ways of dealing with sexual harassment?

■ What can managers do to support and encourage female employees?

The answers to these and other questions are coming up next in chapter 14....

CHAPTER 14

The changes in the demographics of the work force during the past fifty years have been dramatic. While most women were once full-time homemakers, today almost half of the U.S. laborforce is female. The number of mothers with jobs has increased, too. See the comparison in Table 14.1.

Movies and television shows reflect these changes; in recent years, they have provided a wide range of images of women working outside the home. Women on the screen run the gamut from the successful single-mother journalist in "Murphy Brown", to the self-made *Working Girl,* to the down-to-earth mother of three and blue-collar worker in "Roseanne."

The reasons women work are numerous and varied. Some are economic; even married women who would like to stay home often find that two incomes are needed to make house and car payments. But many women are seeking levels of self-fulfillment they find unavailable at home. Broader educational opportunities for women beginning in the 1950s and 1960s allowed greater numbers of women to enter traditionally male fields, such as medicine, law, and engineering. Assisted by the women's movement, women have come to believe that they do not need to give up a satisfying career for marriage and children but can combine all three.

As with any change, there was some resistance to the women's movement. Opponents caused considerable pressure on those advocating the change. The resistance to changing roles for women in the workplace was not limited to males; often women had difficulties seeing themselves and other women as executives, managers, laborers, and so forth.

Nevertheless, it appears that women have won the initial battle in the fight for equal rights. Society has largely accepted the idea that women have a legitimate place in the economic structure and that they have a right to any job for which they are qualified.

Women and business, then, have entered a second phase of the revolution. What remains is for many existing cultural processes, institutions, and assumptions to adjust to the transformation wrought by the women's movement.[1] Women's mass migration to jobs has brought to the attention of business a number of new issues, including career opportunities and advancement for women, parental leave, child care, and sexual harassment.

▼   TABLE 14.1 GROWTH IN WOMEN IN THE WORKFORCE

1960

33 percent of women worked in 1964. In 1959, 18.7 percent of married women in the labor force had children under age 6.

1990

Women comprise 46.8 percent of the workforce, and 57.1 percent of married women in the workforce have children under age 6.

SOURCES: *Doug McClain,* "That Was Then, This Is Now," *Advertising Age,* 30 July 1990, p. 28; Joel Dreyfuss, "Get Ready for the New Work Force," *Fortune,* 23 April 1990, p. 167.

▼ RECRUITING AND PROMOTING FEMALE WORKERS

Modern organizations generally see the value in an effective strategy to recruit, employ, promote, and develop female employees. In recent years, there have been enormous social and governmental pressures to include women as potential employees. The Civil Rights Acts of 1964 and 1991 help protect women against discrimination in hiring and promotion. Affirmative action programs (as discussed in chapter 13) have helped women gain a more equitable proportion of jobs.

Many traditionally male positions are now being filled by females; likewise, men are taking jobs traditionally filled by women, such as nursing, secretarial, and flight attendant positions. Human relations-smart companies aggressively seek competent women outside the organization and provide greater opportunities for potential female managers already within the firm. In the spirit of affirmative action, a business might set a goal of attempting to hire or promote a certain number of qualified women into management positions during the coming year.

Organizations should be careful, however, to avoid setting *quotas*. The *Bakke* case, discussed in chapter 13, indicates the importance of avoiding quotas. To announce a rigid preferential system in which, say, 20 percent of all employees must be female is exclusionary; it is also illegal as well as bad business. Recent Supreme Court decisions have allowed challenges to some affirmative action agreements set up by companies or local governments.

To effectively move women into positions of authority in organizations requires a dual responsibility: companies must actively develop women's management skills, and female employees must learn how to advance their careers.

▼ PROMOTION OPPORTUNITIES IN LINE MANAGEMENT

For women to genuinely participate in organizational power, they must be encouraged and must seek to be offered *line-management* positions. In many organizations, women are more likely to be offered management-level jobs in *staff* roles such as public relations, personnel, accounting, and data processing. Yet responsibility for making high-powered decisions is often in sales, finance, and production. In these more weighty areas, decisions can affect corporate profitability and growth. Titles, nice offices, and inconsequential assignments are only cosmetic in nature and will do little to respond to the demand for power. In many cases, management's commitment to eliminate institutional sexism is most clearly evidenced by the number of women holding significant *line* positions.[2] Women can use a number of strategies to advance their careers. *Working*

■ Why are promotions to line-management jobs preferable to many women?

Woman magazine suggests that in making career decisions, at the least the following should be done:

1. *Develop a step-by-step career plan.* A well-conceived plan gives an outline for success.

2. *Get as much education as possible.* Investing in education can be the single smartest move a career-oriented woman can make.

3. *Be flexible.* Be willing to relocate for a new job or switch to a new career.

4. *Select a predominantly male field.* Salaries are usually higher in male-dominated fields.

Further, in 1992, *Working Woman* suggested the following hottest careers for women:[3]

1. Actuary
2. Bankruptcy attorney
3. Biotech salesperson
4. Certified financial planner
5. Employment attorney
6. Environmental engineer
7. "50-plus" marketer
8. Health designer/architect
9. Home entertainment marketer
10. Home health care specialist
11. Human resources manager
12. Information systems specialist
13. International accountant
14. International entrepreneur
15. Loan specialist
16. Managed health care manager
17. Meteorologist
18. Nurse anesthetist
19. Ombudsperson
20. Physical therapist
21. Physician's assistant
22. Radiology technician
23. Special education teacher
24. Technical writer
25. Telecommunications manager

Following are education requirements and potential salaries for six of these careers:[4]

- *Actuary:* Education—An undergraduate degree in mathematics or economics. Salary—Entry level: $25,000–$29,000; top level: Over $100,000.

- *Environmental engineer:* Education—An undergraduate degree in science or engineering. Salary—Entry level: $27,000–$32,000; top level: $75,000–$100,000.

- *Human Resource Manager:* Education—A business-oriented undergraduate degree. Salary—Entry level: $23,000–$27,000; top level: $100,000–$200,000.

- *Loan Specialist:* Education—A business, banking, or commercial or real estate lending background helps. Salary—Entry level: $45,000–$55,000; top level: $150,000 plus.

- *Meteorologist:* Education—A bachelor's degree in meteorology. Salary—Entry level: $20,000; top level: $55,000–$60,000.

- *Physical therapist:* Education—A bachelor's degree in physical therapy is preferred; however, a certificate from an accredited program is acceptable. Salary—Entry level: $31,000; top level: $75,000.

▼ MENTOR RELATIONSHIPS

Several studies of women who have been highly successful in management positions seem to reveal that women's upward acceleration was largely due to their relationships with bosses who supported them. Such a boss often plays the role of a *mentor:* a wise and trusted counselor; a supporter of his or her subordinates.

- What is a mentor?

The female employee who is interested in advancement can benefit from an older, more experienced employee who shows her the ropes. Women who have worked their way into middle- and upper-management positions serve as mentors to younger women. A woman who is executive vice-president of a large Midwestern advertising agency says that she sees supporting young female employees as an important role. She watches hiring, promotions, and salaries. "It's a mission for me," she says.[5]

Mentor relationships tend to include a bond of affection as long as the protege is dependent. There is often a stormy or tense end of the relationship when the protege feels ready to strike out on her own.

Organizations should attempt to break down sex-based roles to ensure that women—especially those new in management positions—receive opportunities to develop mentor relationships.

▼ ORGANIZATIONAL SUPPORT

In addition to fostering mentor relationships, successful organizations can provide female employees with a manager who performs four essential functions:

1. Provides an effective role model for women to emulate.
2. Helps female subordinates identify alternative ladders to success and helps them design career development programs.

3. Knows the importance of identifying concrete goals and facilitates plans for achieving them.

4. Evaluates and provides systematic, valid, ongoing feedback on the employees' efforts.[6]

▼ WOMEN AS ENTREPRENEURS

For a variety of reasons—more experience, more confidence, changing life-styles, more options, need for a job, and need to work at home, among others—an increasing number of women have launched their own businesses. A recent study indicated that during the second half of 1992, female-owned organizations will employ as many employees as all of the Fortune 500 companies. Some women have even turned their small businesses into big businesses. Fashion designer Liz Claiborne, for example, found her ambitions stifled at the company where she worked, so she started her own apparel company. Sales have grown over the past decade at an annual pace of almost 36 percent, to nearly $2 billion, while profits have increased 42 percent annually, to $205 million. Today, Liz Claiborne is not just one of the country's most successful clothing companies— it is one of its most successful companies, period.[7]

Donna Brooks-Taylor and Paula Robinson opened a communications, marketing, and graphics firm two years ago. When interviewed last year, they admitted to praying a bit. But in the past year, prayer gave w
ay to tough business decisions and tighter monitoring of expenses. This has put their firm on solid ground. "We're flexing our muscles and saying 'This is our business,'" says Brooks Taylor. The company comfortably cleared its revenue goal of half a million dollars for 1991 and this year expects to double its revenue to $1 million.[8]

An increasing number of women have found exceptional opportunities as entrepreneurs.

ACTIVITY: WOMEN AS MANAGERS SCALE (WAMS)

The following items are an attempt to assess the attitudes people have about women in business. The best answer to each statement is your honest *personal opinion*. The statements cover many different and opposing points of view; you may find yourself agreeing strongly with some of the statements, disagreeing just as strongly with others, and perhaps uncertain about others. Whether you agree or disagree with any statement, you can be sure that many people feel the same way you do.

RATING SCALE:

1. Strongly disagree
2. Disagree
3. Slightly disagree
4. Neither disagree nor agree
5. Slightly agree
6. Agree
7. Strongly agree

Using the numbers from 1 to 7 on the rating scale, indicate your personal opinion about each statement in the blank that immediately precedes it. Remember, give your *personal opinion* according to how much you agree or disagree with each item. Please respond to all items.

____ 1. It is less desirable for women than for men to have a job that requires responsibility.

____ 2. Women have the objectivity required to evaluate business situations properly.

____ 3. Challenging work is more important to men than it is to women.

____ 4. Men and women should be given equal opportunity for participation in management training programs.

____ 5. Women have the capability to acquire the necessary skills to be successful managers.

____ 6. On the average, women managers are less capable of contributing to an organization's overall goals than are men.

____ 7. It is not acceptable for women to assume leadership roles as often as men.

____ 8. The business community should someday accept women in key managerial positions.

____ 9. Society should regard work by female managers as valuable as work by male managers.

____ 10. It is acceptable for women to compete with men for top executive positions.

____ 11. The possibility of pregnancy does not make women less desirable employees than men.

____ 12. Women would no more allow their emotions to influence their managerial behavior than would men.

____ 13. Problems associated with menstruation should not make women less desirable than men as employees.

____ 14. To be a successful executive, a woman does not have to sacrifice some of her femininity.

____ 15. On the average, a woman who stays at home all the time with her children is a better mother than a woman who works outside the home at least half time.

____ 16. Women are less capable of learning mathematical and mechanical skills than are men.

____ 17. Women are not ambitious enough to be successful in the business world.

____ 18. Women cannot be assertive in business situations that demand it.

____ 19. Women possess the self-confidence required of a good leader.

____ 20. Women are not competitive enough to be successful in the business world.

____ 21. Women cannot be aggressive in business situations that demand it.

____ Total

SCORING INSTRUCTIONS

1. On the WAMS instrument, circle each reverse-scored item: 1, 3, 6, 7, 15, 16, 17, 18, 20, and 21.

ACTIVITY: WOMEN AS MANAGERS SCALE (WAMS) *continued*

2. Score these items "backwards," i.e., 7 = 1, 6 = 2, 5 = 3, 4 = 4, 3 = 5, 2 = 6, and 1 = 7. Write your new score for each of these items in front of your original number for the statement.

3. Add the scores you now have for all twenty-one statements to obtain a total score for the WAMS.

NORMATIVE DATA

WAMS scores are available for 308 male employees and 114 female employees. This sample covers a wide range of age, education, and job functions for employees in several organizations. There are separate norms for males and females because female respondents as a group have higher WAMS scores than male respondents as a group.

	Males	*Females*
Top 25 percent	118 or above	131 or above
Middle 50 percent	91–117	110–130
Bottom 25 percent	90 or below	109 or below

Thus, a male respondent with a score of 120 would have attitudes toward women as managers that could be classified as more favorable than males in general, and a male respondent with a score of 85 would have attitudes toward women as managers that could be classified as less favorable than males in general. Similar interpretations can be made for female respondents using the normative data for females.

SOURCE: James R. Terborg, Lawrence H. Peters, Daniel R. Ilgen, and Frank Smith, "Organizational and Personal Correlates of Attitudes toward Women As Managers," *Academy of Management Journal* 20(1977):89–100.

Other successful female entrepreneurs have found a specialized marketing niche. Judi Sheppard Missett, CEO and president of Jazzercise, was a professional dancer and dance instructor. She noticed a high dropout rate among homemakers and young mothers in her jazz dance classes. Well ahead of the current fitness boom, she realized there was an untapped market of women who liked the exercise of dance but didn't want professional training. So she developed a casual dance class focusing on fitness, taught in a room without mirrors. It was a success. Eventually, Missett began training other instructors and then set up franchises. Today, her company has thirty-eight hundred franchises worldwide, which, along with her books, records, and mail-order and fitness-gear operations, bring her $13 million in annual revenues.[9]

According to the career survey in *Working Woman,* successful female entrepreneurs enjoy the freedom and excitement of their enterprises and see them as financial opportunities.[10] Yet women still face obstacles to independent business success. More than half of the female owners have service businesses, and another third have retail and wholesale businesses. While these types of businesses require less investment, they also have limited potential for growth and revenues. Female-owned small businesses account for only 12 percent of the total small-business revenues in the United States.[11]

▼ WORKING MOTHERS

In 1978, Title VII of the Civil Rights Act of 1964 was amended to prohibit sex discrimination on the basis of pregnancy. Women affected by pregnancy, child birth, or related medical conditions shall be treated the same for all employment-related purposes, including receipt of benefits under fringe benefit programs, as other persons not so affected but similar in their ability or inability to work. This act has been a great help to women during pregnancy. However, as more women continue to work after having children, parents face the challenge of providing proper care for their children. A number of companies realize that worried parents are not productive workers. Hoping to retain trained employees, they are looking for ways to help parents cope with the stresses on the single-parent family or the family in which both parents work.

Parental Leave

Parental leave is one benefit that some companies are now providing. It allows parents to take a certain amount of time off to care for a newborn or newly adopted child or for very ill children or elderly parents. Legislation to make parental leave a mandatory benefit nationally was introduced in Congress every year since 1985 but died without a vote until 1991. In that year, the Family and Medical Leave Act, which would have required businesses with fifty or more employees to provide up to ten weeks of unpaid family leave, was passed by Congress but vetoed by President George Bush.

Surveys show that most Americans favor parental leave. Nevertheless, business groups such as the U.S. Chamber of Commerce have opposed it, citing the cost and governmental intrusion into business.

Child Care

Single parents or caretaker parents who decide to work face the difficult task of finding quality care for the children at an affordable price. In recent years, some companies have begun working with employees to find solutions to the child care dilemma. Concepts such as in-house day care, job sharing, and *flextime* (where parents arrange their own hours) are helping both two-worker families and single parents.

■ What is flextime?

The Campbell Soup Company has had on-site day care for several years. The company also has a flextime policy in which flexible work hours compensate for child care demands; for example, one parent might work from 7 A.M. to 3:30 P.M., to arrive home when the children are out of school. Campbell also provides a one-month paid maternity leave and a three-month unpaid leave for any worker to care for a new child or sick relative.

To help its employees across the country, IBM began Child Care Referral Service in 1984, which now offers information on child care providers in more than two hundred communities. IBM has also provided money to improve facilities and recruit additional child

Maintaining a career and raising a child requires flexibility.

care providers for its employees. Last year, the company began a program to help with care of elderly relatives, as well.

In addition to these benefits, some companies are trying out other family policies. Some allow two or more employees to share a job, each working part-time; this is called job sharing. Others allow employees to work a reduced schedule to care for children or sick relatives, while staying on a career track. Still others provide group insurance covering nursing home costs for elderly parents.

Many managers believe that a family policy attracts good employees and reduces turnover. "When you make a company a better place to work, you attract better people," says R. Gordon McGovern, president and CEO of Campbell Soup. "My argument is that women are 50 percent of the population, and we should have our share of the best of them working for us."[12]

■ What is job sharing?

▼ SEXUAL HARASSMENT

A pat on the rear end. Unwanted flirtation. Obscene jokes or comments about appearance. Pressure to trade sexual favors for a promotion. These are forms of sexual harassment. As more women have entered the work force, sexual harassment on the job has become a growing problem—primarily for women, but occasionally for men as well.

The Civil Rights Acts of 1964 and 1991 made sexual harassment illegal, as a form of sexual discrimination. But this provision has been difficult to enforce, even after 1980, when the Equal Employment Opportunity Commission published guidelines to help corporations follow the law.

■ What is sexual harassment?

Sexual harassment includes any unwelcome sexual advance.

The EEOC defined *sexual harassment* as

Unwelcome sexual advances, requests for sexual favors, and other verbal or physical contact of a sexual nature constitutes sexual harassment when:

1. Submission to such conduct is made either explicitly or implicitly a term or condition of an individual's employment.
2. Submission to or rejection of such conduct by an individual is used as the basis for employment decisions affecting such individuals.
3. Such conduct has the purpose or effect of unreasonably interfering with an individual's work performance or creating an intimidating, hostile, or offensive working environment.

The 1986 Supreme Court decision in the case of *Meritor Savings Bank v. Vinson* expanded the definition of sexual harassment to include a hostile work environment created by unwelcome flirtation, lewd comments, or obscene jokes.

Based on this case, to make a claim of hostile-environment sexual harassment, a claimant must show that not only was he or she affected and offended by the sexual conduct but that an objective third party—a reasonable person—would also have been offended. Prior to this case, companies had to deal with a notion of sexual harassment that was pretty much in the eye of the beholder.

■ Companies that tolerate sexual harassment pay a price.

A recent reader survey by *Working Woman* discovered that 60 percent of those surveyed indicated they had been sexually harassed in the workplace.[13] The problem is compounded when the source of harassment is one's supervisor. Even when an employee files a sexual harassment charge, prosecution can be difficult; the EEOC, which must investigate all cases before trial, regularly has a year's backlog of cases.[14]

Underlying Causes

Karen Sauvigné, a cofounder of the Working Woman's Institute, sees traditional male and female roles as a major cause of sexual harassment. "Frequently men and women have difficulty relating to each other as co-workers," she says. "The only pattern they have to fall back on in a [work relationship] is one that has sexual overtones. The man is unconsciously acting out what he thinks is expected of him—being the aggressor. And that's exactly what the female defines as inappropriate."[15]

What Companies Can Do

One article estimates that sexual harassment costs a typical Fortune 500 company $6.7 million per year in low morale and productivity, absenteeism, and employee turnover. Many corporate leaders, therefore, "have come to realize that companies that tolerate sexual harassment in the workplace pay a price, in the form of lost productivity, the exit of valuable employees, and expensive and damaging lawsuits."[16]

When a worker is unable to stop sexual harassment alone, he or she should have a way to lodge a formal complaint with the company. Generally, companies handle sexual harassment in the same way as they handle racism or other forms of discrimination.

The tone and attitude of the company can go a long way in preventing sexual harassment, as well. The company should have a clear written policy outlining sexual harassment and the appropriate disciplinary measures. In addition, many companies are now providing training programs on handling sexual harassment. And company officials must make it clear that managers are accountable for dealing effectively with sexual harassment complaints among their workers.

Women face some unique and difficult pressures at work. Supervisors need to be responsive to these special problems. Susan L. Webb in her book *Sexual Harassment in the Workplace: What You Need to Know!* presents six necessary factors for controlling sexual harassment:

1. *Top management's support*—Leaders of organizations must view harassment as a legal and a business problem—one that interferes with productivity. By adopting a serious attitude, top management influences the way people approach the problem.
2. *A written, posted policy*—The written policy should include:
   A. Statement of purpose: to set out the organization's position on sexual harassment.
   B. Legal definition of harassment.
   C. Descriptions of behaviors that constitute harassment.
   D. Importance of the problem.
   E. How employees should handle harassment: how they should confront the harasser and report incidents.

F. How the organization handles complaints.

G. Disciplinary action.

H. Names and numbers of individuals to call to make a complaint.

3. *A procedure for handling complaints*—Give employees an option of going to any of several people with their complaints.

4. *A timetable for handling complaints*—Act quickly and fairly.

5. *Training programs*—Short training programs regarding harassment have been found to be very helpful.

6. *Follow-up*—Keep the concept of harassment on the minds of the employees by occasional memos and other follow-ups.[17]

What Individuals Can Do

The first thing to keep in mind is that the longer sexual advances are allowed to go on, the harder they are to stop. Initially, advances may not be in earnest; the aggressor may make them because he or she thinks it's expected. But if the ritual goes on, personal feelings become involved and an enormous amount of organizational energy can be wasted.

If you are a victim, speak out early—tell the aggressor in a direct, businesslike way that what is going on isn't acceptable. Unfortunately, this is often difficult, especially when the aggressor is your boss. If the problem continues, keep a written record of the advances and your response. Ask other men or women in the office if they have experienced sexual harassment, as well. For further tips about what an individual can do, read the *Another Look* article "Sexual Harassment: The Inside Story" at the end of this chapter.

▼ SUMMARY OF KEY IDEAS

- The role of women in the workplace (and in the home) has changed dramatically over the past fifty years.

- Women are now moving into previously male-dominated fields, such as law, trucking, and engineering, and men are taking jobs that were previously dominated by women.

- Mentor relationships appear to play a vital role in the upward mobility of both female and male workers.

- Women are making significant strides as entrepreneurs.

- Sexual harassment is still a serious, costly problem in many organizations.

- The overall lot of women in the workplace has improved significantly in recent years, and the future looks bright for women at work.

▼ Key Terms, Concepts, and Names

Flextime	Role models
Line-management opportunities	Karen Sauvigné
Mentor relationships	Sex-based roles
Parental leave	Sexual harassment

▼ Questions and Exercises

1. What four essential activities should managers perform to ensure that female employees are provided with the necessary organizational support to be successful? How important are these activities? How do they differ from supports that might be provided for male employees? What *specific* actions should a manager take to create these supports?

2. Describe what actions you would take as a manager to reduce problems of sexual harassment.

▼ Notes

1. Margaret Woodworth and Warner Woodworth, "Women Working," *Exchange* (Spring/Summer 1978):31

2. Ibid., p. 34.

3. Steve Guarnaccia, "The 25 Hottest Careers," *Working Woman*, July 1992, pp. 45–51.

4. Ibid.

5. Jacqueline Giambanco, "Advertising Success in Minneapolis," *Working Woman*, (October 1978), pp. 117–18.

6. Woodworth and Woodworth, "Women Working," p. 35.

7. Nancy Marx Better, "The Secret of Liz Claiborne's Success," *Working Woman*, April 1992, p. 70.

8. Rhonda Richards, "At this Firm, Owners Get Their MBA's by Experience," *USA Today* (June 5, 1989).

9. "The Entrepreneurial Spirit," *Working Woman*, (November 1988, p. 55; Mary Roland, "The Passionate Pioneer of Fitness Franchising," *Working Woman*, November 1988, pp. 56–57.

10. Jane Ciabattari, "Managing Nine Critical Career Turning Points," *Working Woman*, October 1987, p. 94.

11. Roxanne Farmanfarmaian, "Are Women Starving Their Businesses?" *Working Woman*, October 1988, p. 114.

12. Lorraine Dusky, "Companies That Care," *Family Circle*, 25 April 1989, pp. 105–107, 126, 128.

13. Ronni Sandroff, "Sexual Harassment: The Inside Story," *Working Woman*, June 1992, pp. 47–51.

14. Amy Saltzman, "Hands Off at the Office," *U.S. News and World Report* (1 August 1988, pp. 56–57; Ronni Sandroff, "Sexual Harassment in the Fortune 500," *Working Woman*, December 1988, pp. 70–71.

15. "Sexual Harassment—Not at All in a Day's Work," *MGR* (AT&T Long Lines, no. 1, 1980):15.

16. Sandroff, "Sexual Harassment in the Fortune 500," pp. 72–73.

17. Susan L. Webb, *Sexual Harassment in the Workplace: What You Need to Know!* (Seattle: Pacific Resource, 1991).

▼ ANOTHER LOOK: FACTS ON WOMEN

Most of us know by now that women will comprise almost two-thirds of new entrants to the labor force by 2000. But did you also know that women in Alaska are almost three times as likely to own their own business than are women in Mississippi? To better acquaint you with a woman's world, *Management Review* compiled the following list of surprising—and not so surprising—facts.

GETTING DOWN TO BUSINESS ...

■ Almost 60 percent of all women in America are working or looking for work.

... AND GETTING OUT OF BUSINESS

■ More than 40 percent of working baby boom women expect to reduce their job commitments in the next five years because of long work hours and stagnant wages. Almost one-quarter plan to quit work altogether in the next five years.

DANCING ON THE CEILING ...

■ Nearly 80 percent of CEOs acknowledge that there are identifiable barriers to women's advancement.

■ Women most often cited opportunity for growth and development as a reason for leaving a job. Men cited advancement, a

higher level job or money as their reason for leaving.

■ Women in both upper and lower management positions, however, were more likely than men to rate their performance reviews as "fair."

■ Although women account for 40 percent of all managers, only 2 percent of women managers earn more than $50,000 a year compared with 14 percent of men.

BEHIND CLOSED DOORS ...

■ About two-fifths of all major corporations have women on their boards of directors, but only 3 percent to 4 percent of all directorships are held by women.

■ Less than 1 percent of the highest paid officers and directors in the nation's largest 1,000 companies are women. Out of the 4,000 people surveyed, only 19 were women, and only nine of the women were married with children.

TAKING CARE OF BUSINESS ...

■ Women own about one-third of all non-farm sole proprietorships. Nine out of 10 of these businesses are in the service, retail trade, finance, real estate or insurance industries.

■ Although California has the greatest number of women-owned businesses, women from Alaska are more likely to own

their own businesses—there are 13,976 women-owned businesses in an adult women population of 165,000.

MARRIED WITH CHILDREN? WHAT'S THE HURRY?

■ Today, women are marrying later; the average age for a woman's first marriage is 23.6 years old, up from 20.3 in 1960. More women are having children later too; 29 percent of married women under 30 were childless, while fewer than 13 percent were in 1960.

■ Women also are having fewer children. Today, a woman has an average of 1.8 children, compared to 3.7 in the late 1950s at the height of the baby boom.

POSTPARTUM BLUES ...

■ New mothers were more than 10 times more likely to lose their jobs after medical leaves for childbirth than employees taking others kinds of medical leave.

■ About half of all women with children under the age of one work outside of the home. Four out of five single mothers with children under the age of three work.

■ More than one in five married women with a small child at home usually works weekends. Almost one in three unmarried women with children at home works weekends.

ANOTHER LOOK: FACTS ON WOMEN *continued*

CHANGE IS IN THE AIR ...

- For the first time in 20 years, the share of working women who would prefer to stay home with their kids, if they could afford to, rose about 50 percent. In 1986, 33 percent of working women would have preferred to stay at home, but in 1990, 56 percent would have chosen that option if they could.

SHE'S NO JUNE CLEAVER ...

- Less than 11 percent of all women are housewives—defined as married women who are not in the labor force and who have children at home.

TENNIS ANYONE? NOT THESE DAYS ...

- The average working mother spends 44 hours at work and 31 hours on family responsibilities; her spouse spends 47 hours at work and 15 hours helping around the house.

- Only one-third of women who work full time hire household help.

- Not surprisingly, more women than men reported that they experience work-family conflicts and feel pressured by time constraints.

YOU'VE COME A LONG WAY BABY ... OR HAVE YOU?

- Women earn 72 cents for every dollar men make today, a slight improvement from 1955 when women only made 65 cents for every dollar earned by men.

- The median income (in 1989 dollars) for women working full time, year-round is $18,778; the median income for men is $27,430.

- The median income of a college-educated woman aged 25 or older is $21,659, only a few dollars more than what her male counterpart receives with only a high school degree ($21,650).

- The average income of a dual-income family is $36,431; without a wife's income, however, families, earn only $24,556.

ALPHABET ANTICS ...

- Women account for half of all under-graduate business students, about one-third of all M.B.A.s, more than one-third of all Ph.D.s and M.D.s, and more than two-fifths of all J.D.s.
- More women, however are needed in engineering; only 13 percent of masters degrees in engineering are earned by women.

WHEN THE GOING GETS TOUGH, THE TOUGH GO SHOPPING ...

- Three out of four women buy most of their clothes on sale. Yet most women (60 percent) have little or no interest in fashion.

- Shoppers who frequent malls are most likely to be married women with children living at home.

- Women are buying 47 percent of the new cars sold today. And by 2000, that number is expected to jump to 65 percent.

EXERCISE YOUR RIGHT...

- There are only two female senators—Nancy L. Kassebaum (R.-Kan.) and Barbara A. Mikulski (D.-Md.)—a fact that most people discovered during the Thomas-Hill hearings.

- Women were more likely than men to have voted in the 1988 presidential election. More than 58 percent of eligible women voted, compared to 56.4 percent of men.

SOURCE: Karen Matthes, "Facts on Women," *Management Review,* March 1992, pp. 60–61.

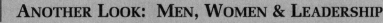

ANOTHER LOOK: MEN, WOMEN & LEADERSHIP

When Kay Unger and Jon Levy joined forces 18 years ago to form Gillian, a women's clothing company in New York, they weren't out to prove anything about leadership.

"I'm interested in making a lot of money but having a lot of fun at the same time," Levy recalls telling Unger. "If that's what you want to do, then let's go into business."

They've met those two goals. Their annual revenues exceed $125 million, they employ 300, and they sell chic career fashions throughout the United States, Canada, Europe, and Australia. And they seem to be having a good time doing it.

But in the process, they've also unwittingly made some points about leadership: that men and women managers can work comfortably together at the top and that their differing styles of leadership can be complementary, producing a synergism that gives the company benefits it would not receive if two men or two women were in those jobs.

Unger and Levy and two other male-female partnerships included in this article symbolize some of the questions that businesses are raising about leadership these days:

Are women's leadership styles different from men's? Are women's ways of leading more effective than the traditional "command-and-control" style? As women continue to start and grow

their own businesses and to advance to senior corporate levels, what changes will they bring to American business?

Until very recently, the general perception of business management was a structure dominated by males whose leadership style was hierarchical, action-oriented, and even quasi-military. The ideal leader was seen as an independent, tough, individualistic hero—like a John Wayne character or the real-life Lee Iacocca.

But now a new generation of women is bringing to business a style often described as more consensus-building, more open and inclusive, more likely to encourage participation by others, and even more caring than that of many males.

Smart companies are making room for a diversity of styles, encouraging the development of women leaders along with the men.

The fortunate businesses are those in which these differing styles become complementary rather than confrontational. Men and women are learning the strengths of each other's approach. Many women are incorporating the best of the traditional styles, such as focus on performance, into their leadership portfolios, while more men are adopting the so-called "soft" approaches that women use effectively.

The timing may be just right. Recent studies show—and an increasing number of

business people are expressing agreement—that women are especially suited to leadership. Moreover, according to the studies, leadership based on greater openness and interaction with people is especially suited to a contemporary work force whose members identify with such traits far more than previous generations did. That is particularly true, the experts say, of today's better-educated work force.

Edward M. Moldt, managing director of the Snider Entrepreneurial Center at the Wharton School of the University of Pennsylvania, says that the women's approach is "one that is right for the times." Today's companies, he says, require leaders who not only are risk takers and visionaries but also are "strong enough people that they're capable of hearing the ideas of others and really empowering them to use some of those ideas in changing businesses and in making them successful."

Women can meet this challenge very well, he suggests, because they are "very comfortable with having to persuade people, to encourage, to motivate," while men are "used to giving orders and having them followed."

Judith Hoy of Learning Systems, a New York consulting firm specializing in management effectiveness, notes that female leadership traits can help companies solve three major problems: the need for better customer service, the demand for

ANOTHER LOOK: MEN, WOMEN & LEADERSHIP *continued*

higher quality, and the need for leadership itself. All require the relationship-building skills at which women excel, Hoy says.

Dealing with these problems also requires the ability to build networks, to listen, to resolve conflict, and to get people to work together, says Hoy. "While these skills are not the sole property of women," she says, "research and experience suggest that women are more likely to have them."

In addition, women can help companies be more competitive because they see business opportunities as a result of their own experience. Gillian has achieved its success in part because its female co-leader, Kay Unger, had the sense to cater to career women like herself. She believes she understands the needs of working women all over the world. "I think we can grow very well in an international market," she says.

As never before, the United States is seeing the emergence of the female leader. It's happening most quickly on the entrepreneurial side, where women start at the top by launching their own companies—more than 4 million of them in the U.S. now.

However, the female leader cannot help but emerge also on the corporate side in this decade and the next as a lower percentage of white males in the workplace forces companies to

dip into the growing pool of women and minorities for executive talent.

A survey of high-level executives by Russell Reynolds Associates, Inc., a New York-based executive recruiting firm, categorized respondents as "leader-style" (that is, visionary, innovative, and strategic in their thinking) or as "manager-style" (concerned with maintaining momentum, balancing interests, stabilizing forces, and implementing tactical plans). The study found that women in both staff and line positions were more likely to be leader-style executives than their male counterparts.

In a *Harvard Business Review* report on a leadership survey that she conducted for the International Women's Forum, in Washington, Judy B. Rosener says she found that the women respondents tended to use what she calls an "interactive" leadership style, in which they not only encouraged others' participation but also attempted "to enhance other people's sense of self-worth and to energize followers." These women leaders, she says, "believe that people perform best when they feel good about themselves and their work."

The study, based on responses from 456 executives—355 women and 101 men—found that the women were also more likely to use what experts call a "transformational" style, getting sub-

ordinates to transform their own self-interests into the goals of the organization.

The male respondents leaned toward the traditional "command-and-control" style. They were more likely to employ a "transactional" leadership, viewing job performance as a series of transactions with subordinates and offering rewards for services rendered or punishment for inadequate performance.

"While men have had to appear to be competitive, strong, tough, decisive, and in control, women have been allowed to be cooperative, emotional, supportive, and vulnerable," says Rosener, a management professor at the Graduate School of Management of the University of California in Irvine. "This may explain why women today are more likely than men to be interactive leaders."

In her book, *Feminine Leadership, or How To Succeed in Business Without Being One of the Boys* (Times Books, 1985), Marilyn Loden, a San Francisco corporate management consultant, wrote: "In some respects, it seems that women managers may be better prepared to cope with the challenges of the future than many traditional male leaders who succeeded in the past. For many of the characteristics being touted as critical for future success—concern for people, interpersonal skills, intuitive man-

ANOTHER LOOK *continued*

agement, and creative problem solving—are qualities that women as a group are encouraged to develop and rely on throughout their lives."

In a position to shape a corporate culture, women business founders say the companies they create are different from most of those headed by men. "The structures that women establish seem to be mechanisms to facilitate team building and fluidity, to empower the entire staff as opposed to creating fiefdoms and territories," entrepreneur Laura Henderson said at a recent symposium sponsored by the National Foundation for Women Business Owners. Henderson is president of Prospect Associates, an $11-million-a-year Rockville, Md., health research and communications firm.

Because they were breaking new ground, the first female executives copied the leadership styles that had proved successful for men, according to Rosener.

"Now a second wave of women is making its way into top management," Rosener says, "not by adopting the style and habits that have proved successful for men but by drawing on the skills and attitudes they developed from their shared experience as women."

What's becoming a thing of the past, says Ellen B. Richstone, are women "who think that the way [they're] going to get to the top is by

being more male than the males." A member of an otherwise all-male corporate inner circle, Richstone, 39, is chief financial officer of Bull HN Information Systems Inc., a computer maker with annual revenues of $2.2 billion. Richstone was hired by the Billerica, Mass., company—a member of Groupe Bull—in 1989 to help reverse its downhill slide; she commands a staff of 700 worldwide.

"My feeling is that the women who will do the best in the long run are the ones who are comfortable being themselves," she says. That means they are "strong professionals," but they feel secure enough to wear dresses instead of masculine-looking suits, and, if they're like Richstone, they'll keep a jar of candy in the office. She has been teased that the candy jar is a "typically female" touch, but she says "it's amazing what a little bit of sweets will do in terms of producing an environment of communication and friendliness."

The two types of leadership, one predominantly masculine and the other predominantly feminine, appear to have grown out of two different kinds of experiences—men's in the military and on the playing field, and women's in managing the home and nurturing husbands and children.

But many business leaders and academic experts are reluctant to encourage new

stereotypes by labeling one form of leadership male and another female.

In a collection of comments in the *Harvard Business Review* by several writers responding to Rosener's article, Cynthia Fuchs Epstein of the City University of New York wrote: "It is up to the leaders of business and other institutions to affirm the humanitarian values that women are associated with but that men also can (and do) express if they are not made to feel embarrassed about showing them. And those qualities of toughness and drive that many men are made to feel comfortable with should be prized in women who wish to express them when they are appropriate. The category is 'people,' not 'men and women.'"

Gillian's Jon Levy describes himself as more "intense and aggressive" and says his partner, Kay Unger, is more low-key. He attributes their differences not to sex but to their personalities and the types of operations they run. Unger oversees design and production, while Levy is responsible for sales, marketing, and finance.

Unger describes Levy as more strict and rigid ("but in a very good way") because his responsibilities require more structure. Because she deals with creative people, Unger says, she is more fluid, spontaneous, and flexible. But she also thinks that she is tougher than her

ANOTHER LOOK: MEN, WOMEN & LEADERSHIP *continued*

partner and that "he has a kinder heart."

Like Unger and Levy, the principals in two other male-female partnerships—Naomi Young and Lawrence J. Gartner in Los Angeles and Cheryl McArthur and Alan Glen in Washington—have created successful businesses by blending different styles of leadership. Also like Unger and Levy, these partners are linked by neither marriage nor romance.

Young and Gartner firmly believe that leadership style has nothing to do with one's sex. The founders of Gartner & Young, a small law firm that represents major corporations in labor matters, they agree that Gartner is more likely to be the consensus builder while Young is more likely to take the command approach.

"It is very complementary to my personality, and it's a style that I've had for a very long time," says Young, who is majority shareholder of the firm. "From a get-somebody's-attention standpoint, it has been beneficial for me to be direct, no-nonsense, get on the table what you want, and get it done." It's an approach that also saves time, she adds.

"Our management styles develop out of personalities and life experiences, and it's what we're comfortable with," says Gartner. He and his partner find that they can trade styles when the situation calls for it—Gartner can be direct when he has to be,

and Young can accommodate and compromise.

"We each have a predominant style, but the other aspects of leadership must be present as tools to use when you need them," explains Young.

McArthur and Glen four years ago founded McArthur/Glen Group, a company that develops and manages upscale outlet shopping centers throughout the country. McArthur sees herself fitting the female leadership mold, describing herself as interactive and as one who encourages participation and tries to share power and information. On the other hand, she is the more aggressive and ambitious of the two partners. "If it had been left up to [Glen], I think we probably would have done only a couple of centers," she says. They now have nine malls up and running, and they expect to complete four more this year.

Glen, more interested in the creation of the centers, says he's "delighted" to leave the details of running the 125-employee organization to McArthur. "This company would never be where it is today if it [had not been] for her ambition and drive. Nor would it have gotten there if it hadn't had my experience as to how to get this kind of stuff going," says Glen. He is 65, and she is 41. She makes it clear he has been her mentor.

They're "like a zipper, fitting very nicely," says McArthur's administrative assistant, Lorri Schoeni. She thinks McArthur is willing to spend more time with employees to work out problems, while Glen is more directive and more interested in the big picture. But both styles get results. "I love the mix; I think it's great," she says.

President of the nearly $500-million-a-year magazine group of Meredith Corp., in Des Moines, Iowa, James A. Autry doesn't fit the picture of the hard-nosed, dispassionate male executive. "It's only marginally easier to be a man and a poet and a writer and be in corporate management than it is to be a woman and be in corporate management," he says. Autry is the author of *Love & Profit: The Art of Caring Leadership* (Morrow, 1991), a book of touching and often amusing essays and poems about management.

"Faulty perceptions have arisen that there's 'soft' management in which you are sensitive and caring and supportive, and there's 'hard' management in which you're tough and draw the lines," Autry says. "I think a lot of the tough-guy stuff is really cowardly management." Managers who take the "hard" approach, he says, are "hiding behind a shell of aloofness and toughness rather than confronting their own emotions and feelings

ANOTHER LOOK *continued*

and rather than confronting other people honestly about theirs."

Perhaps the controversy over whether women's styles of leadership are better than men's or whether there's any difference at all is merely a signal that all leadership is becoming more feminized simply because it makes good business sense.

As researcher Judy Rosener points out, a high proportion of young professional workers is increasingly typical in organizations. "They demand to participate and contribute," she says. "In some cases, they have knowledge or talents their bosses don't have." She sees these kinds of workers as likely to respond more to interactive leaders.

"We're going to be so short of workers by the end of the decade, particularly knowledge workers and information-service workers, that companies that try to manage in the old top-down, hierarchical, drill-sergeant way are just doomed," says Autry.

Given that scenario, men will become freer to use so-called feminine tools of leadership without embarrassment, and women such as Ellen Richstone, who see that "being more male than male" is no longer effective for women leaders—if it ever was—will feel freer to use styles that are more natural to them as individuals, whether "soft" or "tough."

Based on the experiences that shaped their styles, both men and women business leaders, regardless of the size of their companies, have a lot they can teach one another—as well as the members of their own sex—about leadership. As they learn from one another, they can bring strengthened leadership abilities to their companies. Here are suggestions drawn from those interviewed for this article:

IF YOU'RE A WOMAN, CONSIDER BEING MORE DECISIVE

This doesn't mean having a closed mind or being bullheaded, says Jim Autry. But he says that "decisiveness is an area that I think women could probably learn something from men about." Women often lack a sense of timing about when to stop building consensus and gathering information and to make a decision, Autry says.

BE A GOOD LISTENER

Kay Unger, who feels that women leaders tend to be better listeners than men, says: "I think listening is key because I learn from the people who work for me. I learn their ideas. If they know I'm open, I even hear the downside." This kind of information, she says, enables her to keep making changes to improve the organization.

Each month Ellen Richstone meets with a different group of 15 or so non-

managerial employees for round-table discussions. "They're designed for me to get to know people at levels I might never see," says Richstone. The purpose of the round-tables is communication, but Richstone makes a point of listening more than talking.

Listening doesn't always mean agreement, however. Autry says that "listening to you doesn't impose upon me the responsibility to decide it your way—only to listen to you and for you to feel at least that you were heard."

AGAIN, IF YOU'RE A WOMAN, ADD AN ABILITY TO FOCUS ON SHORT-TERM GOALS

Women, says Autry, seem to have a good long-term focus but less ability to lead on short-term crisis problems, such as a cost-cutting program or revenue-generating effort. Male managers, he observes, are "extremely good" at building enthusiasm in employees and coaching them through short-term crises.

BE WILLING TO EXPRESS YOUR EMOTIONS, EVEN TO CRY

That goes for both men and women, says Autry, who adds that when he stopped trying to bottle up all his emotions, he became a better manager. Women often are not as direct and honest as they should be, Autry thinks, partly out of fear of crying and being thought soft.

Another Look: Men, Women & Leadership *continued*

Leaders who cry because they're so proud of something their employees have done or because they have to give a negative appraisal reveal their own humanity, convey that they care about their employees, and inspire excellence.

"I am not talking about management for and by the wimps," he says in his book. "In fact, I am talking about the most difficult management there is, a management without emotional hiding places." If you're going to be on the leading edge of management, he continues, "you sometimes must be on the emotional edge as well."

Don't Let Your Ego Get in the Way

Whether you're a man or a woman, says Jon Levy of Gillian, "the first thing you have to learn in leadership is that there's no room for ego." No one person makes a company successful; it'a team effort and a team attitude, he says. If something's good, "we all take credit. If it's bad, we all take the blame."

Be Yourself

Don't try to force yourself into a certain style that's not natural to you, even if you think it's expected of you. You can learn to draw on other leaders' styles, however, to enrich your choice of tools. Says Larry Gartner: "I build on my strengths in terms of my personality, and it basically comes down to what works best for me."

If you're a business owner hoping that women leaders will emerge in your company along with men leaders, keep in mind that you have to help bring them along.

The following suggestions from the Russell Reynolds Associates study can help you nurture the development of women leaders:

- Look at both staff and line positions for potential leaders. Traditionally, leaders are drawn from line positions with profit-and-loss responsibilities. But the study found that just as many women in staff positions (support functions) as in line positions are leader-oriented.

- Encourage mentoring for women. And create situations that facilitate informal, on-the-job advice for women. Women frequently feel shut out from these kinds of assistance to their career development, says the study.

- Add qualified women to your board of directors. The study found that leader-style women were twice as likely to work in companies with a woman on the board.

Whether a style is "masculine" or "feminine" doesn't matter, contends almost everyone, even those who think women represent leadership styles all their own. The best leadership style depends on the organization, says Judy Rosener. The International Women's

Forum study "shows that a nontraditional leadership style can be effective in organizations that accept it," she says.

And if you're not convinced things are changing, consider that dazzling example of leadership, Gen. H. Norman Schwarzkopf. *Boston Globe* columnist Ellen Goodman recently described him as "caring but, well, commanding."

"This complicated character seems to synthesize conflicting and changing male images," Goodman wrote. "Introspective but decisive, caring yet competent, one of the guys and a leader? Not stuff that always comes in the same male package."

If caring leadership is good enough for the U.S. military, can more of it in business be far behind?

Business people increasingly seem to understand that giving a variety of leaders a chance to grow and shine is good for business.

"The good news is that there is an even richer than expected source of leaders among women executives," says Malcolm MacKay, managing director of Russell Reynolds Associates. "My belief is that the most competitive organizations will take leaders wherever they find them, no matter what sex they are. That's not only the essence of capitalism, it's the law of survival of the fittest."

SOURCE: Sharon Nelton, "Men, Women & Leadership," *Nation's Business,* May 1991, pp. 16–22.

▼ ANOTHER LOOK: SEXUAL HARASSMENT: THE INSIDE STORY

The response was immediate, passionate and overwhelming. Less than a week after the February issue of *Working Woman* reached homes and newsstands, thousands of surveys flooded our offices. They came from as far away as Paris and as close as an office building on the next block. Many were accompanied by pages of letters that detailed painful personal experiences. In some workplaces the survey was photocopied and circulated, the results sent back in batches. A man who had been sexually harassed by his female boss wrote that co-workers insisted he fill out the survey. Less than a month after the magazine hit the newsstand, we had received more than 9,000 responses—and they kept coming.

Clearly, the confrontation between Anita Hill and Clarence Thomas [over allegations of sexual harassment made during the Senate hearings of Thomas's nomination to the U.S. Supreme Court] had an impact on how and why readers answered. It also had an effect on the human-resources executives of the Fortune 500 (the 1,000 companies that make up the top 500 service and 500 industrial corporations). We sent them a simultaneous survey following up a pioneering report, "Sexual Harassment in the Fortune 500," done by this magazine in 1988. This time their responses were somewhat more critical of their compa-

nies' efforts to stop sexual harassment, but, as before, they concluded that the system generally works. Many *Working Woman* readers, on the other hand, insist that filing a complaint still amounts to "career suicide." What's more, they are angry enough about the spectacle of the Thomas hearings to vote their minds in a year when it matters. In this, the first major survey to scrutinize and compare the views of these two groups, several messages came through loud and clear:

■ **Women know what harassment is,** either by legal definition (54%) or intuition (30%). Only 15 percent were not sure about the boundaries between harassment and harmless fooling around. The 106 human-resources executives who responded go even further than most readers in toeing the party line, but there's often a discrepancy between what they say is wrong and how they respond to a real situation.

■ **The higher a woman is in the corporate hierarchy, the more likely she is to be harassed.** More than 60 percent of our readers said they personally have been harassed, and more than a third know a co-worker who has been harassed. However, since only one out of four women reported the harassment and most companies receive fewer than five complaints a

month, it's obvious that the vast majority of women who are harassed don't feel they can safely report a problem.

■ **Women are not at fault.** Provocative dressing and behavior or oversensitivity to sexual jokes is *not* the cause of sexual harassment, say three out of four readers and most of the personnel officers. And over half of the human-resources executives also say that office romances that go sour are not the source of many complaints.

■ **It is an issue that matters.** Seventy-five percent of readers feel sexual harassment is an issue on a par with salary inequities, inadequate child care and prejudice against promoting women. And more than 90 percent think their companies and the government can—and must—do more to prevent and stop abuse. Only one out of five women believes that most complaints are given justice, but more than 70 percent of the personnel managers think they are.

■ **Anita Hill changed the picture.** Part of the clarity about this issue must be credited to the national teach-in on sexual harassment during the confirmation hearings for Clarence Thomas [in 1991].... Fifty-nine percent of readers believe that Anita Hill was telling the truth (compared with only 38

ANOTHER LOOK: SEXUAL HARASSMENT: THE INSIDE STORY *continued*

percent of the corporate executives), and more than half the readers—and a third of the personnel managers—plan to vote against their senator if he or she voted to confirm Thomas.

Certainly the hearings provoked discussion in the workplace. While 37 percent of readers said it was treated as a big joke, almost 40 percent said the confrontation brought the issue out in the open and led women to trade war stories about sexual harassment. Here's what they said.

WHO GETS HARASSED?

The old prey on the young, and the powerful on the less powerful. A female subordinate under 34 being harassed by a male over 35 is the most common scenario, according to both readers and human-resources executives. Almost 30 percent of the incidents occur when the women are 18 to 24 years old—a very large number, considering the small size of this age group in the work force. In 83 percent of the cases, the harasser is in a more powerful position than the harassed. "[As] the youngest and newest nurse in the department, I was eager to please," writes a reader in Hawaii who was harassed by her supervising doctor. "At first [his] remarks were mildly flirtatious. Later he began to be more bold. The one time I was ever

alone with him, he grabbed me and kissed me. The last straw was when he, I and another nurse were in our lab. He casually asked how old I was and [said], 'I wouldn't want to f- - - you, because it would be like f- - - ing one of my daughters.'"

Harassment becomes much more common when women enter some predominantly male workplaces or breach the formerly all-male domain of upper management. "The higher up you climb, the worse the harassment gets," writes an insurance-company executive from Iowa. "Men feel threatened and choose this behavior to deter our advancement." Women in managerial and professional positions, earning over $50,000, as well as those working in male-dominated companies, are more likely to experience harassment.

That's probably why *Working Woman* readers reported higher rates of harassment (60%) than respondents to other surveys, whose rates hover between 25 and 40 percent. Lynn Hecht Schafran of the National Organization for Women's Legal Defense and Education Fund says the *Working Woman* figures are "not out of line with what we see in surveys of professional women." Recent polls of female chemical engineers, lawyers and executives also found that roughly 6 out of 10 women report harassment. "[I have been]

patted, poked and squeezed to death at industry meetings," writes a marketing executive who worked for a Fortune 500 chemical company. "When I was in sales, I was one of only two females in a division of 22. At regional meetings, the guys always went to strip joints. I [went] back to my room."

The incidents that reach the attention of corporate officers are often severe, and the profile today is even worse than the one reported by Fortune 500 executives in 1988. Pressure for dates and/or sexual favors occurred in 50 percent of the cases reported to company executives this year, but in only 29 percent of the cases in the 1988 survey. In 1992 over 34 percent of the reported incidents involved touching or cornering, compared with 26 percent in 1988. And most of today's complaints are valid, according to 68 percent of the executives surveyed—4 percent more than agreed with that statement in 1988.

WHY DO MEN DO IT?

It's not flirtatiousness, hormones or sexual desire, say many readers. The desire to bully and humiliate women is behind most harassment, according to one out of two readers. "The harasser wants a victim, not a playmate, and a woman with modest dress, makeup and comportment is just as likely—maybe even more likely—to be harassed," writes a Washington professor.

ANOTHER LOOK *continued*

A relative few may be responsible for a hefty percentage of harassment cases. Forty-seven percent of the readers who have been harassed have known "chronic harassers," men who bully one woman after another at work. "Most [harassers] share a common goal—intimidation," writes a 29-year-old secretary from Pennsylvania. "If someone is capable of harassing a co-worker or subordinate, they're also likely to take advantage of people in other ways." Her insight is confirmed by Freada Klein, who conducts training sessions on the problem for major corporations. "We've found that workplaces with high rates of sexual harassment also have high rates of racial harassment, discrimination and other forms of unfair treatment."

IF IT HAPPENS TO YOU

When asked what they would advise a close friend or relative to do if she were being sexually harassed at work, 79 percent of readers took an assertive stand: "Let the perpetrator know, loud and clear, that if the behavior doesn't stop, she will turn him in," one respondent replied. But their advice is often a case of "Do as I say, not as I do." Among those who themselves have been harassed, only 40 percent told the harasser to stop, and just 26 percent reported the harassment.

Women are not unaware of the contradiction. Though a public-relations director from Houston advises others to fight back, she admits, "I cannot say absolutely that I would file charges, because *I need that job!* And that makes me *really, really angry.*"

Trying to ignore the problem was the most common tactic (46%). "A disapproving look or turning away is an almost pitiful strategy for a woman to employ," writes a 52-year-old-project director at a small company in Maryland. "But I also was taught never to make a scene, so I sympathize." In fact, a firm "No" *can* work better than ignoring the problem. One out of three women who protested got the harasser to stop, compared with one out of four who tried to ignore or avoid the harasser.

Dr. Rita R. Newman, a psychiatrist and former president of the American Medical Women's Association, advises women to document harassment—in dated, written notes or on cassette or videotape—even if they don't intend to report it. If the situation later escalates, and you're forced to take action, you have contemporaneous documentation, which is looked on quite favorably by the law. Even if you never report the incident, Newman says, gaining some control over the situation through documentation can help preserve self-esteem.

CALCULATING THE DAMAGE

Sexual harassment clearly does hurt women, whether or not they go through the often grueling process of filing a complaint. Readers who were harassed reported such ill effects as being fired or forced to quit their jobs (25%), seriously undermined self-confidence (27%), impaired health (12%) and long-term career damage (13%). Only 17 percent reported no ill effects.

Health problems associated with harassment are similar to those that spring from other stressful situations, such as headache, chronic fatigue, nausea, sleep and appetite disturbances and more frequent colds and urinary-tract infections, says Dr. Diane K. Shrier, professor of clinical psychiatry and pediatrics at New Jersey Medical School at Newark. "Often women and their doctors don't recognize any links between these symptoms and harassment. And yet, when you take a careful history, you'll see the symptoms began as harassment occurred and go away once the situation is resolved."

Emotional turmoil, which usually affects work performance, is also common. "Women may feel that unless they go along with the harasser, they will face the end of their professional lives," says Newman. "So they feel exploited, cheapened and forced to submit. For some, self-esteem is impaired forever."

ANOTHER LOOK: SEXUAL HARASSMENT: THE INSIDE STORY *continued*

Forced career tours also take their toll on women's earning power. "I lost or was forced out of my job each time, while my respective harassers are busily lying, tormenting, embarrassing or firing people as we speak," wrote a former personnel coordinator from Illinois who was harassed on three different jobs over a long career. The harassed may be doubly victimized by being blamed for the results of their harassment. Many readers who complained were told to take a course in "how to deal with difficult people" or given poor marks on their next reviews.

THE ODDS OF GETTING EVEN

If a woman does decide to fight back and report harassment, what are her chances of getting justice? That depends quite a bit on whom you ask. Those who write company policies are much more bullish about how well they work than those who must use them. Only 21 percent of readers agree that complaints are dealt with justly, and over 60 percent say charges are completely ignored or offenders are given only token reprimands. Fifty-five percent who have tried reporting harassment found that nothing happened to the harasser. "For 19 years I have been in the Air Force," writes an information-systems manager. "I have been humiliated by everything from males throwing me up against a

wall, running hands up my skirt, and grabbing my breasts to sexist jokes and nude pictures plastered over my work station. A year ago a major [showed up at] my house at 10:30 P.M. (Fortunately, both of my sons are over six feet.) At work [the major] was always humiliating me by ordering me to straddle the arms of a chair in my skirt and by rubbing his hands up and down my back and sides. [When I complained], I was threatened to stop pursuing my EOT/EEO complaint, 'or else.' I was told that because the major outranked me, his word carried more truth than mine."

The executives responsible for hearing complaints believe a just resolution is much more common; over 80 percent say most offenders in their companies are punished justly. But that number is down from the 1988 survey; then 90 percent of the executives believed offenders were justly punished.

"This is the key contradiction in sexual harassment in the 1990s," says Freada Klein, who analyzed *Working Woman's* 1988 survey. "In every workplace we've surveyed, we find that a majority of employees don't have faith in corporate channels for complaint."

Today 81 percent of Fortune 500 companies report having trained programs on sexual harassment, compared with only 60 percent in the 1988 survey— although only half of

Working Woman readers work for a company with these procedures.

Most Fortune 500 executives believe their own companies are doing a good job in this area. Even if they are, women believe government must help bring about real change. Most think it should ease (78%) and speed up (80%) the complaint-resolution process, increase the 6- to 10-month (depending on the state) statute of limitations for reporting abuses (60%) and increase penalties for companies (66%).

THE ULTIMATE INFLUENCE

More and more, the power of the purse will also promote change. Interestingly, Fortune 500 executives see their companies as much more legally vulnerable than do readers. The 1991 Civil Rights Act gives harassment victims the right to a jury trial and compensatory and punitive damages for financial and emotional harm, with awards based on company size. Congress is expected to pass an amendment that would lift the current cap ($300,000) on these awards, but companies fear that even with limits, sexual-harassment suits will become the "next asbestos." It may cost Corporate America more than $1 billion over the next five years to settle these lawsuits, according to calculations by *Treasury,* a magazine for financial executives. Many

ANOTHER LOOK *continued*

companies may begin to push the burden onto the harassers—by firing them promptly.

Even in that legendary lair of harassment, the construction site, fear of monetary loss can bring about change. A female architect, 39, from Chicago reports that one contractor deals with complaints against harassers by "immediate dismissal, no reassignment, no second chance. Walking through the job site is like walking through an altar boys' convention. The color green is the most powerful motivation in this country."

Behavior can turn around quickly in a workplace once the stakes are raised high enough. "Economic and legal pressures may not immediately change attitudes—that can take decades—but they *can* change behavior," notes Helen Neuborne, executive director of the NOW Legal Defense and Education Fund. And changing behavior is good enough.

SOURCE: Ronni Sandroff, "Sexual Harassment: The Inside Story," *Working Woman,* June 1992, pp. 47–51.

▼ A CASE IN POINT: IS IT SEXUAL HARASSMENT?

The recent attention given to sexual harassment in the press may trigger complaints in your workplace. Do you know what is sexual harassment? To test yourself, see how you do with the situations presented below. Which ones are sexual harassment? How should your company respond in each instance?

TWELVE SCENARIOS

Case #1. For monthly staff meetings, Barry, the department head, always asks Jane to set up the meeting room, arrange for refreshments, and take the minutes. The work group is made up of engineers: Jane, John, Jorge, and Kumar.

Case #2. Jerry is a supervisor. He has been having an affair with Mary, an engineering aide in another department. Jerry has an opening in his department that Mary qualifies for, and he chooses her over another qualified person even though Mary has significantly less experience.

Case #3. Sam is a plant manager at a waste treatment plant. At the facility, calendars with pictures of naked women are posted everywhere. In the lunchroom, there is also a picture of a naked man and woman embracing pasted on a picture of the plant's instrumentation room. The caption on the picture reads, "There is more to life than sludge." The only female employee at the plant, a lab technician, has never complained.

Case #4. When Harriet walks over to the department's computers, she has to pass Larry's door. Larry frequently wheels his chair to the opening, and as he watches her he often says things like, "Hey, sweetie, let me know when you finish so I don't miss the show on your way back."

Case #5. Sylvia is a manager. Tom, a biologist, reports to her. While she and Tom are on a business trip, she tells Tom that she hopes he doesn't snore; they are going to share a room "to keep overhead costs down." Also, he should be aware that she doesn't wear pajamas so he doesn't have to bring any either. Tom refuses to share a room and complains when he goes back to work.

Case #6. George is an accountant. When there are new female employees, he welcomes them by hugging them and kissing them "lightly" on the mouth. He tells them that he is the "social director" for the department and "to fit in all new single women have to date him at least once, ha, ha."

A CASE IN POINT: IS IT SEXUAL HARASSMENT? *continued*

Case #7. Jose, a project manager, is quite "smitten" by Janice, the new department secretary. He sends her notes telling her that she is beautiful, and that he wants to date her. He continues to do so even after she tells him she doesn't want to go out with him. Nothing else happens.

Case #8. Betty is a very shy and quiet person. Some of the jokesters in her department have decided to have fun at her expense and have left "girlie" magazines on her desk to see how she will react.

Case #9. Marty is a new, recently relocated manager. He asks his secretary, Louise, to rent him an apartment because he's too busy with his new job. While Louise is at the apartment checking that everything has been done as requested, Marty shows up and suggests they try out the bed. She refuses. Nothing else happens. Two months later there is a reduction in force and Louise is laid off. The official reason is her undocumented inability to get along with co-workers (which is quite true—she is continually arguing with her co-workers).

Case #10. Harold is a financial analyst. He is a good worker who always gets the job done even if he has to work long hours. One night while working late he went to the employee exercise area to use the equipment. Only he and Jennifer were there. Jennifer was using the treadmill. When she was finished, he cornered her, and ran his hands all over her body. She slapped him. He stopped. He still goes to the exercise room at night. When Jennifer is there, he stares at her. He has never touched or spoken to her again. When Jennifer complained to the human resources department, she discovered that he had been accused of doing the same thing (also without witnesses) a few months earlier. At that time he had been warned not to do anything like it again.

Case #11. Jim, a vice-president, and Jane, a project manager, are at a professional conference. Jim shows up at Jane's room after the day's session is over and says he's lonely. He insists that she is the woman he's been looking for all his life. She invites him to spend the night. Back on the job, they decide it was a bad idea and do not see each other again.

Case #12. Richard is a marketing manager. Ted is a technical writer in his department. Ted is homosexual. Richard continually asks Ted if he wants to date different women in the office. Richard tells Ted there should be a company policy to test people like Ted "because he could have AIDS." When Ted gets angry at statements like these, Richard says, "Careful Ted, don't bite me; you'll give me AIDS."

IS IT HARASSMENT?

Let's look at the 12 cases to see if they are examples of sexual harassment and what action is likely to be taken.

Case #1. The answer to the first case is "No," but it is discriminatory to select women to do these "menial" tasks at each meeting. Barry should be told to rotate the tasks. Some might think this is a small matter, but Barry's behavior could be the basis of a discrimination suit if Jane receives lower raises than the others (or some other treatment).

Case #2. Yes. Jerry said to his manager that he believed Mary had the right attitude for the new assignment and the other job candidate didn't. This other person (whether male or female) could claim that Jerry was guilty of showing favoritism because of his relationship with Mary and Jerry would not be able to show it was not the basis for the decision.

Case #3. Yes. It's a hostile environment, whether the female employee complains or not. All the calendars and pictures should be taken down.

Case #4. Yes, again, it is a hostile environment. Larry should be warned to stop. If he doesn't, he should receive discipline—for instance, a suspension without pay.

Case #5. Yes. Women can be harassers. Sylvia should receive a written warning.

Case #6. Yes. It's not a joke. George should receive a written warning.

Case #7. Yes. It's a hostile or intimidating environment. Jose should receive a written warning.

Case #8. Yes. It is not a joke. The supervisor should verbally warn the jokesters and, if it happens again, there should be discipline.

A CASE IN POINT *continued*

Case #9. Yes. It's harassment and even without the "try out the bed" part, it would be an abuse of power. Employees are not required to do personal tasks the manager should do for himself or herself. Even though it happened just once, and Louise did have difficulty getting along with co-workers, the layoff will be assumed by any investigating agency to be the result of her refusal. Therefore, if she complains about the termination, the company would probably have to rehire her or provide a monetary settlement.

Case #10. Yes. Harold admitted it and, since it had happened before, he should be terminated.

Case #11. No. The behavior was not unwelcome and nothing else happened at work.

Case #12. Yes. While it is not specifically mentioned in the law, harassment based on sexual orientation is frequently found in courts to be sexual harassment. Richard should receive a written warning for a first offense.

BOTTOM LINE

Remember, sexual harassment is not limited to unwelcome sexual advances. Sexual harassment is also verbal or physical conduct of a sexual nature that creates an intimidating or offensive work environment.

SOURCE: Michael Lee Smith, "Is It Sexual Harassment?" *Supervisory Management,* April 1992, pp. 5–6.

▼ A CASE IN POINT: THE JOB MAKES THE WOMAN

Linda Santiago worked in the secretarial pool of a large corporation for eleven years. Five years ago, she would have said that she never wanted to be anything but a secretary. She also would have told you that because she had recently had children, she was thinking of quitting. Secretarial work was not a good enough reason to leave her children at a day-care center each day. In fact, the only reason Santiago continued working was that she enjoyed the association with the other "girls" in the secretarial pool.

In recent years, the corporation that Santiago worked for initiated an aggressive affirmative action program. Santiago, who had always been a very conscientious worker, was offered a promotion. At first, she wavered. It meant leaving her good friends in the secretarial pool for a lonely life among predominantly male managers. Her friends thought she was abandoning them. She worried whether she could handle the new job. But her boss talked her into it and promised to help, reassuring her that he would be her sponsor.

So Santiago was promoted, and now she handles a challenging management job very successfully. Seeing friends is the least of her many reasons to come to work every day, and her ambitions have soared. She wants to go right to the top.

"I have fifteen years left to work," she says. "And I want to move up six grades to corporate vice-president—at least."

QUESTIONS

1. In what ways has Santiago readjusted her expectations? What do you think accounts for this upgrading of goals?
2. How do you think Santiago has changed her self-image?
3. What are some of the primary motivators at work in Santiago's career today? How are they different from what motivated her several years ago?
4. What role did Santiago's boss play in helping her make the transition from the secretarial pool to management?

CHAPTER

15

PERSPECTIVES ON SPECIAL WORK GROUPS

This chapter answers several all-important questions:

- What are the three types of disabilities?

- What is affirmative action for workers with disabilities?

- What are some of the problems alcoholism presents at work?

- What are employee assistance programs, and how are they expanding in their functions within enlightened companies?

- Why do drug testing, AIDS diagnosis, and other personal concerns pose a dilemma for organizations?

- What special pressures do many old and young people and persons with disabilities face at work?

- What kinds of changes and adjustments do old or young people face?

- What stereotypes do many people hold about the old, the young, or persons with disabilities in the workplace?

- Are young people more reckless and irresponsible than older people?

- Are young workers less committed to organizations?

- How might a manager best react to people who face the kinds of pressures described in this chapter?

The answers to these and other questions are coming up next in chapter 15....

CHAPTER 15

We recently watched with agony as a bright student of ours was unable to get employment. She had completed a law degree and passed the bar examination in her state. She had also completed her M.B.A. degree with honors. However, since she was barely four feet tall, most people saw her as a child. She had a very real physical disability. We believe her size caused many organizations to pass over her for employment.

Organizations are made up of all sorts of people, including: people with disabilities that are mental and/or physical, older people, younger people, people with drug- and alcohol-dependency problems, and people who are seriously ill with diseases such as AIDS. All of these people in organizations and those who are trying to get into organizations deserve to be treated equally. They deserve to be respected. They deserve to receive equal wages. Like our law student with great qualifications, they should be given a chance. This chapter will take a look at such people and the forces that affect them in their jobs and their relations with others.

The manager in today's work force needs to consider all workers as individuals—not as members of some category. Today's manager also needs to strive to understand some of the special pressures that may influence the behaviors of these workers.

▼ WORKERS WITH DISABILITIES

Individuals suffer a wide variety of disabilities both physical and mental. Fortunately, public awareness of the difficulties and the courage of people with disabilities is increasing. A few years ago, for example, a disabled athlete ran from Boston to Los Angeles, despite having lost one leg to bone cancer. Upon completion of the grueling transcontinental run, he told news reporters: "I'm not physically disabled. I'm physically *challenged*."

Physical or mental impairments, when severe enough to affect the job, typically affect one or more of the following:

1. Physical appearance
2. Physical functioning (especially motor skills)
3. Mental functioning

Many disabilities can be corrected to the extent that an individual can function almost as well as a person without a disability. Crutches, artificial limbs, wheelchairs, and many other modern technological developments have helped people with physical disabilities function effectively in many jobs.

Changes and Adjustments Faced by Workers with Disabilities

■ Should we have affirmative action for the disabled?

Employees who have physical or mental disabilities often face considerable frustration. The frustration is rooted primarily in not being hired for work that they can do. The problem, in this sense, is similar to that of racial or sex discrimination. Such discrimination can result in lowered self-esteem and psychological adjustment problems.

© 1985. Washington Post Writers Group. Reprinted with permission.

Many organizations have affirmative action programs for workers with disabilities. Legislation has placed considerable emphasis on encouraging companies to hire people with disabilities. This is not a new idea; workers with disabilities have been hired for many years, and most organizations regard such hiring as good business.

Congress passed the Americans with Disabilities Act in 1990 to provide people with disabilities equal opportunity in employment, public accommodations, transportation, government services, and telecommunications. This act was a direct result of statistics showing that a large number of the nation's employable persons with disabilities simply were not getting jobs. For more information on this act, read the Another Look article, "Achieving Access for the Disabled" at the end of this chapter.

Federal law calls for businesses to have affirmative action programs that include the following types of activities:

- Outreach and positive recruitment of people with disabilities.
- Internal communication of the obligation to employ and advance persons with disabilities. Such communication should foster acceptance and understanding of workers with disabilities among other employees and management.
- Development of internal procedures ensuring fair treatment of workers with disabilities.
- Use of all available recruiting sources—state employment and vocational, rehabilitation agencies, workshops, and other institutions that train persons with disabilities.
- Review of employment records to determine the availability of promotable workers with disabilities.
- Accommodation of the physical and mental limitations of qualified employees with disabilities.[1]

Stereotypes and Misconceptions about Workers with Disabilities

A stereotype is a generalization about the nature of people that is often incorrect. Many people have misconceptions and stereotypes

Unfounded stereotypes about workers with disabilities may unfairly restrict their opportunities.

about workers with physical or mental disabilities. Among these are:

- *"They are accident-prone"*—not true. Little evidence exists to indicate that people with physical or mental disabilities have any more accidents than do other people. Some people with disabilities do not have the physical agility to do certain things, but they are often more aware of their own limitations than others may be.

  Studies of accident-proneness seem to indicate that it has little or nothing to do with physical disabilities. Most people who suffer frequent accidents do so because of attitudinal problems, specifically, people find themselves in accidents because they make wrong assumptions about what is about to happen. Similarly, they fail to consider potential hazards.

  People with disabilities are thus not any more accident-prone than any other individuals. In fact, in many cases they may be more careful.

- *"They are offensive to look at"*—not true. "Probably the single greatest difficulty that disabled people have is that they make 'normal us' feel uncomfortable when they are around us. Can you recall as a child, staring at a physically disabled person? Most young people do that at one time or another. This is particularly true when they first see a disabled person."[2]

■ People are uncertain about how people with disabilities will react to questions or comments.

Many people are uncomfortable around people with disabilities because they don't know how they will react to their comments. People feel a degree of sympathy for the individual who has lost a limb or who is crippled or who has a mental impairment—in part, perhaps, because one would hate to have to change places with them. At any rate, this discomfort toward people with disabilities is primarily rooted in a lack of understanding.

Recall, from the chapter on cultural diversity, that getting to know others on a personal basis is one effective way of reducing prejudices. The same might be said with the person with disabilities. As one gets to know the person with a physical or mental disability, one often discovers many more similarities than differences. One is likely to discover that "they" are really very much like "us."

■ *"They can't pull their own weight in the organization"*—not true. A criticism similar to that levied against the older employee is that the person with a disability cannot do a fair amount of work. Again, with modern technological devices and assistance, this misconception is not founded on fact. People with disabilities with certain assistance devices can and do produce a productive day's work. In addition, the awareness of the extra effort that an employer may be putting forth to hire and keep them on is often highly appreciated. The result is highly reliable, loyal workers.

▼ WORKERS WITH ALCOHOL- AND DRUG-DEPENDENCY PROBLEMS

The excessive use of alcohol and drugs continues to be a prevalent and costly problem to many organizations. Estimates show that around 18 million people in the United States have serious drinking problems. And the lives of an estimated 36 million people are adversely affected by alcohol. Drug abuse affects the lives of still more millions of people. How widespread and serious are these kinds of problems in industry?

Alcoholism in the Workplace

Alcoholism is a problem of epidemic proportions in the United States, Canada, and many other countries. Although considerable debate exists over where social drinking ends and alcoholism begins, there is little doubt that alcoholism is a serious problem in the workplace. According to the National Council on Alcoholism, alcoholics are absent from work three times more than average employees and have two to four times more on-the-job accidents than do nonalcoholics.[3]

The problem is not limited to the workplace. The excessive use or abuse of alcohol occurs in colleges, secondary schools, and, in some cases, even elementary schools. It appears in governmental bodies, in churches, and in the home. Although our focus is on the workplace, most of the material presented here is applicable in a much wider arena.

Studies of alcoholism among workers conclude that:

■ Studies of alcoholism conclude that ...

1. Workers who suffer from job stress and organizational frustration frequently turn to alcohol as a tool for unwinding.

▼   TABLE 15.1 THE COSTS OF ALCOHOLISM

ALCOHOLISM REMAINS DANGEROUSLY WIDESPREAD

- Around 18 million Americans have a serious drinking problem
- Annual deaths due to alcohol number about 105,000
- Of all hospitalized patients, 25 percent have alcohol-related problems
- Alcohol is involved in 47 percent of industrial accidents
- Half of all auto fatalities are due to alcohol-related crashes—23,352 in 1988

ITS ANNUAL COSTS ARE STAGGERING

Lower productivity, treatment	$41.7 billion
Costs due to premature death	$28.5 billion
Road accidents, crime and law enforcement	$9.6 billion
TOTAL COSTS	$85.8 billion

SOURCE: "Is Business Bungling Its Battle with Booze?" *Business Week*, 25 March 1991, pp. 76–78.

2. While depression, lack of close personal relationships, guilt feelings, social rejection, and genetic, chemical, mental, and other disorders are associated with excessive drinking, there is also a clear correlation between job stress and high alcohol consumption.

3. While it is widely recognized that excessive drinking can lead to physical or psychological dependence on alcohol, many organizations encourage social drinking. Company activities often revolve around cocktail parties or other drinking socials. Most companies show little concern for the heavy drinker until the employee's work is adversely affected.

4. Alcoholism costs U.S. business between $41.7 billion and $85.8 billion per year in such work-related problems as absenteeism, wasted time and ruined materials, accidents, related health problems, and premature death.[4]

Alcoholic employees often remain on the job for several years after the onset of alcoholism because they are able to camouflage the symptoms of their illness. Symptoms of alcoholism will vary based on the work environment and include those on the following list. Supervisors will be better able to help afflicted employees if they recognize these symptoms early on.

- Avoidance of boss and associates
- Uncharacteristically outgoing or pushy
- Pronounced and frequent changes in work pace
- Elaborate or bizarre excuses for work deficiencies
- Severe financial difficulties
- Increased nervousness, hand tremors, gastric upsets, and insomnia
- Sloppy personal appearance with signs of hangover

- Frequent lapses of efficiency, occasionally causing damage to equipment or creating safety hazards
- Frequent trips to water cooler and break area
- Marked increase in medical claims for accidents and illnesses both on and off the job

Drug Abuse in the Workplace

Many of the same problems faced by alcohol-dependent employees are also faced by those who use habit-forming drugs. Drug abuse is a problem of great concern in the workplace. Most estimates place the number of users of drugs as slightly less than the number of abusers of alcohol. Statistics regarding the use of drugs vary greatly. Further, it is not as easy to identify drug users as it is to identify alcohol users. However, when all drugs, including over-the-counter preparations, cocaine, crack, marijuana, LSD, PCP, peyote, mescaline, "ecstasy," and heroin are considered together, drug abuse becomes an obviously large problem both in and out of our major organizations. Statistics regarding drug abuse are difficult to obtain because drugs, unlike alcohol, are illegal and many users are unwilling to admit or discuss their use. More statistical data appears to be available on cocaine use than on many other drugs. Following are a few facts that help give a better understanding of the impact of drugs on people, organizations, and society:

- Drug problems involve both addiction and illegal actions.

- In 1990, treating the 158,400 infants exposed to cocaine added an estimated $500 million per year to inpatient hospital costs.[5]
- The number of people who had used cocaine within the past month jumped to 1.9 million in 1991, up from 1.6 million in 1990. The number of weekly cocaine users rose nearly a third, with the sharpest rise among people over 35. From the fall of 1990 to the spring of 1991, heroin episodes increased 27 percent.[6]

The costs of drug abuse in the workplace are not as well documented as the costs of alcoholism, but it is believed that they are huge—and definitely growing.

The symptoms of drug abuse are similar to those of alcoholism and also include the following:

- Slurred or incoherent speech
- Dilated eyes
- Uncontrollable laughter or crying
- Sloppy appearance without the smell of alcohol
- Unsteady walk or impaired dexterity
- Wide mood fluctuations

There are many other symptoms depending on the type of drug used. The end result is that the abuser is normally unfit for work.

Drug Testing: The Ethical Dilemma

Although organizations need to know when their people have drug problems, many are torn between this need to know and the

ACTIVITY: DRUGS: HOW MUCH DO YOU KNOW?

A test of what people knew about illicit drugs and their effects would have been a brief exercise a decade ago. Now, the list of questions is uncomfortably long, the answers more disturbing than ever. How much do you know?

1. Name the major drug problem among teenagers today.

2. How fast can a child become an alcoholic?

3. Why are grade-school children drawn to wine coolers?

4. Are some drugs gateways that may lead to further substance abuse?

5. How does today's marijuana compare with the marijuana of a generation ago?

6. Does the use of marijuana cause damage to the brain?

7. Do marijuana and cigarettes inflict about the same lung damage?

8. How did "crack" get its name?

9. How long does alcohol stay in the bloodstream after a round of heavy drinking?

10. How long do traces of marijuana remain in the body after it has been smoked?

11. What does crack look like?

12. What is "crack"?

13. How long does a crack high last?

14. How does marijuana affect mood?

15. How many children ages 12 to 17 say they have tried hallucinogens like LSD, PCP, peyote or mescaline at least once?

16. Can geneticists figure out which people are likeliest to become addicts?

17. What is the price of a single dose of crack?

18. Blotter paper is associated with which drug?

19. Which drug temporarily gives its user abnormal physical strength?

20. What is "ecstasy"?

ANSWERS

1. Alcohol.

2. As quickly as six months. An early start on drinking and an immature brain and body make youngsters vulnerable.

3. Because they look and taste much like soda. (Girls especially like them because they don't look or taste like beer.) But wine coolers average 6 percent alcohol content, compared with 4 percent for beer and 10 to 14 percent for wine. Wine typically is served in smaller amounts, so a 12-ounce cooler delivers more alcohol than a glass of wine.

4. Yes. Researchers say it is rare to find abusers of cocaine, heroin or virtually any addictive drug who did not start with some combination of alcohol, tobacco and marijuana.

5. It is much more potent. The National Institute on Drug Abuse reports that the amount of THC, the active ingredient in marijuana, averaged 1 percent by weight in 1970. Today's dope averages 3 to 3.5 percent. Sinsemilla, an increasingly popular type of marijuana, averages 6.5 percent THC and may contain as much as 10 to 15 percent.

6. Animal studies demonstrate that ingesting the daily equivalent of a joint or two for several years destroys brain cells.

7. Researchers say one to three joints daily produce lung damage and cancer risks comparable with smoking five times as many cigarettes.

8. From the crackling made by the crystals of cocaine when smoked.

9. Alcohol leaves the body in 24 hours or less.

10. Traces of THC show up in the urine 10 to 35 days after marijuana is smoked.

11. Soap-like shavings or broken chalk.

ACTIVITY *continued*

12. It is the street form for methampheta-mine, a class of stimulants also called "speed".

13. Six to 8 minutes.

14. Whatever a person's conscious or uncon-scious emotional state, marijuana magni-fies it. After the initial effect, however, it acts as a depressant.

15. According to the federal 1988 National Household Survey on Drug Abuse, 704,000 youngsters have tried hallucino-gens at least once.

16. No method can reliably predict who will become chemically dependent.

17. Generally $2 to $5 in major urban centers but $25 and up in smaller cities, depend-ing on supply and demand.

18. "Acid," or LSD.

19. Known as angel dust, PCP has painkilling properties that make users extraordinarily difficult to restrain physically.

20. Also known as XTC or Adam (from its chemical acronym MDMA), ecstacy is a hallucinogen currently popular with col-lege students. It appears to cause brain damage.

SOURCE: "How to Beat Drugs," *U.S. News & World Report,* September 1989, pp. 69, 71.

potential for violation of privacy. At the center of the debate is the issue of involuntary drug testing.

Those favoring testing cite the health and safety hazards associat-ed with drug-impaired workers. They see random testing as the best way to identify drug abusers since many who use illegal drugs deny doing so.

Those opposing testing cite fundamental rights to personal priva-cy. They express concern that testing for drug use today could lead to other kinds of testing in the future. Eventually, they fear, genetic screening (using lab tests to determine whether employees have genetic traits that make them susceptible to certain diseases) will be used to discriminate against workers.[7]

■ Mandatory drug testing is a controversial issue.

Policies for Dealing with Alcoholism, Drug Abuse, and Privacy

Many companies have written policies for dealing with alcoholism and drug abuse. Those policies include the following ideas:

■ Alcoholism and drug abuse are diseases that can be successfully treated.

■ Workers will be treated confidentially.

■ Workers will not be forced to accept treatment under the compa-ny treatment program if they can show that they are actively engaged in solving the problem through other means.

Employee Assistance Programs

Employers are increasingly providing assistance to their employees with alcohol or other chemical dependency problems through

■ What are EAPs?

employee assistance programs (EAPs). These programs focus on identifying the problem and providing a system for referring the employee to professional treatment services.

Employee assistance programs are addressing an increasing range of individual problems ranging from substance abuse to marital and family conflicts. EAPs often work closely with company "wellness" programs and employee physical fitness efforts.

The best of these programs allow the employee a great amount of privacy and initiative in resolving personal problems while at the same time relieving supervisors of some headaches by providing employees direct access to support services. While these programs are quite new, they have generally proven to be cost-effective.

Successful EAP programs do the following:

1. Establish a committee with equal representation of labor and management, with a medical representative included if practical.

2. Develop a policy statement that clearly expresses the company philosophy toward problems affecting job performance.

3. Where unions exist, develop a joint labor-management policy that recognizes and acknowledges (1) the serious health and behavioral problems associated with alcoholism and drug abuse and (2) the commitment of both management and labor to helping the company and individuals deal effectively with those problems.

4. Train supervisors in appropriate methods for dealing with alcoholism, drug abuse, and other diseases in the workplace.

For an EAP to be successful, it must be rooted in a firm management commitment to helping employees. For example, the employer must assume the responsibility for confronting an employee with a poor work performance or other symptoms of an alcohol problem. Company policies on alcoholism must be made known to employees, and, when warranted, referral to professional treatment must be made. Once an employee has been referred, the manager may follow up but should otherwise cease involvement. He or she should then let the professional counselors work with the employee.[8]

▼ WORKERS WITH AIDS

A newcomer to the list of human relations concerns is Acquired Immunodeficiency Syndrome (AIDS). The likelihood that a company will have people with AIDS among its employees is ever-increasing. Some businesses are especially vulnerable to fears about the disease. For example, a restaurant's business could be devastated if word got out that a person with AIDS was an employee.[9]

■ Companies avoid actions against the seriously ill (especially employees with AIDS) for fear of being accused of illegal discrimination.

Companies must be careful to avoid taking actions against employees with AIDS that could be ruled discriminatory, lest they be subject to legal action. In many places, employers are forbidden by law to fire or to refuse to hire a person with AIDS unless it can be shown that employment alone or the duties of a specific job will intensify the person's risk of illness and death. Most laws provide for discharge action when the person with AIDS cannot adequately perform the job.[10] However, more important than the legal ramifications of dealing with employees with AIDS should be the simple desire on the part of the organization and its employees to understand, accept, and assist fellow employees with this illness.

Many companies have written policies stating that AIDS and other serious diseases are confidential matters. These require AIDS to be treated discreetly and not made public knowledge.

The American Council of Life Insurance of the Health Insurance Association of America estimates that more than $1 billion was paid for AIDS-related claims in 1989, which were up 83 percent from 1988. Unfortunately, more cost increases are expected. A researcher speaking at a 1990 international AIDS conference reported, "The cost of treating U.S. AIDS patients could soar beyond $11 billion annually by 1994." This will undoubtedly increase medical premiums and costs to U.S. businesses.[11]

U.S. companies, by developing simple yet inexpensive AIDS training programs, can take positive action toward reducing direct costs, limiting and possibly eliminating indirect costs, and increasing social responsibility. The best training programs emphasize sensitivity and provide information to dispel myths and preconceptions about AIDS.

▼ WORKERS WHO ARE OLDER

What is an older worker? Age is a highly relative thing. A recent radio commentary was phrased as a "good-news/bad-news" story. The reporter told the good news: "A recent survey at a major southern university showed that female college students found middle-aged men very attractive." The bad news: "They defined 'middle-aged' as 'about thirty-two.'"

■ How old is old?

A corporate president, Supreme Court justice, or high-ranking political figure in his or her early forties is considered very young. A professional athlete can be washed up at thirty-three, while a medical doctor is just starting a career at that age. So age is indeed relative.

Age has different values in different cultures, too. In Western nations, people tend to pride themselves on being "young and vigorous." Enormous amounts of money are spent by people trying to regain their youth and keep a young appearance. In other cultures, notably the Asian cultures, great value is placed on the "wisdom of age."

There is only one thing age can give you, and that is wisdom.
S. I. HAYAKAWA

Tragically, some highly productive workers are now being "put out to pasture" because they reach a particular numerical age—typically sixty-five years. A lot of talent is wasted when able employees are no longer given opportunities for productive work. Yet this, too, seems to be changing. An increasing activity and even militancy among older people has begun to develop, as illustrated by such movements as the Gray Panthers and the increasing power of such organizations as the American Association for Retired Persons. Many

■ Does mandatory retirement waste organizational resources?

older people are enjoying unprecedented good health and vigor, and they want to continue being productive members of society.

Changes and Adjustments Faced by Older Employees

As workers reach the age of senior citizenship, they face some potentially dramatic adjustments. They experience, for example, changes in their family and social needs and responsibilities. Over the years, they have been responsible for being breadwinners and for raising families. Suddenly they are likely to be more alone, perhaps with only their spouses. Sometimes they feel they are not needed. This can, for some, result in lowered self-esteem.

In addition, with age comes a heightened awareness of the implication of one's own death. Older employees have usually mourned the deaths of many of their peers and associates. Inevitably, workers in their sixties or seventies face this greatest of all changes with apprehension.

Other changes, too, must be faced. Frequently, the older worker considers the possibility of retirement. Although retirement may pose a very pleasant change for many workers, it nevertheless calls for significant adjustments in daily activity. Psychologists tell us that major changes in daily activity are very stressful. Some organizations hold preretirement training sessions with older employees to help get them ready for this significant change in their daily pattern of living.

Finally, the older worker usually experiences some physical infirmities. A natural decline in strength and a rise in physical impairments come naturally with age. For example, loss of hearing, changing sleep patterns, chronic illness, hypertension, arthritis, lack of energy, and loss of sight are common difficulties. As workers age, they encounter more physical problems.

Although such changes and adjustments are normal among older workers, their supervisors need to be sensitive to these changes and also need to be aware of stereotypes about the older worker, which are often misconceptions. Let's take a look at some of these misconceptions and discuss them.

Stereotypes and Misconceptions about Older Workers

Stereotypes applied to older workers, especially those in their sixties or beyond, include the following:

- *"They cannot pull their own weight on the job"*—not true. What is meant by "pulling their own weight" differs among various organizations. Does it mean having physical stamina and the ability to handle heavy work? Or keeping up with clerical or nonphysical activities? Either way, the generalization does not hold up.

  Although older employees do tend to have increasing physical infirmities and often decline in strength, this tends to have rela-

---

■ Changing family responsibilities can lower older people's sense of self-worth.

■ Older workers generally have more physical problems.

■ Most stereotypes of older workers are without foundation.

Old age is when you know all the answers but nobody asks you the questions.
Laurence J. Peter

Older workers face special challenges. Nevertheless, their experience and maturity often make them especially valuable workers.

tively little effect on their work. Mature workers develop a clear understanding of their physical limits and work within them. Furthermore, older workers are generally more stable and less likely to "job hop" than their younger co-workers.

From a physical perspective, older people can almost always lift as much as the upper limit set by law. When laws were demanded requiring machines for many lifting jobs, they were initiated by younger people who felt they were having to work too hard—not by older people.

- *"They resist changes"*—not true. The old adage "You can't teach an old dog new tricks" seems to have been taken too literally. Many people assume that older people cannot learn new tasks quickly, that they tend to be in a rut. The fact is that people of all ages resist changes. There is no evidence that resistance to change is limited to older workers.

- *"They are costly to the organization"*—not true. Some assume that older employees cost the organization more money. Again, there is virtually no support for this statement.

Some older employees have developed expertise and skills that make them extremely efficient on the job. In addition, turnover rates among older employees are significantly lower. As workers face imminent retirement, they have virtually no motivation to change jobs. Older employees tend to stick with current positions and thus eliminate for their organizations the cost of hiring and training workers to replace them.

Older people, in fact, have better attendance records than younger employees. Most studies of worker absenteeism, tardiness, and attendance show that older people create fewer problems for their employers than do other workers. Although inevitable health problems or physical difficulties may cause them to miss work occasionally, most absenteeism in organizations is not a result of sickness. Employees of all ages take time

When your friends begin to flatter you on how young you look, it's a sure sign you're getting older.
MARK TWAIN

off for personal or family reasons, or simply because they want to go to a baseball game or some other activity, more often than because of illness.

In summary, most stereotypes of older employees are without foundation. Older employees tend to face some changes and adjustments in their lives, but such changes are not significantly different from those faced by other people. All people face changes as they evolve through the various phases of live.[12]

▼ WORKERS WHO ARE YOUNGER

Younger workers (workers under the age of twenty-five) are also subject to certain changes and adjustments in their lives as well as to stereotypes and misconceptions held by others.

Changes and Adjustments Faced by Young Workers

■ The awareness that one is not a kid anymore can call for major adjustments.

The young, full-time employee may suddenly realize that he or she is "not a kid anymore." This can be quite an adjustment. As people leave the school environment and go into the full-time work force, they experience some serious changes in their life-styles. They suddenly have responsibilities, need to get up and be someplace at a particular time, and need to produce useful effort on behalf of an organization. All these changes frequently add up to a dramatic change in the life pattern of the young person.

The process of adjusting and conforming to a work routine is further complicated when we consider the uncertainties associated with new work expectations. Many young people begin jobs without fully understanding what is expected of them by their employers. These kinds of things can be clarified by the sensitive supervisor, but inevitably the young employees will make some mistakes or misjudgments early in their work careers.

Nobody can be so amusingly arrogant as a young man who has just discovered an old idea and thinks it is his own.
SYDNEY HARRIS

Finally, some special adjustments are faced by young people who suddenly find that they have a degree of financial independence. They now face more new decisions and problems as they earn and spend their own income—perhaps for the first time.

Stereotypes and Misconceptions about Young Workers

As with older employees, certain stereotypes exist about young workers. Among these stereotypes are the following:

■ *"They are reckless and irresponsible"*—not true. Many people tend to think that young workers go off "half-cocked" and don't think about all of their actions. Some truth may be found in this, but such actions are certainly not limited to young employees.

The air of recklessness and irresponsibility associated with some young adults may arise from inexperience or a lack of

Young people face challenges as they adjust to the adult world of work.

"social graces" or knowledge of organizational protocol. The oft-mentioned statistic that indicates that younger people have more automobile accidents (and are therefore more reckless) than older people is a classic example of a stereotype. If one were to study the ratio of miles driven—that is, the number of accidents compared against the exposure to accidents—little evidence exists that younger people are more reckless, irresponsible, or careless.[13] There is a tendency in our society to remember and talk about the few young people who get in automobile wrecks, belong to gangs, are arrested for disorderly conduct during spring break, and so on. Unfortunately, little is heard or said about the vast majority of young people who act responsibly.

■ *"They are less committed to the organization"*—not true. The assumption is that young people are concerned only with their own interests and care little for organizational accomplishment. No foundation has been found for assuming that this is a general condition among young people. Many young people, in fact, are very committed to certain causes. Such commitment can often be effectively used in a business organization.

The supervisor who is aware of these common misconceptions will be more likely to deal effectively with, and reduce many of the pressures on, the young worker.

Young workers often come to the work environment with a great amount of energy and a desire to put to work what they have learned at school. All too often, work organizations are rigid and provide few opportunities for young people to expend their energy in positive ways or to employ their knowledge. The supervisor who is able to positively challenge young workers is likely to achieve considerable success with them.

▼ MANAGER REACTIONS TO PEOPLE WITH PROBLEMS

A manager is often defined as "a person who achieves organizational goals through the efforts of other people." To achieve their purposes, managers must be able to work with a variety of people with a wide range of special characteristics or problems.

We have discussed several such special human relations challenges in this chapter: old age, youth, people with disabilities, drug or alcohol abuse, and AIDS. The wise manager or supervisor realizes that he or she has a responsibility for helping employees deal effectively with special pressures or problems that may interfere with work. He or she also realizes that the costs of not dealing with these pressures effectively are prohibitive, while the ability to deal with them effectively is both professionally and personally rewarding.

The point of this chapter is that several special work groups have special pressures on them. Managers can recognize some of these problems, including the stereotypes and misconceptions that others hold toward these people, and can help ensure fairness and equality of opportunity for all people. In addition, supervisors can help provide counseling services, when feasible, to help such people to reach maximum satisfaction in their jobs.

▼ SUMMARY OF KEY IDEAS

- The three misconceptions about persons with disability are that they are accident-prone, are offensive to look at, and cannot do their share of work.

- Alcoholism and drug abuse are major problems in the modern workplace; their resolution depends on the coordinated and cooperative efforts of management, labor leaders, and the afflicted workers.

- Alcoholism costs business enormous amounts of money and typically results in higher absenteeism, more on-the-job accidents, and additional health care costs.

- Drug testing and other forms of evaluations by companies pose significant risks to personal privacy. Yet, in some cases, failure to test could be disastrous for the company.

- Employee assistance programs provide employees with treatment opportunities when facing alcohol, drug, or other emotional and physical problems.

- The three misconceptions about older workers are that they cannot pull their own weight on the job, they resist change, and they are costly to the organization.

- Two common misconceptions about young workers assert that they are reckless and irresponsible and that they are less committed to the organization than their more mature counterparts.

▼ KEY TERMS, CONCEPTS, AND NAMES

Affirmative action for persons
  with disabilities
Acquired Immunodeficiency
  Syndrome (AIDS)
Alcoholism

Americans with Disabilities Act
Drug dependence
Stereotypes
Symptoms of emotional
  problems

▼ QUESTIONS AND EXERCISES

1. What stereotypes do you hold toward old, young, and handicapped people? Make a list. Then use this list as a basis for a class discussion. How realistic are these stereotypes?

2. Make a case for or against the statement that "younger workers are more careless, impulsive, and irresponsible than more mature workers."

3. In general, how can a manager best cope with the employment of workers with disabilities? What approach is likely to be most sensitive to the person with disabilities? Describe a general strategy for dealing with people with disabilities.

4. Review the discussion of affirmative action for persons of disability. How could you as a manager implement such a program? Be specific.

5. What are some symptoms of alcohol and drug abuse?

6. How should a manager deal with an obvious case of drug abuse or extreme alcoholism?

7. What are EAPs? What areas might they be involved in? Can you see an expanding role for EAPs? Describe it.

8. Answer the introductory questions at the beginning of this chapter.

▼ NOTES

1. Larry Steinmetz, *Human Relations* (New York: Harper and Row, 1979), p. 295.

2. Stan Kossen, *Supervision* (New York: Harper and Row, 1981), p. 380.

3. Jerry Bell and Pat Bell, "Alcohol in the Workplace," *Professional Safety* 34 (February 1989): 11.

4. Gene Milbourn, Jr., "Alcohol and Drugs," *Supervisory Management* (March 1981).

5. "Tab for Infant Cocaine Exposure: $500 Million," *Modern Healthcare*, 23 September 1991, p. 16.

6. "The War on Drugs Continued," *U.S. News & World Report*, 30 December 1991, p. 21.

7. Katie Hafner with Susan Garland, "Privacy," *Business Week*, 28 March 1988, pp. 61ff.

8. Bell and Bell, "Alcohol in the Workplace," p. 13.

9. "How Business Owners Deal with AIDS in the Workplace," *Profit-building Strategies for Business Owners* 18 (March 1988): 11-12.

10. Henry N. Saad, "AIDS Discrimination in the Workplace," *Small Business Report* 12 (March 1987): 79.

11. Vaughn Alliton, "Financial Realities of AIDS in the Workplace," *HR Magazine*, February 1992, pp. 78-81.

ANOTHER LOOK: ACHIEVING ACCESS FOR THE DISABLED

Kreonite Inc., a Wichita, Kan., company that makes photo-processing equipment, failed to retain its first few disabled employees 18 years ago because "we focused on the disability," says Larry Burd, head of manufacturing.

In the years since, he says, the company has learned to focus instead on disabled employees' abilities and to provide the resources they need to do their jobs. By making a few adjustments in working arrangements and plant conditions—such as improved lighting and Braille markings for visually impaired employees—Kreonite has been able to keep disabled workers on the payroll. The firm's 228 employees now include 26 disabled men and women.

Similarly, Beach Brothers Printing Inc, in Rockville, Md., has retained two autistic employees by giving them extra training and teaching them how to function in a workplace with other employees. One of the workers, now with the firm 10 years, had only a two-word vocabulary when he was hired, says Roger Beach, who owns the firm with his four brothers.

Since then, Beach says, that worker has become more expressive and has built an extensive vocabulary. The rigorous effort was worthwhile, Beach says. "He's a taxpayer."

The voluntarism of business owners like Burd and Beach in providing opportunities for disabled employees is being replaced now by government mandates that combine the worst aspects of federal controls—complexity, vagueness, and the threat of ruin for companies that don't comply.

The Americans with Disabilities Act, which was signed into law in July 1990, requires practically all businesses to make their facilities accessible to disabled employees and customers, and it requires businesses with more than 14 employees to accommodate disabled job candidates in hiring.

The law's scope is spotlighted in *What Business Must Know about the Americans with Disabilities Act,* a book published by the U.S. Chamber of Commerce. The authors state:

"The recently enacted Americans with Disabilities Act ... has the potential to change the face of America. Indeed, it will change the way most businesses conduct their employment practices and will determine what actions they must take to make their facilities accessible to all people."

As this enormous statute takes effect in stages over the next three years, companies must cope with requirements ranging from highly detailed specifications on the width of retail-store aisles, for example, to such vague standards as "readily achievable," "undue hardship," and "reasonable accommodation."

Since passage of the act almost a year ago, federal enforcement agencies involved have drafted detailed regulations in two major areas. The Department of Justice has prepared rules on public access, and the Equal Employment Opportunity Commission (EEOC) has dealt with employment.

Companies that will have to implement the law and the consultants who will advise them had hoped the regulations would provide specific guidance on the many unclear sections of the law.

But although compliance will profoundly alter the way a firm does business, says Nancy Fulco, human-resources attorney for the U.S. Chamber of Commerce, the new regulations give "very little guidance" on how to comply. Fulco says businesses expected the regulations to clear up questions left by the law itself. However, the regulations "don't tell us anything we don't already know," she says.

What is known is coming as a shock to many business people who had not been aware of the sweeping nature of this new law. Here are basic details and key provisions that companies should be aware of as they prepare for implementation of the disabilities law:

EFFECTIVE DATES

The law's provisions take effect at various times over the coming three years:

ANOTHER LOOK *continued*

Jan. 26, 1992: Regulations on access to existing private businesses that serve the public take effect, with these exceptions: The law becomes effective on July 26, 1992, for companies that have 25 or fewer workers and gross annual receipts of $1 million or less, and it takes effect Jan. 26, 1993, for companies with 10 or fewer employees and with gross annual receipts not exceeding $500,000.

July 26, 1992: Effective date for equal-employment rules for employers with 25 or more employees every day for at least 20 weeks per year.

Jan. 26, 1993: Newly built facilities with first occupancy from this date must be accessible to both categories covered by the law—members of the public and covered employees.

July 26, 1994: Equal-employment rules take effect for employers with 15 or more employees every day for at least 20 weeks per year.

CONTROVERSIAL EDICTS

Although the law remains to be implemented, many employers are concerned that enforcement and compliance could lead to protracted litigation. In such cases, companies could be ordered to construct facilities, remove alleged barriers, hire personnel, or take other steps to comply with the law. They also may have to pay plaintiffs' attorneys' fees.

Business apprehension about enforcement of the law is based on such requirements as the one that employers make "reasonable accommodation" to hire qualified disabled job candidates, if such an adjustment causes no "undue hardship" to the company. The regulations, like the law itself, contain no solid benchmark for determining what is reasonable or undue. Says David Copus, a Washington, D.C., employment attorney: "Instead of guidance, the EEOC has given us the case-by-case method," and he suggests that many companies cited for discrimination can expect to make a costly defense in court of their actions.

The public-access rules require that firms remove barriers to the disabled wherever their removal is "readily achievable"— defined as not causing "significant loss of profit" or reduction of efficiency. Zachary Fasman, a Washington attorney specializing in labor and equal-employment matters and an author of the U.S. Chamber publication on the disabilities law, says the wording of this provision is one of the many reasons why businesses will have to "wait for the courts to make up their minds as to how the law will work."

Paul Hearne, president of the Dole Foundation for Employment of People with Disabilities, in Washington, disagrees with forecasts of compliance problems. Firms

creating access for disabled employees and customers will themselves benefit, he says. There are economies of scale involved, Hearne argues, and accommodations not only will help one worker but also will give access to "an entire reliable work force" of disabled individuals who will "enter the marketplace both as employees and as consumers." Hearne also says the long lead times before the law's effective dates will help firms comply.

A DEFINITION OF "DISABLED"

The law bars discrimination against anybody with a physical or mental impairment or with a record of impairment. Also protected are people who are "regarded" as having a disability—for example, a victim of disfiguring burns who is shunned as impaired, or someone who cares for a disabled person.

EMPLOYMENT PROTECTIONS

The equal-employment protections of the disabilities law cover all aspects of the work relationship, including hiring, firing, training, benefits, and promotion.

Under the law, a disabled candidate is considered qualified to be hired or promoted if he or she can carry out the "essential functions" of the job (with or without reasonable accommodation). An employer may have to offer training, or such aids as readers or interpreters, if these steps would enhance

ANOTHER LOOK: ACHIEVING ACCESS FOR THE DISABLED
continued

employment opportunities and not cause undue hardship to the company. To determine potential hardship because of a needed accommodation, the law's rules consider the nature of the accommodation itself, the size of the firm, and its financial condition.

Larry Burd says Kreonite has made a variety of physical changes in its workplace to help employees with disabilities. Workers with poor vision use high-intensity lights and magnified computer screens, for example, to design circuitboards. Burd says some power tools are marked in Braille, as is the company's time clock. "Our manufacturing is all accessible," says Burd.

Accommodations for disabled employees may be less noticeable, however. DH Print, a Riverton, Wyo., manufacturer of dot-matrix printers, has modified work schedules and job functions for some employees, says Joe Dennis, general manager. The affected employees include a supervisor confined to a wheelchair, a blind assembly worker, and eight mentally retarded contract workers who test the firm's products. "You mostly have to use common sense about the access problems," Dennis says, "and make sure the job fits the person's abilities."

In matching candidates to jobs, however, employers may not inquire about candidates' disabilities. Employers may only list the essential tasks of a job and ask whether the person can perform them.

What if a candidate who is denied a job argues that all the work tasks specified are not essential? To defend the essential nature of a job task, the employer may show a written job description prepared before the job was advertised or announced, or show that only a limited number of employees can do the task. The employer also can demonstrate that the tasks are essential by showing that the job exists only for the sake for the task.

Employers may not use pre-employment medical examinations to screen disabled candidates before making a job offer. After offering a job, an employer may require a job-related medical exam if such exams are given to all candidates for the position.

Drug testing is allowed. Current use of illegal drugs is not protected as a disability by the law, but drug users and alcoholics who have been rehabilitated are covered.

Under the disabilities law, an employer does not have to hire a candidate posing a "direct threat"—that is, a high probability of substantial harm—to co-workers' health or safety. But the employer must determine whether a reasonable accommodation would mitigate or eliminate the possibility of harm.

PUBLIC ACCESS

Rules covering equal access to public accommodations fall into two classes. One consists of requirements for existing businesses, which take effect next year; the other encompasses even stricter requirements for new businesses in facilities available for occupancy from Jan. 26, 1993.

The access rules cover all businesses that serve the public, except private clubs, religious institutions, residential facilities covered by fair-housing laws, and owner-occupied inns with fewer than six rooms for rent.

The rules are drawn to ensure that disabled patrons have the same access as other customers to a firm's goods or services. In this vein, companies may not exclude or segregate people with disabilities, by company policy or otherwise. It would be illegal, for instance, to require a blind person to produce a driver's license for identification when cashing a check. The business would have to request another form of identification.

Firms must offer such auxiliary aids as sign-language interpreters or readers when such assistance would help provide service to customers with vision or hearing impairments.

If providing such aids is not feasible, a business must offer alternatives. For instance, a restaurant could

ANOTHER LOOK *continued*

provide Braille menus, or, if that is not possible, its staff could inform blind customers that a menu will be read to them. Likewise, if barrier removal is not readily achievable, the business must offer alternative service, such as curbside or home delivery, or help reaching items on shelves. Businesses may not charge extra money for such alternatives.

Nor may a company make any change to its premises that would make it less accessible to the disabled. If renovations or alterations are made to a building, they must meet the strict standards of access for new construction. Less strict rules apply where access requirements would threaten the character of a designated historic property.

Alterations to so-called "primary function" areas of a business, such as a bank's lobby, must include an accessible path of travel. Any phones, restrooms, or drinking fountains in these areas, if altered, must be accessible if the cost of making specific changes is not "disproportionate" to the whole cost of the alteration. However, the Department of Justice, in its proposed regulations, has not settled on a formula for determining "disproportionate" costs of providing access to altered areas. The department's final rules could cap the cost of an accessible amenity at 10 percent, 20 percent, or 30 percent of the entire alteration expense.

REQUIRED FIXTURES

In all new construction, and where feasible in existing facilities, the new law requires the following features for access by disabled customers:

One designated parking space must be provided for every 25 or fewer spaces in a parking area. A diminishing ratio of accessible spaces is required in parking areas beyond 100 spaces. Hotels, motels, and inns must provide an accessible parking space for each guest room required to be accessible. (Generally, 5 percent of rooms must be accessible to wheelchairs, and another 5 percent must be equipped with devices such as visual alarms for hearing-impaired guests.) These lodging places also must provide some accessible parking for disabled visitors.

Access ramps must be in place wherever the floor level changes more than one-half inch. Elevators are required in buildings of three stories or more and in those that have more than 3,000 square feet of floor space per story. Multilevel shopping centers, malls, and professional offices of health-care providers must have elevators as well.

In retail and grocery stores, checkout aisles must be wide enough for wheelchairs—36 inches at least.

Restaurants must have 5 percent of fixed tables accessible to people in wheelchairs.

In newly built restaurants, sunken or raised dining areas must be accessible. In renovated restaurants, raised dining areas need not be accessible if the same character of dining (for example, service and decor) is available in some accessible area used by all patrons and not just by the disabled.

On floors of accessible routes, carpets can be no higher than one-half inch in pile. Floors of accessible routes must be slip-resistant, though no measurement exists for slip resistance.

Toilet facilities, water fountains, and telephones, if provided, must be accessible in both new construction and alterations. In alterations where access to all toilets is not possible, one unisex toilet for the disabled is allowed instead. Mirrors, urinals, and dispensers must conform to certain height standards.

Public phones on any floor must be accessible to people in wheelchairs. Twenty-five percent of other public phones must have volume controls; when public phones are in clusters of six or more, at least one must have a telecommunicating device for the deaf.

Self-service shelves, counters, and bars must meet rigid standards of access by people in wheelchairs and the visually impaired, and

ANOTHER LOOK: ACHIEVING ACCESS FOR THE DISABLED
continued

all new automated-teller machines must meet the same standards.

Theaters and other places of assembly for 50 or more people must have at least three wheelchair spaces "dispersed throughout" the seating area. The formula diminishes as the number of seats increases. A 150-seat theater would need five spaces for wheelchairs.

Paul Roth, of Roth Theatres in Silver Spring, Md., who owns more than 40 theaters in Maryland, North Carolina, and South Carolina, contends two wheelchair spaces are sufficient in a 150-seat auditorium. He says they should be near the back, on a flat surface, near an emergency exit. His concern is that "five or more" seats and the revenue they bring are lost for each wheelchair space created in any auditorium.

Places of assembly such as movie theaters and meeting halls also must have at least two fixed listening devices for people with hearing impairments. Roth says these devices are "rarely if ever used" and that the regulations should require portable listening devises that could be moved from one auditorium to another.

TAX DEDUCTIONS

Companies that spend money on access for the disabled can take a deduction of up to $15,000 per year, under changes made to the Internal Revenue Code in 1990. Also, small firms that spend between $250 and $10,250 on access may claim a tax credit equal to as much as 50 percent of the cost; the credit is available only to firms with gross receipts under $1 million or with fewer than 30 full-time employees.

In addition to exploring the legal maze of compliance with the new law, many small-business people will be conferring with peers who have experience in providing accommodations for the disabled.

Kreonite's Larry Burd is among those with that experience. He talks to a lot of small-business owners who fear the impact of the Americans with Disabilities Act on their firms. He urges patience. No two challenges are alike, Burd says, and no two solutions are the same. Burd sounds almost reassuring when he says, "We don't have all the answers, but you have to start somewhere,"

Whatever advice small-business people receive, the common denominator of compliance with the new law is summed up in the U.S. Chamber's guide:

"If you are [a company] of *any* size, the Americans with Disabilities Act is bound to have a profound effect on the way you do business."

SOURCE: Bradford McKee, "Achieving Access for the Disabled," *Nation's Business,* June 1991, pp. 31–34.

ANOTHER LOOK: HOW TO CONFRONT—AND HELP— AN ALCOHOLIC EMPLOYEE

Unless you work for a very small company, at least one of your colleagues probably has a drinking problem. And if you're a manager, the odds are that you haven't done anything about it.

Most managers dread the idea of confronting an alcohol abuser. They don't know what to say. In some fields, such as journalism and sales, drinking may seem such an integral part of the job that it seems unfair to single anyone out. And you can almost count on getting the runaround. "No one but alcoholics will talk so much about how little they drink," says Eugene McWilliams, chairman of the National Council on Alcoholism & Drug Dependence.

DELICATE ART

Still, McWilliams and other experts say intervention is often the only way to get an alcoholic into treatment. Fortunately, such tactics are especially effective at work. "The reality that your job is on the line is usually quite an eye-opener," says Carol Cepress, who runs a program that helps business deal with alcoholics at the Hazelden treatment center in Center City, Minn.

But intervention doesn't work if it's not done right. Once you suspect a problem, begin documenting instances in which job performance has fallen short. Absenteeism is one problem characteristic of the alcoholic employee. The drinker may habitually leave the office early or arrive late and take more days off than others. Accidents, errors, and an overall decline in quantity or quality of work are increasingly evident. An alcoholic's mood swings may also lead to a rise in conflicts with other employees.

Once you have marshaled the facts, set up a meeting. But don't get right to the point. That's the last thing the experts recommend. Instead, they advise managers not even to mention drinking, let alone diagnose alcoholism.

Instead, says Susan Swan-Grainger, executive director of Employee Assistance of Central Virginia, which provides EAP services for some 20,000 employees from different companies, "keep the discussion focused on performance." Outline the shortcomings, insist on improvement, and then ask if there is anything you can do to help.

The alcoholic employee will probably promise to improve. But almost inevitably, performance problems will recur, often within just a few weeks. Now, it's time for a tougher session. At this meeting, Swan-Grainger says, still avoid the issue of drinking, and say: "I don't know what's wrong with you, but I want you to see an employee assistance counselor." To give the worker an extra push, Swan-Grainger advises setting up the appointment yourself.

This approach leaves the diagnosis and treatment recommendations to trained counselors. But you can increase the odds of success by "telling them that if performance doesn't improve, they'll be disciplined," says Dr. Gary M. Kohn, the corporate medical director at United Air Lines Inc.

Consider how American Telephone & Telegraph Co. handled Steven, 36, a middle manager in its international operations who was addicted to both alcohol and cocaine. Steven says he was coming into work late every day, often on little or no sleep. Early last year, while exploring a possible transfer within AT&T, he ran up a four-figure balance for personal expenses on his corporate credit card. With this, AT&T nixed the transfer, and his boss urged Steven to see a counselor—without accusing him of anything specific. Steven entered treatment in May and has been sober since. His performance has improved, and he recently got another transfer he wanted.

Many managers put off confronting employees like Steven, often in the belief they're being kind. To the contrary, confrontation may be the kindest course. Steven says that intervention "saved my life." And AT&T seems to have reclaimed a young worker whose gratitude and restored ability could result in years of productive service.

SOURCE: William C. Symonds and Peter Coy, "How to Confront—and Help—an Alcoholic Employee," *Business Week,* 25 March 1991, p. 78.

▼ ANOTHER LOOK: AIDS TRAINING IN THE WORKPLACE

The reality of Acquired Immune Deficiency Syndrome (AIDS) is beginning to hit home in the workplace. AIDS and the fear generated by the fatal disease are becoming unavoidable employment issues.

Many companies have experienced firsthand the panic that can follow a reported in-house case of AIDS. Fear, fueled by misconceptions about AIDS transmission, has ignited customer boycotts, employee walkouts, disruptions in the workplace, and threats of violence.

Multimillion-dollar wrongful dismissal suits and associated negative publicity are examples of the tangible results of fear-motivated mishandling of carriers of the AIDS virus. Organizations must learn how to deal effectively with AIDS, or they must suffer the consequences.

TARGETING MANAGERS

All employees can benefit from AIDS education, but it is particularly important to train managers. Managers are agents of the company; managerial decisions can have considerable impact on the organization. For example, a manager's decision to fire an employee with AIDS might result in legal action against the organization.

Managers also set examples that other employees follow. They should be trained first so they can become part of the training solution, involved in training their own employees.

Much has been written about AIDS and the need for policies and educational programs, but little specific guidance has been provided for training managers about how to conduct AIDS training.

The following three needs assessment tools for HR practitioners may provide that guidance. These materials make it easy to compute and analyze needs assess-

Fear of AIDS

Rate these items on a scale of 1–5 to indicate the extent to which you agree or disagree with each statement. (1=strongly disagree; 5=strongly agree).

1. It may be dangerous for me to work around someone with AIDS.
2. Working with AIDS victims places co-workers in a life-threatening situation.
3. There is a reason to fear employees who have AIDS.
4. AIDS victims pose a threat to their co-workers.
5. There is a reason to single out employees who have AIDS.

Knowledge of AIDS

Please indicate whether you believe each statement below is true or false.

1. AIDS is a highly contagious disease.
2. Most people who contract AIDS die from the disease.
3. AIDS can be contracted when an AIDS victim sneezes or coughs on others.
4. AIDS can be contracted through nonsexual touching such as shaking hands.
5. Persons who share tools or equipment with AIDS victims are likely to contract the disease.
6. AIDS cannot be contracted through face-to-face conversation with an AIDS victim.
7. AIDS can be transmitted when people eat or drink after one another.
8. AIDS can be transmitted only through blood.
9. There is a vaccine to prevent AIDS.
10. AIDS can be contracted from toilet seats.

All items are false except 2 and 6. Assign 1 point for each correct answer.

ANOTHER LOOK *continued*

Consequences of employing AIDS victims

Rate these items on a scale of 1–5 to indicate the extent to which you agree or disagree with each statement. (1=strongly disagree; 5=strongly agree).

I believe that allowing AIDs victims to work in our facility will ...

1. Result in lost sales.
2. Cause us to lose customers.
3. Hurt the company's image.
4. Undermine our ability to provide services to clients.
5. Cause employees to refuse job assignments.
6. Undermine company morale.
7. Result in acts of violence.
8. Increase the number of grievances filed.
9. Disrupt the flow of work.
10. Cause employees to quit.
11. Diminish the ability of other employees to concentrate on their work.

Calculate "reduced revenue" score by adding items 1 through 4. Calculate "workplace disruption" score by adding items 5 through 11.

SOURCES: M. J. Vest, F. P. O'Brien, and J. M. Vest, "Perceived Consequences of Employing AIDS Victims: Development and Validation of a Scale," *Psychological Reports*, 66: 1367–1374. F. P. O'Brien, "Work-Related Fear of AIDS and Social Desirability Response Bias," *Psychological Reports*, 65: 371–378.

ment data and can be useful in developing AIDS training programs.

The three tools are directed primarily at those who are responsible for training supervisors and managers. These tools, with slight modification, are also appropriate for nonmanagerial employees.

Needs assessment, the critical first step in training program design, ensures that the training addresses relevant needs. It is a diagnostic process that determines what managers know and believe about AIDS and it is used to evaluate the causes of managerial fears before training. The causes for managerial fears then become the focus for training program development. After training, needs assessment data are used to evaluate training program effectiveness.

We have developed and validated the needs assessment scales for managers. To test our scales, 248 managers from manufacturing, retail-ing, service, and government participated in validation studies.

The three scales that we developed are as follows:

- Fear of AIDS. This scale assesses managers' fear for themselves and for their employees of contracting AIDS at work.

- Knowledge of AIDS. This scale assesses how informed employees are about the disease.

- Business consequences of AIDS. This assesses managerial beliefs about the bottom-line consequences of hiring or retaining people with AIDS.

Used together, information from these scales can provide the trainer with a comprehensive needs assessment picture.

FEAR OF AIDS

Because AIDS is a deadly disease, it is understandable for employees to have concerns. But much of the fear that employees experience is irrational. It is based on the idea that they can contract AIDS through casual contact.

Training can be effective in alleviating fear because it provides employees with accurate information that will help change their beliefs. Once you change an employee's beliefs, it becomes easier to teach him or her to exhibit appropriate behavior. Without training, employees will continue to be afraid and to act out their

Another Look: AIDS Training in the Workplace *continued*

fears in behaviors that are destructive to the organization.

The Fear of AIDS scale is a short but reliable measure for assessing work-related fear of AIDS. The items on this scale (see box) are representative of the comments made by managers who participated in a series of focus-group interviews.

Scores on the scale range from 5 (low fear) to 25 (high fear). Overall scores on this scale gauge the emotional reactions of employees to AIDS as a workplace issue. Scores that exceed the midpoint value (15), mark the turning point of concern. This is indicative of a high-level, work-related fear of AIDS.

KNOWLEDGE OF AIDS

Training content should not be based on assumptions about what employees know or do not know about AIDS. The media and various private and government agencies have attempted to educate the public about AIDS through television, newspapers, community meetings, and mailings.

As a result, you'd expect most employees to be at least moderately knowledgeable about AIDS. If anything, you'd expect managers, who are generally better educated than their employees, to be informed about AIDS and to understand how people contract it.

Unfortunately, that is not always the case.

Results from our consulting and research suggest that most managers are not well-informed about AIDS. For example, 86 percent of the respondents in our study thought that AIDS can be contracted from toilet seats. Ninety-two percent of the respondents thought that people who share tools or equipment with AIDS victims are likely to contract the disease. Similarly, 92 percent of the respondents thought that AIDS could be contracted from nonsexual touching, such as shaking hands.

Their responses to such items indicated that the managers who participated in our study were grossly misinformed. The results illustrate the importance of conducting needs assessments.

The Knowledge of AIDS scale (see box on page 380) is designed to assess what employees know about AIDS and its transmission. Items listed on the scale are based on documents published by the U.S. Department of Health and Human Services and the Centers for Disease Control.

An overall score on this scale can range from 0 (poorly informed about AIDS) to 10 (well informed about AIDS). Trainers should look at both the overall scores and the responses to individual scale items. Overall scores provide an indication of a person's general level of knowledge about AIDS; responses to specific items

provide useful information in developing training program content.

Items on the Knowledge of AIDS scale are not static. In other words, as new information becomes available, epidemiological trends change, and scientific breakthroughs occur, items may become outdated and require revision. For example, in the mid-1980s when AIDS grew to epidemic proportions, almost all AIDS victims were homosexual men and intravenous drug users. Current government statistics show that women and newly born infants now comprise 50 percent of all recently reported AIDS cases.

When revisions become necessary, you can obtain up-to-date materials from the U.S. Health Services Public Affairs Office or the American Red Cross AIDS Education Office. AIDS support networks and community-based agencies are excellent information sources for local developments.

BUSINESS CONSEQUENCES OF AIDS

In many respects, managers are not much different from other employees. They worry about contracting AIDS. They may become preoccupied with safeguarding their health and the health of others when employees with AIDS are in the workplace. But many managers also experience anxieties over the potentially adverse business consequences associated

ANOTHER LOOK *continued*

with employing carriers of the AIDS virus.

Specifically, managers repeatedly express fears about reduced revenues and workplace disruptions. Workplace disruptions could result from such things as employees refusing job assignments, sudden increases in voluntary turnover, and outbreaks of violence toward people who are thought to have AIDS. Such disruptions can hurt productivity and profitability. The Consequences of AIDS scale was developed to reflect managerial concerns about loss of revenue and disruptions at work.

Each item in this scale (see page 381) represents a potentially undesirable business-related consequence.

Items 1 through 4 address managerial beliefs concerning loss of revenue. Items 5 through 11 assess managerial beliefs about how disruptive it would be to employ AIDS virus carriers.

Scores on the four-item section on reduced revenues range from 4 (few perceived losses) to 20 (many perceived losses). Scores on the work disruption section range from 7 (little disruption) to 35 (great disruption).

Scores on the overall scale range from 11 (few perceived adverse consequences) to 55 (many perceived adverse consequences).

High scores on specific items or sections identify red flag areas for training emphasis. The overall score reflects how strongly a manager believes that employing a person with AIDS will lead to negative consequences for the organization.

Understanding how managers feel about employing AIDS victims could have a direct effect on future organizational viability. In several wrongful dismissal cases, managers have justified their actions based on strongly held personal beliefs that hiring or retraining AIDS victims would have detrimental business consequences. Identifying and changing negative managerial attitudes reduces the likelihood of inappropriate or illegal managerial actions. And that could spare the organization from litigation, negative publicity, and heavy legal expenses.

COMMITMENT TO EDUCATION

Most responsible managers would agree that it makes

sense to have an AIDS policy and an employee training program. Assessing managerial attitudes toward AIDS encourages involvement and commitment to AIDS education. Such buy-in is paramount to training success.

And managers themselves need to learn about AIDS and how to overcome their own fears so that they can talk rationally about the disease with their employees.

Managers can set good examples by displaying positive attitudes and behavior toward AIDS victims. They can refuse to withdraw and allow social pressure within their work groups to rule relationships.

A company may have sincere intentions when establishing an AIDS employment policy. But managers undermine or reinforce those intentions through their own fears, knowledge, and attitudes. AIDS education, underpinned by careful, thoughtful needs assessment, can make the difference.

SOURCE: Jusanne M. Vest, Fabius P. O'Brien, and Michael J. Vest, "AIDS Training in the Workplace," *Training & Development*, December 1991, pp. 59–64.

▼ A CASE IN POINT: KEVIN'S CONCERN

Kevin was asked to leave a small family-owned company after an accident left him with both physical and mental impairments. Although the severity of Kevin's disability could in no way prevent him from leading a normal and useful life, his employer felt insurance premiums would increase, Kevin's work performance would decrease, and Kevin would cause embarrassment not only to the organization but to his peers. Kevin was let go, even though none of these concerns was justified. In fact, this manager's loss would prove to be another's gain.

Following are seven myths about workers with disabilities:

1. *They have a higher turnover.* Perhaps the most frequent reason employers cite for not hiring the person with disabilities is their belief that such people have poor attendance records and a high rate of job turnover. Nothing could be further from the truth.

2. *They are less productive.* Some managers argue that workers with disabilities are not as productive as similarly salaried employees and that their efficiency has to be lower due to their physical and mental limitations. Again, current research does not support these assertions.

3. *They are a greater safety risk.* A misinformed manager might assume that the company's safety records will become jeopardized, resulting in increased insurance costs. This is not the case.

4. *They are too costly.* Some managers insist that the firm will have to incur a great deal of extra expense in making adjustments to the work environment. Due to their loyalty and high motivation, workers with disabilities are often more cost-effective in the long run.

5. *They are too demanding.* A significant number of managers, when pressed, suggest that special privileges and working arrangements given to workers with disabilities will result in hostility and resentment from coworkers.

In reality, workers with disabilities make no more demands than their counterparts and often are close friends of their coworkers.

6. *They would be an embarrassment to the organization.* Systematic examinations in the last several years have clearly indicated that most individuals having direct contact with people with disabilities have relatively favorable perceptions of them.

7. *They won't fit in the organization's work groups.* On the contrary, many companies view employees who have disabilities, due to their often higher educational levels, realistic job expectations, and ability to work independently and longer hours, as a needed addition to the work group.

QUESTIONS

1. What can be learned about workers with disabilities from this case?

2. What could you do to help integrate workers with disabilities into your organization?

3. Think of those you know who have disabilities. Do any of these myths describe them?

COPING WITH
PERSONAL STRESS

This chapter answers several all-important questions:

■ What is stress?

■ Are we all slowly going crazy because of the stress in our lives?

■ What are the major causes of stress?

■ Why are jobs ruining workers' health?

■ How can good relationships with others help reduce personal stress?

■ What is a midlife crisis?

■ How can the knowledge of techniques for reducing stress make our lives more enjoyable?

■ What are some techniques of stress reduction that can help you be a more effective employee?

■ What are some management approaches to reduce stress among organizational employees?

■ What role does your personality play in how you deal with stress?

■ What is burnout and how can you avoid or relieve it?

The answers to these and other questions are coming up next in chapter 16....

CHAPTER 16

John rushes to the plant. There he has several fights with an obstinate union leader and two disenchanted employees who claim that top management isn't concerned about anyone but itself.

After lunch, John returns to his office to dive into his stack of work, when the phone rings. On the other end, his wife says, "Hi, John—you're not going to believe this, but Suzy fell down roller-skating and broke her leg. Could you come quickly and help me take her to the hospital?"

After getting Suzy to the hospital, John rushes back to his office to complete his work, when he realizes that he doesn't have time. Besides, everyone is heading for home. He gives up, tosses his work in a briefcase, and goes to his car.

When John arrives home, his wife greets him with good news: The insurance policy will cover only half of Suzy's cast, and the doctor and cast will total one thousand dollars. At this time John sighs to himself, walks into the family room, turns on the TV, and hopes to forget what is happening to him.

Although few of us have days that include all of these experiences, many of us have similar experiences more frequently than we wish. Our stomachs churn, we worry, we wonder how we can get our work done, and we question why everything seems to happen to us. When such things happen, we experience stress.

▼ TYPES OF STRESS

Most of us recognize that we face various types of stress in our daily work and personal lives. Few of us, however, take time to consider specifically what we are experiencing. Let's look briefly at what stress is and at four terms or conditions related to stress.

■ What is stress?

Stress may be defined as "a mental or emotional disquieting response to a difficult condition or situation." It may be thought of as a state of mental or emotional imbalance caused by a perceived difference between a person's capabilities and what is expected of that person. Extreme forms of stress can lead to physical conditions, such as hives, high blood pressure, stroke, and heart attacks.

Stress is an inherent part of life; it cannot be totally eliminated, nor should it be. Nevertheless, stress symptoms can be warning signals that changes need to be made in a person's life.

■ What are the positive aspects of stress?

Eustress refers to "a positive form of stress that helps a person recognize the need to make minor or major course corrections in his or her personal or professional life, or both." Eustress often precedes or accompanies growth and positive changes in a person's life.

■ What are some types of stress that affect people at work?

"Technostress" is a relatively new term that refers to "a computer-generated form of physical and emotional burnout" that is caused by an inability to adapt to rapidly changing technology.[1] (Technostress will be addressed in more detail in chapter 17.)

Burnout refers to physical or mental exhaustion that results from long-term, unrelieved stress.

Many middle-aged people experience a series of physical and psychological changes known as the *midlife crisis*. Symptoms include

Middle age workers often experience a midlife crisis.

unhappiness, insecurity, depression, indecision, fear and anxiety, conflict, nervousness, and a feeling of entrapment. Dealing with people who experience this very real malady can be challenging for organizations.

When managers experience a midlife crisis, they have particular difficulty making decisions and commitments. They tend to withdraw into themselves.

Help can be provided to the individual through the following:

■ Managers can help people through much work-related stress.

- An effective appraisal system, with special care given to keeping the employee informed of organizational activities
- Counseling programs that help with personal problems in a confidential manner
- Seminars to increase employee awareness of the problems
- Pre-retirement programs that teach people how to cope with the traumatic effects of retirement
- Understanding and patience[2]

▼ UNDERSTANDING THE CAUSES OF STRESS

A variety of occurrences in any given day can cause us stress. In an article entitled "How to Manage Stress," Jennifer Bolch suggests that we can identify sources of stress in our lives by completing five sentences that address areas of our lives we might like to change.[3]

1. Maybe I don't need to … anymore.
2. Maybe I need to … some more.
3. Maybe I need to … sometime soon.
4. Maybe I need to … once again.
5. Maybe I need to … sometimes.

According to Bolch, the first statement simply clarifies what people would like to change, while the second one deals with things they wish to hang on to or don't wish to change. The third statement deals with future goals, while the fourth recalls a resource from the past. The fifth statement clarifies an area where people need more flexibility.

This quiz can bring many areas of one's life into focus and give a better understanding of where one stands in terms of stress. What might cause you to have personal stress? We all need to reflect on our own lives to determine what causes our stress. What things cause stress? Look closely at your life and the lives of your employees, and identify stresses that can be dealt with and reduced.

▼ PERSONAL STRESSORS

Do any of the following stressors have an impact on you?

1. *Ineffective communication.* Stress often results from a lack of communication or from a lack of the right kind of communication at the right time. Each person is a unique individual. We each see the world differently, and we interpret communicative attempts differently. Therefore, we all must be constantly alert to the difficulties of understanding. We should ask questions and be aware of the other person's frame of reference.

   For example, nothing is more stressful than discovering you have arrived at an appointment with your supervisor at the wrong time. You misunderstood the appointment hour, your supervisor is upset, and you are edgy. Accurate communication could completely reduce this cause of stress. To reduce stress, people must do their best to make certain that they "get the message."

2. *Corporate mismanagement.* Various individuals within organizations are affected by the stresses of corporate life. Corporate mismanagement principally concerns people who serve in key positions and who must make decisions. As they make ineffective decisions, use ineffective management techniques, waste time, or see income falling or new products failing, they tend to be filled with stress. Most people fear for their credibility and position. No one wants to fail. The level of stress tends to increase as employees progress up the organizational ladder.

3. *Information overload.* Information overload is a frequent cause of stress among employees. It simply means that an individual or an employee is given too much data in a certain period of time and is unable to deal with it. Letters can't be answered,

■ Stress can be caused by a lack of communication.

■ Stress can result from too much information or unpredictable leader behavior.

phone calls aren't returned, appointments are rushed or missed, and a tremendous amount of stress falls on the employee.

4. *Inconsistent leader behavior.* Nothing causes greater stress with subordinates than to have their leader function in unpredictable ways. Employees are unable to determine the actions or attitudes of the boss. If people receive supportive behavior from a leader in some situations but nonsupportive behavior in others, a great deal of stress is created.

5. *Work overload.* Work overload is a very depressing aspect of life in an organization. A good way to determine if an organization is facing work overload is to measure the amount of the unfinished work. Work overload produces extreme stress when deadline pressures are put on employees. When employees are unable to meet deadlines, they quickly get bogged down and begin to worry. When employees feel bogged down because of too much work, they can't decide what to do first. Which task is the most important? Which deadlines can be missed? Work overload is likely the major stress producer in an organization.

6. *Job change.* As human beings, we believe in a society that is constantly changing. As one type of work becomes extinct, another type becomes important. We are all forced to change, to take new jobs, to move into new societies and environments. All these changes can cause stress. Moving to a new home can cause stress, as can moving to a new job.

7. *Personal problems.* The personal lives of employees can cause severe personal stress. Although employers usually feel that one's personal problems should be left at home, this is rarely the case. Human nature does not allow people to divorce themselves from their personal lives for eight to ten hours a day at the workplace. Any personal problem ranging from troubles with baby-sitters to the breakup of a marriage or relationship can add to the stress of the employee at work. Even college administrators and faculty (who might be expected to know better) often show a callous disregard for the personal problems of colleagues and students.

SOURCE: Wiazard of Id. By permission of Johnny Hart and NAS, Inc.

■ Some people create additional stress in others.

8. *Stress carriers.* Many of us come in contact with people who generate stress within us. These kinds of people are called *stress carriers.* If a supervisor's style of management is stress-producing, subordinates and peers at all levels of the organization feel the effects. Many stress carriers have no idea of the negative impact they have on their co-workers. Other stress carriers are aware of what they are doing and for some reason enjoy creating stress in others.

9. *Company policies, salary, and working conditions.* Company policies, salary, and working conditions often cause stress within management and among employees. If people work under poor lighting, they can't function well. Workers are also stressed when they feel they should receive more money for their work or if company policy restricts them from doing things they feel they must do to be effective.

10. *Powerlessness associated with role changes.* As roles in life change, many people experience an increase in stress. Jane Clarke reports that while women have gained greater educational and career opportunities in recent years, they have also experienced an alarming increase in "panic attacks" often related to "a sense of powerlessness as their roles in life changed."[4]

Stress hinders individual and organizational effectiveness, so employees and managers must learn to handle it. The initial step for easing stress is recognizing its presence. The next section of this chapter deals with techniques for coping with stress.

▼ INDIVIDUAL TECHNIQUES FOR COPING WITH STRESS

The causes of stress are quite apparent, but effective ways to cope with stress are not quite as obvious. The following ideas have proven to be invaluable in dealing with stress and tension. The application of these ideas depends entirely on the people who use them and the situations in which they are used. We do not suggest that each technique will work for every person in every situation, but a variety of techniques are listed so that individuals will be able to choose among them.

1. *Escape for a while.* If you find yourself encountering a stressful situation where you question how you are going to act, *just leave*—escape for the amount of time you need to get back to normal and get composed. This method of dealing with stress can help a person approach problems in a much better emotional condition and in a less stressful way. If you think you might blow up and fight, it is better to escape for a while.

2. *Talk it out.* One of the best ways to reduce stress is to talk to people about your feelings. Don't hold things in or bottle up tension—confide in someone you trust. You can find great relief in sharing your feelings with someone else. Let others know why you are upset, tense, and nervous. Usually, the longer you talk, the more you reduce your stress.

3. *Work off your anger.* If you are in a situation that is producing an enormous amount of stress, play racquet ball, walk around the block, run up and down stairs, jog a mile, or sock a punching bag. Physical activity is a good way to relieve stress. As you start to cool off, you can approach the situation in a more intelligent manner.

4. *Give in occasionally.* In interactions with supervisors and with family members, people find it difficult to accept being wrong. A good way to reduce stress about who is right and who is wrong is simply to give in occasionally. Besides, if you give in, the other person may respond by occasionally giving in to you. In any event, giving in can help reduce stress.

5. *Do something for others.* When you find yourself in a high-stress situation where you are worrying and simply can't get anything done, you can sometimes reduce stress by doing a kind deed or helping someone else. When you are out buying a flower, a card, or carrot sticks to give to someone else, you can forget about your stress.

6. *Take one thing at a time.* Most of us have too many things to do and cannot possibly complete everything. One effective way to deal with this stressful condition is to rank all items that you have to do. Then take one item at a time and complete it. After each item is finished, go on down the list to the next item. Don't worry about any items other than the one you are working on. This helps in a number of ways. It gives you a sense of accomplishment that you are completing some of your responsibilities, and it helps reduce stress because you are involved in completing the item you are working on.

7. *Shun the superperson urge.* Don't go through life under the mistaken assumption that you can do everything for everybody all the time. This is a gigantic producer of stress. Be willing to do as much as you can, but don't accept more. Don't become too involved.

■ Some techniques for dealing with excessive stress include …

Shoe. Reprinted by permission: Tribune Media Services.

8. *Go easy with criticism.* This is extremely important in dealing
   with others. Working with people who do not complete assignments is stress producing. When one expects too much from
   others, one can easily be let down, disappointed, and frustrated.
   It is best to go easy with criticism. Expect the work to be done,
   but don't expect too much.

9. *Make yourself available.* One great cause of stress is worrying
   about how others feel about you. Making yourself available
   gives you the opportunity to hear what people have to say about
   you. As you interact with others, you learn quickly that you
   have no need to be full of stress.

Physical activity is a great way to release stress.

10. *Take time for recreation.* Physical recreation and reduction of mental stress go hand in hand. All employees of an organization should routinely take time each day for recreation. Recreation can take the form of extreme physical activities, such as jogging, or it can take the form of less strenuous activity, such as going to the movies or a concert. Recreation helps take your mind off all the stress-producing activities in your life.

11. *Organize your life.* A highly organized time schedule saves tension as well as helps you accomplish a great deal. Being organized can help save the time necessary to complete more work. (However, being too organized can occasionally also cause stress in your life.)

12. *Establish a nutritious diet.* Include a balance of healthy foods while eliminating or reducing excessive calories, fats, alcohol, caffeine, and other unhealthy substances.

13. *Investigate stress-reduction programs.* Check out employee assistance programs or community agency programs that offer help in reducing stress.

14. *Discover your personality.* How stress affects one depends on certain aspects of personality. Complete and score the following activity entitled "Which Personality Type Are you?" and then read the section on job stress and personality to discover how your personality might be a cause of stress in your life.

▼ JOB STRESS AND PERSONALITY

■ Twelve personality characteristics that relate to stress ...

"Jobs in and of themselves, are not necessarily the cause of stress," says Rosalind Forbes in an article entitled "Job Stress and Personality."[5] Forbes describes twelve personality characteristics and their relationship to stress:

1. *"I want to be left alone."* Introverts are not very social and do not cope well with tensions with other people. They usually do well working alone but are often hampered in team settings. Promotions trigger stress because they usually include assuming supervisory or additional interpersonal responsibilities.

2. *"Look at me; I'm here and I want to join you."* Extroverts are "people who need people" for a variety of reasons. They usually work well in jobs that require teamwork and interpersonal relationships. Extroverts are limited in that they require access to others if they are to perform adequately. Whereas the introvert is happy if left alone, the extrovert must be surrounded with people to maintain a healthy self-identity.

3. *"You'll do it this way or else!"* Rigidly structured individuals are interested in security and are afraid to take risks. They possess characteristics that are highly resistant to change. These people might crack under pressure while attempting to implement an inappropriate but accepted strategy, rather than risking the use of an innovative solution that has not been totally proven. They are stressed by anything that upsets the routine. They sometimes make it to supervisory or managerial positions, where their need for knowing and controlling details causes their employees to work out of fear. Rigid individuals rarely make good managers because they lack the flexibility required for effectively interacting with others.

4. *"Sure, I'm willing to try it."* People with the flexible personality type normally suffer very little job stress. They have healthy, mature egos and can usually adapt to changing situations while tolerating high degrees of stress. Individuals with this personality type can generally delegate authority and work well either alone or in a group.

5. *"Where there isn't any stress, I'll create it."* The stress-prone personality if often both a victim and a carrier of stress. Characterized as hard-driving, work-oriented, performance-conscious, or goal-oriented, individuals in this category constantly overwork and seldom enjoy the benefits of their efforts as they continuously seek greater and often unrealistic goals. They are also highly susceptible to physical repercussions and are three times more likely than others to suffer a coronary in middle age.

6. *"If there is no reason to be concerned, I won't worry about it."* Stress reducers may be as ambitious and work-oriented as stress-prone individuals. However, they are usually more aware of, and confident in, their capabilities and therefore are more patient and less concerned with what others think of their work.

ACTIVITY: WHICH PERSONALITY TYPE ARE YOU?

This questionnaire is designed to help you determine if the personality you bring to work is the reason for most of your stress. Go through all thirty statements and rate yourself as to how you typically feel or react in each situation.

1. Never   2. Seldom   3. Sometimes   4. Frequently   5. Always

1. _____ Meeting new acquaintances is very stressful for me.

2. _____ My spouse or friends think I am hard-driving and work too hard.

3. _____ What happens in my life is determined by fate and circumstances.

4. _____ If given the chance, I prefer to work alone.

5. _____ When a job is not clearly laid out for me, I begin to feel anxious.

6. _____ A negative evaluation about my work makes me depressed for days.

7. _____ I pride myself on accomplishing the most work in my department and being the first to meet quotas.

8. _____ Having to make business decisions is particularly stressful for me.

9. _____ There is little I can do to influence the decisions of those in authority.

10. _____ My work is less productive when I have to interact with others.

11. _____ I rely more on other people's opinions than on my own.

12. _____ I would rather have a steady income I can count on than a stimulating but responsible job.

13. _____ I usually work with frequent deadlines and time pressures.

14. _____ Since it is impossible to try to change a large organization, I tend to go along with things as they are.

15. _____ I tend to withdraw from people rather than confront them with problems.

16. _____ If one method for getting the job done works, I am not likely to change it.

17. _____ I need the praise of others to feel I am doing a good job.

18. _____ Since I do not want to fail, I avoid risks.

19. _____ I seldom feel good about myself.

20. _____ I become particularly upset with any changes in my routine.

21. _____ I personally do not reveal things about myself.

22. _____ I tend to become overly cautious and anxious in new situations.

23. _____ I have a tendency to produce more and more work in less time.

24. _____ Because of my work, I have no opportunity to do the things I really want to do in life.

25. _____ If someone criticizes me, I begin to doubt myself.

26. _____ I pride myself on being orderly, neat, and punctual.

27. _____ I do not like to go to parties or places where there are a large number of people.

28. _____ Luck has a great deal to do with success.

29. _____ I do a great deal of business during a game of golf or in the course of evening dinners with clients.

30. _____ I become particularly upset if I am contradicted.

EVALUATION

If your score is between 134 and 150, you possess personality characteristics that are likely to generate a great deal of stress for you on the job. Your personality causes you to create much of your own stress, and this may limit your ability to function well under pressure.

A score between 114 and 135 indicates there is room for improvement. You are usually unable to handle high amounts of stress for prolonged periods of time.

ACTIVITY: WHICH PERSONALITY TYPE ARE YOU? *continued*

There is a good balance between 74 and 115. You will have to make a conscious effort, however, to keep your behavior on the positive end of the scale when going through stressful situations.

If your score is between 44 and 75, it is not likely that your personality aggravates your reaction to stress. You probably feel that you can handle and control most situations.

A score between 30 and 45 indicates you possess characteristics that defuse much of the stress in your life. You have the qualities that make you a candidate for a leadership position since you function well under pressure.

The statements you just responded to can be used to indicate more than just how you react to stress; they an also identify what personality trait is causing you to react that way.

To identify which personality type you are, the items on the questionnaire are grouped around personality clusters. Add up the score of each cluster and you will see which is more heavily weighted. It is not unusual to have more than one predominant trait.

Cluster	Pertinent Statements
Low/high self-esteem	6, 11, 17, 19, 25
Rigid/flexible	5, 16, 20, 26, 30
Introvert/extrovert	4, 10, 15, 21, 27
Outer-/inner-directed	3, 9, 14, 24, 28
Stress-prone/stress reducer	2, 7, 13 23, 29
Security seeker/risk seeker	1, 8, 12, 18, 22

Once you have determined which characteristics are creating your stress, you can begin changing those aspects of your behavior.

These people are seldom driven by the clock and do not take on extra work just to enhance their image or prestige. Nevertheless, they accomplish much and are more likely to enjoy the fruits of their accomplishments than will their driven, exhausted counterparts.

7. *"If I take a chance, I might fail."* Risk avoiders tend to be overly cautious and afraid to make a decision. These people are driven by feelings of inadequacy, insecurity, and dependency, which inhibit innovative thinking. They avoid new ideas, new jobs, transfers, and even promotions as they seek security while rarely feeling secure.

8. *"Hey, that sounds great! Let's risk it!"* Risk takers create action and provide the fuel for most business and professional endeavors. Usually logical thinkers, people with this personality type consider available facts, weigh alternatives, and take appropriate action. Risk takers have confidence in their decisions and enjoy a high level of success.

9. *"They set me up to fail."* People with an outer-directed personality tend to blame other people, things, or the organization when problems occur. Since they are outer-directed, their self-identities are tied to their work or organization and they have no sense of power or control. To compensate for this problem, their immediate action when faced with failure is to look for someone to blame. Outer-directed people often develop a high level of expertise in generating paperwork since paper can often be used

to cover mistakes and failures. While outer-directed people are capable of success, they are sensitive to criticism, and because they often spend more time working on excuses than solutions, they limit their success potential.

10. *"I'm responsible."* Inner-directed people attribute their failures and successes to their own actions, attitudes, and inner resources. They are more adaptable than outer-directed people but often suffer higher stress levels. In extreme cases, they become preoccupied with details and obsessed with finding why they have not achieved desired results.

11. *"Tell me I'm okay."* Persons with low self-esteem tend to become overwhelmed and show a sharp decrease in performance when under stress. These people seldom succeed in high-pressure business situations and if placed in such situations are likely to suffer severe depression.

12. *"That's all right; I'm okay."* Individuals with high self-esteem can usually deal with frustration and often perform better under pressure. These people have self-confidence based on internal qualities and tend to be optimistic about their ability to achieve desired results. High self-esteem is a vital quality for success in the rough-and-tumble business world.

Forbes's twelve personality types are not all mutually exclusive. When we consider how they might apply to us personally (or to those around us), we often find that many apply to varying degrees. We can refer to these types and develop ideas for building on our strengths and limiting or compensating for our weaknesses in order to reduce negative stress and improve overall performance.

▼ THE BURNED-OUT WORKER

Human relations problems arising from stresses on the job, as well as from social pressures, are increasing. We have been addressing these kinds of pressures for several chapters now. Certain symptoms show up in so-called burned-out workers; workers who have given their all for the company and are now, frankly, very tired of it.

Why do workers burn out? A number of forces are at work here. Sometimes the frustrations emerge from a high achiever's expectations. When a person who has set very high goals suddenly finds that those goals are not achievable, that person may become very frustrated and may burn out.

■ Why do workers burn out?

In other cases, workaholics may be set up as role models—as what workers should try to be like. Nevertheless, the problems of *workaholism*—that is, addiction to one's work—are very severe. They can readily lead not only to worker burnout but to all types of social, family, and other adjustment problems.

Many highly successful people come to feel that they have given their all to their organizations. Some of these people eventually face the reality that life is passing them by. They recognize that they have dedicated virtually all their time and efforts to their

ACTIVITY: THE NWNL WORKPLACE STRESS TEST

Thinking about your work site, how strongly do you agree or disagree with the following statements? For each statement, fill in the circle with a pencil under the response that best describes your work life.

	Response				
	Disagree Strongly	Disagree Somewhat	Neutral or Don't Know	Agree Somewhat	Agree Strongly
SECTION A					
1. Management is supportive of employee's efforts.	O	O	O	O	O
2. Management encourages work and personal support groups.	O	O	O	O	O
3. Management and employees talk openly.	O	O	O	O	O
4. Employees receive training when assigned new tasks.	O	O	O	O	O
5. Employees are recognized and rewarded for their contributions.	O	O	O	O	O
6. Work rules are published and are the same for everyone.	O	O	O	O	O
7. Employees have current and understandable job descriptions.	O	O	O	O	O
8. Management appreciates humor in the workplace.	O	O	O	O	O
9. Employees and management are trained in how to resolve conflicts.	O	O	O	O	O
10. Employees are free to talk with one another.	O	O	O	O	O

	Response				
	Disagree Strongly	Disagree Somewhat	Neutral or Don't Know	Agree Somewhat	Agree Strongly
SECTION B					
11. Workloads vary greatly for individuals or between individuals.	O	O	O	O	O
12. Employees have work spaces that are not crowded.	O	O	O	O	O
13. Employees have access to technology they need.	O	O	O	O	O
14. Few opportunities for advancement are available.	O	O	O	O	O

ACTIVITY *continued*

	Disagree Strongly	Disagree Somewhat	Neutral or Don't Know	Agree Somewhat	Agree Strongly
15. Employees are given little control in how they do their work.	○	○	○	○	○
16. Employees generally are physically isolated.	○	○	○	○	○
17. Mandatory overtime is frequently required.	○	○	○	○	○
18. Employees have little or no privacy.	○	○	○	○	○
19. Performance of work units generally is below average.	○	○	○	○	○
20. Personal conflicts on the job are common.	○	○	○	○	○
21. Consequences of making a mistake on the job are severe.	○	○	○	○	○

	Response				
	Disagree Strongly	Disagree Somewhat	Neutral or Don't Know	Agree Somewhat	Agree Strongly

SECTION C

	Disagree Strongly	Disagree Somewhat	Neutral or Don't Know	Agree Somewhat	Agree Strongly
22. Employees expect the organization will be sold or relocated.	○	○	○	○	○
23. There has been a major reorganization in the past 12 months.	○	○	○	○	○

	Response				
	Disagree Strongly	Disagree Somewhat	Neutral or Don't Know	Agree Somewhat	Agree Strongly

SECTION D

	Disagree Strongly	Disagree Somewhat	Neutral or Don't Know	Agree Somewhat	Agree Strongly
24. Meal breaks are unpredictable.	○	○	○	○	○
25. Medical and mental health benefits are provided by the employer.	○	○	○	○	○
26. Employees are given information regularly on how to cope with stress.	○	○	○	○	○
27. Sick and vacation benefits are below that of similar organizations.	○	○	○	○	○
28. Employee benefits are significantly cut in the past 12 months.	○	○	○	○	○
29. An employee assistance program (EAP) is offered.	○	○	○	○	○
30. Pay is below the going rate.	○	○	○	○	○

ACTIVITY: THE NWNL WORKPLACE STRESS TEST *continued*

	Disagree Strongly	Disagree Somewhat	Neutral or Don't Know	Agree Somewhat	Agree Strongly
31. Employees can work flexible hours.	O	O	O	O	O
32. Employees have a place and time to relax during the workday.	O	O	O	O	O
33. Employer has a formal employee communications program.	O	O	O	O	O

	Response				
	Disagree Strongly	Disagree Somewhat	Neutral or Don't Know	Agree Somewhat	Agree Strongly

SECTION E

	Disagree Strongly	Disagree Somewhat	Neutral or Don't Know	Agree Somewhat	Agree Strongly
34. Child care programs or referral services are available.	O	O	O	O	O
35. Referral programs or day care for elderly relatives are offered.	O	O	O	O	O
36. Special privileges are granted fairly based on an employee's level.	O	O	O	O	O
37. New machines or ways of working were introduced in the past year.	O	O	O	O	O
38. Employer offers exercise or other stress-reduction programs.	O	O	O	O	O

	Response				
	Disagree Strongly	Disagree Somewhat	Neutral or Don't Know	Agree Somewhat	Agree Strongly

SECTION F

	Disagree Strongly	Disagree Somewhat	Neutral or Don't Know	Agree Somewhat	Agree Strongly
39. Work is primarily sedentary or physically exhausting.	O	O	O	O	O
40. Most work is machine-paced or fast-paced.	O	O	O	O	O
41. Staffing or expense budgets are inadequate.	O	O	O	O	O
42. Noise or vibratrion is high, or temperatures are extreme or fluctuating.	O	O	O	O	O
43. Emloyees deal with a lot of red tape to get things done.	O	O	O	O	O
44. Downsizing or layoffs have occurred in the past 12 months.	O	O	O	O	O
45. Emloyees can put up personal items in their work area.	O	O	O	O	O

ACTIVITY *continued*

46. Employees must react quickly
    and accurately to rapidly changing
    conditions.   ◯   ◯   ◯   ◯   ◯

Please check that you have filled in one response for each statement. Thank you for completing the questionnaire.

Work sites that record low stress scores are less likely to suffer the costs associated with high turnover and frequent stress-related illnesses among employees. Scores within ranges were determined by a research.

A. EMPLOYEE SUPPORT AND TRAINING

Low		Medium		High	
0	14.1	14.2	19.6	19.7	40

The Employee Support and Training Scale is composed of 10 measures of how well management communicates with employees and encourages a nonthreatening, comfortable work atmosphere. The scale also reflects the adequacy of training, clearness of direction and fairness of management. A low score on the scale indicates the organization is characterized by behaviors that reduce workplace stress.

B. WORK CONDITIONS

Low		Medium		High	
0	17.8	17.9	22.2	22.3	44

The Work Conditions Scale is composed of 11 items measuring how effectively work loads and employees are managed. A low score indicates management reduces stress by empowering employees, handling personal issues, encurring adequate resources are available and allocating work effectively and equitably.

C. ORGANIZATIONAL CHANGE

Low		Medium		High	
0	2.3	2.4	4.6	4.7	8

The Organizational Change Scale comprises two changes which significantly affect workplace stress: a major reorganization and the expectation that the company will be sold or relocated. A low score indicates fewer stressors related to change.

D. EMPLOYEE BENEFITS

Low		Medium		High	
0	18.3	18.4	22.1	22.2	40

The Employee Benefits Scale is composed of 10 items describing the employee benefits and workplace amenities that are offered by an organization. Employers who provide a wide range of benefits and competitive compensation will record a lower score and lower organizational stress level.

E. PROGRESSIVE PROGRAMS

Low		Medium		High	
0	12.9	13.0	14.2	14.3	20

The Progressive Programs Scale is composed of five advanced programs or activities that help employees cope with job stress. A low score indicates lower workplace stress.

F. JOB DESIGN & PHYSICAL ENVIRONMENT

Low		Medium		High	
0	15.9	16.0	18.8	18.9	32

The Job Design & Physical Environment Scale uses eight characteristics of the organization's working environment that affects stress. The scale reflects type of

ACTIVITY: THE NWNL WORKPLACE STRESS TEST *continued*

work, staffing levels and physical conditions.

GRAND SCORE 0 TO 184

Low		Medium		High	
0	81.1	81.2	101.5	101.6	184

The Grand Score for The NWNL Workplace Stress Test reflects the overall risk that the organization will suffer from the negative effects of job stress.

career pursuits while missing out on many other aspects of life. These people are burned out—they have little left to give.

■ Early warning signs of burnout.

In his article "Coping with Burnout," Kerry L. Johnson says that burnout may be caused by a compulsion for business or financial success.[6] He also says that burnout causes low self-esteem, lowered productivity, and sometimes failed relationships, but that burnout is not inevitable if recognized and treated in early stages. The five stages of burnout, as identified by Randy Kunkel, are headaches, general body fatigue, cutting off of communication to family and friends, overload, and disintegration of values. According to Johnson, burnout can be avoided or alleviated by avoiding a career rut, staying physically active, focusing on nonbusiness relationships, stimulating the intellect, making spiritual discoveries, and consciously improving one's life-style.

▼ MANAGEMENT APPROACHES FOR COPING WITH STRESS AND BURNOUT

I think that maybe in every company today there is always at least one person who is going crazy slowly.
Joseph Heller

Management can reduce stress by bringing employees together in team meetings, using proper management techniques, establishing an effective communication system, and, above all, reducing uncertainty among employees.

Team Meetings

Talking over problems helps people feel better about their co-workers. This tends to reduce the stress they have about their ability or inability to solve problems. Team meetings allow for the employees to get together and discuss problems.

If employees are feeling a tremendous amount of stress, team meetings can be an effective way to reduce the stress. The Bell System allows time for team meetings and interactive meetings. When it changed its organization and various policies, employees felt a tremendous amount of stress. So the company initiated noontime discussion programs where various team members could come together to discuss what was causing stress and how to deal with it.

Some organizations use encounter groups to reduce stress. The members reduce their feelings and emotions by telling others why they are upset. A professional group facilitator should lead the encounter, so that people do not become too upset with what takes place.

Another approach is the deep sensing session. In a deep sensing session, executives meet with employees and communicate face-to-face. This approach should not be just a gripe session, but a situation where problems associated with miscommunication can be cleared up. Usually with this approach a special outside consultant must be brought in to guide and direct the meeting. The consultant can usually direct misunderstandings without evoking too much defensive behavior.

Whether you use a deep sensing group, an encounter group, or team meetings, you can reduce stress by allowing team members within the organization to interact and recognize one another's feelings.

Proper Management: An Alternative to Dealing with Stress

Proper management does a great deal to reduce employee stress. For example, a manager can reduce stress related to time or overwork. Managers should allow the employees enough time to plan and organize and do the tasks they must do. Furthermore, managers should give people specific tasks, let them make decisions, and let them know what is expected of them. Sometimes management by objectives is used: people are allowed to make their own decisions but they also know what is expected of them.

■ Good managers can do much to reduce stress.

Rest breaks during the working day can also help reduce stress. Some organizations call these rest breaks "minivacations." All people need some time during the day to sit down, to daydream, to fantasize, and to deal with feelings.

Teaching people how to cope with stress is important to management. Employees can be taught to cope with difficulties and reduce their own tensions. Managers should help employees upgrade their life goals. If people are working toward strong, positive life goals, they can overcome small stressful circumstances much more quickly and effectively. The organization must help employees establish life goals.

Productive Communication

Effective communication within the organization and among employees is probably the most important asset an organization can have for reducing employee stress. When employees do not receive information, they wonder why, and they tend to become worried and suspicious. An effective communication system allows for

■ Effective communication reduces stress.

"Sorry, Smith. If I let you go home, I'll have to do the same for any employee who had a heart attack."

openness and feedback for all levels and for all people in the organization.

Communication experts have offered many approaches for increasing effective communication within an organization. One approach that is often used is to talk about the achievements of employees and to let word get out that people are doing well and that they are appreciated. This builds high employee expectations, self-esteem, and self-confidence. And it tends to reduce stress.

Also make certain that people understand what they have been asked to do. Managers should continually ask for feedback so that they know what is happening. In the section on communication in chapter 11, many suggestions are made on how to ask for feedback.

A Final Statement

■ As stress is reduced, employees become happier and organizations more productive.

Anything that *can* be done to reduce employee stress *should* be done. More and more companies have established stress-reducing programs to increase productivity and efficiency in employees. Some managers will always support the idea that one must pressure employees to get them to complete their jobs. However, many organizations are now realizing that stress reduction is important. As individuals and organizations learn to alleviate stress and supervisors and employees become happier, organizations become more productive. Team interaction, good management, and effective communication can help reduce uncertainty and help organizations function more effectively with less stress.

▼ SUMMARY OF KEY IDEAS

- The ten stressors are: ineffective communication; corporate mismanagement; information overload; inconsistent leader behavior; work overload; job change; personal problems; stress carriers; company policies, salary, and working conditions; and powerlessness associated with role changes.

- Fourteen techniques of coping with stress are: escape for a while, talk it out, work off your anger, give in occasionally, do something for others, take one thing at a time, shun the superperson urge, go easy with criticism, make yourself available, take time for recreation, organize your life, establish a nutritious diet, investigate stress-reduction programs, and discover your personality.

- Our personalities have much to do with our susceptibilities to stress as well as our reactions to it. A greater awareness of personality types helps us deal more effectively with stress in ourselves and others.

- Burnout is a logical but avoidable response to prolonged stress. It can be avoided or relieved by avoiding career ruts, staying physically active, focusing on nonbusiness relationships, stimulating the intellect, making spiritual discoveries, and consciously improving one's life-style.

- Management can help reduce stress in the work environment by holding team meetings, using proper management techniques, employing effective communication systems, and reducing uncertainty among employees.

▼ KEY TERMS, CONCEPTS, AND NAMES

Burnout	Midlife crisis
Change-produced stress	Personality-produced stress
Coping techniques	Recreation
Criticism	Stress
Environment-produced stress	Stress carrier
Eustress	Team meetings
Information overload	Technostress

▼ QUESTIONS AND EXERCISES

1. Answer the introductory questions at the beginning of the chapter.

2. Give an example of each technique for coping with stress listed in this chapter.

3. Discuss why you agree with or disagree with the way you scored on the stress and personality inventory.

4. Read the following statement by St. Augustine. How does it relate to stress? Does St. Augustine's statement relate to or disagree with the information presented in this chapter on stress?

> For the world is like an olive press, and men are constantly under pressure. If you are the dregs of the oil you are carried away through the sewer, but if you are true oil you remain in the vessel. To be under pressure is inescapable. Pressure takes place through all the world: war, siege, the worries of state. We all know men who grumble under these pressures, and complain. They are cowards. They lack splendor. But there is another sort of man who is under the same pressure, but does not complain. For it is the friction which polishes him. It is pressure which refines and makes him noble.
>
> St. Augustine
> First archbishop of Canterbury
> Seventh century A.D.

5. Compare the ten personal stressors listed in this chapter against your own experiences. What items would you add to the list? What items would you delete?

6. Review Bolch's five statements for identifying sources of stress (see page 390). Complete each statement with at least five different sources of stress.

7. Often one of the best approaches for dealing with stress is simply to escape for a while. As we have reviewed a variety of stress seminars and materials, we have found the following escape techniques (all of them have been advocated by someone or another).

   Check off the ones that appeal to you and then store them in your memory and use them the next time you find yourself in a stressful situation.

CHECKLIST OF TEMPORARY ESCAPE TECHNIQUES

___ Spend time with the books you've been promising to read.
___ Movies.
___ Listen to good music.
___ Work it off.
___ Avoid striving.
___ Give in more often.
___ Create a quiet scene.
___ Use "not now" buttons.
___ Plan your work.
___ Do something for someone else.
___ Write a letter.
___ Take an adult education course.
___ Abolish Monday—leave the house, fix your hair, come home, and read.
___ Take a walk.

___ Talk it out.
___ Cry.
___ Take a bubble bath.
___ Focus on enjoyment.
___ Avoid making too many big changes at once.
___ Be realistic.

___ Tackle one task at a time.
___ Oil door squeaks.
___ Hit a tennis ball against a wall.
___ Engage in 10-minute "pity parties."

▼ NOTES

1. Victoria B. Elder, Ella P. Gardner, and Stephen R. Ruth, "Gender and Age in Technostress: Effects on White Collar Productivity," *Government Finance Review* 3 (December 1987): 17–21.

2. Daniel K. Rosetti, T. J. Surynt, E. N. Maddox, "Understanding and Coping with Employee Midlife Crisis," *SAM Advanced Management Journal* 52 (Autumn 1987): 33–36.

3. Jennifer Bolch, "How to Manage Stress," *Reader's Digest,* July 1980, pp. 81–85.

4. Jane Clarke, "Stress Management: Three Generations," *Business Credit* 90 (November 1988):35–38.

5. Rosalind Forbes, "Job Stress and Personality," *Western's World* 10 (1970): 41–43, 64–67..

6. Kerry L. Johnson, "Coping with Burnout," *Broker World* 8 (December 1988): 88–96.

7. Copyright 1991. Northwestern National Life Insurance Company. Reproduced with permission.

▼ ANOTHER LOOK: STRESS AWARENESS

Becoming aware of stress is a two-fold process. First, try to recognize and identify the things in your life that cause you to feel stress. These stressors may be minor hassles, major lifestyle changes, or a combination of both. Then, once you realize what causes your stress, try to focus on how your body feels under stress. For example, you may know that getting caught in traffic is one of your stressors, but do you know how your body reacts? Are your muscles tense? Is your heart beating faster? Knowing your stressors, and listening to what your body can tell you, can help you become aware of your own individual stress reaction. This awareness, in turn, is the first step in finding solutions to the problem.

RECOGNIZING THE PROBLEM

Minor hassles are those daily annoyances that are a part of day-to-day life. Traffic jams, missed buses, lost car keys, and petty disagreements are rarely earth-shattering events, but their side effects can accumulate. Even these minor irritations can lead to chronic, negative stress and health-related problems, so be aware of situations that "get your blood pressure up."

Major changes are any changes—positive or negative—that effect your lifestyle. Positive changes, like the birth of a new baby or a promotion, can be just

as stressful as negative changes such as the loss of a loved one or being laid off from a job. Most major lifestyle changes require you to adapt to new or unknown situations, which in itself can be stressful.

Stress overload can occur when you find yourself faced with situations beyond your control that have combined to an unmanageable level. At home or in the workplace, there may be times when you feel pulled in so many directions at once that you're not sure what to deal with first. Try to accept the fact that it's virtually impossible to control all of life's variables.

Feeling helpless often results when the cause of your stress is not easily recognizable or manageable. If you (or someone you know) feel as if there's "no way out," or feel overwhelmed or depressed, seek out professional help. Your family physician, your employer, or your state and local health agencies can refer you to a specialist who can help you to cope with these feelings.

FINDING SOLUTIONS

Avoiding hassles can help you to eliminate some of the minor irritations that lead to chronic, negative stress. If rush-hour traffic "drives you up a wall," why not join (or start) a carpool, or try taking public transportation? If rushing to get to work on time makes you anxious, try

getting up earlier, or look into taking a course in time management.

Controlling lifestyle change isn't as difficult as it may sound. When one aspect of your life changes (positively or negatively), do what you can to limit other changes. If you've become a new parent or started a new career, for example, make an effort to continue doing the things that bring your pleasure—don't change your entire lifestyle just because one of the variables is different.

Take a break when your stressors combine to the "I can't cope level." Sometimes you need a little distance from your problems to figure out how to deal with situations effectively. Take a few minutes by yourself to calm down. Sit down, relax, and then decide what needs to be done immediately, what can wait until later, and so on. Take it one step at a time!

Finding help is the best solution when you feel overwhelmed or unable to deal with stress on your own. First, you may wish to see your doctor who can help to rule out any medical reasons for your problem. Then, if no physical problem exists, consider seeing a professional counselor who can help you understand your feelings. Even when you feel "helpless," remember: help is available.

RELAXATION: DEEP BREATHING

Once you've become aware

ANOTHER LOOK *continued*

of stress, it's time to relax! There are many techniques for relaxing (and no one method is better than another), but the most basic is deep breathing. One of the body's automatic reactions to stress is rapid, shallow breathing. Breathing slowly and deeply is one of the ways you can "turn off" your stress reaction and "turn on" your relaxation response.

The Basic Technique Deep breathing is a simple technique that is basic to most other relaxation skills. By inhaling deeply and allowing your lungs to breathe in as much oxygen as possible, you can begin to relieve the tension that can lead to negative stress. And, best of all, deep breathing can be done anywhere and at any time. Try to practice deep breathing for a few minutes three or four times a day, or whenever you begin to feel tense.

Inhale Sit or stand (using good posture) and place your hands firmly and comfortably on your stomach. Inhale slowly and deeply through your nose, letting your stomach expand as much as possible. Many people are "backward breathers"—they tend to tighten their stomachs when breathing in. By placing your hands on your stomach, you can actually feel when you are breathing properly. When you've breathed in as much as possible, hold your breath for a few seconds before exhaling.

Exhale With your hands on your stomach, exhale slowly through your mouth, pursing your lips as if you were about to whistle. By pursing your lips, you can control how fast you exhale and keep your airways open as long as possible. As you exhale, your stomach deflates, while the large muscle under your lungs (the diaphragm) expands. When your lungs feel "empty," begin the inhale— exhale cycle again. Try to repeat this cycle three or four times at each session.

RELAXATION: CLEARING YOUR MIND

Another relaxation technique that can help reduce stress is "clearing your mind." Since your stress response is a physical and emotional interaction, giving yourself a mental "break" can help relax your body as well. When you clear your mind, you try to concentrate on one pleasant thought, word, or image and let the rest of your worries slip away.

The Basic Technique Clearing your mind forms the basis for other relaxation techniques such as meditation. The principle of clearing your mind is really quite simple—by allowing yourself to mentally focus on a single, peaceful word, thought, or image, you can create a feeling of deep relaxation. Clearing your mind helps you take a mental and physical retreat from the "outside world" and helps

balance the stress of everyday life.

Reduce distractions, noise, and interruptions as much as possible as you begin this exercise. Try to set aside 5–10 minute daily to practice clearing your mind.

Sit comfortably, loosen any tight clothing, kick off your shoes, and relax yourself. Then, close your eyes and begin to breathe slowly and deeply....

Mentally focus on one peaceful word, thought, or image. If other thoughts should enter your mind, don't be discouraged—relax, breathe deeply, and try again.

Stretch and exhale as you complete the exercise. With practice, clearing your mind can help you feel refreshed, energetic, and ready to tackle the next challenge!

RELAXATION: STRETCHING

One of your automatic physical responses to stress is muscle tension. A simple, easy way to loosen up tight muscles and combat stress is to do stretching exercises. The following exercises take only a few minutes and can be done at home or at work during coffee or lunch breaks. You might wish to check with a health professional before starting these exercises.

Back Stretch While sitting, stretch forward, rest your body on your lap, and relax your head and neck. Hold for about a minute, then press on your thighs to help yourself sit back up.

ANOTHER LOOK: STRESS AWARENESS *continued*

Neck Stretch   While standing or sitting, slowly tilt your head to the right without moving your shoulders, and then slowly tilt your head to the left. Repeat 5 times toward each side.

Shoulder and Arm Stretch
Hold your hands together with fingers interlaced and stretch overhead with palms upward. Hold about 30 seconds, relax, and repeat 5 times.

Passive Back Stretch   Lie on the floor with your legs on a chair as shown. Relax, pressing your lower back onto the floor. Rest in this position for several minutes.

Leg Stretch   With one foot on a support, slowly lean forward. Bend from your hips, and keep your back straight. Repeat the stretch 5 times on each leg.

Upper Body Stretch   With your feet comfortably apart, reach overhead and stretch to the side. (Try not to move your hips.) Hold for 30 seconds, then switch sides.

SOURCE: Krames Communications, *A Guide to Managing Stress,* Daly City, Calif.: Krames Communications, 1985.

▼ ANOTHER LOOK: WORKPLACE STRESS REVISITED

Your alarm clock went off 20 minutes late. The water in the shower never got above tepid. You burned the toast, spilled juice all over the fridge and didn't notice the cream was sour until it was already in your coffee. You ran over a tricycle backing down the driveway, lost your exact change for the coffee machine under the front seat, and got soaked to the skin running from the parking lot to the office. You clocked in 15 minutes late. And your boss, just returned from a seminar called "Even Newer and More Profound Management Secrets of Attila the Hun," looks ready to practice his newfound skills on you.

Ah, and Mr. Godawful from operations is on the line. He wants to know exactly why the proposal he ordered for a comprehensive

management development program for his six supervisors last Friday afternoon wasn't on his desk at 8 a.m. this morning.

Have a nice day!

The frantic '80s may be behind us, but stress in the workplace is back on the front burner as an organizational concern. After years of "hanging in there," the current argument goes, managers and professionals who've managed to bob and weave through successive ways of down- and right-sizing, acquisitions, consolidations and the wholesale flattening of the opportunity pyramid, are finally starting to lose their grip.

"Employee Burnout: America's Newest Epidemic," a 1991 report based on a survey of 600 full-time employees conducted by Northwestern

National Life Insurance Co. [NWNL] of Minneapolis, is one of the handful of studies credited with fanning the latest flame of concern over stress in the workplace. Among other things, the NWNL study found:

■ One in three Americans seriously thought about quitting work in 1990 because of job stress, and one in three expects to "burn out" on the job in the near future. Fourteen percent quit or changed jobs in the past two years due to job stress.

■ Stress levels are extremely or very high for nearly half of the study respondents. One in three say job stress is the single greatest stress in their lives.

■ Significant burnout occurred in companies

ANOTHER LOOK *continued*

that had substantially cut employee benefits, changed ownership, required frequent overtime or reduced the work force.

■ Seven of 10 workers say job stress lowers their productivity and contributes to frequent health ailments. It also causes them to miss one or more days of work a year.

■ Victims of burnout deserve disability pay from their employers, say 82 percent of respondents.

The "Mitchum Report on Stress in the '90s," published by the New York-based firm Research and Forecasts Inc., found that 26 percent of 501 men and women interviewed in 1990 reported they were under "a lot" of stress in their lives. According to one in five, the predominant source of that stress was "related to work." The groups most prone to report high job stress: Two-career couples and anyone between the ages of 35 and 49.

A survey conducted by the American's Use of Time Project at the University of Maryland found that women who feel "constantly under pressure, trying to accomplish more than they can handle," outnumber men 35 percent to 23 percent. But men and women alike are feeling crunched, concluded the report.

Independent of these and other provocative survey results, companies worry

that more than productivity and spirit are at risk in the stressful workplace. Specifically, they are alarmed about direct dollar costs. The number of stress-related workers' compensation claims being filed across the country is skyrocketing.

In October, *Fortune* magazine reported that even in states like California—where the stress-based compensation claims have been accepted for some time—filings have taken on new dimensions. According to *Fortune,* a former cake decorator for Albertson's, a California supermarket chain, "won compensation in part because she said her supervisor had been 'very curt' with her." Specifically he told her to "get her butt in gear."

In August, *Time* magazine reported two equally unusual work-stress cases. The first occurred in Los Angeles: "At least three cops who witnessed the notorious videotaped beating of a black motorist [Rodney King] last March have filed for worker's compensation, claiming that they suffered anxiety and stress." Meanwhile, in Martinez, [California]: "Crew members of a U.S. Navy train that severed an antiwar protester's legs in 1987 sued him, alleging post-traumatic stress disorder." Neither case has been resolved.

NWNL says that only 6 percent of its disability cases were stress-related in 1982. That proportion grew to 13 percent by the end of 1990.

"We are seeing twice the incidents of stressed disabilities in our caseloads over just 10 years," says Scott Knowlton, disability manager at NWNL.

During the same period, says NWNL's study, stress-related disabilities have become less responsive to rehabilitation. In 1990 only one-third of stress-disabled employees were able to return to work as a result of therapeutic intervention. In 1982 the success rate was 88 percent. At the same time, recovery rates for disabilities stemming from other causes were 80 percent and 78 percent, respectively.

Is it possible that the survivors of the tumult of the late 80s and early '90s are all stressed up and ready to explode? Will any relatively traumatic event in the workplace send them into debilitating burnout?

IT ALL DEPENDS

On the face of it, recent surveys and expert opinions would argue for making the workplace less stressful—and pronto. But as alarming as some of these conclusions seem to be, they are less dramatic when viewed in "context." Specifically, in the context of repeat measures taken over time.

TRAINING Magazine has been tracking organizational downsizing and managerial stress as part of our annual readership survey since 1985. Six out of seven years since then we've asked

ANOTHER LOOK: WORKPLACE STRESS REVISITED *continued*

TRAINING readers about their observations in several areas: changes in organizational structure, such as increases and decreases in levels of management and number of direct reports, consolidations, downsizing efforts, mergers, acquisitions and the like; apparent or perceived changes in middle-manager behaviors, such as working more weekends and longer hours, less patience with subordinates and so forth; and stress symptoms commonly cited by experts, such as passivity, indecisiveness, tiredness, rigid dedication to the organization and so on.

This year, 999 respondents answered the workplace stress-related questions on our readership survey. Table 1 makes it clear that middle managers in some organizations are perceived to be stressed up and stumbling toward burnout. But in the eyes of our respondents, the phenomenon has peaked and is now on a downhill slide; 1986 through 1988 were significantly more stressful than any other period on which we have data. That is, high stress levels were reported in many more organizations during those three years than on any survey since. At the same time, 1991 respondents who do perceive widespread symptoms of stress and burnout tend to represent organizations that share certain characteristics.

■ *Big versus small.* As Table 2 indicates, there seems to

▼ **TABLE 1 MIDDLE-MANAGER STRESS AND BURNOUT***

	MIDDLE MANAGERS APPEAR MORE "STRESSED" UNDER PRESSURE AND CHAFING	MIDDLE MANAGERS SEEM TO BE WORKING CLOSE TO "BURNOUT"
YEAR	% AGREEING	% AGREEING
1985	45	23
1986	54	33
1987	51	31
1988	51	28
1990	42	26
1991	41	25

Readership survey did not include these questions in 1989.
SOURCE: TRAINING Magazine

▼ **TABLE 2 STRESS BY ORGANIZATION SIZE**

NUMBER OF EMPLOYEES IN ORGANIZATION	% REPORTING "MANAGERS APPEAR STRESSED"	% REPORTING "MANAGERS WORKING NEAR BURNOUT"
Fewer than 100	19	17
100 to 499	38	27
500 to 2,499	51	28
2,500 +	50	33
Overall Average	41	25

be a direct relationship between the size of an organization—measured by number of employees—and the likelihood that managers will be seen as stressed up or working toward burnout. The bigger the organization, the higher the score in both of those categories. Other factors, such as "working longer hours," spending more time in the office on weekends" and "being

less patient with subordinates," also tend to increase as organizational size increases.

■ Industry. In addition to organizational size, the industry in which a manager works has an impact on stress and burnout potential. Over seven years, we've seen significant changes that appear closely related to specific events in a given industry. As Table 3 suggests,

ANOTHER LOOK *continued*

▼ TABLE 3 STRESS BY INDUSTRY

INDUSTRY	% REPORTING "MANAGERS APPEAR STRESSED"	INDUSTRY	% REPORTING "MANAGERS WORKING NEAR BURNOUT"
Transportation/ Communications/ Utilities	50	Business Services	30
Manufacturing	48	Manufacturing	29
Wholesale/Retail Trade	46	Transportation/ Communications/ Utilities	28
Finance/Insurance/ Banking	44	Public Administration	28
Business Services	42	Health Services	27
Health Services	36	Finance/Insurance/ Banking	25
Public Adminsitration	33	Wholesale/Retail Trade	24
Educational Services	24	Educational Services	16
Overall Average	41		25

managers in manufacturing, transportation/communications/utilities, and wholesale/retail trade are most likely to be viewed as highly stressed ("under pressure and chafing at it") by our 1991 respondents.

But most industries' perceived stress levels change over the years. In 1988, for example, 69 percent of TRAINING's health-care respondents reported that managers in their organizations seemed stressed. That figure dropped to 43 percent in 1990 and 36 percent in 1991. It's almost certainly no

coincidence that health-care managers in the mid- to late 1980s were, for the first time, actually facing something akin to a free market economy. By now, many—if not most—are learning that the brave new world of competitive health-care delivery is a manageable beast after all.

In manufacturing, on the other hand, the proportion of respondents reporting that managers appear to be stressed has been in the mid-40 percent to low 50 percent range in all six surveys. This may reflect the fact that U.S. manufacturing, in general, is still under a competitive and cost-containment siege.

THE DOWNSIZING EFFECT

As you might expect, events such as organizational downsizing increase reports of apparent stress and stress-related symptoms. In Table 4, we compare 1991 respondents from organizations that have undergone recent, significant consolidation or downsizing to all other respondents. Not surprisingly, we found a number of consistent and statistically significant relationships between downsizing and perceived stress symptoms. Among them:

■ Managers in recently downsized organizations

ANOTHER LOOK: WORKPLACE STRESS REVISITED *continued*

▼   TABLE 4 MIDDLE MANAGERS, STRESS AND DOWNSIZING

MIDDLE MANAGERS IN MY ORGANIZATION	RESPONDENTS FROM ORGANIZATIONS THAT HAVE SIGNIFICANTLY DOWNSIZED OR CONSOLIDATED	RESPONDENTS FROM ORGANIZATIONS THAT HAVE *NOT* SIGNIFICANTLY DOWNSIZED OR CONSOLIDATED
Are preoccupied with their careers.	11%	5%
Are less patient with their subordinates	16	9
Are treated less like members of the management "team" than they once were.	25	14
Are less decisive.	18	11
Act as if they are in less control of what goes on around them.	39	23
Appear more "stressed"; that is, under pressure and chafing at it.	58	35
Seem tired all the time.	18	12
Seem to be working close to "burnout."	35	22
Are more competitive and less cooperative with fellow managers.	15	10
Seem to be working longer hours.	56	39
Come into the office on weekends more frequently.	29	23

are almost twice as likely to be seen as "obsessed with their careers," "less patient with subordinates," "less decisive," and "acting as if they are in less control of what goes on around them."

■ These same manager are also likely to be seen as "being treated less like a part of the management team" than in the past.

■ Managers in recently downsized organizations are not—as you might expect—prone to exhibit "argumentative behavior," unusual "passivity" or

rigid "dedication to the organization."

The symptoms that distinguish respondents from downsized versus non-downsized organizations are similar to those discussed in NWNL's report and other recent studies.

Just as enlightening were respondents' handwritten comments about stress in their organizations. Forty-nine percent of the 134 people who commented on the specifics of stress in their organizations wrote, "Stress has become much higher here lately," and 9 percent

simply concluded, "Stress is out of control here."

SO?

Is organizational stress out of control? Are North American businesses in the midst of a burnout epidemic? It depends on where you look.

In industries that are trapped in spiraling woes, accelerating cost-containment demands and ever-escalating bad news from the marketplace, the answer is probably yes. Right now, for example, you might have a tough time locating a retail manager or savings and loan

ANOTHER LOOK *continued*

officer who *isn't* stressed.

In industries that have passed through the worst of the consolidation craze, crash cost-cutting and recessionary pressures, the answer is unclear. In the telecommunications business, the upheaval started with the mid-'80s deregulation. Now that the dust has settled, a certain veneer of calm has returned. Yet some experts warn that constant moderate pressure on

employees is as damaging and stressful as sudden traumatic events.

From our vantage point—peering through the lens of our data—it's clear that overall reports of stress and burnout are on the decline. But that's little solace to people in organizations still downsizing, belt-tightening and consolidating. In those organizations the pressure is real and apparently taking its toll.

The bottom line is a warning: Be prepared. Employees in many workplaces have been shouldering quite a load. Don't be surprised if the cost of the struggle begins to make itself known. The bill for the '80s is yet to be paid—in more ways than one.

SOURCE: Ron Zemke, "Workplace Stress Revisited," *Training,* November 1991, pp. 35–38.

▼ A CASE IN POINT: BONNE BELL: DRESS IS OPTIONAL

This beauty-aids company bends office rules and adds financial incentives to promote good health among its employees. President Jess Bell brought the spirit of fitness to Bonne Bell. After sponsoring ski and tennis events throughout the 1960s, he started encouraging his employees to ride bikes to work and arranged for them to purchase bikes at cost. Today, the company sponsors races such as the Cleveland Heart-A-Thon and the Cystic Fibrosis Benefit Run.

In 1976, Bonne Bell began its first official fitness program, building tennis and volleyball courts, a track and shower and locker facilities. The company also constructed exercise rooms at both of its office locations in Ohio. To get and keep employees interested, Bonne Bell has set up generous incentives: Workers can use the facilities for free, they get an extra 30 minutes at lunch if they want to exercise, and workout clothes are acceptable attire after lunch. Employees can also pur-

chase running suits and shoes at discount prices. Its newest incentive promises a check for $250 to employees who exercise four days a week from January to June.

Bonne Bell also pays $250 to employees who stop smoking for six months and $5 for each pound (up to 40) a worker loses over six months. Going back to bad health habits cost double: The company requires people who start smoking again to give $500 to the corporate charitable foundation. For every pound gained back within six months of its loss, that donation is $10.

The company has noted many positive changes since the program began. Records of sick days, for example, show much less absenteeism. "Everyone enjoys it," says Connie Schafer, a spokesperson for Bonne Bell. "We've seen people start to take care of themselves." And, she adds, many employees—especially Jess Bell—wouldn't miss Wednesday morning early-bird runs.

A CASE IN POINT: BONNE BELL: DRESS IS OPTIONAL *continued*

QUESTIONS

1. Why do Bonne Bell's programs make "dollars and sense"?
2. If you worked for the ideal organization, what would you like to see it do for

employee stress management?

SOURCE: "Bonne Bell: Dress Is Optional," *Psychology Today,* May 1989, p. 56. Reprinted with permission from *Psychology Today* magazine. Copyright © 1989 (PT Partners, L.P.).

▼ A CASE IN POINT: A PERFECT RECIPE FOR A LAWSUIT

By 1982, John J. O'Brien had worked nearly 10 years for Papa Gino's of America, a New England restaurant chain. As an area supervisor, he was in charge of 28 restaurants and about 500 employees. "I was in line for vice-president and felt a strong loyalty to the company," O'Brien recalls.

Suddenly his life "was cut right in half." Despite repeated requests, he refused to promote a company director's son who was also the godson of the president, contending the man was incompetent. A few weeks later, O'Brien's boss told him that someone—Papa Gino's never identified the person—had seen him take drugs at a party. The company gave O'Brien two choices: take a polygraph test or be fired.

"I was angry that they were putting a machine against my word and my history with the company," O'Brien says. But he took the test. Papa Gino's said it proved he lied and fired him. He sued. For the next three years, O'Brien, a 32-year-old father, couldn't find work. "It was like hell," he says. "I went from $50,000 a year and a lot of good self-image to no employment at all."

In 1985 a federal jury found the polygraph investigation "highly offensive" and awarded damages that eventually totaled $595,000. A federal appeals court upheld the award, as well as findings of defamation and invasion of privacy. Now a renovator of houses in New Hampshire, O'Brien feels the false charge of drug abuse will always be with him. "People in the company avoided me like the plague when they spread that around, and I think I'll always carry the stigma."

QUESTIONS

1. What stress related issues are involved in the case of O'Brien?
2. As a human relations-smart manager, how would you handle a similar situation?
3. How can organizations reduce the potential for lawsuits in such situations?

SOURCE: "A Perfect Recipe for a Lawsuit," *Business Week,* 28 March 1988, p. 63. Reprinted from 28 March 1988 issue of *Business Week* by special permission. Copyright © 1988. By McGraw-Hill, Inc.

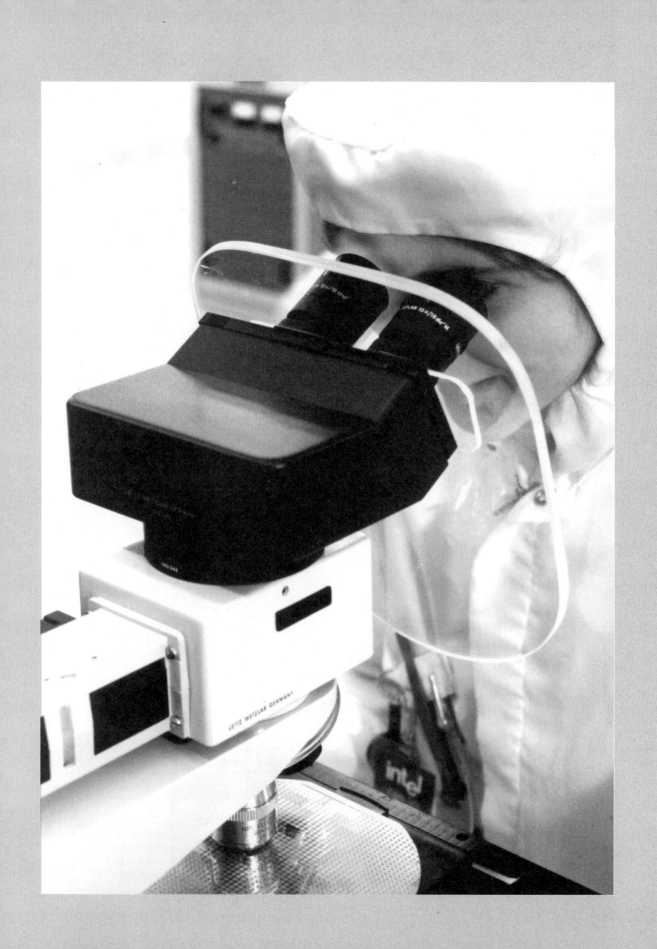

SPECIAL PRESSURES FROM TECHNOLOGICAL CHANGES

This chapter answers several all-important questions:

- How is the computer revolution affecting the lives of people at work?

- Why is such technology necessary?

- What kinds of things are happening to change office and manufacturing jobs?

- Why do many people resist these changes?

- What forms can resistance to technology take?

- What is technostress and what can be done about it?

- What can managers do to reduce employees' resistance to new systems?

- How does emerging technology affect the job market?

The answers to these and other questions are coming up next in chapter 17....

CHAPTER 17

Many of us have a love-hate relationship with so-called high tech. We appreciate the convenience of computerized information processing, the precision of computer-aided design and manufacturing, and the thrill of the chase in a good game of Super Mario. But most of us are more than a little apprehensive of the seeming avalanche of high tech rumbling down onto our daily lives.

A recent letter in a student newspaper expressed some of the anxieties:

> So high technology has plopped down in our laps to stay awhile. We might as well get comfortable with it, or so the experts say. Students were told that those who don't keep pace with computer technology will be intellectually dead in seven years.
>
> Okay, okay. I can accept that. I've even made moderate strides to comply with these doom-saying dictums. Yes, I have cozied up to the computer terminal. I have learned how to read a computer-generated financial report. I can enter data and print it out. I have learned how to perform most word-processing functions, change a daisy wheel, flip a floppy disk and even replace a circuit board on a system.
>
> Yet this only scratches the surface. The burden of technological expectations lies heavily upon the spirit, casting a pall on what is otherwise a bright future.
>
> Some of our hearts have not yet turned into silicon. We cannot fully embrace the high-tech changes in our lives without a few adjustment pains.
>
> With the proliferation of home computers, my genuine empathy lies with laymen who are forced to develop at least a working familiarity with things computorial. I feel particularly tenderhearted toward those of us over 30 who remember what the world was like B.C.—Before Computers.
>
> Even ownership of two common manifestations of integrated circuitry—the video game and cable television—can prove frustrating. A mire of wire puddles around the TV set. Sorting out this mangle sets the mind musing over the bygone era when a television had but one protruding cord.
>
> Remember the Underwood? This is a little like saying, "Remember the Alamo." It is somehow disheartening to realize that incoming freshmen may have never seen this writer's workhorse. T. H. Watkins recently called it "a thing of steel and sinew, a miracle of sturdy contrivance, a paragon of the purely mechanical arts ... the sort of machine that can be hurled bodily across the room, then be picked up and put back to work again."
>
> Yet, longing after days gone by is a romantic activity not altogether consonant with the new information age. It's just that it takes some getting used to.

■ High tech causes concern for many workers.

Indeed, high tech does take some getting used to, and it generates some serious concern for many people at work. Human nature tends to resist change—especially change that could affect job security.

In the nineteenth century, workers in European textile mills destroyed new labor-saving machinery to protect themselves from reduced wages and unemployment. The Luddite movement, named after Ned Ludd, a mythical character who supposedly smashed two newfangled frames belonging to his Leicestershire employer, flourished in the early 1800s.

**"I don't think the data loss was due to a virus.
I think it was just plain stupidity."**

TRAINING Magazine April, 1992, p. 60.

The sweeping advances of modern technology have revived something of a Luddite mentality among those who a few years ago would "fold, spindle, or mutilate" computer cards and who today take delight in a computer breakdown.

Nevertheless, technology, especially in the form of computers, will have increasing impact on our lives. Data processing experts H. L. Capron and Brian K. Williams introduce their text by saying, "The Computer Revolution will be far more sweeping than the Industrial Revolution—and far more sudden. The effects of the computer are seen now in spectacular ways: in the graphics it produces; in its use as an industrial robot; and in its effect on transportation, money, paperwork, commerce, the professions, and our personal lives. Despite computer anxiety, we cannot turn the clock back, nor would we want to. Liberation lies in computer literacy."[1]

■ The computer revolution may be more far reaching than the Industrial Revolution.

Two areas of rapid technological change provide a look at special pressures people feel as they are swept up by organizational changes at an ever-increasing pace. These areas are office automation and robotics. First let's look at the electronic office revolution.[2]

▼ PLUGGING INTO THE ELECTRONIC OFFICE REVOLUTION

"I'll take care of that right away," Kelly said as he rose to leave the conference room.

Within minutes, Kelly was sitting in front of his desktop terminal, the florescent screen a faint glow. He began to type in the following sequence of characters: RUN CALUPDATE.

Seconds later, the integrated annual calendar for managers popped onto the screen. Kelly inserted the new information about his emergency trip to Boston scheduled for the following week. He then scanned the calendar, noting the recent changes in his colleagues' schedules. "That's great," he thought. "Pat will be in Boston on a sales trip at the same time."

Kelly pushed a few more buttons and the electronic bulletin board flashed on the screen. He typed in a message to Pat in the Houston office, asking if she wanted to get together for lunch next week while in Boston. "Just leave me a note on the board if you can make it," he signed off.

Leaning back in his chair, Kelly began to organize his thoughts for the sales memo he was about to draft. He called up the word processor program on his terminal and began to type. When he finished, he routed the memo to the terminals of his seven sales representatives.

Such actions are routine in more and more businesses every day. The "paperless office" is already here for many workers. In fact, the office we just described, a subsidiary of a major aerospace firm, is led by a vice-president who is so committed to a paperless society that he put terminals on everyone's desks. All the scheduling, agenda setting, information gathering, reporting and word processing are done on the same computer. Memos and messages are sent electronically to the office staff. No one dictates anymore. Even the president of the subsidiary types his own letters and memos by drafting and editing them on his own screen.

The office of the future *is* here today. What's behind this big push for automating the office? What are the trends? Why do people resist office automation? What are the effects of technostress? Let's tackle these questions one at a time.

Why the Push to Automate?

Office automation is not new. It started with typewriters. In fact, the word *typewriter* used to refer to the nineteenth-century clerk who wrote down the boss's messages. Eventually, the same term came to refer to the typewriting machine.

Today we continue to shift effort from people to equipment. Within the past decade, however, the pace has picked up considerably. Why? At least four forces drive us toward automation:

1. Increased complexity of business
2. Stagnant employee productivity levels

3. Increased information needs

4. Technological advances

INCREASE COMPLEXITY OF BUSINESS

Nothing's simple anymore. Some experts say that business today has become so multifaceted that the complexity alone poses a major barrier to many who would like to start a venture. Former U.S. Secretary of Commerce Elliot Richardson claims that business has increasingly fallen into the hands of "technocrats"—technical bureaucrats—and is less subject to the initiative of the traditional entrepreneur.

This increased complexity has led to changes in the way businesses are organized. During the first eighty years of the twentieth century, the numbers of managers and layers of management increased significantly to meet the demands of an increasingly complex business environment. In the 1980s, however, the number of managers and layers of management decreased dramatically, largely for two reasons. The first reason was, and is, the dramatic increase in foreign competition that forced businesses worldwide to become more efficient in order to survive. The second reason is the electronic revolution, which radically changed the way we communicate within the office and around the world.

During the late seventies, as a result of the demands for more information and for greater efficiency in the workplace, the number of "information workers" (white-collar employees) surpassed the number of "noninformation workers" (blue-collar employees) in our work force for the first time in history. Today, almost a trillion dollars a year are spent on these information workers. That's almost as much as the federal budget. Seventy-five percent of this estimated cost is for people. Only 25 percent relates to supplies, equipment, and overhead.

■ Complex organizations call for more support staff and more information workers.

Ironically, management has traditionally focused on paring company expenses by reducing manufacturing costs and increasing blue-collar productivity. But with the swift rise in white-collar cost due to increased complexity of tasks, management has now turned its attention to reducing office overhead.

STAGNANT EMPLOYEE PRODUCTIVITY

While blue-collar productivity increased slightly over the years, white-collar productivity remained stagnant. Probably the biggest reason for this stagnation was management's traditional approach to white-collar productivity. In the past, to increase white-collar output management's typical response was to hire *more* workers rather than to make existing workers more productive.

According to experts, by the early 1980s, U.S. businesses spent roughly twenty-four thousand dollars on equipment for each factory worker and thirty-five thousand dollars on equipment for each farmer. During the same period, only two thousand dollars was spent on equipment for the average clerical worker. This was at least one reason, possibly the primary reason, for the low productivity of white-collar workers.

Things changed dramatically in the late eighties as a result of the computer revolution and the drive for greater economies in business. Investments in equipment for white-collar employees increased even as managers looked for ways to reduce overhead (including that associated with white-collar workers) to keep their companies economically viable.

INCREASED INFORMATION NEEDS

■ Increasing government regulation causes some of the increased paperwork.

Today's complex business demands more complex information. Part of this increased demand for information can be attributed to government. According to the White House Office of Management and Budget, the federal government has about five thousand reporting requirements for business, recipients of federal aid, and the general public, who spend a total of 785 million hours a year responding to them.

In addition to government's needs, today's sophisticated management structures require more information. Competing against other big businesses in a global market requires a great deal of relevant data. Not only is more information needed to run today's businesses, but more information is also available to process than in the past. Some experts suggest that what we need now isn't more management information but rather more *information management.* We must learn to effectively use data we already have.

TECHNOLOGICAL ADVANCES

Even as I type this paragraph on my personal computer, engineers and technicians in dozens of laboratories around the world are frantically working on the next generation of computer hardware and software. In less than forty years, the computer has indeed revolutionized the way we do business in both the public and the private sectors. It is highly probable that many more technological advances are on the horizon.

Technology of the so-called work place "office of the future" is already a reality.

What's Happening in Today's Office?

Two major trends are making a big impact on the modern office:

- Increased use of high-technology equipment
- The movement toward telecommuting

HIGH-TECHNOLOGY EQUIPMENT

Let's think for a moment about how information workers do their jobs. Typically, office information is subject to five major functions:

1. Input
2. Process
3. Output
4. Distribution
5. Storage

In the past, information workers used separate pieces of equipment for each of these tasks. For example, a simple memo would be *input* into the office system through dictation equipment. A secretary would use a transcribing machine and a typewriter to *process, output,* and *distribute* the message through the intercompany mail system. And, finally, the memo would be *stored* in a four-drawer metal filing cabinet.

- High tech allows several functions to be integrated into one system.

With the advent of high-technology office equipment, many of these functions are integrated into one machine. Remember Kelly in the example earlier in this chapter? The sales manager inputted, processed, outputted, stored, and distributed his memo to the sales representatives, all on the office computer system. Increasingly, offices of the future will tend toward such equipment integration.

Most of the technology for the office of the future is already here. Word processors are used to speed text processing. Facsimile transmission is used to send important mail electronically. Diskettes are used to store data and text. There is presently only one technological advance missing from the office of the future: voice recognition. Although it is not yet commercially feasible, within the near future you may be able to dictate directly into a word processor that recognizes your voice.

THE ELECTRONIC COTTAGE

Not only is technology changing the way office work is done, it is also changing *where* that work is done. *Telecommuting, the electronic cottage, flexiplace, homework.* All these are buzzwords that describe a growing trend for employees to work at home and link up to offices electronically. Some experts predict that within the next decade, 5 million people could join the telecommuting revolution.

- An increasing number of people are working at home while linking with their office through computers.

Working at home is not new. Before the Industrial Revolution, the home was where people generally worked. In today's industrialized society, however, only about 3 percent of the U.S. labor force works at home. That may be changing. With the advent of computers, the pendulum may just swing back toward working at home once again.

Telecommuting is becoming more common.

Today's telecommuters include stockholders, sales representatives, and even some managers. These people use home computer terminals to communicate over telephone lines with clients, co-workers, and data banks. Through the use of modern technology, the home has become an office-away-from-the-office for the homeworker.

Many telecommuters work for computer companies. Control Data Corporation has more than one hundred employees using terminals to work from their homes in its Alternate Work Site program. These employees are usually computer programmers or systems analysts.

But the concept of the electronic cottage is not confined to computer professionals. The Continental Bank of Chicago recently hired people to transcribe dictation at home on word processing terminals. In New York, some brokers have quit Wall Street to manage stock portfolios at home with terminals connected to the New York Stock Exchange. And more and more, sales representatives are communicating with their home offices through laptop computers.

The electronic cottage offers distinct advantages. At-home workers can avoid time-consuming and costly commuting to the office. Working parents with preschool-age children can tend the children at home, scheduling in the work when appropriate. Finally, sick or disabled workers can continue to produce at home while recuperating.

Telecommuting is not for everyone. It requires self-discipline to get things done in a home environment (and stay away from the refrigerator!). In addition, at-home workers miss out on the social interaction that occurs at the office. Some telecommuters have found the best arrangement is two days at home for every three at the office. Whatever the arrangement, we can be sure that the trend toward telecommuting will continue.

Why Do People Resist Office Automation?

With all the apparent advantages of the electronic office, one might ask why it may exert special pressures on people at work, as our chapter title implies.

When organizations introduce electronic office technology, often referred to as management information systems (MIS), they must consider how such changes will affect human behaviors. Implementing management information systems frequently results in changes to the formal structure of an organization (such as adjustments in department boundaries, individual responsibilities, and communication channels) or to the informal structure (work relations, work group norms, or status). Such changes potentially affect many persons.

Changes in the organization, which may have unforeseeable consequences for people, can lead to resistance to those changes; in a phrase, we fear the unknown. In addition, people may fear that change will affect their status with colleagues. For example, some executives feel that MIS will mean they will be required to type their correspondence, rather than have a secretary do so. If they do not know how to type, they may feel ignorant and embarrassed in front of their colleagues.

People who work with computers for long periods of time can experience eyestrain or muscular discomfort. Those who constantly use computers are experiencing a rising number of cases of carpal tunnel syndrome. This is a wrist problem directly associated with constant keyboard use. Some resistance could arise from a feeling that the worker is little more than an extension of the computer.

All of these situations can create distress and resistance within a work force. Recall that the term *"technostress"* addresses the physical and emotional burnout that result from a person's inability to adapt to new technology. H. L. Capron uses the term *cyberphobia* to describe extreme cases of stress where people "showed actual symptoms of classic phobia; Nausea, dizziness, cold sweat, and high blood pressure" as a result of their "fear, distrust, or hatred of computers."[3] Another factor can be unfamiliarity with new equipment and software. As an employee learns to use new equipment, fears and doubts diminish.

- Effects of human behavior must be considered when installing a management information system.

- Some resistance stems from the fear of losing status.

What Are the Effects of Technostress?

A study of the use of computers in government finance organizations revealed that gender, age, and job title were related significantly to computer anxiety, or technostress. Twenty-three percent of female respondents experienced technostress, compared with 14 percent of male respondents. The percentage of technostressed respondents over age fifty was more than twice that of respondents under age thirty. The percentage of clerical workers classified a technostressed was twice that of professionals.[4]

Technostress has been linked to four major fears. First, some employees fear that as they rely more on computers and less on their job knowledge, their jobs will be "de-skilled" and they will be more

ACTIVITY: OFFICE OF THE FUTURE—HIGH-TECH MATCH

Test your awareness of some common high-tech terms. Match each name in the left hand column with the correct description in the right-hand column. Put the correct letter in each blank. The correct answers follow the quiz.

1. Fax

    a. Feature available on some word processors; automatically checks the spelling in your text against a 50,000- to 100,000-word vocabulary, highlighting potential errors. (Some word processors can even check your grammar.)

2. Microprocessor

    b. Videocassette recorder; used in offices for training, sending of visual messages from headquarters, and employment screening.

3. Spelling checker

    c. Magnetic storage medium used to store text for word processing or data for data processing; generally comes in 5-$^{1}/_{2}$-inch and 3-$^{1}/_{2}$-inch disks.

4. Word processor

    d. Modulator-demodulator; used to enact your terminal to a computer in another location over telephone lines.

5. Robotics

    e. Use of computerized machines to perform human functions; an example is the automated mail cart that circulates through various departments to pick up and drop off mail.

6. Diskette

    f. Integration of a whole series of terminals and computers into one system.

7. Electronic mail.

    g. Often referred to as a computer on a chip.

8. VCR

    h. Common item in modernized offices, sometimes referred to as a screen, monitor or cathode ray tube.

9. Terminal

    i. Shortened form of "facsimile transmission"; a facsimile machine is used to transmit over telephone lines a graphic copy of your message, whether it is words, charts, or maps, to a destination with special receiver equipment.

10. Local area network

    j. Messages that are sent and received through computerized equipment; instead of reading a hard copy of the message, you read the message from a computer screen.

11. CRT

    k. Computer programmed to edit and format text; errors and corrections can be made right on the computer screen, and the hard copy can be printed out at speeds up to five hundred words per minute.

12. Modem

    l. Keyboard and monitor connected to a host computer; can transmit and receive data from the host or central computer.

13. Laser printer

    m. Type of mobile phone; allows personal portable phone service, such as in cars.

ACTIVITY *continued*

14. Call forwarding

n. A way to connect a number of people for a meeting or conference. This can include a small or very large number of people and can be accomplished with either a phone or a video conference.

15. Cellular phone

o. An option for telephone service that allows incoming calls to ring at another extension or phone.

16. Teleconferencing

p. A piece of computer hardware used for output of data. Prints data on various sizes of paper and other options (such as envelopes and labels) with a high quality of print.

ANSWERS

Here are the answers:

1. i	5. e	9. l	13. p
2. g	6. c	10. f	14. o
3. a	7. j	11. h	15. m
4. k	8. b	12. d	16. n

How did you do? If you got ten or more right, you're fairly well plugged in to what's going on in today's rapidly changing office. For those of you who got nine or less, don't worry. That just means you have a lot of exciting challenges ahead as you begin to integrate into the office of the future.

easily replaceable and less secure. Second, other employees have a related fear that computers will replace people and lead to layoffs. Third, workers with low self-esteem fear that they will be unable to use computers. And fourth, some workers fear that the corporate power structure will be threatened as computers allow managers access to information that was previously jealously guarded by subordinates.[5]

Too often, managers and information specialists address the problems of technostress or emotional resistance to computerization by showing employees that such technological advances will reduce costs, increase profits, decrease decision time, permit job streamlining, and improve the flow and accuracy of information. While these arguments in favor of computerization are logical and reasonable, they usually fail to address (and often increase) the emotional concerns of workers. When workers' concerns are not properly addressed, three kinds of resistance often occur.

- Employee resistance cannot be reduced by logic alone.

1. *Aggression*—Attacking the information system in an attempt to make it either inoperative or ineffective.
2. *Projection*—Blaming the system for anything that goes wrong in the organization.
3. *Avoidance*—Withdrawing from or avoiding interaction with the information system, often as a result of frustration.[6]

It appears that the fears leading to technostress are in many cases well-founded and that logical arguments that the computers will

SOURCE: *Shoe.* Reprinted by permission: Tribune Media Services.

help the organization are generally futile. There is presently no easy or foolproof way to solve the problem of technostress, but steps can be taken to overcome the fears or at least alleviate them.

In a report on ways to overcome resistance to computers, Robert E. Callahan and Patrick C. Fleenor recommend the following four steps for overcoming employee fear of computers:

1. Have managers take the lead by buying and using computers to show how they can help performance.
2. Encourage and reward employees who show an interest in computers.
3. Establish a personal computer training center where employees can learn about and practice with computers.
4. Provide thorough employee computer training.[7]

Technostress may be seen as a healthy warning sign that we might be pushing technology without adequate concern for the human element at work. The technology revolution is continuing, as shown by the increasing use of robotics. Great opportunities lie ahead for those who will address ways and means of mobilizing the human resources that are too often neglected.

▼ ROBOTICS: SCIENCE FICTION COMING TO LIFE

Robotics refers to the study, design, and manufacture of robots. Robots are sophisticated machines that perform work in a seemingly human way.

More and more repetitive tasks are being handled by robotic devices. Whole assembly lines manufacture products untouched by human hands. At the same time, major advances are being made in the number and complexity of tasks that can be performed by robots.

The science of robotics poses many real and interesting challenges. One expert comments, "Today our robots are like toys. They

do only the simple things they're programmed to. But clearly they're about to cross the edgeless line past which they'll do the things *we* are programmed to. Already there's so much power in those arcade chips that one might think the toys are playing with our kids. Most robots rolling around these days are mere fakes, remote-controlled by people hiding out of view. A few, though, do some things that real robots ought to do, like sensing the sounds of certain words and acting on those words and phrases. And as they reap the fruits of research, these machines will show more visible signs of having minds."[8]

More Sophisticated Robots

Robots differ from sophisticated mass-production equipment in several ways. First, unlike single-purpose machines that can churn out an enormous volume of one kind of product, the more sophisticated robots can turn out a few specialized items, then can be programmed cheaply and accurately to make a slightly different model or another product altogether. This capability is important to meet current changing market needs. A recent government study found that the vast majority of items purchased by such users as the military, for example, are made in lots of fewer than one hundred.

- Robots go beyond today's mass-production machinery.

Robots have long had the brawn for machine loading, spot welding, spray painting, die casting, material handling, and other strenuous tasks. As technology improves. robots are acquiring control and senses to match.

Robot vision is now used to grade the quality of bacon by comparing the amount of dark meat and white fat. In the future, 3-D vision will enable robots to recognize one part lying on others in a bin of many components. Thus, they will learn to assemble intricate machinery without having to be presented parts with special care. Already certain robots can assemble electrical relays accurately and quickly.

As technology improves, it will be less costly to produce the sense of touch in robots. Tactile ability will enable robots to check the parts they handle, making sure that each is free of defects. Automobile engine valves will no longer be *about* the right size; they will be exact. Quality will improve as a result. Tomorrow's robots will handle items too delicate for today's models; they may shear sheep, pick fruit, and package easily bruised foods. Most robots now use grippers designed for a single job. In the future, they will have the most versatile holding device of all: a hand.

Making robots standard equipment in the work place will bring their cost down as the numbers in use increase. Small businesses will be able to afford to automate their production lines with robots and in turn compete with large manufacturers.[9]

Robots and Our Jobs

For those who overreact to the perils of new technology, robots seem to be an easy target.

■ Each assembly line robot replaces, on average, two people.

Each robot on an assembly line replaces, on average, two people, leaving a single human overseeing every four or five machines. Although the need for productivity improvements in manufacturing is generally accepted, many members of the media, academia, labor groups, and corporate management itself link productivity gains—particularly those attributed to robots—with declining employment levels.

Yet when we look at the real cause of unemployment, it becomes clear that in the long run robots will create jobs, not destroy them. In fact, every new advanced technology developed has created employment. For example, the computer and semiconductor industries, virtually nonexistent a few decades ago, today employ tens of millions of people.

■ High tech creates new jobs.

New jobs created by high tech will not be the same ones we have today. Assembly line jobs will be replaced by jobs in quality control, robot repair, programming, and service industries yet to be invented.

▼ TECHNOLOGY IS HERE TO STAY

Although we have focused on peoples' resistance to the changes created by advances in high technology, it is important to emphasize that these changes, however uncomfortable, are almost always worth the costs. Indeed, technology is growing rapidly because it provides new services in far more efficient ways than ever before possible.

Capron and Williams argue that the computer is no longer a luxury and that "unplugging it would have enormous consequences that most of us are not prepared to live with."[10] They explain that there are at least five reasons why we cannot—indeed, should not—turn back the clock. First, it is human nature to be resentful of service that is not fast. But it is computer nature that provides fast service. Thus, unless we are prepared to do a lot more waiting—for paychecks, grades, telephone calls, travel reservations, and many other things—we need the split-second processing of the computer.

■ Only computers can provide the fast services we demand.

Second, computers are extremely reliable. Though stories about compute mistakes make good newspaper headlines, it is rarely reported that most of the mistakes are not the fault of the computers themselves. True, equipment failures sometimes occur, but most errors supposedly made by computers are really errors made by humans.

■ Computers can do the boring dangerous jobs.

Third, computers are able to perform boring, dangerous, or highly sensitive jobs that people cannot or should not perform such as working with nuclear fuel rods. Granted, computers will eliminate some jobs; automation is a tough issue for society to deal with and always has been. But computers free human beings for other kinds of productivity.

Fourth, because of expanding technology and sophisticated communications, we suffer from an information deluge. Although this can be attributed in part to our computer society, it is the computer that will help control it. To make essential decisions in business and

government, managers need to take into account a variety of information—financial, geographical, logistical, and so on. The computer helps them sort wheat from chaff and make better decisions.

Finally, the computer is an inflation fighter. By holding down labor costs and reducing paperwork, fuel use, and waste, computers lower the cost per individual product or service while increasing productivity, thereby tending to hold down inflation.

■ High tech can keep costs down.

▼ TECHNOLOGY AND THE CHALLENGE TO MANAGEMENT

"It is no secret that advanced computer technologies often fail to achieve the dreams and visions of their designers and backers," says Harvard University researcher Dr. Shoshana Zuboff.[11] Those dreams and visions have not been achieved because managers "have failed to recognize that their organizations need to be fundamentally changed to fully exploit the potential of information technologies."

Computer technologies "have the capacity to translate events, processes, objects and behaviors into data and then display that data" in a process Zuboff calls *informating*. This process approaches real thinking in that it provides not only specific details regarding the inputs and outputs of a process but also information on the process itself. In this way, it sheds "new light on the internal dynamics of the business and client behavior." It thereby helps management better understand how the business operates and where it can be improved.

The catch is that while "informating" provides opportunities for learning and improving the organization, it simultaneously calls for a new type of organization and new styles of management. The technologies give workers and managers greater access to a great amount of information. This represents a major change from the traditional situation in which people fought to retain control of key information. According to Zuboff, success in exploiting the full capacities of new technologies will depend on the ability of top management to "create an organization that celebrates learning, risk taking and creative thinking."

■ Technology often calls for organizational changes.

▼ TECHNOLOGY AND THE FUTURE

"Things are not as nice as in the good old days" is a common expression. "But ...," adds one person who experienced the good old days, "they never really were." Before technostress, there were many other types of stress, some of which have been eliminated or alleviated by technology.

Technology is a mixed bag: even as it brings great advances, it also brings new challenges that must be addressed. Computers have led to the creation not only of new jobs but of entirely new career fields—even as they have led to the elimination of others. Technology has enabled doctors to prolong life extensively and has brought along myriad questions regarding the codes and ethics of life extension. Technology has enabled us to quickly copy and transmit papers, documents, books, and motion pictures, but it has also opened a Pandora's box of ethical issues involving privacy, piracy, and copyrights.

Technology will continue to bring profound changes in the way we live and work. Our challenge is to develop positive ways of dealing with and taking advantage of the exciting new tools that are at our fingertips.

▼ SUMMARY OF KEY IDEAS

- Rapid and profound changes arising from new technology naturally lead to some resistance among people; however, the computer revolution cannot be turned back, for its advantages far outweigh the problems it may create.

- Office automation and robotics are two areas of technology that create special pressures on people at work.

- Automated offices can better meet the needs created by increased complexity of business and government, stagnant productivity levels, increased needs for information, and technological advances.

- Modern organizations seldom need more management information; rather, they need more effective information management.

- Two major high-tech trends in the electronic office are the increased use of sophisticated equipment and the move to more telecommuting.

- The electronic cottage links work-at-home employees to offices through telecommuting, allowing them to avoid time-consuming commuting, to tend children, and to work flexible schedules.

- Technostress is a computer-generated form of burnout resulting from a person's inability to adapt to new technology; it can result in attacks on new technical systems, blaming such systems for all mistakes and failures, and the refusal of employees to use the new technology.

- Because resistance to technological change is generally more emotional than logical, arguing that workers should accept a system because it makes good business sense will seldom reduce resistance.

- Technostress can be treated by (1) having managers take the lead in using new technology; (2) encouraging and rewarding employees who take the lead in using new systems; (3) providing computer centers where employees can experiment with, learn about, and practice with new systems; and (4) providing thorough employee training on new technical systems.

- The development of increasingly sensitive and sophisticated robots is aiding productivity, eliminating monotonous work for people, and creating new high-tech job opportunities.
- New technological developments are providing new jobs, new career fields, new opportunities, and new challenges for people at work.

▼ KEY TERMS, CONCEPTS, AND NAMES

Computer revolution
Electronic cottage
Electronic office
High tech
Informating
Integrated office equipment

Luddites
Management information systems (MIS)
Technostress
Telecommuting

▼ NOTES

1. H. L. Capron and Brian K. Williams, *Computers and Data Processing* (Menlo Park, Calif.: Benjamin Cummings Publishing, 1982), p. 5.

2. The section entitled "Plugging into the Electronic Office Revolution" was adapted from Christopher Jones and Paul R. Timm, "Plugging into the Electronic Office Revolution," *Manage*, July 1982. Used by permission of the authors.

3. H. L. Capron, instructor's guide to accompany *Computers and Data Processing*, 2d ed. (Menlo Park, Calif.: Benjamin Cummings Publishing, 1983), p. 4.

4. Victoria B. Elder, Ella P. Gardner, and Stephen P. Ruth, "Gender and Age in Technostress: Effects on White Collar Productivity," *Government Finance Review* 3 (December 1987): 17–21.

5. Robert E. Callahan and Patrick C. Fleenor, "There Are Ways to Overcome Resistance to Computers," *Office* 106 (October 1987): 78–80.

6. James A. Senn, "Essential Principles of Information Systems Development," *MIS Quarterly* 2 (June 1978): 24.

7. Callahan and Fleenor, "There Are Ways," p. 80.

8. Marvin Minsky, "First Word," *Omni*, April 1983, p. 6.

9. Stanley Polcyn, "Robots and Our Jobs," *Omni*, April 1983, p. 35.

10. Capron and Williams, *Computers and Data Processing*, p. 13.

11. Shoshana Zuboff, "Short-Circuiting New Technology: Old-fashioned Management Styles Hinder Effective Use of Computers," *Los Angeles Times*, 5 June 1988, pp. 3, 6.

▼ ## ANOTHER LOOK: CLIMBING THE TOWER OF TECHNOBABBLE

A few years ago, I accepted a position that thrust me into the world of interactive video (or multimedia, for those on the trendy side of the jargon). Anxious to learn as much as possible about the technology, I attended a conference at which vendors were presenting their latest developments.

I walked into a huge exhibit hall and looked around at all the booths. I didn't know where to begin. After a few minutes, I saw a large crowd around one booth. Everyone was gathered around a young woman who pointed to various computer peripherals and occasionally touched a computer screen as she spoke. I walked to the back of the crowd and began to listen.

"This 386 system has a 40 megabyte voice coil drive with 28-millisecond access time," she said. "We do recommend using a multisync monitor for easy switching from NTSC video to RGB. This model can display CGA to Super VGA with the right cards, and it has been modified with a touch screen. This one's set up with Windows and 2 meg of RAM. It can handle straight DOS if you prefer. Of course, we can emulate InfoWindow. And we have a configuration for OS/2."

Everyone seemed to be nodding in agreement, so I reserved my judgment. The woman continued:

"This is the CD-ROM (High Sierra format) with caddy, and a third-party digital audio card. Of course, we can handle all major brands of LDPs. Courseware authored with all the big hitters—TenCORE. Quest, L 1—is compatible with our system. We used a frame grabber to digitize the still. It only takes up 700 K on the hard drive and we're displaying it at 640 by 480 by 256 colors...."

As I listened, I felt as if I were back in a graduate school statistics class. I felt like Alice in Wonderland. Had I entered an acronym convention by mistake? And what was the deal with windows?

THE RISKING TIDE OF TECHNOBABBLE

I learned a lot at the conference—not just about interactive video, also about how important it is to speak a language that most people can understand. It can be fun at times to slip in a little technobabble—an "interleaved" this or a "magneto-optical" that. But technobabble shouldn't be the norm—unless, of course, you're talking to a fellow technobabbler or to your boss just before your performance review.

Unfortunately, jargon frequently is the norm when professionals discuss interactive video instruction (IVI). In fact, the jargon itself is classified in color-coded books. The Red Book outlines the specifications for compact disc (CD); the Yellow Book, for compact disc–read only memory (CD-

ROM); and the Green Book, for compact disc–interactive (CD-I).

The technical orientation can be a big obstacle to many who might otherwise embrace the technology.

Consider windows.

Once upon a time, everyone knew exactly what the word "window" meant. You remember: "Spring cleaning—time to do the windows." Or, "It's hot in here—how about opening the windows?"

Those days are gone forever. In interactive video circles, when someone mentions windows the conversation might be about computer operating systems, multitasking, or computer hardware.

How can someone entering the interactive video arena keep such things straight?

That's an excellent question.

A BOGUS SOLUTION

Many people have made progress toward translating technical term into English. But with no established standards, the translations are not always compatible with the end-user's or developer's level of understanding. Clearly, the economic impact of this incompatibility could be serious.

In an effort to reduce the use of the technobabble, I propose the formation of a consortium of Businesses Opposed to Generally Useless Syntax. The BOGUS consortium's objective is the

ANOTHER LOOK *continued*

development of an international standard for translating interactive video and relate technical terms into English and other appropriate languages. The larger goal is to allow any IVI Technical term to be used by any level of IVI user or developer.

Of course, it may take some time to form the BOGUS consortium. In the meantime, I have taken the liberty of translating into English a few of the more common interactive video technical terms.

I have developed a translation standard I've dubbed the Peabody Format (named for the famous Peabody Hotel in Memphis, where the inspiration for the BOGUS consortium was found). I have faithfully outlined the Peabody Format in an Off-White Book (I don't think that color is taken), which I will offer to the consortium when it convenes.

In brief, the Peabody Format encompasses three translation levels: 1, 2, and 3 (or, for technobabblers: TL1, TL2, and TL3). The levels are defined as follows:

- Level 1: A definition of an IVI technical term that still remains shrouded in technical mysticism. You might think of Level 1 as a halfway house for hardcore technobabblers.

- Level 2: An intermediate translation of a technical term into its quasi-accurate English counterpart.

- Level 3: The final and complete translation level in which the term has lost all technical connotations and is therefore understandable to most humans.

PEABODY FORMAT TRANSLATIONS

In an effort to ease into the translation standards, technobabblers everywhere should review the translations listed below. Try using the Level 3 version at each appropriate opportunity. One you are comfortable with these examples, feel free to follow the Peabody format and begin translating the technical terms of your choice.

If you're a non-technobabbler, you may want to study the translations below to increase your understanding of friends who are technical gurus. Once you feel comfortable with one level, move to the next.

For each term, I first give the technobabble name and then define it on each of the three levels from the simplest to the most complex. Happy translations!

CD-DA, OR COMPACT DISC—DIGITAL AUDIO

Level 3: More commonly referred to as CD-A or simply CD. In other words, music CDs, like the ones you play on your stereo at home.
Level 2: Stereo-quality digital audio (generally music)

stored on a compact disc in a format that will play on any industry-standard CD player. Not compatible with most computer-based CD-ROM drives, although some drives can play both DC-DA and CD-ROM discs.
Level 1: A 12-centimeter optical disc on which approximately 75 minutes of stereo-quality digital sound may be recorded and played back using a constant linear velocity (CLV) format. The international CLV format for recording CD-DA is known as the Red Book and was established by NV Philips and Sony. CD-DA is generally targeted toward the consumer market and was introduced in 1982.

CD-ROM, OR COMPACT DISC—READ ONLY MEMORY

Level 3: CDs for computers.
Level 2: A 120-centimeter optical disc that is capable of holding 550 to 660 megabytes (about 500 high-density floppy diskettes' worth) of digital information such as text, graphics, digital stills and digital audio, for use with a computer and CD-ROM player. CD-ROM discs are not generally compatible with CD-DA players, although some devices can play both formats.
Level 1: A 12-centimeter optical disc on which up to 660MB of digital information can be stored. The generally accepted standard for encoding and decoding CD-ROM is International Standards Organization (SIO) 9660,

ANOTHER LOOK: CLIMBING THE TOWER OF TECHNOBABBLE
continued

which is a revision of the High Sierra format (so named for the High Sierra Hotel in Nevada, where a now-famous ad hoc committee first met to establish the original CD-ROM standards, now known as the Yellow Book). CD-ROM requires a CD-ROM drive and computer interface to operate. CD-ROM was introduced in 1983.

CD-ROM XA, OR COMPACT DISC—READ ONLY MEMORY, EXTENDED ARCHITECTURE

Level 3: A CD that can hold music, data, and some moving pictures, but won't work on home CD players designed just for music.
Level 2: An extension of the CD-ROM format that allows the user to mix together (interleave) text, graphics, and digital stills with three levels of digital audio in a standard format that allows real-time, seamless playback. The CD-ROM XA format requires a CD-ROM XA player with an interface to a personal computer or other CPU. CD-ROM XA discs are not compatible with CD-DA players, although some devices may play both formats.
Level 1: An expansion of the standards developed for CD-DA and CD-ROM, which was announced in August 1988 by Philips, Sony, and Microsoft. The volume and file structure conform to the ISO 9660 standard, while the character set follows ISO 8859/1. CD-ROM XA is being

marketed as an intermediate step between CD-ROM and CD-I.

CD-ROM XA uses many of the standards set earlier for CD-I, such as the Adaptive Delta Pulse Code Modulation (ADPCM) method for compressed, interweaved audio. Nevertheless, CD-ROM XA is not limited to the CD-I operating system (CD-RTOS) or CPU. Limited-motion digital video (15 frames per second, rather than the standard 30 frames per second) can be archived and played back.

CD-I, OR COMPACT DISC—INTERACTIVE

Level 3: A future upgrade to your home entertainment system, featuring an advanced CD player, which works like a VCR that rewinds instantly.
Level 2: A consumer-oriented product that can play Super HiFi audio, limited full-motion (30 frames per second) video, and computer graphics. CD-I can play any audio CD and some CD-ROMs. Several peripheral devices can be attached for enhanced functionality.
Level 1: A multimedia standard released in March 1987 by Philips and Sony and known as the Green Book. CD-I is a consumer-oriented product that is being prepared for commercial release. It features a stand-alone hardware set (or CPU) called the CD-I Base Case. The Base Case utilizes CD-RTOS (Real Time Operating System) and can process 12-

centimeter optical discs that utilize CD-I, CD-DA or CD-ROM formats.

CD-I is capable of processing four levels of real-time digital audio (one CD-DA and three ADPCM levels), digital stills, limited full-motion digital video, and computer graphics. The Green Book also specifies the File Manager Interface (FMI) for CD-I peripherals and extensions such as high-resolution video processors, RAM, modems, drives, and so forth.

DVI, OR DIGITAL VIDEO INTERACTIVE

Level 3: A technology that allows full-motion video to play on a properly equipped computer without a laser disc player.
Level 2: An all-digital multimedia board and software set that can operate on IBM ATs and Ps/2s or 100-percent IBM compatibles. DVI can process full-motion digital images, digital stills, digital audio, and computer graphics in a compressed format that allows approximately 72 minutes of full-motion digital video to be stored and played from a standard CD-ROM. For motion video to be available in its highest-quality format (Presentation Level), the video must be externally processed.
Level 1: An all-digital multimedia technology, owned by Intel, that was initially researched in 1983 at the

ANOTHER LOOK *continued*

David Sarnoff Research Center.

DVI does not require a specific OS or CPU. The heart of DVI is a proprietary Very Large Scale Integration (VLSI) Video Display Processor (VDP). The VLSI VDP is a two-chip set. VDPI is a type of pixel processor for images in Video Random-Access Memory (VRAM). VDP2 is an output display processor for converting VRAM images to a signal that is usable by a monitor.

Edit Level (real-time) compression is available on all DVI systems, but Presentation Level compression of motion video requires outside processing for 30-frames-per-second playback. Because of the spatial and temporal redundancies in motion video, presentation-level video compression is about 100:1, which allows for approximately 72 minutes of full-motion, digital video on a standard CD-ROM, as opposed to about 1.5 minutes without compression.

ANALOG VIDEO

Level 3: Regular old video.
Level 2: The video format used by a typical camcorder or TV show. Video presented in this format cannot be directly processed by a computer.
Level 1: A representation of light waves through physical variables (such as electrical current) in a manner that theoretically allows infinite continual graduations between levels of the video image. Analog video cannot be directly processed by a typical computer, unlike digital video, which is discontinuous and can be directly processed by a computer.

DIGITAL VIDEO

Level 3: Video for computers.
Level 2: Video images that are represented by numbers. Digital video can be stored on CD-ROM or other optical media, with certain restrictions. It can be manipulated by a computer if it is recorded in a proper format.
Level 1: A video signal represented by binary numbers (the digits 0 and 1) or other on/off schemes in a discontinuous format. Unlike analog audio, digital video can be read and manipulated by a computer if the proper format and equipment are used.

COMPRESSED VIDEO

Level 3: Video for computers (see digital video) that is scrunched up to require less storage space.
Level 2: Digital video that is sampled, stored, and accessed by a computer in a way that takes less space.
Level 1: Video that is digitally encoded and decoded in a manner that requires less storage space. Generally, the greater the compression, the less frequent the sampling of the master and the greater the variation from the master.

DIGITIZE

Level 3: Changing regular old video into computer-usable video.
Level 2: Converting video into a format that can be used by a computer.
Level 1: When referring to video, digitizing describes several processes for converting analog video into digital video. Audio can also be digitized.

BOARDS

Level 3: Computer parts, like the engine or the air conditioner of a car.
Level 2: Internal components of a personal computer system; each provides specific functionality.
Level 1: Integrated electrical circuits, chips, or resistors are mounted on a thin, flat (board-like) structure. Boards are designed to be installed in a personal computer system to add specific functionality. Also referred to as cards.

SOURCE: Bart Dahmer, "Climbing the Tower of Technobabble," *Training & Development,* January 1992, pp. 44–46.

ANOTHER LOOK: TELECOMMUTING: A BETTER WAY TO WORK

Here you sit, again, in the line of stop-and-go traffic crawling into the city. Care to glance about at your fellow commuters? Faces full of slow-brewing rage and resigned despair surround you as you swing around the '77 Impala stalled in the center lane. You'll be 20 minutes late for work, again, and you pray the coffee isn't gone when you get there.

Suddenly it occurs to you that you get to do this all over again tonight. You stifle a scream. Your mind thrashes like a wounded badger, trying to recall one of those stress-reduction exercises from the seminar last year.

The best way to forgo the torments of traveling to and from work in most major cities would be, of course, to avoid the commute altogether. That's the idea behind telecommuting. The concept has been around for years but is just now beginning to make significant inroads into the workplace. Telecommuting means, essentially, doing your job at home or at a satellite location (a small branch office near your home, for instance) instead of working at the main office. In most telecommuting arrangements your work remains the same, your benefits stay in place, your salary is unchanged and the hours you work may be identical. The difference is *where* you work—and sometimes that can make all the difference.

Take Robert Duerr of Philadelphia, for example.

He's the product manager for Atlantic Bell's speech recognition line, and he telecommutes one or two days a week. His official office hours are 8 A.M. to 5 P.M. On days when he goes to the office, he faces a 40-minute drive—provided he's on the road by 6:30 A.M. to avoid traffic. He stays at the office until 6 P.M., again to avoid traffic, and gets home about 40 minutes later if he's lucky.

A telecommuting morning, on the other hand, starts for Duerr at 7:45 A.M. He goes downstairs, starts a pot of coffee and turns on his personal computer. By 8 A.M. he's at work. His phone calls can be forwarded from the office to his home, and he has access to his coworkers through voice mail and elec-

▼ TELECOMMUTING FROM THE ELECTRONIC COTTAGE

Futurist Alvin Toffler's discussion of the "electronic cottage" in his 1980 book *The Third Wave* is probably one of the driving forces behind the introduction of telecommuting to business and government. But one question remains: Has the electronic cottage been built yet?

We've seen prototypes, and all the necessary technology is available. Affordability, however, remains the biggest hurdle to the utopian ideal that many envision. Interactive TV that patches into a huge computer network with multimedia and video-teleconferencing capability, while possible, still depends on large installed bases of high-tech equipment and the right kind of electronic cables. Since only about 25 percent of all Ameri-

cans have personal computers in their homes, a fully functional electronic cottage may still be on the distant horizon. Maybe the more important question is: Do we really need all the fancy technology in order to telecommute?

Gil Gordon, editor of the "Telecommuting Review" newsletter, is a proponent of outfitting a home office with precisely what you need to do your work, no more and no less. The minimum equipment for a telecommuter's home office is a telephone, according to Gordon. You could have more, but first be sure you need it.

A personal computer, when combined with a modem, opens up a world of communications and research capabilities. If *continued ...*

ANOTHER LOOK *continued*

tronic mail. He works until noon, goes out for some lunch, works the rest of the afternoon and shuts down at 5 P.M.

Nancy Apeles, the telecommuting program manager for Los Angeles County, practices what she preaches by telecommuting two days a week. Her round-trip commute to the county government office where she works is about 80 miles, and

she estimates that telecommuting saves her at least 90 minutes in the morning alone. That means she doesn't have to get her son up at 5 A.M. to take him to day care. It also means she has time for exercise; she jogs on the mornings she works at home. Since one of her tasks is legislative analysis, Apeles reads a lot of legislative bills. At home, she

says, she gets through about 26 bills in a day. At the office, because of interruptions, she read about three a day.

If telecommuting is so great, exactly how many people are doing it? Link Resources, a New York-based research and consulting firm, conducts a National Work-at-Home Survey every year. According to the 1991

---

your office has electronic mail, a PC often can connect you to that system. Many voice mail systems also can be accessed from home. According to Karen Gislason, director of the telecommuting and home-based business markets for Bell Atlantic in Philadelphia: "The use of voice messaging services has proven invaluable. In many respects, people feel they are even more 'available' in a telecommuting situation than in the office."

With the advent of fax/modems, faxing documents with your computer can relieve you of the economic burden of buying a fully functional fax machine.

In short, much of the equipment that might be called the foundation of the electronic cottage is becoming affordable for either companies or individuals— whoever is buying the equipment.

At J.C. Penney, about

200 part-time customer-service employees telecommute. To allow these people to take catalog orders over the phone and register those orders in the computer, the company had to run two business telephone lines into each employee's home. One line is for the phone calls, the other transfers data to the main computer. That's one reason why Carl Kirkpatrick, planning and program manager for J.C. Penney's telemarketing division, isn't planning to expand his telecommuting program. While he is satisfied with the original investment, he can't justify more expenditures until the technology becomes more affordable.

Michael Crampton, a director in the telecommunications division of the information systems department of The Travelers, a Hartford, CT-based insurance company, sees the installation of ISDN (integrated services

digital network) lines as a possible solution to Kirkpatrick's current problems. These cables, which are only now becoming available, can transmit video, computer data and telephone calls, all using the same line. If the ideal electronic cottage ever becomes a reality, ISDN lines may be the link between the tele-commuter and the rest of the world.

The affordability of personal computers certainly has been a key reason why telecommuting has caught on in the last 10 years, but voice mail and e-mail are the applications telecommuters mention most often as critical to keeping in touch with their peers and supervisors. The most important technology in any telecommuting program, however, is a commodity that's inexpensive but often hard to come by; good communications between managers and employees.—B.F.

ANOTHER LOOK: TELECOMMUTING: A BETTER WAY TO WORK
continued

version, about 5.5 million part-time and full-time company employees work at home during normal business hours. That's up 38 percent from 1990.

In another study on flexible work arrangements, the Conference Board, also a New York-based research firm, found that 15 percent to 20 percent of the companies it surveyed offered formal telecommuting arrangements to some of their employees. Closer to 80 percent, however, had informal telecommuting as a work option. Informal telecommuting is usually arranged between a supervisor and an employee without the knowledge of upper management or the HR department.

While these arrangements can work out fine, they usually forgo successful elements like a telecommuting agreement, formal training and job analysis.

SOURCE: Bob Filipezak, "Telecommuting: A Better Way to Work?" *Training,* May 1992, pp. 53–56.

▼ A CASE IN POINT: ANSWERING SYSTEMS RETAIN FEMININE TOUCH

Technology may be transforming the job of receptionist, but tradition still counts for something. If a phone call is answered by a machine these days, chances are the recording will be a woman's voice.

An unscientific survey of "automated attendants" and "voice-processing" systems shows that almost all use a female voice. When system providers and users are asked why, the typical answer is, "I never thought about that."

Robert Yellowlees, president of American Telesystems, says many customers "instinctively" choose a female voice. When Spiegel wanted to tape messages, it went to its own operators, "who happen to all be female," says Michael Zivich, telecommunications manager.

The company also uses women because it doesn't want to confuse callers. When it adds its own taped instructions to a recording, it wants to match them with the "canned" voices already in the automated systems it buys. And they're always female.

Using women's voices may seem harmless, but Margaret Hennig, Dean of Simmons College Graduate School of Management, says that, however "unconscious, it simply perpetuates stereotypes." The "cumulative effect" of such small signals, she adds, is to slow women's progress.

Voice-system users of the future, Mr. Yellowlees believes, will be more sophisticated about the image they project, paying more careful attention to gender and tone, just as some advertisers do with voiceovers in commercials.

But for the moment, companies are "trying to simulate what the caller has experienced," he says. With many callers annoyed about a machine answering calls, voice-systems users are eager to avoid backlash with any more surprises—like a male voice.

QUESTIONS

1. How does this case illustrate resistance to change?
2. Do you agree that using women's voices 'perpetuates stereotypes"? Why or Why not?

SOURCE: Jolie Solomon, "Answering Systems Retain Feminine Touch," *Wall Street Journal* 12 July 1989, p. B-1.

▼ A CASE IN POINT: CYBERPHOBIA

In a test measuring *cyberphobia*—meaning fear, distrust, or hatred of computers—managers and students were wired with skin-response measuring devices while they worked at their computers. It was found that nearly one third of these people were cyberphobic and showed actual symptoms of classic phobia: nausea, dizziness, cold sweat, and high blood pressure.

It is believed, in fact, that the problem may be worse than we think. Maybe thousands of cyberphobic people hide their fears because of peer pressure to extol the benefits of computers.

One factor that contributes to cyberphobia among managers is their fear that they don't actually manage anything—that they are merely information keepers who could easily be replaced by the very computers they are learning to use.

QUESTIONS

1. How do you feel about computers? Does the computer revolution cause you concern? Articulate your feelings.
2. What fears might executive-level managers have with regard to computerization?

SOURCE: H. L. Capron, instructor's guide to accompany *Computers and Data Processing,* 2d ed. (Menlo Park, Calif.: Benjamin Cummings Publishing, 1983), p. 4.

THE CHALLENGE: DEVELOPMENT

CHAPTER

18

DEVELOPING STRONGER EMPLOYEES:
YOURSELF AND OTHERS

This chapter answers several all-important questions:

- What are the basic steps for bringing about change in people's lives?

- What is the difference between attitudes and behaviors?

- Why is dissonance important in the process of change?

- What role do trusted people play in the change process?

- What role do life experiences play in the change process?

- What are the differences between training, education, and development?

- What are the differences between the three areas of development focus: job, individual, and organization?

- What is the role of employee development in organizations?

The answers to these and other questions are coming up next in chapter 18....

CHAPTER 18

Phil grew up on a large ranch in a sparsely populated area of the West, where he enjoyed such activities as riding a horse, camping under the stars, and playing with his dog. His father was constantly pushing him to leave home and attend a university: "You'll grow up to be a bum! You've got to go to college and get educated. If you want to be a success in this life, you need to be better than me!"

Phil would ponder his father's statements and usually reply, "I don't want to go to college, I don't need a college education to work on the ranch." When Phil's father could see that his begging wasn't working, he decided to bribe Phil. He offered him a new horse trailer if he would go to college for one semester. His hopes were that Phil would enjoy the university so much that he wouldn't want to come back to the ranch until he finished his education.

Phil decided a horse trailer was worth one semester at college. He entered a large university on the Pacific coast with a gigantic group of first-year students. The smallest class he signed up for had fifty students in it. He did not enjoy being with a lot of people, but he started to have positive experiences.

Just before he took his first examination, a girl named Jennifer started sitting next to him in class. He was a bit embarrassed but said, "Hi, I'm Phil."

She looked at him and said, "Hi, Phil, my name is Jennifer." She looked at Phil's boots and said, "You must be a cowboy."

"Yes, I'm in the rodeo club," he replied.

She in turn said, "I was a rodeo queen in my hometown."

"Well, let's go riding," Phil said.

"I'd love to," Jennifer responded.

While they were horseback riding, they decided to study together for their first test. They studied together and both of them received A's on the test. Suddenly, Phil was starting to get some very positive feelings about attending college. He was getting good grades, and he had met a great girl.

If you want to change and grow, listen to people you trust.

Reprinted by permission: Tribune Media Services.

Furthermore, he met one of the outstanding rodeo stars, who had always been his favorite. The rodeo star told Phil, "You really made a wise decision. Riding and messing around rodeos the rest of your life is not the way to go. You need to have managerial experience, you need a background in business so you can more effectively run the ranch."

Needless to say, Phil said he would stay in college and get his degree. He was very satisfied that his father had bribed him by giving him a horse trailer. After all, he now had a horse trailer, and in a few years he would have a college degree.

▼ GETTING STARTED: BRINGING ABOUT CHANGE

Phil's story illustrates the change process in human beings. There are a variety of ways to bring about change in the lives of people.

The way people act is the result of what they think or the attitudes they hold. Phil came to college because he was bribed by his father. His attitude was that attending college was bad and that staying home on the ranch was good. However, at school he received positive reinforcement or feedback on his schooling experience, which caused him to change his attitude. He liked Jennifer, he aced the test, and a respected person told him that being at school was important. His attitude changed to be in accordance with his behavior. We can diagram this as shown in figure 18.1.

Attitudes are opinions and the positive or negative feelings people associate with those opinions. Attitudes predispose people to behave or act the way they do. For example, if you feel that attending college is good (attitude), then you will likely attend college (behavior).

When managers deal with employees in organizations, the principles are the same. To change someone, begin by dealing with the person's behavior or attitudes. One can try to change the attitude, or one can try to change the behavior.

There are many theories about attitude change. One of the more famous deals with cognitive dissonance (a detailed discussion of

■ The way people act is the result of what they think.

■ Dissonance is the feeling one has when doing something in which one does not believe.

FIGURE **18.1**
A model of change.

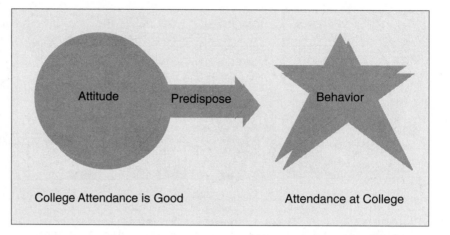

cognitive dissonance appeared in chapter 4). This theory states that if attitudes and behaviors are dissimilar, people experience dissonance. It is difficult to change someone if that person's attitudes and behavior are in agreement. However, if a manager can create within an employee a difference between behaviors and attitudes, the employee will reduce the dissonance by changing either the behavior or the attitude, so the two will match.

Phil came to the university in a dissonant state. His attitudes and behavior were not similar. He was open for change. Two things could happen to reduce his dissonance: (1) he could leave school and retain his attitude that school was bad, or (2) he could change his attitude to "school is good" and stay at school.

■ If we want to change people, we can create dissonance in them.

▼ MAKING CHANGES: IT'S OFTEN SLOW

■ Helping people to change is often a slow process.

Experience with people in organizations shows that after dissonance is created, two major steps can help a person change: (1) introduction to new and credible people and (2) introduction to new experiences. The impact that people and new experiences have on us is exemplified by the story of Phil. Having a rodeo rider he trusted and respected say he was doing the proper thing by being in school had a very positive impact on him. After he met Jennifer and they became friends, she too had an impact on him. These credible people helped him change. Furthermore, the new experiences of being in school, being involved in the rodeo club, and doing well on his test were positive change experiences.

The impacts of experiences and people are not always positive. Suppose Phil came to school and flunked the first test, and as the teacher handed the test back to him she said, "That's one of the poorer scores on the test." Or suppose Jennifer turned to Phil, sniffed the air, and (in a big-city way) said, "You must be a cowboy. Don't you ever clean your boots?" Or suppose Phil didn't become a member of the rodeo club. Or suppose that when Phil met his favorite rodeo star, the cowboy said, "Boy, you've made a big mis-

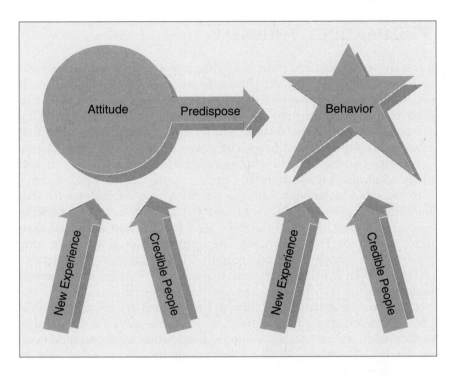

FIGURE **18.2**
How people and experiences affect change.

take, you're just wasting your time going to college. You ought to be out on the rodeo circuit making money." If these things had happened to Phil, his attitude about not going to school might have been strengthened. At the first available opportunity, he might have left school, never to return.

People and experiences have a tremendous impact on us. Figure 18.2 shows how this works. The diagram points out that change can be made by dealing with either the attitude or the behavior. However, new experiences and credible people must be present to bring about change.

If you are concerned about the behavior of an employee and wish to influence that person to do what you perceive as best for the organization, then introduce the employee to as many new experiences and credible people as possible who can reinforce your point of view. For example, let's say one of your male employees is having difficulty accepting his new female boss, and the feedback he is getting from his associates and the people he trusts is that women should be in the home and not on the job. He could snub his new boss completely, and the work of the office might not get completed. If you want to change this employee's attitude and behavior regarding his boss, introduce him to new credible people. Bring in employees who feel that women's rights are extremely important. Remember, this approach won't work unless the male employee trusts and believes in the people who speak to him. Furthermore, give him as many new experiences as possible that point out that the boss's sex does not matter, that what matters is the efficiency of the boss. Make certain the female supervisor provides positive work experiences for the male employee.

■ Changing oneself is as important as changing others.

▼ CHANGING YOURSELF

Even more important than bringing about change among your employees is bringing about change in your own life. The process is essentially the same for you as for anyone else. For example, if you wish to quit cigarette smoking and your experiences with smoking are positive, you probably won't quit. If close friends tell you that smoking the new low-tar brands is okay and evidence doesn't seem to indicate that smoking low-tar brands will harm you, then you will likely be reinforced to continue.

If you wish to change, listen to people you trust that are against smoking and give yourself new experiences with cigarette smoking that are not positive. Visit someone who has smoked a pack of cigarettes a day most of his or her life and who has undergone lung surgery to remove a cancerous growth. This could give you negative reactions, both from the experience of the visit and from the person you visited.

Whatever the situation, whether it be personal or organizational, if you want to change your behavior, you must be aware of the kind of people with whom you associate and the kinds of experiences you are having. They both have a tremendous impact on what you do and what you think.

We have talked about how you get started in bringing about change. You need to be aware of your attitudes and your behaviors and the impact that people and experiences have on you. The next section of this chapter covers how people can continue to reinforce themselves after they make an initial change.

▼ CONTINUING: LEARNING IS A LIFELONG PROCESS

■ Learning is a lifelong process.

After making a change, continued progress and development is important. How does one continue to develop? In his book *Developing Human Resources,* Leonard Nadler offers some good ideas of learning approaches to help people develop more effectively.[1] He advocates three major areas of focus: (1) the job, (2) the individual, and (3) the organization (see figure 18.3).

Each of these areas of focus requires a different type of learning development (see figure 18.4). For development needs associated with the job, Nadler discusses *training*. Training is development associated with learning human and technical skills to make the

FIGURE **18.3**
Areas of focus.
SOURCE: Leonard Nadler, *Developing Human Resources* (San Francisco: Jossey-Bass, 1989).

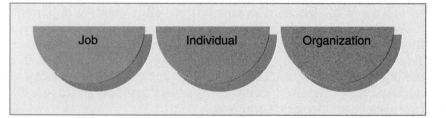

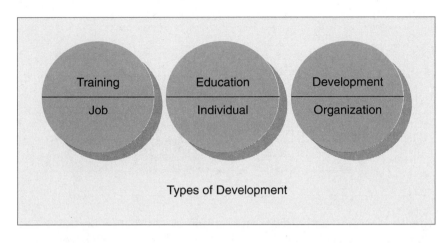

FIGURE **18.4**
Types of development.
SOURCE: Leonard Nadler, *Developing Human Resources* (San Francisco: Jossey-Bass, 1989).

employee more effective on a specific job. Nadler relates individual development in *education.* Education is the development of an employee to be well-rounded and generally developed. Organization *development* means developing employees to be able to adapt and progress with the organization.

These three areas of focus and the three types of learning together create a complete concept of human resource development (see figure 18.5).

■ Human resource development is important for all organizations.

▼ HUMAN RESOURCE DEVELOPMENT

Each person who belongs to an organization can strengthen and develop himself or herself for specific jobs, for individual needs, and for changing organizations. We will now discuss the importance of the three types of human resource development (HRD) and how they can help people maintain themselves.

Training

Training includes activities that improve job performance. It helps make a person more employable or promotable within the organization and teaches basic skills. It is specific learning and focuses

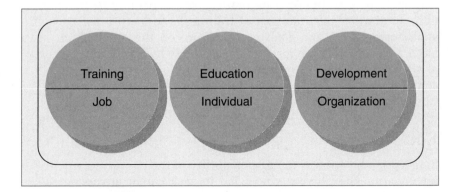

FIGURE **18.5**
The concept of human resource development (HRD).
SOURCE: Leonard Nadler, *Developing Human Resources* (San Francisco: Jossey-Bass, 1989).

FIGURE **18.6**
Contrasting training and education. *SOURCE:* Leonard Nadler, *Developing Human Resources* (San Francisco: Jossey-Bass, 1989).

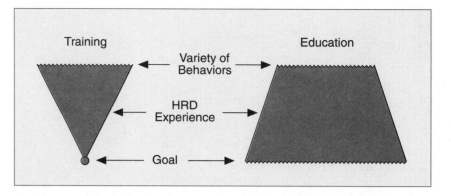

directly on basic activities. For example, a typist may be trained to move from the typing pool to a secretarial position. A laborer could be taught to drive a truck and then to qualify as a driver. Training teaches people new basic techniques and introduces them to new methods related to their jobs. We all need to improve ourselves for our jobs at all times by being as effectively trained as possible.

As mentioned in chapter 17, rapid technological changes place increased demands on management and labor. The rapidly changing workplace requires a work force that has a greater range of skills than were needed a generation ago. A recent research project revealed five key basic skills that employers say are needed in today's workplace and need to be addressed in current training programs:

1. How to learn
2. Listening and oral communications
3. Problem solving and creative thinking
4. Interpersonal
5. Organizational effectiveness and leadership[2]

Each skill area might well be addressed in both education and training programs.

What is the difference between training and education? Nadler explains it as shown in figure 18.6. Training and education use essentially the same varieties of behaviors to reach their goals. They also use the same kinds of human resource development experiences. However, the goals of education and of training are different. Although job training on a particular job can usually be transferred to other similar jobs, the goal of training is to learn a very specific behavior or skill. The goal of education, on the other hand, is to learn a variety of behavior and skills so one can deal with a variety of situations in the organization. Training focuses on a specific job activity, and education focuses on teaching a person to be effective from a broad perspective.

Education

Employee education is the responsibility of the employee, not of the organization. Employees who wish to seek career advancement or

Organizational training prepares workers to handle specific job situations.

even to remain competitive in their current positions will be wise to continue their education. Although a high school diploma was sufficient for most entry-level jobs a generation ago, many employers today are seeking (and finding) applicants with college degrees for most jobs. Many people with less than a college degree are finding it difficult to compete in the high-tech environment of business.

Because of this demand for higher educational levels, a variety of special courses, high school and college programs, and nontraditional learning experiences are available in most parts of the United States and Canada for people who wish to improve their ability to deal with work organizations and life itself. The emphasis has shifted from technical or job-related training only to employee education, which is often experiential and focuses on improving the student's appreciation for life and for people. As employees gain wider experience, more maturity and understanding, and a better appreciation for life and people, they have greater opportunities for advancement. To become educated, as well as trained, should be a goal for every member of society.

Development

The basic function of training is to help people improve their performance on specific jobs. Education is geared to helping people prepare for life in general and for general careers or vocations. Employee development helps employees prepare for individual growth and advancement with growing organizations. It helps employees to better understand and to cope with changes in the organization.

Education and training focus on the individual employee. Employee development, on the other hand, focuses on the organization. Its purpose is to create a work force that is geared to the needs of the

■ What is the ODIE model for organizational development?

organization, oriented to the future, looking for change, and able to adapt to change while maintaining effectiveness and efficiency.

Specific models have been designed to facilitate the achievement of development goals. One such model, a design for organizational development through the involvement of employees (ODIE), focuses on an organization's vision, mission, and goals. It requires that employee groups identify obstacles that keep them from achieving organizational goals, quantify the identified obstacle, set a performance level, and take steps to achieve it.

The ODIE model illustrates that employee development is a serious and essential undertaking for organizations that hope to maintain a competitive edge in the business world as we approach the twenty-first century. Its application is likely to result in improvements in (1) productivity, product or service quality or both, cost containment, business development, and technological advancement; (2) the quality of work life; and (3) organizational development knowledge.[3]

We have pointed out the importance of change in your life and your employees' lives. And we have reviewed the importance of training, education, and development within the organization and within the individual. Now ask yourself, "Am I in a situation where I need to change? If so, how should I go about making change?" What kinds of training do you need to be effective in your job? How can you better educate yourself for your job? Do you need more active involvement with your organization as it grows, develops, and changes? In summary: (1) what do you or your organization need to change? and (2) what do you or your organization need to learn? The one certainty of life is change. Employees who are not willing to change and learn new information will be less likely to succeed as organizations grow and develop in the future. Where do you stand?

▼ SUMMARY OF KEY IDEAS

■ Attitudes affect one's behaviors, thus, to change a person's behavior you often must first change his or her attitude.

■ Although changing a person's behavior is a slow process, the two major steps that can help the process are introducing the person to new and credible people and introducing the person to new experiences.

■ Nadler advocates three areas of development: the job, the individual, and the organization. He combines each of these areas with training, education, and development.

▼ KEY TERMS, CONCEPTS, AND NAMES

Attitude
Credible people

Development
Dissonance

Education
Job training
Leonard Nadler

Organizational development
   through the involvement
   of employees (ODIE)
Organization development
Training

▼ QUESTIONS AND EXERCISES

1. Answer the introductory questions at the beginning of the chapter.
2. Differentiate between training, education, and development.
3. Give a personal example from your life that illustrates the change process.

▼ NOTES

1. Adapted from Leonard Nadler, *Developing Human Resources,* 2d ed. (Austin, Texas: Learning Concepts, 1979), pp. 37–90.

2. Anthony P. Carnavale, Leila J. Gainer, Ann S. Meltzer, and Shari L. Holland, "Workplace Basics: The Skills Employers Want," *Training and Development Journal* 42 (October 1988): 22–30.

3. Peggy Tollison, "Meet 'ODIE,'" *Journal for Quality and Participation* 12 (March 1989): 82–88.

▽ ANOTHER LOOK: TAKING CHARGE OF CHANGE

Certainly today's change is unlike any ever confronted. As George Land, the author of the classic book on growth cycles, *Grow or Die,* says, change is more rapid, more complex, more turbulent, and more unpredictable than ever before....

The radical nature of change today has energized some organizations and paralyzed others. General Electric is pushing for a "boundaryless" state in which "everyone has access to the same information and there are no artificial barriers to keep change away." General Motors, by contrast, appears stunned into slow-motion reactions to a world it cannot believe has changed.

"We now have a crisis mentality," says Charles Kiefer, president of Innovation Associates in Framingham, Massachusetts. "The business environment is so entirely different on a day-to-day basis that whole systems we work in are not up to performing," he says.

"We used to talk about taking 10 or 15 years to fully implement major changes. We don't have that luxury anymore. We have to move faster and develop technologies to accelerate that process."

"The rate of change has accelerated," says Carla O'Dell of O'Dell and Associates, in Houston. "But our ability to manage it and our technologies have not accelerated at the same rate. We're still using the old

1950s and 1960s methodologies for organizational change. The old ways are simply not fast enough for today's problems."

People have always been able to adapt if given enough time, says Gloria Regalbuto, director of corporate professional development for William M. Mercer in Columbus, Ohio.

"That's because gradual, evolutionary change is almost invisible," she continues. "The rules have changed. Things are happening so rapidly that we face a quick series of changes and don't have time to adjust. Obviously we have to look at things differently."

One of the best places to look at things differently these days is the former Soviet Union. Steven Rhinesmith, whose consulting practice is based in Stamford, Connecticut, recently helped establish a department of organizational change at the University of Moscow. He agrees that when it comes to large-scale change, old ways are not working. "Stability has become the enemy of survival," he says.

"We haven't developed a body of knowledge that includes these three crucial skills: diagnosing, introducing, and sustaining change....

"Maybe we need to junk the traditional methods and put our resources into new ones that can change large groups fast. You can't get one change process started

before another one is on your tail.

"If I had to put my money on major breakthroughs in the next 10 years, I'd put it on new change technologies that will affect larger and larger groups of people faster."

Will HR [human relations] professionals be inventing, leading, and facilitating these new technologies? Consultant Michael Doyle, of Michael Doyle and Associates in San Francisco, warns that "most companies are changing without us. HR people need to trust their intuition. They need to move away from a doctor/patient style of doing business and become allies with management."

CONSIDER THE FORCE

Perhaps the first thing to consider when thinking about where change is headed is the forces that are behind it.

Much change today is driven from outside, says Charles Smith, executive vice-president of human resources at Chase Manhattan Bank in New York.

"External change in the banking industry forced us to change. For example, capital markets changed because money was accessible in places other than the United States banking system. Our competition changed. And when that happens you have no choice but to change."

"Recessions, language barriers, a lack of critical thinking skills in the workplace,

ANOTHER LOOK *continued*

reduced resources, and newly merged cultures are all factors driving change in the workplace," says Linda Hodo, director of training and organizational development at Rush Presbyterian St. Luke's Medical Center in Chicago.

"Probably the greatest force driving change right now is the economy," says Elaine Biech, a consultant based in Portage, Wisconsin. "Another force is the realization that organizations have to be more innovative in the future, not only to grow but to survive. Organizations are learning that they have to count on human resources—the people who work for them. They have to change not only the way they manage the business but also the way people think and interact."

ARRESTING RESISTANCE

Anyone who has been involved in change knows that one of the major obstacles to it is people's natural resistance.

"Resistance is a fundamental response to change that seems to be universal," says Gloria Regalbuto. "There is a basic, primal drive in people to keep things the same over time. It creates a feeling of longevity within a system."

Peter Senge, in his book *The Fifth Discipline: The Art and Practice of the Learning Organization,* writes that people both fear and seek change. An organization change consultant whom

Senge quotes puts change in this perspective: "People don't resist change. They resist being changed."

The trick, then, is getting people to choose change rather than resist it. But how do you hurdle a basic primal drive? A first step that many recommend is focusing on achieving results rather than dwelling on resistance.

Charles Smith says that leaders contribute to resistance through their use of language. "There is a lot of charged language referring to change. Such words as future shock, targets, and agents add a dimension that is more contentious than what actually happens in a change situation.

"There's no question that when you get into the change process you'll have resistance. You have to manage resistance but that isn't what is going to help you achieve what you want. You should focus on building on what you want to accomplish rather than on fighting the points of resistance and worrying about future shock, agents, and warriors," says Smith.

Change probably won't happen if people aren't motivated to change. And getting them to be motivated can be difficult if you believe, as Charles Kiefer does, that you can't motivate people; people motivate themselves.

"If people motivate themselves then the approach to motivation has to be very individual," says Kiefer. "You have to find what turns

people on; you have to discover what they care about.

"You can keep people moving by keeping the heat turned up, but if you're looking for a self-reinforcing, enduring effect, you've got to find what people really want to be doing. Then the motivation will be natural."

Karin Kolodziejski, manager of human resources for Network Displays at Tektronix in Wilsonville, Oregon, agrees: "Most of the time we try to convince people that change is going to be better. Instead, we should be trying to pull them into the visioning process.

"We have employee meetings about how a change is going to be better for all of us, but many employees don't buy it. We have to figure out why they don't."

When we go about the task of change, says Elaine Biech, we need to recognize that "it is not a mechanism or an organization that we are changing. We are changing individuals by trying to make them want to change themselves.

"We have to keep rewards in front of them so they don't lose their enthusiasm. If people don't profit from a change, why should they take risks, learn new skills, or do things differently?"

Gloria Regalbuto cautions that not all people react to change in the same way. "You'll get more people to change if you recognize differences in their comfort levels," she says.

"Some people seek change.

ANOTHER LOOK: TAKING CHARGE OF CHANGE *continued*

They love it, and they will be in the avant garde. Others will observe the avant garde and choose a path based on what they see. We call them early adopters. Most people are in this group. Then there are the laggards who won't adopt a change no matter what you do."

PAIN BEFORE GAIN

Some organizations use pain strategically to motivate people to change. Most experts agree that crisis-driven change works and is sometimes necessary, but that it is not enduring.

"Change is faster with pain," says Biech, "because there is a compelling reason to change. When people are told over and over to quit smoking or to lose weight, they don't do it. After they have a heart attack they change their habits instantly.

"We have worked with organizations that have had tremendous pain and have made some great gains very quickly. Of course, that all reaches a plateau as soon as the pain stops. Because pain works only temporarily, you have to implement something to keep the momentum and improvements going."

Smith believes that much of the pain people experience is self-imposed. "I don't think pain is necessary. It happens because people are not adaptable. Our environment challenges us to be adaptable and amenable to change. To the extent that

people try to fight that process, they create an immense amount of pain for themselves.

"Still, change is difficult. It affects things that are very personal, such as people's roles and their opportunities for reward and advancement. Those are issues people don't always deal with successfully."

Kiefer agrees that pain does motivate but that it does not do so effectively. That's because it is temporary and because people don't respond to it well, he says.

"Do you do important things because you want to get away from some sort of pain? No. You do great things because you want to do them. People climb mountains because they want to reach the top, not to avoid pain at the bottom.

"The problem with using pain as the primary motivator for organization change is that once you take enough steps to reduce the pain, your motivation for continued change diminishes."

SEARCH FOR ENERGY

One way to sidestep resistance is to find groups of people in the organization who are already moving in a direction that responds to the change you need to make. The experts refer to this tactic as going where the energy is.

"It is similar to caring for a plant," says Regalbuto. "You

look for where the plant is beginning to flourish and then reallocate resources from dying branches toward the points of energy."

"There are ways to create energy," says Robert Levit, director of corporate HRD for MCI Communications in Washington, D.C. "You could blow up something— create an event that catalyzes people. There is energy in outrage.

"The easiest way is to find people who already manifest what you want and find out how they are doing it. Then make an example of them, give them more visibility, and see what happens."

Karin Kolodziejski thinks turning toward energy is a viable approach to change. At the same time, she believes that you have to ask why the energy isn't in other places.

"If some people in the business have the right idea, you can fuel those people with resources. But unless you understand why other people aren't on the right path, you won't be able to spread what is happening in one place to the rest of the organization.

"In our company, we have had pockets of that kind of excellence for a long time, but sometimes it doesn't spread. It dies and the rest of the organization never gets the value of it."

Jeryl Mitchell, manager of training and development for Gould's Pumps in Seneca Falls, New York, believes

ANOTHER LOOK *continued*

that for the energy theory to work, top management or at least middle management has to drive the change or be involved in it.

"The idea that you identify the energy and run with it regardless of who causes it," says Mitchell, "isn't the best approach. The success and outcome of the change depends more on who is driving it."

READY FOR THE RADICAL?

Radical changes to organizational structures are likely to continue. Do they work?

O'Dell says it isn't something that organizations choose lightly or do willingly, but that radical change can work. She cites as an example motorcycle manufacturer Harley-Davidson. When on the brink of financial disaster, the company successfully restructured.

"Harley-Davidson almost went out of business, but was able to save itself by fundamentally changing everything. The company threw away all the normal hierarchies, all the traditional jobs people had, and all the traditional ways of making decisions. It was literally chaos for a while but it worked. The company is very successful now."

Kolodziejski thinks of the idea of destroying an organization and putting it back together again as typically American. "I like the Japanese method of making radical innovations in incremental steps. But perhaps it

takes tearing down and rebuilding to make change work in our society."

Robert Levit doesn't think structures need to be eliminated and rebuilt but he does see the destructive process of ideas as natural.

"If you look at human creativity and at human energy, it is a constant creative/destructive process. Creation and destruction are always in balance. For every idea accepted, another is lost forever.

"But you don't have to destroy an organization to revitalize it. By setting human energy loose, you naturally will change the organization. You have to liberate the people in it. An organization's leadership has to channel the creative/destructive surge of human energy as it seeks situational solutions to problems."

In changing structures, O'Dell says that any change in structure is only as good as people's willingness to change with it. "If people aren't prepared to deal with change, then no amount of structural change will produce the desired effect. At the same time, just preparing people to deal with change without actually changing the processes that are causing the problems won't get you any positive results either."

Charline Seyfer, technical education coordinator for Sandia National Laboratories in Albuquerque, New Mexico, agrees: "Taking care of the people is most impor-

tant. You can have the most perfect structure in place, but if you've got people who are unhappy or unmotivated, the structure is not going to make that better."

THINK AGAIN

What new methods will work best to help people accept change, motivate themselves, and adapt to future change? What mechanisms will be best for changing organizational structures? The experts are confident that inventive approaches will be developed.

"New approaches to change will be as surprising as the surprises that cause them," says Kiefer. "We will see a lot of experimentation. We are going to find things working that no one ever dreamed would work. And we will find things that always worked in the past not working in the future. It is going to be surprising, astonishing, and exhilarating."

Beich agrees: "People are experimenting now with new technologies. It will be exciting to see what comes out of those experiments," she says.

In searching for new approaches and methods for change, the experts agree that people will have to be open to many new directions rather than relying on a single strategic approach. In other words, linear thinking won't produce the results needed in today's environment.

ANOTHER LOOK: TAKING CHARGE OF CHANGE *continued*

"We are very comfortable with linear thinking, but it is not a good depiction of reality," says Regalbuto. "The development of new methodologies will probably come from systems theory. That is the only theoretical framework I know of that allows you to look at multiple influences. Success will come from our ability to hold the vision of a holistic system in our heads."

Because the pace of change is so rapid, says O'Dell, you can't stick with one specific strategy. You have to look at other options along the way and adapt them to your strategy.

"By the time you hit step two in your 10-step process," says O'Dell, "it is already irrelevant. If you could get to step 10 in the time it's taken you to get through steps one and two, you could use the old methodology successfully."

Biech sees the "popcorn approach" as the future. "That's where you have all these little explosions and popcorn lies all over the place," says Biech. "It looks messy, like people are headed in different directions. And perhaps they are until someone can figure out what the new direction needs to be. You watch which way the kernels are flying and which ones end up the best and then move toward that."

Regalbuto says that future thinking will require people to cast away the idea of focusing on an end goal. It also will require business leaders to allow employees to move in directions that may be risky. Management might not see those choices as viable, but they could chart the future direction for the rest of the organization.

"We need to admit that we don't know what the rules are going to be. We don't know the outcomes. Of course, employees need to trust that you aren't going to punish them for breaking the rules—for doing things differently. That kind of trust relationship is not common. The traditional structure of organizations fights against it."

"We need to change people's consciousness about change," says Michael Doyle. "Change is a process of going from the known to the unknown. So are the processes of learning and planning."

TAKING CHARGE

Where will HR fit in when it comes to making future changes? Will practitioners play the role of change agents, change facilitators, or change chasers?

Kiefer sees the ideal role of HR as one of helping organizations think through the human and organizational components of change and the reasons why businesses require new organizational forms.

"The HR function should not only be a voice at the table but should bring those issues up. The very best HR people are the ones who can broaden the definition of strategy to include organizational strategy," says Kiefer.

Kolodziejski doesn't believe that the title of change agent fits the future role of an HR person. "As long as we think of ourselves as change agents, if implies that we are doing something to the system. But if we engage in a process of joining—in which we really understand the business and are working with the business to accomplish objectives—we are in a better position to influence the future."

"Ideally HR's role is to be a visionary," says Seyfer. "We keep tabs on where things are going and then attempt to get the mechanisms in place to help support the vision when change comes. That's a difficult role because while we're busy getting all of the mechanisms in place to make change work, it can go right past us."

Mitchell sees HR people playing the role of conduit. "We need to be coaches and counselors to line managers as well as working with peer support groups to help drive or facilitate the changes they are about to make in organizations.

"We should be key players in looking at individuals in the organization and at the process of change itself. We need to be active in how people go about communicating the process, recognizing the need to change, and then changing."

ANOTHER LOOK *continued*

Levit warns against change agents becoming fad chasers in pursuit of quick-fix solutions. "The real issue for human resource people is deciding whether they are going to think independently, use new approaches, or just chase fads."

Regalbuto sees HR people more as change facilitators than change agents. "A change agent to me is a person who is dedicated to the end goal. Rather than heading for your anticipated end goal, you provide variety on the way so that there are multiple paths. You keep five or six streams running and make sure that new streams come along so that branching continues.

"The term change agent sounds too much like the person who is going for the end goal. A change facilitator is someone who is looking not for closings but for openings."

SURPRISES AND FAITH

How well will the HR profession perform in this more rapid, more complex, more turbulent, and more unpredictable future? The experts foresee a positive, successful future.

Kiefer believes that those who "have an abiding faith in themselves will be successful. The mark of a great sports team is how its members play when the momentum is

against them, not how they play when they are on top.

"It may be that for the next 10 years the momentum is going to be against us. But I believe that of all the surprises ahead, a wonderful consequence for the United States will be a rebirth of the spirit that pioneered the West. We didn't know where we were going, but somehow we knew it would turn out all right."

Regalbuto also agrees that faith and confidence will play a significant role in making it through the turbulence ahead. "We can't control change. That's not the issue anymore. It is managing the ride, rolling with the flow. That is very different from where we've been and not a place where we are comfortable. It involved a lot of risk.

"We used to say that successful leaders were those who did not perceive failure as failure but as an opening of other avenues. That is the mindset we need. We need to find comfort and security in knowing that if we can make it to step one and step two, then we can probably cope with the unpredictable steps ahead of us."

Levit believes HR professionals will be successful as long as they are willing to look at change with a new perspective. "The belief about change is that it's

some mysterious process that we've studied for a long time. That's not true. It is a new paradigm and if we look in new directions, solutions will appear. We have to open our perceptions to new ways of looking at things. We have to shock people out of a dogmatic slumber."

Mat Juechter, reflecting on the crystallization of contemporary change expressed in all these views, observes that "the obvious but sometimes forgotten fact is that the words *organisms* (humans) and *organizations* (all types), derive from the same root. So when we talk about organizational change, we are really talking about individual change.

"Unless that reality is acknowledged, there will be no proactive change, only reactive or crisis-driven change. What we need, therefore, are more sophisticated practices that help individuals in large numbers critically examine the reality of their present circumstances, and what is truly important to them, so they can move toward the latter with courage, conviction, and clarity. That is what creates lasting change."

SOURCE: Craig Steinburg, "Taking Charge of Change," *Training & Development*, March 1992, pp. 26–32.

▼ Another Look: Thirty Things We Know for Sure about Adult Learning

1. Adults seek out learning experiences in order to cope with specific life-change events. Marriage, divorce, a new job, a promotion, being fired, retiring, losing a loved one and moving to a new city are examples.

2. The more life-change events an adult encounters, the more likely he or she is to seek out learning opportunities. Just as stress increases as life-change events accumulate, the motivation to cope with change through engagement in a learning experience increases. Since the people who most frequently seek out learning opportunities are people who have the most years of education, it is reasonable to guess that for many of us learning is a coping response to significant change.

3. The learning experiences adults seek out on their own are directly related—at least in their own perceptions—to the life-change events that triggered the seeking. Therefore, if 80 percent of the change being encountered is work-related, then 80 percent of the learning experiences sought should be work-related.

4. Adults are generally willing to engage in learning experiences before, after or even during the actual life-change event. Once convinced that the change is a certainty, adults will engage in any learning that promises to help them cope with the transition.

5. Although adults have been found to engage in learning for a variety of reasons—job advancement, pleasure, love of learning and so on—it is equally true that for most adults learning is not its own reward. Adults who are motivated to seek out a learning experience do so primarily (80–90 percent of the time) because they have a use for the knowledge or skill being sought. Learning is a means to an end, not an end in itself.

6. Increasing or maintaining one's sense of self-esteem and pleasure are strong secondary motivators for engaging in learning experiences. Having a new skill or extending and enriching current knowledge can be both, depending on the individual's personal perceptions.

The major contributors to what we know about adult motivation to learn have been Allen Tough, Carol Aslanian and Henry Brickell, Kjell Rubenson and Harry L. Miller. One implication of their findings for the trainer is that there seem to be "teachable moments" in the lives of adults. Their existence impacts the planning and scheduling of training. As a recent study by the management development group of one large manufacturer concluded, "Newly promoted supervisors and managers must receive training as nearly concurrent with promotions and changes in responsibilities as possible. The longer such training is delayed, the less impact it appears to have on actual job performance."

CURRICULUM DESIGN

One developing research-based concept that seems likely to have an impact on our view and practice of adult training and development is the concept of "fluid" versus "crystallized" intelligence. R. B. Catell's research on lifelong intellectual development suggests there are two distinct kinds of intelligence that show distinct patterns of age-related development but function in a complementary fashion. Fluid intellect tends to be what we once called innate intelligence; fluid intelligence has to do with the ability to store strings of numbers and facts in short-term memory, react quickly, see spatial relations and do abstract reasoning. Crystallized intelligence is the part of intellectual functioning we have always taken to be a product of knowledge acquisition and experience. It is related to vocabulary, general information, conceptual knowledge,

ANOTHER LOOK *continued*

judgment and concrete reasoning.

Historically, many societies have equated youth with the ability to insatiably acquire information, and age with the ability to wisely use information. Catell's research suggests this is true—that wisdom is, in fact, a separate intellectual function that develops as we grow older. Which leads to some curriculum development implications of this two-faceted intellect concept:

7. Adult learners tend to be less interested in, and enthralled by, survey courses. They tend to prefer single-concept, single-theory courses that focus heavily on the application of the concept to relevant problems. This tendency increases with age.

8. Adults need to be able to integrate new ideas with what they already know if they are going to keep—and use—the new information.

9. Information that conflicts sharply with what is already held to be true, and thus forces a reevaluation of the old material, is integrated more slowly.

10. Information that has little "conceptual overlap" with what is already known is acquired slowly.

11. Fast-paced, complex or unusual learning tasks interfere with the learning of the concepts or data they are intended to teach or illustrate.

12. Adults tend to compensate for being slower in some psychomotor learning tasks by being more accurate and making fewer trial-and-error ventures.

13. Adults tend to take errors personally and are more likely to let them affect self-esteem. Therefore, they tend to apply tried-and-true solutions and take fewer risks. There is even evidence that adults will misinterpret feedback and "mistake" errors for positive confirmation.

Dr. K. Patricia Cross, author of *Adults As Learners,* sees four global implications for designing adult curriculum in Catell's work. "First, the presentation of new information should be meaningful, and it should include aids that help the learner organize it and relate it to previously stored information. Second, it should be presented at a pace that permits mastery. Third, presentation of one idea at a time and minimization of competing intellectual demands should aid comprehension. Finally, frequent summarization should facilitate retention and recall."

A second neat new idea that influences curriculum design is the concept of adult developmental stages. Jean Piaget, Lawrence Kohlberg and others have seen children as passing through phases and stages for some time. It is only recently, thanks to Gail Sheehy, Roger Gould, Daniel Levinson and others, that we've come to acknowledge that there are also adult growth stages. A subset of this concept is the idea that not only do adults' needs and interests continually change, but their values also continue to grow and change. For that insight, we can thank Clare W. Graves and his pioneering work in value analysis. The implications, though still formative:

14. The curriculum designer must know whether the concepts and ideas will be in concert or in conflict with learner and organizational values. As trainers at AT&T have learned, moving from a service to a sales philosophy requires more than a change in words and titles. It requires a change in the way people think and value.

15. Programs need to be designed to accept viewpoints from people in different life stages and with different value "sets."

16. A concept needs to be "anchored" or explained from more than one value set and appeal to more than one developmental life stage.

A final set of curriculum-design guides comes from the research on learning media preference.

ANOTHER LOOK: THIRTY THINGS WE KNOW FOR SURE ABOUT ADULT LEARNING *continued*

Researchers have for years been asking students if they preferred learning XYZ from a book, a movie, an experience or another person. Though there are limitations to the value of this sort of data, enough of it is accumulating to be of some help to the design effort.

17. Adults prefer self-directed and self-designed learning projects 7 to 1 over group-learning experiences led by a professional. Furthermore, the adult learner often selects more than one medium for the design. Reading and talking to a qualified peer are frequently cited as good resources. The desire to control pace and start/stop time strongly affects the self-directed preference.

18. Non-human media such as books, programmed instruction and television have become popular in recent years. One piece of research found them very influential in the way adults plan self-directed learning projects.

19. Regardless of media, straightforward how-to is the preferred content orientation. As many as 80 percent of the polled adults in one study cited the need for applications and how-to information as the primary motivation for undertaking a learning project.

20. Self-direction does *not* mean isolation. In fact, studies of self-directed learning show self-directed projects involve an average of 10 other people as resources, guides, encouragers and the like. The incompetence or inadequacy of these same people is often rated as a primary frustration. But even for the self-professed, self-directed learner, lectures and short seminars get positive ratings, especially when these events give the learner face-to-face, one-to-one access to an expert.

Apparently, the adult learner is a very efficiency-minded individual. Allen Tough suggests that the typical adult learner asks "What is the cheapest, easiest, fastest way for me to learn to do *that?*" and then proceeds independently along this self-determined route. An obvious tip for the trainer is that the adult trainee has to have a hand in shaping the curriculum of the program.

IN THE CLASSROOM

We seem to know the least about helping the adult maximize the classroom experience. There are master performers in our trade who gladly pass along their favorite tips and tricks, but as Marshall McLuhan observed, "We don't know who discovered water but we can be pretty sure it wasn't a fish." In other words, the master performer is often a poor judge of how one becomes a master performer. There certainly are volumes of opinion and suggestion, but by and large they rest more on theory than hard data. Ironically, some of the strongest data comes from survey studies of what turns off adults in the classroom. Likewise, there is a nicely developing body of literature on what makes for good and bad meetings that has implications for training:

21. The learning environment must by physically and psychologically comfortable. Adults report that long lectures, periods of interminable sitting and the absence of practice opportunities are high on the irritation scale.

22. Adults have something real to lose in a classroom situation. Self-esteem and ego are on the line when they are asked to risk trying a new behavior in front of peers and cohorts. Bad experiences in traditional education, feelings about authority and the preoccupation with events outside the classroom all affect in-class experience. These and other influencing factors are carried into class with the learners as surely as are their gold Cross pens and lined yellow pads.

23. Adults have expectations, and it is critical to

ANOTHER LOOK *continued*

take time up front to clarify and articulate *all* expectations before getting into content. Both trainees and the instructor/facilitator need to state their expectations. When they are at variance, the problem should be acknowledged and a resolution negotiated. In any case, the instructor can assume responsibility only for his or her own expectations, not for those of trainees.

24. Adults bring a great deal of life experience into the classroom, an invaluable asset to be acknowledged, tapped and used. Adults can learn well—and much—from dialogue with respected peers.

25. Instructors who have a tendency to hold forth rather than facilitate can hold that tendency in check—or compensate for it—by concentrating on the use of open-ended questions to draw out relevant trainee knowledge and experience.

26. New knowledge has to be integrated with previous knowledge; that means active learner participation. Since only the learners can tell us how the new fits or fails to fit with the old, we have to ask them. Just as the learner is dependent

on us for confirming feedback on skill practice, we are dependent on the learner for feedback about our curriculum and in-class performance.

27. The key to the instructor role is control. The instructor must balance the presentation of new material, debate and discussion, sharing of relevant trainee experiences and the clock. Ironically, we seem best able to establish control when we risk giving it up. When we shelve our egos and stifle the tendency to be threatened by challenge to our plans and methods, we gain the kind of facilitative control we seem to need to effect adult learning.

28. The instructor has to protect minority opinion, keep disagreements civil and unheated, make connections between various opinions and ideas, and keep reminding the group of the variety of potential solutions to the problem. Just as in a good problem-solving meeting, the instructor is less advocate than orchestrator.

29. Integration of new knowledge and skill requires transition time and focused effort. Working on applications to specific back-on-the-job problems helps with

the transfer. Action plans, accountability strategies and follow-up after training all increase the likelihood of that transfer. Involving the trainees' supervisor in pre- and post-course activities helps with both in-class focus and transfer.

30. Learning and teaching theories function better as a resource than as a Rosetta stone. The four currently influential theories—humanistic, behavioral, cognitive and developmental—all offer valuable guidance when matched with an appropriate learning task. A skill-training task can draw much from the behavioral approach, for example, while personal growth-centered subjects seem to draw gainfully from humanistic concepts. The trainer of adults needs to take an eclectic rather than a single theory-based approach to developing strategies and procedures.

SOURCE: Ron Zemke and Susan Zemke, "Thirty Things We Know for Sure about Adult Learning," *Training* (July 1988), pp. 57–61. Reprinted with permission from the June 1981 issue of *Training: The Magazine of Human Resources Development.* Copyright 1981, Lakewood Publications Inc., Minneapolis, MN (612) 333-0471. All rights reserved.

▼ A CASE IN POINT: MONOTONY REDUCTION IN WORK ASSIGNMENTS

Most employees need some variation in their job assignments. They tend to get bored with the same day-to-day routine. Companies that ignore this need risk losing their employees.

For example, a computer department of one company hired programmers to work on three distinct projects. Each project required specialized training, but many of the programmers' skills were transferable across project lines. Several of the programmers expressed interest in transferring to one of the other projects to broaden their experience. But the supervisors refused to let them go, saying they could not afford to let the programmers off their current projects. In addition, when new job openings appeared on projects, the company filled them with people from the outside, never by advertising them to people on other projects. Despite management's value of developing people, the reality was that once assigned to a project, the employee was stuck. Turnover skyrocketed among programmers who felt they had to go to another company to broaden their experiences.

The programmers' situation is contrasted with an example of a sales manager in the same company who kept a careful record of the career development of her people. She established a system for tracking the job assignments of each person in her department. By doing so, she could easily spot which people might need new assignments to round out their skills and break the monotony. She actively developed her people by trading them in and out of different assignments and even transferring them to other departments to broaden their experience.

QUESTIONS

1. Based on the information presented in this chapter, why does the sales manager's approach make more sense?
2. How would you discover the underlying development problems illustrated in this case?

▼ A CASE IN POINT: EAGER MIKE McHUGH

One Monday morning Mike McHugh, a recent college graduate, walked into the sales office as a new sales trainee. Ron Noel, the zone sales manager for a business machines company, was there to greet him. Noel's area covered three counties, and ten sales representatives reported to him. The large volume of sales in his area was attributed to recent population growth; industries were finding this section of the state very attractive.

Noel has collected several sales reports, catalogs, and pamphlets describing in detail the types of office equipment sold by the company. After a pleasant chat, he gave McHugh the collected material and showed him his assigned desk. Soon afterward, Noel excused himself and did not return. McHugh spent the day reading over the material, and at five o'clock he went home. This was the entire "training program."

QUESTIONS

1. What can be said about Noel's training program?
2. In light of the information presented in the chapter about training, education, and development, does McHugh really need any more training than he received from Noel?
3. If you would suggest more training, what types of training would you suggest? What approach do you think would be most effective?

SOURCE: Jack Halloran/George L. Frunzi, Supervision: *The Art of Management,* 2d ed. (Englewood Cliffs, N.J.: Prentice-Hall, 1986), p. 275. © 1986. Adapted by permission of Prentice-Hall Inc., Englewood Cliffs, N.J.

PERSONAL VALUES, CAREER PLANNING, AND SUCCESS WITH PEOPLE AT WORK

This chapter answers several all-important questions:

- What are the four key components of career planning?

- How can goal planning be kept realistic?

- What are some broad questions to ask yourself in regard to career planning?

- Where can you look for occupational information useful in career planning?

- What is value clarification, and how can it help you develop a good career plan?

- What do organizations expect from their managers?

- What can managers reasonably expect from their companies?

- Why is the clarification of expectations an important step to becoming successful?

- How can you become an effective subordinate by managing your manager?

- How can you better manage yourself, your time, and your tasks?

The answers to these and other questions are coming up next in chapter 19....

CHAPTER 19

If you've read this entire book so far, you will recognize that getting meaningful work accomplished through the efforts of others is a complex business. We hope you now better understand more about human relationships and their effects on people at work.

Managerial leadership is not a job designed for everyone. Directing the work efforts of other employees can be frustrating and difficult. Nevertheless, people feel a great sense of satisfaction when they accomplish organizational work in the spirit of cooperation and teamwork.

There are all kinds of managers: some are highly successful, some are dismal failures, and most are somewhere in between. Since you have had the good sense to select our book as a guide to your study of human relations, we assume that you are a person of discriminating taste and impeccable judgment. You, we suspect, will be satisfied with nothing less than becoming highly successful!

A few key ideas can help you achieve this, and we'll share them with you in the following pages. These ideas are based on our studies of highly successful managers whom we've worked with and observed over the past twenty-five years or so. The highly successful manager has learned to manage his or her career. That manager has learned to do the following:

- Develop clear career plans
- Clarify expectations on the job
- Manage not only subordinates but also bosses
- Manage himself or herself

▼ KEY IDEA 1: CAREER PLANNING

- Having clear, appropriate goals is a prerequisite for job success.

Knowing where you're going, or at least having a pretty good idea of where you'd like to be, puts you way ahead of most people. Most people spend more time planning their annual two-week vacations than they do planning their careers.

Career planning is particularly important because it leads to goal-directed behaviors. In other words, the more conscious one is of one's own goals, the more direct and efficient the pursuit of those goals will be. We have used the terms *goals* and *goal direction* many times in this book. Having clear objectives is a prerequisite to success in most careers. But for goals to effectively guide one, they must also mesh with one's self-appraisal and with the realities of the management job one seeks.

- Career planning has four components:
  Goal selection
  Self-evaluation
  Vision
  Occupational
    information

Career planning has four components: *goals, self-evaluation, vision,* and *occupational information* (see figure 19.1). To develop an effective career plan for yourself, all four elements must be considered very carefully. To set personal goals without considering the nature of the job market or, for that matter, the nature of one's own personality can lead to considerable frustration and disappointment.

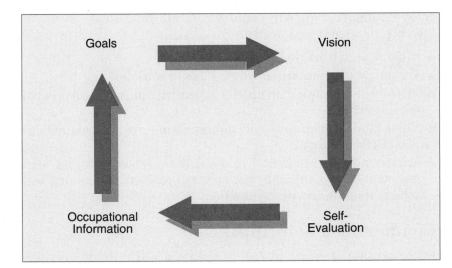

FIGURE **19.1**
Four key components of
career planning.

Developing Personal Goals:
Start with a Dream List

For many people, writing down specific goals is an unfamiliar
process. Yet without tangible objectives, keeping direction in one's
life can be difficult. What do you really want to get out of life?

Goals should be based on what is realistically attainable. But
before we focus on those realistic goals, it can be fun—and useful—
to do some personal brainstorming. Take a piece of paper and write
down virtually *everything you ever* want to accomplish, be, or have.
Typically, people begin by listing such things as a new Mercedes, a
yacht, a few million dollars, and some other tangible items. But keep
writing far beyond that. Try filling up several sheets of paper with
lists of all kinds of things you would like to accomplish or have in
your life. Be sure to include the intangible also: such things as har-
monious family relationships, sense of satisfaction at work, spiritu-
ality, the esteem of others, and so forth. Keep on writing until you
can think of nothing more to put down. Don't be overly critical at
this point—write it *all* down.

If you are like most people, you will find that some conflicts exist
among the goals you have listed. Frequently, people say that they
would like to be major corporate executives, yet somewhere else on
their goal "dream lists" they speak of spending a great deal of time
with their families. Likewise, some people want to be rich and
famous but also seek quiet and privacy.

Obviously, reality poses some limitations on our dream lists. By
listing all of these things, however, one can begin to recognize
where potential conflicts among different objectives emerge. Then
the process becomes one of selecting objectives that have the highest
priority.

As you review your dream list, consider which goals are related to
your career. If you are like most people, you will have many career

■ Personal
brainstorming can
help sort out goals.

■ Career planning starts
with some key
questions.

goals—although some will conflict with others. To help focus further, ask yourself these questions:

- What type of work do I prefer?
- What type of organization would I like to work for?
- What type of position do I prefer (research, line, staff, governmental, industrial)?
- What kind of monetary and noneconomic reward balance do I want from working?
- What kinds of things do I find particularly satisfying in work (accomplishing a difficult task, solving problems, interacting with others, creating something new)?

Conducting a Self-Appraisal

In the process of career planning, one must reflect in considerable depth. Some of the broad questions we posed in the preceding paragraphs can also provide some insights into what you would like to get out of your life. But self-evaluation goes even further than that.

■ One's personal values justify the goals and objectives one sets.

A critical activity for people is to identify and clarify in some way their personal *values.* A personal *value* can be defined as an idea of something that is intrinsically (in and of itself) desirable to you. Values, once clarified and accepted as your own, provide the justification for the goals and objectives you set.

What people say they value most can be divided into eight broad categories (although exceptions could be made to these):

1. Career success (achievement and satisfaction on the job)
2. Family
3. Social life
4. Health and vigor
5. Financial stability or independence
6. Leisure (a comfortable life)
7. Spiritual development
8. Personal development (mental ability, physical skills, and so on)

■ Value clarification is not an easy process.

The process of identifying basic values is not an easy one. Many people feel frustrated when asked to identify core values. In part, this may be because we typically experience value conflicts—our behaviors do not always jibe with what we say we value. Many people say their families are of the greatest importance to them, yet research has shown that fathers spend only about seven minutes a week talking, one-on-one, with each child in their family. Likewise, our relationships with our spouses may be highly valued, yet studies show that the average couple spends only twenty minutes a week with each other, alone, communicating.

Value conflicts are normal. Yet the people who enjoy the greatest life satisfaction work constantly to bring their behaviors into line with their values. The goal-setting process we discussed earlier gains impact when we include value clarifying, too. If you were to spend a few hours carefully defining and describing your core values, you could return to the brainstormed list of goals and sort them out quickly. If, for example, you determine that health and vigor is a *major* value for you, you may decide that the goal of being a top executive in a pressure-packed, stressful industry may *not* be all that is desirable for you.

Just how important is value clarification? In their best-selling book *In Search of Excellence,* Tom Peters and Robert Waterman devote considerable space to describing or illustrating how values affect the "excellent" companies they studied. The points they make about organizational values can readily be applied to personal values. At one point, they summarize:

> Let us suppose that we were asked for one all-purpose bit of advice for management, one truth that we were able to distill from the excellent companies researched. We might be tempted to reply, "Figure out your value system. Decide what your company *stands for.* What does your enterprise do that gives everyone the most pride? Put yourself out ten or twenty years in the future: What would you look back on with the greatest satisfaction?[1]

In the book *Successful Self-Management,* Paul Timm recommends a three-step process for value clarifying:

1. *Name the value.* Call it whatever you like; for example, *financial security, family solidarity, professional excellence, freedom.*

   ■ A three-step process for value clarification.

2. *Describe what that value means to you.* Write this description in the present tense as if you have already achieved it. For example, the value you call physical fitness may be described this way: "I jog one thousand miles a year. I play golf at least twice a month. I feel good and maintain appropriate weight and blood cholesterol level. I get enough sleep and do not let stress grind me down. I am generally optimistic. I am active in many sports." Even if you don't yet accomplish all these things, write them in the present tense. They then become *affirmations*—statements of where you are going.

3. *Write out the value-aligning activities or goals needed to become congruent with your value.* If you see jogging twelve hundred miles a year as a definition of physical fitness, a value-aligning activity will be to jog one hundred miles a month, or an average of twenty-five miles a week. If financial freedom is a value, your value-aligning activities may include a plan for getting out of debt.[2]

The process of value clarification is a powerful one and should be taken seriously. When we take the time and effort to do this, we begin the process of creating a vision.

Creating a Vision

Successful managers and leaders focus their thinking and their people on worthy goals for the future. A vision, in its simplest form, is a view of the future. While the definition is simple, the concept is profound. Wise people have known about the power of the mind—the power of thought—since ancient times. The prophet and teacher Solomon said, "Without a vision, the people perish!" In his book *The Greatest Secret in the World,* Og Mandino said the "greatest secret" is that "we become what we think about most of the time."[3]

Researchers know that vision is a key ingredient in most success recipes. In their extensive study of leadership strategies, Warren Bennis and Burt Nanus found vision to be the first key element associated with the success of the leaders they interviewed.[4]

Vision gives a sense of direction to individuals and to organizations. In turn, it can be formalized in written plans or *mission statements,* which are statements that explain the purpose for which, or reason, an organization exists.

Gathering Occupational Information

■ Where can one find career-planning information?

The fourth side of the career-planning square we have described deals with gathering information about possible opportunities. Many good books are available on career planning that may suggest to you some areas for employment that you had not previously considered.

■ Some people are likely to end up in careers that don't even exist yet.

Become aware of as many possible alternatives as you can. Many people end up in careers they never considered initially. In fact, many attractive careers didn't even exist a few years ago. Rapidly developing technology, as well as specialization within professional fields, have created new and frequently attractive opportunities. Keep abreast of changes and new opportunities by being professionally alert. If your field is business management, read the business magazines and newspapers regularly.

If you're not certain about what field you'd like to work in, spend a few hours in a good university library reading professional magazines from a wide variety of areas. Look for the specialty magazines, such as *Advertising Age* and *Sales and Marketing Management,* as well as publications in engineering, electronics, retailing, and the like.

Keep your mind open, your ear to the ground, your shoulder to the wheel, and your nose to the grindstone. (Do all this, and you'll be a great contortionist!) But seriously, and old clichés aside, it does make sense to be open to a wide variety of career possibilities.

▼ KEY IDEA 2: CLARIFYING EXPECTATIONS

■ Why is clarifying expectations so important?

One theme of this book is the importance of creating better understanding among people by clarifying expectations. Theory X managers miss many opportunities to help subordinates grow because of their unclarified and generally pessimistic expectations of others. Likewise, communicators or motivators who fail to clarify what arouses interest in others operate in a hit-and-miss fashion. The result frequently is wheel spinning and unproductive management.

Successful managers spend time and effort in clarifying what is expected of them as well as what is expected of the organization.

What Organizations Expect of Management Employees

Typically, when people begin new jobs, some uncertainties are involved. The level of uncertainty is especially high for the recent graduate who is going into his or her first full-time employment. Both the new employee and the organization must first come to agreement about what each expects from the other. Typically, companies expect the following kinds of things from their management employees.

REPRESENTATION OF THE COMPANY

Management employees at all levels, be they first-line supervisors or top-level executives, are expected to represent their company on and off the job. We all represent the organizations to which we belong. The people we meet socially, in community activities, as neighbors, or within the scope of our business dealings develop an impression of our company based on our behavior. If we come across as being shifty or suspicious, others may well question the ethics of our corporation. If we are aboveboard, honest, optimistic, and direct about our organization, we reflect a more positive image in the eyes of our friends and neighbors.

Even minor conflicts of interest or seemingly inconsistent behavior can hurt the organization. A few years ago, Lee Iacocca, as head of Chrysler Corporation, was aggressively selling people on the need to buy American automobiles while publicly expressing his preference for Cuban cigars. The contradiction was not lost on one U.S. tobacco manufacturer, who complained in a letter to a national news magazine.

More recently, President George Bush was pictured fishing from a boat powered by a Yamaha outboard. A little thing? Perhaps. But with the increasing competition with Japan, it sent a mixed message.

Managers expect their people to behave in ways that reflect positively on the company. They expect people to avoid activities or behaviors that might compromise or embarrass the organization in the eyes of the public. Although public relations (PR) is often a specialized function within an organization, in a very real sense, all employees are involved in PR. The public judges a company by the people it keeps.

■ The public judges a company by the people it keeps.

A DESIRE FOR SUCCESS

Companies expect their employees to truly want to be successful. Few organizations want to hire people who have negative self-images or severe reservations as to what they can accomplish. Companies who recruit new employees all want to recruit winners. They typically look for people with proven track records. However, past successes are not enough. The ongoing desire to be successful within the organization is a very positive characteristics.

We once had lunch with a highly successful young executive who had formed a small conglomerate with his two brothers. Their growth rate had been highly impressive—all three had become self-made millionaires while still in their twenties. In our conversation, this individual identified his desire to be successful as a key to their organization's growth. All three brothers sincerely wanted their organization to be successful. There was no questioning of each other's desire. Each knew that the other two were working just as hard as he to make the corporation go. Organizational success was the first priority. In fact, this businessman made the point that if he were suddenly given three hundred dollars for some advice or service, he would immediately, and without hesitation, give each of his brothers one hundred dollars. An "all for one and one for all" philosophy guided their business decisions.

A tightly knit family corporation is fairly unique, but the point here is that these men had a true desire to succeed *as an organization,* not just as individuals. This is one key to becoming a highly successful manager.

■ Companies want managers who want to succeed as an organization.

A PROFESSIONAL BUSINESS APPEARANCE

Corporations expect their employees to dress and groom themselves in a way that reflects positively on the company. Many major corporations require men and women to wear business suits and to avoid grooming habits that are too far out of the mainstream of society. Although "dressing for success" may not be stressed too heavily in some companies, few organizations would be satisfied with management representatives who are excessively sloppy or poorly groomed.

The key word here is *appropriateness.* In some organizations and in some industries, casual dress is normal and accepted. Top male executives in the building materials business in Florida wear casual slacks and knit shirts for example.

In rural Saskatchewan or Montana, in Boston, in San Francisco, in Toronto, footwear, outerwear, and accessories are as local as the dialect.

In his series of books on dressing for success, John T. Molloy asserts that people will have a better chance to do a better job at a

SOURCE: "Miss Peach" by Mell Lazarus. 1990 Mell Lazarus.

higher salary if they learn to use clothing as a business tool, beginning with the initial job interview.[5] One should not believe, however, that dress alone can overshadow the importance of proper education and personal development. We would never think to suggest that dress alone could, as Molloy states, "put a boob in the board room," but, as Molloy concludes, "incorrect dress can definitely keep an intelligent, able man out." Such guidelines as to what is appropriate business appearance should be regarded as just that: *guidelines.* People don't need to look like clones.

■ "Dress-for-success" advocates see clothing as a business tool.

TIME SPENT ON THE JOB

Most companies expect their employees to spend a certain amount of time on the job each day. Normally, workers are expected at work at a certain time, and they are also expected to remain there until quitting time. Employees who habitually show up late for work or leave early create the impression of doing less than their fair share. This negative impression may be difficult to overcome, even if the employee is quite successful. Some individuals in sales, for example, accomplish a great deal of work in a short period of time. They meet their company objectives while only working a few hours a day in active sales. Nevertheless, they are regarded with some suspicion. The question is, "If they can attain company objectives working half a day, how much could they do if they worked a full eight-hour day?"

■ People who work short hours are seen as doing less than their share.

The old adage of "An honest day's work for an honest day's pay" still makes sense to most employers. Highly successful managers are typically generous with the time and effort they give to the organization. Clockwatchers seldom succeed.

SOME CREATIVITY

Most organizations expect their management employees to be creative. Creativity here does not necessarily mean coming up with a brand-new concept or idea that changes the entire direction of the corporation. It can, however, mean using ingenuity and initiative to do work in different, more productive, or more effective ways. We have talked throughout this book about the importance of motivating employees to participate in the creative process of doing the work of the organization more effectively. Good managers use creativity. They are not bound to "the way we've always done it" but constantly look for a better way, a more creative way of accomplishing the organization's work.

■ Managers are expected to be somewhat creative in solving organizational problems.

A LONG-TERM COMMITMENT

Perhaps one of the most frustrating experiences for a company is to recruit and hire a potentially valuable team member, only to have that person quit after a few months on the job. Recruiting, training and employee development are costly processes for most organizations. Few employees carry their own weight immediately on joining an organization. The training period costs the company far more than the immediate return that those employees can make to the organization's profitability.

■ Managers should make a long-term commitment to their organizations.

Organizations often spend forty thousand, fifty thousand, or even one hundred thousand dollars on extensive training of employees. Training is very expensive. Ethically, employees are bound to stay with a company at least until they are contributing members of the organization. Don't take a job with a company if you don't intend to give it your best shot for a reasonable period of time.

CUSTOMER SERVICE[6]

Regardless of your job title, position in an organization, or experience, *your number-one task* will *always* be to attract, satisfy, and preserve "customers." And *everyone has customers.*

For many of us, these are easy to identify. They buy something from us. But some people will say, "I don't work directly with customers." Before you accept this idea, take a closer look at just who exactly your customers are.

In organizations, customers take two forms, *internal* and *external.* *Internal* customers are those people, departments, or organizations served by what we do. The only person who might have no internal customers is the individual who works completely alone. For the rest of us, internal customers are a fact of life.

For example, a word processing clerk or copy center worker within a company serves other workers' document-handling needs. A personnel office worker serves employees' needs for benefits information, management's needs for staffing, and company legal people's needs for handling various government paperwork requirements.

As individuals, we all have at least one internal customer: our boss; as managers, we also have internal customers in the form of the people we supervise. They rely on us to meet their needs.

External customers are those people or departments who are the end users of our organization's product or services. This is, of course, the traditional use of the term *customer.*

Arguably, the key to your success is your ability to meet and exceed customer expectations.

What Companies Do Not Expect from a New Manager

■ New employees are not expected to know it all.

Organizations *do not* expect a new employee to know it all. Clearly, new employees do not have a basis for making all the right decisions and performing all the right actions. This is why expensive employee development programs are provided in all major organizations.

By the same token, new employees are not typically expected to produce immediate or profitable results for the company. As we've said, most organizations take a loss in productivity initially on hiring new employees. They hope to regain that initial loss by developing productive contributors to the organization as time goes on, but immediate results are seldom expected.

Having a realistic understanding of these expectations up-front can help avoid problems later. You must also have a realistic picture of what you as an employee can expect from your company.

What Management Employees Can Expect from the Company

Clarifying expectations is a two-way street. Not only must employees understand what is expected of them, but the organization's leaders must understand what employees normally expect from the company. Basic obligations to employees normally include the following.

OPENNESS AND HONESTY IN THE RECRUITING PROCESS

Organizations have an obligation to tell potential employees what the company is all about. The individual being recruited should have an understanding of the company's management philosophy and the nature of the products or services provided by the company, as well as clear statements about what the company expects from its employees. Getting this information during the recruiting process should be the responsibility of both the applicant, who should seek it out, and the potential employers, who should readily provide it.

■ Companies should give applicants a clear picture of the organization before hiring them.

APPROPRIATE AND ADEQUATE TRAINING

Organizations need to provide both their new employees and current employees with the training necessary for them to skillfully complete the tasks to which they've been assigned. Training is not and should not be regarded as a fringe benefit; it is at the heart of the managerial process.

■ Training is at the heart of the management process.

REASONABLE COMPENSATION AND BENEFITS

Organizations have an obligation to provide fair and equitable compensation, as well as reasonable benefit plans.

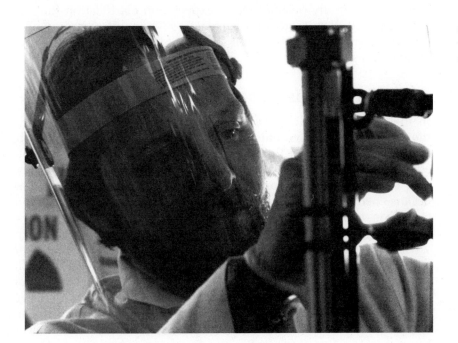

Organizations must provide training to their employees.

■ Employees have a
right to know how
they are doing.

PERFORMANCE REVIEWS AND PERIODIC RAISES

In addition to receiving pay and benefits, employees have a right to
know how well they are doing. The performance review, discussed
earlier as a motivational technique, is widely expected in industry.
People who perform well also expect to receive additional compensation. An individual who produces more is worth more to the organization and therefore should be paid more.

A GOOD WORKING ENVIRONMENT

Corporations have an obligation to provide a safe, healthy, and reasonably pleasant working environment for their employees. Although some tasks must be performed under less-than-desirable conditions, employees who do difficult, dangerous, or unpleasant work
should receive additional compensation.

▼ KEY IDEA 3: MANAGING YOUR BOSS

Nearly everybody has a boss. People at all levels in the organization
report to someone else; even the top executive reports to stockholders and the public. Yet, from university classroom lectures to the
slick paperbacks we find in bookstores, people have focused on how
to develop your "management style" by successfully directing those
beneath you. Little attention has been paid to the other side of the
issue: establishing your career based on your ability to manage *those
who formally manage you.*

Norman C. Hill and Paul H. Thompson wrote an article entitled
"Managing Your Manager: The Effective Subordinate." In it, they
suggested a number of ideas that can be useful as we try to become
highly successful managers.

Building initially on the idea of expectation clarification that we
have already discussed, they suggest some specific areas where
understandings need to be established. We've paraphrased a number
of their ideas in this section.[7]

■ Little attention has
been paid to the
important art of man-
aging your manager.

Resolving Key Issues

In the traditional role, bosses give orders and subordinates carry
them out. Many individuals expect the manager to define the job,
make assignments, and then check to see that the work is completed. When the boss doesn't behave in this manner, frustration arises.
The worker becomes confused. This confusion usually arises
because people have different expectations about job roles that lead
to tension, conflict, missed deadlines, and turnover.

One way to avoid some of these kinds of problems is to sit down
with your boss and talk things out. One successful manager
described doing this: "Whenever I get a new boss, I sit down with
him and ask him to make his expectations explicit. We try to list not
my job activities, but the main purposes of my job. To do that, we
continue each statement of activity with 'in order to …' and try to
complete the sentence. By recording my job purposes, we get a clear

■ Sit down with your
boss and talk things
out.

picture of what I should be accomplishing; and that's what counts—results."

This approach works very well for the individual, but most bosses are not able (or willing) to be nearly that clear about their expectations. In most cases, communication between superiors and subordinates is an ongoing process. Most issues are not resolved in a one-shot conversation.

You can excel in your organization by taking the initiative to resolve certain issues with your boss directly. This will be an ongoing process. The kinds of things that need to be discussed include (1) the content of your job, (2) the degree to which you should take initiative on your job, (3) how to keep the boss informed, and (4) how to ask for help.

■ Repeated conversations are often required.

CLARIFYING JOB CONTENT

Reach an agreement on your responsibilities. Having a clearly written job description is more useful in some companies than in others. If, for example, your company is experiencing unusual growth or a rapidly changing environment, job descriptions may be less useful. In other words, people need to be able to react to changes and be flexible.

■ Job descriptions often need to be flexible.

TAKING INITIATIVE

One manager describes a good subordinate as one who "thinks of the things I would do before I do them. What this means is that he or she tries to adopt my perspective and look at things from my position in the organization."

Some employees think that just reporting back their efforts, even though those efforts may not have succeeded, is enough. But good intentions are no substitute for what the boss needs. The message in this is that individuals need to take initiative on the job. But the degree of initiative taken needs to be talked out with your boss. Some bosses may be threatened by subordinates who anticipate their desires; others welcome the enterprise of such employees.

■ Just reporting back may not be enough.

KEEPING THE BOSS INFORMED

Keeping the boss informed is closely tied to taking initiative, but some aspects deserve separate consideration. Subordinates need to learn how to keep the boss advised on *appropriate* matters. But don't overdo it and report everything. One rule of thumb is to let the boss know about the *progress* being made on a particular project and to avoid reporting all the *activities* engaged in to achieve those results.

Managers need to have negative information as well as positive. Subordinates often like to "cover their tracks." To be a successful manager, don't hesitate to bring *needed* negative and positive information to your boss.

■ Don't overdo your reporting to the boss; report progress, not activities.

■ Tell the boss the bad news, too—when he or she needs to know.

ASKING FOR HELP

Some bosses want to be deeply involved in a project, and they use requests for help as an opportunity to teach their subordinates.

Others only want to see the final product and do not want to be bothered with frequent questions.

A bank manager presented his views on the issue: "Some subordinates will take an assignment, work as hard on it as possible, then come back to you when they get stuck or when it is completed. Other people start coming back to you to do their work for them. People in the second group don't do very well in our bank."

Asking for help too often can undermine the boss's confidence in you. When you're stuck, seek out the help of more experienced people on your own level first.

Also consider the amount of risk involved in a situation. A promising young accountant described his strategy on seeking advice from the boss: "My boss had high expectations from me when he hired me, and I believe I have lived up to them. To ensure that I would perform successfully, I adopted a strategy of taking risks—not gambles, but calculated risks. If a decision involved a high level of risk, I would consult with my boss. However, if a job was not overly risky or of crucial importance, I would do as much of it on my own as I could and not waste my boss's time with the details. I assumed it was important to look out for my boss's welfare, not just my own. If I could make him look good or make his job easier and less time-consuming, then it would benefit me as well. However, when I made a decision that turned out to be a mistake, I told my boss about it and didn't try to cover my errors."

This suggests some important guidelines for deciding when to go to the boss for help and when to handle a situation alone:

- Take risks, not gambles (and recognize the differences between the two).
- Handle the details, but keep the manager informed.
- Check with the boss on decisions that will affect work units outside the department.
- Give the boss a recommendation each time he or she asks for an analysis of a project.
- Ask for an appointment only when you are prepared to suggest some action that should be taken.

Developing Trust with the Boss

Four conditions are necessary for subordinate-superior trust to develop: accessibility, availability, predictability, and loyalty. Let's look at each briefly.

ACCESSIBILITY
An accessible person takes in ideas easily and gives them out freely. If two people are going to develop a productive relationship, they must respect each other's ideas and give those ideas careful thought and consideration. A subordinate who does not respect the boss's ideas will never be trusted and will not obtain needed help to develop his or her own ideas. You don't have to agree, just be respectful of each other's point of view.

(margin notes) ■ Asking for help too often can undermine your boss's confidence in you. ■ Guidelines for when to go to the boss for help. ■ Four conditions for trust are as follows: Accessibility Availability Predictability Loyalty

AVAILABILITY

The subordinate should be attentive and available physically, mentally, and emotionally when the manager is under pressure and needs support.

Don't become upset because the help you may need from the boss is not immediately there. Instead, take an attitude such as the following: "I know you're under a lot of pressure right now trying to complete high-priority projects. This project I'm working on is less important, so I am quite willing to let it wait for a while. In addition, if I can be of help on any of your projects, just let me know. I'm willing to pitch in and help in any way I can."

PREDICTABILITY

Predictability means the handling of delicate administrative circumstances with good judgment and thoroughness. If subordinates have been given appropriate assignments—ones that allow them to develop their personal skills—they will acquire the ability to handle even sensitive situations. However, if a subordinate lacks sensitivity or interpersonal skills and jeopardizes relationships with customers, in the future this subordinate will not be trusted and thus will be of much less value to the boss.

Predictability also means reliability in reaching important deadlines and doing work of high quality. Managers don't like to be let down. Surprises or failures to meet deadlines embarrass them, make them look bad, and do not help build manager-subordinate trust.

■ Embarrassing surprises do not help build trust.

LOYALTY

Personal loyalty to one's boss and to one's subordinate is important. A manager is not likely to trust a subordinate with important information if he or she fears that the information might be used to further the subordinate's own interests at the manager's expense.

But loyalty must also be considered in a broader context. Sometimes loyalty to an immediate supervisor conflicts with loyalty to the organization or to society. What is good for the boss is not always good for the organization and vice versa. When such potential conflicts arise, your personal ethics enter in. One highly regarded middle manager described his strategy: "I'm not a 'yes' man. I know the importance of speaking up and saying what's on my mind. I also know that other people in the organization may have a better perspective than I do. So I follow this rule of thumb: I argue forcefully *one* time for my position. If my boss then does not accept my recommendation, I try to make his decision an effective one through my support and commitment. That is, of course, unless I feel a conflict with my personal values."

■ Loyalty does not mean always saying yes.

Once again, we suggest being up-front with managers. The relationship between two individuals in a superior-subordinate relationship is critical, and mutual expectations must be achieved if the individual is to become a valued subordinate. Herein lies the key to becoming a highly successful manager.

To recap some key thoughts, certain issues should be evident to any worker, regardless of organizational level:

- Very few bosses will do all that is necessary to clarify expectations in a superior-subordinate relationship.
- Most managers will respond favorably to a discussion of the manager-subordinate relationship. However, managers have varying styles, so an individual is well-advised to find out how the boss is *likely* to respond.

▼ KEY IDEA 4: MANAGING YOURSELF

Ultimately, success is a "do-it-yourself" project.

We have talked about the importance of clarifying expectations, creating your personal vision, and finding career-planning information. All of these actions will help you decide what kind of organization—if any—you would best work in.

Regardless of where you work, *how* you work is equally important. And of all the resources you work with, *time* is your most valuable.

Identifying Time-Saving Techniques

■ Leaders pay lip service to time management but fail to help others be productive with time.

It's ironic that some managers pay lip service to time management (after all, "time is money," they are quick to say) but fail to help subordinates be productive with their time. Indeed, the manager may be the employees' worst enemy when it comes to using time.

R. Alec Mackenzie begins his book *The Time Trap* by identifying examples of a few exceptional people who have used time-saving techniques well. Among them, he cites the following:

- A company leader who cut his staff meetings in half and began sticking to an agenda. Immediately, the participants began to accomplish better results in less time.
- An Eastern school superintendent [who] discourages reverse delegation. When someone sends in a problem he thinks should have been handled at a lower level, he returns it with a note asking, "Why are you sending this to me?" If he allows himself to get involved in the daily decisions, he won't have time to manage.
- A Dutch manager [who] does not say yes when his subordinates call to ask if they can come in with a problem. After determining … the problem is not an emergency, he says, "Give me ten minutes (or whatever time he needs) to complete the task I am doing. Then I will come to your office." This saves times, he says, because if he sits down in his own office, the *visitor* is [in] control. If he goes to the subordinate's office, he says, "I'm in control because I can leave at my time."
- Another businessman [who] got tired of a caller who wasted his time on the telephone. One call came at a particularly bad moment. The manager hung up on *himself.* Of course, the caller

assumed the fault was the phone company's—no one would ever think a person would do that to himself.[8]

Supervisors can and should develop time-saving techniques that show others they value time. We need to be *constantly jealous* of our time as well as our subordinates' and co-workers' time. Consistent awareness of time doesn't mean you become a slave to the clock. Quite the contrary. It means you more productively use your time so that you can have more leisure as well as better results.

Working with people can be particularly time-consuming. And working with people is a central task of managers. People are time consumers. And most people are time wasters—to some extent. We need to develop a sensitivity to others that tells us when to spend more time with people and when to cut back.

■ We need to be constantly jealous of our own and others' time.

Time and Task Management Tools and Skills[9]

The best tool for making the most of your time is a planner system. Bookstores and office supply stores are well stocked with a wide variety of planners, to-do list forms, and calendars. While formats differ, the purpose is the same: to help you get organized and better spend your daily 86,400 seconds.

A planner needn't be elaborate or expensive. Some people succumb to the status symbolism of certain planners, but any appropriately designed planner can tremendously boost your power to be productive.

A planner needs five things to make it work for you:

1. A place to list and assign priorities to tasks. We'll show you how to develop a priority task list in just a moment.)
2. A place to record notes and follow-up information.
3. A place for goals and values. Having these incorporated into your planning tool is a powerful way to make sure they are realized.
4. A place for frequently referred-to information, especially addresses, phone numbers, perhaps birthdays, and so forth.
5. Flexibility to meet your needs.

Some people resist planning. Some say they don't like to feel bound by a plan—they want to stay "flexible." Others claim to do all their planning in their heads. And more than a few simply don't see the value to planning. They live by wandering around.

Time management experts claim that as a general rule, spending only 5 percent of the day planning can help managers achieve 95 percent of their goals. Planning prevents managers from doing the wrong things the wrong way at the wrong time, and it forces them to answer the question, 'What really needs to be accomplished?'

Planning is a good idea because it is always best to perform activities sequentially rather than simultaneously. In fact, we *can't* do things simultaneously and do them well. The idea behind time management is determining *how to do things sequentially.*

The Nuts and Bolts of Time and Task Management

Devote a minimum of ten to fifteen minutes a day solely to planning. Use a planner system you like. Then apply the steps described below, and you will see a significant increase in your personal effectiveness. First-time users of a planner report immediate productivity increases of 25 percent or more!

STEP 1. DEVELOP A PRIORITY TASK LIST FOR EACH DAY

Prioritizing tasks helps us sort them out, determine which need to be attacked first and which can be saved for later.

Here's how: List the specific tasks you want or need to spend your time on for a particular day. Using your own shorthand, list the items you wish to accomplish. It might read something like this: "Complete the XYZ report, get stamps, attend Billy's softball game, eat more fish, keep date with Chris."

At this stage, don't be overly concerned with the *importance* of the items; just get in the habit of listing *all* nonroutine tasks that you want to accomplish that day. Don't bother listing all those tasks you do automatically (e.g., brushing teeth, doing the dishes, waiting on customers).

STEP 2. ASSIGN A LETTER PRIORITY TO EACH ITEM ON YOUR LIST

Use A, B, C, or a star and place the letter A next to items that *must* be done. These are critical to you, though you alone determine whether they are critical or not based on your values and goals. Tasks required either by outside forces (e.g., your boss) or internal ones (e.g., a strong personal commitment) will normally receive an A priority. Be careful not to assign A's to *every* task. Giving everything an A defeats the purpose of prioritizing.

Using the letter B to indicate *should-do* items. These tasks aren't quite as critical as the A tasks, yet it is worth spending time to achieve them.

The letter C is for *could-do* items. These tasks are worth listing and thinking about—and, if you complete your A's and B's, worth doing.

A star indicates an item that is *urgent*—something that *must* be done and done *now*. It is both important and vital and must be done right away. Occasionally, such a job occurs during a workday (i.e., a crisis). When you add starred items to your list, drop whatever else you're doing, even an A item, and complete the starred tasks first.

Use a star very sparingly. Normally, urgent tasks are not factored into your dedicated planning time. They pop up and scream "do me now!" Be careful, however, to determine that an item really *is* important before you bump the rest of your plan to squeeze it in. Just because something makes a lot of noise doesn't necessarily mean that it must be done instantly. Don't let a false urgency override an important task you've planned.

STEP 3. ASSIGN A NUMBER TO YOUR TASK

Your plan of attack can be further sharpened by assigning a number to each task. Some people, however, see little value in numbering tasks once the priority letter has been assigned. You can decide what works best for you.

The best use of the numbering system is as a chronological indicator. Ask, "Which task should I do first?" If you have a meeting at two in the afternoon and it's an A item, the meeting may not be A-1 simply because other priorities must be attended to earlier in the day.

STEP 4. USE COMPLETION SYMBOLS: THE PAYOFF

After you complete the tasks listed in your planner, you deserve a reward. This reward takes the form of a completion symbol.

Here are several completion symbols:

- (✔) The check mark symbol indicates that a task has been completed. That should feel good. Many people prefer to make their check marks in red as a reminder of how productive they have been.

- (→) A second symbol, an arrow, is used when a task needs to be rescheduled. Perhaps a meeting has been cancelled or an appointment changed, or the task simply could not be completed because you were wrapped up in another matter.

IMPORTANT: Whenever you use the arrow, be sure to reschedule the task to another day in the planner. Using the arrow and rescheduling the task for another day earns you the right to forget that task for awhile. You'll be reminded of it automatically on the new day on which you scheduled it. And it'll be there when you do your daily personal planning.

(O) A third symbol often used is a circle placed in the margin to the left of the completion symbol column to indicate that the task has been delegated to someone else.

It may be that you've asked your spouse to pick up a book of stamps on the way home from work or assigned a child to clean out the garage. Or it may be a more formal kind of delegation, in which you've asked a colleague or subordinate to complete a task. If several people are reporting to you, you may want to use the circle centered with the initial of the person to whom the task has been delegated. When the task has been completed, you should then place a check mark in the "completed" column.

(X) A fourth symbol is an X, to indicate that a task has been deleted. It may mean that you blew it, and it just didn't get done, or it may mean that you've reconsidered and determined that this task simply isn't worth doing. Remember, you are in charge. If you schedule a task but later decide it really isn't what you want to do—so be it. You X it out.

Incorporating Goals and Values in Your Daily Planning

Your priority task list should provide an overview of your daily activities. But how do these activities tie in with your long-term values and goals?

For most people, they don't. And that's why people often fail to achieve what's really important to them. The challenge is to *make your daily activities consistent with your goals and values.*

The best planner system is more than just a calendar. It should have a place to record your core values and goals.

While planning your daily priority tasks, make sure that the goals and values you previously articulated for yourself are evident. It is very important to refer to them. The more often these are reviewed, the more likely they will become a part of your being. Your daily plan should reflect "the big picture" described in your value clarifying efforts.

BLOCKING OUT TIME WASTERS

Writing down tasks and prioritizing them helps avoid one time waster: lack of focus. This is an internal time waster. External time wasters are another problem. Primarily, these are forces that interrupt you from working your plan. Telephone calls, impromptu meetings, visits from workers, and excessive amounts of junk mail pose interruptions.

■ Don't get so well organized that you can't take some time for others.

There is no foolproof formula to use when such interruptions arise. Indeed, an interruption now, although aggravating, may clarify a worker's task or solidify a relationship that will prevent more serious problems down the road. Let's hope we never become so perfectly organized that we cannot take unplanned time to help another person in need. One of the fastest ways to create employee resentment is to give the impression of being too busy to be accessible. Here is where the *art* of managing comes into play. There are no scientific ways to teach people sensitivity to the needs of others. There are times when you'll need to waste a little time. And there are times to avoid such distractions.

Disruptive incoming mail is easy to handle. When in doubt, throw it out. Rather than let reports, memos, letters, and ads pile up on your desk, ask these questions: "What would happen if I threw this out?" "Will I need to refer to this later?" "Will someone else keep a file copy if, by some chance, I do need to see it?"

■ Handle each piece of mail only once.

Don't let paperwork pile up. Handle each piece of incoming mail only once. Look at it, decide what to do with it, and get it out of sight. Either

- file it,
- respond to it,
- pass it on to someone else, or
- throw it away.

■ Be candid with those who try to waste your time.

People are trickier to deal with than mail. If you determine that someone is wasting your time, be up front about it. Simply say, in a matter-of-fact tone (don't sound accusing or sarcastic):

- "Tom, I'd like to talk with you more about that issue, but I have some other work I need to do first," or
- "Carmelita, I think I understand what you are saying. Can we pursue this more after I've had a chance to think through a few ideas?" or

- (When the interrupter is a telephone caller) "I have someone else here with me. Can we talk this out later?"

Once the interruption is set aside, you can determine whether the issue is worth following up on. If you are concerned, you can initiate contact. If not, you can use selective forgetfulness to let the matter drop.

Delegating to Save Time

A leader's willingness and ability to delegate effectively will have an important bearing on his or her time use. Simply stated, the more we can delegate, the more time we'll have for other activities.

Be aware of your attitudes toward delegation, when you should delegate, your understanding of subordinate attitudes toward accepting delegation, and your skills at assigning tasks. Let's take a closer look at these criteria:

WHY SOME MANAGERS HESITATE TO DELEGATE

Delegating work to others always involves some risk. Sometimes the job doesn't get done as well as you'd like—or doesn't get done at all. A few bad experiences with delegated tasks "dropping between the cracks," and a supervisor can easily become gun-shy. But most managers have no choice. Some work *must* be delegated.

If you are overly hesitant about delegating, your behavior may stem from one of these common reasons supervisors don't delegate:

- *I-can-do-it-myself reasoning.* Sure, you probably can do virtually anything you ask others to do. That's not the issue. The real question isn't whether or not you *can* do it. It's a matter of whether or not you *should.* Is doing it yourself a productive use of your time? If not, delegate.

- *Lack of confidence in subordinates.* If you are hesitant to delegate work to others because you think they'll foul up the job, your problem goes much deeper. Either you are insufficiently aware of what your people can do, or you have failed to provide proper and sufficient training or development opportunities. Your supervisory task here is not to avoid delegating but to *increase* delegating until you find out the limitations of your workers. Then work to upgrade employee capabilities through training and job enrichment.

- *Fear of not getting credit and recognition.* We all like to get credit for our efforts. And to some extent, we fear that someone else— perhaps someone we see as a competitor—will get the honor and glory for a job well done. In reality, supervisors can and should get full credit for the productivity of their entire work section. Top management recognizes that supervisors don't do all the work alone. That's not their job! The supervisor's job is to get meaningful work accomplished *through the efforts of others.* The talent to do so is highly valued. As someone said, "There are no limits to what can be accomplished when we don't care who gets the credit."

> ■ Most supervisors have no choice. Work *must* be delegated.

- *Lack of time, skills, or both at turning work over to others.* Sometimes it seems to take more time to delegate than to do the work yourself. But that is a short-range viewpoint. You could spend quite a bit of time teaching a secretary how to handle routine incoming correspondence initially. But eventually, that secretary will be able to handle what had been a significant time-eating task.

You can spend time and effort now. Or you can keep on spending it forever. It's your choice.

WHY YOU MAY NOT DELEGATE

Most of us have hesitations about delegating in some cases. But if these hang-ups apply to you consistently, you'll have considerable difficulty in being a good supervisor.

To be an effective delegator, a supervisor must be willing to do the following:

- Entrust others with responsibilities.
- Give subordinates the freedom necessary to carry out expanded tasks.
- Spend the time to bring people along from easy to more complex tasks.
- Let subordinates participate increasingly in decisions that affect them.

In short, an effective, time-conscious supervisor *must* delegate in order to strengthen the organization. Without delegation, people are limited to accomplishing only what they can do in a limited time, before exhaustion sets in. With delegation, opportunities for accomplishment are almost unlimited.

HOW DELEGATION CAN SOMETIMES GO WRONG

The most common reasons that delegation sometimes fails to produce the desired results follow, with some suggestions for overcoming the problems.

- *Supervisors fail to keep the communication channels open.* Look for feedback about delegated jobs. Create a climate where the worker can ask you for clarifying instructions or periodically check on how he or she is doing.
- *Supervisors fail to allow for mistakes.* Workers will make mistakes when doing delegated work. Allow for these. Don't jump all over the worker or make him or her feel inadequate. Let him or her learn from the inevitable—and forgiven—mistakes.
- *Supervisors fail to follow up on delegated tasks.* Periodic checking to keep up-to-date on a job conveys a sense of continued interest and also provides communication opportunities.
- *Supervisors fail to delegate enough authority to complete the task.* If you ask one of your workers to research a particular problem that involves interviewing other workers, for example, be sure those other employees know that the interviews are authorized. Often a memo announcing that employee X has been given

such-and-such a task and asking others to cooperate will suffice.

■ *Supervisors don't delegate clearly.* Be sure the expected results or outcome is understood by both boss and worker. Specify the nature of the finished product. Do you want a written report or an oral briefing? Should the worker review parts shortages for the entire year or just for the third quarter? Be specific.

In this chapter, we've stressed the importance of career planning, clarifying organizational and personal expectations, managing the manager, and managing one's own time and tasks. As a closing thought, we encourage you to *now take charge!* You can indeed find a rewarding career in people management and create the skills needed to be *human-relations smart.* Applying the principles we've discussed in this book, you can magnify your efforts and make this a better place for all of us to live and work.

▼ SUMMARY OF KEY IDEAS

■ The highly successful manager learns to develop clear career plans, clarify job expectations, manage both subordinates and superiors, and manage himself or herself.

■ The four components of career planning are goals, self-evaluation (value clarification), vision, and occupational information.

■ Clarifying one's expectations requires understanding what organizations do and do not expect of managers as well as what managers can expect from companies.

■ The art of managing one's superior is often overlooked in management texts but is nonetheless important for successful people at work.

■ Managing upward requires that one understands job responsibilities, takes the initiative, keeps the boss informed, asks for help when needed, and, above all, develops trust with the boss.

■ The four conditions for establishing trust with one's boss involve accessibility, availability, predictability, and loyalty.

■ Managing your own time and tasks is critical to overall success.

■ Prioritizing tasks, writing "to-do" lists, delegating, and accepting responsibility for the use of your most precious resource, time, will make a huge difference in your success.

■ Success is a "do-it-yourself" project.

■ The highly successful manager recognizes the significance of a manager's role, applies human relations principles, and is willing to take charge.

▼ KEY TERMS, CONCEPTS, AND NAMES

A-B-C tasks
Availability of subordinate
   to manager

Career planning
Creativity on the jobs
Dream list

Dress for success	Predictability
Goal selection	Priority task list
Job expectations	Self-appraisal
Long-term commitment	Superior-subordinate trust
Managing your manager	Value-aligning activities
Noneconomic rewards	Value clarification
Occupational information	

▼ QUESTIONS AND EXERCISES

1. What do you expect from your employer (present or future)? Discuss these expectations with a manager. How realistic have you been?

2. Try developing a dream list (as suggested in this chapter). Get as many of your personal goals, wants, or desires as possible down on paper. Do this as a free-flowing, brainstorming activity. Don't be critical or particularly selective at first. Then review what you've written, to identify conflicting items. Determine a priority of goals from this, and then boil the list down to ten long-range and ten short-range objectives.

3. List five sources of occupational information that may be useful to your career planning.

4. How can a person show others that he or she values time?

5. What are some ways to reduce clutter and get organized?

6. How does the A-B-C system work to help organize time?

7. What are some common excuses people offer for not delegating enough?

8. How can a person be a more effective delegator?

9. Answer the introductory questions at the beginning of this chapter.

▼ NOTES

1. Thomas J. Peters and Robert H. Waterman, *In Search of Excellence: Lessons from America's Best-Run Companies* (New York: Harper and Row, 1982), p. 279.

2. For details on value planning, see Paul R. Timm, *Successful Self-Management* (Los Altos, Calif.: Crisp Publications, 1987).

3. Og Mandino, *The Greatest Secret in the World* (New York: Bantam Books), 1982.

4. Warren Bennis and Burt Nanus, *Leaders: The Strategies for Taking Charge* (New York: Harper and Row, 1985), p. 27.

5. John T. Molloy, *Dress for Success* (New York: Warner Books, 1976).

6. Paul R. Timm, *50 Simple Things You Can Do to Save Your Customers* (Hawthorne, N.J.: Career Press, 1992), pp. 2–3.

7. Norman C. Hill and Paul H. Thompson, "Managing Your Manager: The Effective Subordinate," *Exchange* (Fall-Winter 1978).

8. R. Alec Mackenzie, *The Time Trap.* (New York: McGraw-Hill, 1972).

9. Adapted from Paul R. Timm, *Recharge Your Career and Your Life* (Los Altos, Calif.: Crisp Publications, 1990), pp. 124–31.

ANOTHER LOOK: WHICH CORPORATE CULTURE FITS YOU?

"Academy" or "fortress"? "Baseball team" or "club"?

According to one management scholar, those four descriptions of corporate culture are more than mere fodder for gossip around the water cooler. Understanding the culture you work in—and knowing whether it matches your career personality—can affect how far or how easily you scurry up the management ranks.

"We've taught managers how to assess their own abilities but not how to match those with the right company," says Jeffrey Sonnenfeld, director of Emory University's Center for Leadership and Career Change who is researching career paths in different corporate cultures.

A risk-taker, for instance, will thrive at a baseball-team company but fall flat on his face at an academy. But take note, a team player who craves security won't last at a baseball team, says Mr. Sonnenfeld, who is also a professor at Emory.

Analyzing a company's corporate culture doesn't guarantee landing a job or a promotion, career experts and managers agree. But it can illuminate why achievements and a sense of belonging come easier in some settings than in others.

Academies. For the steady climber who wants to thoroughly master each new job and make one company his or her career home, Mr. Sonnenfeld recommends the academy. There, new recruits are invariably young college graduates who are steered through a myriad of specialized jobs.

A classic academy is International Business Machines Corp., where every manager spends at least 40 hours each year in management-training school, with 32 hours devoted to people management.

IBM identifies fast-trackers early on and "carefully grooms them to become expert in a particular function," Mr. Sonnenfeld says. "They'll tell you they're IBMers first and foremost but then add they're an IBMer who cares about data-entry systems or applications technology."

Donald Laidlaw, IBM's director of executive resources and management development and a 37-year veteran of the company, calls himself "an IBM personnel executive." He joined IBM right after college as a sales trainee, then moved from marketing to personnel, mastering 11 jobs at 10 locations. "You don't move ahead until you perform where you are," he says.

Clubs While managers in academies must stand out to move ahead, "those in clubs must strive to fit in," says Mr. Sonnenfeld, describing his second grouping.

"What counts isn't individual achievement but seniority, commitment and doing things for the good of the group," he says. "If you like quick upward mobility and notoriety, clubs aren't for you."

And unlike academies, clubs groom managers as generalists, with initiation beginning at an entry-level job. At **United Parcel Service of America,** Inc., chief executive John W. Rogers and his management committee began their careers as clerks, drivers and management trainees. Instead of becoming narrow specialists, they learned a little of everything from distribution to marketing as they crisscrossed their way up the corporate ladder.

The chief executive, a 32-year UPS veteran, still does his own photocopying, eats lunch in the cafeteria alongside packagers and junior managers, and shares a secretary. "When decisions have to be made, we get everyone's opinion, and the company feels like a family to a lot of us," says John Tranfo, a staff vice president who will soon be celebrating his 40th year at UPS. "In management, we have hardly any turnover," he adds.

Baseball Teams Baseball-team companies, which include accounting and law firms, consulting, advertising and software development, are a different breed entirely. Entrepreneurial in style, baseball teams seek out talent of all ages and experience and reward them by what they produce.

"They don't care how committed you'll be tomorrow," says Mr. Sonnenfeld.

ANOTHER LOOK: WHICH CORPORATE CULTURE FITS YOU? *continued*

"They want cutting-edge results today. And they don't train their employees; either you come in with skills or develop them quickly on the job."

Managers at baseball-team companies perceive themselves as free agents, much like professional athletes. If one company doesn't give them the freedom or rewards they think they deserve, they'll leave for a company that does—or form their own.

Such was the case with Bruce Wasserstein and Joseph Perella, two young investment-banking wizards who made mergers and acquisitions Wall Street's most lucrative business. **First Boston** Corp. paid them more than the firm's top executives. Yet last year they quit to form their own company, **Wasserstein Perella** & Co., because they felt the profits they were producing shouldn't be used to subsidize money-losing operations, like securities trading.

"It took me less than an hour to decide to go with them," says George Hornig, a former First Boston colleague who is now managing director and chief operating officer of Wasserstein Perella. But like most baseball-team managers, he also can't predict where he'll work in the future. "Beyond five years it starts to cloud in my crystal ball," he says.

After working as a consultant at **Booz, Allen & Hamilton** Inc. and as an executive at **Time** Inc.,

Sandra Kresch concludes that "Booz Allen's baseball team meritocracy works better for me. At Time, (where the culture is clubby) who you knew seemed more important than anything you did, and that didn't fit my style." Ms. Kresch is now an independent consultant.

Fortresses   If baseball-team companies value inventiveness, fortresses are concerned with survival. Many fortresses are academies, clubs or baseball teams that have failed in the marketplace and are struggling to reverse their fortunes. Others, including retailing and natural-resources companies, are in a perpetual boom-and-bust cycle.

Fortresses can't promise job security or reward people simply on the basis of how well they perform. The most competent fortress manager may find himself suddenly out of a job when the business he oversees is sold or restructured.

Yet for those who relish the challenge of a turn-around, fortresses can be exciting. "I like the fact that there's adrenaline flowing, because you're doing an overhaul, not just a refining, and you have the chance to really create something," says Bruce McKinnon, senior vice president of **Microbrand Wireless Cable** of New York. In the past six years, he's worked at three other cable-television companies, recruited to each as

"a portable warlord to help them back on track," he says.

Managers who crave security and conviviality may not be able to tolerate fortresses. "No one likes to be told they're overweight, but when you're doing a turnaround you're usually putting everyone on a diet," says Mr. McKinnon. "I elicit strong emotions from subordinates."

Blends and Transitions   Of course, many companies can't be neatly categorized in any one way. Many have a blend of corporate cultures. Within **General Electric** Co., the Kidder Peabody unit and the NBC unit both have baseball-team qualities. But GE's aerospace division operates more like a club, the electronics division is like an academy and the home-appliance unit is a fortress. "All four cells are there," Mr. Sonnenfeld says.

Still other companies are in transition. **Apple Computer** Co. started out as a baseball team but is becoming an academy as it matures. And with deregulation, banks—once the clubbiest of employers—are fast evolving into baseball teams.

Managers of **Chemical Bank** Corp. can no longer count on lifelong employment there or working with people out of the same mold, says Pat Cook, a former senior vice president at the bank. Today, "the old club members who played by all the rules are being outpaced by new hotshots from Wall

ANOTHER LOOK *continued*

Street" recruited to combat competition and takeover tremors, she adds. "There's been a massive plate shifting."

COMPARING BUSINESS CULTURES

The four categories of corporate cultures—Academies, Clubs, Baseball Teams and Fortresses—in general appear to attract certain personalities. Based on surveys of 125 Harvard Business School graduates from the class of 1974, these are some of the traits found within managers who gravitated to a particular corporate culture.

ACADEMIES

- had parents who valued self-reliance but put less emphasis on honesty and consideration
- tend to be less religious
- graduated business school with high grades
- had more problems with subordinates in their first 10 years of work

CLUBS

- had parents who emphasized honesty and consideration
- had a lower regard for hard work and self-reliance
- tend to be more religious
- care more about health, family and security and less about future income and autonomy
- are less likely to have substantial equity in their companies

BASEBALL TEAMS

- described their fathers as unpredictable
- generally had more problems planning their careers in the first 10 years after business school, and worked for more companies during that period than classmates did
- priorities include personal growth and future income
- value security less than others

FORTRESSES

- had parents who valued curiosity
- were helped strongly by mentors in the first year out of school
- are less concerned than others with feelings of belonging, professional growth and future income
- experienced problems in career planning, on-the-job decisions and job implementation

SOURCE: Jeffrey Sonnenfeld and Carol Hymowitz, "Which Corporate Culture Fits You?" *Wall Street Journal* (July 17, 1989), p. B-1.

▼ ANOTHER LOOK: CHOOSING TO BE A TOP PERFORMER

Our success in life is determined by the choices we make. You are going to be making choices that will determine your success as you learn to manage yourself and others. To be effective in making proper choices, you must understand the difference between reacting and responding.

If *react* and *respond* sound like the same things to you, let me explain the difference. You go to the doctor, who gives you a prescription and tells you to come back the next day. When you go back, if he looks worried and tells you he needs to change the prescription because your body is "reacting" to the medicine, you're probably going to be concerned.

On the other hand, if he tells you your body is "responding" to the medicine, you're going to smile because you know you're on your way to recovery. So, to react is negative and to respond is positive—the choice is yours! It's a fact that you can't tailormake the situations in life, but you can tailormake the attitudes to fit those situations before they arise.

RESPOND FOR A BETTER TOMORROW

Now, there are some things you simply are not going to change. If you were born white, you're going to stay white. If you were born black, you're going to stay black. I don't care how much thought you give it, you're not going to add a single cubit to your height. You're not going to change when you were born, where you were born, how you were born or to whom you were born. As a matter of fact, you're not going to change one single whisper that's taken place in the yesterdays of your life.

Tomorrow is a different subject. Regardless of your past, your tomorrow is a clean slate. You can choose what you want to write on that slate. You make that choice each time you decide to respond to negative events or react to those negative events. As a manager, when your employees act in a rude, thoughtless, and inconsiderate manner and are impossible to deal with, please understand you can still choose to respond or react. Your choice will play a major role in your relationship with your people.

Obviously, this doesn't mean that to lead others, you must be "perfect" and never blow your cool. That's not only unrealistic, it is impossible and maybe even undesirable. After all, managers are people, too, and our employees need to know we are human and have feelings. On balance, however, we need to be careful that we choose to respond far more often than we choose to react, and that when we react it is under control and is to the action the person took and not to the employee personally.

My friend, Fred Smith, one of the truly outstanding consultants and management experts in America, gives us some helpful advice on this matter in his excellent book *You and Your Network.* Fred says that when others deal with us in a dogmatic or even in a mean and vicious way, it doesn't necessarily mean they want to hurt us. It could mean, and generally does, that they are acting that way because they are hurting.

If you will remember that every obnoxious act is a cry for help, you are way ahead of the game. Recognizing and accepting this fact makes it much easier for us to take a calmer, more level-headed approach to our functions as managers and as people.

IT'S UP TO YOU

All of life is a series of choices, and what you choose to give life today will determine what life will give you tomorrow. You can choose to get drunk tonight, but when you do, you have chosen to feel miserable tomorrow. You can choose to light up a cigarette today, but when you do you have chosen to die 14 minutes early.

You can choose to eat properly today, and when you do, you have chosen to be healthier tomorrow. You can choose to be overweight, or you can choose to be the right weight. You can choose to be happy or you can choose to be sad....

When a young person chooses to sit up late at night

ANOTHER LOOK *continued*

watching television or socializing, he has chosen to be sleepy in class the next day and, consequently, absorb less of the information he needs to know in order to be successful in the competitive world in which he lives. When we choose to be mean, nasty, and ornery to other people, we have chosen to be treated in a mean, nasty, and ornery fashion by others. By the same token, when we choose to be thoughtful and considerate of others, we've chosen to be treated in a thoughtful and considerate manner.

This list is endless, but the message is the same: *You are free to choose, but the choices you make today will determine what you will have, be, and do in the tomorrows of your life.* You can choose to take the necessary steps to help you succeed as a manager, or you can choose to ignore the experience of successful managers and take the consequences for you and your employees.

We must teach our employees that they are responsible for their attitudes and their conduct and that in life, every choice we make, whether it is good or bad has consequences! Once those consequences are thoroughly understood, it's easier to make the right choice.

THE CHOICE IS YOURS

I choose to respond for one simple reason. I don't have, need, or want ulcers, high blood pressure, a heart prob-

lem, or any of the negative consequences that go with reacting. I have chosen to respond to negative situations in life instead of reacting to those situations. Even if this does not benefit anyone else, I'm persuaded that it is the best thing I can do for me. When it's the best thing for me, then obviously that puts me in a far better position to do my work, which basically is designed to help other people.

Once I was in Kansas City for a lengthy four-hour recording session. I finished at one and had a three o'clock flight to Dallas. We packed and made a mad dash for the airport.

When we arrived, the ticket agent looked at me, smiled and said, "The three o'clock flight to Dallas has been canceled."

To this I enthusiastically responded, "Fantastic."

"Yes," said the agent, "but the next flight doesn't leave until 6:05."

To that I smiled and responded, "Fantastic."

The woman looked at me in complete shock and said, "I'm really puzzled. Why would you say 'fantastic' when I've just told you that you have a four-hour wait in the airport?"

I smilingly said, "Ma'am, it's really very simple. I have never had a chance to spend four hours in the airport in Kansas City, Missouri. Why do you realize that at this moment there are literally tens of millions of people on the face of this earth who not

only are cold but also hungry?

"Here I am in a beautiful facility, and even though it's cold outside, it's comfortable inside. Down the corridor is a nice little coffee shop. I'm going to go there, relax for a few minutes and enjoy a cup of coffee. Then I've got some extremely important work to do. And here I am in one of the nicest buildings in the whole area. It's easily the biggest, most comfortable, rent-free office I've ever had at my disposal. Fantastic."

As a practical matter, I do not know anyone who works for that airline. From the chairman of the board to a single one. However, it is their airline, and if they choose to do so, they can cancel my flight. But they can't cancel my day! It's mine. God Himself gave it to me with written instructions on how I am to use it. He told me to "rejoice and be glad in it."

That, my friend, is exactly the same position you are in. When you respond, you are making real progress toward living a healthier, happier life and developing effective, efficient, and happy employees.

Yes, your past is important, but as important as it is, according to Dr. Tony Campolo, it is not nearly as important to your present as the way you see your future. Ralph Waldo Emerson was right when he said that what lies behind you and what lies before you pale in significance when you learn to

ANOTHER LOOK: CHOOSING TO BE A TOP PERFORMER *continued*

respond and not react to life's daily challenges.

It's been said before and it will be said again: You cannot change the past, but your future is spotless. You can write on it what you will. In order to do so, however, you need to learn to respond to the positive and the negative.

Fortunately, you have far more control than you realize. For example, all of us have on occasion been guilty of saying, "He/She makes me so made!" That simply is not so. As a wise man said, you can't stir the soup unless there's some soup in the pot to stir. Nobody can make you act mad unless there is already some mad in you. Mad reactions are *learned*

behaviors and consequently they can be *unlearned.*

You can watch a person go about his or her daily activities for days or weeks and learn a great deal about him. However, you can watch a person under adverse circumstances for five minutes and see whether he has learned to respond or react. Actually, you can learn more about him a few minutes under trying conditions than you can in days of just watching him involved in daily activities.

Your response or reaction to negative reveals what's inside of you. It exposes your heart and shows the kind of person you really are. The problem is that most people have a tendency to

react instead of respond. They have a tendency to blame everything and everybody for the difficulties and reversals in life.

Most of us have a tendency to blame somebody else for our difficulties, but keep appropriate credit for our success to ourselves. What about you? Do you respond to the negative and make it better, or do you react to the negative and make it worse? To be a Top Performer, you must make the proper choices.

SOURCE: Zig Ziglar, "Choosing to Be a Top Performer," *Executive Excellence* (April 1987). Reprinted with permission of *Executive Excellence,* © 1987.

▼ A CASE IN POINT: BRIDGET GOES BANANAS

As a typist, Bridget was incredible. She seemed to turn out error-free work at an amazing pace. Her attention to detail was admired by all who used her services. She seldom committed even a minor typo.

Last month, Bridget became supervisor over the executive word processing center. It is her first management experience. But already some problems have surfaced. Leslie, a typist with four years experience, went over Bridget's head to complain to Alice Benson, administrative manager, about the "unbelievable nit-picking."

"I can't seem to do anything right, according to Bridget," complained Leslie. "She

checks everything I type! She's driving me nuts, not to mention the fact that my output has slowed down dramatically. Just yesterday, Phil Underwood, that new VP of marketing, made a wisecrack about cobwebs growing on his report before he could get it out of typing."

When Alice asked about Leslie's concerns, Bridget flew off the handle. "We're supposed to be the best typing pool in the company. After all, we type for the top people. The work has to be *perfect!*" She was almost screaming. Then she slumped down in a chair in Alice's office.

A CASE IN POINT *continued*

"Alice, I'm going nuts up there. None of my people seems to care about the quality of the work the way I do. I've been working till nine or ten every night checking work and just trying to keep up. I'm about convinced that being a supervisor just isn't worth it."

QUESTIONS

1. What seems to be a driving need in Bridget's work?

2. If you were Alice, what would you suggest to Bridget?

SOURCE: Paul Timm, *Supervision* (St. Paul: West Publishing, 1992), p. 417. Reprinted by permission. Copyright © 1992 by West Publishing Company. All rights reserved.

▼ A CASE IN POINT: GEORGE LANDEN'S SHORT CAREER

After only eight months on the job, George Landen was looking for a way out. Not that he was incompetent: He had graduated near the top of his M.B.A. class at a leading business school, had been heavily recruited, and had finally accepted a position with a major accounting firm. A successful career had seemed the inevitable next step.

But Landen's short career in public accounting had been more painful than successful. When asked what had gone wrong, Landen shrugged his shoulders. "I guess it's the work itself," he sighed. "You can't get into depth on any problem. Deadlines are so tight that all your work ends up being pretty superficial. I guess that's what they want, but it drives me crazy."

Questioned about his performance, Landen's fellow workers told a different story.

Said one, "Landen's technical competence is impeccable, but he's too quiet—he keeps to himself. It's almost impossible for him to handle his clients and colleagues effectively. If he could break out of his shell, things might be different. But as it is now, I'm afraid that the management wouldn't be the least bit sorry to see him go."

QUESTIONS

1. What problems seem to be at the root of Landen's situation?

2. If you were Landen's manager and wanted to help him stay with the company, what advice would you give him?

SOURCE: Adapted from Gene W. Dalton and Paul H. Thompson, *Novations: Strategies for Career Management* (Glenview, Ill.: Scott, Foresman, 1986), p. 20. Copyright © 1986 by Gene W. Dalton and Paul H. Thompson. Reprinted by permission Scott, Foresman and Company.

GLOSSARY

Accurate Understanding   A valid interpretation of one's own experiences or the experiences of others. To achieve accurate understanding of another's communication, you might restate in your own words what that other person's statement means to you.

Acquired Immunodeficiency Syndrome (AIDS)   A disease transmitted between people through the blood. It is generally transmitted sexually and there is currently no known cure.

Affirmative Action   An active effort to improve the employment or educational opportunities of members of minority groups, the handicapped, and women.

Alcoholism   A complex chronic psychological disorder associated with excessive and especially compulsive drinking. Alcoholism is a major cause of lost efficiency and effectiveness in the work place.

Americans with Disabilities Act   An act passed by Congress in 1990 to provide people with disabilities equal opportunity in employment, public accommodations, transportation, government services, and telecommunications.

Assumptions   Propositions, axioms, or notions that, while unproven are taken for granted or considered true.

Attitude   A feeling or emotion regarding a fact or state.

Autocratic Style   A leadership style characterized by very high leader decisiveness and very low employee participation.

Availability   A condition of being physically, mentally, and emotionally ready to do what is necessary for the good of an organization. An available person is present, qualified, willing, and ready for duty or use. Availability is a general trait associated with successful people.

Bakke Decision   The 1978 U.S. Supreme Court finding that affirmative action quotas that discriminate against whites violate the Civil Rights Act of 1964.

Basic Needs   Fundamental human necessities such as water, food, sleep, and oxygen.

Behavior Modification   A systematic approach to providing tangible or intangible rewards to influence future behavior. Also called operant conditioning, or contingency management.

Behaviorism   An approach to psychology pioneered by John Watson and B. F. Skinner that assumes observed behavior provides the only valid data of psychology.

Belonging Need   A normal psychological longing, yearning, or desire to be accepted by others or to be a member of some group or organization.

Body Language   The subtle body movements and stances that are exhibited by people and provide clues to a person's attitudes, feelings, or inclinations. The interpretation of body language is an imprecise skill. Conclusions should not be drawn based on body language alone but rather should consider other nonverbal as well as verbal communications.

Boss-centered Leadership   A leadership style in which the leader or "boss" makes decisions and then announces them to subordinates; authority is centralized with the leader.

Brainstorming   A group problem-solving technique that involves the spontaneous contribution of ideas from all members of the group.

Burnout   Exhaustion of physical or emotional strength; the combined physical, mental, and emotional exhaustion caused by stress.

Captive Nation   A group such as native Americans or an ethnic minority in another country that is encompassed by some other dominant group of people with whom the members of the captive nation do not easily assimilate.

Career Planning   Giving forethought to one's career by selecting goals, gathering occupational information, and clarifying personal values.

Caring   Showing interest or concern for others; protecting or supervising; paying attention to detail.

Centralized Decision Making   The concentration of decision making to top-level management, when even routine decisions are made by top management.

Chain of Command   The arrangement of organizational authority that determines how many people report to each manager, the span of control of the organization, and the size and number of levels of authority.

Change-Produced Stress   Stress produced by changes in the work environment.

Civil Rights Act of 1964   The federal legislation that prohibits employers, labor unions, and employees from discriminating against persons on the basis of color, religion, sex, or national origin.

Civil Rights Act of 1991   This act amended the Civil Rights Act of 1964 to strengthen and improve federal civil rights laws and to provide damages in cases of intentional employment discrimination.

Civil Rights Movement   The social campaign beginning in the 1960s that served as the catalyst for civil rights legislation.

Clarifying Expectations   Identifying and describing what the company and its employees should expect from one another.

Cognitive Dissonance   An imbalance created in the mind when an experience is inconsistent with what one already "knows"; perceived inconsistency between beliefs and knowledge or behavioral tendency.

Cohesiveness   A sense of teamwork, group morale, and team spirit that characterizes a group and often leads to high productivity; the act or state of sticking together tightly.

Communication   A process by which information is exchanged between individuals through a common system of symbols, signs, or behavior; the ability to gain or relate understanding through the exchange of concepts and ideas.

Communication Climate   The overall climate created by the personal communication styles of all group members determined by subtle verbal and nonverbal behaviors occurring during interpersonal transactions.

Communication Conflict   Caustic, angry, defensive, and sarcastic reactions that occur during communication.

Computer Revolution   The pervasive and increasing use of computers in today's society.

Conflict-managing techniques   The method of understanding all aspects of communication conflict and using the proper approach to keep the conflict from causing problems or escalating.

Conformity   Adherence to norms that often leads to feelings of satisfaction and increased personal value; action in accordance with some specified standard or authority.

Consensus   Group solidarity in sentiment and belief; unanimity; general agreement; the judgment arrived at by most of those concerned.

Consultative Style   A leadership style characterized by fairly high leader decisiveness and some employee participation. The consultative leader welcomes ideas.

Content Reflection   The act of echoing or mirroring back in the form of a question what the other person said to make sure one is understanding.

Continuous Reinforcement   The method in which an individual receives reinforcement every time he or she does the desired behavior. This works best for quick learning when low levels of abilities are in use.

Coping   The process in which people struggle or contend with a problem, often by trial and error, until they achieve some degree of satisfaction.

Coping Techniques   Individual methods for coping with stress, such as taking time for recreation and avoiding criticism.

Corporate Character   The aggregate of features and qualities that distinguishes one corporation from all others.

Credible People   Believable individuals who can influence a person to change. Credible people and new experiences affect attitude.

Criteria   Standards or guidelines phrased as statements that indicate the minimal requirements that any suggestion or proposal must meet to be acceptable; a standard on which a judgment or decision may be based.

Criticism   The act of giving feedback, whether positive or negative, in order to change or compliment a behavior. Positive or constructive evaluative feedback is given in order to attain a desired result or no change at all.

Customer Departmentalization   The process of organizing an enterprise by grouping together similar types of activities and responsibilities into section, divisions, branches, or departments based on the types of customers served.

Defensive Climate   A situation in which the prevailing attitudes, standards, or conditions discourage open communication, undermine trust, and lead participants to feel that they are not appreciated and that their efforts will not be supported.

Derived X   Stan Kossen's list of managerial assumptions that are originally similar to Theory Y, but evolve into a Theory X position owing to negative experiences.

Development   The act or process of helping and encouraging organization members to grow and advance professionally; to go through a process of natural growth, differentiation, or evolution by successive changes.

Development Level   A combination of four characteristics that shows the competence and commitment a person or group has in relation to a specific job to be accomplished.

Developmental Dimensions   The various levels of development. Chris Argyris suggests that people move through seven developmental dimensions or stages as they mature.

Direction and Control   The process of providing guidance and analysis to a system in order to enable it to maintain positive progress toward predetermined goals.

Discrimination   The act of systematically restraining or prohibiting an individual from occupying a position or activity on the basis of sex, religion, race, or national origin.

Dissonance   Inconsistency between the beliefs one holds or between one's actions and one's beliefs.

Dream List   A personal record of all the goals one wishes to attain in a lifetime.

Diversity   The cultural differences among people in the workplace such as looks, beliefs, language or customs.

Drug Dependent   An employee whose repeated over indulgence in drug usage sharply reduces his or her effectiveness and dependability on the job.

Education   The development of an employee into a well-rounded and generally competent individual; to develop mentally, morally, or aesthetically by instruction or other method.

Effective Listening   Listening to show support for the other person and to retain and evaluate information.

Ego Conflict   An intrapersonal stressful situation involving competing or conflicting needs or desires that threaten one's basic sense of being.

Electronic Cottage   A home where work is done by electronically linking up to the office through telecommunicating. Also called flexiplace.

Electronic Office   An office that uses automation and electronic information management systems.

Environment   In business, the context (physical surroundings, setting, or location) in which employees work; the circumstances, objects, or conditions by which one is surrounded and that influence the life of an individual or community.

Environment-produced Stress   Stress caused by a lack of control over one's work environment.

Equal Employment Opportunity Commission (EEOC)   A federal agency established to help carry out affirmative action programs.

Equipment or Process Departmentalization   An organizational process by which a company is organized according to the equipment or process used. Also called process departmentation.

Equity Theory   A theory of job motivation emphasizing the role played by one's belief in the equity or fairness of rewards and punishments associated with one's performance.

Esteem Needs   The human need to be recognized by others and to have clear self-images.

Eustress   Stress arriving from pleasant events

Expectancy Theory of Motivation   A model designed by Victor Vroom that shows relationships between needs and motivation.

Extinguishing Behaviors   The result that tends to occur when reinforcement is withheld; the unrewarded behavior ceases over time.

Favorableness of the Situation   A state defined by Fred Fiedler as "the degree to which the situation enables the leader to exert his influence over his group."

Fixation   The beating of one's head against a brick wall in a futile effort to accomplish a blocked goal; a persistent concentration on achieving a goal. Also called obsession.

Flat Organization   An organization structure in which many people report to a given manager; a broad span of control in which more horizontal communication is likely to occur.

Flexiplace   A home where work is done by electronically linking up to the office through telecommuting. Also called electronic cottage.

Flextime   A system that allows its employees to choose their own times for starting and finishing work within a broad range of available hours.

Frustration   The human response that occurs when one is prevented from accomplishing a desired goal or objective; a deep chronic sense or state of insecurity and dissatisfaction arising from unresolved problems or unfulfilled needs.

Function Departmentation   An organizational process in which specialized needs are met by individual departments such as research and development, finance, personnel, marketing, and manufacturing.

Goal Congruity   The situation that exists when the goals of individuals coincide with the goals of the organization.

Goal-consuming Activity   Actual participation in the goal itself. Also called goal activity. For example, when going to a restaurant and ordering a pizza, the goal activity would be eating the pizza.

Goal-directed Activity   Motivated behavior based on expectations that the goal is, in fact, attainable, worthwhile, and desirable.

Goal Selection   The process of choosing goals that are based on realistic expectations.

Group Structuring   Getting a group together and arranging it so that the members are ready to work.

Hawthorne Experiments   Experiments that were conducted in Western Electric's Hawthorne Plant in the 1920s and that are collectively viewed as the starting point for the human relations movement.

High-Tech   Abbreviation for high-technology; refers to complex modern technology.

Horizontal Communication   Communication among peers in the same work group.

Human Relations Smart   The state in which one is aware of the basics of interpersonal relations and communications that preclude or reduce many stresses in the work place.

Human Values Objective and subjective concepts of the desirable, the goods of life, and life resources.

Hygiene Factors Dissatisfiers that relate to Maslow's lower-level needs. Also called maintenance factors.

Informating The process of actively acquiring, processing, and dispensing information.

Information Overload The stressful condition that prevails when an individual is given too much data in a given period of time and is unable to deal with it.

Integrated Office Equipment Office equipment that allows several functions to be combined by one machine.

Interaction The communication patterns among group members; mutual or reciprocal action or influence.

Intermittent Reinforcement The method in which an individual receives reinforcement for desired behavior at particular intervals or at random times.

Internal Colony See *Captive Nation*.

Interpersonal Communication Communication that maintains close relationships, aids in self-understanding, and personal growth, carefully deals with information, and creates a supportive climate.

Interpretation The meaning one assigns to one's perceptions; a concept of another's behavior or words.

Intrapreneurs Organizations or individuals who seek to expand by exploring new opportunities through new combinations of their existing resources; a person who innovates and takes exceptional risks while functioning within an organization.

Job Burnout A condition affecting the worker who has given his or her all for the company, is now very tired of it, and has lost motivation. This condition is influenced by high unachieved goals.

Job Design The division of an organization's work among its employees.

Job Enrichment A process in which, through talking together, subordinates and their supervisors come to an understanding of how the job could be made more meaningful. This involves delegating more responsibility and having more trust.

Job Expectations Expectations an employee holds regarding his or her job, and expectations the company holds about the employee.

Job Satisfaction Contentment with one's job that does not necessarily include personal motivation.

Job Satisfaction Questionnaire A questionnaire designed to measure employee satisfaction on the job.

Job Training Training that helps employees improve their performance on specific jobs.

Knowledge Familiarity, awareness, or understanding gained through experience or study; the fact or condition of knowing something with familiarity gained through experience or association.

Kye A method of pooling financial resources and providing substantial personal loans to members of the group that is used by Korean-Americans to finance new business ventures.

Laissez-Faire Style A leadership style characterized by very little leader interference or guidance—employees have a free rein.

Leadership Behaviors that keep a group together and working to solve a problem; the office or position held by an individual who guides others.

Leadership Contingency Model A system that helps determine the best leader style by looking at three variables: leader-member relations, task structure, and position power.

Life Balance The concept of placing the various aspects of one's life in a balanced condition.

Line Management Functional managers who are in direct authority of the organization's primary output or product.

Linking-Pin Function The role of a leader as a liaison between workers and top management.

Long-Term Commitment The act of staying with a company until one has become a contributing member of the organization for a reasonable period of time.

Luddites Members of a movement in the early 1800s that protested the use of innovations in European textile mills. Today's Luddites are protesting the use of modern office automation.

Maintenance Activities Activities concerned with how group members perform a task.

Majority A number greater than half of the total. Decisions are made with a majority by identifying the majority and minority points of view and then taking some type of poll or vote.

Maladjusted Worker An employee who is poorly adjusted to his or her work environment.

Management Information Systems (MIS) Office technology that permits the organization of data and contributes to the elimination of paper filing systems, which are replaced by computer files and data bases; computer-based information systems for more effective planning, decision making, and control.

Management by Objectives (MBO) A cyclical system that ties together the company's goals of profit and growth with the workers' needs to contribute and develop personally; a formal set of procedures that establishes and reviews progress toward common goals for managers and subordinates.

Managing Conflict Taking action to deal with conflict with subordinates or managers such as suppression, compromise, or confrontation.

Managing Your Manager   Practicing techniques that enable you to foster understanding with your supervisor.

Maslow's Hierarchy of Needs   A list of universal needs established by Abraham Maslow that includes physiological, safety, belongingness, esteem, and self-actualization needs.

Matrix Organizations   Organizations that use a matrix design organized around functions and projects; an organizational structure in which each employee reports both to a functional or division manager and to a project or group manager.

"Me" Generation   A term based on the assumption that young people are concerned only about self-interests and care little for organizational accomplishments.

Mechanistic View of Organizations   An outlook that compares organizations to machines, in which organizations are broken down into separate special tasks.

Mentor   A wise and trusted counselor or guide, a supporter of his or her subordinates; an employee who develops ideas, supervises others, and assumes responsibility for the work of subordinates.

Message   Symbols combined into units of meaning that are assigned to some experience; a communication in writing, in speech, or by signals; the encoded information sent by the sender to the receiver.

Midlife Crisis   A highly stressful situation usually associated with males in their forties or fifties, in which they seriously question long-held values. This phenomenon sometimes results in dramatic changes in life-styles.

Motivation   The process of providing reasons or motives for exerting effort and causing to act in certain ways.

Motives   Personal wants, interests, and desires that affect perceptions; the factors that cause, channel, and sustain an individual's behavior.

Need for Achievement   The human urge to achieve, which is exerted by challenging and competitive work situations. To a certain point this can be taught and learned.

Need for Affiliation   The human desire to be accepted by others, which is important for job satisfaction.

Need for Power   The human need to win arguments, persuade others, and prevail in every situation.

New Experiences   Experiences introduced for the first time, which can influence a person to change.

Nominal Group   A structured group meeting in which participants alternate among silently thinking up ideas, listing ideas on a flip chart, and voting on ideas.

Noneconomic Rewards   Rewards that are nonmonetary (e.g., good relationships with co-workers, job satisfaction, etc.).

Nonverbal Symbols   Nonlinguistic (not using language) behavior to which people assign meaning.

Occupational Information   Information about possible types of jobs, occupations, or careers.

Open-ended Question   A question that cannot be answered with a simple yes or no statement.

Organic Organizations   Organizations that have loosely defined task activities, have few rules and procedures, and emphasize self-control and horizontal communication. Members communicate across all levels of the organization to obtain information and advice.

Organization   The meaningful way in which people put selected information together, the arrangement of an organization's structure and coordination of its managerial practices and resource use to achieve its goals.

Organizational Climate   The composite impression people get from such things as the work atmosphere, organizational objectives, and corporate philosophy.

Organizational Culture   The set of pervasive understandings, such as norms, values, attitudes, and beliefs, shared by organization members.

Organizational Development   A planned effort that is aided by a change agent (an organizational development specialist) to improve the efficiency and effectiveness of the organization and its people; a long-range effort supported by top management to increase an organization's problem-solving and renewal processes through effective management of organizational culture.

Organizational Development through the Involvement of Employees (ODIE)   A planned program for organizational change that is contingent upon the active involvement of employees at various levels.

Paralanguage   The study of how something is said (now what is said) by the words that are used (also called vocal cues); optional vocal effects (such as tone of voice) that accompany or modify the phonemes of an utterance and that may communicate meaning.

Parental Leave   Work leave granted to either males or females for the purpose of attending to important activities involving children. This is a major expansion of the old maternity leave concept.

Participative Decision Making (PDM)   The process in which several people work on the same problem, sharing ideas and resolving differences in constructive ways.

Participative Style   A leadership style characterized by very high employee participation. This style takes advantage of the subordinates' willingness and ability to work by creating a motivating environment.

Peer-Group Pressures   Stresses in which individuals are influenced by their peers to see life in much the same way as their peers would like them to see life.

Perception   How an individual sees the world through his or her experiences, expectations, and interests; a quick, acute, and intuitive cognition; a common source of communication barriers; a pattern of meaning that comes to the individual through the five senses.

Perception/Truth Fallacy   The erroneous tendency of people to believe that the way they see the world is closer to "the truth" than the way others see it.

Perceptual Expectancy   Mental anticipation about how people, events, or things will be.

Performance Reviews   Formal processes of providing feedback to employees regarding the degree to which their job performances match established performance standards or objectives.

Personal Space   The distance people allow and demand between themselves and others.

Personal Value   One's idea of something that is intrinsically (in and of itself) desirable.

Personality-produced Stress   Stress experienced by an individual because of particular personality characteristics.

Physiological Needs   Human needs related to physiological comfort; one of Maslow's hierarchy of needs.

Plurality   More than half of the whole majority. With a plurality, the acceptable decision is the one supported by the largest number of individuals as determined by some type of poll or vote.

Position Power   A recognized status due to one's position in a company; according to Fred Fiedler, the power that is inherent in the formal position the leader holds.

Positive Role Model   One who teaches by positive example.

Predictability   The capacity for handling delicate administrative circumstances with good judgment and thoroughness; reliability in reaching important deadlines and doing high-quality work; the state of foretelling on the basis of observation, experience, or scientific reason.

Prejudice   A tendency to prejudge others that is often rooted in a misunderstanding of or lack of exposure to different types of people; damage resulting from some judgment or action of another in disregard of one's rights.

Prestige Needs   Needs for the feeling of self-accomplishment and the social and psychological rewards of excelling.

Product Departmentalization   Organization of a company along product or service lines.

Profit Centers   Subgroups responsible for their own decisions; organizational units where performance is measured by numerical differences between revenues and expenditures.

Programmed Limitations   Self-perceptions of what one can or cannot achieve.

Pseudoconflict   A conflict in which people agree on an issue but are unable to communicate the agreement, in which the agreement seems apparent but is not stated.

Quality Circles   Processes in which workers and managers meet on a regular basis to study and solve job-related problems and discuss ways of improving quality control of the products or services the organization produces.

Rationalization   One response to perceived inequity; a coping response whereby the person discounts or tries to explain away how a goal can or cannot be achieved.

Receptiveness to Ideas   The state of being qualified or ready to receive ideas.

Recreation   Refreshment of strengths and sprits after work.

Retention Listening   Listening to retain and evaluate information by doing such things as identifying the speaker's purpose, adapting to it, and developing note-taking skills.

Reverse Discrimination   Discrimination against white males arising from preferential treatment for minorities.

Robotics   The study, design, and manufacture of robots that are able to be reprogrammed to perform more difficult tasks than previous mechanical devices could perform.

Role   The pattern that characterizes an individual's contributions to the group; a socially expected behavior pattern usually determined by an individual's status in a particular society.

Role Model   A person whose behavior in a particular role is imitated or emulated by others.

Safety and Security Needs   Primary drives or desires related to self-preservation and freedom from fear of physical danger.

Secondary Needs   Higher-level human wants and desires such as to be accepted by others, to achieve certain goals, or to have prestige.

Security Needs   Human wants and desires related to protecting oneself from physical or psychological loss.

Selection   The process of sifting through raw data to identify for use key information that holds importance for the individual.

Self-Actualization Need   The human need to maximize one's potential.

Self-Appraisal   The process of looking closely at oneself to evaluate personal strengths and weakness. This process is closely associated with values clarification.

Self-Fulfilling Prophecies   Outcomes that appear to be related to our preconceived expectations. For example, one person's expectations of a second person seem to influence the second person to behave in certain ways to make the expectations reality.

Self-Fulfillment   The process or fact of fulfilling one's ambitions or goals, or satisfying personal needs, through one's own efforts.

Sexual Harassment   Unwanted sexual requests or advances or the creation of a sexually harassing environment through sexual jokes and remarks.

Simple Conflict   The condition in which individuals or groups cannot satisfy their own goals or needs without blocking the goals or needs of some other individuals or groups.

Situational Leadership Theory (SLT)   Paul Hersey and Kenneth Blanchard's leadership model that describes the situational or contingent behaviors of directing, coaching, supporting, and delegating.

Small Group   A gathering of two or more people, yet few enough in number to permit each member the opportunity to communicate directly with all other members.

Small-Group Problem Solving   The activity in which a small group is employed to solve specific problems by stating and analyzing questions, generating ideas, selecting the most useful ideas, and deciding which ideas will be used.

Social Needs   Human wants and desires for belonging, affiliation, love, and acceptance by other people.

Span of Control   The number of people who report to an individual supervisor or manager.

Stereotype   A generalization about the nature of people or groups that is often incorrect or misleading.

Stress   Psychological, physical, or emotional strain or tension.

Stress Carrier   A person who creates stress in another person.

Stroking   In transactional analysis, a verbal approval statement indicating that an individual is valuable and is contributing to the organization.

Subordinate-centered Leadership   A leadership situation characterized by a high degree of subordinate participation in making decisions.

Superior-Subordinate Trust   A state of trust between superior and subordinate developed through accessibility, predictability, and mutual loyalty and respect.

Support Listening   Hearing and attending to what others say with a minimum of emotional or observable reaction.

Supportive Climate   A situation in which the prevailing attitudes, standards, or conditions encourage participants to feel that they have a sense of worth and importance and that their efforts will be supported.

Supportive Relationships   Associations characterized by objective descriptions of problems, a spontaneous climate, a sense of fairness, and openness to divergent viewpoints.

Supportiveness   The degree or extent to which one person or group is willing to aid or sustain another; one of Charles Redding's five components of organizational climate; the degree to which management supports its employees' efforts.

Survival Needs   Human wants or desires associated with the will to live. According to Abraham Maslow and others, these basic needs have dominance over higher-level needs.

Symbol   Something used for or regarded as representing something else.

Symptoms of Emotional Problems   Telltale signs that reveal negative or inappropriate behaviors that are excessive, have acute onset, or noticeably increase over time.

Tall Organization   A common organizational structure in which relatively few people report to one manager and many levels of management exist.

Task Activities   Activities concerned with what group members are doing to accomplish the specific work (or tasks) assigned to the group, as opposed to maintenance activities, which are concerned with holding the group together.

Task Integration   The tying together or coordinating of specialized work (or tasks) of various individuals or groups to ensure that the overall organization goals are met.

Task Specialization   The process of assigning specific work (or tasks) to individuals or groups so that those individuals or groups will become expert in dealing with a specific segment of the organization's overall mission.

Task Structure   The degree to which a task is defined. A clearly designed task is high in structure, while a vaguely designed task is low in structure.

Team Meeting   A meeting that allows employees to get together and discuss problems in order to resolve problems and to reduce stress.

Telecommuting   Using computer terminals to communicate by means of telephone lines with clients, coworkers, and data banks. This process is making it possible for many jobs to be shifted from corporate offices to home offices.

Territory Departmentalization   The organization of a company along territorial or geographical lines.

Theory X   A pessimistic, traditional approach to managing people that was described but not espoused by researcher Douglas McGregor. This approach is based on assumptions that employees have an inherent dislike of work, will avoid work whenever possible, are lazy, are unambitious, avoid responsibility, and prefer to be directed.

Theory Y   An optimistic view of human nature that assumes that people will naturally expend physical and mental effort in work and that they will direct themselves toward objectives if their achievements are recognized and rewarded. This theory, developed (along with Theory X) by Douglas McGregor, holds that people are able and willing to seek responsibility and to apply imagination, ingenuity, and creativity to organizational problems.

Time Departmentalization   The process of organizing an enterprise according to time schedules, as in the use of work shifts.

Timely Information   Information, conveyed when needed, to enable employees to do their jobs properly and to establish a feeling of belonging in the company.

Touch Behavior   Use of the sense of touch to communicate certain kinds of nonverbal symbols.

Training   Development associated with learning human and technical skills to make the employee more effective on a specific job.

Traits Approach to Leadership   A theory based on the underlying assumption that leaders possess certain traits that make them effective leaders.

Transactional Analysis   The process, developed by Eric Berne, of studying interpersonal interactions (or scripts) that explain the parent, adult, and child ego states inherent in all people.

Trust   Belief in and reliance on the ability, strength, and integrity of a person or thing; one of Charles Redding's five components of organizational climate. The degree of trust employees have in management is contingent upon a number of factors including the respect and trust that management holds for employees.

Two-Factor Theory of Motivation   Frederick Herzberg's motivational-hygiene theory, which suggests that people are motivated by one set of higher-level needs (such as achievement and recognition) and satisfied by the fulfillment of another set of lower-level needs (such as pay and working conditions).

Type 1 Criticism   Criticism that is directed at the individual rather than the work, is conducted in a knee jerk fashion often in public, and results in defensiveness and deterioration of performance.

Type 2 Criticism   Criticism that is directed at work performance rather than at the worker, includes a discussion of cause and effect, allows for input from the worker, and is therefore potentially constructive because it may result in improved future performance.

Type 1 Praise   Vague, generalized statements regarding expected performance that is often used as either side of a "sandwich" that contains harsh criticism in the middle. This type of praise is unlikely to have a significant, positive effect on the performance of the receiver.

Type 2 Praise   Specific statements regarding exceptional performance that is given primarily to commend and recognize rather than to cloak some ulterior motive. Type 2 praise is likely to have a positive effect on the performance of the receiver under normal circumstances.

"Uh-Huh" Technique   The method of focusing on the other person and verbalizing support by saying "uh-huh" or some equivalent nonjudgmental comment.

Unanimity   Total agreement that transcends differences and leads to harmony.

Unity of Command   The principle that each employee reports to only one boss.

Upward-Downward Communication   Communication that is vertically directed in an organization and typically follows the formal chain of command.

Values Clarification   The process of identifying and clarifying the relatively permanent personal desires that guide one's behavior and attitudes. This process is closely related to self-appraisal.

Work Ethic   The traditional value that work and hard effort are intrinsically rewarding to the individual's self-worth.

Work Team   An autonomous group of employees who are collectively responsible for their output.

Workaholic   One who is addicted to his or her work.

INDEX